In Łowicz, Poland, a master craftswoman works at the traditional Polish folk art of paper cutting. Using only shears and colored paper, she creates intricate designs like those beside her.

Michal Heron–Woodfin Camp & Associates

Funk & Wagnalls New Encyclopedia

VOLUME 19

NEW JERSEY to ORTHODONTICS

LEON L. BRAM
Vice-President and Editorial Director

ROBERT S. PHILLIPS
Editor-in-Chief

NORMA H. DICKEY
Special Projects Editor-in-Chief

Funk & Wagnalls, Inc.
Publishers since 1876

Funk & Wagnalls
New Encyclopedia
Copyright © MCMLXXI,
MCMLXXV, MCMLXXIX, MCMLXXXIII
by Funk & Wagnalls, Inc.

Edward Haas,
Senior Vice-President, Manufacturing

Steven G. Weinfeld,
Vice-President, Manufacturing

Volumes are published subsequent
to copyright dates to contain
the latest updated information

ISBN 0–8343–0051–6
Library of Congress Catalog
Card Number 72–170933

ahc 4

Funk & Wagnalls New Encyclopedia is liberally provided with **finding devices** that aid in the search for information. The brief descriptions and suggestions that follow are intended to encourage the proper use of these devices so that full use is made of the information resources within these pages.

The **index** in volume 29 should be the starting point in a search for information. If a search is made *without* the use of the index, the following suggestions should be kept in mind:

- If the search is *unsuccessful,* the index should be used to search again. The topic may be discussed in an article that was overlooked. Only after use of the index can a search be considered thorough or completed.

- If the search is initially *successful,* the index should be used to find additional information. A topic may be discussed in several articles; the index can locate the less-obvious ones.

The use and structure of the index is explained in the Guide to the Index, volume 29, pages 6–8.

Cross-references of several types are used frequently within most articles in Funk & Wagnalls New Encyclopedia. Each cross-reference directs the search for information to other articles that contain additional or related information. The types of cross-references and their specific uses are explained in the Guide to Funk & Wagnalls New Encyclopedia, volume 1, pages 10–13, under the subhead, Cross-references.

Bibliography cross-references follow all the major articles in Funk & Wagnalls New Encyclopedia. They direct the search for further information from the articles to appropriate **reading lists** of books and periodicals in the **bibliography** in volume 28. The reading lists may also be used for independent study. A full description of bibliography cross-references and reading lists is found in the Preface and Guide to the Bibliography, volume 28, pages 186–87.

SELECTED ABBREVIATIONS USED IN TEXT*

AC	alternating current	F	Fahrenheit	Nor.	Norwegian
AD	*anno Domini* (Lat., "in the year of the Lord")	Finn.	Finnish	O.E.	Old English
		fl.	flourished	O.Fr.	Old French
		FM	frequency modulation	O.H.G.	Old High German
alt.	altitude			O.N.	Old Norse
AM	*ante meridiem* (Lat., "before noon")	Fr.	French	Op.	*Opus* (Lat., "work")
		ft	foot, feet	oz	ounce(s)
		g	gram(s)	Pers.	Persian
AM	amplitude modulation	gal	gallon(s)	PM	*post meridiem* (Lat., "after noon")
		Ger.	German		
amu	atomic mass unit(s)	GeV	billion electron volts	Pol.	Polish
Arab.	Arabic			pop.	population
Arm.	Armenian	Gr.	Greek	Port.	Portuguese
A.S.	Anglo-Saxon	ha	hectare(s)	q.v.	*quod vide* (Lat., "which see")
ASSR	Autonomous Soviet Socialist Republic	Heb.	Hebrew		
		hp	horsepower	r.	reigned
atm.	atmosphere	hr	hour	R.	River
at.no.	atomic number	Hung.	Hungarian	repr.	reprinted
at.wt.	atomic weight	Hz	hertz or cycle(s) per second	rev.	revised
b.	born			Rom.	Romanian
BC	before Christ	Icel.	Icelandic	Rus.	Russian
b.p.	boiling point	i.e.	*id est* (Lat., "that is")	S	south; southern
Btu	British Thermal Unit			sec.	second(s); secant
		in	inch(es)	SFSR	Soviet Federated Socialist Republic
bu	bushel(s)	inc.	incorporated		
Bulg.	Bulgarian	Ital.	Italian	Skt.	Sanskrit
C	Celsius	Jap.	Japanese	Span.	Spanish
c.	*circa* (Lat., "about")	K	Kelvin	sp.gr.	specific gravity
cent.	century	kg	kilogram(s)	sq	square
Chin.	Chinese	km	kilometer(s)	sq km	square kilometer(s)
cm	centimeter(s)	kw	kilowatt(s)	sq mi	square mile(s)
Co.	Company, County	kwh	kilowatt hour(s)	SSR	Soviet Socialist Republic
cu	cubic	Lat.	Latin		
Czech.	Czechoslovakian	lat	latitude	St.	Saint, Street
d.	died	lb	pound(s)	Sum.	Sumerian
Dan.	Danish	long	longitude	Swed.	Swedish
DC	direct current	m	meter(s)	trans.	translated, translation, translator(s)
Du.	Dutch	mass no.	mass number		
E	east; eastern	MeV	million electron volts		
ed.	edited, edition, editors			Turk.	Turkish
		mg	milligram(s)	Ukr.	Ukrainian
e.g.	*exempli gratia* (Lat., "for example")	mi	mile(s)	UN	United Nations
		min	minute(s)	U.S.	United States
Egypt.	Egyptian	ml	milliliter(s)	USSR	Union of Soviet Socialist Republics
Eng.	English	mm	millimeter(s)		
est.	established; estimated	m.p.	melting point	v.	versus; verse
		mph	miles per hour	Ved.	Vedic
et al.	*et alii* (Lat., "and others")	Mt(s).	Mount, Mountain(s)	vol.	Volume(s)
				W	west; western
EV	electron volt(s)	N	north; northern	yd	yard(s)

* For a more extensive listing, see ABBREVIATIONS AND ACRONYMS. Charts of pertinent abbreviations also accompany the articles DEGREE, ACADEMIC; ELEMENTS, CHEMICAL; MATHEMATICAL SYMBOLS; and WEIGHTS AND MEASURES.

FUNK & WAGNALLS NEW ENCYCLOPEDIA

NEW JERSEY, one of the Middle Atlantic states of the U.S., bordered on the NE by New York State, on the E by the Atlantic Ocean, on the S by Delaware, and on the W and NW by Pennsylvania. The Hudson R. forms part of the state's boundary with New York; Delaware Bay and the Delaware R. form the boundary with Delaware; and the Delaware R. forms New Jersey's boundary with Pennsylvania.

New Jersey entered the Union on Dec. 18, 1787, as the third of the original 13 states. During the American Revolution, it had been the scene of several important events, including George Washington's crossing of the Delaware in December 1776 to defeat the British at Trenton, now the state capital. Manufacturing became the leading economic activity of the state in the late 19th century, and in the early 1980s New Jersey was also known for its resorts along the Atlantic coast and for its productive farms. President Grover Cleveland was born in New Jersey, and President Woodrow Wilson spent most of his adult life here. The state is named for the Isle of Jersey, in the English Channel, the birthplace of Sir George Carteret, who in 1644 became a part owner of what is now New Jersey. New Jersey is known as the Garden State.

LAND AND RESOURCES

New Jersey, with an area of 20,168 sq km (7787 sq mi), is the 46th largest state in the U.S.; 3.1% of its land area is owned by the federal government. The state is roughly rectangular in shape, and its extreme dimensions are about 265 km (about 165 mi) from N to S and about 100 km (about 60 mi) from E to W. Elevations range from sea level, along the Atlantic Ocean, to 550 m (1803 ft), atop High Point in the N. The approximate mean elevation is 76 m (250 ft). New Jersey's coastline is 209 km (130 mi) long.

Physical Geography. The S three-fifths of New Jersey is part of the Atlantic Coastal Plain. Most of its surface is nearly flat, seldom rising to more than 30 m (100 ft); for some distance inland from the Atlantic Ocean elevations are less than 15 m (50 ft). Along the lower Delaware R. and along Delaware Bay are extensive marshes. Large marshes are also found along the Atlantic coast, between the mainland and barrier beaches (low offshore islands). Several bays—such as Great Bay, Barnegat Bay, and Sandy Hook Bay—are also situated between the mainland and the barrier beaches. The SW part of the region has fertile, sandy-loam soil.

Northwest of the coastal plain is a section of the Piedmont Plateau. It is separated from the plain by the fall line (q.v.), which extends NE from the Trenton area to Newark Bay. Underlain mostly by metamorphic rock, mainly gneiss and schist, it is generally a region of low relief, lying at elevations of about 30 to 150 m (about 100 to 500 ft). The Watchung Mts., in the N part of the region, are ridges of diabase rock rising some 60 to 90 m (some 200 to 300 ft) above the general surface level.

To the N of the Piedmont area is a part of the New England Upland, known here as the New Jersey Highlands. Underlain by various crystalline rocks, it rises steeply in such mountains as the Pohatcong, Scotts, and Sparta. Broad, flat-floored valleys are situated between the ridges. Many lakes are in the region.

A section of the Appalachian Valley and Ridge region lies in NW New Jersey. Immediately beyond the New Jersey Highlands is a part of the Great Valley, known locally as the Kittatinny Valley, some 24 km (some 15 mi) wide and underlain by limestone or sandstone and shale. Beyond the valley are the Kittatinny Mts., a crystalline ridge containing some of the highest elevations in the state. The scenic Delaware Water Gap (q.v.) is situated where the Delaware R. flows through the mountains.

Rivers and Lakes. Nearly one-third of New Jersey, mainly in the W and S, drains into the Delaware

The Ford Mansion in Morristown, N.J., served as George Washington's headquarters in the winter of 1779–80, during the American Revolution.

Joseph Tomala, Jr.–Bruce Coleman, Inc.

R. and Delaware Bay. Much of the N part of the state is drained into the Atlantic Ocean via the Passaic, Hackensack, and Raritan rivers. A small N section is drained into the Hudson R. by way of the Wallkill R. Rivers of the Atlantic Coastal Plain are mostly short, and some are swampy in their lower courses; they include the Toms, Mullica, and Great Egg Harbor rivers.

Several lakes lie in the New England Upland region. Among the largest of these are Hopatcong, Mohawk, and Greenwood lakes.

Climate. New Jersey has a temperate climate. Average monthly temperatures in the N range from about −1° C (about 30° F) in January to about 21° to 24° C (about 70° to 75° F) in July; in the S the range is from 0° to 1.1° C (30° to 34° F) in January to about 24° to 25° C (about 75° to 77° F) in July. The coolest temperatures are usually in the higher elevations of the NW; the warmest temperatures along the SE coast. The recorded temperature in the state has ranged from −36.7° C (−34° F), in 1904 at River Vale in the NE, to 43.3° C (110° F), in 1936 at Runyon. Annual precipitation varies between 1220 and 1270 mm (about 48 to 50 in) in most parts of the N and between about 1040 and 1140 mm (about 41 to 45 in) in the S. It is fairly evenly distributed

throughout the year. Parts of the N receive up to about 1270 mm (50 in) of snow per year; the yearly snowfall in the S usually is much less. Violent storms are unusual in New Jersey, but occasionally hurricanes from the Atlantic strike the state.

Plants and Animals. About 40% of New Jersey is covered with forests, which are generally made up of both deciduous and coniferous trees. In the N, oak, birch, beech, maple, and hemlock are intermixed. To the S, oak, white cedar, and pine are common. A unique area is the large Pine Barrens (q.v.) of the Atlantic Coastal Plain region. Mostly scrub pine and oak grow in the sandy soil of the area. Other common plants of New Jersey are goldenrod, wild azalea, dogwood, mountain laurel, daisy, violets, and ferns.

Among the large animals of New Jersey are many white-tailed deer and a few bear (mainly living in the N). Small animals include fox, squirrel, chipmunk, rabbit, woodchuck, opossum, and skunk. Two poisonous snake species, found mainly in the N, are the timber rattlesnake and copperhead. The state's large number of birds include the bluebird, bluejay, cardinal, goldfinch, sparrow, and owl. A variety of shore birds are found in New Jersey, including the gull, heron,

INDEX TO MAP OF NEW JERSEY

Cities and Towns

Absecon . . . D5
Allendale . . . B1
Allenhurst . . . F3
Allentown . . . E3
Allenwood . . . E3
Alloway . . . C4
Alpha . . . C2
Alpine . . . D2
Andover . . . D2
Asbury Park . . . F3
Ashland . . . D4
Atco . . . D4
Atlantic City . . . E5
Atlantic Highlands . . . F3
Audubon . . . C4
Audubon Park . . . B3
Avalon . . . D5
Avenel . . . E2
Avon By The Sea . . . F3
Baptistown . . . D2
Barnegat . . . E4
Barrington . . . B3
Basking Ridge . . . D2
Batsto . . . D4
Bay Head . . . E3
Bayonne . . . B2
Bayville . . . E4
Beach Haven . . . E4
Beachwood . . . E4
Beaver Lake . . . D1
Bedminster . . . D2
Belford . . . E3
Belle Mead . . . D3
Belleville . . . A3
Bellmawr . . . B2
Belmar . . . C4
Belvidere ⊙ . . . C2
Bergenfield . . . C1
Berkeley Heights . . . E2
Berlin . . . D4
Bernardsville . . . D2
Beverly . . . D3
Bivalve . . . C5
Blackwood . . . C4
Blairstown . . . C2
Bloomfield . . . B2
Bloomingdale . . . E1
Bloomsbury . . . C2
Bogota . . . B2
Boonton . . . E2
Bordentown . . . D3
Bound Brook . . . D2
Bradley Beach . . . F3
Brainards . . . C2

Breton Woods . . . E3
Brick . . . E3
Bridgeport ⊙ . . . C4
Bridgeton ⊙ . . . C5
Bridgewater . . . D2
Brielle . . . E3
Brigantine . . . E5
Brooklawn . . . B3
Budd Lake . . . D2
Buena . . . D4
Burlington . . . D3
Butler . . . E2
Buttzville . . . C2
Caldwell . . . E2
Califon . . . D2
Camden ⊙ . . . C4
Candlewood . . . E3
Cape May ⊙ . . . D6
Cape May Court House . . . D5
Carlstadt . . . B2
Carneys Point . . . C4
Carteret . . . E2
Cedar Grove . . . B2
Cedar Knolls . . . D2
Cedarville . . . C5
Cedarwood Park . . . E3
Chatham . . . E2
Chatsworth . . . D4
Cheesequake . . . E3
Cherry Hill . . . B3
Chesilhurst . . . D4
Chester . . . D1
Chesterfield . . . D3
Clark . . . D3
Clarksboro . . . B4
Clarksburg . . . C4
Clayton . . . C4
Clementon . . . D4
Cliffside Park . . . C1
Cliffwood . . . E2
Clinton . . . D2
Closter . . . D2
Cologne . . . D5
Colonia . . . C4
Colts Neck . . . E3
Columbia . . . C2
Columbus . . . D3
Convent Station . . . D2
Corbin City . . . D5
Cranberry Lake . . . D2
Cranbury . . . D3
Cranford . . . E2
Cresskill . . . C1
Deal . . . F3
Deepwater . . . C4

Delair . . . C4
Delanco . . . D3
Delran . . . B3
Demarest . . . C1
Dennisville . . . D5
Denville . . . E2
Deptford . . . B4
Dorchester . . . D5
Dorothy . . . D5
Dover . . . D2
Dumont . . . C1
Dunellen . . . E2
East Brunswick . . . E3
East Hanover . . . E2
East Keansburg . . . E2
East Millstone . . . D3
East Newark . . . B2
East Orange . . . B2
East Rutherford . . . E3
Eatontown . . . E3
Echo Lake . . . E1
Edgewater . . . C2
Edgewater Park . . . D3
Edison . . . E2
Egg Harbor City . . . D4
Elberon . . . E3
Elizabeth ⊙ . . . E3
Elmer . . . C4
Elmwood Park . . . B2
Emerson . . . C1
Englewood . . . C2
Englewood Cliffs . . . C1
English Creek . . . D5
Englishtown . . . E3
Essex Fells . . . B2
Estell Manor . . . A2
Fairfield . . . E3
Fair Haven . . . E3
Fair Lawn . . . C2
Fairview . . . C2
Fanwood . . . E2
Far Hills . . . D2
Farmingdale . . . E3
Flagtown . . . D2
Flanders . . . D2
Flemington ⊙ . . . D3
Florence . . . D3
Florham Park . . . E2
Folsom . . . D4
Fords . . . E2
Forked River . . . E4
Fort Lee . . . C2
Franklin . . . D1
Franklin Lakes . . . B1
Franklin Park . . . D3
Franklinville . . . C4
Freehold ⊙ . . . E3
Frenchtown . . . C2

Garfield . . . E2
Garwood . . . E2
Gibbsboro . . . D4
Gibbstown . . . C4
Gilford Park . . . E4
Gillette . . . E2
Glassboro . . . C4
Glendora . . . B4
Glen Gardner . . . D2
Glen Ridge . . . B2
Glen Rock . . . B1
Gloucester City . . . C4
Great Meadows . . . D2
Green Creek . . . D5
Green Pond . . . E1
Green Village . . . D2
Greenwich . . . C5
Grenloch . . . C4
Greystone Park . . . D2
Groveville . . . D3
Guttenberg . . . C2
Hackensack ⊙ . . . C2
Hackettstown . . . F2
Haddonfield . . . D2
Haddon Heights . . . B4
Hainesport . . . D4
Haledon . . . B1
Hamburg . . . D1
Hamilton Square . . . D3
Hammonton . . . D4
Hampton . . . C2
Harrington Park . . . C1
Harrison . . . B2
Harrisonville . . . C4
Hasbrouck Heights . . . B2
Haworth . . . C1
Hawthorne . . . E3
Hazlet . . . E3
Helmetta . . . E3
Hewitt . . . E1
High Bridge . . . D2
Highland Park . . . E2
Highlands . . . F3
Hightstown . . . D3
Hillsdale . . . D2
Hillside . . . B2
Hi-Nella . . . B4
Hoboken . . . C2
Ho-Ho-Kus . . . B1
Holmdel . . . E3
Hopatcong . . . D2
Hope . . . C2
Hopewell . . . D3
Howell . . . E3
Huntington . . . C4
Interlaken . . . E3
Ironia . . . E3
Irvington . . . B2

Iselin . . . E2
Island Heights . . . E4
Jackson . . . D4
Jamesburg . . . E3
Jersey City ⊙ . . . F2
Keansburg . . . E3
Kearny . . . B2
Keasbey . . . E2
Kendall Park . . . D3
Kenilworth . . . E2
Keyport . . . E3
Kingston . . . D3
Kinnelon . . . E2
Kirkwood . . . B4
Lafayette . . . D1
Lake Hiawatha . . . E2
Lake Hopatcong . . . D2
Lakehurst . . . E3
Lake Mohawk . . . D1
Lakewood . . . E3
Lambertville . . . D3
Landing . . . D2
Lanoka Harbor . . . E4
Laurel Springs . . . B4
Laurence Harbor . . . E3
Lavallette . . . E4
Lawnside . . . B3
Lawrenceville . . . D3
Lebanon . . . D2
Ledgewood . . . D2
Leesburg . . . D5
Leonardo . . . E3
Leonia . . . C2
Liberty Corner . . . D2
Lincoln Park . . . A1
Lincroft . . . E3
Linden . . . B2
Lindenwold . . . B4
Linwood . . . D5
Little Falls . . . B2
Little Ferry . . . B2
Little Silver . . . F3
Livingston . . . E2
Lodi . . . B2
Long Branch . . . F3
Longport . . . D5
Long Valley . . . D2
Lyndhurst . . . B2
Lyons . . . D2
McAfee . . . D1
McKee City . . . D5
Madison . . . E2
Magnolia . . . C4
Mahwah . . . E1
Manahawkin . . . E4
Manasquan . . . E3
Mantua . . . C4
Manville . . . D2

Maple Shade . . . D4
Maplewood . . . E2
Margate City . . . E5
Marlboro . . . E3
Marlton . . . D4
Martinsville . . . D2
Matawan . . . E3
Mauricetown . . . D5
Mays Landing ⊙ . . . D5
Maywood . . . B2
Medford . . . D4
Medford Lakes . . . D4
Mendham . . . E2
Menlo Park . . . B4
Mercerville . . . D3
Merchantville . . . E2
Metuchen . . . D2
Mickleton . . . E3
Middlesex . . . E2
Middletown . . . E3
Midland Park . . . B1
Milford . . . C2
Millburn . . . E2
Millington . . . D2
Milltown . . . E3
Millville . . . C5
Milton . . . D1
Mine Hill . . . D5
Mizpah . . . F3
Monmouth Beach . . . F3
Monmouth Junction . . . D3
Monroe . . . E3
Montclair . . . C2
Montvale . . . D2
Montville . . . E1
Moonachie . . . E2
Moorestown . . . D4
Morris Plains . . . D2
Morristown ⊙ . . . E2
Mountain Lakes . . . D5
Mountainside . . . E2
Mountain View . . . E2
Mount Arlington . . . E2
Mount Ephraim . . . B2
Mount Freedom . . . D2
Mount Holly ⊙ . . . D4
Mount Hope . . . D2
Mount Laurel . . . B2
Mount Royal . . . D4
Mullica Hill . . . C4
Mystic Islands . . . E4
National Park . . . B3
Navesink . . . E3
Neptune . . . F3
Neptune City . . . E3
Netcong . . . D2
Newark ⊙ . . . C4
New Brunswick . . . E3

⊙ County seat

9

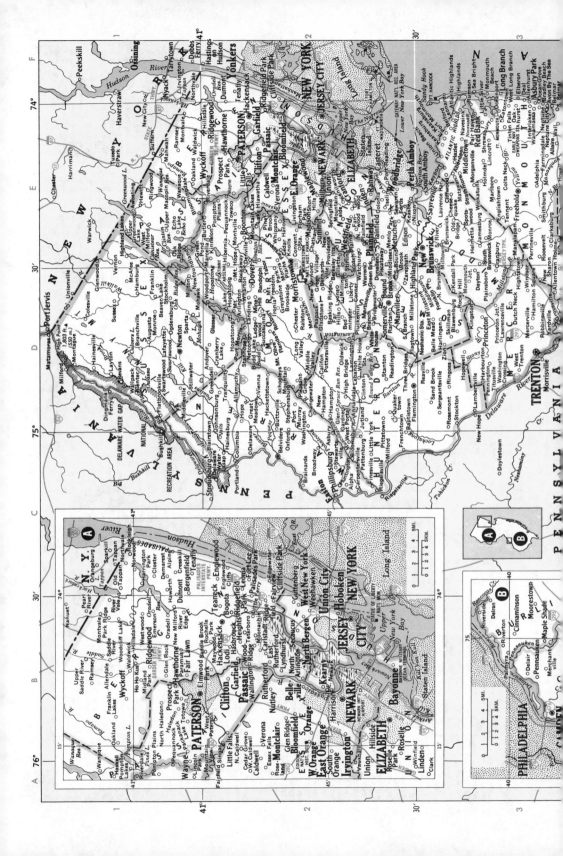

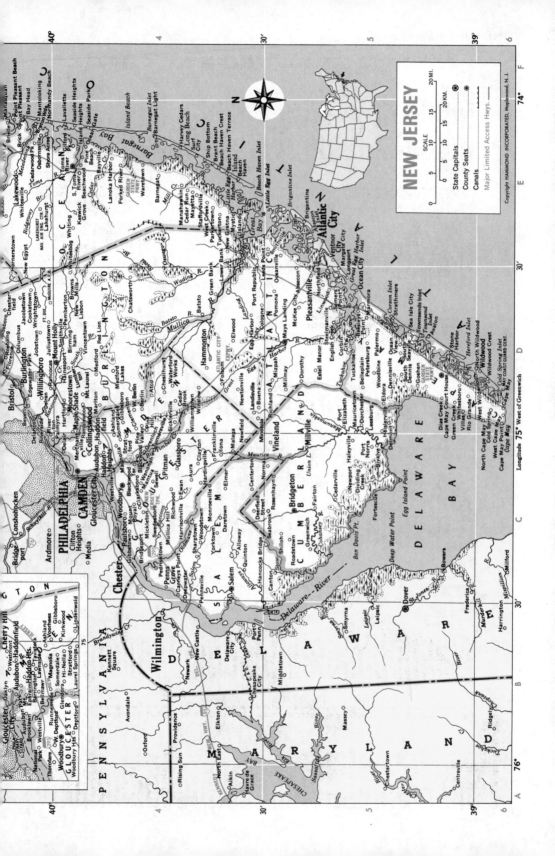

NEW JERSEY

SCALE
0   5   10   15   20 MI.
0   5   10   15   20 KM.

State Capitals ⊛
County Seats ◉
Canals
Major Limited Access Hwys.

74°

N

DELAWARE BAY

Longitude 75° West of Greenwich

PENNSYLVANIA

DELAWARE

MARYLAND

PHILADELPHIA

CAMDEN

CHESAPEAKE BAY

Index to Map of New Jersey

New Egypt ... E 3
Newfield ... D 4
Newfoundland ... D 1
New Gretna ... E 4
New Milford ... B 1
Newport ... C 5
New Providence ... E 2
Newton ⊙ ... D 1
New Vernon ... E 2
Nixon ... C 4
Norma ... C 4
North Arlington ... B 2
North Bergen ... B 2
North Brunswick ... D 3
North Caldwell ... E 2
North Cape May ... C 6
Northfield ... D 5
North Haledon ... B 1
North Plainfield ... E 2
Northvale ... F 1
North Wildwood ... D 6
Norwood ... C 1
Nutley ... B 2
Oakhurst ... E 3
Oakland ... E 1
Oaklyn ... B 3
Ocean City ... D 5
Ocean Gate ... E 4
Ocean Grove ... E 3
Oceanport ... E 3
Ocean View ... D 5
Ogdensburg ... D 1
Old Bridge ... E 3
Old Tappan ... C 1
Oldwick ... D 2
Oradell ... B 1
Orange ... B 2
Osbornsville ... E 3
Oxford ... D 2
Packanack Lake ... B 1
Palisades Park ... C 2
Palmyra ... B 3
Paramus ... B 1
Park Ridge ... E 2
Parsippany ... E 2
Passaic ... B 2
Paterson ⊙ ... E 2
Paulsboro ... C 4
Peapack-Gladstone ... D 2
Pedricktown ... C 4
Pemberton ... D 4
Pennington ... D 3
Pennsauken ... B 3
Penns Grove ... C 4

Pennsville ... C 4
Pequannock ... E 2
Perth Amboy ... C 4
Phillipsburg ... E 3
Pine Beach ... E 4
Pine Brook ... B 1
Pine Hill ... D 4
Piscataway ... D 2
Pitman ... C 4
Plainfield ... E 2
Plainsboro ... D 3
Pleasantville ... D 5
Pluckemin ... E 4
Point Pleasant ... E 4
Pomona ... D 5
Pompton Lakes ... B 1
Pompton Plains ... B 1
Port Monmouth ... E 3
Port Morris ... D 2
Port Murray ... D 2
Port Norris ... C 5
Port Reading ... E 2
Pottersville ... D 2
Princeton ... D 3
Princeton Jct. ... D 3
Prospect Park ... B 1
Rahway ... E 2
Ramblewood ... D 4
Ramsey ... E 1
Raritan ... D 4
Red Bank ... E 3
Red Lion ... D 4
Richland ... D 5
Ridgefield ... F 2
Ridgefield Park ... B 2
Ridgewood ... E 2
Ringoes ... D 3
Ringwood ... E 1
Rio Grande ... D 5
Riverdale ... E 2
River Edge ... B 1
Riverside ... C 2
Riverton ... B 1
River Vale ... B 1
Rochelle Park ... B 2
Rockaway ... E 2
Roebling ... D 3
Roosevelt ... E 3
Roseland ... A 2
Roselle ... B 2
Roselle Park ... B 2
Rosenhayn ... C 5
Roxbury ... D 4
Rumson ... F 3
Runnemede ... B 3
Rutherford ... B 2

Saddle Brook ... B 1
Saddle River ... B 1
Salem ⊙ ... C 4
Sayreville ... E 3
Schooleys Mountain ... D 2
Scotch Plains ... E 2
Sea Bright ... F 3
Seabrook ... C 5
Sea Girt ... D 5
Sea Isle City ... D 5
Seaside Heights ... E 4
Seaside Park ... E 4
Secaucus ... B 2
Sewaren ... E 2
Sewell ... C 4
Ship Bottom ... E 5
Shrewsbury ... E 3
Sicklerville ... D 4
Singac ... D 2
Skillman ... D 3
Smithville ... C 5
Somerdale ... D 4
Somers Point ... D 5
Somerville ⊙ ... D 2
South Amboy ... E 2
South Belmar ... E 3
South Bound Brook ... D 4
South Brunswick ... E 3
South Orange ... A 2
South Plainfield ... E 2
South River ... E 3
South Toms River ... E 4
Sparta ... D 1
Spotswood ... E 3
Springfield ... E 2
Spring Lake ... E 3
Spring Lake Heights ... E 3
Stanhope ... D 2
Stanton ... E 2
Stewartsville ... D 3
Stillwater ... D 1
Stirling ... E 2
Stockholm ... B 1
Stockton ... D 3
Stone Harbor ... D 5
Stratford ... C 4
Succasunna ... D 2
Summit ... E 2
Surf City ... E 4
Sussex ... D 1
Swedesboro ... C 4
Tabor ... E 2
Teaneck ... B 2
Tenafly ... F 2
Teterboro ... B 2

Thorofare ... B 4
Tinton Falls ... E 3
Titusville ... D 3
Toms River ⊙ ... E 4
Totowa ... B 1
Towaco ... E 2
Tranquility ... D 2
Trenton (cap.) ⊙ ... D 3
Tuckerton ... E 4
Union ... E 2
Union Beach ... E 3
Union City ... C 2
Upper Greenwood Lake ... E 1
Upper Saddle River ... B 1
Vauxhall ... A 2
Ventnor City ... D 5
Vernon ... E 1
Verona ... E 2
Vienna ... D 2
Villas ... D 5
Vincentown ... D 4
Vineland ... C 5
Waldwick ... E 1
Wall ... E 3
Wallpack Center ... D 1
Wallington ... B 2
Wanamassa ... E 3
Wanaque ... E 1
Waretown ... E 4
Washington ... D 2
Watchung ... E 2
Waterford Works ... D 4
Wayne ... A 1
Weehawken ... C 2
Wenonah ... C 4
West Caldwell ... A 2
Westfield ... E 2
West Long Beach ... F 3
West Milford ... E 1
Westmont ... B 3
West New York ... C 2
West Orange ... A 2
West Paterson ... B 2
West Trenton ... D 3
Westville ... C 4
Westwood ... B 1
Wharton ... D 2
Whippany ... E 2
Whitehouse Station ... D 2
White House Station ... D 1
Whitesboro ... C 6
Whiting ... E 4
Wickatunk ... E 3
Wildwood ... D 6
Wildwood Crest ... D 6

Williamstown ... D 4
Willingboro ... D 3
Winfield ... B 3
Winslow ... D 4
Woodbine ... D 5
Woodbridge ... E 2
Woodbury ⊙ ... C 4
Woodbury Heights ... C 4
Woodcliff Lake ... B 1
Wood-Lynne ... B 3
Woodport ... D 2
Wood-Ridge ... B 2
Woodstown ... C 4
Wrightstown ... D 3
Wyckoff ... B 1
Yardville ... D 3
Zarephath ... D 2

Other Features

Arthur Kill (strait) ... B 3
Atlantic Highlands ... E 3
Barnegat (bay) ... E 4
Big Flat (brook) ... D 1
Big Timber (creek) ... C 4
Budd (lake) ... D 2
Cohansey (river) ... C 5
Cold Spring (inlet) ... D 6
Cooper (river) ... B 3
Culvers (lake) ... D 1
Delaware (bay) ... C 5
Delaware (river) ... D 2
Delaware Water Gap Nat'l Rec. Area ... C 1
Dix, Fort ... D 4
Earle Naval Weapons Station ... E 3
Edison Nat'l Hist. Site ... A 2
Egg Island (point) ... C 5
Fort Dix ... D 3
Fort Hancock ... F 3
Fort Monmouth ... E 3
Gateway Nat'l Rec. Area ... E 2
Great (bay) ... E 4
Great Egg Harbor (river) ... D 4
Greenwood (lake) ... E 1
Hackensack (river) ... F 1
Hancock, Fort ... F 3
High Point (mt.) ... D 1
Hopatcong (lake) ... D 2
Hudson (river) ... C 1
Island (beach) ... E 4
Kill Van Kull (strait) ... B 2

Kittatinny (mts.) ... D 1
Lakehurst Nav. Air Engineering Center ... E 3
Lamington (river) ... D 2
Little Egg (harbor) ... E 4
Long Beach (island) ... E 4
Lower New York (bay) ... E 2
McGuire AFB ... D 3
Manasquan (river) ... E 3
May (cape) ... C 6
Maurice (river) ... C 4
Metedeconk (river) ... E 3
Millstone (river) ... D 3
Mohawk (lake) ... D 1
Monmouth, Fort ... E 3
Morristown Nat'l Hist. Park ... D 2
Mullica (river) ... D 4
Musconetcong (river) ... C 2
Narrows, The (strait) ... E 3
Navesink (river) ... B 2
Newark (bay) ... B 2
Newark Int'l Airport ... B 2
Oradell (res.) ... B 1
Owassa (lake) ... C 1
Palisades ... D 1
Passaic (river) ... E 2
Paulins Kill (river) ... D 1
Pequest (river) ... D 2
Picatinny Arsenal ... D 2
Pines (lake) ... B 1
Pohatcong (creek) ... C 2
Pompton (lakes) ... B 1
Rancocas (creek) ... D 3
Ramapo (river) ... E 1
Raritan (bay) ... E 3
Raritan (river) ... D 2
Saddle (river) ... B 1
Salem (river) ... C 4
Sandy Hook (spit) ... F 3
Statue of Liberty Nat'l Mon. ... B 2
Swartswood (lake) ... D 1
Tappan (lake) ... C 1
Toms (river) ... D 5
Tuckahoe (river) ... C 5
Union (lake) ... C 5
Upper New York (bay) ... E 2
Wading (river) ... D 4
Wallkill (river) ... D 1
Wanaque (res.) ... E 1
Wawayanda (lake) ... E 1

⊙ County seat

osprey, and duck. Marine life of the Atlantic coast includes oysters, clams, crabs, flounder, bluefish, bass, and menhadon.

Mineral Resources. New Jersey has substantial deposits of several minerals such as stone (including granite, limestone, marble, slate), sand and gravel, clay, zinc, iron ore, and marl. Stone is chiefly found in the N part of New Jersey, and sand and gravel are found in many parts of the state.   H.H.F.

POPULATION
According to the 1980 census, New Jersey had 7,364,823 inhabitants, an increase of 2.7% over 1970. The average population density of 365 people per sq km (946 per sq mi) was higher than that of any other state. Whites made up 83.2% of the population and blacks 12.6%; additional population groups included some 29,507 persons of Asian Indian background, 24,377 persons of Filipino origin, 23,366 persons of Chinese descent, 12,845 persons of Korean extraction, 9905 persons of Japanese ancestry, and 8176 American Indians. Approximately 491,870 persons, or about 6.6% of the population, were of Hispanic (primarily Puerto Rican and Cuban) background. Roman Catholics formed the largest single religious group, constituting nearly two-fifths of the population. Other leading religious groups included Baptists, Episcopalians, Lutherans, and Jews. After California, New Jersey is the most urbanized state in the U.S. In 1980 about 89% of the state's residents lived in areas defined as urban, and the rest lived in rural areas. New Jersey's largest cities were Newark; Jersey City; Paterson; Elizabeth; and Trenton, the capital.

EDUCATION AND CULTURAL ACTIVITY
New Jersey has a comprehensive statewide educational system, a number of interesting historical sites, and a variety of cultural institutions. The state's residents also make use of the extensive cultural and educational facilities of New York City and Philadelphia.

Newark International Airport, one of the three main air terminals serving the New York metropolitan area.
Port Authority of New York and New Jersey

Education. In 1813 a group of New Jersey residents tried to establish a state-supported public school system. Not until 1871, however, did the legislature abolish all fees for instruction in public schools. The first state normal school (now Trenton State College) was founded in Trenton in 1855. In the early 1980s New Jersey had 2401 public elementary and secondary schools with a combined annual enrollment of about 822,000 elementary pupils and 427,000 secondary students. New Jersey also had more than 650 private schools, which together enrolled about 233,600 students.

The state's first institution of higher education, the College of New Jersey, now Princeton University, in Princeton, was founded in 1746. In the early 1980s New Jersey had 62 institutions of higher education with an aggregate annual enrollment of more than 321,600 students. Besides Princeton University, notable schools included Rutgers the State University of New Jersey, in New Brunswick; Princeton Theological Seminary (1812), in Princeton; Fairleigh Dickinson University (1942), in Rutherford; Stevens Institute of Technology (1870), in Hoboken; Rider College (1865), in Lawrenceville; Seton Hall University, in South Orange; Bloomfield College (1868), in Bloomfield; Drew University (1866), in Madison; Upsala College (1893), in East Orange; Kean College of New Jersey (1855), in Union; and William Paterson College (1855), in Wayne. The Institute for Advanced Study, in Princeton, is a noted center for research.

Cultural Institutions. New Jersey has a number of outstanding museums. These include the Art Museum at Princeton University; the Newark Museum, which has a noted collection of Oriental art, and the New Jersey Historical Society Museum, in Newark; the Morris Museum of Arts and Sciences, in Morristown; the Montclair Art Museum, in Montclair; the U.S. Army Communications-Electronics Museum, at Fort Monmouth; and the New Jersey State Museum, part of the state cultural center in Trenton.

The first public library in New Jersey was founded in 1750 in Trenton. In the early 1980s the state had some 330 public libraries.

Historical Sites. Many of New Jersey's historical sites commemorate people and places associated with the American Revolution. Red Bank Battlefield Park, in Woodbury, was the site of Fort Mercer; Batsto Area of the Wharton State Forest, in Batsto, was the site of the ironworks (founded c. 1766) that supplied cannonballs to U.S. forces during the revolution; and Morristown National Historical Park, in Morristown, encompasses the winter headquarters of the Continental Army in

A battle monument marks the spot where Gen. George Washington's Continental artillery opened fire on the Hessians at Trenton, N.J., on Dec. 26, 1776.
Trenton Chamber of Commerce

1777 and 1779–80. Other points of interest include the Princeton Battle Monument, in Princeton; the Trenton Battle Monument, in Trenton; the Historic Towne of Smithville, a restoration of an 18th-century community; and Edison National Historic Site, containing the library, workshop, laboratory, and home of Thomas A. Edison, in West Orange. Among the homes of noted figures are the James Fenimore Cooper House, located in Burlington; the Grover Cleveland Birthplace, located in Caldwell; and the Walt Whitman House, in Camden.

Sports and Recreation. New Jersey's seaside resorts are popular attractions for swimming, fishing, and boating enthusiasts. The leading resorts include Atlantic City, Asbury Park, Ocean City, Wildwood, and Cape May. Horseracing is another popular sport in the state, as are hunting and skiing. The big Meadowlands Sports Complex, in East Rutherford, includes an outdoor stadium, an indoor arena, and a horse racetrack.

Communications. In the early 1980s New Jersey had a communications system that included 39 AM and 36 FM commercial radiobroadcasting stations and 5 commercial television stations. The first radio station in New Jersey, and the second in the U.S., WJZ in Newark, was licensed in

1921; it subsequently was moved to New York City. WATV in Newark became (1948) the state's first commercial television station; it is now public station WNET. The *New Jersey Gazette,* New Jersey's first newspaper, was initially published in 1777 in Burlington. In the early 1980s New Jersey had 27 daily newspapers with a combined daily circulation of about 1,693,000. Influential newspapers included the *Star-Ledger,* in Newark; the *Trenton Times* and the *Trentonian;* the *Courier-Post,* in Camden; the *Record,* in Bergen Co.; and the *Asbury Park Press.*

GOVERNMENT AND POLITICS

New Jersey is governed under a constitution adopted in 1947 and put into effect in 1948, as amended. Two earlier constitutions had been adopted in 1776 and 1844. An amendment to the constitution may be proposed by the state legislature. To become effective, it must be approved by either a three-fifths majority of the legislature at one session or by a simple majority of each house at two successive sessions, and then by a majority of persons voting on the issue in a general election.

Executive. The chief executive of New Jersey is a governor, who is popularly elected to a 4-year term and who is limited to a maximum of two consecutive terms. The president of the Senate succeeds the governor should the latter resign, die, or be removed from office. The governor, with the consent of the Senate, appoints the state's principal executive officials, such as the secretary of state, treasurer, and attorney general.

Legislature. The bicameral New Jersey legislature is made up of a Senate and a General Assembly. The 40 members of the Senate are usually popularly elected to serve 4-year terms; Senate terms beginning in January of the second year following the U.S. decennial census, however, are for only two years. The 80 members of the General Assembly are popularly elected to 2-year terms.

Judiciary. New Jersey's highest court, the supreme court, is made up a chief justice and six associate judges. The appellate division of the superior court has 21 judges, and the superior court itself (the major trial court) has 236 judges. Judges of these courts are appointed by the governor, with the consent of the Senate, to 7-year terms.

Local Government. In the early 1980s, New Jersey had 21 counties, 53 cities, and 234 townships. Each of the counties was governed by an elected board of chosen freeholders.

National Representation. New Jersey elects 2 senators and 14 representatives to the U.S. Congress. The state has 16 electoral votes in presidential elections.

Politics. The Republican and Democratic parties in New Jersey are closely matched, but in presidential elections since 1948 the state's voters have generally favored the Republican nominee. An influential New Jersey Democrat, Peter Rodino (1909–), first elected to the U.S. House of Representatives in 1948, became chairman of the House Judiciary Committee in 1973.

ECONOMY

Since the late 19th century, manufacturing has been the leading economic activity of New Jersey, and in the early 1980s it was the state's leading employer. New Jersey also has a large tourist industry, and many workers are employed by commercial firms. Newark is a major center of the U.S. insurance industry, and the state has several important facilities engaged in the research and development of communications and electronic equipment. A large number of New Jersey residents commute to jobs in the nearby New York City and Philadelphia metropolitan areas.

Agriculture. Farming contributes relatively little to the New Jersey economy, but some agricultural commodities are produced in sizable quantities. The state is usually among the top ten U.S. states in the combined production of tomatoes and other vegetables. The state has some 9000 farms, which have an average size of about 45 ha (about 110 acres). About 72% of the annual farm income is derived from the sale of crops, and the rest comes from sales of livestock and livestock products. The chief crops are soybeans, hay, tomatoes, peaches, and corn. Also produced in large amounts are potatoes, eggplants, onions, peppers, beans, asparagus, apples, cranberries, blueberries, strawberries, and greenhouse and nursery products (especially commercial flowers). The SW counties of Salem, Cumberland, and Gloucester are particularly favored for vegetable production and have helped New Jersey earn its reputation as the Garden State. The principal livestock and livestock products produced in New Jersey are dairy goods, chicken eggs, beef cattle, hogs, chickens, and turkeys. Dairying is centered in the SW part of New Jersey, and poultry raising is important in the E counties.

Forestry and Fishing. Forestry in New Jersey is not an important commercial activity, although some wood pulp and other forestry products are produced. Trees in the state are mostly too small to be of commercial value.

New Jersey firms employ fewer than 400 workers in fishing. The state's yearly fish catch is valued at about $49.9 million. Approximately one-fourth of the clams caught in the U.S. come from New Jersey waters; major clam beds stretch from Barnegat Bay to Cape May. Other shellfish taken

NEW JERSEY

DATE OF STATEHOOD: December 18, 1787; 3d state

CAPITAL:	Trenton
MOTTO:	Liberty and prosperity
NICKNAME:	Garden State
STATE TREE:	Red oak
STATE FLOWER:	Violet
STATE BIRD:	Eastern Goldfinch
POPULATION (1980):	7,364,823; 9th among the states
AREA:	20,168 sq km (7787 sq mi); 46th largest state; includes 826 sq km (319 sq mi) of inland water
COASTLINE:	209 km (130 mi)
HIGHEST POINT:	High Point, 550 m (1803 ft)
LOWEST POINT:	Sea level, at the Atlantic coast
ELECTORAL VOTES:	16
U.S. CONGRESS:	2 senators; 14 representatives

POPULATION OF NEW JERSEY SINCE 1790

Year of Census	Population	Classified As Urban
1790	184,000	0%
1820	278,000	3%
1850	490,000	18%
1880	1,131,000	54%
1900	1,884,000	71%
1920	3,156,000	80%
1940	4,160,000	82%
1960	6,067,000	89%
1970	7,171,000	89%
1980	7,365,000	89%

POPULATION OF TEN LARGEST COMMUNITIES

	1980 Census	1970 Census
Newark	329,248	381,930
Jersey City	223,532	260,350
Paterson	137,970	144,824
Elizabeth	106,201	112,654
Trenton	92,124	104,786
Camden	84,910	102,551
East Orange	77,690	75,471
Clifton	74,388	82,437
Bayonne	65,047	72,743
Irvington	61,493	59,743

CLIMATE

	NEWARK	ATLANTIC CITY
Average January temperature range	−4.4° to 3.9° C (24° to 39° F)	−4.4° to 5° C (24° to 41° F)
Average July temperature range	19.4° to 30° C (67° to 86° F)	18.3° to 29.4° C (65° to 85° F)
Average annual temperature	12.2° C (54° F)	12.2° C (54° F)
Average annual precipitation	1041 mm (41 in)	1143 mm (45 in)
Average annual snowfall	711 mm (28 in)	406 mm (16 in)
Mean number of days per year with appreciable precipitation	122	113
Average daily relative humidity	63%	69%
Mean number of clear days per year	96	96

NATURAL REGIONS OF NEW JERSEY

NEW ENGLAND UPLAND
APPALACHIAN
VALLEY & RIDGE REGION
PIEDMONT
PLATEAU
Delaware R.
ATLANTIC
COASTAL
PLAIN

PRINCIPAL PRODUCTS
OF NEW JERSEY

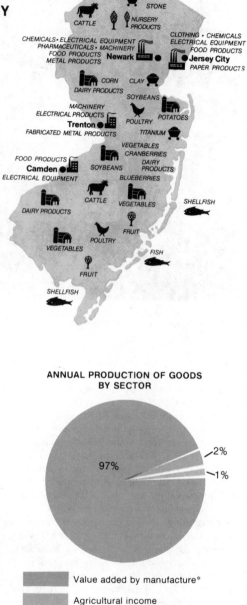

ECONOMY

State budget............... revenue $8.8 billion
                   expenditure $8.5 billion
State personal income tax, per capita $118
Personal income, per capita............ $10,924
Assets, commercial banks (176) ..... $34.3 billion
Labor force (civilian) 3,515,000
     Employed in services   27%
     Employed in manufacturing   23%
     Employed in wholesale and retail trade   19%

	Quantity Produced	Value
FARM PRODUCTS		**$431 million**
Crops		**$309 million**
Vegetables	278,000 metric tons	$70 million
Corn	246,000 metric tons	$28 million
Soybeans	95,000 metric tons	$27 million
Peaches	50,000 metric tons	$23 million
Hay	232,000 metric tons	$19 million
Livestock and Livestock Products		**$122 million**
Milk	220,000 metric tons	$67 million
Cattle	14,000 metric tons	$18 million
Eggs	279 million	$13 million
Hogs	6500 metric tons	$4 million
MINERALS		**$147 million**
Stone	10.3 million metric tons	$55 million
Sand, gravel	9.3 million metric tons	$44 million
Zinc	33,000 metric tons	$27 million
FISHING	**91,000 metric tons**	**$49.9 million**

	Labor and Proprietors' Income
FORESTRY	**$1.9 million**
MANUFACTURING	**$16.4 billion**
Chemicals and allied products	$3.2 billion
Electric and electronic equipment	$2.0 billion
Nonelectric machinery	$1.7 billion
Fabricated metal products	$1.3 billion
Food and kindred products	$1.1 billion
Printing and publishing	$951 million
Instruments and related products	$823 million
Paper and allied products	$693 million
Rubber and plastics products	$656 million
Apparel and other textile products	$644 million
OTHER	**$36.1 billion**
Services	$10.4 billion
Government and government enterprises	$8.1 billion
Transportation and public utilities	$3.0 billion
Finance, insurance, and real estate	$5.0 billion
Wholesale trade	$4.6 billion
Retail trade	$5.0 billion

ANNUAL PRODUCTION OF GOODS BY SECTOR

97%

2%

1%

Value added by manufacture*

Agricultural income

Value of minerals and fish

* The value added by an industry is a measure of the
value created in its products, not counting such production costs as raw materials and power.

Sources: U.S. government publications

A Japanese cargo ship is unloaded at a container-shipping installation at Port Elizabeth, N.J. Access to New York Harbor gives northern New Jersey a large international
shipping trade.   D. Brewster–Bruce Coleman, Inc.

are crab, lobster, oysters, and scallops. Saltwater finfish such as croaker, flounder, bluefish, and weakfish are caught by commercial fishers and processed locally.

Mining. The annual value of the output of the New Jersey mining industry, which employs some 2500 workers, is about $147 million. The leading mineral products are basalt, limestone, granite, and other types of stone; sand and gravel; zinc; and titanium. Also produced in significant amounts are clay, magnesium compounds, peat, greensand marl, and sulfur.

Manufacturing. The leading sector by far of the New Jersey economy is manufacturing, which accounts for about 97% of the yearly value of goods produced in the state. The principal products include chemicals, processed food, electrical and electronic equipment, and nonelectrical machinery. New Jersey is one of the leading U.S. states in chemical production; products include petrochemicals, pharmaceuticals, and basic chemicals such as sulfuric acid. A wide variety of food products are processed in New Jersey; among them are canned and frozen vegetables and fruit, packed meat, and baked goods. Among the electrical and electronic items produced in the state are communications equipment, home appliances, and motors. Other important manufactures of New Jersey include fabricated metal, transportation equipment, printed materials, pottery and fine china, glass, paper goods, clothing, and instruments. The NE part of the state is the leading manufacturing area; another important industrial region, in central and S New Jersey, includes the cities of Trenton and Camden.

Tourism. The tourist industry is an important part of the New Jersey economy. Most visitors are attracted by the state's ocean resorts; Atlantic City, which has large gambling casinos, is particularly popular. Many travelers also are lured by the mountains, lakes, and scenic areas (such as the Delaware Water Gap) of the NW part of the state and by the Pine Barrens of the S. New Jersey maintains some 106 state parks and recreation areas.

Transportation. New Jersey is an important link between the big industrial areas of New York State and New England and the S and W parts of the U.S. The state has about 54,410 km (about 33,810 mi) of roads, including 536 km (333 mi) of Interstate Highways. The New Jersey Turnpike is a major N-S artery for commercial and private vehicles. The state is connected by bridges and tunnels with New York City and by bridges with

Pennsylvania and Delaware. New Jersey is served by about 2590 km (about 1610 mi) of operated railroad track. The seaports at Newark and Elizabeth, both regulated by the Port Authority of New York and New Jersey, are among the most important in the U.S. and have modern facilities for handling containerized freight. Smaller ports are on the Delaware R. at Paulsboro, Camden, Gloucester City, and Trenton. New Jersey has about 270 airports. The busiest by far is Newark International Airport. Many smaller craft use Teterboro Airport.

Energy. The electricity-generating plants of New Jersey have an installed capacity of about 12.6 million kw and produce some 29.4 billion kwh of electricity each year. Approximately 29% of the annual electricity output is generated in facilities using petroleum products, about 22% in coal-burning installations, some 26% in nuclear power plants, and about 23% in facilities consuming natural gas.   W.J.Y.

HISTORY

The Indians of the region that is now New Jersey were known as the Delaware or Leni-Lenape ("original people"). Classified as members of the Algonquian group, the Indians were subdivided into three tribal units—the Minsi, Unami, and Unalactigo.

The Colonial and Revolutionary Periods. The area was claimed by both the Dutch and the English when they began to found colonies on the coast of North America in the early 17th century. The Dutch founded settlements at Fort Nassau (present-day Glouster City) on the Delaware River in 1624, and at Pavonia (now part of Jersey City) in 1630. Swedish settlements on the Delaware were taken over by the Dutch in 1655. Nevertheless, New Jersey was still sparsely settled in 1664, when King Charles II of England granted all the territory between the Connecticut and Delaware rivers to his brother, James, duke of York (later King James II).

British rule. James ousted the Dutch and assigned New Jersey to two close friends, Sir George Carteret and John, Lord Berkeley (d. 1678), who named it after the island of Jersey in the English Channel. Assuming governmental control, the two proprietors issued a constitution known as the Concessions and Agreement of 1665, which provided that freeholders were annually to elect members of an assembly and which offered freedom of religious beliefs. English settlers resisted the proprietors' authority, however, and in 1674 Berkeley sold his half interest to a consortium of Quakers. Boundaries had to be established between Quaker property and the Carteret proprietary, and this resulted in a

division into East and West Jersey. Carteret's estate of East Jersey was auctioned off after his death in 1681. Acquired by William Penn and associates, it was soon subdivided amid conflicting claims. West Jersey, also a Quaker province, had similar problems over land grants.

In 1702 East and West Jersey were united as the royal province of New Jersey. By that date, its population was made up of people from the British Isles, Holland, Belgium, France, and Germany, as well as slaves from Africa and the West Indies.

Conflicts among rival political factions over fiscal and land policies continued to trouble the colony until the eve of the American Revolution. Part of the problem stemmed from the fact that New Jersey shared royally appointed governors with New York until 1738. The first governor appointed for New Jersey alone was Lewis Morris, who served from 1738 until his death in 1746. The economy of colonial New Jersey was based on agriculture, including the breeding of livestock; the area also contained iron mines, and iron manufactures were produced.

The American Revolution. New Jersey's last royal governor was William Franklin, son of Benjamin Franklin. Assuming office in 1763, he remained in power until 1776, when he was deposed by a provincial congress for siding with the British during the Revolution. Sentiment in the province was divided over the revolutionary cause, but New Jersey gradually moved into the patriot camp after 1774. On July 2, 1776, the same provincial congress that deposed Franklin approved a state constitution. The first state governor was William Livingston, who remained in office until his death in 1790.

Several important battles of the Revolution were fought in New Jersey. The Americans were routed at Fort Lee (November 1776) but won victories at Trenton (December 1776), Princeton (1777), Monmouth (1778), and Springfield (1780). George Washington's army encamped at Morristown and other localities within the state. At the war's conclusion, the Continental Congress established the nation's capital at Princeton from June until November 1783.

Early Statehood. Because of a continuing controversy with New York over transportation rights on the Hudson River and over the use of New York Harbor, New Jersey favored a new federal constitution that would protect the rights of the smaller states. At the Constitutional Convention, held in Philadelphia in 1787, the New Jersey delegates led small-state efforts that resulted in the adoption of equal representation in the U.S. Senate.

Alexander Hamilton, the first U.S. secretary of

Atlantic City, a classic resort
community with a new angle:
legalized casino gambling.
City of Atlantic City

the treasury, envisioned the creation of a manufacturing complex along the falls of the Passaic
River and founded the Society for Useful Manufactures in the new community of Paterson.

Under New Jersey's state constitution of 1776
women were granted suffrage, but when a number of women voted in disputed local elections
in 1807, the legislature rescinded this right with
the Suffrage Reform Act.

Industrial New Jersey. The state remained primarily agricultural into the 1820s. Manufacturing
became important after 1840, when Paterson, already a textile center, began manufacturing armaments and locomotives. The American Civil
War provided further impetus for industrialization. By 1900 the population had grown to more
than 900,000, with the greatest increase centered
in Jersey City, Newark, Bayonne, and Passaic. Paterson became a symbol for bitter labor strife in
the early decades of the 20th century, when the
city's factory workers struggled to organize to
improve their work and wage conditions.

Woodrow Wilson, the 28th president of the
U.S., first achieved prominence as president of
Princeton University and as Democratic governor
of New Jersey (1910–12). Wilson established a
record as a reform governor before moving on to

the presidency in the election of 1912. State politics in the post–World War I era was associated
with "bossism" under Frank Hague (1876–1956)
of Jersey City, who was an influential figure in
New Jersey from 1913 to 1947.

After World War II, New Jersey experienced an
industrial and population boom, becoming the
eighth most populous state by 1960. Immigrant
groups in the early 20th century included Irish,
Italians, Jews, and Slovaks; blacks, Puerto Ricans,
and Cubans came in later decades. The construction of a containerization center at Port Newark,
the burgeoning Newark International Airport,
the emerging Meadowlands Sports Complex in
East Rutherford, and the establishment of gambling casinos in Atlantic City brought new jobs
to New Jersey during the 1970s. New Jersey's industrialization continued apace in the early
1980s, but some 40 percent of the state was still
forest or woodlands, and an additional 21 percent was used to grow fruits and vegetables. J.Ju.

*For further information on this topic, see the
Bibliography in volume 28,* section 1177.

NEW JERUSALEM, CHURCH OF THE. *See*
SWEDENBORG, EMANUEL.

NEW LONDON, city, New London Co., SE Connecticut, on the Thames R. near its mouth on

20

Long Island Sound; inc. as a city 1784. It is an industrial city and summer resort and has a deep-water port. Major manufactures include submarines, pharmaceuticals, printed materials, chemicals, and textiles. New London is the site of Connecticut College (1911), a junior college, the U.S. Coast Guard Academy, and a U.S. Navy submarine base. Points of interest include the Lyman Allyn art museum; the Olde Town Mill, a gristmill built in 1650; and the Joshua Hempsted House (1678), a restored colonial house. The annual boat races between Harvard and Yale universities are held here on the Thames. The settlement was laid out by the English colonist John Winthrop and his followers in 1646. During the American Revolution it was an important base for privateers and was attacked and burned in 1781 by British forces led by Benedict Arnold, formerly a general for the colonial forces. In the 19th century the city was a leading shipbuilding center and a whaling port. Pop. (1970) 31,630; (1980) 28,842.

NEWMAN, Barnett (1905–70), American abstract expressionist painter and a prominent exponent of its color-field wing. He is best known for his highly simplified canvases in which a large block of color, or color-field, is broken by one or more vertical lines. In his early works of the 1940s, Newman consciously attempted to reject contemporary American and European influences; his arrangements of loose vertical and horizontal lines and circular forms were intended simply as representations of surfaces and voids. In 1948, with *Onement I* (Newman Collection, New York City), he restricted himself to a solid-color canvas broken by a single contrasting vertical band, a format he was to follow for the rest of his life. By treating the band of color not as a sharply defined stripe but as a rough-edged strip, Newman attempted to create a sense of tension on the canvas, as though the main color-field was ripped or torn apart by the ascending vertical. His work strongly influenced other abstract expressionist painters.

NEWMAN, John Henry (1801–90), English clergyman, who was leader of the Oxford movement, and cardinal after his conversion to the Roman Catholic church; outstanding religious thinker and essayist.

Born on Feb. 21, 1801, Newman was educated at Trinity College, University of Oxford. In 1822 he obtained an Oriel College fellowship, then the highest distinction of Oxford scholarship, and thus was brought into close association with a number of the most illustrious men of the time. In 1826 Newman was appointed a tutor at Oriel and two years later became vicar of Saint Mary's,

the (Anglican) church of the University of Oxford. In this position he exerted a pervasive influence on contemporary religious thought through his learned and eloquent sermons. He resigned his tutorship in 1832 and in the following year made a tour of the Mediterranean region, during which he wrote the famous hymn "Lead, Kindly Light."

Newman returned to England in time to hear the memorable sermon "On the National Apostasy," preached at St. Mary's by John Keble, a fellow Oxonian. This sermon defined the religious issues of the time and marked the inception of the Oxford movement, a movement within the Church of England directed against the growth of theological liberalism and advocating the return to theology and ritual of the period following the Reformation.

Newman, whose own religious thinking had for some time been along similar lines, soon became the acknowledged leader of the Oxford group, a role for which his vital personality, fervent asceticism, and persuasive eloquence preeminently qualified him. He was one of the chief contributors to the *Tracts for the Times* (1833–41), for which he wrote 29 papers, including the famous *Tract 90,* which terminated the series. That final tract provoked a storm of opposition by its claim that the Thirty-nine Articles of the Church of England, which incorporate the creed of the Reformed Church in England, are aimed primarily at the abuses and not the dogmas of Roman Catholicism. The thesis was repudiated by Anglican dignitaries, who almost universally declared against the Oxford movement.

In 1842 Newman retired from Oxford to the neighboring village of Littlemore, where he passed three years in seclusion, writing at this time a formal retraction of the adverse criticisms of the Roman Catholic church that he had made on previous occasions. He also resigned his post as vicar of St. Mary's, and on Oct. 9, 1845, after writing his *Essay on the Development of Christian Doctrine,* which expressed the final crystallization of his ideas, he became a Roman Catholic. A year later he went to Rome, where he was ordained priest and entered the Congregation of the Oratory. On his return to England he introduced the Oratorians there.

Newman spent most of the remainder of his life in the house of the Oratory that he had established near Birmingham. From 1854 to 1858, however, he served as rector of a Roman Catholic university that the bishops of Ireland were attempting to establish in Dublin. The institution failed, but while there Newman delivered a series of lectures, subsequently revised and pub-

Cardinal John Henry Newman   Bettmann Archive

lished as *The Idea of a University Defined* (1873), in which he defined the function of a university as the training of the mind rather than the diffusion of practical information. In response to a charge by the British novelist Charles Kingsley that Roman Catholicism was indifferent to the truth, Newman in 1864 published his masterpiece, *Apologia pro Vita Sua* (Apology for His Life), a memorable account of his spiritual development that is an acknowledged classic both of religious autobiography and English prose. He was elected an honorary fellow of Trinity College, Oxford, in 1877, and Pope Leo XIII created him a cardinal in 1879. He died Aug. 11, 1890. Newman's other important writings include *An Essay in Aid of a Grammar of Assent* (1870), a closely reasoned work on the philosophy of faith. He also wrote the novels *Loss and Gain* (1848) and *Callista* (1856); *The Dream of Gerontius* (1865), a monologue in verse; and *Verses on Various Occasions* (1874).

NEWMARKET, town, in Forest Heath District, Suffolk, E England. Newmarket has some light industry, but is known as a horseracing and horse training center. Races have been held here since the early 17th century. Devil's Dyke, an Anglo-Saxon defensive mound and ditch, traverses one of the racecourses. Pop. (Forest Heath District, 1981) 51,907.

NEWMARKET, industrial town, Regional Municipality of York, SE Ontario, Canada, on the Holland R., near Lake Simcoe. Major manufactures include metal and plastic products, motor-vehicle parts, writing instruments, processed food, and building materials. The site was settled by Quakers around 1800. Pop. (1976) 24,795; (1981) 29,753.

NEW MEXICO, one of the Mountain states of the U.S., bounded on the N by Colorado, on the E by Oklahoma and Texas, on the S by Texas and the Mexican state of Chihuahua, and on the W by Arizona.

New Mexico entered the Union on Jan. 6, 1912, as the 47th state. In the early 1980s, although manufacturing had grown in importance, New Mexico's economy continued to be dominated by mining, crop farming, and ranching. Tourism is also important. Visitors are attracted not only by the scenic beauty of its deserts and mountains but also by the rich Indian and Spanish cultural heritage that distinguishes the state. The region N of Mexico was named Nuevo Mexico by a Spanish explorer in the 1560s. The name was translated and applied to the U.S. territory organized in 1850 and later to the state. New Mexico is called the Land of Enchantment.

LAND AND RESOURCES

New Mexico, with an area of 314,924 sq km (121,593 sq mi), is the fifth largest state in the U.S.; 33.2% of the land area is owned by the federal government. The state is roughly square in shape, and its extreme dimensions are about 630 km (about 390 mi) from N to S and about 565 km (about 350 mi) from E to W. Elevations range from 859 m (2817 ft) at Red Bluff Lake in the SE to 4011 m (13,161 ft) atop Wheeler Peak in the N. The approximate mean elevation in the state is 1737 m (5700 ft).

Physical Geography. New Mexico has great diversity of topographic relief, from desert basins to lofty snowcapped peaks. The E third of the state is part of the Great Plains. The portion of this region lying S of the Canadian R. is known as the High Plains, or Llano Estacado (q.v.). The N portion contains eroded formations such as mesas and buttes. The N central part of the state is occupied by an extension of the Rocky Mts. The gorge of the Rio Grande extends from N to S, dividing this rugged region in half: To the E lie the Sangre de Cristo Mts.; to the W are the Nacimiento Mts. The central and SW parts of the state are occupied by the Basin and Range Region, which consists of a series of mountain ranges interspersed with valleys and desert basins. The NW quadrant of New Mexico is part of the Colorado Plateau, an area of broad valleys and plains, cut by deep canyons and dotted with mesas. The San Juan Basin in the extreme NE of this region is an area of relatively low relief.

Rivers and Lakes. The major rivers of New Mexico rise in the Rocky Mts. region and radiate out-

Religious beliefs are colorfully expressed among the New Mexico Pueblos, as in this ritual dance performed by the Tesuque Pueblos on Christmas day. The Tesuque Pueblos inhabit one of 19 pueblos, or adobe communes, in New Mexico.

Jacques Jangoux–Peter Arnold, Inc.

ward. The state's major river, the Rio Grande, flows S through the center of the state and provides water for the many settlements in its valley. The Pecos R., a tributary of the Rio Grande, rises in the Sangre de Cristo Mts. and flows S. The Canadian R. and its tributaries flow generally E across the NE part of the state. The Chaco and San Juan rivers flow generally W across the NW part of the state. In the SW two rivers that do not rise in the Rocky Mts.—the Gila and San Francisco—are locally important; both flow W. New Mexico has few sizable natural lakes, and most of these are found in the mountain ranges of the N central part of the state. Larger artificial bodies of water include Elephant Butte Reservoir, as well as Conchas Lake, Caballo and Navajo reservoirs, and Lake Sumner.

Climate. New Mexico has a mild, semiarid to arid continental climate. Although topographic diversity causes a wide range of precipitation and temperatures, the climate can be characterized as one of abundant sunshine, low relative humidity, and a wide annual and daily temperature range. The average annual temperature ranges from about 4.4° C (about 40° F) in the mountains of the N central region to about 17.8° C (about 64° F) in the S. The recorded temperature has ranged from −45.6° C (−50° F) in 1951 to 46.7° C (116° F) in 1934. The average annual precipitation ranges from only 254 mm (10 in) in the S and central parts of the state to more than 508 mm (more than 20 in) in the mountainous areas. Most rain falls in thundershowers. Annual snowfall averages from 76 mm (3 in) in the S to 2540 mm (100 in) in the N mountains.

Plants and Animals. More than 6000 species of plants have been identified in New Mexico, ranging from desert plants to alpine vegetation. Various grasses and shrubs are found in the Great Plains region. In the deserts of the S are cactus, mesquite, sagebrush, and, near watercourses, cottonwood and desert willow trees. On lower mountain slopes are desert grasses, creosote bush, juniper, and piñon pine. At higher elevations are forests of yellow, ponderosa, and bristlecone pine, as well as oak, maple, aspen, spruce, and birch. A total of 23% of New Mexico's land area is forest-covered, less than one-third of which is of commercial value.

Because of the diversity of natural environments, New Mexico has a great variety of wildlife. Among the larger mammals are black bear,

INDEX TO MAP OF NEW MEXICO

Cities and Towns

Acoma . . . . B 2
Alamogordo ⊙ . . . . . . C 3
Albuquerque ⊙ . . . . . B 2
Animas . . . . A 4
Anthony . . . . B 3
Anton Chico . . . . C 2
Arroyo Hondo . . . . C 1
Artesia . . . . C 3
Aztec ⊙ . . . . B 1
Bayard . . . . A 3
Belen . . . . B 2
Bernalillo ⊙ . . . . B 2
Blanco . . . . B 1
Bloomfield . . . . A 1
Bluewater . . . . A 2
Buckhorn . . . . A 3
Canjilon . . . . B 1
Capitan . . . . C 3
Carlsbad ⊙ . . . . C 3
Carrizozo ⊙ . . . . C 3
Central . . . . A 3
Chama . . . . B 1
Chimayo . . . . C 2
Cimarron . . . . C 1
Clayton ⊙ . . . . D 1
Clovis ⊙ . . . . D 2
Columbus . . . . B 4
Corona . . . . C 2
Corrales . . . . B 2
Crownpoint . . . . A 2
Cuba . . . . B 2
Deming ⊙ . . . . B 3
Dexter . . . . C 3
Dixon . . . . C 1
Dulce . . . . B 1
Elida . . . . D 3
El Rito . . . . B 1
Encino . . . . C 2
Espanola . . . . B 1
Estancia . . . . B 2
Eunice . . . . D 3
Farmington . . . . A 1
Fort Sumner ⊙ . . . . . . C 2
Gallup ⊙ . . . . A 2
Gamerco . . . . A 2
Glorieta . . . . C 2
Grants ⊙ . . . . B 2
Hagerman . . . . C 3
Hanover . . . . A 3
Hatch . . . . B 3
Hobbs . . . . D 3
Hurley . . . . A 3
Isleta . . . . B 2
Jal . . . . D 3

⊙ County seat

Jarales . . . . B 2
Jemez Pueblo . . . . B 2
La Jara . . . . B 1
La Mesa . . . . B 3
Las Cruces ⊙ . . . . B 3
Las Vegas ⊙ . . . . C 2
La Union ⊙ . . . . B 4
Lemitar . . . . B 2
Lincoln . . . . C 3
Logan . . . . D 2
Lordsburg ⊙ . . . . A 3
Los Alamos ⊙ . . . . B 2
Los Lunas ⊙ . . . . B 2
Loving . . . . C 3
Lovington ⊙ . . . . D 3
Magdalena . . . . B 2
Manuelito . . . . A 2
Maxwell . . . . C 1
Melrose . . . . D 2
Mescalero . . . . C 3
Mesilla . . . . B 3
Milan . . . . B 2
Mora ⊙ . . . . C 2
Moriarty . . . . C 2
Mosquero ⊙ . . . . C 2
Mountainair . . . . B 2
Oil Center . . . . D 3
Paguate . . . . B 2
Pecos . . . . C 2
Penasco . . . . C 1
Portales ⊙ . . . . D 2
Pueblo of Acoma . . . . . B 2
Quemado . . . . A 2
Questa . . . . C 1
Ranches of Taos . . . . . . C 1
Raton ⊙ . . . . C 1
Reserve ⊙ . . . . A 3
Rincon . . . . B 3
Roswell ⊙ . . . . C 3
Rowe . . . . C 2
Roy . . . . C 2
Ruidoso . . . . C 3
San Antonio . . . . B 3
San Felipe Pueblo . . . . . B 2
San Juan Pueblo . . . . . . B 1
San Mateo . . . . B 2
San Rafael . . . . A 2
Santa Fe ⊙ (cap.) . . . . . B 2
Santa Rita . . . . B 3
Santa Rosa ⊙ . . . . C 2
Santo Domingo
  Pueblo . . . . B 2
Shiprock . . . . A 1
Silver City ⊙ . . . . A 3
Socorro ⊙ . . . . B 2
Springer . . . . C 1
Taos ⊙ . . . . C 1
Tatum ⊙ . . . . D 3

Tesuque . . . . C 2
Texico . . . . D 2
Thoreau . . . . A 2
Tierra Amarilla ⊙ . . . . . B 1
Tijeras . . . . B 2
Toadlena . . . . A 1
Truchas . . . . C 1
Truth or
  Consequences ⊙ . . . B 3
Tucumcari ⊙ . . . . D 2
Tularosa . . . . C 3
University Park . . . . B 3
Vaughn . . . . C 2
Velarde . . . . B 1
Wagon Mound . . . . C 1
Watrous . . . . C 2
Zuni . . . . A 2

Other Features

Alamosa (river) . . . . B 3
Animas (river) . . . . B 1
Avalon (lake) . . . . C 3
Aztec Ruins Nat'l
  Mon. . . . . A 1
Bandelier Nat'l Mon. . . . B 2
Black (mt. range) . . . . . . B 3
Blanco (creek) . . . . D 2
Caballo (mts.) . . . . B 3
Caballo (res.) . . . . B 3
Canadian (river) . . . . . . D 2
Cannon AFB . . . . D 2
Capulin Mountain
  Nat'l Mon. . . . . C 1
Carlsbad Caverns
  Nat'l Park . . . . C 3
Carrizo (creek) . . . . D 1
Chaco (river) . . . . A 1
Chaco Culture Nat'l
  Hist. Park . . . . B 1
Chuska (mts.) . . . . A 1
Conchas (dam) . . . . C 2
Conchas (lake) . . . . C 2
Corrumpa (creek) . . . . . D 1
Delaware (creek) . . . . . . C 4
Dry Cimarron (river) . . . D 1
Eagle Nest (lake) . . . . . C 1
Elephant Butte (res.) . . . B 3
El Morro Nat'l Mon. . . . . A 2
Fifteenmile Arroyo
  (creek) . . . . C 2
Fort Bliss Military
  Reservation . . . . B 3
Fort Union Nat'l Mon. . . C 2
Gallinas (mts.) . . . . B 2
Georgia O'Keeffe Nat'l
  Hist. Site . . . . B 1

Gila (river) . . . . A 3
Gila Cliff Dwellings
  Nat'l Mon. . . . . A 3
Great Plains (plains) . . D 2,3
Guadalupe (mts.) . . . . . C 3
Holloman AFB . . . . B 3
Jicarilla Ind. Res. . . . . . B 1
Jornada del Muerto
  (valley) . . . . B 3
Kirtland AFB . . . . B 2
Llano Estacado (plain) . . D 3
McMillan (lake) . . . . C 3
Manzano (mts.) . . . . B 2
Mescalero Apache
  Ind. Res. . . . . C 3
Mimbres (mts.) . . . . B 3
Navajo (res.) . . . . B 1
Navajo Indian Res. . . . . A 1
Pecos (river) . . . . C 2
Pecos Nat'l Mon. . . . . . C 2
Perro (lagoon) . . . . C 2
Pueblo Ind. Res. . . . . B 2, C 2
Puerco (river) . . . . A 2
Red Bluff (lake) . . . . D 4
Rio Grande (river) . . . . . B 2
Rio Hondo (river) . . . . . C 3
Rio Penasco (river) . . . . C 3
Rio Puerco (river) . . . . . B 2
Sacramento (mts.) . . . . . C 3
Salinas Nat'l Mon. . . . . . B 2
Salt (creek) . . . . C 3
Salt (lake) . . . . D 2
San Andres (mts.) . . . . . B 3
San Francisco (river) . . . A 3
Sangre de Cristo (mt.
  range) . . . . C 1
San Juan (mts.) . . . . B 1
San Juan (river) . . . . . . A 1
San Mateo (mts.) . . . . . B 3
Sierra Blanca Pk. (mt.) . . B 3
So. Ute Ind. Res. . . . . . B 1
Sumner (dam) . . . . C 2
Sumner (lake) . . . . C 2
Taylor (mt.) . . . . B 2
Tularosa (valley) . . . . . . B 3
Ute (creek) . . . . D 2
Ute (res.) . . . . D 2
Ute Mountain Ind.
  Res. . . . . A 1
Wheeler Peak (mt.) . . . . C 1
White Sands Missile
  Range . . . . B 3
White Sands Nat'l
  Mon. . . . . B 3
Whitewater Baldy (mt.) . . A 3
Zuni (river) . . . . A 2
Zuni Indian Res. . . . . . . A 2

pronghorn antelope, mountain lion, bobcat, mule and white-tailed deer, and coyote. Barbary sheep from North Africa have been introduced in mountain areas. Other wildlife includes jack rabbit, badger, prairie dog, mink, and beaver. Game birds include prairie chickens, quail, grouse, pheasant, and wild turkey. Rattlesnakes are also present, and the tarantula is found in the SW. Streams contain trout, bass, crappie, and catfish. **Mineral Resources.** New Mexico is rich in minerals, especially energy-related minerals. Coal, petroleum, and natural gas occur in the San Juan Basin and at various places in the Great Plains region. Major uranium sources are in the W part of the state. Potash, found in the SE, and copper, mined in the SW, are also important. Other mineral resources include gold, silver, iron ore, lead, manganese, molybdenum, and zinc.   R.W.D.

POPULATION

According to the 1980 census, New Mexico had 1,302,981 inhabitants, an increase of 28.1% over 1970. The average population density was only 4 people per sq km (11 per sq mi). Whites made up 75.1% of the population and blacks 1.8%. Also residing in the state were some 104,634 American Indians, constituting about 8% of the total population. The principal Indian groups were the Pueblo (see PUEBLO INDIANS), Navajo (see NAVAJO INDIANS), and Apache (q.v.); many of the Indians resided on reservations in the state. Some 476,089 persons, or nearly 37% of the total population, were of Hispanic background. The Spanish-Mexican cultural influence is strong, and many people in the state speak both Spanish and English. Roman Catholics formed the largest single religious group, and the state also had sub-

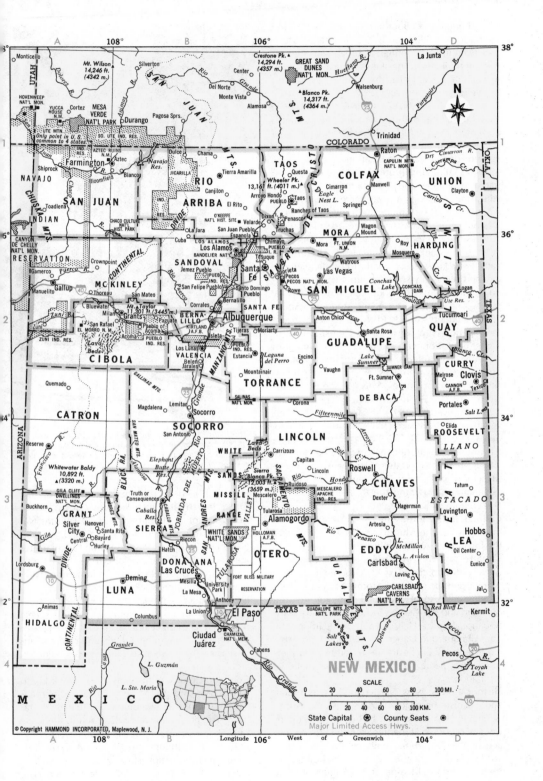

NEW MEXICO

SCALE

| | 20 | 40 | 60 | 80 | 100 MI. |

| 0 | 20 40 | 60 | 80 | 100 KM. |

State Capital ⊛   County Seats ●

Major Limited Access Hwys.

25

stantial numbers of Southern Baptists and United Methodists. In 1980 about 72% of all New Mexicans lived in areas defined as urban, and the rest lived in rural areas. The state's largest cities were Albuquerque; Santa Fe, the capital; Las Cruces; Roswell; Farmington; and Clovis.

EDUCATION AND CULTURAL ACTIVITY

New Mexico has had to overcome the problems presented by a widely scattered and bilingual population in order to proceed with the development of the state's educational system. New Mexico's cultural institutions are largely concentrated in Santa Fe and Albuquerque.

Education. Although a royal decree provided for a public school system for the territory in 1721, it was not until the 1850s that the first permanent schools were founded in New Mexico. The public school system was established in 1891. In the early 1980s New Mexico had 618 public elementary and secondary schools with a combined annual enrollment of about 186,200 elementary pupils and 89,600 secondary students. About 18,400 students attended private schools. In the same period New Mexico had 19 institutions of higher education with a combined enrollment of about 58,300 students. Among the most notable of these schools were New Mexico State University (1888), in Las Cruces; New Mexico Highlands University (1893), in Las Vegas; Western New Mexico University (1893), in Silver City; the University of New Mexico (1889) and the University of Albuquerque (1920), both in Albuquerque; New Mexico Institute of Mining and Technology (1889), in Socorro; Eastern New Mexico University (1927), in Portales; and Saint John's College at Santa Fe (1964) and the College of Santa Fe (1947), both in Santa Fe.

Cultural Institutions. Among the state's major museums are the Museum of New Mexico and the Institute of American Indian Arts Museum, in Santa Fe, and the Art Museum of the University of New Mexico, the Maxwell Museum of Anthropology, and the National Atomic Museum, in Albuquerque. Also of importance are the Roswell Museum and Art Center, in Roswell, and the International Space Hall of Fame, in Alamogordo. The Albuquerque Dance Theater and New Mexico Symphony Orchestra are based in Albuquerque. The Santa Fe Opera has a national reputation.

Historical Sites. New Mexico honors its Indian and Spanish heritage in many historical sites. Acoma Pueblo is believed to be the oldest continually occupied settlement in the U.S. The Palace of the Governors, built by the Spanish in 1610 in Santa Fe, is the oldest public building in the U.S., and the Mission of San Miguel of Santa

The relatively modern fine arts building of the Museum of New Mexico, in Santa Fe, retains the charm of the colonial Spanish past. Each facade is modeled after a historic New Mexico mission church.   UPI

Fe is one of the oldest churches in the country. Other Indian sites include Taos Pueblo; Aztec Ruins National Monument; Chaco Culture National Historical Park; and Gila Cliff Dwellings National Monument. Two important natural sites are Carlsbad Caverns National Park, near Carlsbad, and El Morro National Monument, encompassing Inscription Rock, near Grants.

Sports and Recreation. New Mexico's vast areas of national forests and mountains and its scenic rivers and lakes make it a haven for hunting, fishing, boating, swimming, hiking, and camping enthusiasts. The state also has several major ski areas.

Communications. In the early 1980s New Mexico had 57 AM and 29 FM commercial radiobroadcasting stations and 9 commercial television stations. The first radio station licensed in the state, KOB in Albuquerque, began operation in 1922. KOB-TV in Albuquergue, New Mexico's first commercial television station, began broadcasting in 1948. *El Crepúsculo de la Libertad* (The

Dawn of Liberty), the state's first Spanish-language newspaper, and the *Santa Fe Republican,* the first English-language newspaper, were initially printed in Santa Fe in 1834 and 1847, respectively. In the early 1980 New Mexico had 20 daily newspapers with a total daily circulation of about 273,000; they included the *Albuquerque Journal* and the *Albuquerque Tribune,* in Albuquerque, and *The New Mexican,* in Santa Fe.

GOVERNMENT AND POLITICS

New Mexico is governed under its original constitution, adopted in 1911 and put into effect in 1912, as amended. An amendment to the constitution may be proposed by the legislature or by a constitutional convention. To become effective, an amendment proposed by the legislature must be approved by persons voting on the issue in a general election.

Executive. The chief executive of New Mexico is a governor, who is popularly elected to a 4-year term and who must wait one full term before being eligible for a second term. The popularly elected lieutenant governor succeeds the governor should the latter resign, die, or be removed from office. Other elected state officials include the secretary of state, attorney general, treasurer, auditor, and commissioner of public lands.

Irrigation projects are transforming the parched soil of New Mexico into colorful, productive land.
U.S. Bureau of Reclamation

Legislature. The bicameral New Mexico legislature is composed of a Senate and a House of Representatives. The 42 members of the Senate are elected to 4-year terms, and the 70 members of the House are elected to 2-year terms.

Judiciary. New Mexico's highest court, the supreme court, has five justices elected to 8-year terms. The intermediate court of appeals is composed of seven judges elected to 8-year terms. The major trial courts are the district courts, with a total of 49 judges elected to serve 6-year terms.

Local Government. In the early 1980s New Mexico had 33 counties and 95 incorporated municipalities. Each county is governed by three county commissioners. New Mexico's Indian reservations are managed by elective councils.

National Representation. New Mexico elects two senators and three representatives to the U.S. Congress. The state has five electoral votes in presidential elections.

Politics. Since statehood, in both state and national politics, Democrats and Republicans have been elected in relatively equal numbers. Peter V. Domenici (1932–), a Republican elected to the U.S. Senate in 1972, became chairman of the Senate Budget Committee in 1981.

ECONOMY

Spanish settlers, who first arrived in the region that is now New Mexico in the 17th century, established a self-sufficient farming and ranching economy. Because of the dry climate, nearly all settlement was along the rivers. No major economic change occurred until after the completion, in 1879, of the region's first railroad. In the next few decades cattle ranching grew on a large scale. The mining of gold, silver, and other minerals became important, and agriculture spread to newly irrigated land as more settlers moved to the region. A new aspect was added to the economy when the Los Alamos Scientific Laboratory, established in 1943, developed the world's first atomic bomb. This and other military establishments stimulated the growth of associated private industry.

Agriculture. Agriculture accounts for 21% of the annual value of goods produced in New Mexico. The state has some 14,000 farms, which average 1390 ha (3434 acres) in size. Livestock and livestock products make up about four-fifths of New Mexico's yearly agricultural income. Grazing land is found throughout the state, except in the mountainous areas of the N and W. Most cattle are raised in the E half of the state, especially in the Llano Estacado and the Pecos R. valley. Most sheep are raised in the SE and NW.

Crops account for about one-fifth of New Mexico's annual agricultural income. The leading

NEW MEXICO

DATE OF STATEHOOD: January 6, 1912; 47th state

CAPITAL:	Santa Fe
MOTTO:	*Crescit eundo* (It grows as it goes)
NICKNAME:	Land of Enchantment
STATE SONG:	"O, Fair New Mexico" (words and music by Elizabeth Garrett)
STATE TREE:	Piñon (Nut pine)
STATE FLOWER:	Yucca flower
STATE BIRD:	Roadrunner
POPULATION (1980):	1,302,981; 37th among the states
AREA:	314,924 sq km (121,593 sq mi); 5th largest state; includes 668 sq km (258 sq mi) of inland water
HIGHEST POINT:	Wheeler Peak, 4011 m (13,161 ft)
LOWEST POINT:	859 m (2817 ft), along the shore of Red Bluff Lake
ELECTRICAL VOTES:	5
U.S. CONGRESS:	2 senators; 3 representatives

POPULATION OF NEW MEXICO SINCE 1850

Year of Census	Population	Classified As Urban
1850	62,000	7%
1880	120,000	6%
1900	195,000	14%
1920	360,000	18%
1940	532,000	33%
1950	681,000	50%
1960	951,000	66%
1970	1,017,000	70%
1980	1,303,000	72%

POPULATION OF TEN LARGEST CITIES

	1980 Census	1970 Census
Albuquerque	331,767	244,501
Santa Fe	48,953	41,167
Las Cruces	45,086	37,857
Roswell	39,676	33,908
Farmington	31,222	21,979
Clovis	31,194	28,495
Hobbs	29,153	26,025
Carlsbad	25,496	21,297
Alamogordo	24,024	23,035
Gallup	18,167	14,596

CLIMATE

	ALBUQUERQUE	ROSWELL
Average January temperature range	−4.4° to 8.3° C (24° to 47° F)	−6.1° to 12.8° C (21° to 55° F)
Average July temperature range	18.3° to 33.3° C (65° to 92° F)	17.8° to 35° C (64° to 95° F)
Average annual temperature	13.9° C (57° F)	15° C (59° F)
Average annual precipitation	203 mm (8 in)	279 mm (11 in)
Average annual snowfall	279 mm (11 in)	279 mm (11 in)
Mean number of days per year with appreciable precipitation	58	49
Average daily relative humidity	33%	37%
Mean number of clear days per year	172	176

NATURAL REGIONS
OF NEW MEXICO

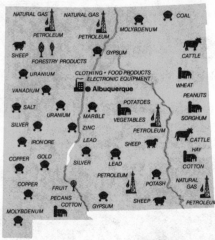

PRINCIPAL PRODUCTS
OF NEW MEXICO

ECONOMY

Sources: U.S. government publications

State budget. . . . . revenue $2.2 billion
expenditure $1.7 billion
State personal income tax, per capita $55
Personal income, per capita $7841
Assets, commercial banks (86) . . . . $5.4 billion
Labor force (civilian). 550,100
   Employed in services   30%
   Employed in government   24%
   Employed in wholesale and retail trade   19%
   Employed in manufacturing   8%

	Quantity Produced	Value
FARM PRODUCTS		**$1.1 billion**
Crops		**$269 million**
Hay	1.0 million metric tons	$97 million
Wheat	286,000 metric tons	$40 million
Cotton	25,000 metric tons	$42 million
Sorghum	261,000 metric tons	$31 million
Corn	230,000 metric tons	$26 million
Livestock and Livestock Products		**$876 million**
Cattle	290,000 metric tons	$413 million
Milk	260,000 metric tons	$84 million
Eggs	378 million	$19 million
Sheep	7400 metric tons	$9 million
MINERALS		**$5.1 billion**
Natural gas . .	33 billion cu m	$2.0 billion
Petroleum. . . .	69 million barrels	$1.6 billion
Coal†	16.8 million metric tons	$645 million
Copper	155,000 metric tons	$346 million

†Value estimated from govt. indications

	Labor and Proprietors' Income
FORESTRY	**$1.1 million**
MANUFACTURING	**$559 million**
Food and kindred products	$65 million
Transportation equipment	$63 million
Electric and electronic equipment.	$57 million
Nonelectric machinery	$54 million
Stone, clay, and glass products	$42 million
Printing and publishing	$41 million
Lumber and wood products.	$39 million
Petroleum and coal products	$33 million
Primary metals	$31 million

OTHER . . . . **$5.6 billion**
  Services. . . . . $1.4 billion
  Government and government
    enterprises. . . . . $2.0 billion
  Transportation and public utilities. . . . . . $653 million
  Finance, insurance, and real estate . . . . $331 million
  Wholesale trade . . . . $378 million
  Retail trade . . . . $816 million

ANNUAL PRODUCTION OF GOODS BY SECTOR

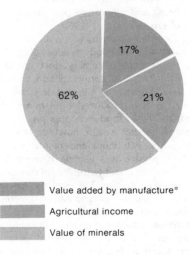

17%

62%

21%

▬ Value added by manufacture*

▬ Agricultural income

▬ Value of minerals

*The value added by an industry is a measure of the
value created in its products, not counting such production costs as raw materials and power.

Sheep grazing near the village of Aztec, in northwestern New Mexico.
Denver and Rio Grande Western Railroad

crops are hay, cotton, sorghum, and wheat. Most of the state's cropland is concentrated in three areas that combine adequate rainfall (for dry farming) or the availability of irrigation water with a sufficiently long frost-free period. These areas are the Llano Estacado, which grows wheat, sorghum, and peanuts by dry farming and cotton by irrigation; the Pecos R. valley (alfalfa and cotton); and the Rio Grande Valley (cotton and pecans). More than half of all cropland is irrigated.

Forestry. Forestry is of minor importance to the New Mexico economy. Small logging camps, scattered in the mountains of the N and W, supply ponderosa and piñon pine and juniper to a number of sawmills.

Mining. The mining industry accounts for 62% of the annual value of goods produced in New Mexico. The principal mineral products are natural gas, petroleum, coal, copper, potash, and uranium. New Mexico is the nation's leading supplier of potash, produced from mines near Carlsbad, and ranks third in copper production. The greatest mineral wealth, however, is in energy resources. Petroleum and natural gas, of which New Mexico is a leading national producer, account for about two-thirds of the state's yearly mineral production. The state also has vast reserves of low-sulfur coal and half of the country's known reserves of uranium.

Manufacturing. Enterprises engaged in manufacturing account for 17% of the annual value of goods produced in New Mexico and employ approximately 42,550 workers. The leading manufactures are food products; electrical and electronic equipment; transportation equipment; nonelectrical machinery; and stone, clay, and glass products. Other manufactures include ap-

parel, wood and lumber products, printed materials, and jewelry. More than half of the state's manufacturing is concentrated in Albuquerque. A number of high-technology military facilities, including Los Alamos Scientific Laboratory, Sandia Laboratories, and the Air Force Special Weapons Center, are located nearby. The making of arts and crafts items is important to certain localities, particularly Taos, Santa Fe, and most Indian communities.

Tourism. Tourism is a major industry in New Mexico. Each year out-of-state visitors produce about $1 billion for the state economy. In addition to Carlsbad Caverns National Park and nine national monuments, which are visited by nearly 2 million tourists annually, the state maintains a system of 38 parks and monuments areas that attract 4 million visitors. Also popular are the national forests, Indian pueblos, and the cities of Albuquerque, Santa Fe, and Taos.

Transportation. Albuquerque is the principal hub in a network of about 121,265 km (about 75,350 mi) of federal, state, and local roads. This includes 1584 km (984 mi) of Interstate Highways that link the state's major cities. Interstate Highways cross the state from E to W and from N to S, the latter following the route of the old Spanish road, the Camino Real, along the Rio Grande Valley to Santa Fe and into E Colorado. New Mexico is also served by 3339 km (2075 mi) of operated railroad track.

The state has approximately 156 airports. Albuquerque International Airport is the busiest facility. Pipelines carry much of New Mexico's natural-gas production to neighboring states.

Energy. The electricity-generating plants in New Mexico have a total capacity of about 5 million kw and produce some 24.7 billion kwh of electricity each year. About 78% of the yearly electricity output is produced by coal-fired thermal power plants, the most important of which is the huge Four Corners project near Farmington. Most of the rest is produced by plants using natural gas.   M.E.B.

HISTORY

Stone Age remains found near Folsom in the northeast part of the state show that human beings have lived in the area of New Mexico for more than 10,000 years. Later Indian cultures practiced farming and irrigation. The Anasazi culture flourished in the San Juan River Basin in the 1st millennium AD. By AD 1300 thousands of Pueblo Indians (q.v.), descendants of the Anasazi, lived in 18 towns along the Rio Grande from Taos south to Isleta (below present-day Albuquerque). The Pueblos were advanced in domestic arts and crafts—pottery, weaving, and home decoration. Some of their adobe dwellings were

five stories high. They domesticated turkeys, and in the fields near their towns they raised corn, beans, and squash and cotton for weaving into blankets. In the 15th century the serenity of their lives was shattered by the arrival of the nomadic Navajo and Apache tribes. The newcomers raided the prosperous Pueblo settlements for food, clothing, tools, and Pueblo children, whom they enslaved, initiating four centuries of warfare between the two groups.

Spanish and Mexican Rule. In 1539 a Spanish expedition under a Franciscan priest, Marcos de Niza (c. 1495–1558), explored present New Mexico, visiting the Zuñi Pueblo. The following year Francisco Coronado ascended the Rio Grande. Spanish colonization of the area began in 1598, and Santa Fe was founded in 1610. The Spanish authorities imposed their rule on the Pueblos and converted many of them to Christianity, but the missionaries' attempts to suppress the Indians' traditional religious customs caused resent-

One of New Mexico's ten national monuments is Chaco Canyon in San Juan Co. Occupying 87 sq km (34 sq mi), it contains the state's largest Indian ruins and represents the summit of Pueblo civilization.
Williams–West Stock, Inc.

31

ment. In 1680 the Pueblos rose in revolt, killing many of the settlers and forcing the rest to flee.

The Spanish reoccupied Santa Fe in 1692. By 1696 they had reconquered the whole area, and the Spanish crown thereafter recognized the Pueblos' title to their ancestral lands. New towns were established in the 18th century. Albuquerque, founded in 1706, had a population of more than 4000 by 1800. Both Spanish and Pueblo communities were exposed to continual raids from the Navajo, Apache, Comanche, and other nomadic Indian peoples in the surrounding region, and enough troops were seldom available to defend the province adequately. Nevertheless, its population continued to grow, numbering 30,000 at the beginning of the 19th century. In 1821, Spain gave up all its American mainland possessions, and New Mexico became a province of the new nation of Mexico.

Mexican rule brought many changes, as Spain had always excluded foreigners from New Mexico. Under Mexico, trade with the U.S. was permitted, and pack trains began to move back and forth along the Santa Fe Trail from Saint Louis, Mo. American merchants and trappers flocked to Santa Fe and Taos. The cultural clash thus began between the "Anglos" (Americans of European origin) on the one hand and the Hispanos (New Mexicans of mixed Spanish and Indian ancestry) and Indians on the other. By this time, those of pure Spanish ancestry were few, but Spanish culture was still dominant. Most natives spoke Spanish and were members of the Roman Catholic church, although the Indians retained their dialects and traditional ceremonies. Relations between natives and Anglos became tense when the new Texas republic tried to seize New Mexico in 1841. Meanwhile, expansionists in the U.S. were demanding the annexation of all the Southwest and California. President James K. Polk declared war on Mexico in 1846 and sent Gen. Stephen Watts Kearny and the Army of the West to invade New Mexico. Kearny took Santa Fe without firing a shot and proclaimed New Mexico part of the U.S. on Aug. 18, 1846.

New Mexico as a U.S. Territory. Some Hispano New Mexicans welcomed the victorious Americans, but Indians at Taos Pueblo revolted and murdered Charles Bent (1799-1847), the governor appointed by Kearny. All Hispano New Mexicans and Pueblo Indians became U.S. citizens by terms of the 1848 treaty ending the war between the U.S. and Mexico, but Congress denied the area statehood and created the territory of New Mexico (including present New Mexico and Arizona) as part of the Compromise of 1850 that brought California into the Union as a state. Dur-

ing the American Civil War a Confederate force from Texas invaded the territory, fought its way up the Rio Grande, captured Santa Fe, and headed north, but was defeated at Glorieta Pass in March 1862 by the Colorado Volunteers, fighting for the Union. This ended the Confederacy's hope of seizing the Southwest and California. Decades of unrest followed as the native New Mexicans tried to adjust their colorful easygoing ways to the driving materialism of the Anglos. In 1863, Congress carved the territory of Arizona out of western New Mexico. The Navajos, Apaches, and Comanches were subdued by U.S. Army units, but the forced removal of the Navajos—their tragic "Long Walk" to a reservation at Bosque Redondo—was a failure; the starving people were returned in 1868 to their San Juan River homeland. Meanwhile, the economy of the territory was stimulated by the coming of Santa Fe and Southern Pacific railroads, by mineral finds, and by the growth of tourism. Nevertheless, most Americans before 1900 thought of New Mexico as an exotic foreign country with a strange language and strange foods and dress, known for lawlessness, cattle wars, and land-grant skulduggery and as the home of outlaws such as Billy the Kid, who was killed in a gunfight at Fort Sumner in 1881. A more attractive notion of New Mexico began to emerge at the turn of the century, when artists from the East began describing the romantic charms of Taos and Santa Fe, and health seekers began moving to Albuquerque to take advantage of its sunny climate.

The 20th Century. New Mexico remained a territory for 62 years, partly because its residents feared the higher taxes that would come with statehood, and partly because Congress feared that democracy would not work in a Spanish-speaking community. The public schools began teaching English in 1898, however, and New Mexico was admitted to the Union on Jan. 6, 1912, as the 47th—and fifth largest—state.

The nation's oldest society found itself plunged into modernity when the secret city of Los Alamos near Santa Fe became the birthplace of the atomic bomb in 1943. Two years later the world's first atomic bomb was exploded near Alamogordo, south of Santa Fe. The state's economy then boomed with the coming of the White Sands Missile Range, Kirtland Air Force Base, and nuclear research installations at Albuquerque. The state's empty desert areas came to life with the discovery of oil and gas and, near Grants, of uranium. The modest tourism of the early 1900s became a major industry, with millions visiting Carlsbad Caverns National Park annually. Others flocked to Santa Fe to experience the Spanish colonial atmosphere. In the 1980s, while enjoying a rapid growth as part of America's prosperous Sun Belt, New Mexico continues to attach great importance to preserving its characteristic cultural heritage.   M.Sp.

For further information on this topic, see the Bibliography in volume 28, section 1216.

NEW ORLEANS, city and port, seat of, and coextensive with, Orleans Parish, SE Louisiana, on the Mississippi R., N of its mouth on the Gulf of Mexico; inc. as a city 1805. Long known for its unique and vivid cultural blend, New Orleans is now a major commercial and manufacturing center of the South and the second busiest port in the U.S.

Economy. The city's economy has traditionally been dominated by shipping, including both river barge and ocean vessel traffic. Extensive dock facilities are located along the Mississippi R., the Gulf Intracoastal Waterway, and the Mississippi-Gulf Outlet (a deep channel opened in 1963). Exports from the city's vast hinterland include grains, cotton, and food and petroleum products. Imports, many of which come from Latin America, include bananas, cocoa, coffee, and bauxite. The city's industrial base is highly diversified and encompasses more than 800 manufacturing operations. The leading industries include shipbuilding, petroleum refining, food processing, and the manufacture of clothing, construction materials, wood products, primary metals, and petrochemicals. Tourism is also very important to the city's economy.

The Urban Landscape. The precinct of the original settlement is distinguishable today as the Vieux Carré, also known as the French Quarter. The picturesque houses that line the narrow streets of this section are built in a style that combines French and Spanish influences. At the heart of the Vieux Carré is Jackson Square, around which are located Saint Louis Cathedral (1851) and the Cabildo and Presbytère, former government buildings begun in the late 18th century. Dixieland jazz is still played on Basin and Bourbon streets, where it originated in the early 20th century. To the W of the Vieux Carré is Canal Street, the main thoroughfare of the modern commercial district. The Louisiana Superdome, a large enclosed stadium, is on the edge of this district. To the W of this lies the Garden District, an area of many fine 19th-century homes. On the N side of the city is the extensive City Park, which borders on Lake Pontchartrain.

Cultural and Educational Institutions. Among the city's cultural institutions are the New Orleans Museum of Art, a symphony orchestra, and an opera association. Jazz festivals and the annual

A favorite tourist attraction in New Orleans is the French Quarter. Pictured here is Jackson Square, where street artists ply their trade.

New Orleans Tourist and Convention Commission

Mardi Gras celebration are other aspects of the city's cultural life. Education began in New Orleans in 1728, when Ursuline nuns opened a convent school for girls. Among the numerous institutions of higher learning today are Tulane University of Louisiana, Loyola University in New Orleans (1912), Southern University in New Orleans (1956), Xavier University of Louisiana (1915), and the University of New Orleans (1956).

History. Small villages of the Quinipissa and Tangipahoa Indians were located in the vicinity of present-day New Orleans when the site was first visited by a European explorer, the Frenchman Robert Cavelier, sieur de La Salle, in 1682. The site was visited in 1699 by another French explorer, Jean Baptiste Le Moyne, sieur de Bienville. Recognizing the importance of the location, he established a settlement here in 1718 after he had become governor of the Louisiana Territory. He named it Nouvelle Orléans, for the duc d'Orléans, regent of France. In 1722 the town was made the capital of the French colony. Following the partition of Louisiana between England and Spain in 1767, New Orleans became the capital of Spanish Louisiana. A rebellion (1768–69) against Spanish rule was quickly suppressed. In 1800 New Orleans was secretly ceded to France; in 1803 it was formally ceded to France and then, by the terms of the Louisiana Purchase, to the U.S. In 1812 Louisiana became a state with New Orleans as its capital. (The city was the state capital from 1812 to 1830 and again from 1831 to 1849.) In 1815, at the close of the War of 1812, the city was defended from a British attack by American forces led by Gen. Andrew Jackson in a confrontation known as the Battle of New Orleans. Between 1810 and 1850 steamboat traffic on the Mississippi River made the city one of the busiest ports in North America; by 1852 New Orleans was the third largest city in the U.S.

During the American Civil War the city was a major port and military center for the Confederacy and was an early objective of Union troops. It was captured by a Union fleet in 1862 and remained a Union stronghold for the rest of the war. After the war, shipping activities declined, but by 1900 they had begun to increase again. The period following World War II was marked by commercial and industrial growth and the completion of major public works programs. New Orleans was the site of a world's fair in 1984. Pop. (1970) 593,471; (1980) 557,515. W.B.K.

NEW ORLEANS, BATTLE OF, name of two battles fought near New Orleans, La., one in the War of 1812 and the other in the American Civil War.

The Battle of New Orleans of the War of 1812 was fought on Jan. 8, 1815, between about 6500 American troops, mostly irregulars, under the command of the American general Andrew Jackson and a British force of about 7500, commanded by the British general Sir Edward Pakenham (1778–1815). The British planned to attack New Orleans and thereby gain access to the entire Mississippi Valley. The entrance of British troops into the Gulf of Mexico in the autumn of 1814 prompted Jackson's arrival at New Orleans on Dec. 1, 1814. Later that month a fleet of 50 British vessels made a surprise landing at Lake Borgne, east of New Orleans, after which some 2000 British troops walked across the swamps to the banks of the Mississippi just below New Orleans. Jackson hastily fortified the area. After a number of skirmishes during late December and early January, Jackson, with the valuable aid of the French pirate Jean Laffite, won the decisive battle in less than a half hour on January 8. Jackson's improvised fortifications proved highly effective, and the American force suffered only 71 casualties while inflicting more than 2000; Pakenham was one of the 289 British dead. The overwhelming defeat caused the British to abandon further combat projects, and they soon embarked for England. The battle had no effect on the war. Peace terms had already been agreed on in the Treaty of Ghent, signed on Dec. 24, 1814; at the time of the battle, however, the treaty had not yet been ratified by the U.S. Senate.

The Battle of New Orleans of the American Civil War occurred as a result of the federal government's plan to seize New Orleans, one of the most important cities in the South. A naval squadron under the Union admiral David Farragut, carrying troops led by Benjamin Butler, appeared in the lower Mississippi River in the spring of 1862. To prevent the capture of New Orleans, the Confederates placed a heavy chain cable across the river near the city; New Orleans was also defended by forts Jackson and Saint Philip. After several days of firing on the forts, Farragut succeeded in cutting the chain and passing the forts during the earliest hours of April 24. The Union forces sank or captured 9 of the 17 Confederate vessels; emerging virtually without damage to their own ships, they proceeded to New Orleans. The city, inadequately protected by only 3000 Confederate troops, fell on April 25, was occupied by federal troops on May 1, and was held for the duration of the war. The loss of New Orleans, gateway to the Mississippi River and Valley and chief city and port of the Confederacy, was catastrophic.

NEWPORT, city, seat of Newport Co., SE Rhode Island, a port on Rhode (also called Aquidneck)

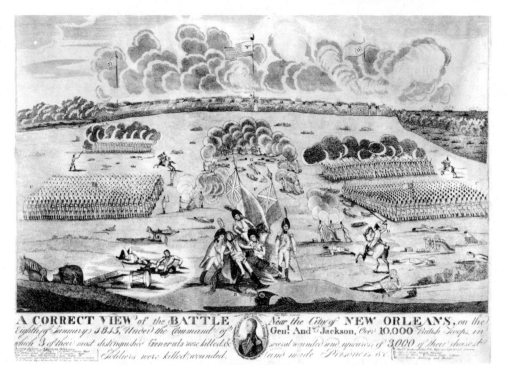

A CORRECT VIEW of the BATTLE *Eighth of January 1815, Under the Command of* Near the City of NEW ORLEAN'S, on the Gen! And Jackson, Over 10.000 British Troops, in *which 3 of their most distinguished Generals were killed &* *several wounded and upwards of 3000 of their choisest* Soldiers were killed wounded. and made Prisoners &c

The defeat of the British at the Battle of New Orleans on Jan. 8, 1815, 15 days after the signing of the peace treaty of Ghent. Granger Collection

Island, near the mouth of Narragansett Bay; inc. as a city 1784. It is a popular summer resort and a yachting center, site of the America's Cup Race (q.v.), 1930–83. Manufactures include boats and electronic equipment, and a fishing industry is based here. The U.S. Naval War College (1885), the Naval Education and Training Center, the Naval Underwater Systems Center, Salve Regina-The Newport College (1934), and the International Tennis Hall of Fame and Tennis Museum are in the city. Among the many notable structures here are the Friends Meeting House (1699); Trinity Church (1726); Redwood Library and Athenaeum (1748–50); Touro Synagogue (1763), the oldest synagogue in the U.S.; and several large mansions, including The Breakers (1895), Château-Sur-Mer (1852), The Elms, Marble House (1892), and Rosecliff (1902).

The community was founded as a "new port" by Antinomians (religious refugees from Massachusetts Bay Colony) in 1639 and grew as a trade and shipbuilding center and a haven for Quakers (who arrived here in 1657) and Sephardic Jews (1658). It was occupied (1776–79) by the British during the American Revolution. In the late 19th century Newport became a fashionable resort for the wealthy, most of whom had given up their mansions by the mid-20th century. The city was cocapital of Rhode Island until 1900, when Providence became the sole capital. Noted jazz and folk-music festivals were held here in the 1950s and '60s; the Newport Jazz Festival was revived in 1981. Pop. (1970) 34,562; (1980) 29,259.

NEWPORT, town and seaport, administrative center of Newport Borough, Gwent, SE Wales, and the adjacent county of Mid Glamorgan, on the Usk R., near its mouth on the Bristol Channel. Newport is a major steel-producing center of Great Britain. It is also a commercial and transportation center of SE Wales. Its port, improved in the 1970s, handles imports of ore and timber and exports of iron, steel, and machinery. Located here is Saint Woolos's Church, a cathedral since 1921, and a notable museum and art gallery. Newport received a charter granting trade privileges in 1385. In 1839 it was the scene of the Chartist riots of political reformers. The town developed as a coal-exporting and industrial center in the 19th century. Pop. (Newport Borough, 1981) 133,698.

NEWPORT BEACH, city, Orange Co., S California, on Newport Bay and the Pacific Ocean; inc.

1906. Parts of the city, which has a fine, protected harbor, are located on Balboa Island and Lido Isle. The Corona Del Mar district and Balboa Peninsula are noted for their ocean beaches. Besides being a resort and a residential center, Newport Beach has industries that manufacture boats, marine supplies, and electronic equipment. The community, which grew in the 1860s and '70s as a shipping center for hides, tallow, grain, and lumber, was known as McFadden's Landing from 1873 to 1892, when the name Newport was adopted. Extensive harbor improvements were undertaken in the 1930s. Pop. (1970) 49,582; (1980) 62,556.

NEWPORT NEWS, independent industrial city, SE Virginia, at the mouth of the James R.; inc. as a city 1896. With nearby harbors it forms the Port of Hampton Roads, one of the principal commercial ports in the U.S. Important industrials here include shipbuilding and ship repairing, seafood processing, and petroleum refining; aerospace and electronic equipment, chemicals, textiles, and metal items also are produced. Newport News is the site of Christopher Newport College (1960); the Mariners Museum, with a collection of artifacts depicting life at sea; the War Memorial Museum of Virginia, containing exhibits on the two world wars; the Peninsula Nature and Science Center, encompassing a planetarium, a natural history museum, an aquarium, and a zoo; and the Victory Arch (1919), a memorial to U.S. armed forces.

The site of present-day Newport News was settled about 1620 by Irish colonists. The settlement was fortified by federal troops during the American Civil War; in 1862 the battle between the ironclad ships *Monitor* and *Merrimack* took place off Newport News. Major industrial development did not begin here until the early 1880s, when the city became a railroad terminus. The shipbuilding industry was started here in 1886, and the city now contains one of the world's leading shipyards. In 1958 the city of Warwick was consolidated with Newport News. Pop. (1970) 138,177; (1980) 144,903.

NEW ROCHELLE, city, Westchester Co., SE New York, on Long Island Sound, a residential and commercial community near New York City; inc. as a city 1899. It has some light industry and extensive outdoor-recreation facilities. The College of New Rochelle (1898) and Iona College (1940) are here. Of interest is the home of the political theorist Thomas Paine, preserved as a national historic shrine. The community, settled by French Huguenots in 1688, is named for La Rochelle, France. It was a summer resort in the 19th century. Pop. (1970) 75,385; (1980) 70,794.

NEW SOUTH WALES, state, SE Australia, bounded on the N by Queensland, on the E by the Tasman Sea, on the S by Victoria, and on the W by South Australia. The chains of the Great Dividing Range extend across the state parallel to the coast. The highest elevation is Mt. Kosciusko (2228 m/7310 ft), near the Victoria border. The chief rivers are the Murray, Darling, and Murrumbidgee. The capital city is Sydney. Area, 801,600 sq km (309,500 sq mi), including Lord Howe Island; pop. (1981 est.) 5,183,300.

Mining is one of the most important industries. The chief mining products are gold, silver, coal, copper, tin, lead, zinc, and cobalt. Gold was first worked in 1851 near Bathurst. It is found in nearly all parts of New South Wales, but the most important districts are Bathurst, Lachlan, Mudgee, Peel, and Uralla. Silver (discovered in 1883) and lead mining are concentrated mainly at Broken Hill in the Albert mining district. The main coal-bearing rocks extend over a large area around the seaport of Sydney.

The area under cultivation in the early 1980s totaled about 5.3 million ha (about 13.1 million acres). Principal crops are wheat, corn, barley, oats, potatoes, tobacco, and rice. Cane sugar and grapes are also grown, wine and sugar constituting important products. Citrus fruits are raised in considerable number, oranges predominating. Grazing and livestock raising are major industries. Forest area in New South Wales is estimated at 16.3 million ha (40.3 million acres).

The chief manufactures are iron and steel, textiles, electrical appliances, automobiles, furniture, chemicals, and clothing.

Executive power in New South Wales is nominally vested in a governor appointed by the British crown; actual power is exercised by a premier and cabinet. The state legislature consists of a parliament of two houses, namely, the legislative council, which has 45 members popularly elected to 9-year terms, and the legislative assembly of 99 members who are popularly elected to 3-year terms.

New South Wales, the oldest colony of Australasia, was named in 1770 by the British explorer Capt. James Cook.

NEWSPAPERS, publications usually issued on a daily or weekly basis, the main function of which is to report the news. Newspapers also provide commentary on the news, advocate various public policies, furnish special information and advice to readers, and sometimes include features such as comic strips, cartoons, and serialized books. In nearly all cases and in varying degrees, they depend on the publication of commercial advertising for their income.

Despite the development of motion pictures early in the 20th century, of radiobroadcasting in the 1920s, and of television in the 1940s, newspapers remain a major source of information on matters ranging from details of important news events to human-interest items. In the U.S., for example, about 1750 daily newspapers print a total of 63 million copies, and almost every copy is read by at least two persons. More than 7000 weekly newspapers are also published, with a combined circulation of more than 40 million. Newspaper publishers in the U.S. estimate that nearly 8 out of 10 adult Americans read a newspaper every day.

Throughout the world, newspapers are a significant force for informing people and helping to mold their opinions. In Great Britain and Western Europe, major newspapers such as the *Times* of London and the *Journal de Geneve* of Geneva have managed to maintain a long tradition of press freedom and diversification despite wars, dictatorships, and other efforts at intimidation of a free press. Other developed countries such as Japan also have a strong newspaper tradition. Newspapers are important in Communist countries as well, but in those nations the press is carefully controlled by the government. *See* PRESS, FREEDOM OF THE.

In the Third World countries of Asia, Africa, and Latin America, newspapers range from government-controlled organs to lively publications run by independent editors. Newspaper expansion has been limited in many developing nations, however, because of the countries' high illiteracy rate.

Early History. Before the development of movable metal type in the mid-15th century and for some time thereafter, news was disseminated by word of mouth, by written letters, or by public notices. Not until 1609 were the earliest known newspapers published. These papers, printed in northern Germany, were called *coranto*s, and they dispensed "tydings," often about events in other countries. The word *news* was not coined until a century later.

Within 20 years newspapers were being published in Cologne, Frankfurt, Berlin, and Hamburg, Germany; Basel, Switzerland; Vienna; Amsterdam; and Antwerp, Belgium. The Amsterdam papers, printed in both English and French, soon found their way to London, where the first newspaper was published in 1621, and to Paris, where a newspaper was begun in 1631. By 1645 Stockholm had a court paper, which is still published.

Early newspapers were small in size, usually consisting of only one page. They had neither headlines nor advertising and looked more like newsletters than today's broadsheet papers with their bold headlines and numerous pictures.

British Newspapers. The first continuously published English newspaper was the *Weekly News* (1622–41). The earliest newspapers in England printed mostly foreign news, but in 1628 the first papers giving domestic news were begun by clerks who reported the debates of the English Parliament. These papers were called diurnals.

Censorship (q.v.) was a problem faced by the fledgling English press throughout much of the 17th century. Beginning in the 1630s, under King Charles I, heavy restrictions (including licensing) were placed on the press; these restrictions continued during the civil wars of the 1640s. In the mid-1600s, under the government of Oliver Cromwell, limitations on the press were continued. With the restoration of King Charles II in 1660, licensing provisions and other restrictions were gradually ended, and the English press was able to publish in an atmosphere of considerable freedom as long as it refrained from criticizing the government. In 1702 the first daily newspaper in England, the *Daily Courant,* was founded in London.

The abolition of the government tax on newspapers in 1855 brought about a general reduction in their prices and an increase in their circulation. Prices were further reduced at the end of the 19th century when cheaper paper and improved printing machinery became available. As circulation grew, so did the practice of advertising, giving publishers an important source of revenue apart from that obtained by sales. These developments finally resulted in the general establishment of the halfpenny daily newspaper in Great Britain at the beginning of the 20th century.

HISTORY OF AMERICAN NEWSPAPERS

Not until 1690 was anything resembling the early European newspapers printed in the American colonies. In that year a three-page paper called *Publick Occurrences* was published in Boston, but it was suppressed by the government after one issue.

Colonial Newspapers. The first continuously published American newspaper was the *Boston News-Letter,* established in 1704 by John Campbell (1653–1728). The paper, which was censored by the governor of the Massachusetts Bay Colony, contained financial and foreign news and also recorded births, deaths, and social events. In 1721 James Franklin (1697–1735) founded the *New England Courant* in Boston; his staff included his younger brother Benjamin Franklin who in 1723 went to Philadelphia, where he subsequently published the *Pennsylvania Gazette*

The Boſton News-Letter.

Selections from Iſſues of 1704-1707.

Windſor, September 14, 1704.

THis day Captain *Trevor,* Commander of Her Majeſty's Ship the *Triton,* arrived here; being ſent Expreſs by Sir *George Rooke* from the Fleet, with Letters to *His Royal Highneſs,* dated on Board the *Royal Catherine* off of Cape St. Vincent, Auguſt 27, O. S. 1704. Which contain the following Account.

On the 9th Inſtant, returning from watering our Ships on the *Coaſt of Barbary* to *Gibraltar,* with little Wind Eaſterly, our Scouts to the Windward made the Signals of ſeeing the Enemy's Fleet, with little, according to the Account they gave, conſiſted of 66 Sail, and were about 10 Leagues to Windward of us. A Council of Flag-Officers was called, wherein it was determined to lie to the Eaſtward of *Gibraltar* to receive and engage them; But perceiving that Night, by the Report of their Signal-Guns, that they wrought from us, we followed them in the Morning with all the Sail we could make.

On the 11th we forced one of the Enemy's Ships aſhore near *Fuengerole;* the Crew quitted her, ſet her on Fire, and ſhe blew up immediately, We continued ſtill purſuing them; and the 12th, not hearing any of their Guns all Night, nor ſeeing any of their Scouts in the Morning, our Admiral had a Jealouſie they might make a Double, & by the help of their Gallies ſlip between us and the Shore to the Weſtward; ſo that a Council of War was called, wherein it was reſolved, That in caſe we did not ſee the Enemy before Night, we ſhould make the beſt of our way to *Gibraltar;* but ſtanding in to the Shore about Noon we diſcovered the Enemy's Fleet and Gallies to the Weſtward, near *Cape Malaga,* going away large. We immediately made all the Sail we could after them, and continued the Chace all Night.

On Sunday the 13th in the Morning, we were within 3 Leagues of the Enemy, who brought to with their Heads to the Southward, the Wind being Eaſterly, formed their Line, and lay to receive us. Their Line conſiſted of 53 Ships & 24 Gallies; they were very ſtrong in the Center, & weaker in the Van and Rear, to ſupply which, moſt of the Gallies were divided into thoſe Quarters. In the Center was Monſieur de *Thouleuſe* with the White Squadron; in the Van the White and Blue; and in the Rear the Blue; each Admiral had his Vice and Rear-Admirals. Our Line conſiſted of 53 Ships; the Admiral & Rear-Admirals *Bings* & *Dilks* being in the Center, Sir *Cloudeſly Shovel* and Sir *John Locke* led the Van, and the *Dutch* the Rear.

The Admiral ordered the *Swallow* and *Panther,* with the *Lark* and *Newport,* and 2 Fire-ſhips, to lie to the Windward of us, that in caſe the Enemy's Van ſhould puſh through our Line with their Gallies and Fire-ſhips, they might give them ſome diverſion.

We bore down upon the Enemy in order of Battel, a little after 10 a Clock, when being about half Gun-ſhot from them, they ſet all their Sails at once, and ſeemed to intend to ſtretch a-head, and weather us, ſo that our Admiral, after firing a Chace Gun at the French Admiral to ſtay for him, of which he took no notice, put the Signal out, & began the Battel, which fell very heavy on the *Royal Catharine,* the *St. George,* and the *Shrewſbury.* About 2 in the afternoon, the Enemy's Van gave way to ours, & the Battel ended with the Day, when the Enemy went away by the help of their Gallies to the Leward. In the Night the Wind ſhifted to the Northward, & in the Morning to the Weſtward, which gave the Enemy the Wind of us: We lay by all Day within 3 Leagues of one another, repairing our Defects, & at Night they filed & ſtood to the Northward.

On the 15th in the Morning the Enemy was got four or five Leagues to the Windward of us; but a little before Noon we had a Breeze of Wind Eaſterly, with which we bore down on them till 4 a Clock Afternoon: It being too late to Engage, we brought to, and lay by with our Heads to the Northward all night.

On the 16th in the Morning, the Wind being ſtill Eaſterly, hazy Weather, and having no ſight of the Enemy, or their Scouts, we filed and bore away to the Weſtward, ſuppoſing they would have gone away for *Cadiz;* but being adviſed from *Gibraltar,* and the *Coaſt of Barbary,* that they did not paſs the *Streights,* we concluded they had been ſo ſeverely treated, as to oblige them to return to *Thoulon.*

Rhode-Iſland, Octob. 5. On Sunday laſt arrived here one *Benjamin Church,* who Sailed hence Maſter of a ſmall Sloop bound for *Antigua,* the 8th of Auguſt laſt, and on the 18th, in the Lat. of 34, met with the ſame Storm that the *Jamaica Fleet* met with on ſaid day, which overſet the Sloop, and the people kept on the Bowſprit from Saturday till Monday when the Sloop righted, but loſt her Maſt, and through their Induſtry they freed her, the Wind hanging Eaſterly, they drove aſhore on *Cape May,* and ſo ſaved all their lives.

Philadelphia, Auguſt 3. Yeſterday arrived here Capt. *Puckle* from *London* about 14 weeks paſſage.

Selections of news items from America's first continuously published newspaper, the Boston News-Letter.

and the *General Magazine.* Although both these publications failed, Franklin later enjoyed much success as a writer, editor, and publisher (before becoming a diplomat and statesman).

The first New York City newspaper, founded in 1725, was called the *Gazette;* it was soon followed by several others including the *New York Weekly Journal,* edited by the German-American printer John Peter Zenger. When Zenger published criticism of the British colonial governor of New York and his administration, he was arrested and jailed on charges of seditious libel. Zenger was tried and found not guilty, and his case created an important precedent for the tradition of a free press in America.

Revolutionary Period. In 1750 there were 12 newspapers in the American colonies, which then had a total population of about 1 million. By 1775 the population had increased to 2.5 million, and the number of newspapers had jumped to 48. They were published weekly, contained only four pages each, and typically had a circulation of no more than 400 copies. The papers printed more essays than news and were distinctly libertarian in tone, anticipating the American Revolution. When the British Stamp Act of 1765 imposed a heavy tax on paper, the prerevolutionary press denounced the act and refused to pay

the tax. Even though the Stamp Act was repealed in 1766, it had united many editors and publishers in support of the cause of independence. The American patriot Samuel Adams, who often edited the *Boston Gazette,* organized the Committees of Correspondence, comprising agents who kept track of events throughout the colonies. In 1776 the patriot papers carried on their front pages the Declaration of Independence.

During the war, newspapers brought accounts of military developments to an increasing number of readers, while business generated by the war brought advertising to the papers. The surviving papers thus emerged from the Revolution greatly strengthened. This stronger press, however, soon found itself deeply divided—first, when the Articles of Confederation were ratified and, later, when the new U.S. Constitution was adopted. On one side of most issues were the conservative Federalists; on the other side were the agrarian Republicans, or Democratic-Republicans. On one issue, however, the newspapers of the country were united: support of the 1st Amendment to the Constitution, adopted in 1791 as part of the Bill of Rights, which declared that "Congress shall make no law . . . abridging the freedom of speech, or of the press." The amendment also guaranteed freedom of religion, the right of assembly, and the right to petition Congress. The 1st Amendment has been under fire many times during the succeeding years, but it has remained the cornerstone of the free press in the U.S. It has guaranteed American newspapers as great or greater freedom than the press of any other nation in the world.

The Alien and Sedition Acts (q.v.) of 1798 called into question the freedom of the press. The Sedition Act provided that a person could be fined or imprisoned for "any false, scandalous and malicious writing . . . against the government of the United States, or either house of the Congress . . . or the said President." The law, supported by the Federalists, was used to jail editors who opposed their party, but was not invoked against editors who attacked such Democratic-Republicans as Thomas Jefferson. Reaction against this repressive law helped to elect Jefferson president in 1800, and the act was allowed to lapse when it expired in 1801.

Penny Press. The first daily newspaper in the U.S., the *Pennsylvania Evening Post and Daily Advertiser,* had begun daily publication in 1783 in Philadelphia. By 1800, 20 daily papers were in operation, and the number continued to increase in the first three decades of the 19th century as the Industrial Revolution spread, spawning a new working class in the nation's growing cities.

Until the 1830s newspapers were concerned almost entirely with business and political news; thus they appealed largely to the privileged classes. Benjamin Henry Day changed all that in 1833, when he published the first edition of the *New York Sun,* creating the penny press that would dominate U.S. journalism throughout the rest of the 19th century. In the *Sun,* Day expanded the definition of news to include crime and violence, feature stories, and entertainment items. The modern newspaper with its appeal to a mass audience was born, and the newspaper cost only 1 cent.

An instant success, the *Sun* was soon followed by the *New York Herald,* the *New York Tribune,* and the *New York Times.* The penny press spread to other eastern cities and across the country as well, as the nation expanded westward. Newspaper circulation quickly climbed into the tens of thousands. Technological advances that made possible the production of cheap paper from wood pulp and the development of fast rotary presses to replace the traditional flatbed press also contributed to the rapid expansion of U.S. newspapers.

From the Mid-1800s to the 20th Century. The American Civil War brought a new dimension to the American press. The first telegraph line was strung from Washington, D.C., to Baltimore, Md., in 1844, and by the time the war began in 1861, most of the East and South were connected by telegraph. News could now be transmitted

Horace Greeley, founder of the New York Tribune *in 1841, was one of the leading editors of the mid-19th century.* UPI

Adolph S. Ochs was the publisher of the New York Times *from 1896 until his death in 1935. He stressed nonpartisan, almost clinical, news reporting.*
International News Photos

quickly. At least 150 reporters covered the war and sent back their dispatches by telegraph.

In 1848 another significant development had occurred. Six New York City newspapers had joined together to share the cost of bringing news to New York by telegraph from Washington and Boston. This informal organization soon became the Associated Press (AP), the country's first news agency. After the Civil War, the AP expanded rapidly, serving newspapers with many different political views. The AP was thus forced to present news in a nonpartisan, objective manner, a standard that is still sought by many U.S. papers.

The middle and later years of the 19th century are particularly noted in the history of journalism for the work of a number of outstanding publishers and editors. One of them was James Gordon Bennett, who in 1835 founded the *New York Herald,* which he made into one of the most widely read newspapers of the time, at first by emphasis on lurid and scandalous news items and later by an unprecedentedly thorough coverage of foreign news. The most distinguished editor of the period—noted for editorials in which he supported the rights of labor and of women, fought slavery, and backed the Union cause in the Civil War—was Horace Greeley, who founded the *New York Tribune* in 1841. The *New York Times* was acquired in 1896 by Adolph Simon Ochs. In his hands it became one of the

William Randolph Hearst, head of the far-flung Hearst newspaper chain, directed his syndicate until his death in 1951 at the age of 88.   UPI

of dailies, however, has declined greatly in recent years. The principal reasons for the discontinuation of many dailies appear to have been loss of advertising revenue to competing papers or to television and other media; labor difficulties; and rising costs of equipment, labor, and material. Most remaining papers are profitable, well printed, and illustrated with clear photographs and drawings. Developments in paper, presses, engraving, and electronic, computer-assisted typesetting have all improved the quality of newspapers. The decline in the number of dailies has also been marked by a move toward consolidation, as newspapers that were losing money have been purchased by publishers of successful papers in the same city, who then merged them with their own newspaper properties. The tendency toward newspaper chains—ownership of a number of newspapers by a single company—that began with Hearst and Edward Wyllis Scripps in the late 1800s has also increased considerably. Three more news agencies—United Press, International News Service, and Universal News—were begun; in 1958 they were consolidated into United Press International (UPI).

Another 20th-century trend was the develop-

The New York Mirror, a major tabloid newspaper, ceased publication in 1963. A pressman inspects the last edition of the newspaper.   Wide World Photos

world's foremost newspapers, remarkable for the thoroughness of its reporting of all aspects of the daily news, both foreign and domestic.

As newspapers began to compete more and more with one another to increase circulation in order to obtain more advertising, a different type of journalism was developed by the publishers Joseph Pulitzer and William Randolph Hearst. Pulitzer, in the New York World, and Hearst, in the San Francisco Examiner and the New York Morning Journal, transformed newspapers with sensational and scandalous news coverage, the use of drawings, and the inclusion of more features such as comic strips. After Hearst began publishing color comic sections that included a strip entitled The Yellow Kid, this type of paper was labeled "yellow journalism."

Further technological advances helped to encourage the growth of newspapers. The development of the first Linotype machine in the mid-1880s speeded up typesetting by making possible the automatic casting of type in lines. Rotary presses were also improved, and newspaper circulation in large cities climbed into the hundreds of thousands.

20th-Century Developments. By 1900, daily newspapers in the U.S. numbered 2326. Large cities had several papers each, and most smaller cities had at least two newspapers. The number

A newsroom of the Chicago Tribune, one of America's major newspapers.   CHICAGO TRIBUNE

ment of tabloid newspapers. The tabloid differs from the standard paper in its size, the depth of its news coverage, and the number of illustrations; the tabloid is usually about half the size of a standard paper, reports news in more condensed or shortened versions, and offers many more illustrations.

MODERN NEWSPAPERS

Most U.S. cities today have only one newspaper publisher. In more than 170 American cities, a single publisher produces both a morning and an evening paper; in other cities a single evening newspaper is published. Fewer than 30 cities have competing papers with different ownerships. Newspapers today average about 65 pages in length during the week and more than 200 pages for Sunday editions. About two-thirds of this space is taken up by commercial advertising, and one-third is reserved for news and features.

Although most daily papers have a monopoly in their cities and surrounding metropolitan areas, their news departments compete with radio and television reporters in their areas. The papers also compete for advertising with radio, television, and magazines. Some newspaper publishers, however, own radio and television stations, often in the same city where their papers are published.

Circulation. The Wall Street Journal, a specialized publication aimed primarily at business executives, but which also carries much news of general interest, has the largest circulation in the nation, with more than 1.8 million copies sold daily. The largest general-interest newspaper is the New York Daily News, a tabloid paper with a daily circulation of about 1.5 million. Fewer than 100 newspapers have circulations of more than 100,000, with the average paper selling 50,000 copies a day. Some daily papers have circulations of only a few thousand.

Organization and Activities. Major newspapers such as the Wall Street Journal, New York Daily News, New York Times, Washington Post, Los Angeles Times, and Chicago Tribune have large, specialized staffs. In addition to a news staff of hundreds of reporters and editors, the bigger papers also have sizable staffs in their advertising, circulation, and production departments. The publisher oversees all the operations, usually with the aid of an executive editor in charge of the news department, an editorial-page editor who supervises the commentary pages, and a business manager responsible for advertising, circulation, and production of the newspaper.

For a typical large paper, the main news staff is located on one huge, unpartitioned floor of the newspaper plant. The staff usually includes "metro" or local reporters, photographers, artists, and editors who cover news of the city and suburban areas under the direction of the metropolitan editor. Other groups report and edit national news and foreign news. Additional staff members are concerned with business news, sports, and cultural events. Overseeing these editors and reporters are the executive editor, a managing editor who handles the day-to-day operations of the news staff, and various assistant managing editors.

Major newspapers also have Washington, D.C., bureaus covering news about the president, government departments and agencies, and the U.S. Congress; reporters stationed in large cities around the country; and foreign correspondents in important world capitals. In addition to receiving reports from their own staffs, newspapers also subscribe to the AP and the UPI, such foreign news agencies as Britain's Reuters and France's Agence France Presse, and newspaper syndicates that distribute features. The *New York Times, Washington Post,* and *Los Angeles Times,* among others, have established their own wire services to sell their news reports to papers both in the U.S. and abroad.

Some reporters cover a "beat" such as city hall, the police department, or the courts; some are general-assignment reporters covering a variety of news events; still others are primarily investigative reporters often involved with stories about corruption in government, business, or labor. Many reporters cover only daily events—meetings of a city council, press conferences, fires, and accidents—while others work for weeks to develop in-depth articles.

Each day a newspaper's editors decide what news and features to use. Because of space limitations, they generally select only those stories dealing with the most interesting and important events and developments. Reporters on large papers write their own stories on computerized electronic typewriters that display the articles on video terminals at their desks. The stories are then edited by copy editors, who also write the headlines. Placement of articles and illustrations is determined by layout editors working with "dummies" (or representations) of pages on which space has already been blocked out for the day's advertising. Some features such as syndicated columns and crossword puzzles are run every day in approximately the same place in the paper.

Newspaper editorial and comment pages generally have their own editor who is not part of the news department. A large paper will have several editorial writers. The editorials reflect the views of the publisher or owner on public issues; other writers usually are selected to provide a balance of political and social views. Many of the best-known writers of commentary and analysis are based in Washington, D.C., and their columns are syndicated to hundreds of newspapers around the country. Among the most widely syndicated columnists are Jack Anderson (1922–   ), who specializes in investigative reporting; Art Buchwald (1925–   ), who combines humor and

Most newspaper advertising is now made up electronically. Shown here is the composing room at the Minneapolis Star and Tribune.   Minneapolis Star and Tribune

Mainichi Shimbun

Pravda

Even in languages unfamiliar to Western eyes, the front pages of all newspapers share certain resemblances. Left: With vertical headlines, a front page of a Japanese newspaper, the Mainichi Shimbun *Right: In Cyrillic characters, a front page of the Volgograd edition of* Pravda, *the official newspaper of the Soviet Communist party.*

satire with political comments; and Joseph Kraft (1924–   ) and James J. Kilpatrick (1920–   ), who offer serious political commentary. Editorial pages also often feature cartoonists, who use humorous drawings to comment on political and social events, as well as a selection of letters from readers.

To cope with the competition of instant news reports on radio and television, newspapers have become more analytical; they now provide extensive background information on the news, particularly since the expansion of television news in the 1960s. Most newspaper editors are no longer content to give their readers simply an account of the news; they also try to provide a reasoned explanation for events.

Although newspapers have grown greatly in size and circulation since the penny press innovations of 150 years ago, they remain publications aimed at a mass readership. In addition to the serious news of the day, the newspaper, whether large or small, contains something to appeal to most men, women, and children. Surprisingly, many people buy newspapers more for the advertising than for the news.

Newspapers no longer cost 1 cent. Today most sell for 20 or 25 cents a copy, but advertising still accounts for about 75 percent of newspaper revenues. The biggest cost in the publication of

large papers is newsprint, which amounts to approximately one-third of the total budget.

Newspaper Chains. The growth of newspaper chains has been a major element in 20th-century journalism. The 20 largest newspapers companies account for almost half the daily circulation in the U.S.—more than 30 million of the 63 million copies sold each day. These 20 companies own more than 404 dailies. The largest of the chains is the Gannett Co., which owns some 80 newspapers with a circulation totaling more than 3.6 million. Second to Gannett is Knight-Ridder Newspapers, with 34 papers and a circulation of almost 3.5 million. Many newspaper groups are publicly owned, and their stocks can easily be purchased. Some critics see a danger to the free press in the expansion of newspaper chains, but the owners of the chains contend that they generally improve a newspaper after they buy it.

The Power of the Press. Although total newspaper circulation has remained virtually unchanged since the early 1970s, newspapers are still a powerful force in American society. In 1971, for example, the *New York Times* began publishing the Pentagon Papers. When the government tried to prevent their publication, the U.S. Supreme Court upheld the right of the newspaper to print this material. The Pentagon Papers gave Americans a look behind the scenes at govern-

43

ment planning and policies that led to the U.S. role in the Vietnam War and caused many citizens to demand an end to U.S. involvement in Southeast Asia.

Perhaps the foremost example of the power of the press came about in 1974 when President Richard M. Nixon resigned his office after revelations about the Watergate (q.v.) scandal involving his administration, which had first been brought to public attention by the *Washington Post.* The Watergate affair also led to a renewal of investigative reporting by many newspapers throughout the country.

Trends and Developments. During the last two decades newspapers have made more technological advances than at any time since the development of the automatic typesetting machines and fast rotary presses in the late 19th century. The huge, clacking machines that laboriously set lines of type in lead for almost a century have disappeared from newspaper plants. Replacing them are sophisticated electronic typesetting systems that use computers to store information and turn words into lines of type. In today's newspaper plant, the reporters and editors, working on keyboards hooked into computers, have also become the typesetters. The printers who once set type with machines now work at light tables arranging proofs of stories and pictures into newspaper pages. Increased use of electronic typesetting and data transmission has made possible the development of national newspapers with decentralized printing facilities, such as *USA Today.*

The freedom enjoyed by newspapers in the U.S. has been attacked in recent years in cases involving access to court and government records, such as the Pentagon Papers case. The press and its freedom, however, have emerged from these attacks with the 1st Amendment substantially intact. In the last 20 years the courts have greatly expanded the latitude allowed the press by holding that public figures cannot be libeled under the law unless a publication prints information about them knowing the material to be false, and using it with malicious intent. At the same time, the courts have widely expanded the definition of a public figure.

Disputes have also arisen over the rights of journalists to protect the anonymity of their sources. Some states have passed shield laws offering such protection. Although newspapers vigorously oppose any outside censorship, the papers may use self-censorship in cases involving national security or criminal prosecution.

Newspaper publishers are now experimenting with the use of computers and television to transmit news, advertising, and other information directly into homes. Some people believe that the newspaper of the future will not be printed but will be an electronic information service instantly available in every home.

For additional information on individuals mentioned, see biographies of those whose names are not followed by dates.   J.Du.

For further information on this topic, see the Bibliography in volume 28, sections 17.

NEWT, also eft, common name applied generally to many small, semiaquatic salamanders of the family Salamandridae. The many species in this family are widely distributed throughout the temperate regions of the northern hemisphere. Slender and active, newts are usually about 8 to 10 cm (about 3 to 4 in) long when adult. The common newt of the eastern and central U.S. is *Diemictylus viridescens,* a tannish-green species, spotted on the sides with blotches of red surrounded by black and spotted below with black. This amphibian inhabits thickly vegetated ponds and streams and feeds on aquatic snails and insects. The female attaches its sticky eggs individually to aquatic plants; the newly hatched larvae are equipped with gills that become rudimentary when the larvae are about 2.5 cm (about 1 in) long. At this time, the larvae, which are reddish-orange with black spots and are known as red efts, leave the water and spend the next few years on land, living under stones and logs in damp, wooded regions. The larvae eventually return to the water, develop the adult coloration, and spend the rest of their lives in an aquatic habitat. Another common American species is the giant newt, *Taricha torosa,* which attains a

The common red-spotted newt, or red eft (Diemictylus viridescens), *in its terrestrial stage of development. The red eft lives on land for two or three years, then becomes permanently aquatic, changing in color from bright red to green.*   Dr. E. R. Degginger

length of more than 15 cm (6 in). Among the common European species are the spotted newt, *Triturus vulgaris,* the crested newt, *Triturus cristatus,* the male of which develops a crest during the breeding season, and the palmate newt, *Triturus mipes.*

NEW TESTAMENT. *See* BIBLE.

NEW THOUGHT, idealistic movement in religious and philosophical thinking that developed in the U.S., particularly in New England, early in the second half of the 19th century. This movement, from which evolved various theosophic and psychotherapeutic systems, such as the so-called Higher Thought, Mental Science, Metaphysical Healing, and Practical Christianity, has numerous affinities with the transcendental philosophy of the American philosophers Amos Bronson Alcott, Ralph Waldo Emerson, and Henry David Thoreau and with the mystical doctrines of Platonism.

The chief tenets of New Thought are that God is omnipotent and omnipresent, spirit is the ultimate reality, true human selfhood is divine, divinely attuned thought is a positive force for good, disease is mental in origin, and right thinking has a healing effect. The therapeutic theories of New Thought received particular emphasis in the Divine Science Church, which taught that God is the sole reality, sickness is the result of the failure to realize this truth, and healing is accomplished by the affirmation of the oneness of the human race with God. The first exponent of metaphysical healing in the U.S. was Phineas Parkhurst Quimby. Another practitioner was John Bovee Dods (1795–1862), who also wrote several books expounding the thesis that disease originates in the electrical impulses of the nervous system and is curable by a change of belief. The mental science of the Swedenborgian minister Warren Felt Evans (1817–89), a follower of Quimby's, also contributed to the development of this movement. New Thought is customarily differentiated from Christian Science and medical psychotherapy.

NEWTON, city, Middlesex Co., NE Massachusetts, on the Charles R., a residential and commercial community near Boston; inc. as a city 1873. It comprises some 13 villages, including Chestnut Hill, Newton, Newton Centre, Newton Lower Falls, and West Newton. Machinery, paper, concrete products, and printed materials are produced. Boston College (1863), Andover Newton Theological School (1807), several junior colleges, and the Longwood Cricket Club (a noted tennis center) are here. The community was settled in 1639 as part of Cambridge. Known first as Cambridge Village and then as New Cambridge,

it was renamed Newtowne in 1691 (shortened to Newton in 1766) mainly to distinguish it from Cambridge. The coming of the railroad in 1834 fostered its growth as a suburb of Boston. Pop. (1970) 91,263; (1980) 83,622.

NEWTON, Sir Isaac (1643–1727), English mathematician and physicist, who brought the scientific revolution of the 17th century to its climax and established the principal outlines of the system of natural science that has since dominated Western thought. In mathematics, he was the first person to develop the calculus (q.v.). In optics, he established the heterogeneity of light (q.v.) and the periodicity of certain phenomena. In mechanics, his three laws of motion became the foundation of modern dynamics, and from them he derived the law of universal gravitation. *See* GRAVITATION; MECHANICS.

Newton was born on Jan. 4, 1643, at Woolsthorpe, near Grantham in Lincolnshire. When he was three years old, his widowed mother remarried, leaving him to be reared by her mother. Eventually, his mother, by then widowed a second time, was persuaded to send him to grammar school in Grantham; then, in the summer of 1661, he was sent to Trinity College, University of Cambridge.

After receiving his bachelor's degree in 1665, and after an intermission of nearly two years caused by the plague, Newton stayed on at Trinity, which elected him to a fellowship in 1667; he took his master's degree in 1668. Meanwhile, he had largely ignored the established curriculum of the university to pursue his own interests: mathematics and natural philosophy. Proceeding entirely on his own, Newton investigated the latest developments in 17th-century mathematics and the new natural philosophy that treated nature as a complicated machine. Almost immediately, he made fundamental discoveries that laid the foundation of his career in science.

The Fluxional Method. Newton's first achievement came in mathematics. He generalized the earlier methods that were being used to draw tangents to curves (similar to differentiation) and to calculate areas under curves (similar to integration), recognized that the two procedures were inverse operations, and—joining them in what he called the fluxional method—developed in the autumn of 1666 what is now known as the calculus. The calculus was a new and powerful instrument that carried modern mathematics above the level of Greek geometry. Although Newton was its inventor, he did not introduce it into European mathematics. Always morbidly fearful of publication and criticism, he kept his discovery to himself, although enough was

Sir Isaac Newton   National Portrait Gallery, London

known of his abilities to effect his appointment in 1669 as Lucasian Professor of Mathematics at the University of Cambridge. In 1675 the German mathematician Gottfried Wilhelm Leibniz arrived independently at virtually the same method, which he called the differential calculus. Leibniz proceeded to publish his method, and the world of mathematics not only learned it from him but also accepted his name for it and his notation. Newton himself did not publish any detailed exposition of his fluxional method until 1704.

Optics. Optics (q.v.) was another of Newton's early interests. In trying to explain how phenomena of colors arise, he arrived at the idea that sunlight is a heterogeneous mixture of different rays—each of which provokes the sensation of a different color—and that reflections and refractions cause colors to appear by separating the mixture into its components. He devised an experimental demonstration of this theory, one of the great early exhibitions of the power of experimental investigation in science. His measurement of the rings reflected from a thin film of air confined between a lens and a sheet of glass was the first demonstration of periodicity in optical phenomena. In 1672 Newton sent a brief exposition of his theory of colors to the Royal Society in London. Its appearance in the *Philosophical Transactions* led to a number of criticisms that confirmed his fear of publication, and he subsequently withdrew as much as possible into the solitude of his Cambridge study. He did not publish his full *Opticks* until 1704.

The *Principia*. In August 1684 Newton's solitude was interrupted by a visit from Edmund Halley, the British astronomer and mathematician, who discussed with Newton the problem of orbital motion. Newton had also pursued the science of mechanics as an undergraduate, and at that time he had entertained rudimentary notions about univeral gravitation. As a result of Halley's visit, he returned to these studies. During the following two and a half years he established the modern science of dynamics by formulating his three laws of motion. From their application to orbital motion as defined by Kepler's laws (q.v.), he derived the law of universal gravitation, a law that bound terrestrial and celestial motion together in a synthesis of stunning generality. The publication of the *Philosophiae Naturalis Principia Mathematica* in 1687 marked an epoch in the history of science; it also ensured that its author could never regain his privacy.

The *Principia*'s appearance also involved Newton in an unpleasant episode with the English philosopher and physicist Robert Hooke, who claimed that Newton had stolen from him a central idea of the book: that bodies attract each other with a force that varies inversely as the square of their distance. Although historians do not take seriously the charge of plagiarism, Hooke never ceased to feel that he had been wronged.

In the same year, 1687, Newton helped to lead Cambridge's resistance to the efforts of King James II to Catholicize it. After the English Revolution, which drove James from England, the university elected Newton one of its representatives in the Convention Parliament. The following four years were filled with intense activity, as, buoyed by the triumph of the *Principia,* he tried to put all his earlier achievements into their final form. In the summer of 1693 Newton exhibited symptoms of a severe emotional disorder. Although he regained his health, his creative period had come to an end.

Newton's connections with the leaders of the new regime in England led to his appointment as warden (and later master) of the Royal Mint in London, where he lived after 1696. In 1703 the Royal Society elected him president, an office he held for the rest of his life. As president, he undertook to force the immediate publication of the astronomical observations of the Astronomer Royal, John Flamsteed, which Newton needed to perfect his lunar theory. He conducted the resulting conflict with Flamsteed in an insensitive and tyrannical manner. He also engaged in a violent dispute with Leibniz over priority in the invention of the calculus. Newton used his position as president of the Royal Society to have a committee of that body investigate the question; he himself secretly wrote the committee's report, which charged Leibniz with deliberate plagiarism. Newton also compiled the book of evidence that the society published. The bitter aftermath of the quarrel lingered nearly until his death, on March 31, 1727, at Kensington. R.S.We.

For further information on this person, see the section Biographies in the Bibliography in volume 28.

NEWTON'S LAWS OF MOTION. *See* MECHANICS.

NEW WESTMINSTER, city, SW British Columbia, Canada, on the Fraser R., near Vancouver; inc. 1860. The city maintains one of the largest freshwater ports on the Pacific coast and is the headquarters for the Fraser R. fishing fleet. Major manufactures include wood, metal, and paper products, processed food, boats, alcoholic beverages, and machinery. New Westminster is the site of a junior college; the Regimental Museum, containing a collection of military artifacts; Irving House Historic Centre and Museum; and the National Lacrosse Hall of Fame. The community was the capital of colonial British Columbia from 1859 to 1866. It was called Queensborough until 1859. Pop. (1976) 38,393; (1981) 38,550.

NEW YEAR'S DAY, first day of the year, January 1 in the Gregorian calendar. In the Middle Ages most European countries used the Julian calendar and observed New Year's Day on March 25, called Annunciation Day and celebrated as the occasion on which it was revealed to Mary that she would give birth to the Son of God. With the introduction of the Gregorian calendar in 1582, Roman Catholic countries began to celebrate New Year's Day on January 1. Scotland accepted the Gregorian calendar in 1600; Germany, Denmark, and Sweden about 1700; and England in 1752. Traditionally the day has been observed as a religious feast, but in modern times the arrival of the New Year has also become an occasion for spirited celebration and the making of personal resolutions about future conduct. The Jewish New Year is called Rosh Hashanah, or the Feast of Trumpets, and is prescribed by the Old Testament as a holy Sabbath. It is celebrated on the first and second days of Tishri (generally September). The Chinese celebrate New Year's Day sometime between January 10 and February 19 of the Gregorian calendar. It is their most important holiday.

NEW YORK, one of the Middle Atlantic states of the U.S., bordered on the N by Ontario and Québec provinces, Canada; on the E by Vermont, Massachusetts, and Connecticut; on the SE by the Atlantic Ocean; on the S by New Jersey and Pennsylvania; and on the W by Pennsylvania and Ontario. Several boundaries are formed by bodies of water, including Lake Ontario and the Saint Lawrence R., in the N; Lake Champlain and the Poultney R., in the NE; the Hudson and Delaware rivers, in the SE; and Lake Erie and the Niagara R., in the W.

New York entered the Union on July 26, 1788, as the 11th of the original 13 states. New York has long been a leader in the political, cultural, and economic life of the U.S. Despite some economic difficulties in the 1970s and the early '80s, particularly in New York City and other urban areas, the state was among the U.S. leaders in such important sectors as manufacturing, commerce, foreign trade, communications, and finance. New York is the birthplace of four U.S. presidents—Martin Van Buren, Millard Fillmore, Theodore Roosevelt, and Franklin D. Roosevelt. In addition, President Grover Cleveland spent most of his life in the state. New York, named in the 1660s for the duke of York, later James II of England, is called the Empire State.

LAND AND RESOURCES

New York, with an area of 127,189 sq km (49,108 sq mi), is the 30th largest state in the U.S.; 0.8% of its land area is owned by the federal government. The mainland portion of New York is shaped roughly like a right triangle; Long Island forms an extension in the SE. The extreme dimensions of the mainland are about 515 km (about 320 mi) from E to W and about 500 km (about 310 mi) from N to S; Long Island extends about 195 km (about 120 mi) from E to W. Elevations begin at sea level, along the Atlantic Ocean in the SE, and range up to 1629 m (5344 ft), atop Mt. Marcy in the NE. The approximate mean elevation is 305 m (1000 ft). The state has a coastline of 204 km (127 mi).

Physical Geography. New York's geography is diverse, encompassing seven major regions. The Saint Lawrence Lowland region, in the N, is made up of a narrow lowland corridor along the St. Lawrence R. plus an area bordering Lake Champlain. The terrain is flat to gently rolling and becomes hillier to the S. Most of the region is underlain by sandstones and limestones and has a mixture of limy and acidic soils.

The Adirondack Upland in NE New York takes in about one-quarter of the state. Much of it is rugged, and many peaks, including Mt. Marcy, rise to more than 1220 m (more than 4000 ft). The oldest and some of the hardest rocks in the state underlie this upland. Soils in the region are generally thin, stony, and acidic.

The Eastern Great Lakes Lowland region, bor-

The Nelson A. Rockefeller Empire State Plaza in Albany, capital of New York, was built in the 1960s and '70s. The modern government buildings are in sharp contrast to the old capitol, seen at the far end of the complex. Jessica Ehlers–Bruce Coleman, Inc.

dering Lakes Erie and Ontario, is generally flat close to the lakes and somewhat rolling to hilly farther away. Between Rochester and Syracuse are thousands of drumlins—low hills shaped somewhat like eggs—formed by the glaciers that once covered the region. The lowland is underlain by sedimentary rocks, mainly limestone, sandstone, and shale. Resistant strata in the southward-dipping layers have produced a series of E to W escarpments in the region. Niagara Falls was formed where the Niagara R. plunges over one of the escarpments. Soils of the region are generally limy and are quite fertile.

Occupying nearly half of the state, the Appalachian Plateau region, in the S, has three main divisions. The Catskill Mts., with elevations ranging to about 1280 (about 4200 ft), form the E part of the region. In central New York is the lowest part, with deep valleys formed by glaciers. Here are the famous Finger Lakes. To the W, the plateau is higher, although cut by deep valleys. The Appalachian Plateau is underlain by sedimentary rocks, principally sandstone, shale, and limestone, and by extensive salt deposits. Soils tend to be deep and acidic; in the major river valleys are rich alluvial soils.

The Hudson-Mohawk Lowlands region is in the central and E parts of New York. Between the Appalachian Plateau and the New England Up-

land region is the narrow Hudson Valley. Near its S end the lowlands extend SW through the Wallkill Valley. The Mohawk Valley lies NW of the Hudson, mainly between the Adirondacks and the Appalachian Plateau. At the extreme NW of the region is an isolated upland with an elevation of about 610 m (about 2000 ft), the Tug Hill Plateau, located between the Adirondacks and the Eastern Great Lakes Lowland. Geologically, the upland is an outlier of the Appalachian Plateau with similar sedimentary rocks. Soils in the Hudson-Mohawk Lowlands vary from the fertile alluvial deposits found in the river valleys to limy, moderately fertile soils that developed on glacial till.

Three main subdivisions make up the New England Upland region. The Taconic Mts. lie along New York's E border. Farther to the S, the spectacular Hudson Highlands extend SW across the Hudson R. The third subdivision is composed of the crystalline Manhattan hills, which are relatively low and make up most of Westchester Co. and Manhattan Island.

Long Island and Staten Island represent most of New York's share of the Atlantic Coastal Plain. The N part of Long Island is composed of low hills rising to about 90 m (about 300 ft), and in the S is a low, flat plain. Soils tend to be sandy and lacking in natural fertility.

Rivers and Lakes. New York has many rivers and lakes. The Great Lakes–St. Lawrence Basin drains much of W and central New York, including the Finger Lakes, the Tug Hill Plateau, and parts of the Adirondacks, plus the extreme N part of the state. Besides the St. Lawrence, some of the better known rivers in this area are the Genesee, Black, Niagara, and Oswego. The Hudson R. drains parts of the Adirondacks and areas E and W of the river. Its main tributary is the Mohawk. The Allegheny R. and a few other streams drain SW New York. The central part of the state S of the Finger Lakes is drained by the Susquehanna R. and its tributaries, such as the Chemung, Cohocton, Chenango, and Unadilla rivers. The Catskill Mts. are drained principally by the Delaware R. and its tributaries. Picturesque waterfalls are found along several of New York's rivers. The best known is Niagara Falls. The upper Hudson R. and the Genesee R. form several smaller falls.

New York contains a large number of lakes, many of which are frequented by summer vacationers. Three large lakes—Champlain, Erie, and Ontario—are only partly in the state. Wholly within New York are Lake Oneida and the Finger Lakes, near Syracuse; the Saranac lakes, Lake Placid, Blue Mountain Lake, Cranberry Lake, Lake George, Raquette Lake, and Tupper Lake, all in the Adirondacks; and Chautauqua Lake, in the SW. In addition to these natural bodies of water,

New York contains several large artificial reservoirs, notably in the Catskill Mts.

Climate. New York's climate is humid continental, reflecting its position in the belt of the mid-latitude westerlies. The considerable climatic variation within the state results mainly from differences of terrain, elevation, and proximity to large water bodies. In general, the SE part of the state has the highest mean monthly temperature, and the uplands of the NE the lowest. Mean annual precipitation ranges from about 890 to 1145 mm (about 35 to 45 in) in most parts of New York and is relatively evenly distributed over the course of a year. Most of the state receives abundant snowfall. East of Lake Erie and along Lake Ontario are belts of especially heavy snowfall, and the Tug Hill Plateau receives some of the greatest annual accumulations of snow of any area in the U.S. east of the Rocky Mts. The recorded temperature in New York has ranged from $-46.7°$ C ($-52°$ F), in 1934 at Stillwater Reservoir in the Adirondacks, to $42.2°$ C ($108°$ F), in 1926 at Troy in the E. Aside from thunderstorms and heavy snowfalls, New York is struck by few damaging storms. Hurricanes occasionally strike Long Island and the SE section of the state's mainland.

Plants and Animals. About 61% of the land area of New York is covered with forest, most of it regrowth on cutover land. Northern hardwoods,

Montauk Point, a promontory at the tip of the southern peninsula of Long Island, is equipped with a 51.2-m (168-ft) stone lighthouse. New York State Dept. of Commerce

including birch, sugar and red maple, and basswood, intermixed with conifers such as hemlock and white pine, are characteristic of much of the Appalachian Plateau forests. In the SE, oaks are dominant, and in the higher Adirondacks spruce and fir dominate, often mixed with northern hardwoods such as ash. Among the many wild flowers of New York are azalea and other rhododendron, black-eyed Susan, buttercups, violets, orchids, and mountain laurel.

New York's larger animals include white-tailed deer and black bear, the former widespread over the state and the latter living mainly in more remote regions of the Adirondacks and the Appalachian Plateau. Among the state's common smaller animals are beaver, rabbit, woodchuck, fox, raccoon, weasel, squirrel, and chipmunk. Game birds include pheasant, grouse, partridge, quail, and wild duck. Some of the other more common birds are robins, sparrows, warblers, crows, bluebirds, and woodpeckers. The fresh and marine waters of New York are inhabited by large numbers of fish. Freshwater varieties include black bass, pickerel, pike, whitefish, crappie, and trout. Among the saltwater fish are marlin, tuna, bluefish, striped bass, and flounder. The Long Island coast is noted for clams.

Mineral Resources. New York has varied mineral resources, mainly nonmetallic. These include limestone, found principally S of Lake Ontario, in the Hudson-Mohawk Lowlands, and in the St. Lawrence and Black river valleys. Other minerals are salt, which underlays much of central and W New York; gypsum, found S of Lake Ontario; talc, located in the N; slate, occurring at the Vermont border; garnets, deposited in the S Adirondacks; clay, situated especially in the Hudson Valley; emery, located in the SE; and stone and sand and gravel, found in many parts of the state. Natural-gas deposits are in W New York, and relatively small amounts of petroleum are in the SW. Metallic minerals occurring in New York include lead, zinc, iron, and silver, situated mainly in and near the Adirondack Mts.   H.H.F.

POPULATION

According to the 1980 census, New York had 17,558,072 inhabitants, a decrease of 3.7% from 1970. During this period New York was one of the few states to lose population; the statewide population loss, however, is largely explained by the decrease in population of New York City. The average population density was 138 people per sq km (358 per sq mi). More than half the state's population was concentrated in the New York City metropolitan area. Whites made up 79.5% of the population and blacks 13.7%; more blacks live in New York (about 2.4 million) than

in any other state. Additional population groups included some 148,104 persons of Chinese descent, 60,511 persons of Asian Indian background, 38,117 American Indians, 34,157 persons of Korean origin, 33,956 persons of Filipino extraction, and 24,524 persons of Japanese ancestry. Approximately 1,659,250 persons, or 9% of the total population, were of Hispanic background; a majority of these were persons of Puerto Rican origin living in the New York City metropolitan area. New York's ethnic and racial diversity has resulted in a religious diversity as well. The state had larger groups of Roman Catholics (about 36% of the total population) and Jews (about 12%) than any other state. Other major religious groups included Episcopalians, Methodists, and Presbyterians. In 1980 about 85% of New Yorkers lived in areas defined as urban and the rest lived in rural areas. The state's biggest cities were New York, the largest city in the U.S.; Buffalo; Rochester; Yonkers; Syracuse; and Albany, the capital.

EDUCATION AND CULTURAL ACTIVITY

New York's numerous institutions of higher education, its fine museums, its noted performing-arts groups, and its communications media have made the state, and particularly New York City, one of the most important cultural centers in the world.

Education. The New York legislature passed a bill in 1784 creating a board of regents to oversee education in the state. In 1812 legislation was passed to establish a statewide system of public elementary schools, and in 1867 such schools were made tuition-free. By the 1860s the state also had a number of free high schools. In the early 1980s, New York had 4143 public elementary and secondary schools. The public schools each year enrolled a total of about 1.8 million elementary pupils and 1 million secondary students. In addition, about 584,000 students annually attended private elementary and secondary schools.

The first institution of higher education in the state was King's College (now Columbia University), in New York City, which was incorporated under a royal charter in 1754. In the early 1980s New York had 293 institutions of higher education with a combined annual enrollment of about 992,240 students. Besides Columbia University, which encompasses Barnard College, notable schools included New York University, the Juilliard School, Rockefeller University, Yeshiva University, Pratt Institute (1887), Fordham University, Wagner College (1883), Saint John's University, and the New School for Social Research (1919), in New York City; the U.S. Military Academy, in West Point; Cornell University and Ithaca

INDEX TO MAP OF NEW YORK

Cities and Towns

Adams ... J 3
Addison ... F 6
Afton ... J 6
Akron ... C 4
Albany (cap.) ⊙ ... N 5
Albion ⊙ ... D 4
Alden ... C 5
Alexandria Bay ... J 2
Alfred ... E 6
Allegany ... C 6
Altamont ... M 5
Amenia ... N 7
Amherst ... C 4
Amityville ... E 3
Amsterdam ... M 5
Angola ... C 5
Apalachin ... H 6
Arcade ... D 5
Ardsley ... H 1
Arlington ... N 7
Athens ... N 6
Atlantic Beach ... A 4
Attica ... D 5
Auburn ⊙ ... G 5
Aurora ... G 5
Au Sable Forks ... N 2
Averill Park ... O 5
Avoca ... F 6
Avon ... E 5
Babylon ... D 2
Bainbridge ... J 6
Baldwin ... B 4
Baldwinsville ... H 4
Ballston Spa ⊙ ... N 5
Balmville ... M 7
Batavia ⊙ ... D 5
Bath ⊙ ... F 6
Bayport ... E 2
Bay Shore ... E 2
Bayville ... B 2
Beacon ... N 7
Bedford Hills ... D 1
Bellerose ... A 3
Bellmore ... B 3
Bellport ... F 2
Belmont ⊙ ... E 6
Bergen ... E 4
Big Flats ... G 6
Binghamton ⊙ ... J 6
Black River ... J 3
Blasdell ... C 5
Bolivar ... D 6
Bolton Landing ... N 3
Boonville ... K 4
Brant Lake ... N 3
Brentwood ... E 2
Brewerton ... H 4
Brewster ... D 1
Broadalbin ... M 4
Brockport ... D 4
Brocton ... B 6
Bronx ⊙ ... D 2
Bronxville ... J 1
Brooklyn ⊙ ... C 2
Brownville ... H 3
Buchanan ... D 1
Buffalo ⊙ ... B 5
Caledonia ... E 5
Cambridge ... O 4
Camden ... J 4
Camillus ... H 4
Canajoharie ... L 5
Canandaigua ⊙ ... F 5
Canastota ... J 4
Canisteo ... E 6
Canton ⊙ ... K 1
Carmel ⊙ ... D 1
Carthage ... J 3
Cassadaga ... B 6
Castile ... D 5
Castleton-on-Hudson ... N 5
Catskill ⊙ ... N 6
Cattaraugus ... C 6
Cazenovia ... J 5
Cedarhurst ... A 4
Celoron ... B 6
Centereach ... E 2

⊙ County seat

Center Moriches ... F 2
Central Islip ... E 2
Champlain ... N 1
Chateaugay ... N 1
Chatham ... N 6
Chautauqua ... A 6
Chazy ... N 1
Cheektowaga ... C 5
Chenango Bridge ... J 6
Chester ... B 1
Chittenango ... J 4
Churchville ... E 4
Cincinnatus ... H 5
Clarence ... C 5
Clarkson ... E 4
Clayton ... H 2
Clifton Park ... N 5
Clifton Springs ... F 5
Clinton ... K 4
Clyde ... G 4
Cobleskill ... L 5
Cohoes ... N 5
Colden ... C 5
Cold Spring ... C 1
Colonie ... N 5
Conesus ... E 5
Cooperstown ⊙ ... L 5
Corinth ... N 4
Corning ... F 6
Cornwall on Hudson ... C 1
Cortland ⊙ ... H 5
Coxsackie ... N 6
Croton Falls ... D 1
Croton-on-Hudson ... C 1
Crown Point ... N 3
Cuba ... D 6
Dannemora ... N 1
Dansville ... E 5
Deer Park ... D 2
Delhi ⊙ ... L 6
Delmar ... N 5
Depew ... C 5
Deposit ... K 6
Derby ... B 5
De Ruyter ... J 5
De Witt ... H 4
Dexter ... H 2
Dobbs Ferry ... H 1
Dolgeville ... L 4
Dryden ... H 6
Dundee ... F 5
Dunkirk ... B 5
Earlville ... J 5
East Aurora ... C 5
East Greenbush ... N 5
East Hampton ... G 2
East Hills ... B 3
East Meadow ... B 3
East Moriches ... F 2
East Northport ... E 2
Eastport ... F 2
East Rochester ... F 4
East Rockaway ... A 4
East Syracuse ... H 4
Eden ... C 5
Eggertsville ... C 5
Elbridge ... G 5
Elizabethtown ⊙ ... N 2
Ellenville ... M 7
Elma ... C 5
Elmira ⊙ ... G 6
Elmira Heights ... G 6
Elmont ... A 3
Elmsford ... J 1
Endicott ... H 6
Endwell ... H 6
Fairport ... F 4
Fairview ... N 7
Falconer ... B 6
Farmingdale ... B 3
Fayetteville ... J 4
Fernwood ... N 4
Fishkill ... N 7
Floral Park ... A 3
Florida ... B 1
Fonda ⊙ ... M 5
Fort Ann ... N 4
Fort Covington ... M 1
Fort Edward ... O 4
Fort Plain ... L 4
Frankfort ... K 4
Franklinville ... D 6
Fredonia ... B 6
Freeport ... B 4
Frewsburg ... B 6
Friendship ... D 6
Fulton ... H 4
Gansevoort ... N 4
Garden City ... B 3
Geneseo ⊙ ... E 5
Geneva ... G 5
Glasco ... M 6
Glen Cove ... A 3
Glens Falls ... N 4
Gloversville ... M 4
Golden's Bridge ... D 1
Goshen ⊙ ... B 1
Gouverneur ... K 2
Gowanda ... B 6
Grand Gorge ... L 6
Grand Island ... B 5
Granville ... O 4
Great Neck ... A 3
Greece ... E 4
Greene ... J 6
Green Island ... N 5
Greenport ... F 1
Greenwich ... O 4
Greenwood Lake ... B 1
Groton ... H 5
Hagaman ... M 5
Hamburg ... C 5
Hamilton ... J 5
Hammondsport ... F 6
Hampton Bays ... F 2
Hancock ... K 7
Harriman ... C 1
Harrison ... J 1
Hastings on Hudson ... H 1
Haverstraw ... C 1
Hawthorne ... H 1
Hempstead ... B 3
Herkimer ⊙ ... L 4
Hermon ... K 2
Herrings ... J 2
Heuvelton ... K 1
Hewlett ... A 4
Hicksville ... B 3
Highland ... M 7
Highland Falls ... C 1
Hillburn ... C 2
Hilton ... E 4
Holley ... D 4
Homer ... H 5
Honeoye Falls ... F 5
Hoosick Falls ... O 5
Hopewell Junction ... N 7
Hornell ... E 6
Horseheads ... G 6
Houghton ... D 6
Hudson ⊙ ... N 6
Hudson Falls ... O 4
Huntington ... B 2
Huntington Station ... B 3
Hurley ... M 7
Hyde Park ... M 7
Ilion ... K 5
Inwood ... A 4
Irondequoit ... E 4
Irvington ... H 1
Island Park ... B 4
Islip ... E 2
Ithaca ⊙ ... G 6
Jamaica ⊙ ... D 2
Jamestown ... B 6
Jericho ... B 3
Johnson City ... J 6
Johnstown ⊙ ... M 4
Jordan ... H 4
Katonah ... D 1
Keeseville ... O 2
Kenmore ... C 5
Kerhonkson ... M 7
Kinderhook ... N 6
Kings Park ... E 2
Kings Point ... A 3
Kingston ⊙ ... M 7
Lackawanna ... B 5
Lake Carmel ... D 1
Lake Erie Beach ... B 5
Lake George ⊙ ... N 4
Lake Katrine ... M 7
Lake Placid ... N 2
Lake Pleasant ⊙ ... M 4
Lake Success ... A 3
Lake View ... B 5
Lakewood ... B 6
Lancaster ... C 5
Larchmont ... J 1
Lawrence ... A 4
Le Roy ... E 5
Levittown ... B 3
Lewiston ... B 4
Liberty ... L 7
Lima ... E 5
Lindenhurst ... E 2
Little Falls ... L 4
Little Valley ⊙ ... C 6
Liverpool ... H 4
Livingston Manor ... L 7
Livonia ... E 5
Lockport ⊙ ... C 4
Long Beach ... B 4
Lowville ⊙ ... J 3
Lynbrook ... A 3
Lyon Mountain ... N 1
Lyons ⊙ ... G 4
Macedon ... F 4
McGraw ... H 5
Mahopac ... D 1
Malone ⊙ ... M 1
Malverne ... A 3
Mamaroneck ... J 1
Manchester ... F 5
Manhasset ... A 3
Manlius ... J 5
Marathon ... J 6
Marcellus ... H 5
Marcy ... K 4
Marlboro ... M 7
Massapequa ... B 3
Massapequa Park ... B 3
Massena ... L 1
Mastic Beach ... F 2
Mattituck ... F 2
Maybrook ... B 1
Mayfield ... M 4
Mayville ⊙ ... A 6
Mechanicville ... N 5
Medina ... D 4
Melrose Park ... H 5
Menands ... N 5
Merrick ... B 4
Mexico ... H 4
Middleburgh ... M 5
Middle Hope ... M 7
Middleport ... C 4
Middletown ... B 1
Millbrook ... N 7
Millerton ... O 7
Mill Neck ... B 2
Milton ... M 7
Milton ... N 4
Mineola ⊙ ... B 3
Mineville ... O 2
Minoa ... H 4
Mohawk ... L 4
Monroe ... C 1
Montgomery ... B 1
Monticello ⊙ ... L 7
Montour Falls ... G 6
Moravia ... H 5
Morrisonville ... N 1
Morrisville ... J 5
Mount Kisco ... D 1
Mount Morris ... E 5
Mount Vernon ... H 1
Naples ... F 5
Nassau ... N 5
Newark ... G 4
Newark Valley ... H 6
New Berlin ... K 5
Newburgh ... C 1
New City ⊙ ... B 1
Newfane ... C 4
New Hartford ... K 4
New Hyde Park ... A 3
New Paltz ... M 7
New Rochelle ... J 1
New Windsor ... C 1
New York ⊙ ... C 2
New York Mills ... K 4
Niagara Falls ... C 4

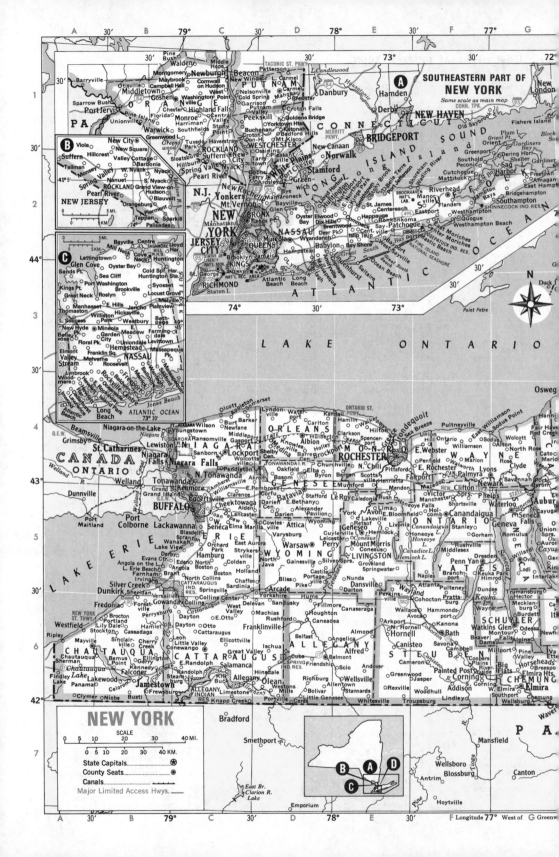

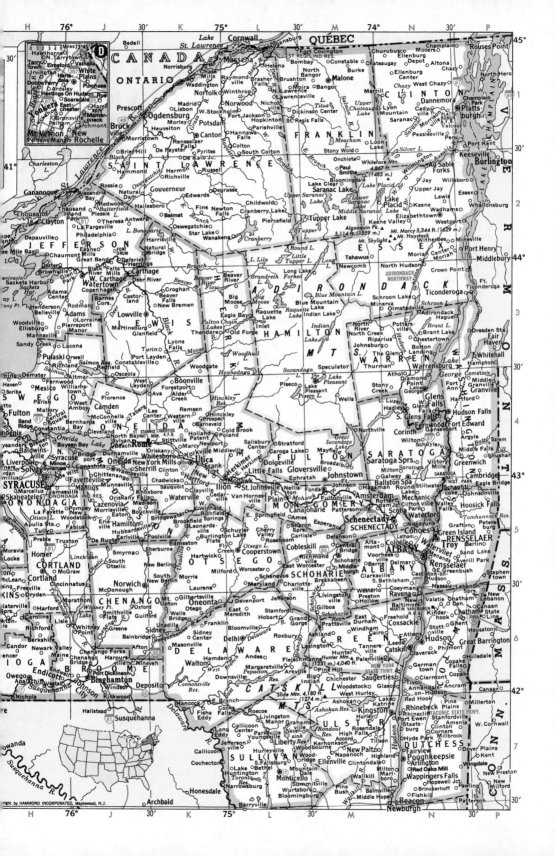

Index to Map of New York

Niskayuna . . . . N 5
Norfolk . . . . K 1
North Boston . . . . C 5
North Chili . . . . E 4
North Collins . . . . C 5
Northport . . . . E 2
North Syracuse . . . . H 4
North Tarrytown . . . . . . H 1
North Tonawanda . . . . . C 4
Northville . . . . M 4
Norwich ⊙ . . . . J 5
Norwood . . . . L 1
Nunda . . . . E 5
Nyack . . . . B 2
Oakfield . . . . D 4
Oceanside . . . . B 4
Ogdensburg . . . . K 1
Olcott . . . . C 4
Olean . . . . D 6
Oneida . . . . J 4
Oneonta . . . . K 6
Orchard Park . . . . C 5
Oriskany . . . . K 4
Ossining . . . . D 1
Oswego ⊙ . . . . G 4
Ovid ⊙ . . . . G 5
Owego ⊙ . . . . H 6
Oxford . . . . J 6
Oyster Bay . . . . B 3
Painted Post . . . . F 6
Palmyra . . . . F 4
Patchogue . . . . E 2
Pawling . . . . N 7
Pearl River . . . . B 2
Peekskill . . . . D 1
Pelham . . . . H 1
Pelham Manor . . . . H 1
Penfield . . . . F 4
Penn Yan ⊙ . . . . F 5
Perry . . . . D 5
Peru . . . . N 1
Phelps . . . . F 5
Philmont . . . . N 6
Phoenix . . . . H 4
Piermont . . . . B 2
Pine Bush . . . . B 1
Pittsford . . . . E 4
Plainview . . . . B 3
Plattsburgh ⊙ . . . . O 1
Pleasantville . . . . D 2
Port Byron . . . . G 4
Port Chester . . . . J 1
Port Ewen . . . . N 7
Port Henry . . . . O 2
Port Jefferson . . . . E 2
Port Jervis . . . . A 1
Portville . . . . D 6
Port Washington . . . . . . A 3
Potsdam . . . . K 1
Poughkeepsie ⊙ . . . . . N 7
Pulaski . . . . H 3
Purchase . . . . J 1
Randolph . . . . C 6
Ravena . . . . N 6
Red Hook . . . . N 7
Rensselaer . . . . N 5
Rhinebeck . . . . N 7
Richfield Springs . . . . . . K 5
Ripley . . . . A 6
Riverhead ⊙ . . . . F 2
Riverside . . . . F 6
Rochester ⊙ . . . . E 4
Rockville Centre . . . . . . B 4
Rome . . . . J 4
Ronkonkoma . . . . E 2
Roosevelt . . . . B 3
Roscoe . . . . L 7
Roslyn . . . . A 3
Rouses Point . . . . O 1
Rye . . . . J 1

⊙ County seat

Sackets Harbor . . . . H 3
Sag Harbor . . . . G 2
Saint George ⊙ . . . . . . C 3
Saint Johnsville . . . . . . L 5
Salamanca . . . . C 6
Salem . . . . O 4
Sands Point . . . . A 3
Saranac Lake . . . . M 2
Saratoga Springs . . . . . N 4
Saugerties . . . . M 6
Sauquoit . . . . K 5
Sayville . . . . E 2
Scarsdale . . . . J 1
Schenectady ⊙ . . . . . . M 5
Schoharie ⊙ . . . . M 5
Schuylerville . . . . N 4
Scotia . . . . N 5
Scottsville . . . . E 4
Scriba . . . . H 4
Sea Cliff . . . . A 3
Seneca Falls . . . . G 5
Sherburne . . . . K 5
Sherrill . . . . J 4
Sidney . . . . K 6
Silver Creek . . . . B 5
Skaneateles . . . . H 5
Sloan . . . . C 5
Sloatsburg . . . . C 2
Smithtown . . . . E 2
Sodus . . . . G 4
Sodus Point . . . . G 4
Solvay . . . . H 4
Southampton . . . . G 2
South Corning . . . . F 6
South Fallsburg . . . . . . L 7
South Glens Falls . . . . . N 4
Southold . . . . F 2
Southport . . . . G 6
Spencerport . . . . E 4
Spring Valley . . . . A 2
Springville . . . . C 5
Stamford . . . . L 6
Stillwater . . . . N 5
Stony Brook . . . . E 2
Stony Point . . . . C 1
Stottville . . . . N 6
Suffern . . . . A 2
Syosset . . . . B 3
Syracuse ⊙ . . . . H 4
Tarrytown . . . . H 1
Thomaston . . . . A 3
Ticonderoga . . . . N 3
Tillson . . . . M 7
Tonawanda . . . . B 4
Troy ⊙ . . . . N 5
Trumansburg . . . . G 5
Tuckahoe . . . . H 1
Tupper Lake . . . . M 2
Unadilla . . . . K 6
Union Springs . . . . G 5
Utica ⊙ . . . . K 4
Valatie . . . . N 6
Valhalla . . . . J 1
Valley Stream . . . . A 3
Vestal . . . . H 6
Victor . . . . F 5
Voorheesville . . . . M 5
Walden . . . . B 1
Wallkill . . . . M 7
Walton . . . . K 6
Wampsville ⊙ . . . . J 4
Wanakah . . . . C 5
Wantagh . . . . B 3
Wappingers Falls . . . . . N 7
Warrensburg . . . . N 3
Warsaw ⊙ . . . . D 5
Warwick ⊙ . . . . B 1
Waterford . . . . N 5
Waterloo ⊙ . . . . G 5
Watertown ⊙ . . . . J 3
Waterville . . . . K 5
Watervliet . . . . N 5

Watkins Glen ⊙ . . . . . . G 6
Waverly . . . . G 7
Wayland . . . . E 5
Webster . . . . F 4
Weedsport . . . . G 4
Wellsville . . . . E 6
Westbury . . . . B 3
West Carthage . . . . J 3
West Elmira . . . . G 6
Westfield . . . . A 6
West Glens Falls . . . . . . N 4
Westhampton . . . . F 2
Westhampton Beach . . . F 2
West Point . . . . C 1
West Seneca . . . . C 5
Whitehall . . . . O 3
White Plains ⊙ . . . . J 1
Whitesboro . . . . K 4
Williamson . . . . F 4
Williamsville . . . . C 5
Williston Park . . . . A 3
Wilson . . . . C 4
Wolcott . . . . G 4
Woodmere . . . . A 4
Woodstock . . . . M 6
Yonkers . . . . H 1
Yorktown Heights . . . . . C 1
Yorkville . . . . K 4
Youngstown . . . . C 4

Other Features

Adirondack (mts.) . . . . . M 3
Algonquin (peak) . . . . . M 2
Allegany Ind. Res. . . . . . C 6
Allegheny (res.) . . . . C 6
Allegheny (river) . . . . . . C 6
Ashokan (res.) . . . . M 7
Ausable (river) . . . . N 2
Batten Kill (river) . . . . . O 4
*Bear (mt.) . . . . C 1
Beaver (river) . . . . K 3
Black (river) . . . . K 3
Blue Mountain (lake) . . M 3
Brookhaven National
  Lab . . . . E 2
Camp Drum . . . . J 3
Canandaigua (lake) . . . F 5
Canisteo (river) . . . . F 6
Cannonsville (res.) . . . . K 6
Catskill (mts.) . . . . L 6
Cattaraugus Ind. Res. . C 5
Cayuga (lake) . . . . G 5
Champlain (lake) . . . . . O 1
Chautauqua (lake) . . . . A 6
Chazy (lake) . . . . N 1
Chenango (river) . . . . . J 6
Cohocton (river) . . . . . . F 6
Conesus (lake) . . . . E 5
Cranberry (lake) . . . . . . L 2
Delaware (river) . . . . . . K 7
East (river) . . . . C 2
*Eleanor Roosevelt
  Nat'l Hist. Site . . . . . . N 7
Erie (lake) . . . . B 5
Fire Isl. Nat'l.
  Seashore . . . . F 2
Fishers (island) . . . . G 1
Fort Niagara . . . . C 4
Fort Stanwix Nat'l.
  Mon. . . . . K 4
Fulton Chain (lakes) . . . K 3
Gardiners (island) . . . . G 2
Gateway Nat'l. Rec.
  Area . . . . C 3
Genesee (river) . . . . E 5
George (lake) . . . . N 4
Grass (river) . . . . K 1

* Not on map

Great Sacandaga
  (lake) . . . . M 4
Great South (bay) . . . . . E 2
Greenwood (lake) . . . . . B 2
Griffiss AFB . . . . K 4
*Home of Franklin D.
  Roosevelt Nat'l. Hist.
  Site . . . . N 7
Honeoye (lake) . . . . F 5
Hudson (river) . . . . N 7
Hunter (mt.) . . . . M 6
Indian (lake) . . . . M 3
Jones (beach) . . . . B 4
Keuka (lake) . . . . F 5
Long (island) . . . . E 2
Long (lake) . . . . M 2
Long Island (sound) . . . E 2
Manhattan (island) . . . . C 2
Marcy (mt.) . . . . N 2
Martin Van Buren
  Nat'l. Hist. Site . . . . . N 6
Mohawk (river) . . . . L 5
Montauk (point) . . . . . . H 2
Moose (river) . . . . K 3
Neversink (res.) . . . . . . L 7
New York State Barge
  (canal) . . . . C 4
Niagara (river) . . . . B 4
Oil Spring Ind. Res. . . . D 6
Oneida (lake) . . . . J 4
Onondaga Ind. Res. . . . H 5
Ontario (lake) . . . . F 3
Orient (point) . . . . G 2
Oswegatchie (river) . . . K 2
Oswego (river) . . . . H 4
Otisco (lake) . . . . H 5
Otsego (lake) . . . . L 5
Owasco (lake) . . . . G 5
Peconic (bay) . . . . F 2
Pepacton (res.) . . . . L 6
Placid (lake) . . . . N 2
Plattsburg AFB . . . . N 1
Poosepatuck Ind. Res. . F 2
Raquette (lake) . . . . L 3
Raquette (river) . . . . L 1
Rondout (res.) . . . . M 7
Sagamore Hill Nat'l.
  Hist. Site . . . . B 2
Saint Lawrence (lake) . . K 1
Saint Lawrence (river) . J 2
Saint Regis (river) . . . . . L 1
Saint Regis Ind. Res. . . M 1
Salmon (river) . . . . H 3
Salmon (river) . . . . M 1
Saranac (lakes) . . . . . . M 2
Saranac (river) . . . . N 1
Saratoga (lake) . . . . N 4
Saratoga Nat'l. Hist.
  Park . . . . N 4
Schoharie (creek) . . . . . M 6
Schroon (lake) . . . . N 3
Seneca (lake) . . . . G 5
Seneca (river) . . . . G 5
Shelter (island) . . . . G 1
Shinnecock Ind. Res. . . G 2
Skaneateles (lake) . . . . H 5
Slide (mt.) . . . . L 6
Staten (island) . . . . C 3
Statue of Liberty Nat'l.
  Mon. . . . . C 3
Susquehanna (river) . . . H 6
Thousand (islands) . . . . H 2
Tioughnioga (river) . . . . H 6
Tonawanda Ind. Res. . . D 4
Tupper (lake) . . . . M 2
Tuscarora Ind. Res. . . . B 4
Unadilla (river) . . . . K 5
Upper Saranac (lake) . . M 2
Valcour (island) . . . . . . N 1
Whiteface (mt.) . . . . N 2
*Women's Rights Nat'l
  Hist. Park . . . . G 5

College (1892), in Ithaca; Rensselaer Polytechnic Institute (1824), in Troy; Skidmore College (1911), in Saratoga Springs; Bard College (1860), in Annandale-on-Hudson; Hamilton College (1812), in Clinton; Hobart-William Smith Colleges (1822), in Geneva; Colgate University, in Hamilton; Union College, in Schenectady; Vassar College, in Poughkeepsie; Syracuse University, in Syracuse; Sarah Lawrence College, in Yonkers; and the University of Rochester, in Rochester. In addition, two extensive public systems of higher education—the State University of New York and the City University of New York—enrolled large numbers of students.

Cultural Institutions. New York City is the foremost cultural center of the U.S. The most famous museums and cultural institutions of the city include the Metropolitan Museum of Art, the Museum of Modern Art, the Whitney Museum of American Art, the Solomon R. Guggenheim Museum, the Frick Collection, the Pierpont Morgan Library, the Jewish Museum, the Museum of the American Indian, the American Museum of Natural History, the New York Zoological Park (Bronx Zoo), the New York Botanical Garden, the Brooklyn Botanic Garden, and the Brooklyn Museum. Other major museums in the state include the Albright-Knox Art Gallery, in Buffalo; the New York State Museum (1836), in Albany; the International Museum of Photography, in Rochester; the National Baseball Hall of Fame and Museum, in Cooperstown; the Corning Museum of Glass, in Corning; and the Hudson River Museum, in Yonkers.

New York CIty is the major U.S. center for the performing arts. Lincoln Center for the Performing Arts, a complex of several large buildings, is the home of such major groups as the Metropolitan Opera Company, the New York City Opera, the New York Philharmonic-Symphony Orchestra, and the New York City Ballet. Other well-known performing arts groups of the city include the American Ballet Theatre, the Dance Theatre of Harlem, the Brooklyn Philharmonic Symphony Orchestra, and numerous theatrical organizations, such as the Manhattan Theatre Club, the New York Shakespeare Festival, and the Negro Ensemble Company. In addition, the midtown section of Manhattan around Broadway is famous for its many theaters. The Buffalo Philharmonic and the Rochester Philharmonic are noted orchestras based outside New York City.

New York has many important specialized and general libraries. Leading research centers include the New York Public Library and the Columbia University libraries, in New York City, and the Cornell University libraries, in Ithaca. The pa-

pers of President Franklin D. Roosevelt are housed in a library in Hyde Park.

Historical Sites. New York contains a wide range of historical sites. Among the historical homes are those of the political writer Thomas Paine, in New Rochelle; the statesman Alexander Hamilton, in New York City; Chief Justice John Jay, in Mount Kisco; the women's rights advocate Susan B. Anthony, in Rochester; the writer Washington Irving, in Tarrytown; President Martin Van Buren, in Kinderhook; President Theodore Roosevelt, in New York City and in Oyster Bay; and President Franklin D. Roosevelt and his wife Eleanor Roosevelt, in Hyde Park. Other notable historical sites are Fort Stanwyx National Monument, near Rome, and Saratoga National Historical Park, near Stillwater, both of which were scenes of important patriot successes against the British in 1777 during the American Revolution; Castle Clinton National Monument, at the S tip of Manhattan Island, including the structure through which some 8 million immigrants passed from 1855 to 1890; and Statue of Liberty National Monument, on an island in New York Harbor, containing the famous copper statue donated by the French in the 1880s.

Sports and Recreation. New York's mountains, lakes, rivers, beaches, and parks offer opportunities for outdoor activities such as hiking, camping, swimming, boating, fishing, hunting, and winter sports. Famous Thoroughbred racetracks in the state are Aqueduct, in New York City; Belmont Park, in Elmont; and Saratoga Race Course, in Saratoga Springs. An automobile racetrack is in Watkins Glen. The New York Yankees baseball club, which uses Yankee Stadium in the Bronx (New York City), is one of the world's most famous professional sports teams. Other major league teams in the state include the New York Jets and the Buffalo Bills (football); the New York Knickerbockers (basketball); the New York Mets (baseball); and the New York Rangers, New York Islanders (based in Uniondale), and Buffalo Sabres (ice hockey). Madison Square Garden Center, in New York City, is a noted site for sports and entertainment events and for conventions.

Communications. New York has a highly developed communications system, which, in the early 1980s, included 161 AM and 120 FM commercial radiobroadcasting stations and 31 commercial television stations. The first radio station in the state, WGY in Schenectady, started broadcasting in 1922. WNBT (now WNBC-TV) in New York City, the first commercial television station in the U.S., went into operation in 1941. The three biggest U.S. television networks—ABC, CBS, and NBC—have their headquarters in New

A scene at Fort Ticonderoga, N.Y., a landmark from the American Revolution that has been restored and is maintained as a historic monument. On May 10, 1775, the American soldiers Ethan Allen and Benedict Arnold captured the fort from the British in a surprise attack.

New York State Dept. of Commerce

York City, as does the noncommercial Public Broadcasting Service. The *Gazette,* which was New York's first newspaper, began publication in New York City in 1725. In the early 1980s, New York had 79 daily newspapers, with a total daily circulation of about 7.9 million. The *New York Times* is one of the world's leading newspapers. Other influential dailies include the *Times-Union,* published in Albany; the *Buffalo Evening News; Newsday,* published in Nassau Co.; the *New York Daily News,* the *New York Post* (one of the oldest newspapers in the U.S.), and the *Wall Street Journal*—all published in New York City; the *Democrat & Chronicle,* published in Rochester; and the *Syracuse Herald-Journal.* New York City also is the leading book and magazine publishing center in the U.S.

GOVERNMENT AND POLITICS

New York is governed under a constitution adopted in 1894 and put into effect in 1895, as amended. Three earlier constitutions had been adopted in 1777, 1822, and 1846. Amendments to the constitution may be proposed by the state legislature or by a constitutional convention. To become effective, an amendment must be approved by a majority of persons voting on the issue in an election.

Executive. The chief executive of New York is a governor, who is popularly elected to a term of four years and who may be reelected any number of times. The same regulations apply to the lieutenant governor, who succeeds the governor should the latter resign, die, or be removed from office. Other elected state officials include the attorney general and comptroller.

Legislature. The bicameral New York legislature is made up of a Senate and an Assembly. The 60 members of the Senate and the 150 members of the Assembly are popularly elected to 2-year terms.

Judiciary. New York's highest tribunal, the court of appeals, is made up of a chief judge and six associate judges. All are appointed by the governor, with the consent of the Senate, to serve 14-year terms and may not serve past the age of 70. The state's intermediate appellate courts, the four appellate divisions of the supreme court, have a total of 24 permanent judges, who are chosen from among the members of the supreme court. New York's major trial court, the supreme court, includes 287 judges elected to 14-year terms. Each county, except for the five that make up New York City, has a county court. New York City is served by a criminal court and a civil court.

Local Government. New York has 62 counties, 62 cities, 931 towns, and 556 villages. Counties outside New York City are governed by a board of supervisors or by a county legislature; in some, an elected county executive has considerable power. New York City is governed by a mayor, city council, and board of estimate; among the members of the last-named are the presidents of the five boroughs, or counties, that make up the city. Such regional bodies as the Port Authority of New York and New Jersey and the Metropolitan Transportation Authority have influence over aspects of local affairs in New York City.

National Representation. New York elects 2 senators and 34 representatives to the U.S. Congress. The state has 36 electoral votes in presidential elections.

Politics. New Yorkers have played a prominent role in national politics since the founding of the U.S. In the early 1980s, Democrats and Republicans were fairly evenly matched in the state, with the majority of New York City voters being Democrats and the rest of the state generally having a greater proportion of Republicans. Increasingly important as a swing bloc during the 1970s and '80s were the voters living in the suburbs of New York City. Although New York's share of electoral votes has declined from a peak of 47 in the 1930s and '40s, the state remains a major battleground in presidential elections.

ECONOMY

New York was the preeminent U.S. state in commerce and manufacturing from the early 19th century until the late 1960s, when it began to be surpassed by California. In the early 1980s it continued to be a leading component of the U.S. economy and remained first in many branches of economic activity. The New York City area, the state's most important economic hub, contained the world headquarters of some of the nation's biggest corporations, was one of the world's principal centers of finance and international trade, and had highly influential broadcasting,

Pleasant Valley in Dutchess Co., north of New York City, is typical dairy country. New York State Dept. of Commerce

Apples, shown here being harvested, are grown extensively in many parts of New York State, and they form one of the state's major agricultural crops.
August Upitis–Shostal Associates

publishing, and advertising industries. Despite a decline in the New York City region, manufacturing was the state's principal economic activity. Farming, transportation, trade, and tourism were other important sectors of the state economy.

Agriculture. New York's annual farm income in the early 1980s was estimated at $2.4 billion; sales of livestock and livestock products accounted for 71% of the income and the sale of crops for the remainder. The state has about 48,000 farms, which have an average size of 78 ha (192 acres). Dairying is the principal agricultural pursuit in New York, and dairy farms are located in most parts of the state. Sales of beef cattle are the second leading source of farm receipts, and considerable income also is derived from the sale of chickens, chicken eggs, turkeys, ducks (raised principally on Long Island), hogs, and sheep. The leading crops produced in New York include corn, oats, wheat, hay, potatoes, onions, lettuce, snap beans, tomatoes, and cabbage. In addition, the Finger Lakes region and Chautauqua Co. are important producers of wine grapes, and the SE shore of Lake Erie and the plain adjacent to Lake

Ontario are well known as fruit-growing regions. New York is a leading producer of apples and tart cherries as well as of maple syrup.

Forestry. New York has a relatively unimportant forestry industry, even though more than half of the state is covered with woodland. About three-quarters of the timber cut each year is made up of hardwoods. The wood harvest is used mainly in the construction of buildings and for the production of paper.

Fishing. Although not noted as a fishing state, New York ranks among the top 15 states in the U.S. in terms of the value of the annual catch, which was estimated at $45.1 million in the early 1980s. Most of the commercial fishing takes place in Long Island Sound. The principal species taken include menhaden, flounder, whiting, clams, oysters, and scallops.

Mining. New York's yearly mineral output in the early 1980s was valued at about $572 million. In order of value, the most important minerals produced are stone, salt, sand and gravel, and petroleum. New York ranks among the leading states in the production of emery; garnet; salt; talc, soapstone, and pyrophyllite; titanium concentrates; and wollastonite. Other important mineral products include natural gas, lead, zinc, mercury, silver, clay, and gypsum.

Manufacturing. The most important sector of the New York economy is manufacturing, which accounts for some 95% of the annual value of goods produced in the state. New York manufacturing establishments employ about 1.6 million persons, and the annual value added by manufacture is more than $50 billion. The chief categories of fabricated goods are printed materials, instruments and related products, nonelectrical machinery, and electrical and electronic equipment. New York is the leading state in producing printed materials, such as periodicals and books. The New York City area is the leading printing center, but major plants also are located in such cities as Binghamton, Buffalo, Elmira, and Schenectady. Instruments and related products include cameras and films, optical and medical equipment, and measuring devices. Rochester is a noted center for producing photographic and optical equipment; other centers of instrument production include Buffalo and New York City. Nonelectrical machinery manufactured in the state includes machine tools and office equipment. New York is well known for developing and producing electrical and electronic equipment. Electrical products include motors, generators, and lighting equipment, and electronic devices fabricated in New York include computers and communications equipment. New York City, Rochester, Buffalo, Schenectady, and Long Island are major centers of these industries.

New York is an important source of other manufactured goods. New York City is a leading U.S. producer of clothing, especially women's apparel, and Rochester, Syracuse, and Troy also have important clothing industries. The Binghamton area has shoe factories. Buffalo has iron and steel and flour mills. Aircraft are manufactured on Long Island, and motor-vehicle parts are produced in several parts of the state. Other major manufactures of New York include chemicals, pharmaceuticals, toiletries, processed food, beverages, fabricated metal, and paper, glass, rubber, and plastic goods.

Tourism. New York contains many areas of natural beauty and interest for the tourist. These include Niagara Falls, the Thousand Islands of the St. Lawrence R., the gorges of the Genesee R. country, the Finger Lakes region, the beaches of Long Island, and the hiking trails and picturesque lakes of the Adirondack and Catskill mountains (much of which are in the Adirondack and Catskill forest preserves). Large numbers of people, many from foreign countries, also travel to New York City for sightseeing or to attend conventions. Many tourists visit such historical sites in the state as the home of President Theodore Roosevelt in Oyster Bay and the home of Franklin D. Roosevelt in Hyde Park. New York maintains 147 state parks and recreation areas.

Transportation. New York is served by an extensive system of transportation facilities. The state functions as a crossroads for traffic in the northeastern U.S. and as an entry and exit point for international commerce. New York has about 176,125 km (about 109,440 mi) of roads, including 2292 km (1424 mi) of Interstate Highways. The Governor Thomas E. Dewey Thruway is a major limited-access highway linking the New York City area with Albany, Syracuse, Rochester, and Buffalo. Among the noted vehicular bridges of the state are the George Washington Bridge, spanning the Hudson R. between New York City and New Jersey; the Brooklyn Bridge, built across the East R. between the New York City boroughs of Brooklyn and Manhattan; the Verrazano-Narrows Bridge, constructed across the Narrows channel between the boroughs of Brooklyn and Staten Island; and the Peace Bridge, joining Buffalo with Canada. New York is served by about 7410 km (about 4605 mi) of operated railroad track. Heavily traveled commuter lines carry workers to and from New York City, which also has one of the world's largest subway systems. The state's first railroad made its initial run in 1831 between Albany and Schenectady. The Port of New York, which includes major facilities in New Jersey, is the leading seaport of the U.S. The interior of the state is served by such important waterways as the Hudson R., the New York State Barge Canal System (which includes parts of the famous Erie Canal), and the St. Lawrence Seaway. Albany is an important port on the Hudson; Ogdensburg is a major port on the St. Lawrence R.; and Buffalo and Oswego are leading Great Lakes ports. New York has 486 airports. The busiest are John F. Kennedy International Airport and La Guardia Airport, both in New York City, and Greater Buffalo International Airport.

Energy. In the early 1980s electricity-generating facilities in New York had an installed capacity of 31.4 million kw and annually produced 108.6 billion kwh of electricity, the fifth highest amount of the 50 states. About 35% of the electricity was generated in plants burning refined petroleum. Installations using coal accounted for about 13%, hydroelectric installations for about 24%, and nuclear power plants for about 18%. Big hydroelectric projects are on the Niagara and St. Lawrence rivers. W.J.Y.

NEW YORK

DATE OF STATEHOOD: July 26, 1788; 11th state

CAPITAL:	Albany
MOTTO:	*Excelsior* (Ever upward)
NICKNAMES:	Empire State; Excelsior State
STATE SONG:	"I Love New York" (words and music by Steve Karmen)
STATE TREE:	Sugar maple
STATE FLOWER:	Rose
STATE BIRD:	Bluebird
POPULATION (1980):	17,558,072; 2d among the states
AREA:	127,189 sq km (49,108 sq mi); 30th largest state; includes 4483 sq km (1731 sq mi) of inland water
COASTLINE:	204 km (127 mi)
HIGHEST POINT:	Mt. Marcy, 1629 m (5344 ft)
LOWEST POINT:	Sea level, at the Atlantic coast
ELECTORAL VOTES:	36
U.S. CONGRESS:	2 senators; 34 representatives

POPULATION OF NEW YORK SINCE 1790

Year of Census	Population	Classified As Urban
1790	340,000	12%
1820	1,373,000	12%
1850	3,097,000	28%
1880	5,083,000	56%
1900	7,269,000	73%
1920	10,385,000	83%
1940	13,479,000	83%
1950	14,830,000	86%
1960	16,782,000	85%
1970	18,241,000	86%
1980	17,558,000	85%

POPULATION OF TEN LARGEST CITIES

	1980 Census	1970 Census
New York	7,071,639	7,895,563
Buffalo	357,870	462,768
Rochester	241,741	295,011
Yonkers	195,351	204,297
Syracuse	170,105	197,297
Albany	101,727	115,781
Utica	75,632	91,373
Niagara Falls	71,384	85,615
New Rochelle	70,794	75,385
Schenectady	67,972	77,958

CLIMATE

	NEW YORK	ROCHESTER
Average January temperature range	−3.3° to 3.9° C (26° to 39° F)	−8.3° to −0.6° C (17° to 31° F)
Average July temperature range	20° to 29.4° C (68° to 85° F)	15.6° to 27.8° C (60° to 82° F)
Average annual temperature	12.8° C (55° F)	8.9° C (48° F)
Average annual precipitation	1016 mm (40 in)	787 mm (31 in)
Average annual snowfall	737 mm (29 in)	2184 mm (86 in)
Mean number of days per year with appreciable precipitation	121	154
Average daily relative humidity	64%	71%
Mean number of clear days per year	107	61

NATURAL REGIONS OF NEW YORK

ST. LAWRENCE LOWLAND

ADIRONDACK UPLAND

EASTERN GREAT LAKES LOWLAND

HUDSON-MOHAWK LOWLANDS

Mohawk R.

APPALACHIAN PLATEAU

Hudson R.

NEW ENGLAND UPLAND

ATLANTIC COASTAL PLAIN

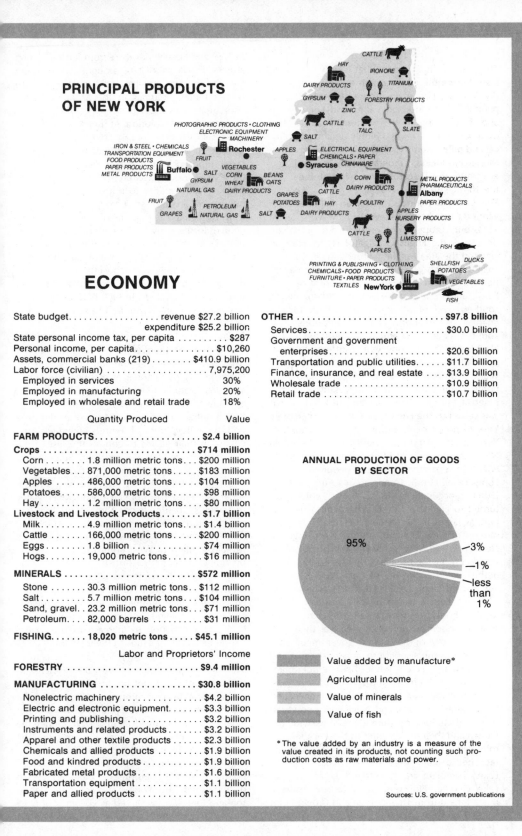

PRINCIPAL PRODUCTS OF NEW YORK

Map labels:
CATTLE, HAY, IRON ORE, TITANIUM, DAIRY PRODUCTS, GYPSUM, FORESTRY PRODUCTS, ZINC, CATTLE, TALC, SLATE, PHOTOGRAPHIC PRODUCTS · CLOTHING, ELECTRONIC EQUIPMENT, MACHINERY, SALT, Rochester, APPLES, ELECTRICAL EQUIPMENT, CHEMICALS · PAPER, IRON & STEEL · CHEMICALS, TRANSPORTATION EQUIPMENT, FOOD PRODUCTS, FRUIT, Syracuse, CHINAWARE, PAPER PRODUCTS, METAL PRODUCTS, Buffalo, SALT, VEGETABLES, CORN, BEANS, CORN, METAL PRODUCTS, PHARMACEUTICALS, GYPSUM, WHEAT, OATS, DAIRY PRODUCTS, Albany, NATURAL GAS, DAIRY PRODUCTS, GRAPES, CATTLE, PAPER PRODUCTS, FRUIT, POTATOES, HAY, POULTRY, APPLES, GRAPES, PETROLEUM, NURSERY PRODUCTS, NATURAL GAS, SALT, DAIRY PRODUCTS, CATTLE, LIMESTONE, APPLES, FISH, PRINTING & PUBLISHING · CLOTHING, SHELLFISH, DUCKS, CHEMICALS · FOOD PRODUCTS, POTATOES, FURNITURE · PAPER PRODUCTS, VEGETABLES, TEXTILES, New York, FISH

ECONOMY

State budget.................. revenue $27.2 billion
                              expenditure $25.2 billion
State personal income tax, per capita $287
Personal income, per capita............... $10,260
Assets, commercial banks (219) .... $410.9 billion
Labor force (civilian) 7,975,200
    Employed in services   30%
    Employed in manufacturing   20%
    Employed in wholesale and retail trade 18%

OTHER .... **$97.8 billion**
Services........................... $30.0 billion
Government and government
  enterprises...................... $20.6 billion
Transportation and public utilities...... $11.7 billion
Finance, insurance, and real estate .... $13.9 billion
Wholesale trade .... $10.9 billion
Retail trade .... $10.7 billion

	Quantity Produced	Value
FARM PRODUCTS.....................		**$2.4 billion**
Crops		**$714 million**
Corn	1.8 million metric tons...	$200 million
Vegetables...	871,000 metric tons.....	$183 million
Apples	486,000 metric tons.....	$104 million
Potatoes.....	586,000 metric tons......	$98 million
Hay.........	1.2 million metric tons....	$80 million
Livestock and Livestock Products........		**$1.7 billion**
Milk.........	4.9 million metric tons....	$1.4 billion
Cattle	166,000 metric tons.....	$200 million
Eggs.........	1.8 billion.............	$74 million
Hogs........	19,000 metric tons.......	$16 million
MINERALS		**$572 million**
Stone........	30.3 million metric tons...	$112 million
Salt.........	5.7 million metric tons...	$104 million
Sand, gravel..	23.2 million metric tons...	$71 million
Petroleum....	82,000 barrels	$31 million
FISHING.......	18,020 metric tons	**$45.1 million**

		Labor and Proprietors' Income
FORESTRY		**$9.4 million**
MANUFACTURING		**$30.8 billion**
Nonelectric machinery		$4.2 billion
Electric and electronic equipment.......		$3.3 billion
Printing and publishing		$3.2 billion
Instruments and related products		$3.2 billion
Apparel and other textile products		$2.3 billion
Chemicals and allied products		$1.9 billion
Food and kindred products		$1.9 billion
Fabricated metal products............		$1.6 billion
Transportation equipment		$1.1 billion
Paper and allied products		$1.1 billion

ANNUAL PRODUCTION OF GOODS BY SECTOR

95%
—3%
—1%
—less than 1%

- Value added by manufacture*
- Agricultural income
- Value of minerals
- Value of fish

*The value added by an industry is a measure of the value created in its products, not counting such production costs as raw materials and power.

Sources: U.S. government publications

HISTORY

The Indians who lived in what is now New York State before the coming of the Europeans were divided into two main groups: the Algonquian peoples of the Hudson Valley and Long Island and the Iroquois in the western area. The Iroquois Confederacy was a highly organized political and military entity, originally consisting of the Mohawk, Oneida, Onondaga, Cayuga, and Seneca tribes; the Tuscaroras were admitted early in the 18th century.

The Colonial Period. The Italian explorer Giovanni da Verrazano discovered New York Bay in 1524, but European colonization did not begin until after the English navigator Henry Hudson claimed the area for the Netherlands in 1609. In 1624 the Dutch West India Co. established a settlement at Fort Orange (near present-day Albany) and in 1625 at New Amsterdam on the southern end of Manhattan Island. In 1629, a charter of freedoms and exemptions was adopted as an inducement for settlement. The New Netherland colony, which suffered from Indian attacks and mismanagement in its early years, achieved a measure of peace and economic stability under Peter Stuyvesant, who governed it from 1647 to 1664. In the latter year it was seized by the English and was renamed New York in honor of its proprietor, James, duke of York, brother of King Charles II. James made New Jersey, which had been part of New Netherland, a separate colony and acquired eastern Long Island from Connecticut. After a brief Dutch reoccupation (1673–74), the colony returned to English control. When James became king as James II, he formed the short-lived Dominion of New England, uniting New England, New York, and New Jersey (1688). The following year, on receiving the news that James had been dethroned, the citizens of New York rebelled and named Jacob Leisler (1640–91) as governor. Although Leisler was hanged for treason when royal authority was reinstated in 1691, the representative assembly he established was thereafter retained as part of the colony's government. Subsequent governors sought to carry out crown and parliamentary decrees while the assembly managed to strengthen its control over purse strings.

Schenectady was destroyed by a French and Indian attack in 1690, and New York continued to be a battleground during the wars with the French and their Indian allies in the decades that followed. In the war of 1754–63, the French established a major base at Fort Ticonderoga on Lake Champlain and penetrated as far south as Lake George. Not until Lord Jeffrey Amherst ousted them from Ticonderoga and Crown Point in 1759 was New York secure from further French attacks. The Peace of 1763 brought an end to the French presence and signaled a rapid move into former Indian holdings in the Mohawk Valley and Great Lakes regions.

The American Revolution. At the Stamp Act Congress held in New York in 1765, representatives of nine American colonies met to protest new taxes imposed by the British Parliament. When the New York legislature refused to provide housing and supplies to British military personnel in 1767, it was dissolved by act of Parliament; a newly elected legislature proved more cooperative. In the early 1770s a split developed between the radicals who opposed British rule and the mercantile aristocracy who remained loyal to the Crown. When Massachusetts rose in rebellion in April 1775, New York sent a volunteer force to aid the rebels. In October, the last royal governor, William Tryon, fled to safety aboard a British warship.

On July 9, 1776, a new legislature approved the Declaration of Independence, and the former royal province became the state of New York. Nevertheless, by October of that year the British army had occupied New York City, Long Island, and lower Westchester Co. The city served as British military headquarters from then until the end of the Revolution. The British were less successful in their efforts to control the rest of the state. The surrender of Gen. John Burgoyne at Saratoga in 1777 was a major setback for them and helped bring France into the war on the American side. The upper Hudson River valley remained in patriot hands throughout the war, and the Hudson River itself was guarded by cannons at West Point. Benedict Arnold sought to reveal the plans of West Point in a plot aborted by the capture of his British accomplice Maj. John André, at Tarrytown in 1780.

New York in the New Nation. At the war's conclusion, the state returned to agricultural pursuits and to developing its commercial activities. New York's determination to increase its use of the harbor area and the Hudson River shipping lanes led to friction with New Jersey, and its claim to Vermont caused a conflict with the residents of that area until Vermont became a state in 1790.

Considerable opposition to ratification of the federal constitution developed in New York, but it was finally approved in July 1788. Under the new government, New York City became the first U.S. capital and the scene of George Washington's inaguration as president in 1789. Washington's first appointees included such distinguished New Yorkers as Alexander Hamilton and John Jay. Jay served as governor of New

York from 1795 to 1801. Another New Yorker, Aaron Burr, served as vice-president under Thomas Jefferson.

Renewed naval warfare between Britain and France soon embroiled the U.S. Although New York shipping was affected by British and French depredations, western New York opposed the war with Britain that broke out in 1812, which once again made a battleground of the area along the Canadian border.

The Empire State. After the War of 1812 Gov. De Witt Clinton, recognizing that a transportation link with the upper Ohio Valley was essential, pressed for construction of a canal across the state, stretching from the confluence of the Hudson and Mohawk rivers west to Lake Erie. The state legislature authorized construction of the Erie Canal in 1817, and it was completed in 1825. The canal was a commercial and financial success and provided the impetus for the rapid settlement of western New York by former New Englanders and by a rising tide of immigrants from Europe.

The opening of the West, an increased maritime trade, and rapid industrialization soon made New York City the leading seaport in the nation. Between 1825 and the American Civil War, New York City emerged as the major manufacturing center in textiles, as the nation's cotton mart, and as the center for banking, imports, insurance, the stock exchange, and for ready-made clothing. Also during this period transportation facilities developed rapidly; a network of turnpikes was introduced, and railroad lines were constructed that extended from New York City to Chicago. The growth encouraged immigration to New York from Ireland, Germany, and Canada. By the time of the Civil War, however, the number of immigrants had decreased, and business opportunities had increased. As a result of New York's close ties with the cotton market, popular sentiment opposed a war against the seceded Southern states. Although New Yorkers served and suffered in every major battle of the Civil War, the inauguration of a military draft led to the New York City draft riots of July 1863.

U.S. Presidents Martin Van Buren, Chester A. Arthur, Grover Cleveland, Theodore Roosevelt, and Franklin D. Roosevelt were all New Yorkers. Other New York figures with national political reputations were Governors Alfred E. Smith, Herbert H. Lehman, Thomas E. Dewey, and Nelson Rockefeller, Senator Robert F. Wagner, and New York City mayor Fiorello La Guardia.

Until the 1960s New York was the most populous state in the Union, with a diverse and cosmopolitan population. In the 1970s and '80s, however, the state began to experience an economic decline. New York City in particular has suffered from unemployment, chronic financial problems, decaying neighborhoods, and a declining population, although it remained the nation's center for stock exchange activities, advertising, banking and finance, and retail merchandising and served as headquarters for major national and international corporations. It was also a major center for the publishing, fashion, and entertainment industries and for the arts in general. Although heavily urbanized and industrialized, New York is still an important agricultural area. Until late in the 19th century, New York led the nation in grain and butter production. Today, its major agricultural activities center on the dairy and cattle industry, apple orchards, maple syrup production, onions, beets, potatoes, and viniculture. No longer the dominant import center or the most populous state in the nation, New York nevertheless retains the general importance to warrant its traditional designation as the Empire State.　　　　J.Ju.

For further information on this topic, see the Bibliography in volume 28, sections 1172–73.

NEW YORK, CITY UNIVERSITY OF. *See* CITY UNIVERSITY OF NEW YORK.

NEW YORK, POLYTECHNIC INSTITUTE OF, professional undergraduate and graduate school with campuses in Brooklyn, the Bronx, and Farmingdale, N.Y. The institute is the result of a merger in 1973 of the Polytechnic Institute of Brooklyn and the School of Engineering and Science of New York University, both founded in 1854. The institute offers programs in engineering, science, history of science, management, operations research, meteorology, transportation planning, oceanography, humanities, and social sciences. It awards bachelor's, master's, engineer's, and doctor's degrees.

NEW YORK, STATE UNIVERSITY OF, state-supported institution of higher learning, the largest in the world, comprising 64 colleges (including 30 2-year community colleges) and centers throughout the state. The university is governed by a board of trustees, but the community colleges are locally administered. The university was established in 1948 by an act of the New York state legislature.

Four-year and graduate degree programs are offered in agriculture, business administration, ceramics, dentistry, engineering, forestry, home economics, industrial and labor relations, law, liberal arts and sciences, maritime service, medicine, nursing, optometry, pharmacy, professional museum work, public administration, social work, teacher education, and veterinary medicine. The degrees of bachelor, master, and doctor are conferred. Two-year programs in nursing and liberal-arts studies and technical courses in agricultural, business, industrial, and medical technology are also offered.

NEW YORK BAY, inlet of the Atlantic Ocean, SE New York, at the mouth of the Hudson R. Enclosed by New Jersey and the New York City boroughs of Staten Island, Manhattan, and Brooklyn, it consists of Upper New York Bay and Lower New York Bay, which are connected by a short strait called the Narrows (q.v.).

NEW YORK CITY, most populous city and a major port of the U.S., SE New York State, on the Hudson and East rivers and New York Bay (an arm of the Atlantic Ocean); inc. 1898. One of the world's leading commercial, financial, and cultural centers, New York City is subdivided into five boroughs that are coextensive with five counties of New York State. In descending order of area, the boroughs are Queens (Queens Co.), Brooklyn (Kings Co.), Staten Island (Richmond Co.), the Bronx (Bronx Co.), and Manhattan (New York Co.) (see separate articles on each borough). Almost all of the Bronx is situated on the mainland, but the other boroughs are situated on, or comprise, islands: Brooklyn and Queens are located on the W end of Long Island, Staten Island encompasses the island of Staten Island, and Manhattan is primarily made up of Manhattan Island. (Manhattan also includes a small exclave in the Bronx mainland.) The city's boroughs include several small islands, of which only Roosevelt Island, in the East R., is densely inhabited. City Island, in the Bronx, also has a substantial population.

Economy. New York is a financial, commercial, manufacturing, and tourist center. A national focus of road, rail, water, and air transportation, it also contains the headquarters of many major corporations. The financial district of Lower Manhattan, which is centered on Wall and Broad streets, includes the New York Stock Exchange and a U.S. Federal Reserve bank, as well as other prominent banking, brokerage, and financial-services institutions. Much domestic and international trade is conducted in New York City's offices, including those in the twin towers of Lower Manhattan's World Trade Center, one of the world's tallest structures. John F. Kennedy International Airport, in Queens, is a major air cargo terminal, and large amounts of freight pass through the city's port facilities; nearby ports in New Jersey, however, now handle much of the

Part of New York City's imposing skyline, including the 110-story twin towers of the World Trade Center—among the tallest buildings in the world.
Port Authority of New York and New Jersey

Vehicular traffic is barred from parts of Central Park for some hours each day, during which only bicycles and pedestrians are permitted.   Photo Researchers, Inc.

freight that formerly passed through New York. Wholesale and retail trade are important to New York's economy. The city is particularly noted for its many retail outlets, including large department stores and specialty shops. Fifth and Madison avenues, in Manhattan, are especially famous for their fine shops.

As a manufacturing center, New York is a national leader in such sectors as the production of clothing (notably in the Garment District of Midtown Manhattan on the West Side), printed materials, and processed food. Other principal products include wood, paper, and metal goods; machinery; chemicals; and textiles. Many manufacturing concerns have left New York since the 1960s, largely because of the high cost of operating in the city. In specialized service activities, however, the city remains strong. Both the advertising and communications industries have major concentrations in New York; the leading national television and radio networks have headquarters in the city, as do many prominent book and magazine publishers. The *New York Times* is

noted as one of the world's best daily newspapers. Tourism and conventions are also important to the city's economy, and numerous hotels and convention facilities are located in Manhattan.

The Urban Landscape. Manhattan S of 14th St. grew by the accretion of small, independent hamlets during the period from the city's founding to the early 19th century. Consequently, this area is characterized by irregularly laid-out districts such as City Hall Plaza and Greenwich Village. North of 14th St., a grid plan (est. 1811) prevails, with named or numbered avenues running roughly N and S, and mostly numbered streets running E and W—superimposed on such irregular roads as Broadway, which predates the plan. Central Park, designed by the American landscape architects Frederick Law Olmsted and Calvert Vaux (1824–95), has dominated the grid from 59th to 110th streets since the 1850s. Olmsted also created other fine landscapes in the city, including Morningside Park, overlooking Harlem in NW Manhattan; and Riverside Park, along the upper Hudson shore of Manhattan. His son, Frederick Law Olmsted, Jr. (1870–1957), continued the tradition with designs such as Fort Tryon Park, in N Manhattan. Among the most distinct of Manhattan's numerous neighborhoods are Chinatown and SoHo, the latter largely an artists' community—both located S of Greenwich Village; the Upper East Side, an elegant residential area; and Harlem, a largely black and Hispanic section, N of 96th St. Manhattan is linked to New Jersey by the George Washington Bridge and the Holland and Lincoln tunnels and to Staten Island by a regular ferry service.

The city's other boroughs are much less regular in plan, having been formed by the coalescence of numerous historically separate towns and villages. Staten Island, because of its relative isolation, is the most rural of the boroughs and remains, to some extent, more a collection of towns than a single urban area. It has, however,

grown considerably since being linked to Brooklyn, in 1964, by the Verrazano-Narrows Bridge, one of the world's longest suspension bridges. Brooklyn is the most populous borough; its diversified neighborhoods include elegant Brooklyn Heights, middle-class ethnic enclaves such as Sheepshead Bay, and the impoverished Brownsville section. Prospect Park, at the heart of the borough, is another major design project of Frederick Law Olmsted. Brooklyn is connected to Manhattan across the East R. by the Brooklyn, Manhattan, and Williamsburg bridges and by the Brooklyn Battery Tunnel. In Queens, neighborhood consciousness is particularly strong—residents tend to identify themselves as citizens of Astoria, Corona, Kew Gardens, or Flushing, for example, rather than of Queens—and as in all the boroughs of New York, many neighborhoods have a distinguishing ethnic population. Notable

The Park Slope neighborhood, an attractive residential section of Brooklyn. Located on Long Island, Brooklyn is the most populous of the five boroughs. Among its well-known districts are Coney Island, the famous seashore recreational area; aristocratic Brooklyn Heights, overlooking the East River; and Bedford-Stuyvesant, with more than 400,000 residents, one of the biggest black communities in the U.S.
Leo DeWys, Inc.

Horse-drawn carriages, popular with tourists, wait for customers at 59th St., near one of the entrances of Manhattan's plush Plaza Hotel. For many, a ride through nearby Central Park and its environs in an open carriage is an indispensable part of a visit to New York City.   Rapho–Photo Researchers, Inc.

in Queens are Forest Hills Gardens, designed by Frederick Law Olmsted, Jr., and Flushing Meadows Corona Park, which was the site of the 1939 and 1964–65 New York world's fairs. Queens is connected to Manhattan by the Queens Midtown Tunnel and the Queensboro (59th St.) Bridge and to the Bronx by the Throgs Neck, Bronx Whitestone, and Triborough bridges. The Bronx, like New York's other boroughs, has a diversity of neighborhoods, ranging from a devastated area of many abandoned buildings in the S to Riverdale, a section in the W including large homes and luxury apartment buildings. In the center of the borough is Bronx Park; the New York Zoological Park (known as the Bronx Zoo) and the New York Botanical Garden are contained within Bronx Park.

Points of Interest. New York City, and particularly Manhattan, boasts many distinguished architectural sites. Skyscrapers dominate the skyline; the Flatiron Building, completed in 1902, was one of the first in the city. Others include the Empire State Building (1931), the group of

buildings that constitute Rockefeller Center (begun 1931), and Citicorp Center (1978). Older structures include Gracie Mansion (late 18th cent.), now the mayor's residence, and City Hall (1802–11). Among the city's well-known religious edifices are Saint Patrick's Cathedral, the Cathedral of Saint John the Divine, Temple Emanu-El, and Trinity Church. Other places of interest include the Statue of Liberty on Liberty Island; Ellis Island, the point of entry of numerous immigrants to the U.S.; and the UN complex, along the East R. in Midtown Manhattan. Major sports facilities in the city include Yankee Stadium, in the Bronx; Shea Stadium, in Queens; and Madison Square Garden, in Manhattan.

Cultural and Educational Institutions. As the undisputed cultural center of the U.S., New York City is rich in first-rate museums, art galleries, and performing arts organizations. Among the leading art museums are the vast Metropolitan Museum of Art, the Cloisters (a replica of a monastery incorporating medieval architectural elements, including five French cloisters and a

67

NEW YORK CITY

Spanish chapel), the Museum of Modern Art, the Frick Collection, the Solomon R. Guggenheim Museum, and the Whitney Museum of American Art—all of which are in Manhattan—and the Brooklyn Museum, in Prospect Park, Brooklyn. Other museums include the American Museum of Natural History with the adjacent Hayden Planetarium, the Museum of the City of New York, the International Center of Photography, the Cooper-Hewitt Museum, the Jewish Museum, the Museum of the American Indian, and the American Craft Museum—all in Manhattan—and the Brooklyn Children's Museum, in Brooklyn. The city's major libraries include the New York Public Library, with some 10 million volumes, the library of Columbia University, and the Pierpont Morgan Library, which has rare books and manuscripts. To the S of Central Park in Midtown Manhattan lies Times Square, the hub of the city's theater district. The more than 30 legitimate theaters here form the heartland of the American stage. Near the SW corner of Central Park is Lincoln Center for the Performing Arts, a monumental cluster of buildings that includes the Metropolitan Opera House; Avery Fisher Hall, home of the New York Philharmonic-Symphony Orchestra; the New York State Theater, where the New York City Ballet and New York City Opera perform; and the Juilliard School. Institutions of higher education in New York include Columbia University, Barnard College, New York University, Pratt Institute (1887), Cooper Union for the Advancement of Science

and Art, City University of New York, Fordham University, Saint John's University, Rockefeller University, Union Theological Seminary, and the Manhattan School of Music (1917).

History. The first European to visit the New York Bay area was Giovanni da Verrazano, an Italian navigator in the service of France, who landed here in 1524. Henry Hudson, whose expedition sailed under the Dutch flag, discovered and explored the Hudson River in 1609, and in 1613 Adriaen Block, also sailing for the Dutch, was forced to winter on Manhattan Island after his boat caught fire. The island was not permanently settled by non-Indians, however, until 1624, when, under the auspices of the Dutch West India Co., the colony of New Amsterdam was established on Manhattan's southern tip. During the mid-17th century, further colonization of Manhattan Island took place, and other settlements were begun in the Bronx, Brooklyn, Queens, and Staten Island. In 1664 Peter Stuyvesant, then governor, surrendered the colony to the English. It was retaken by the Dutch a few years later but was finally ceded to the English in 1674 by the Treaty of Westminster. The settlement, now renamed New York, grew, favored by its sheltered harbor. Thus, the impetus to the city's growth was mercantile, with coastwise, riverine, and oceanic trade all contributing. New York played an important role in events leading to the American Revolution; in 1765 the Stamp Act Congress was held in the city. After the Battle of Long Island (1776), New York was occu-

New York City as it looked in the early 1900s can be seen in this original photograph of the teeming marketplace of Mulberry St. in lower Manhattan.
National Archives

68

pied by British troops until the end of the Revolution. The U.S. Congress met in New York in 1785–89, and George Washington was inaugurated as the first U.S. president here in 1789.

The community continued to grow, but its great expansion occurred after the completion of the Erie Canal in 1825. The canal opened the great markets of the west, and New York became a major center of commodity exchange, banking, marine insurance, and manufacturing. Emigrants, particularly from Germany and Ireland, began to arrive in large numbers. From the mid-19th century until well into the 20th century, the city government was under control of a Democratic party machine, known as the Tammany Society (q.v.). By the late 19th century the population was swelled by emigrants from southern and eastern Europe as well as from China. In 1898, with the act of consolidation, the five-borough city was created—the stage having been set by the great age of bridge construction that was initiated by the achievement of John A. Roebling and Washington A. Roebling (1837–1926): the beautiful, wire-enlaced Brooklyn Bridge (1883). Other bridges soon followed, and in 1904 construction of the interborough subway systems was begun. This complex public transportation network integrated the boroughs into the pattern recognizable today. In the period during and after World War II, the city received numerous black migrants, largely from the southern states. Emigration from Puerto Rico and from other parts of the Caribbean and Latin America became important by the 1950s. Racial conflicts developed in New York, as in many other large U.S. cities, during the 1960s.

The city government was reorganized by a city charter that became effective Jan. 1, 1963; the citywide electorate chooses a mayor for a 4-year term to head a centralized city government. Elected borough presidents sit on the Board of Estimate along with the mayor, comptroller, and city council president. Municipal budget problems culminated in the mid-1970s, when special financial entities (such as the Municipal Assistance Corporation) were created to keep the city from defaulting on its loans. New York's government finances were improved in the late 1970s and early '80s, in part because outlays for city services were closely regulated. Land area, 780 sq km (301 sq mi). Pop. (1970) 7,895,563; (1980) 7,071,639.   G.W.C.

For further information on this topic, see the Bibliography in volume 28, sections 1174–75.

NEW YORK PUBLIC LIBRARY, group of about 90 noncirculating research libraries and circulating neighborhood branch libraries in the boroughs of Manhattan, the Bronx, and Staten Island, in New York City. (Each of the other two boroughs, Brooklyn and Queens, maintains its own public library system.) The New York Public Library provides circulating books and other material, reference services, and research facilities free of charge.

Founding and Organization. The library's full name is the New York Public Library, Astor, Lenox and Tilden Foundations. It was founded in 1895 with funds from a trust left by the American political leader Samuel J. Tilden, enabling the consolidation of collections in two existing research libraries that had been endowed by private fortunes—those of the German-American merchant and financier John Jacob Astor and the American philanthropist and bibliophile James Lenox (1800–80). The Central Building, erected and still maintained by the city, was dedicated as a free research library in 1911. The new nonprofit corporation later contracted with the city to build and operate circulating libraries in three of the city's boroughs. Andrew Carnegie, the American steel magnate and philanthropist, provided the money to build the first 39 branches of the library.

The New York Public Library is unlike other public libraries in that it operates both circulating and research libraries. The latter have larger collections than the circulating branches, but their materials must be used in library reading rooms. An amount covering the operating expenses of the system's more than 80 circulating branches is contributed to the Astor, Lenox and Tilden Foundations corporation annually by New York City. The research libraries, however, are supported mostly by the private donations of individuals, foundations, and businesses; in addition, the federal, state, and city governments have awarded various grants to the research libraries in recent years.

Central Building. The administrative center of the research libraries, and the largest library of the system, is the Central Building, a well-known New York City landmark; the imposing marble structure covers two blocks from 40th to 42d streets on Fifth Ave., in Manhattan. Cataloging and acquisition (*see* LIBRARY: *Technical Services*) for the research libraries are done in the Central Building.

The Research Libraries. The research libraries include, besides the Central Building, the Annex on Manhattan's West Side; the Performing Arts Research Center at the Lincoln Center for the Performing Arts, Inc. (q.v.); and the Schomburg Center for Research in Black Culture, in Harlem. Together, these constitute one of the greatest libraries in the world, containing more than 6 million books and more than 16 million manuscripts, recordings, prints, and other items. They are organized into 20 subject divisions and special collections, covering virtually every field of knowledge in every language.

The Branch Libraries. The branch libraries of the system are as diverse as the city neighborhoods they serve. The Mid-Manhattan Library, across Fifth Ave. from the Central Building, is the system's main resource for college students. Its collection, much of which is available for circulation, is housed on open shelves.

All book ordering and cataloging for the branches are done at Mid-Manhattan, which also houses the Union Catalog indicating the location of all materials available in the various branches. Other branches include the large borough library centers that provide reference as well as circulating material, the Library and Museum of the Performing Arts, the Young Adults Library at Donnell Library Center, the Library for the Blind and Physically Handicapped, and several libraries throughout the city providing for particular vocational, ethnic, or language needs.

NEW YORK STATE BARGE CANAL SYSTEM, waterway system, upper New York State. Its principal sections are the Erie Canal, linking Lake Erie and the Hudson R.; the Oswego Canal, linking the Erie Canal and Lake Ontario; the Cayuga-Seneca Canal, linking the Erie Canal and Lakes Cayuga and Seneca; and the Champlain Canal, linking Lake Champlain and the Hudson R.

NEW YORK UNIVERSITY, privately controlled institution of higher learning, in New York City, chartered in 1831, and opened for instruction the following year as the University of the City of New York. The present name was adopted in 1896. Most divisions of the university, graduate and undergraduate, are located at Washington Square in downtown Manhattan, which was the university's original site.

In 1973 the university sold its campus in the Bronx to the Bronx Community College. Divisions of the university that were on the Bronx campus were changed as follows: the University College of Arts and Science became the Washington Square College and University of Arts and Science; the school of engineering and science was merged with the Polytechnic Institute of Brooklyn; and the Hall of Fame for Great Americans was placed under jurisdiction of Bronx Community College.

The New York University medical center in midtown Manhattan includes University Hospital, student residence halls, the school of medicine, and the institute of rehabilitation medicine.

Nearby is a public-health laboratory occupied jointly by university and municipal services. Also in the vicinity is the university's Brookdale Dental Center, which includes the college of dentistry, a dental clinic, and an institute for dental research.

The Institute of Fine Arts, a division of the graduate school of arts and science, is located in uptown Manhattan near the Metropolitan Museum of Art. Courses in art history and art conservation are offered.

The Elmer Holmes Bobst Library and Study Center, opened in 1973, is one of the largest open-stack libraries in the U.S. It serves the entire university, administering the separate libraries maintained by several of the institutes and divisions.

NEW YORK WORLD'S FAIR. See EXHIBITIONS AND EXPOSITIONS.

NEW ZEALAND, self-governing country, in the South Pacific Ocean, a member of the Commonwealth of Nations, situated SE of Australia. It comprises two large islands—North Island and South Island—and numerous smaller islands, including Stewart Island, to the S of South Island. The area of New Zealand is 268,676 sq km (103,736 sq mi). Associated with New Zealand are Ross Dependency (in Antarctica) and the Cook Islands, Niue, and Tokelau (in the Pacific Ocean).

LAND AND RESOURCES

New Zealand is a generally mountainous country with several large regions of plains. Two-thirds of the area is between about 200 and 1070 m (about 650 and 3500 ft) above sea level; the country has more than 220 named mountains exceeding 2286 m (7500 ft) in height.

North Island has a very irregular coastline, particularly on its N extremity, the Auckland Peninsula. In the vicinity of the city of Auckland the peninsula is only about 10 km (about 6 mi) wide. The principal mountain ranges of North Island extend along the E side. A volcanic range in the N central region has three active volcanic peaks: Mt. Ruapehu (2797 m/9175 ft), the highest point on the island; Mt. Ngauruhoe (2291 m/7515 ft); and Tongariro (1968 m/6458 ft). Mt. Egmont (2518 m/8260 ft), a solitary, extinct volcanic cone, is situated near the W extremity of the island. North Island has numerous rivers, most of which rise in the E and central mountains. The Waikato R. (435 km/270 mi long), the longest river of New Zealand, flows N out of Lake Taupo (606 sq km/234 sq mi), the largest lake in New Zealand, and empties into the Tasman Sea in the W. Numerous mineral hot springs are in the Lake Taupo district.

Wellington, capital of New Zealand, has a large, deep harbor that helps to make it one of the country's principal seaports. Fritz Prenzel–Bruce Coleman, Inc.

South Island has a more regular coastline than that of North Island; in the SW, however, the coast is indented by deep fjords. The chief mountain range of South Island is the Southern Alps, a massive uplift extending in a SW to NE direction for almost the entire length of the island; 17 peaks in the range exceed 3048 m (10,000 ft) in elevation. Mt. Cook (3764 m/12,349 ft), the highest point in New Zealand, rises from the center of the range, which also has a number of glaciers. Most of the rivers of South Island, including the Clutha R. (338 km/210 mi long), the longest river of the island, rise in the Southern Alps. The Clutha is formed by the confluence of two branches originating, respectively, in Lake Hawea (124 sq km/48 sq mi) and Lake Wanaka (194 sq km/75 sq mi) and empties into the Pacific Ocean. The largest lake is Lake Te Anau (342 sq km/132 sq mi) in the S part of the Southern Alps. The Canterbury plains in the E and the Southland plains in the extreme S are the only extensive lowland areas of South Island.

Climate. New Zealand lies within the Temperate Zone; the climate is generally mild, and seasonal differences are not great. The N end of the Auckland Peninsula has the warmest climate; the coldest climate occurs on the SW slopes of the Southern Alps. Rainfall is generally moderate to abundant and, except in a small area in the S central part of South Island, exceeds 508 mm (20 in) annually. The heaviest rainfall (about 5590 mm/about 220 in) occurs around Milford Sound on the SW coast of South Island. The average temperature at Auckland varies between 19° C (66.2° F) in January and 10.6° C (51° F) in July; the average rainfall is 1245 mm (49 in). In Dunedin, on the SE coast of South Island, the average January and July temperatures are 14.7° C (58.5° F) and 4.2° C (39.5° F), respectively; the annual rainfall is 762 mm (30 in).

Geology. The islands, which emerged late in the Tertiary period, contain a notably complete series of marine sedimentary rocks, some of which date from the early Paleozoic era. Much of the topography of New Zealand has resulted from warping and block faulting. Volcanic action also played a part in the formation of the islands, especially on North Island, where the process continues to the present time. Geysers and mineral hot springs occur in the volcanic area, and earthquakes, although usually minor, are fairly frequent here.

Natural Resources. The land is the most important resource of New Zealand. It is ideal for crop farming, dairy farming, and the raising of sheep, all of which predominate in the economy. Forest products are also important. Numerous mineral deposits are found throughout the main islands, including coal, gold, pearlite, sand and gravel, limestone, bentonite, clay, dolomite, and magnesite. Great natural-gas fields are on the North Island and off its SW coast. Deposits of uranium and thorium are believed to be present on the islands, because these minerals have been found in isolated boulders.

Plants. New Zealand plant life is remarkable in that of the 2000 indigenous species, about 1500 are found nowhere else in the world; examples of such unique plants are the golden kowhai and the scarlet pohutukawa. North Island has predominantly subtropical vegetation, including mangrove swamps in the N. The forest, or so-called bush, of North Island is principally evergreen with dense undergrowth of mosses and fern. Evergreen trees include the kauri, rimu, kahikatea, and totara, all of which are excellent timber trees. The only extensive area of native grassland on North Island is the central volcanic plain. The E part of South Island for the most part is grassland up to an elevation of about 1525 m (about 5000 ft). Most of the forest is in the W. It is made up principally of native beech and is succeeded by alpine vegetation at high altitudes.

Animals. With the exception of two species of bat, no indigenous mammals are native to New Zealand. The first white settlers, who arrived early in the 19th century, found a type of dog and a black rat, both of which had been brought by the Maori (see the Population section below) about 500 years earlier and are now almost extinct. The only wild mammals at present are descended from deer, rabbits, goats, pigs, weasels, ferrets, and opossums—all of which were imported. No snakes and few species of annoying insects inhabit New Zealand. The tuatara, a lizardlike reptile with a vestigial third eye, is believed to be a prehistoric survival.

New Zealand has a large population of wild birds, including 23 native species. Among the native species are songbirds, including the bellbird and tui, and flightless species, including the kiwi, kakapo, takahe, and weka. The survival of the flightless birds is attributed to the absence of predatory animals. The sparrow, blackbird, thrush, skylark, magpie, and myna are well-acclimated imported species. New Zealand abounds in a great variety of seabirds and numerous migratory birds.

The rivers and lakes have a variety of native edible fish, including whitebait, eel, lamprey, and freshwater crustaceans, particularly crayfish. Trout and salmon have been imported. The surrounding ocean waters are the habitat of the snapper, flounder, blue cod, hapuku, tarakihi, swordfish, flying fish, shark, and whale, as well as edible shellfish, such as the oyster, mussel, and toheroa.

POPULATION

More than 90% of New Zealanders are of British descent. Approximately 9% (about 290,000) are Maori (q.v.), a Polynesian group with some Melanesian admixture whose ancestors migrated to New Zealand about the 14th century. The Maori have adapted themselves to the society and work in all types of industry and the professions. The remainder of the population includes mostly persons of continental European or Asian birth or descent.

Population Characteristics. The population of New Zealand (UN est. 1981) was about 3,130,000, giving the country an average population density of about 12 persons per sq km (about 30 per sq mi). Nearly three-quarters of the population (including more than 95% of the Maori) resided on North Island, however. About 75% of the people lived in urban areas, and more than half of these in the four largest cities and their environs (see Principal Cities section below).

Political Divisions. New Zealand is divided into 13 administrative areas, which replaced the 9 former provincial districts. On North Island the areas include Northland, Central Auckland, South Auckland–Bay of Plenty, East Coast, Hawke's Bay, Taranaki, and Wellington; on South Island, Marlborough, Nelson, Westland, Canterbury, Otago, and Southland.

Principal Cities. The chief cities of New Zealand, with 1980 estimated populations, are Auckland, a seaport and distribution center for the dairy region (146,000); Christchurch, the wheat and grain center (169,300); Wellington, the capital city and center of interisland and coastal shipping (135,900); Hamilton, a center for dairy farming (91,800); and Dunedin, a wool and gold center (81,000).

Religion and Language. Approximately 90% of the population are Christian. The major denominations are the Church of England, Presbyterian,

INDEX TO MAP OF NEW ZEALAND

Cities and Towns

Akaroa	B 3
Alexandra	A 4
Ashburton	B 3
Auckland	B 2
Balclutha	B 4
Blenheim	B 3
Bluff	A 4
Christchurch	B 3
Collingwood	B 3
Dannevirke	C 3
Dargaville	B 2
Dunedin	B 4
Feilding	B 3
Gisborne	C 2
Gore	A 4
Greymouth	A 3
Hamilton	B 2
Hastings	C 2
Hawera	B 2
Hokitika	A 3
Huntly	B 2
Invercargill	A 4
Kaiapoi	B 3
Kaikoura	B 3
Kaitaia	B 2
Karamea	B 3
Lower Hutt	C 3
Marton	C 3
Masterton	C 3
Moerewa	B 2
Morven	B 4
Motueka	B 3
Napier	C 2
Nelson	B 3
New Plymouth	B 2
Oamaru	B 4
Palmerston North	C 3
Picton	B 3
Pukekohe	B 2
Rangiora	B 3
Ross	B 3
Rotorua	C 2
Roxburgh	A 4
Runanga	A 3
Stratford	C 2
Taupo	C 2
Tauranga	C 2
Te Araroa	C 2
Te Awamutu	B 2
Te Kuiti	B 2
Temuka	B 3
Thames	C 2
Timaru	B 3
Tokanui	A 4
Tuatapere	A 4
Waihi	C 2
Waikari	B 3
Wairoa	C 2
Wanaka	A 3
Wanganui	B 3
Wellington (cap.)	C 3
Westport	B 3
Whakatane	C 2
Whangarei	C 2

Other Features

Aspiring (mt.)	A 3
Canterbury (bight)	B 3
Clutha (river)	B 4
Cook (mt.)	A 3
Cook (strait)	B 3
East (cape)	C 2
Egmont (cape)	B 2
Egmont (mt.)	B 2
Farewell (cape)	B 3
Foveaux (strait)	A 4
Great Barrier (island)	C 2
Hauraki (gulf)	C 2
Hawke (bay)	C 2
Islands (bay)	C 1
Kaipara (harbor)	B 2
Mahia (pen.)	C 2
Maria van Diemen (cape)	B 1
North (cape)	B 1
North (island)	B 2
Otago (pen.)	B 4
Palliser (cape)	C 3
Pegasus (bay)	B 3
Plenty (bay)	C 2
Ruapehu (mt.)	B 2
South (cape)	A 4
South (island)	B 4
Southern Alps (mts.)	A 3
Stewart (island)	A 4
Tasman (bay)	B 3
Taupo (lake)	C 2
Te Anau (lake)	A 4
Three Kings (islands)	B 1
Waikato (river)	B 2

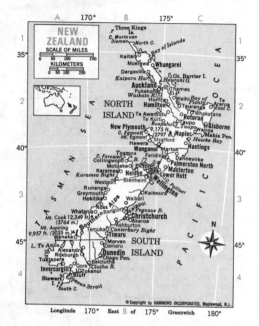

Roman Catholic, and Methodist. Most of the Maori are members of the Ratana and Ringatu Christian sects. Jews constitute a small minority.

English is the official language. The Maori speak Maori, a Polynesian language, but they learn English as a second language.

Education. Education is free and compulsory for children between the ages of 6 and 15 years, but children may enter school at 5 and continue until they are 19. In some areas free kindergartens are maintained for children between three and five years of age. The primary course consists of infant classes during the first two years and six annual grades designated standards 1, 2, 3, and 4 and forms I and II. Free secondary education is available to all children who have completed form II or who have attained the age of 14. On the completion of the third or fourth year of secondary education, pupils who do not desire to enter a university may take the examination for the so-called school certificate, that is, a certifi-

cate attesting completion of the secondary course. The prerequisite for admission to university study is either completion of a 4-year course at an approved secondary school or the passing of the university entrance examination.

Elementary and secondary schools. The number of schools in New Zealand mounted steadily during the 1960s. All types of schools increased in number except the Maori village schools. The decline in the number of Maori schools was due in part to the consolidation of a number of small schools into central schools and in part to the fact that a growing number of Maori students were attending public primary schools. According to latest available figures, in the early 1980s New Zealand had about 2800 public and private primary schools with about 20,400 teachers and an annual enrollment of about 506,600 students. Some 400 public and private secondary schools, with approximately 13,525 teachers, were annually attended by some 226,350 students. In addition, about 145,100 students attended vocational schools.

Universities and colleges. The university system in New Zealand in the early 1980s comprised six separate universities and a university college of agriculture. The seven institutions were the University of Auckland (1882), Waikato University (1964, at Hamilton), the Victoria University of Wellington (1897), Massey University (1926, at Palmerston North), the University of Canterbury (1873, at Christchurch), the University of Otago (1869, at Dunedin), and Lincoln College (1878,

Cathedral Square in Christchurch, New Zealand's largest city. Situated on the eastern coast of South Island, Christchurch is the hub of the country's grain trade.

New Zealand Consulate General

near Christchurch), a constituent agricultural college of the University of Canterbury. Under the Universities Act of 1961 a university grants committee advises the government on the needs of university education and research and also allocates the grants of money that it recommends for appropriation by the parliament. The six universities and the agricultural college had a combined annual enrollment in the early 1980s of about 57,140 students. Several teachers colleges were also in operation, and an extensive adult-education program throughout the country was conducted by the National Council of Adult Education.

Culture. The earliest cultural tradition in New Zealand was that of the Maori. The literature consisted of history, tales, poems, and myths handed down by oral tradition. The indigenous art of New Zealand was also Maori. European settlers, particularly the English, brought with them their own traditions, colored by an unsettled, expatriate sentiment that was a strong influence in the cultural life of the country until the early 20th century but that has since given way to a more confident, nationalistic spirit.

The arts, literature, and music were given great stimulus by the Queen Elizabeth II Arts Council of New Zealand, created in October 1963 to foster artistic and cultural undertakings of all kinds and to make them accessible to the public.

Libraries and museums. The National Library Act of 1965 established the National Library of New Zealand by combining several library systems. The National Library Service in Wellington comprises five major divisions with a total collection of about 4 million volumes. The Auckland Public Library contains about 1 million volumes, including Maori works. Other leading libraries include the Dunedin Public Library (380,000 volumes), the Canterbury University Library in Christchurch (500,000 volumes), and the Wellington Public Library (431,000 volumes). All government records of permanent value are preserved in the National Archives in Wellington.

Art galleries and museums are found in most large cities, but the oldest institutions are in Auckland. The Auckland City Art Gallery, founded in 1888, and the Auckland Museum, opened in 1852, contain notable collections, and the National Art Gallery (1936) in Wellington is noted particularly for its Australian and New Zealand paintings. Outstanding natural history and ethnological collections are found in the National Museum, in Wellington; Canterbury Museum, in Christchurch; and Otago Museum, in Dunedin.

Literature. Soon after Europeans became aware of New Zealand, the orally transmitted myths and legends of the Maori were supplemented on a more factual level by accounts of the country

74

given in the writings of the early voyagers, especially Capt. James Cook, who visited New Zealand in 1769. Later, the early settlers, including the British author Samuel Butler, contributed some graphic descriptions of pioneer life. On the whole, however, the early New Zealanders felt too geographically remote and too cut off from their cultural tradition to write, and until very recent times, Katherine Mansfield, herself an expatriate, was the only New Zealand writer with an international reputation. The economic depression of the 1930s, which was particularly harsh in New Zealand, brought a sense of national identity, and since then poets, short-story writers, and novelists have flourished. These include the novelist Sylvia Ashton-Warner and the detective-story writer Dame Ngaio Marsh (1899–1982).

Art. Until recently, the art of the Maori was regarded as having only ethnological value. The settlers brought little in the way of artistic skills or inclinations. As a consequence very little feeling for art existed in New Zealand before World War II. Since that time, however, an upsurge of interest in art and in the crafts (especially pottery) has occurred. The art of the Maori, particularly their elaborate painted wood carvings, has been reassessed and has strongly influenced other New Zealand artists.

ECONOMY

The national economy of New Zealand is largely dependent on the export of wool, meat, and dairy products. Any negative fluctuation in world prices and demand affects the economy. In the 1960s an unexpected decline of the world demand for wool seriously affected the balance of payments of New Zealand. In 1979–80 the estimated national budget included revenue of about $6.5 billion and expenditure of about $7.5 billion.

Agriculture. Modern methods and machinery are used extensively on New Zealand farms, and the productivity of the country is consequently among the highest in the world. The land is ideally suited for dairy farming and for raising sheep and beef cattle because winter housing for livestock is unnecessary and grass grows nearly the whole year round. Annual output of the main crops in the early 1980s included wheat, 325,000 metric tons; corn, 187,000 tons; barley, 295,000 tons; and oats, 64,000 tons. Other important crops were apples, pears, tobacco, potatoes, and peas. The livestock population of New Zealand included about 68.7 million sheep, some 8.4 million head of cattle, and approximately 540,000 pigs. Farm horses have been almost completely replaced by tractors.

Sheepherding in a fertile valley near Mt. Cook, in the Southern Alps. Wool is New Zealand's most important commodity. New Zealand Consulate General

A view of the Remarkable Mts. on Lake Wakatipu, at Queenstown, on South Island, New Zealand. The mountains, exceptionally craggy and sierran, extend southward from the Kawarau River to the Hector Mts. The Queenstown district is popular with vacationers, who go there to enjoy skiing, hunting, fishing, boating, and other pastimes.
Morton Beebe and Associates–
Photo Researchers, Inc.

Forestry and Fishing. Timber production in 1979 was about 9 million cu m (about 318 million cu ft). Other forestry products produced annually in the same year were approximately 260,000 metric tons of newsprint and about 371,000 tons of other paper and paper board. Most of the native forests were denuded in the early years of colonization. An extensive reforestation program has utilized imported varieties of fast-growing trees instead of native New Zealand trees, most of which are slow-growing. A stand of a North American species of pine in the Kaingaroa State Forest, reputedly the largest planted forest in the world, is exploited at plants owned and operated jointly by the government and private industry.

The most important freshwater and marine species taken are crayfish, oysters, snapper, tarakihi, hapuku, flounder, and sole. In 1979 the catch of the fisheries was approximately 110,000 metric tons, of which crayfish and oysters accounted for about half. Much of the fishing is done by motor trawlers.

Mining. In the 1970s the mineral output of New Zealand increased substantially, as newly discovered deposits of petroleum and natural gas were exploited. Other minerals produced in significant quantities include coal, gold, silver, limestone, iron ore, bentonite, silica sand, and pumice.

Manufacturing. In the late 1970s about 309,000 persons were employed in manufacturing. The principal manufactures were meat and dairy products, paper and paper products, machinery, clothing, lumber, motor vehicles, electrical machinery, refined petroleum, and printed materials. Manufacturing has increased steadily, but New Zealand has insufficient workers and raw materials to support much heavy industry. Auckland is the principal manufacturing center.

Energy. About three-quarters of New Zealand's annual electricity is produced by hydroelectric facilities, and most of the rest is generated in plants burning coal or refined petroleum. In addition underground steam on North Island is used to produce substantial amounts of electricity. Major hydroelectric facilities are on the Waikato R., on North Island, and on the Clutha and Waitaki rivers, on South Island. In the early 1980s New Zealand had an electricity-generating capacity of about 5.9 million kw, and its annual output totaled approximately 22 billion kwh.

Currency and Banking. Under the Decimal Currency Act of 1964 a system of decimal currency was introduced in New Zealand in 1967, with the dollar as the monetary unit. The previous basic unit was the New Zealand pound. The New Zealand dollar is divided into 100 cents (1.3 NZ$ equal U.S.$1; 1982).

In addition to the Reserve Bank of New Zealand, which has the sole power of issue, several commercial banks and trustee savings banks operate, as does the Post Office Savings Bank. The Post Office Savings Bank, the Reserve Bank, and the Bank of New Zealand, which is the largest of the commercial banks, are owned and operated by the government. The government also takes part in commercial credit through the State Advances Corp., which lends money at low interest to farmers, home builders, and individuals in business.

Foreign Trade. The value of exports for New Zealand in the early 1980s totaled approximately $5.6 billion annually. Great Britain, the U.S., Japan, and Australia are important customers. New Zealand is the largest exporter of dairy products in the world and is second only to Australia in the export of wool. Other important exports include lamb, mutton, and beef. Imports in the early 1980s totaled about $5.7 billion annually. Chief imports are manufactured goods, heavy machinery, petroleum, chemicals, iron, steel, and textiles. Imports come mainly from Australia, Great Britain, the U.S., Japan, and Singapore. New Zealand tariffs are low; about half of the manufactured goods are imported into the country free of duty.

Transportation and Communications. Public transport facilities are good even in remote districts. In the early 1980s New Zealand had about 93,350 km (about 58,005 mi) of roads and 4550 km (2830 mi) of railroads. About 1.3 million passenger cars were in use. Ships provide fast overnight service between North Island and South Island and along the coasts. The country's principal ports are Auckland, Wellington, Tauranga, and Lyttelton (near Christchurch). Air transport is widely used, with numerous airfields located throughout the country to serve private pilots. Air New Zealand is the leading airline. All mail, telephone, radio, and cable services are owned by the Post and Telegraph Department. In the early 1980s about 1.7 million telephones were in use. Radios numbered more than 2.7 million, and New Zealanders had about 900,000 television receivers.

Labor. Of a total labor force of about 1,230,000 persons in the late 1970s, about 11% were engaged in agriculture and 25% in manufacturing. More than 290 unions of industrial workers had a combined membership of about 487,000. The standard of living was high, and, as the labor force was insufficient to meet the demand, little unemployment existed.

GOVERNMENT

Executive action nominally is taken in the name of the governor-general, who is appointed by the British sovereign. The governor-general usually works in concert with the Executive Council, which is composed of the governor-general, the prime minister, the ministers heading the various governmental departments, and ministers without portfolio (that is, without departmental responsibility). The principal administrative body in New Zealand is the cabinet, which consists of the prime minister and the ministers in charge of departments.

Health and Welfare. All workers, including those on farms, are guaranteed a 2-week annual paid vacation. A straight deduction from wages finances social security benefits, which include hospitalization and medical care, children's allowances, unemployment benefits, and pensions for disabled workers, widows, the blind, and all persons over the age of 65.

Legislature. New Zealand has a unicameral parliament, which is known as the House of Representatives. A second house, the Legislative Council, was abolished in 1950. The House of Representatives is composed of 88 European (that is, non-Maori) and 4 Maori members; all members are elected by universal adult suffrage for 3-year terms. The prime minister and other ministers usually are selected from among the parliamentary members of the majority party. The government may continue in office only so long as it retains the confidence of the House of Representatives.

Political Parties. The principal political organizations are the Labour party and the National party. The former favors a limited degree of nationalization and strong credit controls. The program of the latter strongly supports free enterprise and opposes state socialism. Both parties advocate increased social security benefits and government assistance for housing and land settlement.

Local Government. New Zealand is divided into 104 counties. Some small offshore islands, however, are not incorporated into any county. The counties exercise authority mainly in areas of scattered population. Where population is denser, local government is conducted by boroughs, independent town districts, or cities. In the late 1970s the country had 135 boroughs and cities.

Judiciary. The highest court in New Zealand is the court of appeal, which exercises appellate jurisdiction only. Decisions of the court are final unless leave is granted to appeal to the Privy Council in Great Britain. The principal trial courts are the high court and the district courts. Justices of the peace in some cases may try minor criminal charges. Specialized courts determine questions relating to labor disputes, workers' compensation, and land valuation in cases of condemnation.

Defense. In the early 1980s the army, navy, and air force of New Zealand were coordinated under the ministry of defense. The army numbered about 5670 regular personnel. Regular navy personnel totaled about 2750. The air force had about 4200 regular members.

HISTORY

New Zealand was discovered and named in 1642 by the Dutch mariner Abel Janszoon Tasman. The British explorer Capt. James Cook visited the islands in 1769 and took possession of them for Great Britain, but nearly 75 years elapsed before the British government recognized his claim.

Moriori and Maori. The inhabitants of New Zealand at the time of Tasman's visit were the Maori, who about the 14th century had immigrated to North Island, probably from Tahiti, in a fleet of large canoes. Maori oral history credits the discovery of New Zealand to Kupe, a Maori navigator who came by canoe in the middle of the 10th century. At that time the islands were uninhabited, but before the Maori immigration a dark-skinned race, the Moriori, of whose origin nothing is known, settled on the eastern coast of North Island to hunt the moa, a wingless bird about 3.7 m (12 ft) tall, which is now extinct. Some of these people were absorbed into the Maori population; the remainder were driven out and allowed to settle in the Chatham Islands, where the last survivor is said to have died in the mid-20th century. The Maori spread out along the coast and the rivers on both the main islands, although they were more numerous on the North Island.

Butter emerges from a giant churn at the Morrinsville Dairy Factory. New Zealand exports fine dairy products worldwide. New Zealand Consulate General

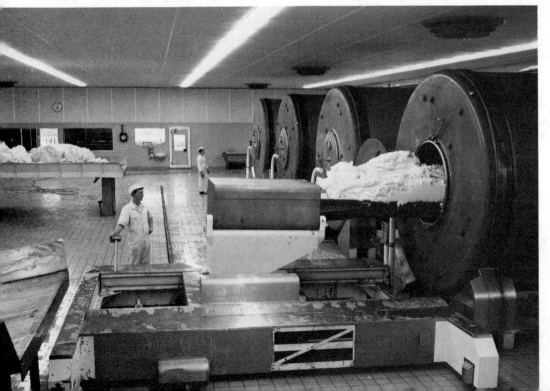

Early in the 19th century British missionaries and whalers, despite fierce opposition from the Maori, established settlements and trading posts in New Zealand, chiefly among the Bay of Islands on North Island. Systematic immigration began in 1839–40 under the auspicies of the New Zealand Co., which had been organized in London.

British Sovereignty. By the terms of the Treaty of Waitangi, signed in 1840 by a British representative and 50 Maori chieftains, Great Britain formally proclaimed sovereignty over the islands and agreed to respect the landownership rights of the Maori, who placed themselves under the protection of the British government. At the same time New Zealand was made a dependency of New South Wales, Australia. In 1841 it was constituted a separate crown colony.

Colonization continued apace during the ensuing decades. Disputes between the newcomers and the Maori over land claims led ultimately to violent Maori uprisings between 1845 and 1848 and between 1860 and 1870. After that date, however, colonial authorities pursued a conciliatory policy that resulted in the establishment of permanent peace between the European and native populations. The discovery of alluvial gold in 1865 caused a new influx of immigrants, many of whom settled down to farming when the deposits of gold were exhausted. Sheep raising and gold mining were the main sources of the country's wealth in the latter part of the 19th century. The introduction of refrigerated ships in 1882 enabled New Zealand to export fresh meat, thus stimulating settlement and more intensive farming in the country.

Parliamentary Government. A central government with an elective parliament and a cabinet was established in New Zealand in 1856. During most of the 19th century, political power was held alternately by liberals, who instituted male suffrage and compulsory education, and by conservatives, mainly large landholders. In 1891, following the failure in the previous year of a maritime strike, trade union leaders gave their support to the liberal faction. A series of Liberal party governments continued uninterruptedly in power until 1912, enjoying labor support until a separate Labour party was organized in 1910. These governments, first under the journalist John Ballance (1839–93) and, after his death, under Richard John Seddon (1845–1906) and Sir Joseph George Ward (1856–1930), effected a program of land reform and social legislation that gained New Zealand worldwide recognition. Large speculative landholdings were broken up under the provisions of a number of statutes that enabled the government to acquire large hold-

ings for subdivision and authorized the purchase of small landholdings on long-term mortgages. In addition, other legislation established minimum rates of pay and provided for the compulsory arbitration and settlement of labor disputes. In 1893 New Zealand became the first country to grant woman suffrage. During this period of liberal-labor dominance the foundation of the social security system was laid.

Early 20th Century. In 1907 New Zealand officially was designated a dominion, although its form of government was unchanged. The conservatives, campaigning as the Reform party, regained power in 1912.

During World War I a coalition of the Reform and Liberal parties governed the country. In the war New Zealand furnished 124,211 men for the British forces, of whom 100,444 served overseas. These troops fought in Egypt and in the Gallipoli, or Dardanelles, campaign of 1915; the Australian and New Zealand Army Corps became known popularly as Anzac. In 1916 New Zealand units organized as a separate division arrived in France in time for the Battle of the Somme, and the Mounted Rifles later served in the campaign in Palestine. The losses of New Zealand in World War I exceeded 16,000 men killed and 40,000 wounded.

The collapse of a speculative land boom that had flourished after the war was an important cause of the economic depression from 1921 to 1926. The economic distress was aggravated by the worldwide depression beginning in 1930. In the parliamentary elections of 1935 the Labour party won a majority over the National party, which had been formed in 1931 by a coalition of the Liberal and Reform parties. The new government, under the labor leader Michael Joseph Savage (1872–1940), nationalized parts of the economy and expanded social security.

World War II and Asia. With the start of the war in 1939, New Zealand imposed wage and price controls and generally emphasized financial stability rather than social progress. New Zealand contributed a larger percentage of the population to the armed services than any of the Allies except Great Britain. The army saw service in Greece, Cyprus, North Africa, Italy, and the Pacific. The air force was active in all theaters. The casualties of New Zealand exceeded 11,600 dead and 15,700 wounded.

The power of the Labour party came to an end on Nov. 30, 1949, when the National party emerged victorious in general elections. The new government promulgated a program more favorable to private enterprise.

In the arena of foreign affairs New Zealand

participated (1950) in the Colombo Plan (q.v.) for Southeast Asia and in 1952 concluded the so-called ANZUS mutual-defense pact with Australia and the U.S. With seven other countries, New Zealand signed the Southeast Asia collective-defense treaty on Sept. 8, 1954 (see SOUTHEAST ASIA TREATY ORGANIZATION). New Zealand forces served with UN forces in Korea and Cyprus, and token forces from the country have served in other areas of conflict.

The Economy in the 1960s. The Labour party was returned to power in the general elections of November 1957. Its accession coincided with the onset of the economic crisis that was to color the 1960s, a crisis due in part to a decline in payments for exports, notably wool. The National party regained parliament in 1960 and, under the leadership of Prime Minister Keith J. Holyoake, retained its majority in 1963 and 1966. Balance-of-payments difficulties and inflationary stress induced the Holyoake government to maintain many of the economic controls imposed by Labour, but it did ease import restrictions.

The 1970s. Early in 1972 Holyoake retired, and in elections held in November Labour swept back to power, and the party leader Norman Eric Kirk (1923-74) became prime minister. In January 1973, Kirk met with Prime Minister Gough Whitlam (1916-) of Australia and pledged closer cooperation between their nations. In the same year New Zealand established diplomatic ties with the People's Republic of China.

When Kirk died in 1974, Wallace Edward Rowling (1927-) succeeded him as prime minister. In 1975 the National party returned to power under Robert Muldoon (1921-); it won reelection by a narrow margin in 1978 and 1981 and tried with limited success to cope with New Zealand's worsening economic problems. The elections of July 1984 returned control of parliament to the Labour party, and party leader David Lange (1942-) became prime minister.

For further information on this topic, see the Bibliography in volume 28, section 1247.

NEY, Michel, Duc d'Elchingen, Prince de la Moskova (1769-1815), marshal of France, born in Saarlouis. He enlisted as a cavalryman in the French army and in 1796 was made general of brigade. On the establishment of the empire by Napoleon Bonaparte, he was made marshal of France and in 1805 was created duke of Elchingen. He distinguished himself in the invasion of Russia in 1812 and was named prince of Moscow. In 1815, after the capitulation of Paris, when Napoleon returned to France after escaping from Elba, Ney was sent to oppose Napoleon's advance. Instead Ney deserted the Bourbon monarchy and with his army joined Napoleon's forces. On June 16, 1815, at Quatre-Bras, a village in Belgium, Ney was defeated by the British general Arthur Wellesley, 1st duke of Wellington, in a preliminary battle of the Waterloo campaign. When the marshal returned to Paris, he was tried, condemned to death for high treason, and shot.

NEZ PERCÉ, leading North American Indian tribe of the Sahaptin linguistic stock. The tribe formerly occupied a large territory in southeastern Washington, northeastern Oregon, and central Idaho. The name Nez Percé (Fr., "pierced nose") given by French explorers, derived from the tribe's practice of wearing nose pendants.

The Nez Percé followed an economy based on fishing, especially salmon, and on vegetable staples such as the bulbs of the camas plant, wild roots, and berries. After about 1700 they also kept horses and hunted buffalo. In winter they lived along riverbanks in villages of long houses built of bark, mats, and skins; in summer they camped in the mountains and in the great upland camas meadows. They practiced some weaving and the decorating of buffalo skins with paint and porcupine quills. Their principal religious ceremony was a dance in honor of the Guardian Spirit, their presiding deity. War dances were also performed. The entire tribe was divided into more than 40 bands, each led by a popularly selected chief. Marriage was generally outside the band or group. In response to the tribe's request for instruction in Christianity, a Protestant mission was established among the Nez Percé at Lapwai, Idaho, in 1837.

In 1855 the Nez Percé made a treaty with the U.S., ceding the greater portion of their territory to the U.S. government and receiving a reservation that included the Wallowa Valley in Oregon. When gold was discovered in the region, the tribe was forced to agree to surrender all its lands and to return to a reservation at Lapwai. A band led by Chief Joseph, whose Indian name was Hinmaton-Yalaktit, refused to accept the agreement, and in 1877 he was victorious in a battle with federal troops. Joseph then led his band, which included women and children, on a retreat of more than 1600 km (about 1000 mi), and although pursued by federal troops that greatly outnumbered them, the Indians won several engagements. About 50 km (about 30 mi) from the safety of the Canadian border, however, Joseph and his band were captured. They were sent to the Indian Territory where many died. Some of the survivors were later permitted to return to Idaho, where the majority of the tribe now lives on the Nez Percé reservation. Joseph and the remainder were sent to Colville reservation in northern Washington.

NGO DINH DIEM. *See* DIEM, NGO DINH.

NGUEMA, Francisco Macías, also called Nguema Biyogo Masie (1924–79), first president of Equatorial Guinea (1968–79). Born in Nsegayong, Río Muni, the son of a famed sorcerer, Nguema became a civil servant in the Spanish colonial government. In the 1960s he emerged as the spokesman for the Fang majority, and in October 1968, having won the preindependence elections, he became president of the new republic. Four years later, he appointed himself president for life. Nguema proved a despotic, brutal ruler. During his regime, the country's educated class was eradicated, some 80,000 people were reported to have been killed, about one-third of the population fled into exile, and the economy collapsed. Following the murder of a family member, he was overthrown in August 1979, quickly tried, and executed.

NGUYEN VAN THIEU. *See* THIEU, NGUYEN VAN.

NHA TRANG, city and seaport, SE Vietnam, capital of Phu Khanh Province, on the rugged South China Sea coast at the mouth of the Song Cai. Nha Trang was chiefly a religious center and beach resort until its port facilities were modernized in the 1970s. Timber is an important export. The Oceanographic Institute of Vietnam (1922) is here, and four Buddhist shrines, built during the 7th to 12th centuries, are nearby landmarks. The community was established by the 3d century AD. It was under French rule from 1862 to 1954 and was part of South Vietnam from 1954 to 1976. During the Vietnam War, a U.S. military base was here. Pop. (est.) 216,200.

NIACIN. *See* VITAMIN.

NIAGARA, river, W of New York and SE Ontario, Canada, about 55 km (about 34 mi) long. It issues from Lake Erie at Buffalo, N.Y., and flows N to Lake Ontario, forming part of the U.S.-Canadian boundary. Near its head the river divides into two channels, between which lies Grand Island, N.Y. The channels merge just beyond the island, and the river soon passes over Niagara Falls. The Whirlpool Rapids are a few miles N of the cataract. During its course the Niagara, which is the main drainage outlet of the four upper Great Lakes, makes a descent of about 99 m (about 326 ft), about one-half of which occurs at the waterfall. The river is navigable except in the region of the waterfall and rapids.

NIAGARA FALLS, city, Regional Municipality of Niagara, SE Ontario, Canada, a port on the Niagara R. opposite Niagara Falls, N.Y. (to which it is connected by bridges); inc. 1904. Principal manufactures include processed food, machinery, abrasives, chemicals, silverware, metal goods, and alcoholic beverages. The city is a popular tourist center overlooking the Canadian, or Horseshoe, Falls (*see* NIAGARA FALLS). Points of interest include Queen Victoria Park, adjacent to the cataract, containing the Oakes Garden; Niagara Falls Museum (1827), one of the oldest museums in North America, featuring displays of art and historical materials; Lundy's Lane Historical Museum, including exhibits pertaining to early local history; and Marineland, with an aquatic theater and a game farm; the Niagara International Centre, which contains Skylon, a tall tower with an observation deck overlooking the falls. Mt. Carmel College and the Niagara Parks School of Horticulture are here. Originally called Elgin, the community was merged with Clifton in 1856 and was given its present name in 1881. In 1963 the city greatly expanded in area when it was merged with Stamford township. Pop. (1976) 69,423; (1981) 70,960.

NIAGARA FALLS, city, Niagara Co., W New York, on the Niagara R., opposite Niagara Falls, Ont.; inc. as a city 1892. It is a major tourist center situated at the American Falls; the principal attractions are included in New York State Niagara Reservation (1885). Among the city's many manufactures are chemicals, machinery, forest products, and processed food; much hydroelectric power also is produced. Niagara University (1856) is nearby.

The French built a fort on the site of the city in 1745. The British captured the region in 1759, and the U.S. settlement of Manchester was founded here in 1806. Held by the British during the War of 1812, the community in 1848 was renamed Niagara Falls, Niagara being an Indian word for "at the neck." The first large hydroelectric facilities here were built in the 1890s. In the late 1970s and early '80s it was reported that chemical wastes dumped (1947–52) in the area of the unfinished Love Canal here may have injured persons living near the canal site. Pop. (1970) 85,615; (1980) 71,384.

NIAGARA FALLS, great waterfall on the Niagara R., in W New York and SE Ontario, Canada. One of the world's most memorable natural sights, it consists of two cataracts: the Canadian, or Horseshoe, Falls (49 m/161 ft high), on the Canadian side of the river, and the American Falls (51 m/167 ft high), on the U.S. side. The waterfalls are separated by Goat Island, N.Y. The crestline of the crescent-shaped Canadian Falls, which carries about nine times more water than the U.S. cataract, is about 790 m (about 2592 ft) long, and the fairly straight crest of the American Falls measures about 305 m (about 1001 ft). A small

Niagara Falls, one of the most spectacular natural wonders of the world, borders New York State and Canada.
New York State Dept. of Commerce

section of the American Falls near Goat Island is also known as Bridal Veil Falls.

Niagara Falls was formed about 12,000 years ago, when glaciers retreated N, allowing water from Lake Erie to flow over the Niagara Escarpment, a ridge that extends from S Ontario to Rochester, N.Y. Since that time, erosion has slowly pushed the waterfall about 11 km (about 7 mi) upstream, forming the Niagara Gorge. At present the Canadian Falls is receding at an average yearly rate of about 1.5 m (about 5 ft), and the American Falls is being cut away at an annual pace of about 15 cm (about 6 in). The Canadian Falls erodes at a faster rate mainly because it carries more water. In 1954 a considerable portion of the American Falls broke off, creating a large talus, or rock slope, at the base of the cataract. In order to study ways of preventing further rockfalls and to remove some of the talus, the American Falls was "shut off" for several months in 1969 by a dam build between the U.S. mainland and Goat Island.

Niagara Falls is a great tourist attraction, luring millions of visitors each year. The falls may be viewed from parks located on either side of the river, from observation towers, from boats, from Goat Island, and from the Rainbow Bridge, located a short distance downstream. Visitors also may enter the Cave of the Winds, situated behind a curtain of falling water near the base of the American Falls.

Samuel de Champlain, a French explorer, probably visited Niagara Falls in 1613. Father Louis Hennepin, a Flemish monk, is known to have visited the waterfall in 1678; he later published an eyewitness description of it.

The Niagara's large volume of flow, averaging about 5520 cu m (about 194,940 cu ft) per second, plus its steep drop, give the river great power potential. The waterpower probably was tapped first in 1757, when Daniel Chabert Joncaire built a sawmill on the upper river. In 1853 work started on a hydraulic canal to divert the waters of the upper river to drive machinery in mills and factories situated below Niagara Falls. In 1875 the first flour mill powered by the canal water was opened, and in 1881 the first hydro-electric generator was installed along the water-way. The first large-scale hydroelectric facility, the Edward Dean Adams Power Plant, was opened on the U.S. side in 1896.

In 1950 the U.S. and Canada signed a treaty fixing the amount of water that could be diverted from the river for power generation, and soon thereafter two major hydroelectric projects were constructed. The Canadians built the twin Sir Adam Beck-Niagara generating stations (completed 1958; capacity, with associated pumped-storage facility, 1,815,000 kw) at Queenston, Ont. The Power Authority of the State of New York constructed the Robert Moses-Niagara Power Plant (completed 1963; capacity, with associated pumped-storage facility, 2,400,000 kw) near Lewiston, N.Y. Both projects, each located about 6 km (about 4 mi) below Niagara Falls, are driven by water diverted just above the falls and con-veyed by underground conduits and canals to turbines. Much of the hydroelectricity is con-sumed by industries in the nearby cities of Niag-ara Falls, N.Y., and Niagara Falls, Ont.

NIAMEY, city, capital of Niger, SW Niger, on the Niger R. A river port and road and trade center, Niamey is the S terminus of a short railroad NW to Tillabery. The city manufactures pottery and bricks, leather goods, textiles, charcoal, metal products, soft drinks, and milled grain. Livestock, hides and skins, grain, vegetables, and locally made mats and textiles are exported.

A French fort since 1902, Niamey succeeded Zinder as capital of the military territory. From 1927 to 1958 it served as capital of the autono-mous Niger Territory. Founded at an unknown time as Niamma, it was later called Niame until the arrival of the French. Pop. (1977) 225,300.

NIBELUNGENLIED, medieval German epic poem of unknown authorship, written in Middle High German in the early 13th century. The poem is a composite of Norse and Teutonic mythology and the early history of the kingdom of Burgundy. Several other versions exist of the material con-tained in the *Nibelungenlied* (Song of the Nibe-lungs). The principal one is the Icelandic prose epic *Volsunga Saga* (Saga of the Volsungs), which emphasizes the mythological and primi-tive elements of the material common to both; the *Nibelungenlied* stresses the historical mate-rial. Parts of both the *Nibelungenlied* and the *Volsunga Saga* were combined by the 19th-cen-tury German composer Richard Wagner for his operatic tetralogy *Der Ring des Nibelungen.*

The hero of the *Nibelungenlied* is Siegfried (Sigurd), a German warrior and hero. He kills two Burgundian chiefs of the Nibelung family and takes their magic sword, their hoard of gold, upon which in dying they put a curse, and their *tarnkappe,* a cape that makes its wearer invisible. He goes to Worms, the Burgundian capital, to court the beautiful Kriemhild, sister of the Bur-gundian king Gunther. Hagen, a wily and treach-erous councilor of Gunther, plans to gain possession of the Nibelung hoard and tells Gun-ther and his brothers that Siegfried has killed other Burgundian monarchs and is not to be trusted. Siegfried wins Gunther's confidence, however, by aiding the Burgundians in a war against the Saxons. Gunther agrees to a marriage between Siegfried and Kriemhild on condition that Siegfried first help him to win Brunhild, queen of Iceland. Siegfried and Gunther go to Iceland, where rendered invisible by his cape, Siegfried overcomes Brunhild in physical com-bat; thinking it is Gunther who has beaten her, she consents to marry him. Siegfried marries Kriemhild, and Gunther marries Brunhild.

Hagen persuades Gunther to let him kill Sieg-fried, winning the consent of the king by point-ing out that although Siegfried is only his vassal he is generally regarded as Gunther's superior. Gunther's hatred of Siegfried is also aroused be-cause Brunhild has discovered that she was tricked into marrying the Burgundian king, and despises him. Through treachery Hagen slays Siegfried at a royal hunt; Kriemhild swears to avenge Siegfried's death. She is powerless, how-ever, because Hagen seizes the Nibelung hoard that Kriemhild inherited and with which she in-tended to raise a strong following. Hagen sinks the hoard into the Rhine River at a secret spot. Thirteen years later Kriemhild marries Etzel (At-tila), king of the Huns, and goes to live at his court. Years later she lures Hagen, Gunther, and their followers to the court of Attila and has them all killed. She herself is killed by a German hero who was horrified at the murder of the Bur-gundians. The hoard of the Nibelungs remains at the bottom of the Rhine; the secret of its loca-tion died with Hagen.

NICAEA, the name of two ancient cities. The more important of the two, now İznik, Turkey, was in Bithynia on the eastern shore of Lake As-cania. It was founded by Antigonus I, king of Macedonia, in the 4th century BC, and later flour-ished under the Romans. It is famous in ecclesi-astical history for the two Councils of Nicaea (*see* NICAEA, COUNCILS OF). The other Nicaea was on the site of the modern city of Nice in France.

NICAEA, COUNCILS OF, two ecumenical coun-cils of the Christian church, held at Nicaea (now İznik, Turkey), a city of ancient Bithynia, in Asia Minor.

NICARAGUA

First Council of Nicaea. Held in 325, this first ecumenical council was convened by Constantine I, emperor of Rome, to settle the Arian dispute concerning the nature of Jesus Christ (*see* ARIANISM). Of the 1800 bishops in the Roman Empire, 318 attended the council. The Nicene Creed, which defined the Son as consubstantial with the Father, was adopted as the official position of the church regarding the divinity of Christ. The council also fixed the celebration of Easter on the Sunday after the Jewish Pesach, or Passover, and granted to the bishop of Alexandria, Egypt, authority in the East in the fashion of Rome's quasi-patriarchal authority, which was not, as sometimes erroneously stated, the same as that of the pope. In this granting of authority lay the origin of the patriarchates throughout the church.

Second Council of Nicaea. Held in 787, the second of the councils at Nicaea was the seventh ecumenical council. It was convened by Irene, empress of the East, and attended by 350 bishops, most of whom were Byzantine. In spite of strong objections by the iconoclasts, the council validated the veneration of images and ordered their restoration in churches throughout the Roman Empire.

NICARAGUA, largest republic of Central America, bounded on the N by Honduras, on the E by the Caribbean Sea, on the S by Costa Rica, and on the W by the Pacific Ocean. The area of Nicaragua is 130,000 sq km (50,193 sq mi).

LAND AND RESOURCES

The Nicaraguan highlands, with a mean elevation of about 610 m (about 2000 ft), cross Nicaragua from the NW to the SE. Several mountain ranges, the highest of which, the Cordillera Isabelia, reaches an elevation of more then 2100 m (more than 6890 ft), cut the highlands from E to W. In the W is a great basin, or depression, containing two lakes, Nicaragua, the largest in Central America, and Managua. The two are connected by the Tipitapa R. A chain of volcanoes, which are a contributory cause of local earthquakes, rises between the lakes and the Pacific coast. In the E, the Caribbean coastal plain known as the Costa de Mosquitos (Mosquito Coast) extends some 72 km (some 45 mi) inland and is partly overgrown with rain forest. The four principal rivers in the country, the San Juan, Coco (Wanks), Grande, and Escondido, empty into the Caribbean.

Climate. The coastal regions of Nicaragua have a tropical climate with a mean average temperature of 25.5° C (78° F). In the higher altitudes in the interior, the temperature varies between 15.5° and 26.5° C (60° and 80° F). The rainy season extends from May to October, and along the Caribbean coast the annual rainfall averages 3810 mm (150 in).

Natural Resources. The natural resources of Nicaragua are primarily agricultural. Deposits of volcanic material have enriched the soil, which is extremely fertile. About half the land is covered with forests. The country has some deposits of gold, silver, and copper.

Plants and Animals. The vegetation of Nicaragua is of a tropical and subtropical nature. Dense rain forests are found along the Caribbean coast and on the E slopes of the highlands. Such trees as oak, pine, cedar, balsam, mahogany, and wild rubber, along with some 50 varieties of fruit trees, abound.

Nicaragua's wild animals incude puma, deer, several species of monkeys, and alligators as well as a variety of other reptiles. Parrots, hummingbirds, and wild turkeys are abundant.

POPULATION

About 70% of the Nicaraguan population is mestizo (people of mixed white and Indian descent), 17% is white, and the remainder is Indian or black.

Population Characteristics. The population of Nicaragua (1981 UN est.) was 2,820,000, giving the country an overall population density of about 22 persons per sq km (about 56 persons per sq mi). Approximately 60% of the population is concentrated in the W part of the country, and about 50% is urban.

Political Divisions and Principal Cities. Nicaragua is divided into 16 departments, which contain more than 134 municipalities. Managua (q.v.), with a population (1978 est.) of 517,700, is the capital and commercial center. León (pop., est., 73,800) is an important religious and cultural center. Granada (50,100) is the terminus of the railway from the main port of entry, Corinto (16,500), on the Pacific coast.

Language and Religion. Spanish is the official language of Nicaragua. About 95% of the Nicaraguan people are Roman Catholic; most of the remainder are Protestant.

Education. In the early 1980s primary and secondary education was free and compulsory in Nicaragua, but many children did not attend classes because of a lack of facilities. About 472,200 pupils were enrolled in the country's primary schools but only about 137,000 pupils attended the secondary and vocational schools. Approximately 34,700 students attended Nicaraguan institutions of higher education, including the National Autonomous University of Nicaragua (1812), in León, and the Central American University (1961), in Managua.

A street scene in Granada, one of Nicaragua's largest cities, situated at the foot of the volcano Mombacho, on Lake Nicaragua.　Photo Researchers, Inc.

Culture. As in other Latin American countries, the culture of Nicaragua reflects Spanish cultural patterns, influential since the colonial period, combined with an ancient Indian heritage. Nicaraguans hold many colorful celebrations to commemorate local saints' days and ecclesiastical events. The marimba is extremely popular, and ancient musical instruments such as the *chrimía* (clarinet), *maraca* (rattle), and *zul* (flute) are common in rural areas. Dances from colonial times survive today, as do fine examples of colonial architecture.

ECONOMY

The economy of Nicaragua grew at a substantial rate until the late 1970s, when civil unrest disrupted economic activity. Agriculture is the chief economic activity, but several modern manufacturing industries have been established, especially in and near Managua. The government plays a major role in Nicaragua's economy. In 1979 the estimated national budget included revenue of $376 million and expenditure of $341 million.

Agriculture. In the early 1980s agriculture in Nicaragua employed approximately 45% of the labor force. The principal commercial crops are coffee and cotton. Other crops include sugarcane, maize, sorghum, rice, beans, bananas, and oranges. Nicaragua is one of the leading cattle-raising countries in Central America. In the early 1980s the country had about 2.4 million head of dairy and beef cattle.

85

INDEX TO MAP OF NICARAGUA

Cities and Towns

Acoyapa ....B 3
Alamikamba ....B 2
Andrés..............C 1
Barra de Rio Grande ..C 2
Bilwaskarma ....C 1
Bluefields ....C 3
Boaco ....B 2
Bocay ....B 1
Bonanza ....B 2
Bragman's Bluff
  (Puerto Cabezas) ...C 1
Cabo Gracias a Dios ..C 1
Camoapa............B 2
Chichigalpa..........A 2
Chinandega..........A 2
Ciudad Dario........A 2
Comalapa...........B 2
Condega............A 2
Corinto ....A 2
Cuicuina ....B 2
Cuyu Tigni ....C 1
Diriamba ....A 3
El Gallo ....B 2
El Jicaral ....A 2
El Jicaro ....A 2
El Limon ....B 2
El Realego...........A 2
El Sauce ....A 2
El Viejo ....A 2

Esquipulas..........B 2
Esteli ....A 2
Granada ....B 3
Greytown (San Juan
  del Norte) ....C 3
Jalapa ....A 2
Jinotega............B 2
Jinotepe............A 3
Juigalpa............B 2
La Conquista........A 3
La Cruz ....B 2
Laguna de Perlas.....C 2
La Libertad ....B 2
La Paz.............A 2
La Paz de Oriente.....B 3
León ....A 2
Managua (cap.)......A 2
Masatepe...........A 3
Masaya ....A 3
Matagalpa..........B 2
Mateare ....A 2
Morrito.............B 3
Moyogalpa..........B 3
Muy Muy ....B 2
Muy Muy Viejo ......B 2
Nagarote ....A 2
Nandaime ....B 3
Ocotal ....A 2
Palsagua...........B 2
Playa Grande ....A 2
Poteca.............B 2

Prinzapolka..........C 2
Puerto Cabezas
  (Bragman's Bluff) ...C 1
Quilali ....B 2
Rama...............B 2
Rivas ....B 3
San Carlos ....B 3
San Francisco........B 3
San Jorge ....B 3
San Juan del Norte
  (Greytown).........C 3
San Juan del Sur ....A 3
San Miguelito ....B 3
San Pedro..........B 2
San Rafael del Norte ..B 2
San Rafael del Sur ....A 3
San Ramón..........B 2
Santa Cruz ....B 2
Santo Domingo.......B 2
Santo Tomás........B 3
Siuna..............B 2
Somotillo...........A 2
Somoto ....A 2
Telpaneca..........A 2
Terrabona..........B 2
Teustepe...........B 2
Tipitapa............B 2
Trinidad............A 2
Tunki ....B 2
Waspán............B 1
Yablis..............C 2

Other Features

Caribbean (sea) ......C 2
Coco (Segovia or
  Wanks) (river) ......B 1
Cosegüina (point).....A 2
Costa de Mosquitos
  (reg.) ....B 2
Dariense (mts.).......B 2
Dipilto (mts.)........A 2
Escondido (river) .....C 2
Grande (river).......B 2
Great Corn (island) ...C 2
Huapi (mts.) ....B 2
Isabelia (mts.).......B 2
Kukalaya (river) ......C 2
Little Corn (island) ....C 2
Managua (lake).......B 2
Miskitos (cays) ....C 1
Monkey (point) ......C 3
Nicaragua (lake) .....B 3
Ometepe (islands) ....B 3
Perlas (lagoon).......C 2
Salinas (bay).........A 3
San Juan (river) ......B 3
Solentiname (islands)..B 3
Tuma (river) ....B 2
Waspuk (river) ......B 1
Wawa (river) ....B 1
Zapatera (island) .....B 3

Forestry and Fishing. Nicaragua has considerable areas of usable timber. Lumbering is carried on along the principal rivers that flow into the Caribbean.

Commercial fishing was taken over by the government in 1961, and by the late 1970s the annual catch of both freshwater and saltwater fish exceeded 15,800 metric tons. The principal commercial fish are shrimp and crayfish.

Manufacturing and Energy. Some 11% of the economically active population in Nicaragua is engaged in manufacturing, chiefly in producing cement, chemicals, petroleum products, and consumer goods. The country has coffee-processing plants and sugar-refining mills, as well as textile mills that process domestic cotton.

In the 1980s Nicaragua had an installed electricity-generating capacity of about 380,000 kw, and annual production was some 988 million kwh. About 60% of the electricity was produced in thermal facilities and most of the rest in hydroelectric installations.

Currency and Foreign Trade. The córdoba, consisting of 100 centavos, is the basic monetary unit of Nicaragua (10.1 córdobas equal U.S.$1; 1982). In 1980 exports were valued at about $450 mil-

Valuable mahogany is readied for movement downstream to a processing plant. OFAR

NICARAGUA

0 25 50 75 100 MI.
0 25 50 75 100 KM.

HONDURAS

CARIBBEAN

PACIFIC
OCEAN

SEA

COSTA RICA

A Long. West of 86° Greenwich   B   84°   C

lion. Main exports included coffee, cotton, meat, chemicals, and sugar. Imports, including raw materials for industry, machinery, and consumer goods, were valued at about $887 million. Principal trading partners included West Germany, Venezuela, Japan, the U.S., and Costa Rica.

Transportation and Communications. Nicaragua has about 18,200 km (about 11,300 mi) of roads, of which 384 km (239 mi) are part of the Pan-American Highway. The country is served by 373 km (232 mi) of railroad track, and steamers operated on Lake Nicaragua. Domestic and international air travel is provided by LANICA, the state airline.

In the early 1980s Nicaragua had about 58,000 telephones, 600,000 radios, and 170,000 television receivers. Major daily newspapers included *Barricada, La Gaceta Diaro Oficial, Nuevo Diario,* and *La Prensa,* all published in Managua; and *El Centroamericano,* published in León.

GOVERNMENT

In 1979 the newly formed Government of National Reconstruction abrogated Nicaragua's 1974 constitution and issued a bill of rights. Many government institutions were in the process of being reorganized in the early 1980s, and elections in November 1984 brought a return to civilian rule.

Executive. Nicaragua was governed by a junta from 1979 until November 1984, when elections for a president and vice-president were held.

Legislature. Under the Government of National Reconstruction, the main legislative organ was the 47-member Council of State. A new 96-seat National Assembly took office in 1984.

Political Parties. Nicaragua's leading political party is the Sandinist National Liberation Front, founded in 1962. Most other parties that contested the 1984 elections were Sandinist allies; some opposition groups boycotted the voting.

Judiciary. The highest tribunal of Nicaragua is the supreme court, which sits in Managua. The country also has several lesser courts.

Defense. In the late 1970s the National Guard, which then served as Nicaragua's police force and army, had about 8000 members. In the early 1980s the government planned to establish a new military force of about 5000 soldiers.

HISTORY

The coast of Nicaragua was sighted by Christopher Columbus in 1502, but the first Spanish expedition of conquest, under Gil González Dávila (c. 1470–c. 1528), did not arrive until 1522; it established several Spanish settlements. A second conquistador, Francisco Fernández de Córdoba (1475–1526), founded Granada in 1523 and León in 1524.

Colonial Times. Nicaragua was governed by Pedrarias Dávila from 1526 to 1531, but later in the century, following a period of intense rivalry and civil war among the Spanish conquerors, it was incorporated into the captaincy-general of Guatemala. Colonial Nicaragua enjoyed comparative peace and prosperity, although freebooters, notably English navigators such as Sir Francis Drake and Sir Richard Hawkins, continually raided and plundered the coastal settlements. In the 18th century the British informally allied themselves with the Miskito—an Indian people intermarried with blacks—severely challenging Spanish hegemony. For a period during and after the middle of the century the Mosquito Coast was considered a British dependency. The so-called Battle of Nicaragua at the time of the American Revolution, however, ended British attempts to win a permanent foothold in the country.

Independence. Agitation for independence began at the beginning of the 19th century, and Nicaragua declared itself independent of Spain in 1821. A year later it became part of the short-lived Mexican empire of Agustín de Iturbide, and in 1823, after Iturbide's downfall, it joined the United Provinces of Central America (with Guatemala, Honduras, El Salvador, and Costa Rica).

Factional strife between the Liberals, centered in the city of León, and the Conservatives, centered in Granada, became characteristic of Nicaraguan politics. The Liberals fought to establish an independent nation and in 1838 declared Nicaragua an independent republic. Civil strife continued, however, and in 1855 William Walker, an American adventurer with a small band of followers, was engaged by the Liberals to head their forces. He captured and sacked Granada in 1855 and in 1856 became president of Nicaragua. By seizing property belonging to a transport company controlled by Cornelius Vanderbilt, Walker incurred the latter's enmity. Vanderbilt backed the conservative opponents of Walker, who was forced to flee the country in 1857.

U.S. Intervention. In 1893 a successful revolution brought the Liberal leader José Santos Zelaya (1853-1919) to power. He remained president for the next 16 years, ruling as a dictator. Zelaya was forced out in 1909, after Adolfo Díaz (1874-1964) was elected provisional president. Following a revolt against his government in 1912, he asked the U.S. for military aid to maintain order, and U.S. marines were landed. According to the Bryan-Chammoro Treaty of 1916, the U.S. paid $3 million to Nicaragua for the right to build a canal across the country from the Atlantic to the Pacific Oceans, to lease the Great and Little Corn islands, and to establish a naval base in the Gulf of Fonseca. The agreement aroused protest in several Central American countries and resulted in anti-American guerrilla warfare in Nicaragua. A force of American marines remained in Nicaragua until 1925. Rebellions began when the marines left, and the American force returned in 1926. An election was held under American supervision in 1928, and Gen. José María Moncada (1871-1945), a Liberal, was chosen president.

The triumphant return home of Orlando José Tardencillas in March 1982. A Nicaraguan soldier captured in El Salvador, he had been taken to the U.S. to provide evidence of Nicaraguan interference in El Salvador; instead, at a State Department news conference, he repudiated his initial statement, which he said had been coerced by his Salvadoran captors.　　　　　Michel Philippot–Sygma

One Liberal leader, however, Augusto Sandino, refused to acquiesce in the presence of U.S. marines and for several years engaged in a guerrilla war against them. The marines were finally withdrawn in 1933, leaving Anastasio Somoza in charge as commander of the National Guard. Somoza managed to have Sandino killed and was elected president in 1937. During the next 20 years, although not always president, he maintained virtual control of Nicaragua.

Somoza Family Rule. Nicaragua declared war on the Axis powers on Dec. 9, 1941. In June 1945 it became a charter member of the UN. Nicaragua joined the Organization of American States in 1948 and the Organization of Central American States, created to solve common Central American problems, in 1951. In 1956 Anastasio Somoza, who had resumed the presidency, was assassinated. He was succeeded by his son, Luis Somoza Debayle (1922–67), who first served out his father's term and was then elected in his own right. For four years after the end of his tenure, close associates, rather than the Somozas themselves, held the presidency. Then, in 1967, Anastasio Somoza Debayle (1925–80), younger son of the former dictator, was elected president. A military-minded autocrat, he soon faced opposition, which he repressed with the aid of the National Guard.

In August 1971 the legislature abrogated the constitution and dissolved itself. In elections to a constituent assembly in February 1972, Somoza's Liberal party won decisively. In May, Somoza stepped down to the post of chief of the armed forces; political control was assumed by a triumvirate of two Liberals and one Conservative. On Dec. 23, 1972, the city of Managua was virtually leveled by earthquake; about 6000 were killed and 20,000 injured. Martial law was declared, and Somoza in effect became chief executive again. He was formally elected president in 1974.

Sandinist Revolt. In early 1978 Pedro Joaquín Chamorro (1924–78), editor of the Managua newspaper *La Prensa* and long the most vocal of Somoza's opponents, was assassinated. Somoza was accused of complicity in the act, and a wave of violence ensued. The opposition to Somoza, which by September had turned into a virtual civil war, was spearheaded by the Sandinist National Liberation Front, a guerrilla group founded in 1962 and named for Augusto Sandino. Although the National Guard temporarily crushed the insurrection, the Sandinists later resumed the conflict, and by April 1979 a full-scale civil war was again ravaging the country. Trying to prevent another Communist regime (in addition to Cuba) in the Hemisphere, the U.S. subsequently urged Somoza to resign in favor of a moderate coalition. He finally stepped down on July 17, flying to exile first in Miami, Fla., then in Paraguay, where he was assassinated the following year.

The Sandinists named a junta to govern the country. Facing enormous difficulties, they tried, initially with U.S. aid, to stimulate the economy, but the U.S. soon became wary of their left-wing policies and, accusing them of abetting rebels in El Salvador, cut off its aid in 1981 and began to support an anti-Sandinist guerrilla movement. In 1982, Nicaragua signed an aid pact with the USSR. As military pressure against the Sandinist regime intensified, curbs on press and political freedoms were relaxed. In elections held in November 1984, the Sandinist presidential candidate, Daniel Ortega Saavedra (1946–), won by a wide margin, and the Sandinists also captured a legislative majority.

For further information on this topic, see the Bibliography in volume 28, section 1127.

NICARAGUA, LAKE, lake, SW Nicaragua. It is about 160 km (about 100 mi) long and has a maximum width of about 72 km (about 45 mi). Roughly oval in shape and covering about 8030 sq km (about 3100 sq mi), it is the largest lake in Central America. The chief port is Granada. The lake contains the island Zapatera in the N, the Solentiname Islands in the S, and between them the island Ometepe, on which are the twin volcanoes Concepción and Maderas.

NICE, city, SE France, capital of Alpes-Maritimes Department, on the Mediterranean Sea, at the foot of the Maritime Alps. The chief resort of the French Riviera, the city is built around a bay, and the old and new parts of Nice are separated by a small stream, the Paillon. Embankments and promenades, including the Promenade des Anglais, line the sea frontage, and a boulevard extends along the bay shore. The city and bay are protected from severe climatic changes by the mountains on the N. Nice has an active commercial port and a variety of manufacturing industries. It also is a cultural center, with a university (1965) and several museums, including museums devoted to works of the 20th-century artists Henri Matisse and Marc Chagall. The dry, mild climate has made Nice a leading winter and summer resort. It is the site of Roman ruins and of the 17th-century monastery of Cimiez.

Probably founded by the Greeks as Nicaea about the 5th century BC, Nice became a well-known trading colony in the ancient world. Taken by the Romans in 154 BC, it subsequently changed rulers several times and suffered damage during many wars. In 1388 it acknowledged the supremacy of the house of Savoy, and in 1796 it was ceded to France by Sardinia, which was at that time ruled by the duke of Savoy. Nice was returned to Sardinia in 1814, and in 1860 was re-incorporated into France after a plebiscite. Pop. (1982) 338,486.

NICENE CREED, in Christian theology, confession of faith.

The first creed so named was adopted at the first Council of Nicaea in AD 325 to settle a controversy concerning the persons of the Trinity. It was intended to cover debated questions as to the divinity of Christ, and it introduced the word *homoousios* (Gr., "of the same substance") to correct the error of the homoiousian ("of like substance") party. To it were added several clauses against Arianism (q.v.).

A later creed that is popularly known as the Nicene Creed is more properly called the Niceno-Constantinopolitan of Constantinopolitan Creed. It is based on a 4th-century creed that was made under the influence of the bishop of Jerusalem, St. Cyril, and edited in a Nicene sense. It is contained in the *Ancoratus* of St. Epiphanius of Salamis and is traditionally but erroneously attributed to the first Council of Constantinople, which met in 381. Of the 178 words in the original of this second "Nicene Creed," only 33 are positively taken from the creed of AD 325. The second creed is received as ecumenical by the Eastern and Roman communions and by the majority of the Reformed churches. It employs the singular form of the words used for expressing assent, "I believe," "I hope," "I confess." At the Council of Toledo (589), the Western church added the *filioque* clause and inserted the preposition "in" before the words "one holy Catholic and Apostolic Church." In the *Book of Common Prayer,* the preposition "in" is omitted, and by an accident the word "holy" does not appear; the phrase reads there "I believe one Catholic and Apostolic Church."

NICHIREN (1222-82), Japanese Buddhist monk of the Kamakura period (1185-1333), who helped establish Buddhism (q.v.) in Japan. At a time in Japan's history when Buddhist teachings were diffuse and conflicting, Nichiren sought the true teaching of the historical Buddha, which would serve as a central, unifying doctrine. After 20 years of careful study, he concluded that authentic Buddhism could be found only in the Lotus Sutra, or Lotus Scripture, text, and he denounced all other forms of Buddhism. For his audacity he was expelled from his monastery and was subjected to hostility and persecution from both religious and civil authorities. In 1271 he was arrested and condemned to die, but his sentence was subsequently commuted.

NICHOLAS, Saint (fl. 4th cent.), Christian prelate, patron saint of Russia, traditionally associated with Christmas celebrations. The accounts of his life are confused and historically unconfirmed. According to tradition he was a native of Patara, formerly a city in the ancient district of Lycia, Asia Minor (in what is now Turkey). He entered the nearby monastery of Sion and subsequently became archbishop of the metropolitan church in Myra, Lycia. He is said to have been present at the first Council of Nicaea. At the end of the 11th century some Italian merchants transported his remains from Myra to Bari, Italy, where his tomb is now a shrine.

Nicholas is the patron saint of children, scholars, virgins, sailors, and merchants, and in the Middle Ages he was regarded by thieves as their patron saint as well. Legend tells of his surreptitious gifts to the three daughters of a poor man, who, unable to give them dowries, was about to abandon them to a life of sin. From this tale has grown the custom of secret giving on the Eve of St. Nicholas. Because of the close proximity of dates, Christmas and St. Nicholas's Day are now celebrated simultaneously in many countries. Santa Claus, the designation for the jolly, bearded figure of folklore who is credited with bringing gifts to children on Christmas Eve, is an American corruption of the Dutch San Nicolaas. His feast day is December 6.

NICHOLAS I, Saint (c. 825-67), known as Nicholas the Great, pope (858-67) who strengthened the Holy See. His most significant act was his upholding of the bishops' right of appeal to the Vatican against the authority of their superiors when he supported Rothad (d. 869), bishop of Soissons, against Hincmar (806-82), archbishop of Reims. Much of his pontificate was devoted to preventing the proposed divorce of Lothair (d. 869), king of Lorraine, who sought to remarry; Nicholas excommunicated the bishops who supported Lothair. Nicholas sided with St. Ignatius (c. 800-77), patriarch of Constantinople, against his powerful rival Photius, particularly after the former's deposition in 858; this resulted, in 867, in his own deposition by a synod summoned by Photius. Nicholas died without knowing of this action and of the ensuing schism between the Eastern and Western churches. His feast day is November 13.

NICHOLAS III (1210?-80), pope (1277-80), who concentrated on freeing the Papal States (q.v.) from the influence of foreign rulers. Born into a wealthy Guelph family in Rome (*see* GUELPHS AND GHIBELLINES), Giovanni Gaetano Orsini was named cardinal in 1244 and served as a papal diplomat. He was elected pope on Nov. 25, 1277.

While pope, Nicholas thwarted the ambitions of the Sicilian king Charles I of Anjou by not renewing his offices of Roman senator and vicar of Tuscany. In 1278 he induced Rudolf I of Habsburg to surrender dominion over the province of Romangna to the papacy. He later struck a balance between the two rulers to protect his own realm.

In 1279 Nicholas issued a bull that temporarily reunified the Franciscans (see FRANCISCANS OR ORDER OF FRIARS MINOR) after an internal dispute over the interpretation of perfect poverty. Nicholas was the first pope in a century to live in Rome on a regular basis, and he made the Vatican the permanent papal residence.

NICHOLAS V (1397–1455), pope (1447–55), called the Great Humanist, who strengthened the alliance between the papacy and the Holy Roman Empire. Born Tomaso Parentucelli in Sarzana, Italy, on Nov. 15, 1397, he served as tutor in two Florentine households, where he met the leading humanist scholars of his day. He himself became a participant in the humanist movement.

Using his political influence, Nicholas made the Concordat of Vienna with Frederick III in 1448, by which the Germans remained faithful to the Roman Catholic church, and Frederick was assured the crown of the Holy Roman Empire. The coronation of Frederick in 1452 marked the last crowning of an emperor to take place in Rome. Nicholas obtained the resignation of the last antipope, Felix V in 1449, thus ending the Council of Basel (see BASEL, COUNCIL OF).

One of Nicholas's achievements was the restoration of Rome and the Vatican. He made Rome a center for metalsmiths, tapestry makers, and other artisans. Artists such as the Florentine painter Fra Angelico were commissioned to embellish the Vatican's buildings. He also established the Vatican Library and contributed many books to its collection.

NICHOLAS I (1796–1855), emperor of Russia (1825–55), third son of Emperor Paul I (1754–1801), born in Tsarskoye Selo (now Pushkin). On the death of his eldest brother, Emperor Alexander I, Nicholas came to the throne after suppressing the Decembrist revolt, staged by reform-minded army officers who favored the accession of his brother Constantine. His domestic policy was autocratic and his foreign policy aggressive. He introduced military descipline into the civil service, tried to prevent the spread of revolutionary ideas by rigid censorship and strict state control of universities, and sought to promote the Russian language and religion among his non-Russian subjects. He waged war successfully against Iran (1826–28) and Turkey (1828–29). During 1830–31 Nicholas crushed Polish revolts against Russian authority and abolished the Polish constitution. In 1849 he aided Austria in the suppression of uprisings in Hungary. His schemes to add more Turkish territory to his domain alarmed the Western European powers and led to the Russian defeat in the Crimean War.

NICHOLAS II (1868–1918), emperor of Russia (1894–1917); one of the major European leaders of the pre–World War I era, he was deposed by the Russian Revolution of 1917.

The eldest son of Emperor Alexander III, Nicholas was born at Tsarskoye Selo (now Pushkin) on May 18, 1868. Educated privately, he was married in 1894 to Alix of Hesse-Darmstadt (1872–1918), a German princess who took the name Alexandra when she converted to Russian Orthodoxy. In the same year his father died, and he succeeded to the throne. Believing firmly in his duty to preserve absolute power in the Russian monarchy, he opposed any concessions to those favoring more democracy in government, but had little talent for leadership himself. He tended to rely for advice on his wife, to whom he was devoted, and was influenced by her mystical beliefs. Nicholas's interest in Russian expansion in the Far East was one of the contributory causes of the disastrous Russo-Japanese War (1904–05), which in turn helped touch off the Russian Revolution of 1905. Forced by the revolution to assent to constitutional monarchy, he nevertheless continued to believe he was responsible only to God.

Nicholas II and Empress Alexandra with their son Alexis Nikolayevich in 1913. Nicholas and his family were executed in 1918. Bettmann Archive

An advocate of international cooperation, Nicholas sponsored the Hague Conferences (q.v.), which created the Permanent Court of Arbitration and formulated rules for the humane conduct of war, but failed to check Europe's growing arms race. Despite his personally friendly relations with his cousin, William II of Germany, their two countries were on opposite sides when World War I broke out in 1914.

Russia's defeats and the suffering caused by the war among the people were blamed on Nicholas, especially after he assumed personal command of the army in 1915. Forced to abdicate in March 1917, he was held captive by the Bolsheviks until executed, along with his family, at Ekaterinburg (now Sverdlovsk) on the night of July 16–17, 1918.

NICHOLAS, in Russian Nikolai Nikolayevich (1856–1929), Russian grand duke and army officer, born in Saint Petersburg (now Leningrad); he was a nephew of Emperor Alexander II and was educated for the military service. As a member of the Russian general staff he distinguished himself during the war with Turkey (1877–78). Becoming inspector general of the cavalry in 1895, he introduced training and organizational reforms in the cavalry schools. In 1905 he was appointed commander in chief of the St. Petersburg military district and made president of the newly created council for national defense. At the outbreak of World War I he was appointed commander in chief of the Russian army. The following year Emperor Nicholas II personally took command of the Russian armies, and the grand duke was made commander in the Caucasus region. In 1917, after the Russian Revolution, the grand duke went into exile in Paris, where he spent his remaining years.

NICHOLAS OF CUSA (1401–64), German cardinal, scholar, mathematician, scientist, and philosopher. As a doctor of canon law, he wrote (1433) in defense of the conciliar theory that asserted the supremacy of church councils over the pope. Later, however, he reversed his position and became an ardent supporter of the papacy. In 1450 he was made bishop of Brixen, or Bressanone, an ecclesiastical principality. The Habsburg archduke Sigismund (1426–96) strongly opposed the appointment because of Cusa's proposals for reform. Sigismund briefly imprisoned Cusa, and, as a result, the archduke was excommunicated.

Cusa was learned not only in theology but also in mathematics, science, and philosophy. An opponent of Scholasticism, he argued that true wisdom lies in the recognition of human ignorance and that knowledge of the deity is possible only through intuition, a higher state of intelli-

gence. Cusa anticipated the teachings of Giordano Bruno, and he suggested a reform of the calendar later carried out by Pope Gregory XIII. His theory on the rotation of the earth predated that of Copernicus by nearly a century. Cusa also became involved in scientific experimentation, diagnostic medicine, botany, cartography, and manuscript collecting. Among his discoveries were 12 comedies by the Roman playwright Plautus.

NICHOLAS OF VERDUN (c. 1130–c. 1205), French artisan, the last of the great medieval goldsmiths. Active in Tournai, Cologne, and Vienna, he created shrines, chalices, candlesticks, figurines, and other gold and silver objects decorated with jewels and precious stones, enamels, and metalwork. His style was particularly notable for its sensitive, lively, and unusually realistic portrayal of human figures. Two signed masterpieces are extant. The pulpit front (1181) at Klosterneuberg, near Vienna, contains 51 enamel plaques illustrating scenes from the Old and New Testaments. The Shrine of Saint Mary (1205, Tournai Cathedral) is a gold-and-silver reliquary encrusted with 1500 precious stones and 4 rock-crystal finials.

NICHOLSON, Ben (1894–1982), English painter and sculptor, born in Denham. His father, Sir William Nicholson, was famous for his portraits, illustrations, and posters, executed mostly in woodcut. The younger Nicholson, who studied painting in England, France, and Italy, had his first one-man show in London in 1922. His work progressed from impressionism through cubism to a phase influenced by the neoplastic painter Piet Mondrian, in which Nicholson constructed shallow reliefs made of basic geometric forms painted white or in neutral tones, such as *White Relief* (1935, Tate Gallery, London) and *Painted Relief* (1939, Museum of Modern Art, New York City). Eventually he evolved his own style of delicately colored and purely composed abstract paintings, always based on real objects or landscapes, as for example, *November 1956 (Pistoia)* (1956, Art Institute of Chicago).

NICKEL, metallic element, symbol Ni, in group VIII of the periodic table (*see* PERIODIC LAW); at.no. 28, at.wt. 58.70. It was used as coinage in nickel-copper alloys for several thousand years, but was not recognized as an elemental substance until 1751 when the Swedish chemist Baron Axel Frederic Cronstedt (1722–65) isolated the metal from niccolite ore.

Occurrence and Production. Nickel occurs as a metal in meteors. Combined with other elements it occurs in minerals such as garnierite, millerite, niccolite, pentlandite, and pyrrhotite; the latter two minerals are the principal ores of nickel. Most of the world supply of nickel is mined in Canada; a rich deposit of nickel was discovered in 1957 in northern Québec. New Caledonia, the Soviet Union, and Australia are next in importance as nickel producers. World production of nickel in 1980 totaled about 771,440 metric tons. The U.S. has no large deposits of nickel; about 13,240 metric tons are produced annually, part of which is a by-product of copper refining. Approximately 92 percent of the nickel that is used in the U.S. is imported.

Nickel ores usually contain impurities, chief among which is copper. Sulfide ores, such as pentlandite and nickeliferous pyrrhotite, are usually smelted in a blast furnace and shipped in the form of a matte of copper and nickel sulfide to refineries, where the nickel is removed by various processes. In the electrolytic process, the nickel is deposited in pure metallic form after the copper has been preferentially removed by deposition at a different voltage and in a different electrolyte. In the Mond process, copper is removed by dissolution in dilute sulfuric acid, and the nickel residue is reduced to impure metallic nickel. Carbon monoxide is passed over the impure nickel, forming nickel carbonyl, $Ni(CO)_4$, a volatile gas. The nickel carbonyl is heated to 200° C (392° F) and decomposes, depositing pure metallic nickel.

Properties. Nickel is a silver-white, hard, malleable, ductile metal, capable of taking a high polish. It is magnetic below 345° C (653° F). It exists in five stable isotopic forms. Metallic nickel is not very active chemically. It does not oxidize upon exposure to air and does not tarnish. It is soluble in dilute nitric acid and becomes passive (nonreactive) in concentrated nitric acid; it does not react with alkalies.

Nickel melts at 1555° C (2831° F), boils at about 2837° C (about 5139° F), and has a sp.gr. of 8.90.

Uses. Nickel is used as a protective and ornamental coating for metals, particularly iron and steel, that are susceptible to corrosion. The nickel plate is deposited by electrolysis in a nickel solution. Finely divided nickel absorbs 17 times its own volume of hydrogen and is used as a catalyst in many processes, including the hydrogenation of oils.

Nickel is used chiefly in the form of alloys. It imparts great strength and corrosion resistance to steel. Nickel steel, containing about 2 to 4 percent nickel, is used in automobile parts such as axles, crankshafts, gears, valves, and rods; in machine parts; and in armor plate. Some of the important nickel-containing alloys are German

silver, Invar, Monel metal, Nichrome, and Permalloy. The nickel coins of currency are an alloy of 25 percent nickel and 75 percent copper.

Compounds. Nickel forms divalent (nickelous) and trivalent (nickelic) compounds. The important compounds are divalent. Most of the salts of nickel, such as nickel chloride, $NiCL_2$, nickel sulfate, $NiSO_4$, and nickel nitrate, $Ni(NO_3)_2$, are green or blue in color, and they are usually hydrated. Nickel ammonium sulfate, $NiSO_4 \cdot (NH_4)_2SO_4.6H_2O$, is used in nickel-electroplating solutions. Nickel compounds are often identified by adding an organic reagent, dimethylgloxime, which reacts with nickel to form a red, flocculent precipitate.

NICKLAUS, Jack William (1940–), American professional golfer, born in Columbus, Ohio. He began playing golf at the age of 10, and at the age of 16 won his first major tournament, the Ohio Open. His next important tournament victory was in 1959, when he won the U.S. amateur championship, a feat he repeated two years later. Between 1959 and 1961, when he turned professional, Nicklaus had won all but one of the 30 amateur matches in which he had competed. In 1972 he tied the record of the American golfer Bobby Jones of having won 13 major titles. Also in 1972, he became, and is still, the top career money winner in golf. By 1981 Nicklaus had won two U.S. amateurs, three U.S. Opens, five Masters, four Professional Golfers' Association titles, and three British Opens.

NICOBAR ISLANDS, group of 19 islands, in the Indian Ocean, between the Bay of Bengal and the Andaman Sea. The islands form, with the Andaman Islands to the N, a union territory called the Andaman and Nicobar Islands, in India. The islands, formed by the peaks of a submerged mountain range, extend some 322 km (some 200 mi) in a NW to SE direction. Great Nicobar is the largest and southernmost of the islands. The chief occupations are fishing, woodworking, and handicrafts, and the chief products are coconut, coffee, rice, and rubber.

The Nicobar Islands were annexed by Great Britain in 1869. During World War II, they were held (1942–45) by the Japanese. Area of Nicobar Islands, about 1625 sq km (about 625 sq mi). Pop. of Andaman and Nicobar islands (1981 prelim.) 188,254.

See ANDAMAN ISLANDS.

NICOLA PISANO. See PISANO.

NICOLLE, Charles Jules Henri (1866–1936), French physician and microbiologist, who demonstrated that typhus was transmitted by the body louse. Nicolle was born in Rouen and educated at the University of Rouen. In 1903, after practicing medicine and working at the Pasteur Institute in Paris under the Russian bacteriologist Élie Metchnikoff and the French bacteriologist Pierre Paul Émile Roux, he was appointed director of the Pasteur Institute in Tunis, Tunisia. He subsequently became professor of bacteriology at the Collège de France. Nicolle's discovery in 1909 that the body louse is the chief vector of typhus made possible the prevention of typhus epidemics by eliminating lice. He was awarded the Nobel Prize in physiology or medicine in 1928.

NICOLLS, Richard (1624–72), first English governor of New York, born in Bedfordshire. During the English Revolution he commanded a cavalry troop in the Royalist forces, and after the defeat of Charles II, king of England, followed the royal family into exile. After the restoration of the monarchy he was commissioned to take New Amsterdam from the Dutch. The town surrendered to Nicolls's forces on Sept. 8, 1664, and he governed the colony as deputy for James, duke of York, later James II, king of England, for four years. He adopted a policy of gradual transition from Dutch to English law and government, renamed the colony and town New York, and formulated the legal code known as the Duke's Laws, which remained in force from 1665 to 1683. Nicolls resigned in 1668 and returned to England. He was killed during a war with the Netherlands in the naval battle of Southwold Bay.

NICOMEDIA. See İZMIT.

NICOSIA (Gr. *Levkosía;* Turk, *Lefkoşa*), city, capital of Cyprus, on the Pedias R., in the N part of the island. It is mainly a commercial and administrative center and has some small-scale manufacturing industries. Products include processed food, clothing, textiles, and footwear. The city is served by an international airport. Selimye Mosque (1209–1325), formerly the Cathedral of Saint Sophia, is a major landmark. Also of interest are the Cyprus Museum, the Cyprus Historical Museum and Archives, and the Folk Art Museum.

One of the world's oldest cities, Nicosia was the center of an independent kingdom as early as the 7th century BC. Known in ancient times as Ledra, it came under Byzantine rule in the early 4th century AD and passed to Guy of Lusignan (d. 1194), the Latin king of Jerusalem, in 1192. The Lusignan kings held Nicosia until it was captured in 1489 by the Venetians. The city passed to the Ottoman Turks in 1571 and to the British in 1878. It was made capital of British-ruled Cyprus in 1925. Nicosia became the capital of independent Cyprus in 1960 and was the scene of the clashes between Turkish and Greek Cypriots in the 1970s. Pop. (1980 est.) 161,000.

NICOTIANA, genus of annual and perennial herbs and, more rarely, shrubs of the family Solanaceae (*see* NIGHTSHADE). The genus, which contains more than 100 species, is native to the western hemisphere; several species are widely cultivated in gardens in warm temperate regions of the world, both for ornament and as crop plants for commercial use. The genus was named after the 16th-century French diplomat Jean Nicot (1530?–1600), who introduced it into France. Nicotiana plants have sticky, hairy, bitter foliage and are poisonous; the leaves are large, simple, and alternate. The white, yellow, green, or violet flowers are borne in panicles or racemes; they have a large, tubular, five-cleft calyx, a large, funnel-shaped, five-lobed corolla from the interior of which a long tube arises, five stamens, and a solitary pistil. The flowers are usually closed during the day and open at night. The fruit is a two-celled, many-seeded capsule. The most valuable nicotiana species is tobacco (q.v.).

NICOTINE, colorless, oily, liquid alkaloid, $C_{10}H_{14}N_2$, that constitutes the principal active chemical constituent of tobacco (q.v.). Nicotine is used in agriculture as an insecticide and in chemistry as a source of nicotinic acid, which is obtained by the oxidation of nicotine. Tobacco smokers absorb small amounts of nicotine from inhaled smoke, and they may feel certain physiological effects as a result. In small doses nicotine serves as a nerve stimulant, especially upon the autonomic nervous system, promoting the flow of adrenaline and other internal secretions. In larger doses, nicotine paralyzes the autonomic nervous system by preventing the transmission of nerve impulses across the spaces between adjoining nerve cells. Still larger doses of nicotine may cause convulsions and death. The effects of nicotine upon the nervous system vary among individuals. In some persons nicotine hastens the formation of gastric ulcers.

NICOTINIC ACID. See VITAMIN.

NICTHEROY. See NITERÓI.

NIDAROS. See TRONDHEIM.

NIEBUHR, Barthold Georg (1776–1831), German historian and statesman, born in Copenhagen, and educated at the University of Kiel in Germany. He entered the Danish civil service in 1799, resigning in 1806 to accept a similar post from the Prussian government. He was made professor of history at the University of Berlin in 1810. From 1816 to 1823, Niebuhr was Prussian ambassador to the Vatican. He uncovered the *Institutes of Gaius,* the first important work to be discovered concerning Roman private law, in the Cathedral of Verona in 1816. In 1820 he found and edited fragments of the works of the Roman historian Livy and the Roman orator and philosopher Marcus Tullius Cicero. After 1823 he taught in Bonn. Niebuhr is the author of *History of Rome* (3 vol., 1811–32; trans. 1828–42) and of many historical treatises. His works had a profound influence on the modern critical approach to the study of history.

NIEBUHR, H(elmut) Richard (1894–1962), American Protestant theologian, born in Wright City, Mo., and educated at Elmhurst College, Elmhurst, Ill.; Eden Theological Seminary, Webster Groves, Mo.; and Yale Divinity School. Ordained in the Evangelical Synod of North America, he served a pastorate for two years and then joined the faculty of Eden Theological Seminary in 1919. He served as president of Elmhurst College from 1924 to 1927. In 1931 he joined the faculty of Yale Divinity School, where he spent the rest of his teaching career; at retirement he was Sterling Professor of Theology and Christian Ethics. Unlike his brother Reinhold, he was noted for his technical expertness as a theologian. His major works, however, indicate his concern with questions that also claimed the attention of his brother. They examine the basis of denominationalism in the U.S., the interrelationship between human beings and the culture within which they live, and the role of Christian faith in the transformation of that culture. These books include *The Social Sources of Denominationalism* (1929), *The Meaning of Revelation* (1942), *Christ and Culture* (1951), *Radical Monotheism and Western Culture* (1960), and *The Responsible Self* (posthumously pub. 1963).

NIEBUHR, Reinhold (1892–1971), American Protestant theologian, whose social doctrines profoundly influenced American theological and political thought.

Born in Wright City, Mo., June 21, 1892, he was educated at Elmhurst College, Elmhurst, Ill.; Eden Theological Seminary, Webster Groves, Mo.; and Yale Divinity School. In 1915 he was ordained in the ministry of the Evangelical Synod of North America and made pastor of the Bethel Evangelical Church of Detroit. He held that post until 1928, at which time he joined the faculty of the Union Theological Seminary, New York City, where he taught for 30 years. At the time of his retirement (1960) he held a chair of ethics and theology; he also served as dean (1950–55) and vice-president (1955–60). After retiring he continued at Union as a lecturer.

An outstanding, although not a systematic, theologian, Niebuhr was notable primarily for his examination of the interrelationships between religion, individuals, and modern society. Outside the field of theology, he took a keen interest

Reinhold Niebuhr   Union Theological Seminary

in trade union and political affairs. He was an active member of the Socialist party in the 1930s, waged a vigorous fight against isolationism and pacifism before and during World War II, and in 1944 helped to found the Liberal party in New York State. He received the U.S. Presidential Medal of Freedom in 1964 and was made a member of the American Academy of Arts and Letters. He died on June 1, 1971.

Niebuhr indicated his overriding interest in what has been called theological anthropology, a concern with the nature of man as a contact point for religion and society, in such major works as *Moral Man and Immoral Society* (1932), *Interpretation of Christian Ethics* (1935), and *The Nature and Destiny of Man* (2 vol., 1941, 1943). A penetrating critic of society, he also published *Faith and History* (1949), *Christian Realism and Political Problems* (1953), *The Self and the Dramas of History* (1955), and *Structure of Nations and Empires* (1959). In addition he edited *Christianity and Society,* a quarterly, and the biweekly periodical *Christianity and Crisis.*

NIELLO. See INLAY.

NIELSEN, Carl August (1865–1931), most famous composer of Denmark, whose works were internationally significant. Born at Nørre Lyndelse, near Odense, he studied with the noted Danish composer Niels Gade (1817–90) in Copenhagen at the Royal Conservatory, where he taught from 1915. He also conducted the Royal Opera in Copenhagen and was violinist in the Royal Chapel Orchestra. Nielsen is best known for his six symphonies, which reflect his increasing concern for counterpoint (interweaving of melodic lines); chromatic harmonies (having chords foreign to the given key), which melt into nonchromatic harmonies at points of climax; and conflicting tonal centers. His other works include the early cantata *Hymnus Amoris* (1869), to his own text translated into Latin; two operas, *Saul and David* (1901) and *Maskarade* (1906); chamber music; and Danish hymns and school songs. He wrote a memoir, *My Childhood* (1927; trans. 1953). Nielsen died in Copenhagen.

NIEMEYER SOARES FILHO, Oscar (1907–   ), Brazilian architect, born in Rio de Janeiro. After he graduated from the University of Brazil in 1935, Niemeyer worked with the Swiss-French architect Le Corbusier on the revolutionary designs for the Brazilian Ministry of Education and Health building, which was completed in 1936. In 1941 Niemeyer received his first important commission in community designing, in a suburb of Belo Horizonte. Among the buildings he designed was the Church of Saint Francis, so radical in its structure that consecretion was delayed until 1959, although the church was completed in 1943. The boldness and imagination that Niemeyer exhibited in all his work gained him an international reputation as one of the leading modern architects. Although highly varied, his work generally has an open, airy quality in which volumes and empty space are integrated in unusual patterns. Buildings held aloft by concrete or steel pilotis, or stilts, are distinctive features of his designs. Niemeyer served on the board of design consultants to the UN. He was the chief designer of the government buildings in Brasília, the capital of Brazil.

NIEMÖLLER, Martin (1892–1984), German Lutheran pastor, whose anti-Nazi activities made him a symbolic figure in his church's struggle against Hitler.

Niemöller was born on Jan. 14, 1892, in Lippstadt, Westphalia. After serving as a German submarine commander during World War I, he studied theology in Münster and in 1924 was ordained a minister of the church in Westphalia. Appointed in 1931 as pastor at Berlin-Dahlem, he at first welcomed National Socialism but soon became its implacable foe because of its anti-Semitic, pagan views.

Niemöller was an organizer and leader of the Confessing Church, a group of German Protestant Christians that opposed Hitler's policies. On July 1, 1937, he was arrested by the Gestapo and incarcerated first at the concentration camp at Sachsenhausen and later at Dachau, being freed only in early 1945 as World War II was coming to

an end. After the war he became a leader in the rebuilding of the German Protestant church and in opposing atomic weapons and German rearmament. Niemöller served (1961–68) as one of the presidents of the World Council of Churches. He died in Wiesbaden, March 6, 1984.   J.D.G.

NIETZSCHE, Friedrich Wilhelm (1844–1900), German philosopher; one of the most influential modern thinkers.

Nietzsche was born on Oct. 15, 1844, in Röcken, near Leipzig. He studied philology at the University of Bonn under the German classical philologist Friedrich Wilhelm Ritschl (1806–76). Nietzsche became professor of classical philology at the University of Basel in 1869.

Early Influences. While a student, Nietzsche discovered the writings of the German philosopher Arthur Schopenhauer and was profoundly influenced by his metaphysical doctrine of the supremacy of the will. Another significant event in Nietzsche's life was his meeting, about 1870, with the German composer Richard Wagner at the latter's villa on the Lake of Lucerne, Switzerland. The two men agreed in their aesthetic and philosophical opinions, and for a time Nietzsche was an enthusiastic proponent of Wagnerian music drama.

As Nietzsche gradually formulated his own distinctive philosophy, however, he began to doubt the doctrines of both Schopenhauer and Wagner, perceiving in the pessimism of the former a mystical negation of the dynamic life impulse, and in the voluptuous art of the latter a narcotic for an effete and decadent age. The process of Nietzsche's alienation from Wagner climaxed about 1874 in a violent quarrel, and thereafter they were enemies. In 1889, after a period of sustained and intensive work during which he produced some of his most important writings, Nietzsche suffered a mental collapse. He was taken to his mother's home near Weimar and was cared for by his sister until his death on Aug. 25, 1900.

Philosophical Work. Nietzsche's work is aphoristic and deliberately unsystematic in form. His significance in philosophy rests on his incisive, psychologically acute criticism of morality, language, and art and his attempt to formulate an approach to values radically different from that of traditional ethical and religious systems. He held that all life expresses a will to power. The highest values are those that represent the highest levels of strength and vitality. Nietzsche did not, however, understand such values primarily in terms of political or physical power; they are most fully realized in great artistic and intellectual achievements. They are the values that bold,

Friedrich Wilhelm Nietzsche on his deathbed (from a 19th-cent. charcoal drawing by Hans Olde).
Bettmann Archive

masterful, self-assertive individuals (such as the ancient Greeks and Renaissance Italians) have created for themselves. Against this "master's morality," Nietzsche set the "slave morality" created by the weak, mediocre, and timid, who, incapable of heroic individualism, have banded together and set up moral standards based on humility, patience, and pity, traits that ensure their own safety and tranquillity. This morality, by exalting conformity and mediocrity, expresses the will to power of those lacking in strength and their resentment of those who are stronger. Appropriate for most human beings, slave morality becomes dangerous only when it is imposed on strong, creative, independent individuals. Christianity, Nietzsche argued, had done this, with results that are ultimately detrimental to civilization and art.

Nietzsche's thought, culminating in the ideal of the Übermensch ("overman," or "superman"), can be traced in *Human, All-Too-Human* (1878), *The Joyful Wisdom* (1882), *Thus Spoke Zarathustra* (1883), *Beyond Good and Evil* (1886), *On the Genealogy of Morals* (1887), and *The Will to Power* (pub. posthumously, 1901). The first complete English translation of Nietzsche's writings was published between 1909 and 1913.

See also EXISTENTIALISM.

NIGER, river in W Africa, rising in Guinea and flowing for about 4180 km (about 2600 mi) through Mali, Niger, and Nigeria to the Gulf of Guinea. The Benue, which joins the Niger at Lokoja in Nigeria, is its chief tributary. The Niger delta (about 36,300 sq km/14,000 sq mi in area) is the largest in Africa; it has a coastline of nearly 190 km (about 120 mi). Port Harcourt is located on the delta. The Niger also forms a vast interior delta in central Mali. The river is navigable almost all year as far upstream as Lokoja; it is seasonally navigable in other areas.

The upper Niger was a core area of the old empires of Mali and Songhai; during this time Timbuktu, at the great bend of the river, was a major cultural and commercial center. Western geographers long sought to establish the course of the Niger. The Scots explorer Mungo Park determined in 1796 that the river flows E, and in 1830 the English brothers Richard Lander (1804–34) and John Lander (1807–39) proved that the Niger empties into the Gulf of Guinea.

NIGER, REPUBLIC OF (Fr. *République du Niger*), republic in W Africa, bounded on the N by Algeria and Libya, on the E by Chad, on the S by Nigeria and Benin, and on the W by Upper Volta and Mali. It has a total area of 1,267,000 sq km (489,191 sq mi).

LAND AND RESOURCES

Niger may be divided into three zones, the northern, central, and southern. The N zone, covering more than half of the total area of the republic, lies within the Sahara (q.v.). It is a highland region of plateaus and mountains and, except in scattered oases, has little vegetation. In this zone is Banguezane (1900 m/6234 ft), the highest elevation in the country. The central zone, known as the Sahel, is semiarid and lightly wooded. The S zone is a fertile, forested area that benefits from adequate rainfall and, in the SW, from the periodic overflow of the Niger R., virtually the only river in the country. On the SE, the nation borders on one of the largest lakes of the continent, the shallow Lake Chad.

Climate. The climate of Niger is hot and, in most areas, dry. Rainfall, negligible in the N, increases to 813 mm (32 in) a year in the S. In the S a rainy season lasts from June to October. The average annual temperature at Niamey is 29.4° C (85° F).

Plants and Animals. The N desert of Niger has little vegetation. In the S are extensive savanna grasslands and, in the lowlands, a variety of trees, including baobab, tamarind, kepok, and a species of mahogany. Animal life includes elephant, buffalo, antelope, giraffe, and lion.

Natural Resources. Niger has diverse mineral resources, most of which remain to be exploited. Large deposits of high-grade uranium ore are found in the N. Other minerals present include coal, tin, phosphate, iron ore, and copper.

POPULATION

The majority of the population of Niger is composed of black peoples, primarily Hausa and Djerma, who are subsistence farmers in the S. Of the remaining quarter of the population, most are Tuareg and Fulani, peoples who follow a nomadic life.

Population Characteristics. The population of Niger (1981 UN est.) was 5,480,000. Overall popula-

97

A simple, ancient device to draw water from a well. Despite some modernization, much of Niger's population hews to the old ways. Wide World Photos

tion density was only 4 persons per sq km (about 11 per sq mi), but approximately 90% of the population is concentrated near the S border.

Political Divisions and Principal Cities. Niger is divided into 7 departments and 32 districts. Niamey, the capital, had a population (1977 est.) of 225,300. Zinder (58,400), Maradi (45,900), and Tahoua (31,300) are the other principal towns.

Religion and Language. About 90% of the people of Niger are Muslims. Most of the remainder adhere to traditional beliefs, and a small Christian minority also exists.

French is the official language, but Hausa is the language of local trade. Other African languages, such as Fulani, Tamachek, and Djerma, are also used extensively.

Education. Schooling in Niger is free but not compulsory. Because of a shortage of teachers and the wide dispersion of the population, only 10 to 15% of the school-age children receive an education. In the late 1970s some 187,000 pupils annually attended primary schools, and about 22,000 pupils were enrolled in secondary schools. Students in a technical school totaled about 330. Advanced training is given at the University of Niamey (1971).

Culture. Islamic influences from North Africa have had a powerful effect on the culture of Niger. Municipalities in Niger have state-run librar-

ies, and several private organizations maintain libraries. The National Museum of Niger, in Niamey, includes both a library and a museum.

ECONOMY

The great majority of the people of Niger are subsistence farmers or pastoralists. In spite of the general aridity of the country, agriculture provides most of the national income. Agriculture has largely recovered from the effects of the disastrous Sahel drought of the early 1970s. Manufacturing enterprises are mostly very small. In 1979–80 the estimated national budget showed a balance of revenue and expenditure, at about $340 million each.

Agriculture and Fishing. Stock raising is the principal agricultural activity. In the early 1980s the annual livestock population included about 3.2 million cattle, 2.6 million sheep, and 350,000 camels. Peanuts are a major export crop. Millet, sorghum, cassava (manioc), and rice are grown for local consumption. Annual production in the early 1980s included millet (1.4 million metric tons), cassava (210,000), peanuts (100,000), and sorghum (380,000).

Fishing is conducted in Lake Chad and the Niger R., and the catch is consumed locally.

Mining and Manufacturing. In the W central part of Niger, salt and natron are mined as well as tin. Large uranium deposits are being exploited in N

Women selling peanuts at a street market in Zinder, southern Niger. United Nations–Andrew Holbrooke

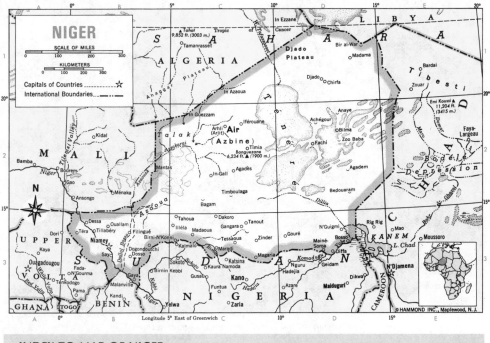

INDEX TO MAP OF NIGER

Cities and Towns

Agadès . . . . .C 2
Arhli (Arlit). . . . . .C 2
Bilma . . . . .D 2
Birni-N'Konni . . . . .B 3
Bosso . . . . .D 3
Chirfa. . . . . .D 1
Dakoro. . . . . .C 3
Diffa. . . . . .D 3
Djado . . . . .D 1
Dogondoutchi. . . . . .B 3
Dosso . . . . .B 3

Fachi . . . . .D 2
Filingué . . . . .B 3
Gaya . . . . .B 3
Gouré . . . . .D 3
Iférouane. . . . . .C 2
Illéla . . . . .C 3
In-Gall . . . . .C 2
Madama . . . . .D 1
Magaria . . . . .C 3
Mainé-Soroa . . . . .D 3
Mantas. . . . . .B 2
Maradi . . . . .C 3
N'Guigmi . . . . .D 3

Niamey (cap.) . . . . .B 3
Ouallam . . . . .B 3
Say. . . . . .B 3
Tahoua . . . . .C 3
Tanout. . . . . .C 3
Téra . . . . .B 3
Tessaoua. . . . . .C 3
Tillabéry. . . . . .B 3
Timboulage . . . . .C 2
Timia . . . . .C 2
Zinder . . . . .C 3
Zoo Baba . . . . .D 2

Other Features

Aïr (Azbine) (plat.) . . . . .C 2
Assakarai (dry river). . . .C 2
Azaoua (reg.) . . . . .B 2
Bagam (well). . . . . .C 2
Banguezane (mt.) . . . . . .C 2
Dallol Bosso (river). . . . .B 3
Komadugu Yobe
  (river). . . . . .D 3
Rima (river). . . . . .C 3
Talak (reg.). . . . . .C 2
Ténéré (desert). . . . . . . .D 2

Niger. Reserves are estimated at more than 100,000 metric tons, and approximately 3700 metric tons were produced in 1979. Industry is limited mainly to food processing and construction.

Currency and Banking. The unit of currency in Niger is the CFA franc (312 CFA francs equal U.S.$1; 1982). It is issued by the Central Bank of the West African States. Several savings banks operate in the country.

Foreign Trade. In the early 1980s Niger annually exported goods amounting to some $435 million, with uranium accounting for the bulk of the value. Imports totaled about $498 million. About three-quarters of all exports went to France. Other major trading partners include Nigeria, Italy, Germany, and the Ivory Coast.

Transportation and Communications. Niger has some 8220 km (about 5110 mi) of motor roads, of which only about 3100 km (about 1925 mi) are serviceable throughout the year. International airports serve Niamey, Maradi, and Zinder, and the country has about 20 smaller public airfields. The government radio station broadcasts in several languages, and a number of daily and weekly newspapers are published.

GOVERNMENT

Until the military coup of April 15, 1974 (see History below), Niger was governed under the 1960 constitution. Since that time the Supreme Military Council, headed by a president, has been the main government body of the country. A council of ministers is appointed by the president of the military council.

Executive. Under the 1960 constitution, the head of state of Niger was a president, who was elected for a 5-year term. He was assisted by a council of ministers whom he selected. Niger was essentially a one-party state. The Niger Pro-

Some nomad women of Niger, hooded in the traditional Muslim fashion, set out for home on their camels after a visit to town (in the background).

gressive party (Parti Progressiste Nigérien, or PPN) controlled the government until it was suspended in 1974.

Legislature. According to the 1960 constitution, legislative authority in Niger was vested in the national assembly, which consisted of 60 deputies, elected by universal suffrage for 5-year terms.

Judiciary. District courts and courts of conciliation are located throughout Niger. An appeals court and the supreme court are in Niamey, but the supreme court was suspended in 1974.

Health and Welfare. Niger, in cooperation with world health services, is attempting to control such widespread diseases as smallpox, yaws, and helminthiasis. The government enforces the provisions of some labor and health legislation, but most welfare services are left to the complex, traditional tribal and family social system.

Defense. The army of Niger included about 2150 persons in the early 1980s. The gendarmerie consisted of about 2000 men, including 1000 national guardsmen. Niger has bilateral defense agreements with France.

HISTORY

During the Middle Ages the Niger region was on the central caravan route from North Africa to the Hausa states and the empires of Mali and Songhai. The area was therefore penetrated early by Muslim missionaries. The Hausa states were dominant in southern Niger from the 10th century until the early 19th century, when they were conquered by the Fulani under Usuman dan Fodio. Songhai was for a thousand years the supreme power in the western part of the country, while the Kanem-Bornu Empire (q.v.) exerted a powerful influence in the east. In the 14th century the Tuareg populated the Aïr Plateau, where they subsequently established the sultanate of Agadès.

The first Europeans to enter the area were the Scottish surgeon and explorer Mungo Park and the German explorers Heinrich Barth and Eduard Vogel (1829–59). The French settled the area about 1890. It was made a military territory in 1900, an autonomous territory in 1922, and an overseas territory in 1946. Proclaimed an autonomous republic of the French Community in 1958, Niger became fully independent on Aug. 3, 1960.

In 1960 Hamani Diori (1916–) was elected president by the legislature. In 1964 the government crushed a rebellion aimed against the Diori regime, and in April 1965 the president survived an assassination attempt. He was reelected in 1965 and 1970. Niger was one of six sub-Sahara nations affected by a 5-year drought, which was broken by summer rains in 1973. Accused of corruption and of mishandling the famine, Diori was overthrown in a military coup d'etat in April 1974. Since the coup, Niger has been ruled by a

Supreme Military Council, headed by Lt. Col. Seyni Kountché (1931–). His first priority was economic recovery after the drought, and to that effect a new agreement with France was concluded in 1977. Plots and coup attempts occurred during Kountché's first years in power, but by 1980 he was confident enough to release former President Diori from detention. Most cabinet posts in the government were gradually filled by civilians, and in the early 1980s the economy was growing.

For further information on this topic, see the Bibliography in volume 28, section 1012.

NIGERIA, FEDERAL REPUBLIC OF, republic of W Africa, bounded by Niger on the N, by Chad and Cameroon on the E, by the Gulf of Guinea on the S, and by Benin on the W. The most populous country of Africa, Nigeria has an area of 923,768 sq km (356,669 sq mi). Its name is derived from that of its major river, the Niger.

Initially composed of a number of ethnically based kingdoms and states, the area of modern Nigeria was brought under British rule by 1906. It became an independent state on Oct. 1, 1960. Following a period of tension among its ethnic groups, especially the Yoruba of the SW, the Ibo of the SE, and the Hausa and Fulani of the N, Nigeria was ruled by the military from 1966 to 1979. During 1967–70 peoples of the SE attempted—without ultimate success—to secede from Nigeria by forming the Republic of Biafra (q.v.). Civilian rule was restored following presidential elections in 1979.

LAND AND RESOURCES

Much of Nigeria consists of a low plateau cut by rivers, especially the Niger and Benue. Most of the country is suitable for agriculture. Its major economic resources are its massive petroleum and natural-gas deposits.

Physiographic Regions. Nigeria can be divided into four distinct geographical regions. Along the coast is a belt of mangrove forests and swamps, stretching some 16 km (some 10 mi) inland in most places. This region is cut by numerous lagoons and creeks. In the Niger delta region, the coastal belt extends some 100 km (some 60 mi) inland. Beyond the coast is a broad, hilly, forested belt, which gradually rises to the rocky terrain of the Jos and Bauchi plateaus. Beyond these plateaus is a region of savanna, which stretches to a semidesert zone in the extreme N. A great plain, marked by occasional outcroppings of granite, the savanna region is Nigeria's main agricultural area. In the E is the Adamawa Massif, which borders Cameroon and in which is Nigeria's highest point, Mt. Dimlang (Vogel Peak), 2042 m (6700 ft) high.

Rivers and Lakes. The Niger R. and its tributaries—principally the Benue, Kaduna, and Sokoto rivers—drain most of Nigeria. In the NE, the rivers drain into Lake Chad. Navigation is restricted by rapids and seasonal fluctuations in depth.

Climate. Nigeria has two distinct climatic zones. Along the coast the equatorial maritime air mass influences the climate, which is characterized by high humidity and heavy rainfall. To the N the tropical continental air mass brings dry, dusty winds (harmattan) from the Sahara; the temperature varies considerably with the season, as does rainfall, which is far less than in the S.

Vegetation and Animal Life. Vegetation zones in Nigeria parallel the climatic zones. In the S, the

The banks of the Niger near the city of Jebba. The Niger, about 4180 km (about 2600 mi) long, is the principal river of Nigeria and one of the longest in Africa.
Marc & Evelyne Bernheim–Woodfin Camp & Associates

well-watered zone is partly covered by dense tropical forests that contain hardwoods such as mahogany and obeche. Oil palms are particularly plentiful. In the plateau and savanna regions, forests give way to grasslands and such hardy trees as the baobab and the tamarind. In the extreme NE, semidesert vegetation prevails. Crocodiles and snakes are found in the swamps and rain forest zones. Most large animals have disappeared from heavily populated areas. Some antelope, camels, and hyenas live in the N.

Mineral Resources. Iron-ore deposits are widespread in the savanna region of Nigeria as are salt deposits. Tin and columbite are found in the plateau area. Great deposits of petroleum and natural gas are located in the Niger delta and offshore in the bights of Benin and Bonny (Biafra).

POPULATION

With more than 250 ethnic groups, Nigeria is a complex linguistic, social, and cultural mosaic. More than half the population consists of the Hausa and Fulani peoples of the N, the Yoruba of the SW, and the Ibo of the SE. Other ethnic groups include the Edo, Ijaw, and Ibibio of the S, the Nupe and Tiv of the central part of the country, and the Kanuri of the NE.

Population Characteristics. The size and distribution of Nigeria's population have been a matter of great political controversy within the country. UN estimates suggest a total population of 79,680,000 in 1981. The most recent officially

sanctioned census, taken in 1963, recorded 55,670,055 persons. The results of a 1973 census were not accepted by the government. About one-half of the population live in the N, and most of the other half are in the SE and SW. Within these broad regions, however, population distribution is extremely uneven. The rate of population increase during 1975–79 was about 3.2% per year. Although more than two-thirds of the people are engaged in farming, Nigeria has a long urban tradition and is one of the most urbanized countries in Africa.

Principal Cities. Lagos, Nigeria's largest city, had a population (1980 est., greater city) of about 6 million. Other cities with more than 225,000 inhabitants include Ibadan, Kano, Ogbomosho, Oshogbo, Ilorin, Abeokuta, Port Harcourt, Ilesha, Onitsha, and Zaria. Numerous communities have more than 100,000 inhabitants. Plans were announced in the late 1970s to move Nigeria's capital to the centrally located federal capital territory, but in 1982 Lagos retained its long-held status as the seat of the national government.

Language. English and Hausa are the official languages of Nigeria. Hausa, a lingua franca in W Africa, is the most widely used language, followed by Yoruba, Ibo, Kanuri, and Tiv.

Religion. About 45% of Nigeria's people are Muslim, the bulk of whom live in the Hausa, Fulani, and Kanuri areas in the N. Some 49% of the Nigerians are Christians, with Roman Catholicism

The streets of Lagos, the largest city and chief port of Nigeria, are congested with automobiles, bicycles, and pedestrians. United Nations

Traditional Hausa village architecture in northern Nigeria. The Hausa are one of the principal ethnic groups of Nigeria.   Marc & Evelyne Bernheim–Woodfin Camp & Associates

centered in the SE and Methodism and Anglicanism being most influential in the SW. Traditional religions are practiced by the remaining 6% of the population.

EDUCATION AND CULTURAL ACTIVITY

Within the boundaries of modern Nigeria are some of the earliest educational and artistic traditions in W Africa. Superimposed on these are the influences of British colonial rule and European missionary educational systems. Since the mid-1970s an increasingly self-confident federal government has sought to rapidly modernize Nigeria, using Western education as a major tool. Revenue from the sale of crude petroleum has helped to finance such modernization.

Education. Old Koranic schools are widespread throughout the N, and missionaries brought Western education to the coastal areas as early as the 1830s. Until the 1970s, enrollment in Western-oriented schools was significantly higher in the S. In 1976 free primary education was established throughout Nigeria. By the early 1980s, some 11.5 million pupils were enrolled each year in primary schools, and more than 1.2 million students attended secondary schools. The educational system is based on a British model. Primary

schooling takes six years to complete. Highly competitive examinations are required for entry into the 5-year secondary or technical school system. Western higher education, begun in 1948 with the founding of the University of Ibadan, is found throughout the country. Other major institutions include Ahmadu Bello University (1962), in Zaria; the University of Ife (1961), in Ile-Ife; the University of Lagos (1962); and the University of Nigeria (1960), in Nsukka. In the late 1970s, British-style universities were augmented by a growing system of American-influenced teachers and technical colleges.

Cultural Life. Nigeria has a long and rich tradition of plastic arts and literature. Terra-cotta sculptures were made by Nok artists of N Nigeria as early as 500 BC, and Ife terra-cottas and Benin bronze work, first made about AD 1200, are world famous. Today, traditional folk art is augmented by Western-influenced graphics, painting, and sculpture. Traditional oral literature has had a significant impact on such world-famous Nigerian writers as Amos Tutuola (1920–), Wole Soyinka (1934–), and Chinua Achebe. Parallel to the rich modern literature, most often written in English, is a written vernacular litera-

Fulani woman in a marketplace of northern Nigeria. The Fulani are one of the major ethnic groups of the country. United Nations

ture, augmented by professional theater companies and dance groups. *See* AFRICAN ART AND ARCHITECTURE; AFRICAN LITERATURE.

Cultural Institutions. The National Museum in Lagos has a rich collection of art from all periods. Museums in Benin City, Ibadan, Ife, Ilorin, Jos, and Kaduna also are outstanding. In recent years the Nigerian government has made a concerted effort to prevent the removal of significant Nigerian art from the country and has sought the return of art taken out during the colonial era. Major collections of books and documents are housed in the National Library of Nigeria (in Lagos) and the National Archives (in Ibadan) as well as in university libraries.

Communications. The first Nigerian newspaper was established in the 1830s in Lagos. Since then a large number of daily and weekly newspapers, published in African languages and in English, have been established. Some 20 English-language daily newspapers were issued in the early 1980s. Even though the federal government has an interest in several newspapers, including Nigeria's largest, the *Daily Times* of Lagos, government censorship and control has been minimal. The national government has been active in broadcasting since 1957, when a chain of radio stations was established. In 1976 the federal government established control over all television stations, placing them under a National Television Authority. Radio and television programs are broadcast in English as well as in major Nigerian

languages. Some 5,250,000 radios and 450,000 television receivers were in use in the late 1970s.

GOVERNMENT

The central reality of Nigeria's political life since independence in 1960 has been the rivalry and suspicion between the traditional, Muslim, Hausa and Fulani domination in the north and the modern, Westernized south led by Yoruba and Ibo politicians. Following military rule during 1966–79, civilian government was restored on Oct. 1, 1979, under a constitution promulgated in 1978. This constitution was suspended following a military coup on Dec. 31, 1983.

Executive. Under the 1978 constitution, the president, who is elected to a 4-year term by direct popular vote, is both head of state and head of government. The constitution stipulates that the president must receive an overall plurality of the national vote while attaining a minimum of one-quarter of the vote in at least two-thirds of the 19 states that make up Nigeria. After the 1983 coup, executive powers were vested in the 19-member Supreme Military Council.

Legislature. The 1978 constitution provides for a National Assembly, consisting of a Senate of 95 members and a House of Representatives of 449 members, as the national legislature of Nigeria. Senators and representatives are to be elected to 4-year terms by direct popular vote.

Judiciary. The highest tribunal of Nigeria is the supreme court. It is made up of a chief justice

In the inland plateau of Nigeria, round, thatched structures are used to store grain. British Information Services

A view of the old section of the city of Kano in northern Nigeria, showing traditional mud-brick architecture.
Shostal Associates

and up to 15 other judges, all appointed by the country's president. Other important courts include the federal court of appeal, the federal high court, and a high court in each state. In addition, some states have Islamic courts and courts based on traditional law.

Local Government. At independence, Nigeria was divided into three regions—the north, ruled by the Hausa and Fulani traditional aristocracy; the west, dominated by the Yoruba; and the east, controlled by the Ibo. In 1966 the country was divided into a number of small states. Under the 1978 constitution Nigeria is divided into 19 states and a federal capital territory. The governor of each state as well as members of its house of assembly are elected for 4-year terms by direct popular vote.

Political Parties. Before independence, Nigeria's political life was dominated by the Northern People's Congress (NPC); the National Convention of Nigerian Citizens (NCNC), an Ibo-led party that was prominent in the SE; and the Action Group (AG), which was controlled by Yoruba politicians and directed the government of the SW. At independence, the NPC and AG formed a coalition and ruled Nigeria until 1966.

Severe ethnic rivalries led to military coups in 1966 and the abolition of political parties. In the elections of 1979 the relatively new, northern-based National Party of Nigeria gained the greatest national support. Other major parties were the Unity Party of Nigeria, the Nigerian People's party, the Greater Nigeria People's party, and the People's Redemption party.

Defense. At independence the national military of Nigeria was composed of a small British-trained and -equipped army, navy, and air force. The regional police forces rivaled the military in numbers. In the late 1960s, during the attempted secession of the region of SE Nigeria known as Biafra, all police functions were centralized in the federal government, and the national military was greatly expanded and modernized. In the early 1980s, the military had about 146,000 members, making it one of the largest armed forces in Africa.

International Organizations. Nigeria is a member of the UN, the Organization of African Unity, the Commonwealth of Nations, the Organization of Petroleum Exporting Countries, the Economic Community of West African States, and several other major international associations.

INDEX TO MAP OF NIGERIA

States

	Aku ....B 2	Jebba................A 2	Sokoto...............B 1	
	Akure...............B 2	Jos...................B 2	Warri...............B 2	
Anambra ....B 2	Asaba ....B 2	Kabba ....B 2	Wukari...............B 2	
Bauchi..............B 1	Baro.................B 2	Kaduna ....B 1	Yan ....C 1	
Bendel..............B 2	Bauchi...............B 1	Kano ....B 1	Yelwa................A 1	
Benue ....B 2	Benin City...........B 2	Katsina...............B 1	Yola.................C 2	
Borno................B 1	Birnin Kebbi ....A 1	Koko ....B 2	Zaria................B 1	
Cross River.........B 2	Bonny ....B 3	Lagos (cap.) ....A 2	Zungeru..............B 2	
Federal Capital Terr. ...B 2	Brass................B 3	Lokoja ....B 2	
Gongola ....C 2	Burutu ....B 2	Maiduguri ....C 1	**Other Features**
Imo..................B 2	Calabar ....B 2	Makurdi...............B 2	
Kaduna ....B 1	Dikwa................C 1	Mushin................A 2	
Kano ....B 1	Donga................C 2	New Bussa ....A 1	Adamawa (reg.) ....C 2
Kwara ....A 2	Ede ....A 2	Nguru ....C 1	Benin (bight)..........A 3
Lagos................A 2	Enugu................B 2	Nnewi................B 2	Benue (river)..........B 2
Niger ....B 1	Forcados.............B 2	Nsukka...............B 2	Chad (lake)...........D 1
Ogun ....A 2	Geidam ....C 1	Offa ....A 2	Cross (river)..........B 2
Ondo ....A 2	Gummi................B 1	Ogbomosho ....A 2	Dimlang (mt.) ....C 2
Oyo ....A 2	Gusau................B 1	Okene ....B 2	Gongola (river)........C 1
Plateau ....B 2	Hadejia ....C 1	Ondo ....B 2	Hadejia (river)........B 1
Rivers ....B 3	Ibadan ....A 2	Onitsha ....B 2	Kaduna (river).........B 2
Sokoto...............B 1	Ibi ....B 2	Oshogbo ....B 2	Kainji (lake)..........A 1
	Ife ....A 2	Owerri ....B 2	Kebbi (river) ....A 1
	Ijebu-Ode ....A 2	Owo ....B 2	Komadugu Yobe
	Ikom ....B 2	Oyo ....A 2	(river)..............C 1
Cities and Towns	Ilesha................B 2	Panyam ....B 2	Niger (delta)..........B 3
	Ilorin ....A 2	Port Harcourt ....B 3	Niger (river)..........B 2
Aba ....B 2	Iseyin................A 2	Sapele................B 2	Sokoto (river) ....B 1
Abeokuta............A 2	Iwo..................A 2	Shaki................A 2	
Ado-Ekiti ....B 2			

ECONOMY

Nigeria traditionally has been an agricultural country, providing the bulk of its own food needs and exporting a variety of agricultural goods, notably palm oil, cacao, and peanuts. By the 1970s, however, petroleum supplanted cash crops as the major source of foreign exchange.

National Output. Influenced by constantly rising petroleum revenues, Nigeria's gross domestic product (GDP) rose dramatically from about $4.9 billion in 1970 to about $44.6 billion in 1979. The per capita GDP was estimated at $600 in 1979.

Labor. The Nigerian labor force included more than 28 million persons in the early 1980s. Despite the overwhelming importance of petroleum to the country's economy, about two-thirds of the work force is engaged in agricultural activities.

Agriculture. Most Nigerians are subsistence farmers, producing sorghum, millet, and cattle in the N and maize, rice, and yams in the S. Cassava, legumes, and tomatoes are raised throughout Nigeria, as are poultry, goats, and sheep. Large amounts of plantains and sugarcane also are produced. Palm oil became an export crop to Europe in the early 19th century. Cacao and peanuts later grew in importance, surpassing palm oil as export crops in the early 1950s. Cotton, raised in the N, began to be grown for domestic use in the early part of the 20th century. Domestic consumption of cotton, palm oil, and peanuts outstripped production in the early 1970s, leading to the importation of these products. Most of Nigeria's agricultural goods are grown on small, family farms. Large plantations were discouraged until

the 1950s, but since then they have been significant in the production of rubber, palm oil, and cacao.

Fishing. About two-thirds of Nigeria's annual fish catch comes from the country's rivers and lakes, with most of the rest being taken from the Gulf of Guinea. Lake Chad is a major source of fish. In addition, small amounts of fish are raised commercially on farms. The total catch in 1979 was about 535,000 metric tons.

Mining. Nigeria is one of the world's leading producers of crude petroleum; output was about 71.2 million metric tons in 1981. Nigerian oil has a low sulfur content, making it particularly attractive to American and European buyers seeking to reduce air pollution. Much natural gas also is recovered in Nigeria. In addition, tin and columbite are mined in the Jos Plateau area, and coal is produced in the Onitsha region. Small amounts of limestone, salt, lignite, and iron ore also are mined.

Manufacturing. Scattered throughout Nigeria are small family businesses producing traditional craft goods—pottery, carvings, ornamental cloth, and leather goods—and more modern consumer goods, such as bricks and other building materials, milled grain, and beverages. In the 1970s, large-scale enterprises were established, mostly in the S. They include motor-vehicle assembly plants, petroleum refineries, and factories producing textiles, rubber goods, aluminum, iron and steel, and petrochemicals.

Energy. In the early 1980s, about 60% of Nigeria's electricity was produced each year in hydroelectric facilities, and almost all the rest was gener-

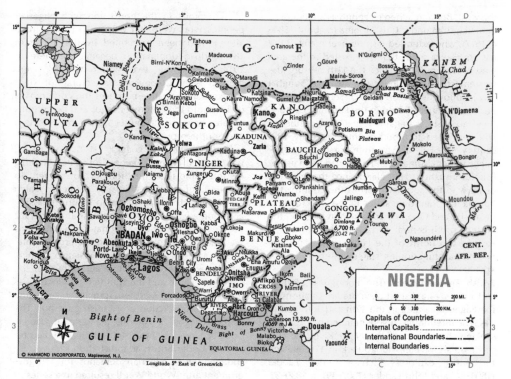

Longitude 5° East of Greenwich

ated in thermal plants. The country had an installed electricity-generating capacity of about 1.9 million kw, and yearly production was some 5 billion kwh. Output had more than tripled since 1970.

Transportation. Nigeria depends heavily on its nationwide network of roads. Approximately 20% of Nigeria's 108,000 km (about 67,110 mi) of roads are all-weather arteries. In the late 1970s expressways linking Lagos to Ibadan and Benin City were built. Railroads have declined in importance because of competition from Nigeria's road system. The country has about 3500 km (about 2175 mi) of operated railroad track. The main seaports are at Lagos, Port Harcourt, Warri, Calabar, Bonny, and Burutu. International airports are located at Lagos and Kano, and smaller airfields serve all 19 state capitals. Nigerian Airways, the government-owned airline, offers international service.

Currency and Banking. The national currency of Nigeria is the naira, which is divided into 100 kobo (0.66 naira equal U.S.$1; 1982). Currency and banking are supervised by the Central Bank of Nigeria (1958). A number of European and American banks have offices in Nigeria; since 1976, all banks operating in the country have been required to have ownership that is at least 60% Nigerian.

Commerce. Much of the internal trade of Nigeria revolves around the sale of foodstuffs and domestically produced consumer goods. Open-air markets, operated by women, and small general stores, some owned by Lebanese, are widespread. Modern department stores are found in the large cities. Onitsha, Aba, Kano, and Ibadan are the major commercial centers.

Foreign Trade. In 1980 Nigeria's imports cost about $15 billion, and its exports earned about $27 billion. Sales of crude petroleum accounted for some 95% of the export earnings. Major imports included motor vehicles and parts, machinery, and chemicals. Nigeria's principal trade partners are the U.S., Great Britain, West Germany, France, and Japan.   J.T.Sa.

HISTORY

Little is known about the history of Nigeria in ancient times, but archaeologists have discovered evidence of a Neolithic (c. 800 BC–AD 200) culture at Nok, southwest of the city of Jos in central Nigeria.

Early States. The northern part of the present territory of Nigeria was the site of organized states during the Middle Ages. By the 8th century, the region southwest of Lake Chad was part of the Kanem-Bornu Empire (q.v.), which in 1086 adopted Islam. By about 1300 Bornu was a flourishing center of Islamic culture, rivaling Mali in the west. Bornu reached its zenith as an independent kingdom under Idris Alooma (r. about 1580–c. 1617), who extended his rule over many of the eastern Hausa states that had existed in the area west of Kanem-Bornu since the 11th century; the western states fell under the sway of Songhai (q.v.). Following the breakup of Songhai and the decline of Kanem-Bornu in the late 16th century, the Hausa states regained their independence and continued to flourish until the early 19th century. The Fulani, who then burst into prominence under Usuman dan Fodio, had been established throughout Hausaland since the late 16th century. In the southern part of the country, the Yoruba had their own states in the west, centering on Ife and Oyo; the Edo ruled in Benin in the present south-central parts; and the Ibo in the east, in and north of the Niger delta. All these people had functioning states before or around AD 1400.

British Encroachment. The Portuguese, British, and others established slave-trading stations in the Niger delta area in the 17th and 18th centuries. The interior was first penetrated by explorers seeking the source of the Niger River, notably the Scottish traveler Mungo Park in 1795–96 and the British explorers Richard Lemon Lander (1804–34) and John Lander (1807–39) in 1830–31. In the 19th century palm oil became so important an article of commerce that the delta region was known as oil rivers. A British consul was sent to Calabar and later to Lagos, where British traders were firmly established. In 1861 Great Britain took full possession of Lagos Island.

After the conclusion of several treaties with native chiefs, the British Oil Rivers Protectorate was established in southern Nigeria. In 1886 the Royal Niger Co. was granted a charter under which it governed the territory of the protectorate, raising an armed constabulary and establishing government services. The name of the protectorate was changed in 1893 to the Niger Coast Protectorate. The kingdom of Benin in the southwest was added to the area in 1897 and, after further expansion in the southeast, the region became the Protectorate of Southern Nigeria in 1900. The charter of the Royal Niger Co. was revoked in the same year, and the Protectorate of Northern Nigeria was proclaimed.

The Protectorates. Neither of the two protectorates was under full British control at the time of its establishment. The entire area of present Nigeria was, however, acknowledged to be British under agreements made between Great Britain, Germany, and France that divided much of Africa into so-called spheres of influence. British troops engaged in military conflicts with followers of

Muslim emirs in the north and with Nigerian peoples who were still engaged in slave trade after it had been prohibited by the British in 1807. British domination became complete in 1914, when the two administrations were merged as the Colony and Protectorate of Nigeria. For administrative purposes the country was divided into the Colony of Lagos and two groups of provinces in the protectorate, the Northern and Southern provinces.

Frederick Dealtry Lugard, 1st Baron Lugard, was the first governor-general of united Nigeria. He left some local functions of government to the traditional tribal chiefs or councils, which acted under the supervision and with the assistance and advice of British administrators. In 1922 the League of Nations mandate of Cameroons was added, administratively, to the protectorate. In the same year the Nigerian legislative council, which had limited legislative authority over the Colony of Lagos and the Southern provinces, was inaugurated; the Northern provinces remained under the jurisdiction of a British governor. The former League of Nations mandate of Cameroons became a UN trust territory in 1946 and remained under British administration.

Independence. Nigerian demands for self-government after World War II resulted in a series of short-lived constitutions. The first, in 1947, established provincial legislatures with limited native participation in the government. By succeeding constitutional changes, Nigeria was provided with a federal type of government, and the provinces were consolidated into three regions (Eastern, Western, and Northern), each with a measure of autonomy. In 1954 Nigeria became a federation and each region was given the option, dependent on certain safeguards for the federation, to assume a self-governing status. Internal self-government was granted to the Eastern and Western regions in 1957 and to the Northern Region in 1959.

On Oct. 1, 1960, Nigeria became independent within the Commonwealth of Nations. On October 7 it was admitted to membership in the UN. The first prime minister, Sir Abubakar Tafawa Balewa, headed a coalition government representing the major parties of the Northern and Eastern regions. The governor-general was Nnamdi Azikiwe, who became president when Nigeria adopted a republican form of government on Oct. 1, 1963. Meanwhile, on Feb. 11–12, 1961, the northern section of the former British Cameroons voted to become a part of Nigeria.

Internal Strains. From the early days of independence, ethnic antagonisms and religious and political differences seriously strained the unity of

Amid pomp and ceremony combining Western uniforms and traditional African transportation, Nigerians celebrate their independence in October 1960. **Wide World Photos**

the federation. In 1962 a major political crisis developed in the Western Region, which was dominated by the Yoruba and their political party, called the Action Group. The Action Group, which had constituted the chief opposition bloc to the ruling coalition in the federal parliament, split in two during the year. Its parliamentary leader, who had expressed fear of a federal plot to break the party's power, was indicted for treason in 1963 and sentenced to ten years' imprisonment. Meanwhile, as the result of a referendum held in mid-1963 in two districts of the Western Region where non-Yoruba peoples were a majority, a Mid-West Region was formed.

Civil War. Political bickering and corruption that left young officers increasingly impatient finally culminated in a military coup in January 1966. Prime Minister Balewa and two regional premiers were killed. A military government was established by the army commander Maj. Gen. Aguiyi-Ironsi (1925–66), who abolished the federal system. In July a countercoup, led by Northern officers, overthrew and killed Ironsi. His successor, Maj. Gen. Yakubu Gowon, revived the federation. During this period many Ibo who were living in the north were killed or returned as refugees.

Relations between the federal government and the Ibo continued to deteriorate. In May 1967 the federal government announced its intention to split the Eastern region into three states, which would leave the Ibo without access to the sea and cut them off from the region's oil-rich areas. The Eastern region then seceded and proclaimed itself the Republic of Biafra. Civil war broke out in July and lasted for two and a half years before Biafran resistance was overcome in January 1970. *See also* BIAFRA, REPUBLIC OF.

Oil Wealth. As life in the Eastern Region returned to normal, Nigeria enjoyed four years of rapid economic growth, fueled by expanding oil revenues, as Nigeria became the fifth largest producer of petroleum in the world. Continued military rule, however, despite promises of return to a civilian government, led to renewed political instability. Gowon was ousted on July 29 in a bloodless coup led by Brigadier Murtala Ramat Muhammad (1937–76). Muhammad was himself assassinated in an unsuccessful coup attempt on Feb. 13, 1976. His successor, Lt. Gen. Olusegun Obasanjo (1937–   ), presided over the preparations for return to civilian rule, which culminated in the promulgation of a new constitution and in the election of a new president, Alhaji Shehu Shagari (1925–   ), in the summer of 1979.

The Shagari government, like its predecessors, attempted to use Nigeria's oil income to fuel an ambitious development program; in addition,

Shagari sought to implement a "green revolution" that would stimulate agricultural productivity and lessen the nation's increasing dependence on food imports. The weakening of the oil market in the early 1980s dealt a crippling blow to these efforts. Revenues from oil exports, which exceeded $20 billion in 1980, declined to $10 billion in 1982, and Nigeria was unable to repay its short-term debts. With foreign exchange scarce, Nigeria could no longer afford essential imports, and the nation's economy, already weakened by persistent mismanagement and corruption, sank into severe recession.

In January 1983 the government ordered the expulsion of all unskilled foreigners. At least 1 million people were forced into exile, although many soon returned. That August, Shagari won reelection to a second presidential term; his political organization, the National Party of Nigeria, also showed commanding strength in subsequent voting for the federal legislature and for state offices. Nigeria's economic position continued to worsen, however, and on Dec. 31, 1983, Shagari was deposed in a military coup led by Maj. Gen. Muhammad Buhari (1942–).

For further information on this topic, see the Bibliography in volume 28, section 1027.

NIGHTHAWK, common name for either of two goatsuckers in the genus *Chordeiles,* found throughout North America. Nighthawks somewhat resemble the closely related whippoorwill, *Caprimulgus vociferus,* and are about 25 cm (10 in) long with a wingspread of almost 60 cm (about 2 ft). They feed on insects, which they usually catch on the wing at dusk. The common nighthawk, *Chordeiles minor,* is speckled in shades of black, gray, and tan and has a broad white band across the throat and on each wing. The male has an additional white band traversing the tail. The cry of this bird is a high-pitched nasal note. It also produces a hollow, booming sound with its wings as it dives directly downward through the air in pursuit of food, thereby acquiring such popular names as bullbat and mosquito hawk. The other species of nighthawk, *C. acutipennis,* is common in the southwestern U.S. *See* GOATSUCKER; WHIPPOORWILL.

NIGHTINGALE (O.E. *nihtegale,* "nightsinger"), common name for any passerine bird in the genus *Luscinia* of the thrush family, Turdidae (*see* THRUSH). Nightingales are known for the exquisite nocturnal song of the male, which is especially fine during the breeding season. Native to the Old World, the birds are about 15 cm (about 6 in) long, and both sexes are russet brown above, shading into a light, reddish chestnut on the rump and tail, and grayish white below. The

bill, legs, and feet are brown. The common nightingale of western Europe, *L. megarhynchos,* builds its nest in thickets; the birds migrate individually to winter in Africa. The name nightingale is extended to a number of other songbirds, particularly the Japanese nightingale, *Leiothrix lutea.* This is a brownish bird with a yellow breast, a red bill, and red feet; it is kept as a cage bird in the U.S.

NIGHTINGALE, Florence (1820–1910), British nurse, hospital reformer, and humanitarian.

Born in Florence, Italy, on May 12, 1820, Nightingale was raised mostly in Derbyshire, England, and received a thorough classical education from her father. In 1849 she went abroad to study the European hospital system, and in 1850 she began training in nursing at the Institute of Saint Vincent de Paul in Alexandria, Egypt. She subsequently studied at the Institute for Protestant Deaconesses at Kaiserswerth, Germany. In 1853 she became superintendent of the Hospital for Invalid Gentlewomen in London.

After the Crimean War broke out in 1854, Nightingale, stirred by reports of the primitive sanitation methods and grossly inadequate nursing facilities at the large British barracks-hospital at Üsküdar (now part of İstanbul, Turkey), dispatched a letter to the British secretary of war, volunteering her services in the Crimea. At the same time, unaware of her action, the minister of war proposed that she assume direction of all nursing operations at the war front. Shortly thereafter she set out for Üsküdar accompanied by 38 nurses. Under her supervision, efficient

Florence Nightingale

nursing departments were established at Üsküdar and later at Balaklava in the Crimea. Through her tireless efforts the mortality rate among the sick and the wounded was greatly reduced.

At the close of the war in 1860, with a fund raised in tribute to her services, Nightingale founded the Nightingale School and Home for Nurses at Saint Thomas's Hospital in London. The opening of this school marked the beginning of professional education in nursing.

Florence Nightingale's contributions to the evolution of nursing as a profession were invaluable. Before she undertook her reforms, nurses were largely untrained personnel who considered their job a menial chore; through her efforts the stature of nursing was raised to a medical profession with high standards of education and important responsibilities. She received many honors from foreign governments and in 1907 became the first woman to receive the British Order of Merit. She died in London on Aug. 13, 1910. In 1915 the Crimean Monument in Waterloo Place, London, was erected in her honor. Her writings include *Notes on Nursing* (1860), the first textbook for nurses, which was translated into many languages. Among her other writings are *Notes on Hospitals* (1859) and *Notes on Nursing for the Labouring Classes* (1861).

For further information on this person, see the section Biographies in the Bibliography in volume 28.

NIGHTSHADE, common name for both a family of plants, Solanaceae, and the genus *Solanum* of mostly weedy plants. The Solanaceae family has about 75 genera and 2000 species and includes crop and garden plants, such as potato, tomato, petunia, tobacco, and eggplant, as well as many poisonous plants. The poisonous nightshades contain alkaloids of three major types: tropane, found in belladonna, jimsonweed, and henbane; pyridine, in tobacco; and steroid, in some members of the genus *Solanum*.

Included in the genus are such common weeds as horse nettle, *S. carolinense,* a spiny, perennial herb of the south-central to eastern U.S.; European bittersweet, *S. dulcamara;* silverleaf nightshade, *S. elaeagnifolium,* a whitish herb of prairies of the southwestern states and Mexico; black nightshade, *S. nigrum,* an annual, self-seeding herb found in disturbed soils of eastern and central North America; and buffalo bur, *S. rostratum,* a spiny weed of the Great Plains and eastward. Also in this genus are the common potato, *S. tuberosum,* eggplant, *S. melongena,* and Jerusalem cherry, *S. pseudo-capsicum.*

All the plants in this family bear flowers that have five sepals, five petals, five stamens, and a

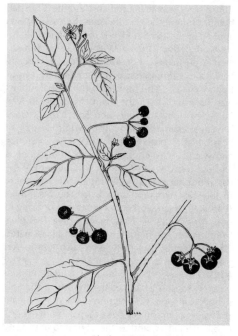

Black nightshade, Solanum nigrum

solitary pistil that in most species ripens into a berry. In horse nettle, the flowers are white or pale violet and the berry yellow; in European bittersweet, the flowers are blue or purple and the berry red; in silverleaf nightshade, the flowers are violet or blue and yellow and the berry orange; and in black nightshade, the flowers are white and the berry black. Buffalo bur has yellow flowers and a spiny fruit or bur resulting from the persistence of the spiny calyx about the berry as it ripens.

The foliage and unripe fruit of most nightshades contain dangerous levels of a steroid alkaloid, solanine. The ripe berries are the least toxic part of these plants but may be deadly under some circumstances. Solanine is also found in potato sprouts and the green spots of some potatoes. A toxic dose of any of these will usually result in severe digestive upset. This may be accompanied by trembling, weakness, difficulty in breathing, or paralysis. Potato sprouts should be removed before using the tubers for food. Potato vines, sprouts, and rotten potatoes should not be used as forage for livestock. Solanaceae are in the order Polemoniales (*see* PHLOX).

NIHILISM (from Lat. *nihil,* "nothing"), designation applied to various radical philosophies, usually by their opponents, the implication being that adherents of these philosophies reject all positive values and believe in nothing.

The term was first used to describe Christian heretics during the Middle Ages. In Russia it was applied in the 1850s and '60s to young intellectuals who, influenced by Western ideas, repudiated Christianity, considered Russian society backward and oppressive, and advocated revolutionary change. The best-known fictional nihilist was Bazarov, one of the main characters in Ivan Turgenev's novel *Fathers and Sons* (1862). Conservatives claimed that nihilism would destroy all possibility of orderly and purposeful existence and was directly contrary to real human needs and desires, but the novelist N. G. Chernyshevshy and other radicals called it a necessary phase in the transformation of Russia. The Narodniks (Populists), who worked for a peasant uprising in the 1870s, and the Narodnaya Volya (People's Will) movement, members of which assassinated Czar Alexander II in 1881, were also considered manifestations of nihilism.

NIIGATA, city, Japan, capital of Niigata Prefecture, N Honshu Island, at the mouth of the Shinano R. Opened to foreign trade in 1859, Niigata is a leading port on the Sea of Japan, with exports of oil, machinery, and textiles. Located in the city is Niigata University (1949). Pop. (1980 prelim.) 457,783.

NIIHAU, island, NW Hawaii, near Kauai. The chief industries are livestock raising and the growing of rushes from which mats are pleated. The island is privately owned. The main village is Puuwai. Area, 186 sq km (72 sq mi); pop. (1980) 226.

NIJINSKY, Vaslav (1890–1950), Russian ballet dancer and choreographer, born in Kiev of Polish parents, and educated at the Imperial Dancing Academy, Saint Petersburg (now Leningrad). He made his first public appearance in 1907 with the St. Petersburg Imperial Ballet. He later went to Paris and after 1909 was a member of the original Ballets Russes under the direction of the Russian ballet producer Sergey Diaghilev. Nijinsky soon attained the rank of premier danseur. He was the first to portray the leading roles in *Le spectre de la rose, Petrushka, Shéhérazade, Les sylphides, The Afternoon of a Faun,* and *The Rite of Spring.* His unconventional choreography for the two last-named ballets aroused lively comment and many protests when the ballets were first performed.

Ranking among the great male dancers of all time, Nijinsky had remarkable technical powers; his grands jetés, for example, created the illusion that he was suspended in midair. His spectacular career ended in 1918 when he became the victim of schizophrenia, from which he never fully recovered.

NIJMEGEN, city, E Netherlands, in Gelderland Province, on the Waal R., near West Germany. It is an inland shipping center, and its industries include the manufacture of bricks, chemicals, leather goods, cigars, silverware, cutlery, and electrical equipment. Principal landmarks in Nijmegen include the 13th-century Groote Church; the Kam Museum, containing Roman antiquities; and the 16th-century Renaissance town hall. The city is the site of the Roman Catholic University of Nijmegen (1923).

Nijmegen is built on the site of a Roman camp and for many years was a residence of the Carolingian emperors. It was a free imperial city and a member of the Hanseatic League. A peace treaty between the Netherlands, France, Spain, and the Holy Roman Empire was concluded (1678–79) here. Pop. (1980) 147,614.

NIKE, in Greek mythology, goddess of victory, daughter of the Titan Pallas and the river Styx. Nike fought on the side of the god Zeus in his battle against the Titans, and in Greek art she is sometimes represented as supported by the hands of Zeus and the goddess Athena. She is otherwise represented as winged and carrying a wreath or palm of victory. The *Nike of Samothráki,* or *Winged Victory* (Louvre, Paris), is one of the finest pieces of Hellenistic sculpture.

Nijinsky performing in the ballet Giselle *in 1910.*
Bettmann Archive

NIKOLAIS, Alwin (1912–), American choreographer, who developed a dance theater of abstract forms, colors, and lights. Born in Southington, Conn., he worked as a theater pianist and puppet master before studying modern dance with such choreographers as the German-American Hanya Holm. In 1948 he became director of the Henry Street Playhouse, New York City. Nikolais choreographed, designed, composed the music, and engineered the lighting for such works as *Masks, Props and Mobiles* (1953), *Structures* (1970), and *Cross-Fade* (1975).

NIKOLAYEV, city, capital of Nikolayev Oblast, Ukrainian SSR, in SW European USSR, at the confluence of the Southern Bug and Ingul rivers. A leading port on the Black Sea and an important shipbuilding center, the city has an excellent harbor kept open in winter by icebreakers. Manufactures include agricultural and construction machinery. Nikolayev was founded in 1788 near the site of an ancient Greek settlement and became a Russian naval base. During World War II the Germans occupied (1941–44) and badly damaged the city. Pop. (1980 est.) 449,000.

NIKON (1605–81), patriarch of Moscow and all Russia and initiator of a series of liturgical reforms that led to a major schism in the Russian Orthodox church. A married priest in Moscow for ten years, Nikon, after his wife died, became a monk and was eventually elevated to the positions of archbishop of Novgorod (1649) and patriarch (1652). Enjoying the friendship of Czar Alexis, he affirmed the absolute superiority of the church over the state and swore the czar to obedience. Nikon proceeded to establish an opulent patriarchal court that rivaled the czar's. At the same time, he undertook to correct Russian liturgical practices by making them conform to the contemporary usage of the Greek church. His reforms included making the sign of the cross with three (instead of two) fingers and a revision of all liturgical books. Through these reforms, he believed, Russia would become the spiritual as well as the political bulwark of orthodoxy.

Several leading members of the clergy and millions of the faithful rejected the reforms, however, and the resulting schism of so-called Old Believers weakened the church in its relations with the government and led to the development of numerous antiinstitutional sects. The opposition to Nikon's reforms was based in part on unenlightened conservatism, but also on the belief that Russia, after the Turkish conquest (1453) of Constantinople, should no longer be bound by the example of the Greek church. Nikon's authoritarian and arbitrary methods intensified the opposition. When the czar was in Poland (1654–56), Nikon served as coruler and alienated the boyars and other state officials. The czar was finally persuaded to depose him in 1658, and Nikon retired to a monastery, but his reforms were confirmed by the Great Council of Moscow (1666–67). J.Me.

NILE, river of Africa, the longest river in the world. From Lake Victoria in E central Africa, it flows generally N through Uganda, Sudan, and Egypt to the Mediterranean Sea, for a distance of 5584 km (3470 mi). From its remotest headstream, the Luvironza R. in Burundi, the river is 6671 km (4145 mi) long. The river basin has an area of more than 2,590,000 km (1,000,000 sq mi).

The source of the Nile is one of the upper branches of the Kagera R. in Tanzania. The Kagera follows the boundary of Rwanda northward, turns along the boundary of Uganda, and drains into Lake Victoria. On leaving Lake Victoria at the site of the now-submerged Ripon Falls, the Nile rushes for 483 km (300 mi) between high rocky walls and over rapids and cataracts, at first NW and then W, until it enters Lake Albert. The section between the two lakes is called the Victoria Nile. The river leaves the N end of Lake Albert as the Albert Nile, flows through N

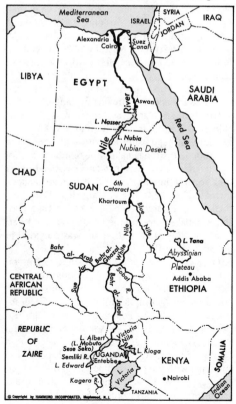

NILE, BATTLE OF THE

Uganda, and at the Sudan border becomes the Bahr al-Jabal. At its junction with the Bahr al-Ghazal, the river becomes the Bahr al-Abyad, or the White Nile. Various tributaries flow through the Bahr al-Ghazal district. At Khartoum the White Nile is joined by the Blue Nile, or Bahr al-Azraq. These are so named because of the color of the water. The Blue Nile, 1529 km (950 mi) long, gathers its volume principally from Lake Tana, in the Ethiopian Highlands; it is known here as the Abbai. From Khartoum the Nile flows NE; 322 km (200 mi) below that city, it is joined by the Atabarah (Atbara) R. The black sediment brought down by this river settles in the Nile delta and makes it extraordinarily fertile. During its course from the confluence of the Atabarah through the Nubian Desert, the great river makes two deep bends. Below Khartoum navigation is rendered dangerous by cataracts, the first occurring N of Khartoum and the sixth near Aswan. The Nile enters the Mediterranean Sea by a delta that separates into two main channels, the Rosetta and the Damietta.

In 1858 the British explorer John Hanning Speke reached Lake Victoria and in 1862 discovered Ripon Falls. Two years later the British explorer Sir Samuel White Baker discovered Lake Albert; the German explorer Georg August Schweinfurth then explored (1868–71) the W feeders of the White Nile. In 1875 the British-American explorer Sir Henry Morton Stanley sailed around Lake Victoria. In 1899 Stanley, in tracing the course of the Semliki R., discovered Lake Edward and the Ruwenzori Range.

The Makwar Dam was built across the Blue Nile S of Khartoum shortly after World War I, providing storage water for cotton plantations in the Sudan. It is today called the Sennar Dam, for the nearby town. Aswan Dam was heightened for a second time in 1936 and its storage capacity increased. In 1971 the Aswan High Dam was dedicated; its large reservoir is called Lake Nasser. At Jabal Awliya, on the White Nile S of Khartoum, another storage reservoir was provided in a dam built in 1937.

NILE, BATTLE OF THE, naval action fought on Aug. 1–2, 1798, during the Napoleonic Wars, between the British and the French in Abu Qir Bay, about 24 km (about 15 mi) northeast of Alexandria, Egypt. In 1798 a French fleet of 17 ships under the command of Vice Admiral François Paul Brueys d'Aigailliers (1753–98) had sailed from Toulon, France, with Napoleon Bonaparte and the army with which Napoleon intended to conquer Egypt, before attacking the British in India. From June to August, British Rear Adm. Horatio Nelson and his fleet of 14 ships searched the

central and eastern Mediterranean Sea for the French fleet, and on the afternoon of August 1 he found the enemy ships anchored in Abu Qir Bay.

Brueys stationed his vessels in a line near one shore of the bay. Expecting the British to fight as they came in from the sea, he ordered the guns on the seaward side of his ships prepared for action, neglecting those on the landward side. The battle began about sunset. Nelson, risking the shallows and the reefs near shore, maneuvered part of his fleet between the French ships and the land and kept part to seaward of the French, who were thus attacked on two sides simultaneously. In addition to being outmaneuvered, the French were short of men, many of their crews having gone to shore earlier in the day to obtain supplies of water. In a few hours all of the French vessels, except four that were captured or destroyed in later engagements, either surrendered or were destroyed; several of the British ships were badly damaged. The British casualties were about 200 killed and 700 wounded; the French lost more than 5000 killed, wounded, or taken prisoner.

The Battle of the Nile was one of the most decisive engagements in naval history. Nelson's victory cut off Napoleon's line of communication with France, a circumstance that eventually caused him to abandon his expedition to the Middle East. The victory also gave Great Britain control of the entire Mediterranean Sea and was instrumental in inducing various European powers to join Great Britain in a new coalition (1799) against France.

NILES, village, Cook Co., NE Illinois, on the Chicago R., near the city of Chicago; settled around 1832, inc. 1902. Manufactures include machinery, electronic equipment, and tools and dies. Niles is the site of a half-size reproduction (1933) of the Leaning Tower of Pisa. Pop. (1970) 31,432; (1980) 30,363.

NILES, city, Trumbull Co., NE Ohio, on the Mahoning R., near Warren; inc. as a city 1895. Manufactures include steel, specialty metals, and motor-vehicle equipment. President William McKinley was born here and is commemorated by a large memorial, which houses the McKinley Library and a museum. The community was founded in 1806 as an ironworking center called Heaton's Furnace. In 1834 it was renamed Nilestown (shortened to Niles in 1843) for Hezekiah Niles (1777–1839), a noted journalist. Pop. (1970) 21,581; (1980) 23,088.

NILSSON, Birgit (1918–), Swedish soprano, considered the foremost Wagnerian soprano of her time. Born near Malmö, she studied voice at the Royal Academy of Music, Stockholm, making her first public appearance in *Macbeth,* by the Italian composer Giuseppe Verdi, in 1948. She gained international fame for her roles in operas by the German composer Richard Wagner at the Bayreuth Festival in West Germany in 1954. Her first American appearance was in 1956 in Los Angeles. Her debut at the Metropolitan Opera, New York City, in 1959 was as Isolde in Wagner's *Tristan und Isolde.*

NIMEIRY, Gaafar Muhammad al- (1930–), president of the Sudan (1969–). Born in Omdurman, the son of a Muslim postman, Nimeiry chose an army career and graduated from the Sudanese military college in 1952. He was deeply influenced by the Nasser revolution (1952) in Egypt and was implicated in several coup attempts before he succeeded (May 1969) in establishing himself as chairman of the Sudanese Revolutionary Command Council. A fervent nationalist, Nimeiry crushed both the conservative Ansar religious faction (in 1969) and the indigenous Communist party, after their coup attempt (1971) failed. Elected president in 1971, his major achievement was the ending (1972) of a 17-year-old civil war between the north and the south, thus stabilizing a united Sudan.

NÎMES, city, S France, capital of Gard Department, on a plain in the Cévennes Region. It is a farm-trade and manufacturing center; products include textiles, clothing, processed food, brandy, footwear, machinery, and chemicals. The city is known for its many well-preserved Roman structures. These include a large arena (1st cent. AD), which is still in use; the Maison-Carrée (1st cent. AD), built in a Greek style as a temple and now housing a museum of Roman sculpture; and a temple of Diana (2d cent. AD). Near the city are the Tour Magne, a tower probably built in the 1st century BC, and the Pont du Gard (19 BC), a famous aqueduct. Also of note are the Cathedral of Saint Castor (begun 11th cent.) and museums of archaeology, fine art, and local history.

Once a Gallic settlement, Nîmes was annexed by the Romans in 121 BC and, as Nemausus, became a prosperous cultural and commercial center. Damaged by the Visigoths in the 5th century AD, the city passed to the counts of Toulouse in the 10th century and to the French crown in the 13th century. Nîmes was a stronghold of Protestantism during the Reformation. After a period of decline, it grew as an economic center in the 19th century. Pop. (1982) 129,924.

NIMITZ, Chester William (1885–1966), American naval officer, born in Fredericksburg, Tex., and educated at the U.S. Naval Academy. During World War I he was chief of staff to the commander of the submarine force of the Atlantic Fleet. In 1938, after advancing through the ranks, he was appointed rear admiral. In December 1941, after the Japanese attack on Pearl Harbor and the entry of the U.S. into World War II, Nimitz was appointed commander in chief of the Pacific Fleet, with the rank of four-star admiral. He was advanced to the position of admiral of the fleet in 1944. Nimitz's accomplished planning of strategy, bold tactics (as in the Battle of Midway), and brilliant use of his staff and forces were largely responsible for the successes of the U.S. Navy in the Pacific theater during the war. He was chief of naval operations from December 1945 to December 1947, when he retired. In 1949 he headed the UN commission for India and Pakistan.

NINEVEH (anc. *Ninua*), former city in northern Iraq that served as the capital of the Assyrian Empire at its height (c. 705–612 BC). Located at the confluence of the Tigris and Khosr rivers, the city in antiquity was an important junction for commercial routes crossing the Tigris. Nineveh was first settled in Neolithic times before 6000 BC and was inhabited almost without a break until after AD 1500. Its most prominent surviving features include two large mounds, Quyunjik and Nebi Yunus, and the remains of the city walls (about 12 km/7.5 mi in circumference).

In the 2d and 3d millennia BC Nineveh was known primarily as a religious center. The healing powers of its statue of the goddess Ishtar were renowned as far away as Egypt. The Assyrian king Sennacherib (r. 705–681 BC) moved the capital to Nineveh shortly after he came to the throne. The ancient city was then laid out anew with broad boulevards, wide squares, parks and gardens, and a magnificent edifice of more than 80 rooms called the Palace Without a Rival. The city's area was expanded to about 730 ha (about 1800 acres), and massive defensive walls were added. Drinking water for the inhabitants was brought in from some 50 km (more than 30 mi) away by a system of canals and aqueducts. Later Nineveh housed an extensive scientific, administrative, and literary library collected by King Ashurbanipal.

The sack of the city by the Babylonians and Medes in 612 BC effectively put an end to the Assyrian Empire; and, although some of its sections were later inhabited, Nineveh never regained its former importance.   J.A.B.

NINGBO, also Ning-po, city, E China, in Zhejiang (Chekiang) Province, a major fishing port and an industrial center on the Yong (Yung) R. The port has an outer harbor for oceangoing vessels downstream at Zhenhai (Chen-hai) and is linked by canal to Shanghai and other cities of the populous Yangtze R. (Chang Jiang) delta. Manufactures of Ningbo include processed food, textiles, machinery, tools, and fishing equipment.

An important foreign trade center as early as the 5th century AD, the city was given the name Liampo by Portuguese merchants who began trading here in 1545. It was one of the original treaty ports opened to foreign commerce in 1842 but was eclipsed as a foreign trade port later in the 19th century by the development of Shanghai. The city was known as Ninghsein from 1911 to 1949, when it was renamed Ningbo. Pop. (est.) 350,000.

NINGSIA HUI AUTONOMOUS REGION, also Ningxia Hui, N central China. It encompasses a semiarid plateau region with desert areas in the N. The Huang He (Huang Ho or Yellow R.) flows across the central part of the region and furnishes water for irrigation. Coal is mined in the E. Modern industry is relatively undeveloped and only one railroad crosses the region. The Hui (Chinese Muslims) constitute about one-third of the population; Mongolians are a significant minority in the N. Yinchuan (Yinchwan) is the capital. Area, about 60,000 sq km (about 23,200 sq mi); pop. (1982) 3,900,000.

NIOBE, in Greek mythology, daughter of Tantalus, and the queen of Thebes. Her husband, King Amphion, was a son of the god Zeus and a great musician. Niobe bore him six handsome sons and six beautiful daughters. Although she was happy, Niobe exhibited the same arrogance toward the gods that her father had shown (see ATREUS, HOUSE OF). Thus, she commanded the people of Thebes to worship her instead of the goddess Leto, who had only two children. The gods heard her words on far-off Mount Olympus and resolved to punish her. Leto's children, Apollo, god of prophecy and a master archer, and Artemis, goddess of the hunt, fired their arrows with deadly aim, killing all of Niobe's children. The grief-stricken Niobe was turned into a stone that was forever wet with her tears.

NIOBIUM or **COLUMBIUM,** metallic element, symbol Nb, in group Vb of the periodic table (see PERIODIC LAW); at.no. 41, at.wt. 92.906. This rare metal was discovered in 1801 by the British chemist Charles Hatchett (1765-1847). It is gray, lustrous, ductile, and malleable. It occurs, associated with the similar element tantalum (q.v.), in various minerals, the most important of which is called columbite or tantalite, depending on which of the two elements predominates. Although niobium is found in many parts of the world, a large proportion of the world production comes from Nigeria and Zaire.

Niobium burns when heated in air and combines with nitrogen, hydrogen, and the halogens. It resists the actions of most acids. Its principal use is as an alloying element in stainless steel, to which it lends additional corrosion resistance, particularly at high temperatures. Pure niobium has excellent characteristics as a construction material in nuclear power plants.

Niobium melts at 2468° C (4474° F), boils at 4927° C (8901° F), and has a sp.gr. of 8.57.

NIPIGON, LAKE, lake of central Ontario, Canada, near Thunder Bay. Studded with several large islands, the lake is about 115 km (about 70 mi) long and has an area of 4848 sq km (1872 sq mi). It is fed by numerous streams and is drained, in the S, by the Nipigon R.

NIRENBERG, Marshall Warren (1927-), American biochemist and Nobel laureate, who is credited with experiments that made possible the solving of the genetic code. Born in New York City and educated at the University of Florida in Gainesville, Nirenberg earned a Ph.D. degree in biochemistry from the University of Michigan in 1957. He was a postdoctoral fellow of the American Cancer Society, joining the National Institutes of Health in Bethesda, Md., in 1957 and remaining there to perform research in the genetic code, protein synthesis, and nucleic acids. In 1962 he became director of the biochemical genetics section of the National Heart Institute. Nirenberg shared the 1968 Nobel Prize in physiology or medicine with the American scientist Robert W. Holley and the Indian-born chemist Har Gobind Khorana for their pioneering independent research in how certain genes determine the formation of certain enzymes. See also GENETICS.

NIRVANA (Skt., "extinguishing"), in Indian religious philosophy, a transcendent state free from suffering and individual phenomenal existence, an ultimate religious goal most frequently identified with Buddhism (q.v.). The word is derived from a verb meaning "to become cool," or "to blow out," as in the extinguishing of a candle. The connotation is that only in nirvana are the flames of lust, hatred, greed, and ignorance extinguished. With the attainment of nirvana, the otherwise endless cycle of rebirths is broken (see TRANSMIGRATION). Its nature has been much debated in Western scholarship, some scholars maintaining that it involves total annihilation and others interpreting it as eternal bliss. Both views are problematic, for nirvana is ultimately indescribable and can only be known directly. Mahayana Buddhists in East Asia interpret nirvana not as an external goal, but as one's own innermost nature, which needs only to be recognized.

They speak of it as Buddhahood, suchness, and emptiness.

See also HINDUISM; JAINISM; MYSTICISM.   J.P.M.

NIŠ, city, E Yugoslavia, in Serbia, on the Nišava R. It is an important railway center, with railway repair facilities, and also a leading industrial center, with production of leather goods, tobacco products, and armaments. The University of Niš (1965) is here.

The city, an important center in ancient Roman times, was the birthplace of the Roman emperor Constantine I. It fell in succession to the Huns, Bulgars, Hungarians, Byzantines, Serbs, and Ottoman Turks and was almost constantly in Turkish possession from the 15th century until it was retaken by the Serbs in 1878. Niš was a capital of Serbia until 1901. It was occupied by the Germans during World War II. Pop. (est.) 193,500.

NISHAPUR, town, NE Iran, in Khurasan Province, in a beautiful and fertile valley, near Meshed. Cotton, grains, and fruits are the most important products. The town was the birthplace, and contains the grave, of the Persian poet Omar Khayyám. Pop. (est.) 59,100.

NISHINOMIYA, city, Japan, in Hyogo Prefecture, SW Honshu Island, on Osaka Bay, near Osaka. A rail junction, the city is a major sake-brewing center, and vegetable oils are also produced here. It is the site of the Hirota Shrine, Kobe Women's College, Kwansei Gakuin University (1889), a baseball stadium, and a racecourse. Pop. (1980 prelim.) 410,329.

NITER.   *See* SALTPETER.

NITERÓI, residential and industrial city, SE Brazil, in Rio de Janeiro State, on Guanabara Bay, opposite the city of Rio de Janeiro (with which it is connected by the Presidente Costa e Silva Bridge). Manufactures include ships, steel, machinery, processed food, and textiles. Fluminense Federal University (1960) is here. The community was founded in 1671. Its name, adopted in 1836, is derived from an Indian term for "hidden water." It was the capital of Rio de Janeiro State from 1835 to 1975, except for the period from 1894 to 1903. Pop. (1980 prelim.) 400,140.

NITRATES.   *See* NITRIC ACID.

NITRIC ACID, colorless, corrosive liquid, HNO_3. Medieval alchemists called it aqua fortis (strong water). Commercially, nitric acid is made by the action of sulfuric acid on sodium nitrate, also known as Chile saltpeter. It is also made by the catalytic oxidation of ammonia. Nitric acid is a strong acid and a strong oxidizing agent. When dropped on the skin, the acid produces a yellow coloration because of the reaction of the acid with certain proteins to form yellow xanthoproteic acid. The concentrated nitric acid used commercially contains about 71 percent HNO_3; the rest is water. Fuming nitric acid, which is widely used commercially, consists of nitric acid with gaseous nitrogen peroxide in solution. It is red or brown in color and more active than colorless nitric acid. Ordinary and fuming nitric acid have wide application. They are used in chemical synthesis, in the nitration of organic materials to form nitro compounds, and in the manufacture of dyes and explosives. Nitric acid melts at $-42°$ C ($-44°$ F) and boils at 83° C (181° F).

The salts of nitric acid are called nitrates. Potassium nitrate, or saltpeter, and sodium nitrate are the nitrates of greatest commercial importance. Nearly all nitrates are soluble in water; one of the exceptions is bismuth subnitrate, $BiONO_3 \cdot H_2O$, which is used in medicine for treating intestinal disorders. Amitol, a powerful explosive, is a mixture of ammonium nitrate and trinitrotoluene (TNT). The reaction of nitric acid with organic compounds yields many important nitrates, such as nitroglycerin and nitrocellulose. Calcium, sodium, potassium, and ammonium nitrates are used in fertilizers to provide a source of nitrogen for plant growth.

NITRIDES, group of inorganic compounds, each composed of nitrogen and another, more electropositive element (tending to release electrons; *see* ELECTRICITY)—usually, however, excluding the halogens and hydrogen. Alkali-metal nitrides such as sodium nitride, Na_3N, decompose at low temperatures and react with water vapor to form ammonia and the metal hydroxide. Nitrides of such elements as boron and silicon, however, are hard, stable at high temperatures, and resistant to chemical attack; for this reason they are used in making crucibles and as abrasives. The metallurgical process called nitriding, used for surface-hardening steel, involves heating the steel in the presence of ammonia. The steel must be an alloy that contains an element, usually aluminum, that forms a nitride. Steel so treated has increased resistance to wear and to the formation of cracks.

NITRITES.   *See* FOOD PROCESSING AND PRESERVATION.

NITROCELLULOSE.   *See* CELLULOSE.

NITROGEN, gaseous element, symbol N, in group Va of the periodic table (*see* PERIODIC LAW); at.no. 7, at.wt. 14.007. It was isolated by the British physician Daniel Rutherford (1749–1819) in 1772 and recognized as an elemental gas by the French chemist Antoine Laurent Lavoisier about 1776. The free gas composes about four-fifths (78.03 percent) by volume of the atmosphere.

Properties. Nitrogen is inert and serves as a diluent for oxygen in burning and respiration processes. It is an important element in plant nutrition; certain bacteria in the soil convert atmospheric nitrogen into a form, such as nitrate, that can be absorbed by plants, a process called nitrogen fixation (q.v.). Nitrogen in the form of protein (q.v.) is an important constituent of animal tissue. The element occurs in the combined state in minerals, of which saltpeter, KNO_3, and Chile saltpeter, $NaNO_3$, are commercially important products.

Nitrogen is a colorless, odorless, tasteless, nontoxic gas. It can be condensed into a colorless liquid, which can in turn be compressed into a colorless, crystalline solid. Nitrogen exists in two natural isotopic forms, and four radioactive isotopes have been artificially prepared.

Nitrogen is obtained from the atmosphere by passing air over heated copper or iron. The oxygen is removed from the air, leaving nitrogen mixed with inert gases. Pure nitrogen is obtained by fractional distillation of liquid air; because liquid nitrogen has a lower boiling point than liquid oxygen, the nitrogen distills off first and can be collected.

Nitrogen melts at $-210.01°$ C $(-346.02°$ F), boils at $-195.79°$ C $(-320.42°$ F), and has a density of 1.251 g/liter at 0° C (32° F).

Uses. Nitrogen is chemically inert and combines with other elements only at very high temperatures or pressures. It is converted to an active form by passing through an electric discharge at low pressure. The nitrogen so produced is very active, combining with alkali metals (q.v.) to form azides; with the vapor of zinc, mercury cadmium, and arsenic to form nitrides; and with many hydrocarbons to form hydrocyanic acid and cyanides, also known as nitriles. Activated nitrogen returns to ordinary nitrogen in about one minute.

In the combined state nitrogen takes part in many reactions; it forms so many compounds that a systematic scheme of compounds containing nitrogen in place of oxygen was created by the American chemist Edward Franklin (1862–1937). In compounds nitrogen exists in all the valence states between -3 and $+5$. Ammonia, hydrazine, and hydroxylamine represent compounds in which the valence of nitrogen is -3, -2, and -1, respectively. Oxides of nitrogen represent nitrogen in all the positive valence states. Nitrous oxide, N_2O, a colorless gas, is prepared by heating ammonium nitrate. It is popularly called laughing gas because it tends to cause hysterical laughter in individuals who inhale it. Mixed with oxygen it is used as an anesthetic in minor operations. Nitric oxide, NO, a colorless gas, is produced commercially by the oxidation of ammonia in the presence of a catalyst. Nitrogen trioxide, N_2O_3, a blue liquid or a red-brown gas, is the acid anhydride of nitrous acid. Nitrogen dioxide, NO_2, a yellow liquid or red-brown gas, is the acid anhydride of nitric acid. Nitrogen pentoxide, N_2O_5, is a white solid.

Among other important nitrogen-containing compounds are amines, azo and diazo compounds, cyanates, cyanogen, fulminates, nitro compounds, nitric acid and nitrates, nitrous acid and nitrites, and urea.

NITROGEN CYCLE, natural cyclic process in the course of which atmospheric nitrogen enters the soil and becomes part of living organisms, before returning to the atmosphere. Nitrogen (q.v.), an essential part of the amino acids (q.v.), is a basic element of life. It also makes up 79 percent of the earth's atmosphere, but gaseous nitrogen must be converted to a chemically usable form before it can be used by living organisms. This is accomplished through the nitrogen cycle, in which gaseous nitrogen is converted to ammonia or nitrates. The high energies provided by lightning and cosmic radiation serve to combine atmospheric nitrogen and oxygen into nitrates, which are carried to the earth's surface in precipitation. Biological fixation (see NITROGEN FIXATION), which accounts for the bulk of the nitrogen-conversion process, is accomplished by free-living, nitrogen-fixing bacteria; symbiotic bacteria living on the roots of plants (mostly legumes and alders); blue-green algae; certain lichens; and epiphytes in tropical forests.

Nitrogen "fixed" as ammonia and nitrates is taken up directly by plants and incorporated in their tissues as plant proteins. The nitrogen then passes through the food chain from plants to herbivores to carnivores (see FOOD WEB). When plants and animals die, the nitrogenous compounds are broken down by decomposing into ammonia, a process called ammonification. Some of this ammonia is taken up by plants; the rest is dissolved in water or held in the soil, where microorganisms convert it into nitrates and nitrites in a process called nitrification. Nitrates may be stored in decomposing humus or leached from the soil and carried to streams and lakes. They may also be converted to free nitrogen through denitrification and returned to the atmosphere.

In natural systems, nitrogen lost by denitrification, leaching, erosion, and similar processes is replaced by fixation and other nitrogen sources. Human intrusion in the nitrogen cycle, however, can result in less nitrogen being cycled, or in an overload of the system. For example, the cultivation of croplands, harvesting of crops, and cut-

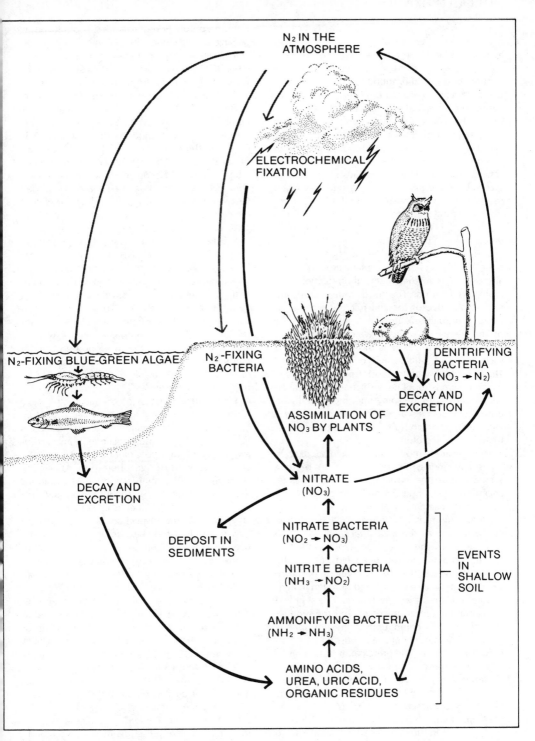

N₂ IN THE ATMOSPHERE

ELECTROCHEMICAL FIXATION

N₂-FIXING BLUE-GREEN ALGAE

N₂-FIXING BACTERIA

DENITRIFYING BACTERIA
($NO_3 \rightarrow N_2$)

DECAY AND EXCRETION

ASSIMILATION OF
NO_3 BY PLANTS

DECAY AND EXCRETION

NITRATE
(NO_3)

DEPOSIT IN SEDIMENTS

NITRATE BACTERIA
($NO_2 \rightarrow NO_3$)

NITRITE BACTERIA
($NH_3 \rightarrow NO_2$)

EVENTS IN SHALLOW SOIL

AMMONIFYING BACTERIA
($NH_2 \rightarrow NH_3$)

AMINO ACIDS,
UREA, URIC ACID,
ORGANIC RESIDUES

In the nitrogen cycle, bacteria, blue-green algae, and lightning convert atmospheric nitrogen to a usable form that plants can absorb through roots and animals can obtain through feeding. Wastes of plants and animals return nitrogen to the soil, and denitrifying bacteria recycle it back into the air. E. O. Wilson et al., *Life on Earth*, 2d ed., 1978, Sinauer Associates, Inc.

ting of forests all have caused a steady decline of nitrogen in the soil. (Some of the losses on agricultural lands are replaced only by applying energy-expensive nitrogenous fertilizers manufactured by artificial fixation.) On the other hand, the leaching of nitrogen from overfertilized croplands, cutover forestland, and animal wastes and sewage has added too much nitrogen to aquatic ecosystems, resulting in reduced water quality and the stimulation of excessive algal growth. In addition, nitrogen dioxide poured into the atmosphere from automobile exhausts and power plants breaks down to form ozone (q.v.) and reacts with other atmospheric pollutants to form photochemical smog (q.v.).   R.L.S.

NITROGEN FIXATION, biological or industrial process by which molecular atmospheric nitrogen (q.v.) is converted into a chemical compound that is essential for plant growth and is also used in industrial chemical production.

Biological Fixation. The most widely used and most productive of the soil microorganisms capable of nitrogen fixation are symbiotic bacteria of the genus *Rhizobium*, which colonize and form nodules on the roots of leguminous plants such as clover, alfalfa, and peas (*see* LEGUME). These bacteria obtain food from the legume, which in turn is supplied with abundant nitrogen compounds. Soils are sometimes inoculated with a particular species of *Rhizobium* to increase a legume crop, which is often planted to replenish the nitrogen depleted by other crops.

Much smaller amounts of nitrogen are fixed in the soil by nonsymbiotic (free-living) bacteria such as the aerobes, which function in the presence of oxygen, and bacteria of the genera *Klebsiella* and *Bacillus,* which function without oxygen. Some forms of blue-green algae also fix nitrogen, such as the alga *Anabaena,* which, in symbiosis with the water fern *Azolla pinnata,* is said to markedly increase rice yields, as was the case in paddies in the Thai Binh region of northern Vietnam. The need for fixed nitrogen in agriculture today is far greater than can be supplied by natural biological processes, and the production of nitrogen compounds from atmospheric nitrogen is a major chemical industry.

Industrial Fixation. The principal industrial nitrogen-fixation process today is the production of ammonia (q.v.) by passing a mixture of atmospheric nitrogen and hydrogen over a metallic catalyst (*see* CATALYSIS) at 500°–600° C (932°–1112° F). Ammonia is then oxidized to form nitric acid, which is in turn combined with ammonia to yield ammonium nitrate, used primarily in explosives and fertilizers (*see* FERTILIZER). In another method, cyanamide, which is used as a fertilizer

or in the production of cyanides, is produced by passing atmospheric nitrogen over heated calcium carbide in the presence of a catalyst.

NITROGLYCERIN, powerful explosive, formula $C_3H_5(NO_3)_3$, derived from glycerin by treatment with a mixture of concentrated sulfuric and nitric acids. It is a heavy, oily, colorless or light-yellow liquid, of sp.gr. 1.60, with a sweet, burning taste. It gives two crystalline forms, one melting at 2.8° C (37° F), the other at 13.5° C (56.3° F). It solidifies at 12° C (53.6° F). Nitroglycerin burns quietly when heated in air, but explodes when heated above 218° C (424° F) or when heated in a closed vessel. It is very sensitive to shock and therefore dangerous to transport. Although discovered in 1847, nitroglycerin was not used as an explosive (*see* EXPLOSIVES) until the Swedish engineer and inventor Alfred Nobel used it in making dynamite in 1866. Nitroglycerin is a common explosive today and is usually mixed with an inert, porous material such as sawdust. When detonated, it produces about 10,000 times its own volume of gas. It is 8 times as powerful as gunpowder (q.v.) in proportion to relative weight, and 13 times as powerful in proportion to relative volume. Nitroglycerin is used medically, in doses of 0.2 to 0.6 mg, as an agent to cause dilation of blood vessels.

NITROSAMINES, group of chemicals that have caused cancer in some animals under laboratory conditions. No compelling evidence has been found that they cause cancer in humans, but awareness of this possibility has involved the U.S. Department of Agriculture (USDA) and the Food and Drug Administration (FDA) in various regulatory maneuvers without, as yet, any outright banning of the chemicals concerned. The chemicals that are suspect are not the nitrosamines themselves but the nitrites that have long been used to cure and preserve meats and other foods. The nitrites can combine with natural amines and amides in the food or in the human body to form nitrosamines.

Awareness of this potential problem with nitrites has existed since the early 1960s, but it drew increased attention in 1973, when nitrosamines were found in fried bacon. A USDA study led, in 1978, to a regulation calling for a reduced level of nitrite use in curing. This created some difficulties over how to label meats that had not been cured in the traditional manner. In the meantime, a study suggested that nitrites themselves could be carcinogenic, but these results were subsequently cast in doubt. In 1980 the FDA and USDA decided not to place a ban on nitrites, although continuing to urge a reduction in their use.

NITROUS OXIDE. *See* NITROGEN.

NIUE, coral island, South Pacific Ocean, situated E of Tonga, about 260 sq km (about 100 sq mi) in area. The largest village and best port is Alofi on the W coast of the island. Major exports include copra, woven goods, honey, and fruit. The island also has uranium deposits. Niue was discovered in 1774 by the British explorer James Cook, who called it Savage Island because of the hostile reception he had received. It was annexed by New Zealand in 1901 and became self-governing in free association with New Zealand in 1974. Pop. (1979) 3578.

NIXON, Richard Milhous (1913–), 37th president of the U.S. (1969–74), and the only one to have resigned from office.

Nixon was born in Yorba Linda, Calif., on Jan. 9, 1913. His parents were poor, and his early life was one of hard work and study. He was a gifted student, finishing second in his class at Whittier College (1934) in Whittier, Calif., and third in his class at Duke University Law School (1937). Unable to find a position with a Wall Street (New York City) law firm after his graduation, Nixon returned to Whittier to practice. There he met Thelma Catherine (Pat) Ryan (1912–), whom he married in 1940. Nixon enlisted in the U.S. Navy in 1942 and served as a supply officer in the South Pacific during World War II. He left the service as a lieutenant commander.

Back in Whittier in 1946, Nixon was persuaded by a group of southern California Republicans to challenge Democratic congressman Jerry Voorhis (1901–84). Nixon campaigned vigorously, tabbed the liberal Voorhis as a dangerous left-winger, and won by 16,000 votes. In 1948 and 1949 Nixon achieved a national reputation in the U.S. House of Representatives as a member of the Committee on Un-American Activities during its investigation of what became known as the Hiss case. In 1950 Nixon ran for the U.S. Senate against Congresswoman Helen Gahagan Douglas (1900–80), whom he labeled the "Pink Lady" for what he alleged to be her pro-Communist sympathies. He won the election, but his campaign tactics were widely criticized.

Vice-President. In 1952 the Republicans nominated Nixon to be the running mate of presidential candidate Dwight D. Eisenhower. When it was disclosed that as a senator Nixon had accepted an $18,000 fund for "political expenses" from California businessmen, he was nearly dropped from the Republican ticket. Nixon's televised self-defense, called the "Checkers" speech because of a sentimental reference to his dog Checkers, saved his political life. As vice-president, Nixon emerged as a vigorous Republi-

can spokesman during the Eisenhower years, campaigning in a cut-and-thrust style that contrasted with Eisenhower's nonpartisan aloofness. In nonelection years, Nixon toured the country trying to bolster Republican party finances and spirit. He also developed foreign affairs credentials by visiting numerous other countries, including the Soviet Union, where an impromptu "kitchen debate" with Nikita S. Khrushchev made worldwide headlines in July 1959. As undisputed party leader at the end of Eisenhower's second term, Nixon easily won the presidential nomination in 1960. Against the articulate, wealthy, and politically well-connected John F. Kennedy, however, the Nixon edge in experience and prominence melted away. Kennedy won with a narrow popular-vote margin of 113,000 votes out of 68.8 million cast.

Returning to California, Nixon sought to revitalize his political career by challenging Gov. Edmund G. (Pat) Brown (1905–) in the 1962 gubernatorial race. Defeated, Nixon angrily announced his withdrawal from active politics. He moved to New York City and began a lucrative law practice. He continued, however, to speak out on foreign policy issues, address Republican fund rallies, and maintain his strong influence in the party. By 1968 he was poised again to try for the presidency, this time as a more seasoned and temperate "new Nixon." With Spiro T. Agnew as the vice-presidential candidate, the Republican campaign made skillful use of television, benefited from national dissatisfaction with the war in Vietnam, and profited from factional divisions in the Democratic camp. Nixon defeated Hubert H. Humphrey with a popular-vote majority of about 500,000 votes.

President. At the pinnacle in 1969, President Nixon organized the White House to protect his energy and time. He left routine matters and most administrative affairs to such powerful aides as H. R. Haldeman (1926–), John Ehrlichman (1925–) and Charles Colson (1931–). This allowed him time for what had become his absorbing interest: international affairs. With Henry A. Kissinger as his most trusted foreign policy adviser, Nixon redefined the American role in the world, suggesting limits to U.S. resources and commitments. "After a period of confrontation," he declared in his inaugural address, "we are entering an era of negotiation." He ordered a gradual withdrawal of the 500,000 U.S. troops in South Vietnam. The withdrawal took four years, however, during which the war raged and U.S. casualties mounted. Nixon authorized a U.S. incursion into Cambodia in 1970 and the bombing of Hanoi and the mining of Haiphong Harbor in 1972. These actions were unpopular, but he credited them with helping to bring about a negotiated settlement by which all U.S. forces were withdrawn and all known U.S. prisoners of war released before the end of March 1973.

Nixon's greatest innovation was his approach to the People's Republic of China. Sensing that the time was right to make an overture to China, Nixon sent Kissinger to confer secretly with Chinese premier Zhou Enlai in July 1971. Nixon's own 1972 summit meeting in China was a diplomatic triumph that left the president's critics, accustomed to his fervent anti-Communism, astonished and off-balance. Within a few weeks, Nixon was in Moscow to negotiate the first step in a strategic arms limitation agreement. Born in that session was the era of détente, a search for accommodation between the two superpowers and an effort to reduce the danger of nuclear war.

Other parts of the world were not neglected. In the strategically vital Middle East, Nixon established links with Egypt while maintaining the U.S. commitment to Israel. After the Yom Kippur War of 1973, the U.S. replaced the Soviet Union as the dominant influence in Egypt.

At home, Nixon adopted the so-called New Federalism, a program designed to end what he said was the Democratic habit of "throwing money at problems." Congress passed part of the plan—revenue sharing with states and cities—and appropriated some $30 billion for local needs. While espousing the fiscal conservatism traditional to his party, Nixon held to no set economic course. After first advocating a balanced budget, he turned to deficit financing. Having decided against wage and price controls to battle rising inflation rates, he reversed himself dramatically in August 1971. He imposed controls, with limited success, in four phases extending into 1974. Nixon's economic policies were bold but inconsistent, and, partly because of rapidly rising energy costs, he was unable to avert a recession in 1974.

On racial matters, Nixon generally adopted a passive stance toward efforts by American blacks to achieve educational, economic, and social equality. He personally opposed busing but insisted that the law be upheld in cases where the courts required it.

The Nixon response to rising urban crime rates included demands for stricter law enforcement and less "coddling" of criminals and radical activists. The leading voice for this politically popular theme of "law and order" was Attorney General John N. Mitchell, the president's former

President Richard M. Nixon in 1972.

law partner and campaign manager. Nixon's four Supreme Court appointees, men whom he called "strict constructionists," brought a more conservative cast to the Court. They were Chief Justice Warren Burger and Justices Harry Blackmun, Lewis Powell, Jr., and William Rehnquist.

Watergate and Resignation. Up for reelection in 1972, Nixon was fresh from the Peking and Moscow triumphs and enjoying the peak of his popularity. He defeated the Democratic senator George S. McGovern (1922–) by the second largest majority in U.S. history. Only one small cloud appeared on the horizon. The attempted burglary and wiretapping of the Democratic National Committee headquarters on June 17, 1972, at the Watergate complex had been traced to men hired by some of the president's closest advisers. Newspaper reporters took the slender thread found at the Watergate burglary and followed it to the White House. Through determined reporting, a larger picture of political corruption was uncovered. Illegal campaign contributions, political "dirty tricks," and irregularities in Nixon's income taxes were unearthed as the story grew during 1973. Testimony before the Senate Select Committee on Presidential Campaign Activities, chaired by Senator Sam Ervin, Jr. (1896–), revealed that extensive tape recordings existed of conversations held in Nixon's office. The various investigations, including that by Archibald Cox (1912–), who was appointed special prosecutor for the case in May 1973, began to focus on the release of these vital tapes.

Public trust in Nixon's leadership plummeted after he had Cox dismissed in October 1973. To compound the president's problems, Vice-President Agnew, facing bribery charges, resigned in the same month. In his choice of a replacement, Nixon settled on a popular U.S. congressman certain of quick confirmation: Gerald R. Ford of Michigan, who was sworn in on Dec. 6, 1973.

A federal grand jury named the president in March 1974 as an unindicted coconspirator in a conspiracy to obstruct justice in the Watergate investigation. Attorney Leon Jaworski (1905–), who replaced Cox as special Watergate prosecutor, continued to press for the White House tapes, while the House Judiciary Committee began to investigate the case for impeachment.

Nixon tried to reestablish his authority with trips to the Middle East and the Soviet Union in the summer of 1974. But the Watergate net closed around him tighter upon his return. On July 24, the Supreme Court unanimously ruled that the president had to turn over the last and most self-incriminating tapes. One of these, recording his order to the Federal Bureau of Investigation to halt its investigation of the Watergate break-in, was conclusive evidence—the so-called smoking gun—of Nixon's primary role in a cover-up. The Judiciary Committee recommended impeachment to the full House of Representatives. On the evening of August 8, Nixon went on nationwide television to announce his decision, unprecedented in U.S. history, to resign. At noon on August 9, Gerald Ford took the oath of office as Nixon was being flown to retirement in California.

Pardoned by his successor "for all offenses against the United States which he . . . committed or may have committed" in office, Nixon in retirement kept a low profile but presented his memoirs both as TV interviews and in book form.

H.S.S.

For further information on this person, see the section Biographies in the Bibliography in volume 28.

NIZHNY TAGIL, city, Russian SFSR, in E European USSR, on the Tagil R. Located in the E foothills of the Ural Mts., the city is an important metallurgical center. Other manufactures include railroad equipment, heavy machinery, and chemicals. Founded in 1725 as a mining community, Nizhny Tagil grew rapidly during World War II. Pop. (1980 est.) 400,000.

NKOMO, Joshua (1917–), Zimbabwean nationalist leader. Born in Matabeleland, the son of a lay preacher and teacher, Nkomo was trained as a social worker. Entering politics in 1952, he led a succession of banned nationalist movements, the last of which, the Zimbabwe African People's Union (ZAPU), he still heads. Imprisoned (1964–74) by Ian Smith's white minority government, he symbolized the struggle for black majority rule in Rhodesia. In 1976 he joined Robert Mugabe to form the Patriotic Front, which fought a guerrilla war against Smith's regime in the late 1970s. When majority rule was achieved in 1980, Nkomo lost the elections to Mugabe, but became minister for home affairs in Mugabe's cabinet. He was dismissed in 1982, charged with plotting to overthrow the government of Zimbabwe.

NKONGSAMBA, city, W Cameroon, at the E foot of the volcanic Manengouba massif. A road and trade center, Nkongsamba is the terminus of the railroad to the port of Douala and is surrounded by coffee and banana plantations. Industries in the city include sawmilling, palm-oil processing, and brewing.

Nkongsamba has a teachers college and technical schools. The railroad was built to the city, then called Samba, in 1912 under German administration. Occupied by the British in 1914, the city came under French rule in 1916 and in 1923 became an administrative center, succeeding nearby Baré. Pop. (est.) 71,000.

NKRUMAH, Kwame (1909–72), first prime minister (1957–60) and president (1960–66) of Ghana. He was born on Sept. 21, 1909, at Nkroful in what was then the British-ruled Gold Coast, the son of a goldsmith. Trained as a teacher, he went to the U.S. in 1935 for advanced studies and later continued his schooling in England, where he helped organize the Pan-African Congress in 1945. Nkrumah returned to his homeland in 1947 and became general secretary of the newly founded United Gold Coast Convention but split from it in 1949 to form the more radical Convention People's party (CPP).

After his "positive action" campaign created disturbances in 1950, Nkrumah was jailed, but when the CPP swept the 1951 elections, he was freed to form a government, and he led the colony to independence as Ghana in 1957.

A firm believer in African liberation, Nkrumah pursued a radical pan-African policy, playing a key role in the formation of the Organization of

African Unity in 1963. As head of government, he was less successful, and as time passed he became increasingly dictatorial. He formed (1964) a one-party state, with himself as president for life, and actively promoted a cult of his own personality. Finally overthrown by the military in 1966, he spent his last years in exile, dying in Bucharest, Romania, on April 27, 1972.

For further information on this person, see the section Biographies in the Bibliography in volume 28.

NOAH, in the Old Testament, son of Lamech, tenth in descent from Adam, and, as survivor with his family of the flood (*see* DELUGE), the father of all humanity (see Gen. 6–9). According to the biblical account, Noah was spared for his piety when God, angered at the corruption of the world, destroyed it with a flood lasting 40 days and 40 nights. Noah had been warned to build the ark, a great ship, and to take on board with him his wife, his three sons, Shem, Ham, and Japheth, his sons' wives, and two mated specimens of every species of animal on earth. In an episode after the flood, Noah is portrayed as having discovered winemaking and becoming helplessly drunk (see Gen. 9:20–27). Noah is said to have lived 950 years (see Gen. 9:29). Similar heroes of flood stories are found in Babylonian, Greek, and other cultures (*see* DEUCALION).

NOBEL, Alfred Bernhard (1833–96), Swedish chemist, inventor, and philanthropist, born in Stockholm. After receiving an education in Saint Petersburg (now Leningrad) and in the U.S., where he studied mechanical engineering, he returned to St. Petersburg to work under his father, developing mines, torpedoes, and other explosives. In a family-owned factory in Heleneborg, Sweden, he sought to develop a safe way to handle nitroglycerin (q.v.), after a factory explosion in 1864 that killed his younger brother and four other people. In 1867 Nobel achieved his goal; by using an organic packing material to reduce the volatility of the nitroglycerin, he produced what he called dynamite. He later produced ballistite, one of the first smokeless powders. At the time of his death he controlled factories for the manufacture of explosives in many parts of the world. His will provided that the major portion of his $9 million estate be set up as a fund to establish yearly prizes for merit in physics, chemistry, medicine and physiology, literature, and world peace. (A prize in economics has been awarded since 1969.) *See* NOBEL PRIZES.

NOBELIUM, metallic, radioactive element, symbol No, member of the actinide series (q.v.) in group IIIb of the periodic table (*see* PERIODIC LAW); at.no. 102, at.wt. of most stable known iso-

tope, 259. Nobelium is not found in nature but is produced artificially in the laboratory. Separate discovery of the element was first claimed in 1957 by scientific groups in the U.S., Great Britain, and Sweden, but the first confirmed discovery, of nobelium-254, took place in 1958 at the Lawrence Radiation Laboratory in Berkeley, Calif. Scientists created the isotope by bombarding curium-244 with carbon-13 ions. A total of nine isotopes are now known; the longest lived, nobelium-259, has a half-life (*see* RADIOACTIVITY) of about 1 hour. The element is named for the Swedish inventor and philanthropist Alfred Bernhard Nobel. Chemically, the properties of nobelium are unknown, but because it is an actinide of the transuranium elements (q.v.), its properties should somewhat resemble those of the rare earth elements.

NOBEL PRIZES, awards granted annually to persons or institutions for outstanding contributions during the year previous to the grant in the fields of physics, chemistry, physiology or medicine, literature, international peace, and economics. The yearly prizes are awarded from the interest accruing from a trust fund provided by the testament of the Swedish inventor and philanthropist Alfred Bernhard Nobel.

According to the will, "The capital (provided by conversion of residue property into money) shall constitute a fund, the interest accruing from which shall be annually awarded in prizes to those persons who shall have contributed most materially to the benefit of mankind during the year immediately preceding. The said interest shall be divided into five equal amounts, to be apportioned as follows: One share to the person who shall have made the most important discovery or invention in the domain of Physics; one share to the person who shall have made the most important Chemical discovery or improvement; one share to the person who shall have made the most important discovery in the domain of Physiology or Medicine; one share to the person who shall have produced the most distinguished work of an idealistic tendency; and finally, one share to the person who shall have done most to promote the Fraternity of Nations and Abolition or Diminution of Standing Armies and the Formation and Increase of Peace Congresses. The prizes for Physics and Chemistry shall be awarded by the Swedish Academy of Science in Stockholm; that for Physiology or Medicine by the Caroline Medico-Surgical Institute in Stockholm; the prize for Literature by the Academy in Stockholm and that for Peace by a Committee of five persons to be elected by the Norwegian Storting. I declare it to be my express

NOBEL PRIZES

NOBEL PRIZE WINNERS

YEAR	LITERATURE	CHEMISTRY	PHYSICS	PHYSIOLOGY OR MEDICINE	PEACE
1901	Sully Prudhomme, René François Armand (Fr.)	Van't Hoff, Jacobus H. (Neth.)	Roentgen, Wilhelm C. (Ger.)	Behring, Emil Adolph von (Ger.)	Dunant, Jean Henri (Switz.); Passy, Frédéric (Fr.)
1902	Mommsen, Theodor (Ger.)	Fischer, Emil H. (Ger.)	Lorentz, Hendrik A. (Neth.); Zeeman, Pieter (Neth.)	Ross, Sir Ronald (G.B.)	Ducommun, Elie (Switz.); Gobat, Charles A. (Switz.)
1903	Björnson, Björnstjerne (Nor.)	Arrhenius, Svante A. (Sw.)	Curie, Pierre (Fr.); Curie, Marie (Fr.); Becquerel, Antoine H. (Fr.)	Finsen, Niels (Den.)	Cremer, Sir William R. (G.B.)
1904	Mistral, Frédéric (Fr.); Echegaray y Eizaguirre, José (Sp.)	Ramsay, Sir William (G.B.)	Rayleigh John W. (G.B.)	Pavlov, Ivan P. (Russ.)	Institute of International Law
1905	Sienkiewicz, Henryk (Pol.)	Baeyer, Adolf von (Ger.)	Lenard, Philipp (Ger.)	Koch, Robert (Ger.)	Suttner, Bertha von (Aust.)
1906	Carducci, Giosuè (It.)	Moissan, Henri (Fr.)	Thomson, Sir Joseph John (G.B.)	Golgi, Camillo (It.); Ramón y Cajal, Santiago (Sp.)	Roosevelt, Theodore (U.S.)
1907	Kipling, Rudyard (G.B.)	Buchner, Eduard (Ger.)	Michelson, Albert A. (U.S.)	Laveran, Charles L.A. (Fr.)	Moneta, Ernesto T. (It.); Renault, Louis (Fr.)
1908	Eucken, Rudolf C. (Ger.)	Rutherford, Ernest (G.B.)	Lippmann, Gabriel (Fr.)	Ehrlich, Paul (Ger.); Metchnikoff, Elie (Russ.)	Arnoldson, Klas P. (Sw.); Bajer, Fredrik (Den.)
1909	Lagerlöf, Selma O.L. (Sw.)	Ostwald, Wilhelm (Ger.)	Marconi, Marchese G. (It.); Braun, Karl F. (Ger.)	Kocher, Emil T. (Switz.)	Beernaert, Auguste M. (Belg.); Estournelles de Constant, Baron d' (Fr.)
1910	Heyse, Paul von (Ger.)	Wallach, Otto (Ger.)	Waals, Johannes D. van der (Neth.)	Kossel, Albrecht (Ger.)	International Peace Bureau
1911	Maeterlinck, Maurice (Belg.)	Curie, Marie (Fr.)	Wien, Wilhelm (Ger.)	Gullstrand, Allvar (Sw.)	Asser, Tobias M.C. (Neth.); Fried, Alfred H. (Aust.)
1912	Hauptmann, Gerhart (Ger.)	Grignard, Victor (Fr.); Sabatier Paul (Fr.)	Dalén, Nils Gustaf (Sw.)	Carrel, Alexis (Fr.)	Root, Elihu (U.S.)
1913	Tagore, Sir Rabindranath (Ind.)	Werner, Alfred (Switz.)	Kamerlingh Onnes, Heike (Neth.)	Richet, Charles R. (Fr.)	Lafontaine, Henri (Belg.)
1914	Not awarded	Richards, Theodore W. (U.S.)	Laue, Max von (Ger.)	Barany, Robert (Aust.)	Not awarded
1915	Rolland, Romain (Fr.)	Willstätter, Richard (Ger.)	Bragg, Sir William Henry (G.B.); Bragg, Sir William L. (G.B.)	Not awarded	Not awarded
1916	Heidenstam, Verner von (Sw.)	Not awarded	Not awarded	Not awarded	Not awarded
1917	Gjellerup, Karl (Den.); Pontoppidan, Henrik (Den.)	Not awarded	Barkla, Charles G. (G.B.)	Not awarded	International Committee of the Red Cross
1918	Not awarded	Haber, Fritz (Ger.)	Planck, Max Karl E.L. (Ger.)	Not awarded	Not awarded
1919	Spitteler, Carl (Switz.)	Not awarded	Stark, Johannes (Ger.)	Bordet, Jules (Belg.)	Wilson, Woodrow (U.S.)
1920	Hamsun, Knut (Nor.)	Nernst, Walther H. (Ger.)	Guillaume, Charles E. (Fr.)	Krogh, (Schack) August (Den.)	Bourgeois, Leon V.A. (Fr.)
1921	France, Anatole (Fr.)	Soddy, Frederick (G.B.)	Einstein, Albert (U.S.)	Not awarded	Branting, Karl H. (Sw.); Lange, Christian L. (Nor.)
1922	Benavente y Martínez, Jacinto (Sp.)	Aston, Francis W. (G.B.)	Bohr, Niels Henrik D. (Den.)	Hill, Archibald V. (G.B.); Meyerhof, Otto (Ger.)	Nansen, Fridtjof (Nor.)
1923	Yeats, William Butler (Ire.)	Pregl, Fritz (Aust.)	Millikan, Robert A. (U.S.)	Banting, Sir Frederick G. (Can.); Macleod, John James R. (G.B.)	Not awarded
1924	Reymont, Wladyslaw S. (Pol.)	Not awarded	Siegbahn, Karl M.G. (Sw.)	Einthoven, Willem (Neth.)	Not awarded
1925	Shaw, George Bernard (G.B.)	Zsigmondy, Richard (Ger.)	Franck, James (Ger.); Hertz, Gustav (Ger.)	Not awarded	Dawes, Charles G. (U.S.); Chamberlain, Sir (Joseph) Austen (G.B.)
1926	Deledda, Grazia (It.)	Svedberg, The (Sw.)	Perrin, Jean Baptiste (Fr.)	Fibiger, Johannes (Den.)	Briand, Aristide (Fr.); Stresemann, Gustav (Ger.)
1927	Bergson, Henri Louis (Fr.)	Wieland, Heinrich O. (Ger.)	Compton, Arthur H. (U.S.); Wilson, Charles T. (G.B.)	Wagner von Jauregg, Julius (Aust.)	Buisson, Ferdinand (Fr.); Quidde, Ludwig (Ger.)
1928	Undset, Sigrid (Nor.)	Windaus, Adolf (Ger.)	Richardson, Sir Owen (G.B.)	Nicolle, Charles Jean H. (Fr.)	Not awarded
1929	Mann, Thomas (Ger.)	Harden, Sir Arthur (G.B.); Euler-Chelpin, Hans von (Sw.)	Broglie, Louis Victor de (Fr.)	Hopkins, Sir Frederick G. (G.B.); Eijkman, Christian (Neth.)	Kellogg, Frank B. (U.S.)
1930	Lewis, Sinclair (U.S.)	Fischer, Hans (Ger.)	Raman, Sir Chandrasekhara (Ind.)	Landsteiner, Karl (U.S.)	Söderblom, Nathan (U.S.)

NOBEL PRIZE WINNERS

YEAR	LITERATURE	CHEMISTRY	PHYSICS	PHYSIOLOGY OR MEDICINE	PEACE
1931	Karlfeldt, Erik Axel (Sw.)	Bosch, Karl (Ger.) Bergius, Friedrich K.R. (Ger.)	Not awarded	Warburg, Otto H. (Ger.)	Addams, Jane (U.S.) Butler, Nicholas M. (U.S.)
1932	Galsworthy, John (G.B.)	Langmuir, Irving (U.S.)	Heisenberg, Werner (Ger.)	Sherrington, Sir Charles S. (G.B.) Adrian, Edgar D. (G.B.)	Not awarded
1933	Bunin, Ivan Alekseevich (USSR)	Not awarded	Dirac, Paul Adrien M. (G.B.) Schrödinger, Erwin (Aust.)	Morgan, Thomas H. (U.S.)	Angell, Sir Norman (G.B.)
1934	Pirandello, Luigi (It.)	Urey, Harold C. (U.S.)	Not awarded	Minot, George R. (U.S.) Murphy, William P. (U.S.) Whipple, George H. (U.S.)	Henderson, Arthur (G.B.)
1935	Not awarded	Joliot-Curie, Irène (Fr.) Joliot-Curie, Frédéric (Fr.)	Chadwick, Sir James (G.B.)	Spemann, Hans (Ger.)	Ossietzky, Carl von (Ger.)
1936	O'Neill, Eugene Gladstone (U.S.)	Debye, Peter Joseph W. (U.S.)	Anderson, Carl D. (U.S.) Hess, Victor F. (Aust.)	Dale, Sir Henry Hallett (G.B.) Loewi, Otto (U.S.)	Saavedra Lamas, Carlos (Arg.)
1937	Martin du Gard, Roger (Fr.)	Haworth, Sir Walter N. (G.B.) Karrer, Paul (Switz.)	Davisson, Clinton J. (U.S.) Thomson, Sir George P. (G.B.)	Szent-Györgyi von Nagyrapolt, Albert (U.S.)	Cecil, Edgar A. (G.B.)
1938	Buck, Pearl (Sydenstricker) (U.S.)	Kuhn, Richard* (Aust.)	Fermi, Enrico (It.)	Heymans, Corneille (Belg.)	Nansen International Office for Refugees
1939	Sillanpää, Frans Eemil (Fin.)	Butenandt, Adolph* (Ger.) Ružička, Leopold (Switz.)	Lawrence, Ernest O. (U.S.)	Domagk, Gerhard* (Ger.)	Not awarded
1940	Not awarded	Not awarded	Not awarded	Not awarded	Not awarded
1941	Not awarded	Not awarded	Not awarded	Not awarded	Not awarded
1942	Not awarded	Not awarded	Not awarded	Not awarded	Not awarded
1943	Not awarded	Hevesy, Georg von (Hung.)	Stern, Otto (U.S.)	Doisy, Edward A. (U.S.) Dam, Carl Peter H. (Den.)	Not awarded
1944	Jensen, Johannes V. (Den.)	Hahn, Otto (Ger.)	Rabi, Isidor I. (U.S.)	Erlanger, Joseph (U.S.) Gasser, Herbert S. (U.S.)	International Committee of the Red Cross
1945	Mistral, Gabriela (Chile)	Virtanen, Artturi I. (Fin.)	Pauli, Wolfgang (U.S.)	Fleming, Sir Alexander (G.B.) Chain, Ernst Boris (G.B.) Florey, Sir Howard W. (G.B.)	Hull, Cordell (U.S.)
1946	Hesse, Hermann (Switz.)	Northrop, John H. (U.S.) Sumner, James B. (U.S.) Stanley, Wendell M. (U.S.)	Bridgman, Percy W. (U.S.)	Muller, Hermann J. (U.S.)	Mott, John R. (U.S.) Balch, Emily G. (U.S.)
1947	Gide, André (Fr.)	Robinson, Sir Robert (G.B.)	Appleton, Sir Edward V. (G.B.)	Cori, Carl F. (U.S.) Cori, Gerty Theresa R. (U.S.) Houssay, Bernardo A. (Arg.)	Friends Service Council (G.B.) American Friends Service Committee (U.S.)
1948	Eliot, T(homas) S(tearns) (G.B.)	Tiselius, Arne V.K. (Sw.)	Blackett, Patrick M.S. (G.B.)	Müller, Paul (Switz.)	Not awarded
1949	Faulkner, William (U.S.)	Giauque, William F. (U.S.)	Yukawa, Hideki (Japan)	Hess, Walter R. (Switz.) Moniz, Antonio C. (Port.)	Boyd Orr, John (G.B.)
1950	Russell, Bertrand A.W. (G.B.)	Diels, Otto Paul H. (W. Ger.) Alder, Kurt (W. Ger.)	Powell, Cecil F. (G.B.)	Hench, Philip S. (U.S.) Kendall, Edward C. (U.S.) Reichstein, Tadeus (Switz.)	Bunche, Ralph J. (U.S.)
1951	Lagerkvist, Pär F. (Sw.)	Seaborg, Glenn T. (U.S.) McMillan, Edwin M. (U.S.)	Cockcroft, Sir John D. (G.B.) Walton, Ernest T.S. (Ire.)	Theiler, Max (S. Afr.)	Jouhaux, Léon (Fr.)
1952	Mauriac, François (Fr.)	Martin, Archer John P. (G.B.) Synge, Richard L.M. (G.B.)	Bloch, Felix (U.S.) Purcell, Edward M. (U.S.)	Waksman, Selman A. (U.S.)	Schweitzer, Albert (Fr.)
1953	Churchill, Sir Winston (G.B.)	Staudinger, Hermann (W. Ger.)	Zernike, Frits (Neth.)	Lipmann, Fritz A. (U.S.) Krebs, Hans Adolf (G.B.)	Marshall George C. (U.S.)
1954	Hemingway, Ernest (U.S.)	Pauling, Linus (U.S.)	Born, Max (W. Ger.) Bothe, Walter (E. Ger.)	Enders, John F. (U.S.) Weller, Thomas H. (U.S.) Robbins, Frederick C. (U.S.)	United Nations High Commissioner for Refugees
1955	Laxness, Halldór Kiljan (Iceland)	Du Vigneaud, Vincent (U.S.)	Lamb, Willis Eugene, Jr. (U.S.) Kusch, Polykarp (U.S.)	Theorell, (Axel) Hugo (Sw.)	Not awarded

YEAR	LITERATURE	CHEMISTRY	PHYSICS	PHYSIOLOGY OR MEDICINE	PEACE
1956	Jiménez, Juan Ramón (Sp.)	Hinshelwood, Sir Cyril (G.B.) Semenov, Nikolai N. (USSR)	Shockley, William B. (U.S.) Brattain, Walter H. (U.S.) Bardeen, John (U.S.)	Richards, Dickinson W. (U.S.) Cournand, André F. (U.S.) Forssmann, Werner (W. Ger.) Bovet, Daniel (It)	Not awarded
1957	Camus, Albert (Fr.)	Todd, Alexander Robertus (G.B.)	Lee, Tsung Dao (U.S.) Yang, Chen Ning (U.S.)		Pearson, Lester B. (Can.)
1958	Pasternak, Boris L.† (USSR)	Sanger, Frederick (G.B.)	Cherenkov, Pavel A. (USSR) Frank, Ilya M. (USSR) Tamm, Igor Y. (USSR)	Beadle, George W. (U.S.) Lederberg, Joshua (U.S.) Tatum, Edward L. (U.S.)	Pire, Dominique G. (Belg.)
1959	Quasimodo, Salvatore (It.)	Heyrovsky, Yaroslav (Czech.)	Segrè, Emilio G. (U.S.) Chamberlain, Owen (U.S.)	Ochoa, Severo (U.S.) Kornberg, Arthur (U.S.)	Noel-Baker, Philip J. (G.B.)
1960	Léger, Alexis Saint-Léger (Fr.)	Libby, Willard F. (U.S.)	Glaser, Donald A. (U.S.)	Burnet, Sir Macfarlane (Austral.) Medawar, Sir Peter B. (G.B.)	Luthuli, Albert J. (S. Afr.)
1961	Andric, Ivo (Yugosl.)	Calvin, Melvin (U.S.)	Hofstadter, Robert (U.S.) Mössbauer, Rudolf L. (W. Ger.)	Békésy, Georg von (U.S.)	Hammarskjöld, Dag (Sw.) Pauling, Linus C. (U.S.)
1962	Steinbeck, John Ernst (U.S.)	Perutz, Max F. (G.B.) Kendrew, John C. (G.B.)	Landau, Lev D. (USSR)	Crick, Francis Harry C. (G.B.) Watson, James D. (U.S.) Wilkins, Maurice H.F. (G.B.)	
1963	Seferiàdes, George (Gr.)	Ziegler, Karl (W. Ger.) Natta, Giulio (It.)	Wigner, Eugene P. (U.S.) Mayer, Maria G. (U.S.) Jensen, Johannes Hans D. (W. Ger.)	Hodgkin, Alan L. (G.B.) Huxley, Andrew F. (G.B.) Eccles, Sir John C. (Austral.)	International Committee of the Red Cross League of Red Cross Societies
1964	Sartre, Jean-Paul† (Fr.)	Hodgkin, Dorothy O. (G.B.)	Townes, Charles H. (U.S.) Basov, Nikolai G. (USSR) Prochorov, Alexander M. (USSR)	Bloch, Konrad E. (U.S.) Lynen, Feodor (W. Ger.)	King, Martin Luther, Jr. (U.S.)
1965	Sholokhov, Mikhail A. (USSR)	Woodward, Robert B. (U.S.)	Schwinger, Julian S. (U.S.) Feynman, Richard P. (U.S.) Tomonaga, Shin'icherō (Japan)	Jacob, François (Fr.) Lwoff, André (Fr.)	United Nations Children's Fund
1966	Agnon, Shmuel Yosef H. (Israel)	Mulliken, Robert S. (U.S.)	Kastler, Alfred (Fr.)	Huggins, Charles B. (U.S.) Rous, (Francis) Peyton (U.S.)	Not awarded
1967	Asturias, Miguel Angel (Guatemala)	Eigen, Manfred (W. Ger.) Norrish, Ronald G.W. (G.B.) Porter, George (G.B.)	Bethe, Hans A. (U.S.)	Granit, Ragnar (Sw.) Hartline, Haldan K. (U.S.) Wald, George (U.S.)	Not awarded
1968	Kawabata Yasunari (Japan)	Onsager, Lars (U.S.)	Alvarez, Luis W. (U.S.)	Holley, Robert William (U.S.) Khorana, Har Gobind (U.S.) Nirenberg, Marshall W. (U.S.)	Cassin, René (Fr.)
1969	Beckett, Samuel (Ire.)	Barton, Derek H.R. (G.B.) Hassel, Odd (Nor.)	Gell-Mann, Murray (U.S.)	Delbrück, Max (U.S.) Hershey, Alfred D. (U.S.) Luria, Salvador E. (U.S.)	International Labor Organization (U.S.)
1970	Solzhenitzyn, Aleksandr I. (USSR)	Leloir, Luis Federico (Arg.)	Alfvén Hannes O.G. (Sw.) Néel, Louis Eugène F. (Fr.)	Axelrod, Julius (U.S.) Euler, Ulf S. von (Sw.) Katz, Sir Bernard (G.B.)	Borlaug, Norman E. (U.S.)
1971 1972	Neruda, Pablo (Chile) Böll, Heinrich (W. Ger.)	Herzberg, Gerhard (Can.) Moore, Stanford (U.S.) Stein, William H. (U.S.)	Gabor, Dennis (G.B.) Bardeen, John (U.S.) Cooper, Leon N. (U.S.) Schrieffer, John R. (U.S.)	Sutherland, Earl Wilbur, Jr. (U.S.) Edelman, Gerald M. (U.S.) Porter, Rodney R. (G.B.)	Brandt, Willy (W. Ger.) Not awarded
1973	White, Patrick V.M. (Austral.)	Anfinsen, Christian B. (U.S.) Fischer, Ernst O. (W. Ger.) Wilkinson, Geoffrey (G.B.)	Esaki, Leo (Japan) Giaever, Ivar (U.S.) Josephson, Brian D. (G.B.)	Frisch, Karl von (W. Ger.) Lorenz, Konrad (Aust.) Tinbergen, Niko(laas) (Neth.)	Kissinger, Henry A. (U.S.) Tho, Le Duct (N. Vietnam)
1974	Johnson, Eyvind (Sw.) Martinson, Harry (Sw.)	Flory, Paul J. (U.S.)	Hewish, Antony (G.B.) Ryle, Sir Martin (G.B.)	Claude, Albert (U.S.) de Duve, Christian (Belg.) Palade, George E. (U.S.)	MacBride, Sean (Ire.) Sato Eisaku (Japan)
1975	Montale, Eugenio (It.)	Cornforth, John W. (Austral.) Prelog, Vladimir (Switz.)	Bohr, Aage N. (Den.) Mottelson, Ben R. (Den.) Rainwater, James (U.S.)	Baltimore, David (U.S.) Dulbecco, Renato (U.S.) Temin, Howard M. (U.S.)	Sakharov, Andrei (USSR)

NOBEL PRIZE WINNERS

YEAR	LITERATURE	CHEMISTRY	PHYSICS	PHYSIOLOGY OR MEDICINE	PEACE
1976	Bellow, Saul (U.S.)	Lipscomb, William N., Jr. (U.S.)	Richter, Burton (U.S.) Ting, Samuel C.C. (U.S.)	Blumberg, Baruch S. (U.S.) Gajdusek, Daniel C. (U.S.)	Corrigan, Mairead (Ire.) Williams, Betty (Ire.)
1977	Aleixandre, Vincente (Sp.)	Prigogine, Ilya (Belg.)	Anderson, Philip W. (U.S.) Mott, Sir Nevill F. (G.B.) Van Vleck, John H. (U.S.)	Yalow, Rosalynn Sussman (U.S.) Guillemin, Roger (U.S.) Schally, Andrew (U.S.)	Amnesty International
1978	Singer, Isaac Bashevis (U.S.)	Mitchell, Peter (G.B.)	Penzias, Arno A. (U.S.) Wilson, Robert W. (U.S.) Kapitza, Peter Leonidovich (USSR)	Nathans, Daniel (U.S.) Smith, Hamilton O. (U.S.) Arber, Werner (Switz.)	Begin, Menachem (Israel) Sadat, Anwar al- (Egypt)
1979	Elytis, Odysseus (Gr.)	Brown, Herbert C. (U.S.) Wittig, Georg (W. Ger.)	Weinberg, Steven (U.S.) Glashow, Sheldon L. (U.S.) Salam, Abdus (Pak.)	Cormack, Allan McLeod (U.S.) Newbold, Godfrey (G.B.)	Mother Teresa (India)
1980	Miłosz, Czeslaw (U.S.)	Berg, Paul (U.S.) Gilbert, Walter (U.S.) Sanger, Frederick (G.B.)	Cronin, James W. (U.S.) Fitch, Val L. (U.S.)	Dausset, Jean (Fr.) Snell, George (U.S.) Benacerraf, Baruj (U.S.)	Pérez Esquivel, Adolfo (Arg.)
1981	Canetti, Elias (G.B.)	Fukui, Kenichi (Jap.) Hoffmann, Roald (U.S.)	Bloembergen, Nicolaas (U.S.) Schawlow, Arthur Leonard (U.S.) Siegbahn, Kai (Sw.)	Hubel, David H. (U.S.) Sperry, Roger W. (U.S.) Wiesel, Torsten N. (Sw.)	Office of the UN High Commissioner for Refugees
1982	Garcia Márquez, Gabriel (Col.)	Klug, Aaron (G.B.)	Wilson, Kenneth G. (U.S.)	Bergstrom, Sune K. (Sw.) Samuelsson, Bengt I. (Sw.) Vane, John R. (G.B.)	Myrdal, Alva (Sw.) Garcia Robles, Alfonso (Mex.)
1983	Golding, William (G.B.)	Taube, Henry (U.S.)	Chandrasekhar, Subrahmanyan (U.S.) Fowler, William A. (U.S.)	McClintock, Barbara (U.S.)	
1984	Seifert, Jaroslav (Czech.)	Merrifield, R. Bruce (U.S.)	Rubbia, Carlo (It.) van der Meer, Simon (Neth.)	Jerne, Niels K. (Den.-G.B.) Kohler, Georges J. F. (W. Ger.) Milstein, Cesar (Arg.-G.B.)	

An asterisk (*) indicates that the cash prize was originally declined by the Nobelist; the medal and diploma alone were awarded to Gerhard Domagk in 1947 and to Richard Kuhn and Adolph Butenandt in 1949.
A dagger (†) indicates that the prize was declined by the Nobelist but he remained listed as the winner of the award.

Top row, left to right: Obverse of the medals for physics and chemistry, medicine or physiology, and literature; reverse of the medals for physics and chemistry; reverse of the medal for medicine or physiology. Bottom row, left to right: reverse of the medal for literature; reverse of the medal for peace; obverse of the medal for peace.
Swedish Information Service

desire that, in the awarding of prizes, no consideration whatever be paid to the nationality of the candidates, that is to say, that the most deserving be awarded the prize, whether of Scandinavian origin or not."

The fund is controlled by the board of directors of the Nobel Foundation, which serves for 2-year periods and consists of five members: four elected by representatives of the awarding bodies mentioned in the will, and the fifth appointed by the Swedish government. In addition to a cash award, each winner also receives a gold medal and a diploma bearing his or her name and field of achievement. The judges often have divided the prize for achievement in a particular field among two or three persons. Prizes may also be withheld for a year, but if not distributed, the money reverts to the original fund. To further the purposes of the foundation, separate institutes have been established, in accordance with Nobel's will, in Sweden and Norway for advancement of each of the five original fields for which the prizes are awarded. The first Nobel Prizes were awarded on Dec. 10, 1901.

In 1969, to commemorate its 300th anniversary, the national bank of Sweden endowed the Alfred Nobel Memorial Prize in economics, to be awarded, as are the other prizes, by the Swedish Academy of Science.

NOBEL PRIZE WINNERS IN ECONOMICS	
1969	Frisch, Ragnar (Nor.)
	Tinbergen, Jan (Neth.)
1970	Samuelson, Paul A. (U.S.)
1971	Kuznets, Simon (U.S.)
1972	Hicks, Sir John R. (G.B.)
	Arrow, Kenneth J. (U.S.)
1973	Leontief, Wassily (U.S.)
1974	von Hayek, F. A. (Aust.)
	Myrdal, Gunnar (Sw.)
1975	Kantorovich, Leonid (USSR)
	Koopmans, T.C. (U.S.)
1976	Friedman, Milton (U.S.)
1977	Meade, James (G.B.)
	Ohlin, Bertil (Sw.)
1978	Simon, Herbert A. (U.S.)
1979	Schultz, Theodore W. (U.S.)
	Lewis, Arthur (U.S.)
1980	Klein, Lawrence R. (U.S.)
1981	Tobin, James (U.S.)
1982	Stigler, George J. (U.S.)
1983	Debreu, Gerard (U.S.)
1984	Stone, Richard (G.B.)

On the accompanying pages are the names of the Nobel Prize winners in the five categories. See also articles on individual recipients.

For further information on this topic, see the Bibliography in volume 28, section 1.

NOBILITY, body of persons within a state possessing various special hereditary privileges, rights, and honors, including titles; an aristocratic or patrician class. The nobilities of the various modern states of Europe came into existence when feudalism (q.v.), a social system based on land tenure, succeeded the imperial government of Rome after the Germanic invasions. During the unsettled social and economic conditions that followed the fall of the Roman Empire, some men acquired land, usually by conquest. These men then granted parts of their holdings to others, over whom they thereafter exercised certain rights, including taxation and the administration of justice, 'and from whom they were entitled to various services. Those who granted the land were known as lords and those who accepted it were known as vassals. The lords of a nation formed its nobility, their rank depending on the extent of their possessions. The preposition *de* in the names of French nobles and *von* in the names of German nobles (both meaning "of" or "from") express the idea of land ownership that is fundamental to the feudal concept of nobility.

Since the French Revolution the tendency in European countries has been strongly toward the abolition of hereditary titles. In France the nobility was first deprived of its special rights and privileges, and then, in 1790, all hereditary titles were abolished by decree. Napoleon, however, created a new nobility, granting titles and estates to those who had served him well, especially in military affairs. After Napoleon's downfall Louis XVIII, king of France, restored to the prerevolutionary nobility its former privileges, rights, and honors. The Second Republic (1848–52) once more abolished nobility in France, but Napoleon III restored the aristocratic class. Under the Third Republic (1871–1945) the nobility was once more abolished. In contemporary France, persons who have inherited titles may use them as part of their family name, but they possess none of the special rights or honors of the former nobility. In Germany titles of nobility existed from early medieval times until they were abolished when the region became a republic in 1918; after 1918, members of the former nobility were permitted to use titles only as part of a name. In Russia titles of nobility similar to those of the nations of Western Europe were instituted by Emperor Peter I; all such titles were abolished by the Revolution of 1917. In Spain titles of nobility still exist. Members of the higher nobility bear the title of grandee; the lesser nobles are known as *los titulados de Castilla*. In Italy, Belgium, and Portugal, only courtesy titles exist.

In Great Britain the sovereign still grants titles of nobility. The British nobility is divided into an upper nobility and a lower nobility. The upper consists of all those who hold a hereditary rank above that of a baronet; it includes those with titles of duke, marquis, earl, viscount, and baron. Among the lower nobility are those holding the rank of baronet, knight, and esquire. The upper nobility makes up the British peerage, and its members have the right to hereditary seats in the House of Lords. Life peers can also be created. They hold the rank for their own lives only; the title does not descend to their children. The Appellate Jurisdiction Act of 1876 gave the Crown the right to give judges the rank of lord of appeal and grant them life peerages. The Life Peerages Act of 1958 gave the Crown the right to create other life peers besides judges, and about ten are now created each year. All life peers have the right to vote in the House of Lords.

No nobility exists in the U.S.; Article I, Section 9, of the U.S. Constitution specifies that no title of nobility shall be granted by the U.S., and in addition it forbids any person holding government office from accepting any such title from a foreign ruler without the express consent of Congress. A private American citizen who accepts a title of nobility automatically resigns his or her citizenship.

NOBLE GASES, also inert gases, group of six gaseous chemical elements constituting the 0 group of the periodic table (*see* PERIODIC LAW). They are, in order of increasing atomic weight, helium, neon, argon, krypton, xenon, and radon (qq.v.).

For many years chemists believed that these gases, because their outermost shells were completely filled with electrons, were inert—that is, that they would not enter into chemical combinations with other elements or compounds. This is now known not to be true, at least for the three heaviest inert gases—krypton, xenon, and radon. In 1962, Neil Bartlett (1932–), a British chemist working in Canada, succeeded in making the first complex xenon compound. His work was confirmed by scientists at Argonne National Laboratory in Illinois, who made the first simple compound of xenon and fluorine (xenon tetrafluoride) and later succeeded in making radon and krypton compounds. Although krypton compounds were made with considerable difficulty, both xenon and radon reacted readily with fluorine, and additional reactions to produce other compounds of xenon and radon could be accomplished.

The forces between the outermost electrons of these three elements and their nuclei are diluted by distance and the interference of other electrons. The energy gained in creating a xenon or radon fluoride is greater than the energy required for promotion of the reaction, and the compounds are chemically stable, although xenon fluorides and oxides are powerful oxidizing agents. The usefulness of radon compounds is limited because radon itself is radioactive and has a half-life of 3.82 days. The energy gain is also greater in the case of krypton, but only slightly so. Compounds of helium, neon, or argon, the electrons of which are more closely bound to their nuclei, are unlikely to be created.

NŌ DRAMA. *See* JAPANESE DRAMA.

NOETHER, (Amalie) Emmy (1882–1935), German mathematician, noted for her work in abstract algebra. Born of a mathematical family, she audited university courses because at that time women were not allowed to attend German universities; nevertheless she was granted a Ph.D. in 1907 by the University of Erlangen. When the Nazis came to power, Noether went to the U.S., where she lectured at Bryn Mawr College and the Institute for Advanced Study at Princeton, N.J. Her work on the theory of invariants was used by Albert Einstein in formulating some of his relativistic concepts.

NOGUCHI, Hideyo (1876–1928), Japanese bacteriologist, who was the first to obtain pure cultures of *Trepanema pallidum,* the spirochete that causes syphilis, and to demonstrate the syphilitic origin of certain forms of general paralysis. Born in Fukushima and educated at Tokyo Medical College, he immigrated to the U.S. in 1901 and studied and taught in the pathology laboratory of the University of Pennsylvania from 1901 to 1903. The following year he joined the staff of the Rockefeller Institute for Medical Research (now Rockefeller University) in New York City, becoming a member of the institute in 1914. He developed one of the first tests to diagnose syphilis and made important contributions to the study of other infectious diseases. Noguchi died of yellow fever while studying the disease in Africa. He was knighted by the kings of Spain and Denmark in 1913 and by the king of Sweden in 1914; he was awarded the Japanese Order of Merit in 1915.

NOGUCHI, Isamu (1904–), American sculptor, son of the poet Yone Noguchi (1875–1947), born in Los Angeles, and educated at Columbia University. In 1927–28 he worked in the Paris studio of the Romanian sculptor Constantin Brancusi. He then traveled and studied in England, China, and Mexico. He won the national competition to decorate the Associated Press Building in Rockefeller Center, New York City, with a huge relief sculpture of stainless steel, executed in 1938. During his voluntary internment in a California nisei camp during World War II, Noguchi continued to experiment with materials and forms. He also carved the graceful marble *Kouros* (1944–45,

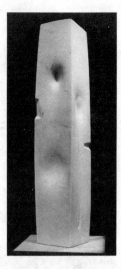

Integral, *by Isamu Noguchi, made of Greek marble, is in the Whitney Museum, New York City.* Collection of Whitney Museum of American Art, New York

Metropolitan Museum, New York City), an abstract interpretation of archaic Greek sculpture. After the war he designed stage sets and costumes for the modern dancer Martha Graham, and for George Balanchine's New York City Ballet. Noguchi's works characteristically present polished abstract forms that blend subtle Oriental respect for materials with the most refined sophistication of Western art. After 1950 his largest projects were outdoor spaces, designed on the aesthetic principles of Japanese gardens, in which large abstract sculptures were precisely sited to achieve balanced relationships between them, their defined space or garden, and the architecture surrounding them. Outstanding examples are the Garden of Peace (1956–58, UNESCO Building, Paris), the Water Garden (1964–65, Chase Manhattan Bank Plaza, New York City), and the Billy Rose Art Garden (1965, Jerusalem). Throughout his career Noguchi has also designed interior furnishings, including his extremely popular paper lamps in a variety of forms.

NOLAND, Kenneth (1924–), American abstract painter. Working principally in the medium of thinned acrylic paint applied directly to raw canvas, he produces paintings whose brilliantly juxtaposed colors create a sense of optical vibration. His main motifs are concentric circles, diagonal chevrons, and long parallel stripes, often including large blank areas of canvas. He is known for his unusual diamond-shaped and elongated rectangular canvases.

NOLDE, Emil (1867–1956), one of the foremost German expressionist painters, whose masklike heads, contorted brushwork, and raw, strident colors were intended to give the viewer a visual

A prospector extracts gold from alluvium during the Nome, Alaska, gold rush.　　　Bettmann Archive

and emotional shock. His original name was Emil Hansen. Nolde was influenced primarily by Vincent van Gogh, Edvard Munch, and James Ensor, whose tortured visions and color experiments he carried to new frontiers. A trip to New Guinea in 1913–14 crystallized his taste for the primitive, for brutal distortions of form, and for contrasting colors. His style changed little throughout his career, and he concentrated principally on landscapes and on interior scenes with human figures. His landscapes, such as *March* (1916, Kunstmuseum, Basel), were brooding and ominous, and his peopled scenes, such as *The Reveler* (1919, Städtische Gallerie, Hanover), present human faces as grotesque masks of crude basic emotions. In works such as the triptych *Life of Maria Aegyptica* (1912, Kunsthalle, Hamburg), he attempted to revive religious imagery in expressionistic treatments of New Testament scenes. He also produced an important body of expressionist watercolors and engravings.

NOME, city, S Seward Peninsula, NW Alaska, a port on Norton Sound (an arm of the Bering Sea); inc. 1900. It is a commercial, transportation, and tourist center of a mining region noted for its gold production. The city's Inuit (Eskimo) inhabitants produce a variety of handicrafts for sale. The community was founded during the rush of prospectors to the area following the discovery of gold at nearby Anvil Creek in 1898. It was called Anvil City until 1900, when it was renamed for nearby Cape Nome; in that year it had some 20,000 inhabitants, but the population decreased drastically in the following years. The city was badly damaged by fire in 1905 and 1934. Gold mining in the region was revived in the late 1970s. Pop. (1970) 2357; (1980) 2301.

NOMINALISM (Lat. *nominalis,* "of or pertaining to names"), in medieval Scholastic philosophy, doctrine that abstractions, known as *universals,* are without essential or substantive reality, and that only individual objects have real existence.

These universals, such as *animal, nation, beauty, circle,* were held to be mere names, hence the term *nominalism.* For example, the name *circle* is applied to things that are round and is thus a general designation; but no concrete identity with a separate essence of roundness exists corresponding to the name. The nominalistic doctrine is opposed to the philosophical theory called extreme realism (*see* REALISM), according to which universals have a real and independent existence prior to and apart from particular objects regardless of whether any mind is aware of them or knows about them.

Nominalism evolved from the thesis of Aristotle that all reality consists of individual things; the extreme theory of realism was first enunciated by Plato in his doctrine of universal archetypal ideas. The nominalist-realist controversy became prominent in the late 11th and 12th centuries, the nominalist position being expounded by the Scholastic Roscelin, and the realist by the Scholastics Bernard of Chartres (d. about 1130) and William of Champeaux (c. 1070–1121).

The issue between nominalism and realism was not only philosophical but also theological, for Roscelin maintained that the Trinity (Father, Son, and Holy Spirit), conceived in the traditional theology of the church as constituting a unity of one divine nature, cannot be understood, according to the individualizing method of nominalism, except as three distinct and separate gods, a doctrine known as tritheism. The church was therefore irreconcilably opposed to nominalism. The implications for ethics were also far-reaching. If there is no common nature for all individuals, then there is no "natural law" that governs all people; actions are morally right or wrong not because they are in accordance with or against human nature but only because they are commanded or forbidden by God.

A theory intermediate between nominalism and realism is that of conceptualism, in which universals, although they have no real or substantive existence in the external world, do exist as ideas or concepts in the mind and are thus something more than mere names. Another alternative theory is moderate realism, which locates universals in the mind but also admits a real basis in particular objects. The defense of nominalism undertaken by the 14th-century English Scholastic philosopher William of Ockham prepared the way for various modern nominalistic theories such as those of instrumentalism, pragmatism, semantics, and logical positivism.

See also SCHOLASTICISM.   J.D.C.

NOMINATION, in politics, the formal selection and presentation of a candidate for an elective office. Four principal methods of nomination have been used in the U.S.: nomination by political convention, by primary election, by caucus, and by petition. Before 1800 candidates for office were nominated at caucuses of leading citizens. By 1800 members of Congress chose candidates for president and vice-president in party caucuses, which enabled them to control party policy. Local party leaders, however, resented such concentration of power in Congress and insisted upon sharing in the selection of major candidates. Beginning in 1831 the system of nominating presidential and vice-presidential candidates at conventions became standard procedure, with delegates from local party organizations convening periodically for this purpose.

NONALIGNED NATIONS, loose association of countries that have no formal commitment to either of the two power blocs in the world, led by the U.S. and the Soviet Union. It consists of mostly developing non-Western nations, with a broad spectrum of political institutions, ranging from leftist to ultraconservative and from democratic to dictatorial. The formation of the group may be traced to the division of the world into Communist and capitalist blocs after World War II and the subsequent end of colonialism; it was initiated by leaders of countries that had been recently freed of foreign control and rejected renewed ties to any big power. Prominent among these leaders were Prime Minister Jawaharlal Nehru of India and Presidents Sukarno of Indonesia, Gamal Abdel Nasser of Egypt, Kwame Nkrumah of Ghana, Sékou Touré of Guinea, and Tito of Yugoslavia.

Nonalignment is distinct from neutrality in that it implies an active participation in international affairs and judgment of issues on their merits rather than from predetermined positions. Thus, a large majority of the nonaligned nations opposed the U.S. during the Vietnam War and the USSR after its invasion of Afghanistan. In practice, however, many nonaligned nations lean heavily toward one or the other of the power blocs, and their claim to nonalignment is challenged. The absence of a formal alliance is a fundamental element for acceptance in the group. The nonaligned nations see themselves as an important buffer between the power blocs, decreasing the possibility of a major confrontation. Any pretension of being a "force," however, is tempered by their weaknesses, both economic and military, that have necessitated foreign assistance, at times on a large scale.   S.B.

NONCONFORMISTS, name given to sectarian English Protestants who have refused to conform to the regulations governing ceremonies and doctrines of the Church of England. It is used in a restricted sense to denote the clergy who were ejected from the Church of England in 1662 for their refusal to submit to the conditions of the Act of Uniformity; the act required that all clergy in England receive Episcopal reordination regardless of what Protestant sect they belonged to before this act.

NONO, Luigi (1924–), Italian composer, known for his advanced techniques and his musical expressions of political convictions. Born in Venice, he studied with the Italian composers Gian Francesco Malipiero and Bruno Maderna (1920–). Nono won international acclaim for his twelve-tone cantata *Il canto sospeso* (The Suspended Song, 1956). In the 1960s he turned to electronic music. To denounce exploitation of the working class he used recordings made in iron foundries for the mixed-media work *La fabbrica illuminata* (The Illuminated Factory, 1964). His opera *Intolleranza* (1960; rev. 1970), dedicated to his father-in-law, the Austrian composer Arnold Schoenberg, protests an inhuman political system.

NOOTKA, group of closely related North American Indian tribes constituting one of the two major divisions of the Wakashan stock, the other being the Kwakiutl. The Nootka inhabit the west coast of Vancouver Island in southern British Colombia. They are maritime tribes with an economy based chiefly on fishing. Their principal food is salmon, which is smoked for storage. Whaling was practiced in the past. The Nootka hunt deer and mountain goats and gather berries. They live in permanent villages of long, rectangular, cedar plank houses, each accommodating several families. Cedar is also used to make boxes, and canoes are hollowed out of cedar tree trunks. Carved and painted totem poles are made from logs and erected in front of the houses as heraldic posts. Bark and root mats and baskets are manufactured. Clothing formerly was made of skins and bark or was woven from the hair of dogs and mountain goats. Nephrite, a form of jade, was widely used in the making of ceremonial and utilitarian objects, and the possession of copper plaques is still important as a measure of wealth and prestige.

Nootka religion is celebrated in elaborate winter ceremonies, characterized by the custom of the potlatch in which the host distributes gifts to guests. Nootka dead are placed in boxes secured high in the trees. The leaders of the Nootka hold power through hereditary rank. Prestige depends on displays of wealth and lavish distributions of gifts. Social rivalry is important in the life of these tribes, and fame is acquired or increased com-

petitively, according to the number of celebrations provided by an individual and the lavishness in bestowing property. The Nootka formerly numbered about 6000; they now total about 1600.

NORAD, acronym for North American Air Defense Command. *See* DEFENSE SYSTEMS.

NORDENSKJÖLD, (Nils) Adolf Erik, Baron (1832–1901), Swedish explorer, geographer, and geologist. He led the first successful navigation of the Northeast Passage (q.v.). In the mid-19th century he made several expeditions to the island of Spitsbergen, off the coast of Norway, producing valuable geological information. His expedition through the Northeast Passage began in July 1878, when his ship, the *Vega,* steamed out of Tromsø, Norway, and headed northeast into the Arctic Ocean. From September until July 1879, the ship was iced near the Bering Strait; it reached Alaska on July 22, returning to Stockholm in April 1880 via China, Ceylon (now Sri Lanka), and the Suez Canal. In 1883 he was the first to break the ice barriers off the southeast coast of Greenland.

NORDENSKJÖLD, (Nils) Otto Gustaf (1869–1928), Swedish geographer and explorer. A nephew of the explorer Adolf Erik, Baron Nordenskjöld, he made important expeditions to both the north and south polar regions. In 1895–97 an expedition to Patagonia and Tierra del Fuego resulted in significant new knowledge of glacial geology. In October 1901 he sailed on the *Antarctic* to Snow Island, off the Graham Coast of Antarctica, from where he explored and surveyed many previously unknown areas, and where he spent the winter of 1902–03, after his ship was crushed in the pack ice.

NORDHAUSEN, city, W East Germany, in Erfurt District, on the Zorge R., near the city of Erfurt. Manufactures include textiles, machinery, and glass. Founded by 1000, Nordhausen was a free city from the mid-13th century until 1803, when it became part of Prussia. During World War II, the city was the site of a notorious German concentration camp and one of the largest underground V-2 rocket plants in Germany. About 50 percent of the city was destroyed during the war. Pop. (1980 est.) 46,691.

NORDIC COUNCIL, common advisory council of the Nordic countries (Denmark, Finland, Iceland, Norway, and Sweden), consisting of parliamentary delegations and appointed cabinet representatives of each. It was founded in Copenhagen in 1953 by Denmark, Iceland, Norway, and Sweden; Finland joined in 1956. The council holds annual sessions of five to ten days (there have also been special sessions) in the five Scandinavian capitals on a strict rotation basis. Of the 78 elected representatives, Denmark has 16, Finland 17, Iceland 6, and Norway and Sweden 18 each. The Faeroe Islands are represented by 2 members, and Ahvenanmaa (Åland Islands) by 1. Members serve for one session only but may be reelected. The council's work falls mainly in the social, economic, and cultural (including communications) fields, its main objectives being to increase inter-Scandinavian cooperation and to coordinate national laws and practices. Resolutions take the form of recommendations to the five governments and are usually acted upon favorably.

NORDKYN, CAPE. *See* NORTH CAPE.

NORD-OSTSEE KANAL, also Kiel Canal, artificial waterway, N West Germany, linking the North Sea and the Baltic Sea. The canal extends in a NE direction across the state of Schleswig-Holstein from Brunsbüttelkoog, near the mouth of the Elbe R., to Kiel, on the Baltic. Constructed between 1887 and 1895 and subsequently enlarged, it is about 97 km (about 60 mi) long, 102 m (335 ft) wide, and 11 m (36 ft) deep. The canal shortened the distance between the North and Baltic seas by about 322 km (about 200 mi) and eliminated the difficult passage around Jutland. It was internationalized by the Treaty of Versailles in 1919.

NORFOLK, county, E England; Norwich is the administrative center. Norfolk comprises a lowland area bounded on the N and E by the North Sea. It is primarily agricultural, producing grains, vegetables, and flower bulbs; livestock and poultry raising are also important. Norwich is the county's principal manufacturing center and Great Yarmouth the chief resort and fishing port. The area was included in the Anglo-Saxon kingdom of East Anglia. During the Middle Ages Norfolk had a thriving wool industry. Area, 5368 sq km (2073 sq mi); pop. (1981) 693,490.

NORFOLK, independent city, SE Virginia; founded 1682, inc. as a borough 1736, as a city 1845. It is situated at the mouth of the James, Elizabeth, and Nansemond rivers, near the outlet of Chesapeake Bay on the Atlantic Ocean; with the cities of Portsmouth and Newport News it forms the port of Hampton Roads (q.v.), one of the greatest natural harbors in the world.

Norfolk is a major national seaport and an important military center, having one of the world's largest concentrations of naval installations as well as important U.S. Marine, Coast Guard, and NATO facilities. An Armed Forces Staff College is also here. The Norfolk Naval Shipyard is across the Elizabeth R., in Portsmouth. A network of railroads and highways converge on the Norfolk-Portsmouth Harbor, making it the leading grain-

Vessels anchored in Hampton Roads, at the U.S. Naval Base in Norfolk, Va., one of the world's largest naval installations. Norfolk Convention & Visitors Bureau

shipping point on the East Coast. Combined with Newport News, it is one of the world's largest coal-exporting ports. Norfolk has shipbuilding, automobile-assembling, chemical, plastic, and food-processing industries. It has an international airport and is linked to the Delmarva Peninsula by the 28-km (17-mi) long Chesapeake Bay Bridge-Tunnel (1964).

Norfolk is the seat of Old Dominion University (1930), Norfolk State University (1935), Virginia Wesleyan College (1961), and Eastern Virginia Medical School (1964). The city is also the site of the Chrysler Museum.

Nearby are many of the state's notable ocean recreation areas. Norfolk's tourist attractions include the extensive Gardens-by-the-Sea, an annual International Azalea Festival, and the Douglas MacArthur Memorial, a restored 1850 courthouse that includes the general's burial crypt.

The town was laid out in 1682. Its early growth was based on the West Indies trade and the shipping of products from the plantations of Virginia and North Carolina. During the American Revolution it suffered both a British naval bombardment (early 1776) and an attack by colonial troops (it had been a rallying point for Tory forces); every building except Saint Paul's Church (1739) was destroyed. Rebuilt after the war, Norfolk became an important shipbuilding and maritime center. A severe epidemic of yellow fever in 1855, however, seriously retarded its development. It was captured by Union forces early in the American Civil War (May 1862). Its enormous military growth began during World War I. The city is named for Norfolk, England. Pop. (1970) 307,951; (1980) 266,979.

NORFOLK, John Howard, 1st Duke of, also known as Jack of Norfolk (c. 1430–85), English nobleman and military commander, who took part, on the Yorkist side, in the Wars of the Roses (*see* ROSES, WARS OF THE). He was knighted by King Edward IV shortly after his accession in 1461, and although he was created a baron by the Lancastrian Henry VI on his restoration in 1470, Howard did not abandon the Yorkist cause; he fought in France for King Edward in 1475. Upon Edward's death in 1483, however, he supported Edward's younger brother, Richard, duke of Gloucester, later King Richard III, who usurped the throne from Edward's son. Richard III made Howard duke of Norfolk and earl marshal of England in 1483. He was killed with Richard in the battle at Bosworth. *See* BOSWORTH FIELD, BATTLE OF.

NORFOLK, Thomas Howard, 2d Duke of (1443–1524), English military commander and courtier, the only son of John Howard, 1st duke of Norfolk. He was created earl of Surrey in 1483 when his father was made duke of Norfolk. At the Battle of Bosworth Field, where his father was killed, he was wounded and taken prisoner. As he had fought on the losing side, his titles were attainted and he was imprisoned until 1489. On his release his earldom was restored; he was placed in command of the defense of the Scottish border and soon recognized as the chief general in England. In 1513 he led the forces that defeated the invading Scots at Flodden Field (q.v.), and in the following year he became duke of Norfolk. When King Henry VIII went to the Field of the Cloth of Gold in 1520, Norfolk was left to guard the kingdom. The following year he presided at the trial for treason of his friend Edward Stafford, 3d duke of Buckingham, on whom he passed a sentence of death. He retired in 1523.

NORFOLK, Thomas Howard, 3d Duke of (1473–1554), English nobleman and court intriguer, the eldest son of Thomas Howard, 2d duke of Norfolk. He commanded the English vanguard at Flodden Field (q.v.) and was made earl when his father regained the family dukedom. On the death of his father he succeeded to the dukedom and became the most powerful peer in England. Norfolk led the party opposed to the policies of the lord chancellor, Cardinal Thomas Wolsey. He favored Henry VIII's divorce from Catherine of Aragón and his marriage to Anne Boleyn, who was Norfolk's niece. As Henry's pliant tool, however, he also presided at Anne's trial and execution in 1536. That same year he repressed the rebellion of the Pilgrimage of Grace, a protest against the confiscation of monastic properties, from which he profited handsomely. In 1540 Norfolk arrested Henry's secretary, Thomas Cromwell, earl of Essex, who had lost favor with the king. With the execution of his niece, Catherine Howard, Henry's fifth wife, in 1542, Norfolk lost his influence at court. When his son, the poet Henry Howard, earl of Surrey, was arrested for treason, Norfolk was charged with complicity; and was condemned and attainted with his son. His son was executed in 1547, but the subsequent death of the king prevented Norfolk's execution. He remained a prisoner until the accession of Mary I in 1533, when his lands and titles were restored.

NORFOLK, Thomas Howard, 4th Duke of (1536–72), English soldier and politician, son of Henry Howard, earl of Surrey. Thomas inherited the dukedom from his grandfather the 3d duke of Norfolk. In 1559 he commanded an English army sent to Scotland, and in 1568 he became president of the commission appointed by Elizabeth

I, queen of England, to investigate the affairs of Mary, queen of Scots. The following year he was arrested and imprisoned, by order of Elizabeth, for plotting to marry Mary, who was at that time in his custody. After his release in 1570 he began negotiations with Philip II of Spain in regard to a plan for a Spanish invasion of England. The plot was discovered in 1571, and he was arrested and beheaded the following year.

NORFOLK ISLAND, island, SW Pacific Ocean, located E of Australia and administered as an Australian external territory. Kingston, a popular tourist center for Australians and New Zealanders, is the chief settlement and main port. Grain, vegetables, fruit, and flowers are produced on the island. Norfolk Island was discovered in 1774 by the English explorer Capt. James Cook. It was a British penal colony from 1788 to 1813 and again from 1825 to 1855. Descendants of the HMS *Bounty* (q.v.) mutineers were relocated here in 1856 from Pitcairn Island. Norfolk Island was separated from New South Wales and made an Australian territory in 1913. Area, about 34 sq km (about 13 sq mi); pop. (1981 est.) 2175.

NORMAL, town, McLean Co., central Illinois, adjoining Bloomington; inc. 1865. It has an economy based largely on the huge Illinois State University, founded in 1857 as Illinois State Normal University (from which the town's name is derived). Manufactures include rubber, wood, and paper products. The community was founded about 1850 and grew with the school. Pop. (1970) 26,396; (1980) 35,672.

NORMAL SCHOOLS. *See* TEACHER TRAINING.

NORMAN, city, seat of Cleveland Co., central Oklahoma; inc. as a city 1902. It is the seat of the University of Oklahoma (1890) and the commercial center of an agricultural area. Manufactures include electric appliances, health-food supplements, and oil-field equipment. Nearby Lake Thunderbird is a local recreation center. The community, founded in 1889 during the Oklahoma land rush, is named for its surveyor, Abner E. Norman. Pop. (1970) 52,117; (1980) 68,020.

NORMAN ARCHITECTURE, building style developed by the Normans in the Middle Ages in northern France, England, southern Italy, and Sicily. *See* ROMANESQUE ART AND ARCHITECTURE.

NORMAN CONQUEST. *See* ENGLAND: *History.*

NORMANDY, region and former province of France, bordering on the English Channel. In area it corresponds approximately to the modern departments of Seine-Maritime, Eure, Orne, Calvados, and Manche; its former capital was Rouen. Normandy is an agricultural region known for its dairy industry.

Under Roman domination the region formed part of Gallia Lugdunensis (Celtic Gaul). With the Frankish invasions it was made a constituent part of the kingdom of Neustria. It came to be known as Normandy about 911, when Charles III, king of France, turned it over to Rollo (860?-931?), the leader of a menacing band of Viking raiders. In 1066 a descendant of Rollo, William II, duke of Normandy, led an invasion of England and established himself there as William I, king of England. Normandy remained an English possession until conquered in 1204 by Philip II Augustus, king of France. During the Hundred Years' War, the region was held at various times by both French and English forces; it was finally recovered by the French in 1450. The Channel Islands, which were once a part of Normandy, remained in the possession of England.

Normandy was the location of the Allied invasion of German-occupied France during World War II.

NORMAN FRENCH LANGUAGE AND LITERATURE, French dialect that developed in Normandy after Viking (or Norse) invaders settled the region around 911, and the literature written in it. During the three centuries after the Norman Conquest of England in 1066, French culture predominated in England; this culture, transmitted by the conquerors and their descendants, is often referred to as Anglo-Norman. Norman French (with the later admixture of Parisian, or standard French), was the official language of the law courts, the church, and polite society in England. A considerable body of Anglo-Norman prose and poetry was produced; much literature was also brought over from France.

In adopting French as a medium of communication the Normans retained for purposes of literary expression many Scandinavian words, which are still, although in a greatly changed form, characteristic of this French dialect; the largest such class is that of proper names of persons and places. During the early period Norman French played a significant part both in French literature and in the development of Middle English and English literature.

Among the most important works written in the dialect are historical accounts, for it was in Normandy that histories in the vernacular (as opposed to Latin) first made their appearance. Geoffrey Gaimar (fl. 12th cent.), an Anglo-Norman poet and historiographer, wrote *Estorie des Engles* (History of the English), narrating the heroic achievements of the Anglo-Normans. Wace, another 12th-century Anglo-Norman chronicler, wrote *Roman de brut,* or *La geste des bretons* (Heroic Achievements of the Bretons). From 1160 to 1174, Wace produced *La geste des normands*

(Heroic Achievements of the Normans), also called *Roman de rou,* comprising 17,000 decasyllabic and octosyllabic lines.

Other 12th-century works include the *Cumpoz* (an ecclesiastical calendar) and *Bestiaire* of the Norman poet Philippe de Thaon or Thaün; the laws of William I the Conqueror; versions of the romances, including the *Chanson de Roland* (Song of Roland); and the *Chançun de Guillelme* (Song of William), which probably belongs to the end of the 11th century.

The 13th century was by far the most flourishing epoch. Among the poets belonging to this period are Fantosme, who wrote a chronicle of the invasions of the Scots in 1173–74; Angier, author of a life of St. Gregory the Great; and Guillaume de Berneville, who wrote a life of St. Gilles. The English martyr Thomas à Becket, the legendary English knight Bevis of Hampton (Boeve de Haumtone), St. Auban, and others are the subjects of anonymous poems. Also of interest are versions of the *Pèlerinage de Charlemagne* (Pilgrimage of Charlemagne), and the mystery play of Adam, as well as a *Fabliau du Héron.* The 14th century, marking the decline of Norman French literature, is noted for the *Contes moralisées* (Moral Tales) by the Anglo-Norman author Nicole Bozon and versions of biblical legends.

After the decline of this literature, French continued to be the language of pleadings in the law courts of England until as late as the mid-16th century. By the end of the 18th century, lawcourt French had completely died out with the exception of a few terms still retained in courts on the Channel Islands.

NORMANS. *See* NORMANDY.

NORRIS, Frank (1870–1902), American novelist, born in Chicago, and educated at the University of California and Harvard University. He was a newspaper correspondent during the South African and the Spanish-American wars. Norris's novels, influenced by the French naturalistic novelist Émile Zola, are brutally realistic, describing and analyzing sordid human motives and environments. The most important are *McTeague* (1899), a powerful story of the tragedy caused by greed in the lives of ordinary people; a trilogy, "The Epic of Wheat," depicting the human dramas arising from the raising, selling, and consumption of wheat, of which two novels, *The Octopus* (1901) and *The Pit* (1903), were written; and *Vandover and the Brute* (1914), a story of degeneration. Other novels include *Moran of the Lady Letty* (1898), *A Man's Woman* (1900), and *Blix* (1900). A volume of Norris's letters was published in 1956.

NORRIS, George William (1861–1944), U.S. senator and reformer, known as the creator of the Tennessee Valley Authority.

Norris was born July 11, 1861, in Sandusky Co., Ohio, and educated at Baldwin University (now Baldwin-Wallace College) and the Northern Indiana Normal School. He settled in Furnas Co., Nebr., in 1885, and entered the practice of law; from 1895 to 1902 he was judge of the 14th Nebraska District Court. From 1903 to 1913 he was a Republican member of the U.S. House of Representatives. During this period Norris was the leader of the group of congressmen who, by effecting a change in the House rules in 1910, ended the arbitrary rule of the Speaker of the House in a House revolt against Joseph Gurney Cannon. In 1912 Norris was elected to the U.S. Senate. For some years he was a member of the midwestern isolationist bloc that opposed the entry of the U.S. into World War I and later attacked the Versailles Treaty.

Norris favored federal regulation of public utilities and led a campaign that culminated in 1933 in the passage of the act that he wrote, creating the Tennessee Valley Authority (q.v.). The first TVA dam to be completed was named for him. Among other laws or acts sponsored by Norris are the 20th Amendment to the U.S. Constitution, popularly known as the Lame Duck Amendment (q.v.), and the Norris-La Guardia Anti-Injunction Act of 1932, by which the power to issue injunctions in labor disputes was restricted. Norris's disregard for the limitations of party politics, as shown by his support for many policies initiated under the New Deal program,

Frank Norris   Bettmann Archive

eventually deprived him of the support of the Republican party. In 1942, when he sought re-election as an Independent, he was defeated by the regular Republican candidate. Norris was the author of an autobiography, *Fighting Liberal* (pub. posthumously, 1945). He died Sept. 2, 1944, in McCook, Nebr.

NORRIS-LA GUARDIA ANTI-INJUNCTION ACT. *See* CLAYTON ANTITRUST ACT; NORRIS, GEORGE WILLIAM.

NORRISTOWN, borough, seat of Montgomery Co., SE Pennsylvania, on the Schuylkill R.; inc. 1812. It is a manufacturing and commercial center. Major products include machinery, textiles, chemicals, metal goods, processed food, and printed materials. The Montgomery County Historical Society Museum, containing a collection of folk art, is here, and Valley Forge State Park is nearby. The site of Norristown was once a part of the Norris Plantation, a tract of land bought in 1704 by Isaac Norris (1671–1735), a Quaker merchant and a mayor of Philadelphia. Pop. (1970) 38,169; (1980) 34,684.

NORRKÖPING, city, SE Sweden, in Östergötland Co., on the Bråviken (an inlet of the Baltic Sea), near Stockholm. It is an important seaport, accessible to oceangoing vessels via the Lindö Canal (completed 1961), and one of Sweden's principal commercial and manufacturing centers. Textiles, chemicals, paper, electrical equipment, and furniture are major manufactures. Hedvig's Church (1675) is a historic landmark here. Norrköping was established around 1350 and became a textile center in the 17th century. It was badly damaged by fire in 1719. Pop. (1980 est.) 119,238.

NORSEMEN. *See* VIKINGS.

NORSE MYTHOLOGY. *See* SCANDINAVIAN MYTHOLOGY.

NORTH, Frederick, 2d Earl of Guilford, called Lord North (1732–92), British statesman, born in London and educated at Eton College and the University of Oxford. In 1754 he was elected a member of the House of Commons, where he served for almost 40 years. He was appointed to the Privy Council in 1766 and became chancellor of the Exchequer in 1767; three years later he became prime minister of Great Britain. In the latter post he was subservient to the wishes of King George III, carrying out measures for the taxation of the American colonies that he personally believed unwise. At the outbreak of the American Revolution in 1776, he advocated arranging an early peace; by 1779 he no longer believed in the possibility of a British victory over the Americans, but was persuaded by the king to continue supporting the war. In 1782, after the surrender of the British forces in America, he resigned. In the following year North formed a coalition with Charles James Fox, who had formerly led the Whig opposition to North's administration, and with whom he succeeded in overthrowing the ministry of William Petty, 2d earl of Shelburne. Thereafter, North was a member of the opposition to the ministry of William Pitt, the Younger. He was created earl of Guilford in 1790.

NORTH AMERICA, 3d largest of the 7 continents, including Canada (the 2d largest country in area in the world), the U.S. (4th), and Mexico (13th). The continent also includes Greenland (Kalâtdlit-Nunât), the largest island, as well as the small French overseas department of Saint Pierre and Miquelon and the British dependency of Bermuda (both made up of small islands in the Atlantic Ocean). It is sometimes defined to include some two dozen countries in Central America and the West Indies, which are treated separately in this encyclopedia. North America, with about 328 million inhabitants (1981 est.), is the 4th most populous continent; the U.S. ranks 4th and Mexico 11th in population among the world's countries. Canada and the U.S. have highly developed modern economies, and Mexico, although less developed, contains some of the world's greatest deposits of petroleum and natural gas.

CHIEF POLITICAL DIVISIONS OF NORTH AMERICA

Political Unit	Political Status
Bermuda	British dependency
Canada	Independent state within the Commonwealth of Nations
Greenland	Internally self-governing part of Denmark
Mexico	Republic
Saint Pierre and Miquelon	French overseas department
United States of America	Republic

Together with Central America, the West Indies, and South America, North America makes up the western hemisphere of the earth. The name America is derived from that of the Italian navigator Amerigo Vespucci, who may have visited the mainland of North America in 1497–98.

THE NATURAL ENVIRONMENT

North America is roughly wedge shaped, with its broadest expanse in the N. Most of its bulk is in the middle latitudes, with a considerable N section in the Arctic and a narrow part around the tropic of Cancer. The continent sprawls E-W across some 176° of longitude, from about long 12° W at Nordost Rundingen (Northeast Foreland) in NE Greenland to about long 172° E at the W extremity of Attu Island, Alaska. Its N-S

139

A mountainous view of central Mexico. At left is the dormant volcano Iztaccíhuatl, popularly called the Sleeping Woman; and at right, Popocatépetl, which contains pure sulfur deposits in its largest crater. Mexican National Tourist Council

extent is some 69°, from about lat 83° N at Cape Morris Jesup in E Greenland to about lat 14° N in S Mexico. North America is bordered on the N by the Arctic Ocean; on the E by the Atlantic Ocean; on the S by the Gulf of Mexico, Central America, and the Pacific Ocean; and on the W by the Pacific Ocean. The area of the continent is approximately 23.5 million sq km (about 9.1 million sq mi).

The outline of North America is exceedingly irregular; some extensive coastal reaches are relatively smooth, but by and large the coastline is broken and embayed, with many prominent offshore islands. The continent has three enormous coastal indentations—Hudson Bay in the NE, the Gulf of Mexico in the SE, and the Gulf of Alaska in the NW. There are many small islands near the E and W coasts, but the most prominent islands are in the far N.

Geological History. According to a widely accepted theory, almost all of North America is situated on the North American plate, an enormous platform considered one of about a dozen major units constituting the structural mosaic of the earth's crust. It is thought that North America was once joined to modern-day Europe and Af-

rica and that it began to break away about 170 million years ago, in the Jurassic period, with the process of continental drift accelerating about 95 million years ago, in the Cretaceous period. As North America drifted W at a rate of about 1.25 cm (0.5 in) per year, the plate underlying the Pacific Ocean is believed to have thrust under the North American plate, thereby causing widespread folding, evident today in a series of high mountains along the W coast. As the Atlantic Ocean widened, it caused extensive faulting along the E coast, resulting in the creation of mountains and offshore islands.

Physiographic Regions. North America can be divided into five major physiographic regions. The E half of Canada, as well as most of Greenland and sections of Minnesota, Wisconsin, Michigan, and New York in the U.S., are part of the Canadian Shield (or Laurentian Plateau), which is a plateau region underlain by ancient crystalline rocks. The region has poor soil, and dense forests cover much of its S part. A second region is made up of a coastal plain in most of the eastern U.S. and Mexico. In the U.S. the coastal plain is bordered on the W by a third region, comprising a relatively narrow cordillera of mountains and hills, notably the rounded Appalachian Mts. A fourth region consists of the central portion of the continent, from S Canada to SW Texas, which encompasses an extensive lowland that has experienced alternating periods of submergence beneath the sea and uplift, with the result that it is deeply covered with layers of sedimentary rock. It is not an uninterrupted flatland, but includes much undulating and even hilly terrain, such as the Ozark Plateau. The W portion is made up of the Great Plains, which slope upward to the foot of the Rocky Mts.

The fifth, and westernmost, region of North America, taking in most of Mexico, is an active zone of mountain building; its recent geological history is dominated by crustal movements and volcanic activity. Adjacent to the Great Plains in the U.S. and Canada are the Rocky Mts., which are geologically related to the Sierra Madre Oriental range of Mexico. To the W is an area of scattered basins and high plateaus, including the Interior Plateau of British Columbia in Canada, the Colorado Plateau and the Great Basin of the U.S., and the vast central plateau of Mexico. Along the Pacific coast are a number of lofty mountain systems, extending from the Alaska Range to the Sierra Madre Occidental and Sierra Madre del Sur of Mexico. In between are such

ranges as the Coast Mts. of British Columbia and the Cascade Range, the Coast Ranges, and the Sierra Nevada of the U.S. Interspersed are some low-lying areas, notably the fertile Central Valley of California. The highest point in North America, Mt. McKinley, or Denali (6194 m/20,320 ft), is situated in the Alaska Range, and the lowest point, 86 m (282 ft) below sea level, is in Death Valley, Calif., a part of the Great Basin.

Drainage. The Continental, or Great, Divide, which mainly runs along the crest of the Rocky Mts., splits North America into two great drainage basins. To the E of the divide, water flows toward the Arctic Ocean, Hudson Bay, the Atlantic Ocean, and the Gulf of Mexico, and to the W, rivers flow toward the Pacific Ocean.

Two prominent drainage systems—the Great Lakes-Saint Lawrence R. system and the Mississippi-Missouri river system—dominate the hydrography of E and central North America. The five Great Lakes (Superior, Michigan, Huron, Erie, Ontario) drain NE to the Atlantic Ocean via the relatively short St. Lawrence R. Most of the central part of the U.S. and a small part of S Canada are drained S to the Gulf of Mexico by the Mississippi R. and its tributaries, notably the Missouri R., the longest river in North America. A great many short, but often voluminous, rivers

Mt. McKinley, the highest peak in North America, in the Alaska Range of the Rocky Mts. Its ice-capped summit is 6194 m (20,320 ft) above sea level. National Park Service

St. George, one of the small islands of Bermuda, is noted for its white sand beaches, blue waters, and colorful plants and coral rocks.　Bermuda News Service

flow to the Atlantic and Gulf of Mexico along the well-watered E coasts of Canada, the U.S., and Mexico. The N interior of the continent is drained by the great Mackenzie R. system of W Canada and by the numerous rivers that flow into Hudson Bay. To the W of the Continental Divide are relatively few major rivers (notably the Colorado, Columbia, Fraser, and Yukon) and many short, large-volume streams.

The S half of North America contains only a few large natural lakes, but Canada and the northern U.S. have a vast number of sizable lakes. Lake Superior, the world's biggest freshwater lake, and 10 of the next 25 largest natural lakes are found in this region. Lake Mead, on the Colorado R. in the U.S., is a large artificial lake, and Great Salt Lake, in Utah, is noted for its highly saline water.

Climate. Although North America has considerable climatic variety, five principal climatic regions can be identified. The N two-thirds of Canada and Alaska, as well as all Greenland, have subarctic and arctic climates, in which long, dark, bitterly cold winters alternate with brief, mild summers. Most of the region, which re-

ceives relatively little precipitation, is covered with snow and ice during much of the year. A second climatic region is made up of the E two-thirds of the U.S. and S Canada. It is characterized by a humid climate in which all four seasons are evident, and weather changes are frequent. The S part of this region has a warmer average temperature. A third region includes the W interior of the U.S. and much of N Mexico. It is mostly mountain and desert country, generally receiving small amounts of precipitation, but with significant local variations due to altitude and exposure. A fourth climatic region is made up of a narrow zone along the Pacific Ocean from S Alaska to S California. It has relatively mild but wet winters and almost rainless summers. Most of S Mexico has a tropical climate, with year-round warmth and considerable precipitation, especially in summer.

Vegetation. The natural vegetation of North America has been significantly modified by human activity, but its general nature is still apparent over much of the continent. The most notable forest is the taiga, or boreal forest, an enormous expanse of mostly coniferous trees (especially spruce, fir, hemlock, and larch) that covers most of S and central Canada and extends into Alaska. In the eastern U.S. a mixed forest, dominated by deciduous trees in the N and by various species of yellow pine in the SE, has mostly been cleared or cut over, but a considerable area has regrown since the 1940s. In the W portion of the continent, forests are primarily associated with mountain ranges, and coniferous trees are dominant. In California, the redwood and giant sequoia grow to enormous size. A great mixture of species characterizes the tropical forests of Mexico.

The vegetation cover in the drier parts of the continent is made up mainly of grassland and shrubland. The central plains and prairies of the U.S. and S Canada were originally grass covered, but much of the natural flora has been replaced by commercial crops. The dry lands of the west-

ern U.S. and N Mexico are sparsely covered with a variety of shrubs and many kinds of cactus. Beyond the tree line in the far N is a region of tundra, containing a mixture of low-growing sedges, grasses, mosses, and lichens.

Animal Life. The native wildlife of North America was once numerous and diverse, but the spread of human settlement has resulted in contracting habitats and diminishing numbers. In general, the fauna of North America is similar to that of the N areas of Europe and Asia. Notable large mammals include several kinds of bear, the largest being the grizzly; bighorn sheep; bison, now only in protected herds; caribou; moose, called elk in Europe; musk-ox; and wapiti. Large carnivores include the puma and, in southernmost regions, the jaguar; the wolf and its smaller relative, the coyote; and, in the far N, the polar bear. One species of marsupial, the common

VEGETATION

MID-LATITUDE FOREST
- Coniferous Forest
- Broadleaf Forest
- Mixed Coniferous and Broadleaf Forest
- Woodland and Shrub (Mediterranean)

MID-LATITUDE GRASSLAND
- Short Grass (Steppe)
- Tall Grass (Prairie)

TROPICAL FOREST
- Tropical Rainforest
- Light Tropical Forest

TROPICAL GRASSLAND
- Wooded Savanna

DESERT AND DESERT SHRUB

TUNDRA AND ALPINE

PERMANENT ICE

© Copyright HAMMOND INCORPORATED, Maplewood, N.J.

opossum, is indigenous to the continent. A few of the many reptiles are poisonous, including the coral snake, pit vipers such as the rattlesnake and copperhead, and the Gila monster and beaded lizard of the southwestern U.S. and Mexico, the only poisonous lizards in the world. A great variety of finfish and shellfish live in the marine waters off North America, and many kinds of fish are found in its freshwater rivers and lakes.

Mineral Resources. North America has large deposits of many important minerals. Petroleum and natural gas are found in great quantity in N Alaska, W Canada, the S and W conterminous U.S., and E Mexico; huge beds of coal are in E and W Canada and the U.S.; and great iron-ore deposits are in E Canada, the northern U.S., and central Mexico. Canada also has major deposits of copper, nickel, uranium, zinc, asbestos, and potash; the U.S. contains great amounts of copper, molybdenum, nickel, phosphate rock, and uranium; and Mexico has large reserves of barite, copper, fluorite, lead, zinc, manganese, and sulfur. All three countries have significant deposits of gold and silver.

THE PEOPLE

North America was sparsely populated until relatively recent times. With the conspicuous exception of the inhabitants of the Mexican heartland (the plateaus and valleys around present-day Mexico City), the aboriginal peoples of the continent were few in number, geographically scattered, and culturally diverse. The settlement of the continent by Europeans began an almost total change in its human geography; the aborigines were decimated and displaced, and the living patterns of most were greatly altered. The contemporary population of North America is mostly European in background, but the continent's population also contains various other important elements.

Ethnography. About one-half of Canada's inhabitants trace their ancestry to the British Isles, and another third are of French background; the latter live mostly in Québec Province. The country also has significant numbers of persons of German, Italian, Polish, Russian, and Scandinavian descent. The population of the U.S. is more diverse than Canada's. Persons of at least part Brit-

View of Mt. Rundle, near Banff, in the province of Alberta, Canada. The peak was named for Robert Terrill Rundle, a 19th-century British missionary. Canadian Consulate

Guarding the Quetzalcoatl temple at Teotihuacán, not far from Mexico City, is this rock-hewn feathered serpent, an emblem characteristic of the arts of the Mexican people.
Aeronaves de Mexico

ish and Irish background form the largest group, with about half of the country's inhabitants. Blacks, who trace their ancestry to Africa, make up about 12% of the population, Germans about 29%, and persons of Hispanic background about 6%. The country also has large numbers of people of Italian, French, Polish, Russian, Dutch, and Scandinavian ancestry. Persons of Asian origin— primarily Japanese, Chinese, Filipinos, Asian Indians, Koreans, and Vietnamese—make up only about 1.5% of the population of the U.S. and Canada, but in the 1970s and early 1980s the number of Asians increased significantly through immigration.

Native Americans—Indians and Inuit (Eskimo)—number about 1.4 million in the U.S. and about 300,000 in Canada. It is believed that the ancestors of the Indians migrated from Asia to North America via a prehistoric land bridge across the modern Bering Strait, off Alaska, beginning about 20,000 years ago, and that the forebears of the Inuit migrated from Asia by boat some 6000 years ago. Some 30,000 Inuit live in Greenland.

About two-thirds of the people of Mexico are mestizos, persons of mixed Indian and European (mainly Spanish) descent. Approximately one-fourth of the population is of relatively pure Indian ancestry, and some 10% is of unmixed European descent.

Demography. In 1980, the U.S. census recorded 226,504,825 inhabitants, Mexico (1980) 67,405,700; Canada (1981) 24,343,181; and Greenland (1981 est.) 50,643. Most of the population was concentrated in the E half of the U.S. and adjacent parts of Ontario and Québec, the W

coast of the U.S., and the central plateau of Mexico. In the early 1980s nearly 80% of the inhabitants of Canada, the U.S., and Greenland were defined as urban, as were about two-thirds of all Mexicans. The principal urban areas were on the U.S. Atlantic coast from Boston to Washington, D.C., around the shores of Lakes Erie and Ontario, at the S end of Lake Michigan, in N and S California, and greater Mexico City. The largest cities included Mexico City, Guadalajara, and Monterrey, in Mexico; New York City, Chicago, Los Angeles, Philadelphia, Houston, and Detroit, in the U.S.; and Montréal, Toronto, Winnipeg, Calgary, and Edmonton, in Canada. Away from the metropolitan areas, most of North America had only a sparse to moderate population density. In Mexico the overall population density was approximately 35 persons per sq km (approximately 90 per sq mi); in the U.S., about 24 per sq km (62 per sq mi); and in Canada, some 2.4 per sq km (some 6.3 per sq mi). The great majority of Canadians lived in a relatively narrow band along the S boundary.

In both Canada and the U.S. the rate of population increase has declined since the 1950s. The Canadian population increased by about 1.1% per year during 1975–79, when the annual growth rate for the U.S. was just 0.8% and for Greenland, 1.2%. Mexico, however, had one of the world's highest rates of population increase, 3.6% per year, and its crude birth rate (about 42 per 1000 persons annually in the 1970s) was more than twice as great as that of the rest of the continent. The crude death rate for the three countries remained at about the same level, 7 per 1000 people each year.

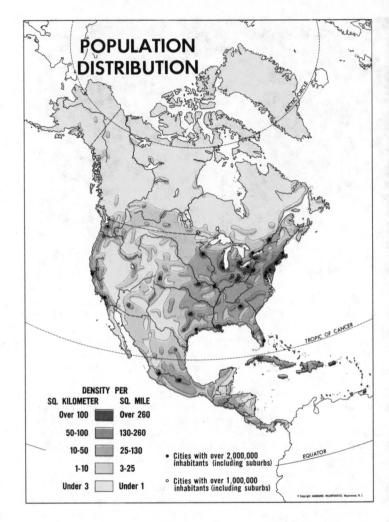

POPULATION DISTRIBUTION

DENSITY PER	
SQ. KILOMETER	SQ. MILE
Over 100	Over 260
50-100	130-260
10-50	25-130
1-10	3-25
Under 3	Under 1

● Cities with over 2,000,000 inhabitants (including suburbs)

○ Cities with over 1,000,000 inhabitants (including suburbs)

© Copyright HAMMOND INCORPORATED, Maplewood, N. J.

Intercontinental migration to North America was significant in the 1970s and early 1980s, with large numbers of Asians and Europeans going to the U.S. and Canada. In addition, many persons moved from South American and Caribbean countries to the U.S. The largest population movements, however, were within North America, from Mexico to the U.S. and from the northeastern U.S. to S and W parts of the country.

Language. English is the principal language for some 90% of the people of the U.S. and for about two-thirds of all Canadians. Spanish is spoken by the majority of Hispanic persons in the U.S., and French is the chief tongue for about one-quarter of the Canadian population. Many of the Indians and Inuit of the U.S., Canada, and Greenland use their traditional languages. Spanish is the dominant language of Mexico, but several million Mexicans speak an Indian language.

Religion. Christianity is the major religion of North America. The great majority of Mexicans are Roman Catholics, and some 45% of Canadians and 30% of U.S. inhabitants profess Roman Catholicism. About 28% of Canada's people are Protestants and some 11% are Anglicans, and Protestants make up about two-fifths of the U.S. population. Canada and the U.S. also have substantial communities of Jews and Eastern Orthodox Christians.

Cultural Activity. Cultural life in the U.S. and Canada is highly developed and diversified, with the mass media (radio, television, motion pictures, newspapers) playing an important role. Almost all cities support theatrical organizations and art museums, and musical groups are widespread. Traditional cultural patterns are more evident in the rural areas of Mexico, but its cities have a variety of modern cultural institutions.

PATTERNS OF ECONOMIC DEVELOPMENT

The economic activities of North America are extraordinarily diverse. The U.S. and Canada have sophisticated modern economies, and in the early 1980s Mexico was in the midst of a dynamic period of change, with major developments in power, transportation, and manufacturing superimposed on a comparatively undeveloped agricultural economy.

Agriculture. Farming is relatively more important in Mexico than in the other North American countries and provides employment for about 40% of the labor force (compared with some 5% in the U.S. and Canada). Subsistence farming is still important throughout Mexico, especially in the S; commercial agriculture is well developed in many areas, however, particularly in the central plateau and in the N. The leading commodities are corn, wheat, and beans, which are raised mostly for domestic consumption, and cotton, cattle, coffee, and sugar, which are produced largely for export.

Agriculture in the U.S. and Canada is dominated by highly mechanized farms, which produce immense quantities of crops, livestock, and livestock products. The Great Plains of the central U.S. and the Canadian Prairie provinces (Alberta, Manitoba, Saskatchewan) are major world producers of grain (particularly wheat but also barley, oats, rye, and grain sorghum), oilseeds, and livestock (dairy and beef cattle and sheep). Perhaps the world's finest large farming area is the Corn Belt, that part of the U.S. Middle West from W Ohio to E Nebraska, which is the world's largest producer of corn, as well as a major supplier of other grains, soybeans, cattle, and hogs. Farming in California yields a huge amount of high-value irrigated crops, notably fruits and vegetables. Florida and Texas also are great producers of fruits and vegetables, and potatoes are grown in vast quantities in Idaho, Washington State, Oregon, Maine, North Dakota, and SE Canada. Other outstanding agricultural products include cotton, broiler chickens, dairy products, and sugarcane.

Forestry and Fishing. Forestry is an important sector of the Canadian economy, especially in British Columbia, Ontario, and Québec Province. Notable forest-products industries also flourish in the western U.S. (particularly in Washington,

Agriculture is a major economic activity of the north-central and northwestern U.S. These fields of wheat are in south-central Washington.   Washington State Dept. of Commerce

Oregon, and California) and in the southeastern U.S.

Fishing is the leading economic activity in Greenland but is a relatively unimportant sector in Canada, the U.S., and Mexico, even though the catch is large and some coastal areas are dependent on revenues from sales of finfish and shellfish. Besides the waters near Greenland, major fishing grounds are off the N Pacific coast, off the N Atlantic coast, and off the S Atlantic and Gulf of Mexico coasts. In addition, large tuna fleets are based in S California and W Mexico.

Mining. The extraction of minerals is an increasingly important economic activity in the U.S., Canada, and Mexico. The U.S. has been the world's third largest petroleum producer for many years, Canada has been a major producer since the late 1940s, and Mexico became a world leader in oil production in the late 1970s. The U.S. ranks first among world natural-gas producers and also leads in mining coal, produced particularly in the vast Appalachian fields. Iron ore has long been a major product of both the U.S. and Canada, primarily from deposits around the

W end of Lake Superior. More recently, much iron ore has been produced in the Québec Province-Labrador border area of E Canada. Among the other minerals that have been recovered in quantity in North America are copper, silver, lead, zinc, nickel, sulfur, asbestos, uranium, phosphate rock, and potash.

Manufacturing. Manufacturing has long been a leading economic sector of the U.S. The principal concentrations of factories have been located in the urban areas of a manufacturing belt extending roughly from Boston to Chicago. Since the 1950s, however, manufacturing has expanded considerably in other parts of the country, particularly in the big cities of California and in the SE states. Output is extremely diversified, with emphasis on primary and fabricated metals, processed food, machinery, electronic and aerospace equipment, motor vehicles, chemicals, textiles, clothing, paper, and printed materials. Manufacturing also is a principal economic activity in Canada. Factories are situated primarily in the cities of Ontario, Québec Province, British Columbia, and Alberta; Toronto and Montréal

The Carlsbad Caverns in New Mexico contain vast underground chambers adorned with gleaming stalactites and stalagmites. The caves, among the largest in the world, are the principal feature of Carlsbad Caverns National Park. New Mexico Dept. of Development

The Badlands of North Dakota display fantastically shaped rock masses forming sheer cliffs and precipitous valleys. Badlands Natural History Assn.

are the leading manufacturing centers. Canadian firms produce a wide variety of goods, especially processed food and beverages, transportation equipment, paper and other forest products, primary and fabricated metals, chemicals, and electrical and electronic equipment.

Manufacturing has become an increasingly important part of the Mexican economy since the 1940s. Although not as highly developed as in the U.S. and Canada, factories in Mexico produce a broad spectrum of goods, notably chemicals, clothing, processed food, motor vehicles and motor-vehicle parts, construction materials, and electrical and electronic equipment. Mexico City is by far the leading manufacturing center, but several other cities, including Monterrey and Guadalajara, have important concentrations of factories.

Energy. North America consumes great quantities of energy. Canada depends much more on hydroelectricity than do the U.S. and Mexico, but it also makes heavy use of petroleum and natural gas. The enormous consumption of energy in the U.S. required, in the early 1980s, great imports of petroleum and natural gas to bolster the considerable domestic output of coal, petroleum, natural gas, and hydroelectric and nuclear power. Mexico's energy production expanded considerably in the 1970s and early '80s, primed by the increased domestic recovery of petroleum and natural gas.

Transportation. The transportation network of North America is extremely well developed in most parts of the conterminous U.S. and in southernmost Canada. A remarkable system of limited-access Interstate Highways was built in the U.S. beginning in the 1950s, and the country in addition has a wide-ranging network of other all-weather roads. The rail network also is well established; it is critical for many types of freight transport but is a relatively unimportant passenger carrier. Air traffic grew considerably after 1945, and an expansive network of routes was created. Inland waterways, particularly the St. Lawrence Seaway-Great Lakes system and the Mississippi-Missouri river system, are important freight-transportation routes. Central and N Canada and Alaska have only limited surface transportation facilities and depend heavily on air service. The interior transportation systems of Mexico are unevenly developed. All three countries have extensive modern facilities for handling oceangoing vessels.

Trade. The U.S. is by far the leading trade partner for both Canada and Mexico, which in turn are significant, but not dominant, trade partners of the U.S. The main exports of the U.S. are machinery, motor vehicles, foodstuffs, chemicals, and

Autumn comes to New England, producing a spectacular display of foliage color that brings tourists in large numbers to the northeastern U.S. Rapho–Photo Researchers, Inc.

aircraft. Canada mainly ships motor vehicles, machinery, metal and metal ore, forest products, chemicals, and foodstuffs, and the principal exports of Mexico are crude petroleum, coffee, and metal ore. At the start of the 1980s the value of Canada's annual exports exceeded that of its imports, whereas the U.S. and Mexico paid more for imports than their exports earned. The U.S. was the world's leading trading country in terms of the total value of imports and exports.   T.L.M.

HISTORY

According to archaelogical evidence, human settlement in North America dates from 100,000 to 40,000 years ago. At some point in that span of time a type of Mongoloid people is thought to have migrated to the continent from Asia, most likely over a land bridge across what is now the Bering Strait. From these beginnings human habitation is supposed to have slowly spread south and eastward.

These earliest inhabitants were Stone Age people, who lived by hunting and gathering, using implements not unlike those known from Southeast Asia. They were later supplanted by other migrants with more advanced tools. These people are believed to be the earliest ancestors of the North American Indians that inhabited the continent at the time when Europeans first arrived. *See* ARCHAEOLOGY.

Greenland, geologically a part of North America, was the first part of the western hemisphere reached by Europeans. According to Icelandic sagas, it was first explored and settled by Eric the Red. The first European to discover any part of the continental mainland was probably Bjarni Herjólfsson, an Icelandic trader, who sighted it about 986. Some time afterward, Leif Ericson, the son of Eric the Red, made a voyage to a land he called Vinland or Wineland, believed to have been somewhere between Labrador and New England. This account was partly substantiated by the 1963 discovery of a Viking-type settlement site at L'Anse-aux-Meadows, Newf., that was determined to be from about 1000.

Age of Exploration. Consecutive discovery and exploration in North America began with the voyage made in 1492 by Christopher Columbus in the service of Spain. His three small ships

INDEX TO MAP OF NORTH AMERICA

Aberdeen, S.Dak. ... J 5
Abilene, Tex. ... J 6
Acapulco, Mexico ... H 8
Aguascalientes, Mexico ... H 7
Aklavik, N.W.T. ... E 3
Akron, Ohio ... K 5
Alabama (state), U.S. ... K 6
Alaska (gulf) ... D 4
Alaska (pen.), Alaska ... C 4
Alaska (range), Alaska ... C 3
Alaska (state), U.S. ... C 3
Albany (cap.), N.Y. ... L 5
Alberta (prov.), Canada ... G 4
Albuquerque, N.Mex. ... H 6
Alexander (arch.), Alaska ... E 4
Amarillo, Tex. ... H 6
Anchorage, Alaska ... D 3
Andros (island), Bahamas ... L 7
Anguilla (island) ... M 8
Anticosti (island), Que. ... M 5
Antigua and Barbuda ... M 8
Appalachian (mts.), U.S. ... K 6
Arizona (state), U.S. ... G 6
Arkansas (river), U.S. ... J 6
Arkansas (state), U.S. ... J 6
Athabasca (lake), Canada ... H 4
Athabasca (river), Alta. ... G 4
Atlanta (cap.), Ga. ... K 6
Augusta, Ga. ... K 6
Augusta (cap.), Maine ... M 5
Austin (cap.), Tex. ... J 6
Axel Heiberg (island), N.W.T. ... J 1
Baffin (bay) ... M 2
Baffin (island), N.W.T. ... L 2
Bahamas ... L 7
Bangor, Maine ... M 5
Banks (island), N.W.T. ... F 2
Barbados ... N 8
Barbuda (island) ... M 8
Barrow (point), Alaska ... C 2
Bathurst (island), N.W.T. ... H 2
Baton Rouge (cap.), La. ... J 6
Beaufort (sea) ... D 2
Beaumont, Tex. ... J 6
Belize ... K 8
Belle Isle (strait), Canada ... N 5
Belmopan (cap.), Belize ... K 8
Bering (sea) ... A 3
Bering (strait) ... B 3
Bermuda (islands) ... M 6
Billings, Mont. ... H 5
Birmingham, Ala. ... K 6
Bismarck (cap.), N.Dak. ... H 5
Bitterroot (range), U.S. ... G 5
Boise (cap.), Idaho ... G 5
Boothia (gulf), N.W.T. ... J 2
Boothia (pen.), N.W.T. ... J 2
Boston (cap.), Mass. ... L 5
Boulder, Colo. ... H 5
Brandon, Man. ... H 4
Brazos (river), Tex. ... J 6
Bristol (bay), Alaska ... B 4
British Columbia (prov.), Canada ... F 4
Brooks (range), Alaska ... C 3
Brownsville, Tex. ... J 7
Buffalo, N.Y. ... L 5
Burlington, Vt. ... L 5
Butte, Mont. ... G 5
Cabot (strait), Canada ... N 5
Calgary (cap.), Alta. ... G 4
California (gulf) ... G 7
California (state), U.S. ... G 6
Camagüey, Cuba ... L 7
Campeche, Mexico ... J 8
Campeche (bay), Mexico ... J 8
Canada ... H 4
Canadian (river), U.S. ... H 6
Canaveral (cape), Fla. ... K 7
Cape Breton (island), N.S. ... N 5
Caribbean (sea) ... K 8
Carlsbad, N.Mex. ... H 6
Carson City (cap.), Nev. ... G 6
Cascade (range), U.S. ... F 5
Casper, Wyo. ... H 5
Cayman (islands) ... K 8
Cedar Rapids, Iowa ... J 5
Charleston, S.C. ... L 6
Charleston (cap.), W.Va. ... K 6
Charlotte, N.C. ... K 6
Charlottetown (cap.), P.E.I. ... M 5
Chattanooga, Tenn. ... K 6
Chesapeake (bay), U.S. ... L 6
Cheyenne (cap.), Wyo. ... H 5
Cheyenne (river), U.S. ... H 5
Chicago, Ill. ... K 5
Chihuahua, Mexico ... H 7
Churchill, Man. ... J 4
Churchill (river), Canada ... J 4
Cincinnati, Ohio ... K 6
Ciudad Juárez, Mexico ... G 6
Cleveland, Ohio ... K 5
Clipperton (island) (Fr.) ... E 8
Coast (mts.), B.C. ... E 4
Coast (ranges), U.S. ... F 5
Coatzacoalcos, Mexico ... J 8
Cochrane, Ont. ... K 5
Cocos (island), Costa Rica ... J 9
Cod (cape), Mass. ... L 5
Colón, Panama ... L 9
Colorado (river), Tex. ... J 7
Colorado (river), U.S. ... G 6
Colorado (state), U.S. ... H 6
Columbia (cap.), S.C. ... K 6
Columbia (river), U.S. ... F 5
Columbus, Ga. ... K 6
Columbus (cap.), Ohio ... K 5
Concord (cap.), N.H. ... L 5
Connecticut (state), U.S. ... L 5
Corpus Christi, Tex. ... J 7
Corrientes (cape), Mexico ... G 7
Costa Rica ... K 8
Cuba ... L 7
Culiacán, Mexico ... G 7
Dallas, Tex. ... J 6
Davis (strait) ... N 3
Dawson, Yukon ... D 3
Dayton, Ohio ... K 5
Daytona Beach, Fla. ... K 7
Dease (strait), N.W.T. ... G 3
Decatur, Ill. ... K 6
Delaware (state), U.S. ... L 6
Denali (McKinley) (mt.), Alaska ... C 3
Denmark (strait) ... R 2
Denver (cap.), Colo. ... H 6
Des Moines (cap.), Iowa ... J 5
Detroit, Mich. ... K 5
Devon (island), N.W.T. ... K 2
District of Columbia, U.S. ... L 6
Dominica ... M 8
Dominican Republic ... M 8
Dover (cap.), Del. ... L 6
Duluth, Minn. ... J 5
Durango, Mexico ... H 7
Edmonton, Alta. ... G 4
Ellesmere (island), N.W.T. ... K 1
El Paso, Tex. ... H 6
El Salvador ... J 8
Erie (lake) ... K 5
Erie, Pa. ... K 5
Eugene, Oreg. ... F 5
Eureka, Calif. ... F 5
Evansville, Ind. ... K 6
Fairbanks, Alaska ... D 3
Farewell (cape), Greenland ... P 4
Fargo, N.Dak. ... J 5
Flagstaff, Ariz. ... G 6
Flattery (cape), Wash. ... F 5
Flin Flon, Man. ... H 4
Flint, Mich. ... K 5
Florida (state), U.S. ... K 7
Florida (straits) ... K 7
Fort Albany, Ont. ... K 4
Fort Collins, Colo. ... H 5
Fort-George, Que. ... K 4
Fort Liard, N.W.T. ... F 3
Fort McMurray, Alta. ... G 4
Fort McPherson, N.W.T. ... E 3
Fort Nelson, B.C. ... F 4
Fort Norman, N.W.T. ... F 3
Fort Peck (lake), Mont. ... H 5
Fort Resolution, N.W.T. ... G 3
Fort Simpson, N.W.T. ... F 3
Fort Smith, Ark. ... J 6
Fort Smith, N.W.T. ... G 3
Fort Worth, Tex. ... J 6
Fort Yukon, Alaska ... D 3
Foxe (basin), N.W.T. ... L 3
Foxe (chan.), N.W.T. ... L 3
Foxe (pen.), N.W.T. ... L 3
Frankfort (cap.), Ky. ... K 6
Fraser (river), B.C. ... F 4
Fredericton, N.B. ... M 5
Frederikshåb, Greenland ... N 3
Fresno, Calif. ... G 6
Galveston, Tex. ... K 7
Gary, Ind. ... K 5
Georgia (state), U.S. ... K 6
Gila (river), U.S. ... G 6
Godhavn, Greenland ... N 3
Godthåb (Nûk), (cap.), Greenland ... N 3
Goose Bay, Newf. ... M 4
Gracias a Dios (cape), Nicaragua ... K 8
Grand Bahama (island), Bahamas ... L 7
Grande-Prairie, Alta. ... G 4
Grand Falls, Newf. ... N 5
Grand Forks, N.Dak. ... J 5
Grand Island, Nebr. ... J 5
Grand Junction, Colo. ... H 6
Grand Rapids, Mich. ... K 5
Great Abaco (island), Bahamas ... L 7
Great Bear (lake), N.W.T. ... F 3
Greater Antilles (islands) ... K 7
Great Exuma (island), Bahamas ... L 7
Great Falls, Mont. ... G 5
Great Inagua (island), Bahamas ... L 7
Great Salt (lake), Utah ... G 6
Great Slave (lake), N.W.T. ... H 3
Green Bay, Wis. ... J 5
Greenland ... P 2
Greenland (sea) ... T 2
Greensboro, N.C. ... K 6
Greenville, Miss. ... K 6
Greenville, S.C. ... K 6
Grenada ... M 8
Guadalajara, Mexico ... H 7
Guadeloupe (island) ... N 8
Guadalupe (island), Mexico ... G 7
Guantánamo, Cuba ... L 7
Guatemala ... J 8
Guatemala (cap.) ... J 8
Haiti ... L 8
Halifax (cap.), N.S. ... M 5
Hamilton, Ont. ... K 5
Harrisburg (cap.), Pa. ... L 5
Hartford (cap.), Conn. ... L 5
Hatteras (cape), N.C. ... L 6
Havana (cap.), Cuba ... K 7
Havasu (lake), U.S. ... G 6
Hecate (strait), B.C. ... E 4
Helena (cap.), Mont. ... G 5
Hermosillo, Mexico ... G 7
Hispaniola (island) ... L 7
Holguín, Cuba ... L 7
Honduras ... K 8
Honduras (gulf) ... K 8
Houston, Tex. ... J 7
Hudson (bay), Canada ... K 3
Hudson (strait), Canada ... L 3
Huron (lake) ... K 5
Idaho (state), U.S. ... G 5
Idaho Falls, Idaho ... G 5
Illinois (state), U.S. ... K 6
Indiana (state), U.S. ... K 6
Indianapolis (cap.), Ind. ... K 5
Inuvik, N.W.T. ... E 3
Iowa (state), U.S. ... J 5
Jackson (cap.), Miss. ... K 6
Jacksonville, Fla. ... K 6
Jamaica ... L 8
James (bay), Canada ... K 4
Jefferson City (cap.), Mo. ... J 6
Juan de Fuca (strait) ... F 5
Julianehåb, Greenland ... P 3
Juneau (cap.), Alaska ... E 4
Juventud (island), Cuba ... K 7
Kalâtdlit-Nunât (Greenland) ... P 2
Kamloops, B.C. ... G 4
Kansas (state), U.S. ... J 6
Kansas City, Mo. ... K 6
Kentucky (state), U.S. ... K 6
Ketchikan, Alaska ... E 4
Key West, Fla. ... K 7
Kingston (cap.), Jamaica ... L 8
Kingston, Ont. ... L 5
Klamath Falls, Oreg. ... F 5
Knoxville, Tenn. ... K 6
Kodiak (island), Alaska ... C 4
Kotzebue, Alaska ... B 3
Labrador (reg.), Newf. ... M 4
Labrador (sea) ... N 4
Lansing (cap.), Mich. ... K 5
La Paz, Mexico ... G 7
Laramie, Wyo. ... H 5
Laredo, Tex. ... J 7
Las Cruces, N.Mex. ... H 6
Las Vegas, Nev. ... G 6
Lawton, Okla. ... J 6
León, Mexico ... H 7
León, Nicaragua ... K 8
Lesser Antilles (islands) ... M 8
Lethbridge, Alta. ... G 4
Lexington, Ky. ... K 6
Liard (river), Canada ... F 3
Limón, Costa Rica ... K 8
Lincoln (cap.), Nebr. ... J 5
Lincoln (sea) ... M 1
Little Rock (cap.), Ark. ... J 6
London, Ont. ... K 5
Long Beach, Calif. ... F 6
Los Angeles, Calif. ... G 6
Louisiana (state), U.S. ... K 6
Louisville, Ky. ... K 6
Lower California (pen.), Mexico ... G 7
Lynchburg, Va. ... K 6
Mackenzie (mts.), Canada ... E 3
Mackenzie (river), N.W.T. ... F 3
McKinley (Denali) (mt.), Alaska ... C 3

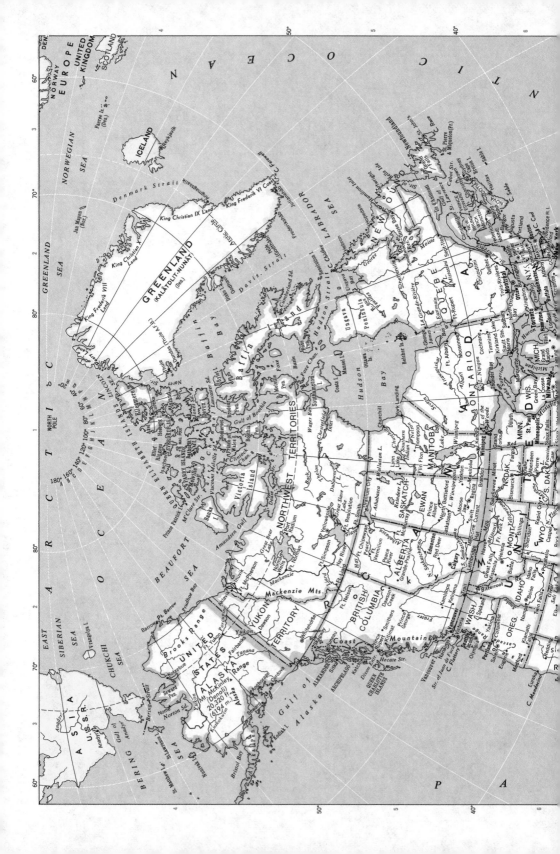

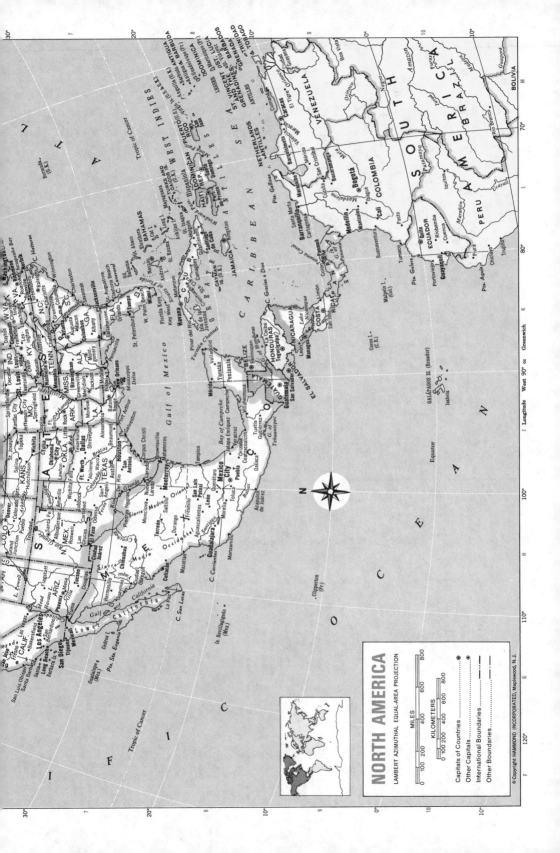

NORTH AMERICA

LAMBERT AZIMUTHAL EQUAL-AREA PROJECTION

Capitals of Countries .... ⊛
Other Capitals .... ◉
International Boundaries .... —·—·—
Other Boundaries .... —·—·—

MILES
0   100 200   400   600   800

KILOMETERS
0 100 200 400   600   800

© Copyright HAMMOND INCORPORATED, Maplewood, N.J.

Index to Map of North America

Macon, Ga. — K 6
Madison (cap.), Wis. — K 5
Maine (state), U.S. — M 5
Managua (cap.), Nicaragua — K 8
Manitoba (prov.), Canada — J 4
Manitoba (lake), Man. — H 4
Manzanillo, Mexico — H 8
Martinique (state), U.S. — M 8
Maryland (state), U.S. — L 6
Massachusetts (state), U.S. — L 5
Matamoros, Mexico — J 7
Matanzas, Cuba — K 7
Mayaguana (island), Bahamas — L 7
Mazatlán, Mexico — H 7
Mead (lake), U.S. — G 6
Medford, Oreg. — F 5
Medicine Hat, Alta. — H 4
Melville (lake), N.W.T. — G 2
Memphis, Tenn. — K 6
Mérida, Mexico — K 8
Meridian, Miss. — K 6
Mesa, Ariz. — G 6
Mexicali, Mexico — G 6
Mexico — H 7
Mexico (gulf) — K 7
Mexico City (cap.), Mexico — J 7
Miami, Fla. — L 7
Michigan (lake), U.S. — K 5
Michigan (state), U.S. — K 5
Milwaukee, Wis. — K 5
Minneapolis, Minn. — J 5
Minnesota (state), U.S. — J 5
Mississippi (delta), La. — K 7
Mississippi (river), U.S. — J 6
Mississippi (state), U.S. — K 6
Missoula, Mont. — G 5
Missouri (river), U.S. — J 5
Missouri (state), U.S. — J 6
Mistassini (lake), Que. — L 4
Mobile, Ala. — K 6
Mona (passg.) — M 8
Moncton, N.B. — M 5
Monroe, La. — K 6
Montana (state), U.S. — H 5
Monterrey, Mexico — J 7
Montgomery (cap.), Ala. — K 6
Montpelier (cap.), Vt. — L 5
Montréal, Que. — L 5
Moose Jaw, Sask. — H 4
Morelia, Mexico — H 8
Nares (strait) — L 2

Nashville (cap.), Tenn. — K 6
Nassau (cap.), Bahamas — L 7
Nebraska (state), U.S. — J 5
Nelson (river), Man. — J 4
Netherlands Antilles — M 8
Nevada (state), U.S. — G 6
New Brunswick (prov.), Canada — M 5
Newfoundland (prov.), Canada — M 4
New Hampshire (state), U.S. — L 5
New Jersey (state), U.S. — L 5
New Mexico (state), U.S. — H 6
New Orleans, La. — K 7
New York, N.Y. — L 5
New York (state), U.S. — L 5
Nicaragua — K 8
Nicaragua (lake), Nicaragua — K 8
Nipigon (lake), Ont. — K 5
Nome, Alaska — B 3
Norfolk, Va. — L 6
North Battleford, Sask. — H 4
North Carolina (state), U.S. — L 6
North Dakota (state), U.S. — H 5
North Platte (river) — H 5
North Saskatchewan (river), Canada — G 4
Northwest Territories (terr.), Canada — G 3
Nova Scotia (prov.), Canada — M 5
Nuevo Laredo, Mexico — J 7
Núk (cap.), Greenland — N 3
Oahe (lake), U.S. — J 5
Oakland, Calif. — F 6
Oaxaca, Mexico — J 8
Ogden, Utah — G 6
Ohio (river), U.S. — K 6
Ohio (state), U.S. — K 5
Oklahoma (state), U.S. — J 6
Oklahoma City (cap.), Okla. — J 6
Olympia (cap.), Wash. — F 5
Omaha, Nebr. — J 5
Ontario (lake) — L 5
Ontario (prov.), Canada — K 4
Oregon (state), U.S. — F 5
Orizaba, Mexico — J 8
Ottawa (cap.), Canada — L 5
Ottawa (river), Canada — L 2

Panama — K 9
Panama (canal) — L 8
Panamá (cap.), Panama — L 9
Panama (gulf) — L 9
Panama — L 9
Parry (chan.), N.W.T. — G 2
Peace (river), Canada — G 4
Peace River, Alta. — G 4
Pecos (river), U.S. — H 6
Pennsylvania (state), U.S. — L 5
Pensacola, Fla. — K 6
Peoria, Ill. — K 5
Philadelphia, Pa. — L 6
Phoenix (cap.), Ariz. — G 6
Pierre (cap.), S.Dak. — H 5
Pittsburgh, Pa. — L 5
Platte (river), Nebr. — H 5
Pocatello, Idaho — G 5
Porcupine (river) — D 3
Port Arthur, Tex. — J 7
Port-au-Prince (cap.), Haiti — L 8
Portland, Maine — M 5
Portland, Oreg. — F 5
Port Radium, N.W.T. — G 3
Powell (lake), U.S. — G 6
Prince Albert, Sask. — H 4
Prince Edward Island (prov.), Canada — M 5
Prince George, B.C. — F 4
Prince Rupert, B.C. — F 4
Prince of Wales (island), N.W.T. — J 2
Providence (cap.), R.I. — L 5
Provo, Utah — G 6
Prudhoe (bay), Alaska — D 2
Puebla, Mexico — J 8
Pueblo, Colo. — H 6
Puerto Rico — M 8
Québec (cap.), Que. — L 5
Québec (prov.), Canada — L 4
Queen Charlotte (islands), B.C. — E 4
Queen Elizabeth (islands), N.W.T. — J 1
Querétaro, Mexico — J 7
Raleigh (cap.), N.C. — L 6
Rapid City, S.Dak. — H 5
Red (river), U.S. — J 6
Red (river), U.S. — J 5
Red Deer, Alta. — G 4
Regina (cap.), Sask. — H 4
Reindeer (lake), Canada — H 4
Reno, Nev. — G 6

Revillagigedo (islands), Mexico — G 8
Rhode Island (state), U.S. — M 5
Richmond (cap.), Va. — L 6
Rio Grande (river) — H 7
Roanoke, Va. — L 6
Rochester, N.Y. — L 5
Rock Springs, Wyo. — G 4
Rocky (mts.) — F 4
Roswell, N.Mex. — H 6
Sable (cape), N.S. — M 5
Sable (island), N.S. — N 5
Sacramento (cap.), Calif. — F 6
Saint Augustine, Fla. — K 7
Saint John (cap.), N.B. — M 5
St. John's (cap.), Newf. — N 5
Saint Lawrence (gulf) — M 5
Saint Lawrence (island), Alaska — A 3
Saint Lawrence (river) — L 5
Saint Louis, Mo. — K 6
Saint Lucia — M 8
Saint Paul (cap.), Minn. — J 5
Saint Petersburg, Fla. — K 7
Saint Pierre and Miquelon (islands) (Fr.) — N 5
Saint Vincent and the Grenadines — M 8
Salem (cap.), Oreg. — F 5
Saltillo, Mexico — H 7
Salt Lake City (cap.), Utah — G 6
San Antonio, Tex. — J 7
San Diego, Calif. — G 6
San Francisco, Calif. — F 6
San Jose, Calif. — F 6
San José (cap.), Costa Rica — K 9
San Juan (cap.), Puerto Rico — M 8
San Lucas (cape), Mexico — G 7
San Luis Potosí, Mexico — H 7
San Salvador (cap.), El Salvador — J 8
Santa Barbara (islands), Calif. — F 6
Santa Fe (cap.), N. Mex. — H 6
Santiago de Cuba, Cuba — L 8
Santo Domingo (cap.), Dom. Rep. — L 8

Saskatchewan (prov.), Canada — H 4
Saskatoon, Sask. — H 4
Sault Ste. Marie, Ont. — K 5
Savannah, Ga. — K 6
Savannah (river), U.S. — K 6
Schefferville, Que. — L 4
Scranton, Pa. — L 5
Seattle, Wash. — F 5
Sept-Îles, Que. — M 4
Seward, Alaska — C 3
Seward (pen.), Alaska — B 3
Sheridan, Wyo. — H 5
Shreveport, La. — J 6
Sierra Nevada (range), Calif. — F 6
Sioux City, Iowa — J 5
Sioux Falls, S.Dak. — J 5
Sitka, Alaska — E 4
Slave (river), Canada — G 4
Snake (river), U.S. — G 5
Somerset (island), N.W.T. — J 2
South Carolina (state), U.S. — K 6
South Dakota (state), U.S. — H 5
Southampton (island), N.W.T. — K 3
South Platte (river) — H 6
South Saskatchewan (river), Canada — G 4
Spokane, Wash. — F 5
Springfield, Mo. — J 6
Springfield (cap.), Ill. — K 6
Sudbury, Ont. — E 3
Superior (lake) — J 6
Sydney, N.S. — M 6
Tacoma, Wash. — F 5
Tallahassee (cap.), Fla. — L 6
Tampa, Fla. — K 7
Tampico, Mexico — H 7
Tanana (river), Alaska — D 3
Tegucigalpa (cap.), Honduras — K 8
Tehuantepec, Mexico — J 8
Tennessee (state), U.S. — K 6
Texarkana, Tex. — J 6
Texas (state), U.S. — H 6
Thule, Greenland — L 6
Thunder Bay, Ont. — J 8
Tijuana, Mexico — J 5
Timmins, Ont. — K 7
Toledo, Ohio — C 3
Toluca, Mexico — E 3
Topeka (cap.), Kans. — G 6

Toronto (cap.), Ont. — K 5
Torreón, Mexico — H 7
Trenton (cap.), N.J. — L 5
Trinidad, Colo. — H 6
Trinidad and Tobago — N 8
Trois-Rivières, Que. — L 5
Tucson, Ariz. — G 6
Tulsa, Okla. — J 6
Turks and Caicos (islands) — L 7
Ungava (pen.), Que. — L 3
United States — H 5
Uranium City, Sask. — G 6
Utah (state), U.S. — K 7
Valladolid, Mexico — F 4
Vancouver, B.C. — F 5
Vancouver (island), B.C. — J 8
Veracruz, Mexico — J 5
Vermont (state), U.S. — F 5
Victoria (cap.), B.C. — G 2
Victoria (island), N.W.T. — J 8
Villahermosa, Mexico — L 6
Virginia (state), U.S. — M 8
Virgin Islands (islands), U.S. — K 7
Waco, Tex. — J 6
Washington (state), U.S. — E 3
Washington, D.C. (cap.), U.S. — J 6
West Indies (islands) — H 6
West Palm Beach, Fla. — L 6
West Virginia (state), U.S. — L 8
Whitehorse (cap.), Yukon — J 5
Wichita, Kans. — J 4
Wichita Falls, Tex. — H 4
Wilmington, N.C. — K 5
Windward (passg.) — J 5
Winnipeg (cap.), Man. — H 5
Winnipeg (lake), Man. — F 5
Winnipegosis (lake), Man. — G 3
Wisconsin (state), U.S. — H 5
Woods (lake) — K 7
Wyoming (state), U.S. — C 3
Yakima, Wash. — E 3
Yellowknife, N.W.T. — G 6
Yellowstone (river), U.S. — H 5
Yukon (river) — K 7
Yukon Territory (terr.), Canada — C 3
Yuma, Ariz. — G 6

sailed from Palos, Andalusia, on August 3, and on October 12 reached San Salvador (Eng. Watling Island) in the Bahamas. Before returning to Europe, Columbus also discovered Cuba and Hispaniola. On Hispaniola he established the first Spanish settlement in the Americas. Columbus made three additional voyages between the years 1493 and 1502. *See also* CENTRAL AMERICA.

In 1497 an Italian navigator in English service, John Cabot, discovered Cape Breton Island; in 1498 he also sailed along the Labrador, Newfoundland, and New England coasts, and possibly as far south as Delaware Bay. The Portuguese navigator Gasper Corte-Real made a voyage in 1500 to the North American coast between Labrador and southeastern Newfoundland. In 1513 Juan Ponce de León, the Spanish governor of Puerto Rico, discovered Florida. Four years later the Spanish soldier Francisco Fernández Córdoba (d. 1518) discovered the Yucatán, and in 1518

Juan de Grijalva (1489?–1527), a nephew of the Spanish soldier Diego Velázquez, explored the eastern coast of Mexico, which he called New Spain. The following year the Spanish conquistador Hernán Cortés invaded Mexico; he conquered it during the next two years.

Spanish Conquests. Spanish conquest of the southern portion of the continent was substantially facilitated by the strife prevailing among the native peoples of the region. Internal turbulence had been especially acute in the Aztec Empire, the rich domain that fell to Cortés in 1521. In many respects the culture of this people, numerically and politically the most powerful in North America, transcended that of the invaders. The Aztecs, however, were hated by many of the tribes under their sovereignty, and some of these tribes became willing allies of Cortés. Through this circumstance and superiority in weapons, Spanish victory was ensured. The Maya, another

An artist's conception of Francisco Coronado, a 16th-century Spanish explorer, leading an expedition in search of the fabled kingdom of Quivira in the Midwest.
Bettmann Archive

155

great Mexican people, living mainly on the Yucatán Peninsula, were disunited also and incapable of offering effective resistance to the Spanish. Although tens of thousands of natives of Mexico and Central America were exterminated during the period of Spanish conquest and rule, the Aztec, Maya, and various other peoples survived and multiplied. Their descendants constitute a large majority of the present-day population of these areas.

The region now known as Baja California was discovered by Cortés in 1536. Among other important Spanish leaders of exploring expeditions during the first half of the 16th century were Pánfilo de Narváez and Álvar Núñez Cabeza de Vaca, who explored parts of Florida, the northern and eastern coasts of the Gulf of Mexico, and parts of northern Mexico between 1528 and 1536; Hernando de Soto, who discovered the Mississippi River in 1541; and Francisco Vásquez de Coronado, who explored large areas in the southwestern part of the present-day U.S. between 1540 and 1542.

By 1600 the Spanish had subjugated the natives of the larger West Indian islands, of the Florida Peninsula, and of southern Mexico (New Spain). For administrative purposes the colonies founded by the Spanish in these areas were grouped in the viceroyalty of New Spain. After consolidating their control of New Spain, the Spanish authorities gradually pushed northward, completing the conquest of Mexico and taking over large areas in the south of what is now the U.S. The colonial policy of Spain in North America was identical in all important respects with its South American colonial policy, that is, ruthless economic exploitation. Regarding the colonies merely as a source of wealth, the Spanish rulers imposed confiscation taxation and maintained a monopoly of colonial trade. The Spanish government even forbade commercial intercourse among its American colonies. This oppressive economic policy and a concomitant political tyranny created among the people of Latin America a spirit of discontent that finally flared into open rebellion.

French and English Colonization. While Spain was consolidating its position in southern North America, France and England explored and settled the continent from Canada southward. England and Spain had been generally allied in international politics during the early part of the 16th century, and as a result the English did not then attempt to compete with Spain for territory on the continent. France, the chief rival of Spain for hegemony on the European continent, entered the race for colonial empire somewhat be-

latedly, but its territorial acquisitions in the New World were nonetheless important. In 1524 the Florentine navigator Giovanni da Verrazano, sailing in French service, followed the North American coast from Cape Fear northward to a point usually identified as Cape Breton. In the course of this voyage he discovered what are now called Narragansett and New York bays. In three voyages between 1534 and 1542 the French explorer Jacques Cartier discovered the Gulf of Saint Lawrence, the Saint Lawrence River, and the Indian village that later became the site of Montréal. France claimed most of the northern part of the continent on the basis of these discoveries. Because of domestic turmoil resulting from the Protestant Reformation, the French were forced to suspend colonial activity for more than half a century. Beginning in 1599, they established fur-trading posts along the St. Lawrence River. Numerous French Jesuit priests came thereafter to the St. Lawrence region, seeking to convert the Indians to the Roman Catholic faith, and various French explorers found and claimed for France new and widely separate sections of the continent. Among the most notable of these explorers were Samuel de Champlain, who founded Québec in 1608 and explored what is now northern New York; the Jesuit missionary Claude Jean Allouez (1622–89), who opened up new territory about Lake Superior; and the Jesuit missionary Jacques Marquette and the explorer Louis Jolliet, who in 1673 together explored the upper Mississippi River as far south as present-day Arkansas. One of the most noted French pioneers in North America was Robert Cavelier, sieur de La Salle, who in 1682 navigated the Mississippi from its junction with the Ohio River to the Gulf of Mexico. In the name of France he took possession of the entire Mississippi Valley, naming it Louisiana after King Louis XIV of France.

The English crown laid claim to the North American continent on the strength of the Cabot voyage of 1497–98, but for nearly a century made no attempts at colonization. The earliest colony in North America was established in 1583 near the present city of Saint John's, Newf., by the English navigator and soldier Sir Humphrey Gilbert, but the settlers returned to England the same year. The first permanent British colony on the continent was Jamestown, which was established in Virginia in 1607. In 1620 Plymouth Colony was founded on the shores of Cape Cod Bay, and Massachusetts Bay Colony was established between 1628 and 1630 on the shores of Massachusetts Bay. After 1630 the English systematically colonized the entire Atlantic seaboard between French Acadia and Spanish Florida. In

The First Sermon Ashore, *a romantic depiction of Plymouth Colony in 1621 by J. L. G. Ferris. About half of the settlers died during the first winter.* Bettmann Archive

addition, in 1664 the English annexed the Dutch colony of New Netherland, founded in 1624, which they renamed New York, and the settlements on the Delaware River that the Dutch had seized from Swedish colonists in 1655. The English colonies grew rapidly in population and wealth. For details, *see* UNITED STATES OF AMERICA: *History.*

At the beginning of the last decade of the 17th century, most of the North American continent from Canada to the Gulf of Mexico was occupied by the French and English colonial empires. The French colonies were widely scattered. The principal settlements were grouped in Canada and near the mouth of the Mississippi River, and a line of trading and military posts along the Ohio and Mississippi rivers connected the two regions. The English colonial holdings consisted of 12 colonies extending along the Atlantic seaboard. A 13th, Georgia, was chartered in 1733.

War and Revolution. As a consequence of efforts to expand westward beyond the Alleghenies, the English eventually came into conflict with the French in the Ohio Valley. In 1689 the two powers began a worldwide struggle for military and

colonial supremacy. In North America the conflict was fought in four successive phases: King William's War, which lasted from 1689 to 1697; Queen Anne's War, from 1702 to 1713; King George's War, from 1744 to 1748; and the French and Indian War, from 1754 to 1763. Reverses suffered in the French and Indian War and in its European extension, the Seven Years' War, forced the French to capitulate. By the Treaty of Paris of 1763 France was forced to yield to Great Britain all its holdings in Canada and also all of Louisiana east of the Mississippi. France had previously ceded to Spain, its ally, New Orleans and all French territory west of the Mississippi.

The outstanding event of the two decades from 1763 to 1783 on the continent was the economic, political, and military conflict between Great Britain and its 13 colonies along the Atlantic seaboard south of Canada. Generally called the American Revolution, this conflict terminated in the establishment of the United States of America. The success of the 13 colonies in freeing themselves from the oppressive rule of their parent country soon had repercussions among the Spanish colonies in the Americas. Inspired by their victory and also by the outcome of the French Revolution, and taking advantage of the involvement of Spain in the Napoleonic Wars, in 1810 the Spanish colonies in the Americas began a struggle for independence. Mexico revolted against Spain in that year but did not actually become free until 1821. During the late 19th and early 20th centuries Canada also succeeded in obtaining from Great Britain a full degree of self-government.

U.S. Expansion. Other outstanding developments marked the history of North America in the 19th century, and they continued in the 20th century. The first involved the increasing importance of the U.S., marked by the nation's unparalleled growth in population and wealth, and its concomitant territorial growth; its resolution of many internal economic and political problems, particularly those of slavery and national unity; and its emergence toward the end of the 19th century as a world power.

The U.S. territorial expansion, sometimes called the "winning of the West," was marked by merciless warfare against the Indians who resisted encroachment on their domains. Except in scattered areas, particularly in the southern Appalachians, the Indians living east of the Mississippi River had been eliminated as an effective force by the final decade of the 18th century. Some of the tribes had withdrawn westward, but the great majority had been decimated or completely destroyed. To a large degree the tragic fate of the aborigines of eastern North America was a result of the involvement of their various tribes and nations in the wars and political rivalries among the colonizing powers, particularly the French and English. Many thousands of Indians, however, perished in the futile localized attempts to wrest their ancestral lands from the usurpers. In 1637 the Pequot, one of the great tribes of the New England region, was virtually eliminated in the course of such an action. Later in the century the Wampanoag sachem Philip organized a confederation of New England tribes for struggle against the English colonists. During the ensuing conflict, King Philip's War, fought in 1675 and 1676, the Indians inflicted numerous severe defeats on their adversaries but were finally overcome, primarily as the result of treachery within their own ranks, and they were nearly exterminated.

Between 1832, when the Sac and Fox chief Black Hawk initiated a war in defense of tribal lands east of the Mississippi River, and 1877, when the Nez Percé tribe of Oregon was vanquished, the Indians of the Great Plains, the Southwest, and the Rocky Mountains contested

An example of 19th-century abstract art by Sioux Indians, painted on buffalo hide. Museum of Primitive Art

almost every major U.S. move westward. Much of this armed opposition to U.S. authority originated among the Sioux, one of the chief peoples of western North America. Sioux resistance reached a memorable climax at the Battle of the Little Bighorn, fought in Montana on June 25, 1876. In this battle a large force of Indian braves under the command of the Sioux chiefs Crazy Horse, Sitting Bull, and Gall (1840?–94) annihilated a U.S. Army detachment numbering some 260 men. *See* LITTLE BIGHORN, BATTLE OF THE.

Meanwhile, the U.S. government had, by treaty arrangements, land purchases, and the establishment of reservations, obtained the cooperation of some tribes and reduced the hostility of others. After the creation in 1849 of the Bureau of Indian Affairs, an agency of the U.S. Department of the Interior, the lot of the Indians in the U.S. slowly and gradually improved. Both in the U.S. and Canada, however, the overwhelming majority of Indians continue to live on reservations. In many of these areas, which represent a poorly integrated fusion of Indian civilization with that of whites, the economic plight of the Indians is serious.

In addition to acquisitions of contiguous territory in the 19th and 20th centuries, the U.S. obtained other regions in North America. These regions were Alaska, discovered in 1741 by the Danish navigator Vitus Bering while in the service of Russia, and sold by Russia to the U.S. in 1867 for $7 million; Puerto Rico, ceded by Spain in 1898 after the Spanish-American War; the Panama Canal Zone, acquired in 1903, but ceded to Panama in 1979; and the Virgin Islands of the United States, purchased from Denmark in 1917 for $25 million.

Hemispheric Developments. A second important development in the history of the continent in the 19th and especially in the 20th century was the participation of the North American nations in the movement manifest throughout the western hemisphere for economic cooperation, for the attainment of peace and mutual understanding, and for solidarity against potential aggressors. In this movement the U.S. played a leading part. The principal display of hemispheric solidarity in the 19th century was the proclamation in 1823 by U.S. President James Monroe of the Monroe Doctrine (q.v.), which stated the intention of the U.S. not to permit European control of territory in the Americas beyond that existing at the time. The only serious intracontinental conflict was the so-called Mexican War of 1846–48 between the U.S. and Mexico. During the 20th century a tendency toward mutual friendship has been apparent among the nations of the western hemisphere. A notable expression of the desire for peace and understanding among the nations of North and South America was the establishment in 1910 of the Pan-American Union. In World War I almost all the nations of the western hemisphere either declared war on or broke diplomatic relations with the Central Powers. In World War II most of these nations acted similarly toward the Axis powers.

One of the most important demonstrations of hemispheric solidarity was the Inter-American Defense Conference of 1947, which promulgated the Inter-American Treaty of Reciprocal Assistance, also known as the Rio Treaty. Signed in September 1947 by the U.S., Mexico, and 17 Central and South American nations, the treaty provides for amicable settlement of disagreements between nations of the western hemisphere, as well as for joint defense against aggression on the region extending from the Bering Sea to the South Pole. In 1948 the Organization of American States (OAS) was formed to implement the Rio Treaty and to serve as a collective security system.

Hemispheric cooperation was temporarily furthered by the Alliance for Progress, which was established in 1961. The alliance, which was accepted by the U.S. and 19 Latin American nations at Punta del Este, Uruguay, consisted of a 10-year development plan to raise the economic and social levels of the area and to strengthen its democratic institutions. After the original 10-year period, however, the alliance showed mixed results, and it gradually ceased to function.

The existence after 1959 of a Communist regime in Cuba tended to mar the solidarity of hemispheric activities. In 1962 at Punta del Este, the OAS voted to exclude Cuba "from participation in the Inter-American system" because of that nation's alignment with the countries of the Communist bloc. Subsequently the U.S., announcing that it had discovered Soviet missile bases in Cuba, blockaded the island and demanded the removal of the bases. The Soviet Union complied and removed the weapons by the end of the year.

Particularly friendly and cooperative since the War of 1812 have been the relations between the U.S. and Canada. No military installations aimed at defense against each other have existed since that time on the entire border between the two nations. The U.S. and Canada collaborated closely in the fight against the Axis powers during World War II. In the postwar period, usually referred to as the era of the cold war, the Canadian and American governments initiated plans for joint defense against possible aggression from the Soviet Union across the Arctic regions.

Despite some temporary differences and irksome problems, cooperation and friendship have also, on the whole, characterized U.S.-Mexican relations, especially in the last quarter of the 20th century.

For further information on this topic, see the Bibliography in volume 28, sections 1103–1230.

NORTHAMPTON, borough, administrative center of Northamptonshire, central England, on the Nene R. Northampton is an important market center and is known for its footwear and leather industries. Other manufactures include machinery and electronic equipment. In Northampton are Saint Sepulchre's Church, an early 12th-century round church; a Roman Catholic cathedral (begun 1864); and several museums. A settlement of Anglo-Saxon origins, Northampton was occupied by the Danes in the 9th century. It received its first charter in 1189, at which time it was a prosperous commercial community. In 1675 a fire destroyed most of the town. Shoe manufacturing developed here in the 18th century. Pop. (1981) 156,848.

NORTHAMPTON, city, seat of Hampshire Co., W Massachusetts, on the Connecticut R.; inc. as a city 1883. It is a residential and manufacturing center. Major products include brooms and brushes, optical instruments, photographic equipment, cutlery, soft drinks, caskets, and printed materials. Northampton is the site of Smith College (1871), the Clarke School for the Deaf, and a number of historic homes. The community, settled in 1654 and named for Northampton, England, remained mainly a farming center until the mid-19th century, when manufacturing became important. Calvin Coolidge lived in the city and served as its mayor (1910–11) before becoming U.S. president. Pop. (1970) 29,664; (1980) 29,286.

NORTHAMPTONSHIRE, county, central England; Northampton is the administrative center. Northamptonshire has an undulating terrain. It is essentially an agricultural county, with livestock raising predominating. Iron ore is mined in the N, and iron and steel are manufactured at Corby. Northampton is known for the production of footwear and clothing. Part of the Anglo-Saxon kingdom of Mercia in the 7th century, Northamptonshire was probably made a county during the subsequent Danish rule. Area, 2367 sq km (914 sq mi); pop. (1981) 527,532.

NORTH ATLANTIC TREATY ORGANIZATION (NATO), regional defense alliance, formed under Article 9 of the North Atlantic Treaty that was signed on April 4, 1949. The original signatories were Belgium, Canada, Denmark, France, Great Britain, Iceland, Italy, Luxembourg, the Netherlands, Norway, Portugal, and the U.S. Greece and Turkey were admitted to the alliance in 1952, West Germany in 1955, and Spain in 1982. NATO's purpose is to enhance the stability, well-being, and freedom of its members by means of a system of collective security.

Background. In the years after the end of World War II, many Western leaders found the policies of the Soviet Union threatening to stability and peace. The forcible installation of Communist governments throughout Eastern Europe, territorial demands by the Soviets, and their support of guerrilla war in Greece and regional separatism in Iran appeared to many as the first steps of World War III. Such events prompted the signing of the Dunkirk Treaty (1947) between Britain and France, pledging common defense against aggression. Subsequent events, including the rejection by Eastern European nations of the Economic Recovery Program (Marshall Plan) and the creation of Cominform (1947), led to the Brussels Treaty (1948), signed by most Western European countries. Among the goals of that pact was the collective defense of its members. The Berlin blockade that began in March 1948 led to negotiations between Western Europe,

Canada, and the U.S. that resulted in the framing of the North Atlantic Treaty.

Treaty Provisions. The treaty consists of a preamble and 14 articles. The preamble states the purpose of the treaty: to promote the common values of its members and to "unite their efforts for collective defense." Article 1 calls for peaceful resolution of disputes. Article 2 pledges the parties to economic and political cooperation. Article 3 calls for development of the capacity for defense. Article 4 provides for joint consultations when a member is threatened. Article 5 promises the use of the members' armed forces for "collective self-defense." Article 6 defines the areas covered by the treaty. Article 7 affirms the precedence of members' obligations under the UN Charter. Article 8 safeguards against conflict with any other treaties of the signatories. Article 9 creates a council to oversee implementation of the treaty. Article 10 describes admission procedures for other nations. Article 11 states the ratification procedure. Article 12 allows for reconsideration of the treaty. Article 13 outlines withdrawal procedures. Article 14 calls for the deposition of the official copies of the treaty in the U.S. Archives.

Structure. The highest authority within NATO is the North Atlantic Council, composed of permanent delegates from all members, headed by a secretary-general. It is responsible for general policy, budgetary outlines, and administrative actions. Subordinate to the council are the Secretariat, various temporary committees, and the Military Committee. The secretary-general runs the secretariat, which handles all the nonmilitary functions of the alliance. The temporary committees deal with specific assignments of the council. The Military Committee consists of the chiefs of staff of the various armed forces; it meets twice a year. Between such meetings the Military Committee, in permanent session with representatives of the members, defines military policies. Below the Military Committee are the various geographical commands: Allied Command Europe, Allied Command Atlantic, Allied Command Channel, and the Regional Planning Group (for North America). These commands are in charge of deploying armed forces in their areas.

History. The outbreak of the Korean War in 1950 intensified NATO activities and led to the adoption of a so-called forward defense policy that sought to avert a possible Soviet invasion into Germany. This led to suggestions that West Germany be allowed to rearm and join the alliance—suggestions bitterly resisted by the French until 1955. Another proposal—for a joint European Defense Community—was also opposed by France. In the late 1950s the emergence of a So-

The nations that are members of NATO meet regularly during the year to discuss "stability and well-being in the North Atlantic area." UPI

viet ICBM (intercontinental ballistic missile) threat to the U.S. raised doubts about the American commitment to Europe, but these were assuaged by President John F. Kennedy's stand after the building of the Berlin Wall in 1961.

France, under President Charles de Gaulle, withdrew from all military bodies of NATO in 1966, calling for a removal of U.S. influence from Europe. Increasing American involvement in Vietnam during the 1960s led to reductions in U.S. force levels in Europe until 1973. This example and the policy of détente persuaded most members to cut their defense budgets until the mid-1970s, when the increase in Soviet forces in Europe induced NATO countries to initiate a variety of rearmament programs, as stated in the Long Term Defense Program of 1977. In 1979 the decision was reached to deploy a new generation of tactical nuclear cruise and ballistic missiles to counter the increase in Soviet missile capacity. The Soviet invasion of Afghanistan in December of that year gave further impetus to NATO rearmament plans.

Achievements. Over the years the existence of NATO has led to closer ties between its members and to a growing community of interests. The treaty itself has provided a model for other collective security agreements. Although it cannot be proved, it is possible that NATO has dissuaded the Soviet Union from attempting direct assault on Western Europe. On the other hand,

the rearmament of West Germany and its admission to the alliance in 1954 (effective in May 1955) were the apparent causes of the establishment of the Warsaw Pact in 1955.

Despite disagreement among its members about how to handle various problems, most Western observers still see NATO as an umbrella of security for Western Europe, as well as a forum for the discussion of outstanding issues.   E.N.L.

For further information on this topic, see the Bibliography in volume 28, section 191.

NORTH BATTLEFORD, city, W Saskatchewan, Canada, at the confluence of the North Saskatchewan and Battle rivers, near Battleford; inc. 1913. It is a commercial and distribution center for the surrounding grain-producing and ranching area. Manufactures include forest products and construction materials. Nearby is Battleford National Historic Park, which includes buildings of an old Northwest Mounted Police post. The community was settled with the arrival of the railroad around 1903. Pop. (1976) 13,158; (1981) 14,030.

NORTH BAY, manufacturing city, seat of Nipissing District, SE Ontario, Canada, on Lake Nipissing and Trout Lake; inc. as a city 1925. Major manufactures include forest products, mining equipment, clothing, soft drinks, and explosives. Tourism and nearby Canadian Forces military installations are also important to the city's economy. Nipissing College is here. The community, laid out in 1882 with the arrival of the railroad, is named for its location on the north bay of Lake Nipissing. Pop. (1976) 51,639; (1981) 51,268.

NORTH BERGEN, township, Hudson Co., NE New Jersey, on the Hudson R., near Jersey City; inc. 1861. It is a residential and transportation hub with some industry. The village of Bergen was established by Dutch colonists around 1630. It is considered the first municipality in what is now New Jersey. In 1688 the community of North Bergen was separated from Bergen. Several communities, such as Hoboken, Weehawken, and Secaucus, were later set off from North Bergen. Pop. (1970) 47,751; (1980) 47,019.

NORTHBROOK, village, Cook Co., NE Illinois, a suburb of Chicago, near Lake Michigan; inc. as a village 1923. It is primarily residential and has insurance-company offices and some manufacturing industries. A botanical garden is nearby. The community, settled in 1838, was called Shermer's Station after the arrival of the railroad in 1871. The present name was chosen in a contest in 1922. Pop. (1970) 25,422; (1980) 30,778.

NORTH CAPE, promontory, N Norway, at lat 71° 10' N. Often referred to as the most northerly point of Europe, it is not on the continent but on the island of Magerøya. The northernmost point of the continent itself is nearby Cape Nordkinn.

NORTH CAROLINA, one of the South Atlantic states of the U.S., bordered on the N by Virginia, on the E by the Atlantic Ocean, on the S by South Carolina and Georgia, and on the W by Tennessee.

North Carolina entered the Union on Nov. 21, 1789, as the 12th of the 13 original states. It was principally a farming state until the 1920s, when such manufactures as textiles, furniture, and tobacco products began to dominate the economy. In the early 1980s, however, agriculture remained an important economic activity, as were forestry and tourism. Two 19th-century U.S. presidents, James K. Polk and Andrew Johnson, were born in the state, and another, Andrew Jackson, was born in the border area between North and South Carolina. North Carolina is named for Charles I and Charles II of England. North Carolina is known as the Tar Heel State.

LAND AND RESOURCES

North Carolina has some of the most striking contrasts in physical geography of any state in the E half of the U.S. It has an area of 136,412 sq km (52,669 sq mi), making it the 28th largest of the U.S. states; 6.5% of its land area is owned by the federal government. North Carolina is roughly rectangular in shape, and its extreme dimensions are about 815 km (about 505 mi) from E to W and about 305 km (about 190 mi) from N to S. Elevations range from sea level, along the

Atlantic Ocean, to 2037 m (6684 ft), atop Mt. Mitchell in the W part of the state. The approximate mean elevation is 213 m (700 ft). North Carolina has a coastline of 484 km (301 mi).

Physical Geography. About two-fifths of North Carolina is part of the Atlantic Coastal Plain, a region formed mainly by the gradual uplifting of the ancient seafloor next to the continent. The plain is underlain by soft, unconsolidated sedimentary beds such as sand and clay. Within about 80 km (about 50 mi) of the coast the surface of the plain is especially flat. Swamps and marshes are widespread; the Great Dismal Swamp, which extends into Virginia, is in the NE. Broad, shallow sounds such as Albemarle Sound and Pamlico Sound lie between the coast and a line of offshore sandy islands called the Outer Banks. Other islands are closer to the shore. On the islands are Cape Hatteras, Cape Lookout, and Cape Fear. Inland the elevation of the Coastal Plain rises gradually to about 90 m (about 300 ft). A line of sand hills extends along part of the inner Coastal Plain boundary.

Bordering the Coastal Plain on the W is a section of the Piedmont Plateau region, which also covers about two-fifths of North Carolina. These two regions are separated by the fall line, where rivers descend over rapids as they flow from the more elevated Piedmont onto the Coastal Plain. Consolidated rocks underlie the Piedmont. Inland from the fall line is a narrow band of reddish sandstones and shales, followed by a broader belt composed mainly of slate and then by a still broader belt of hard crystalline rocks such as granite and gneiss. Elevations increase steadily inland from about 90 m (about 300 ft) to about 460 m (about 1500 ft) at the inner margin of the Piedmont.

The westernmost region of North Carolina, the Blue Ridge, includes more than 40 peaks rising above 1829 m (6000 ft). The region's rocks, such as gneiss and quartzite, are very hard. Mountains are mostly rounded in shape, but steep-sided gorges also occur. The Great Smoky Mts. are the best-known part of this region. Several basins are in the Blue Ridge region. The city of Asheville is in the largest of these basins.

Rivers and Lakes. Most of the large rivers of North Carolina flow SE across the Piedmont Plateau and the Coastal Plain to the Atlantic. These include the Roanoke, which rises in Virginia, the Tar, the Neuse, and the Cape Fear. Some rivers, such as the Catawba and the Yadkin (Pee Dee), flow into South Carolina before continuing toward the Atlantic. In the Blue Ridge region most rivers flow toward the W or N. Rivers such as the French Broad flow to the Tennessee R.

Sheep grazing on the rolling hills near Banner Elk, in northwestern North Carolina. Agriculture and livestock make substantial contributions to the state's income.
Clyde H. Smith–Peter Arnold, Inc.

system beyond North Carolina, and the New R. flows N toward the Ohio R.

North Carolina's natural lakes are small. Most, including the largest, Mattamuskeet, are in the Atlantic Coastal Plain. Several large artificial lakes have been formed by dams on rivers. These include Lake Gaston, on the Roanoke R.; High Rock Lake and Lake Tillery, on the Yadkin R.; Lake Norman, on the Catawba R.; and Fontana Lake, on the Little Tennessee R. A number of picturesque waterfalls are in the Blue Ridge region.

Climate. Important climatic differences exist within North Carolina. The Coastal Plain and Piedmont Plateau regions are just within the N limit of the humid subtropical climate area. In the Blue Ridge the climate is humid continental. The state's climates are affected by distance from the Atlantic and by elevation. As a result, winters are cold and summers cool in the Blue Ridge and at other higher elevations. The Piedmont Plateau and Coastal Plain have mild winters, because they are relatively low in elevation, are close to the Atlantic, and are protected by high mountains from the cold winter air of the interior of North America. Rainfall in North Carolina comes

at all times of the year, but in greater amounts in late winter and in summer. Precipitation is higher in the Blue Ridge than in the other regions. The SW corner of the state has some of the greatest yearly precipitation totals of the eastern U.S. Snowfall is at times heavy in the Blue Ridge, but the rest of the state receives little snow. Northward-moving hurricanes occasionally strike the coast, particularly between Cape Hatteras and Cape Fear. The recorded temperature in North Carolina has ranged from −33.9° C (−29° F), in 1966 on Mt. Mitchell in the W, to 42.8° C (109° F), in 1940 at Albemarle in the center and in 1954 at Weldon in the NE.

Plants and Animals. The Atlantic Coastal Plain has forests of shortleaf, longleaf, loblolly, and Virginia pine. They are part of the much larger Southeastern Pine Forest of the U.S. Hardwood trees such as cypress grow in the wet areas, including the Great Dismal Swamp. In the Piedmont Plateau region the forest is a mixture of pines and hardwoods, mainly varieties of oak. Lower Blue Ridge slopes are covered with oak, hickory, tulip, poplar, and other hardwood trees. On somewhat higher slopes these give way to birch, beech, maple, and hemlock; above about 1770 m (about 5800 ft) are spruce and balsam-fir forests. The mountain forests have a rich understory of rhododendron and azalea. Other flowering plants of North Carolina include camellia, dogwood, and orchid.

Virginia deer, opossum, raccoon, squirrel, and fox are widespread in North Carolina. Black bear still survive in Coastal Plain forests and are common in parts of the Blue Ridge, especially Great Smoky Mountains National Park. Ducks, geese, and other waterfowl migrate along the Atlantic flyway in the coastal section of the state. Common freshwater fish of North Carolina's rivers and lakes include bass, catfish, crappie, perch, shad, and trout. Among the marine animals living in North Carolina's coastal waters are bluefish, flounder, herring, mackerel, menhaden, oysters, shrimp, and scallops.

Mineral Resources. North Carolina has deposits of a variety of minerals. Among the more important are limestone, phosphate rock, sand and gravel, clay, talc, lithium, feldspar, mica, olivine, asbestos, and various gemstones.   D.J.P.

POPULATION

According to the 1980 census, North Carolina had 5,881,813 inhabitants, an increase of 15.7% over 1970. The average population density was 43 people per sq km (112 per sq mi). Whites made up 75.8% of the population and blacks 22.4%; additional population groups included some 64,519 American Indians, 4718 persons of Asian Indian background, 3581 persons of Korean extraction, 3186 persons of Japanese descent, and 3170 persons of Chinese ancestry. North Carolina had the largest American Indian population of any state E of the Mississippi R.; the Cherokee (q.v.) and Lumbee are the state's principal Indian groups. Approximately 56,600 persons in North Carolina were of Hispanic background. Baptists form the state's largest religious group. North Carolina is one of the least urbanized states in the nation; in 1980 about 48% of all North Carolinians lived in areas defined as urban and the rest lived in rural areas. The state's largest cities were Charlotte; Greensboro; Raleigh, the capital; Winston-Salem; and Durham.

EDUCATION AND CULTURAL ACTIVITY

North Carolina has notable educational and cultural institutions and a number of interesting historical sites. Of special interest are the handicrafts, music, and pageantry of the people of the mountainous W part of the state.

Education. The first school in North Carolina was set up in the early 18th century, but a public school system began to be established only in 1839. In 1795 the University of North Carolina at

Chapel Hill had become the first state university in the U.S. to hold classes.

In the early 1980s, North Carolina had 2032 public elementary and secondary schools. About 785,900 elementary pupils and 343,500 secondary students were enrolled in these schools each year. About 58,600 of the state's schoolchildren attended private schools.

In the same period, North Carolina had 126 institutions of higher education, which had a combined annual enrollment of about 287,540. Besides the University of North Carolina at Chapel Hill, notable schools included the University of North Carolina at Charlotte (1965), at Greensboro (1891), and at Wilmington (1947); North Carolina State University at Raleigh (1887); Appalachian State University (1899), at Boone; East Carolina University (1907), at Greenville; Western Carolina University (1889), at Cullowhee; Bennett College (1873) and Guilford College (1837), at Greensboro; Davidson College (1837), at Davidson; Duke University, at Durham; Lenoir-Rhyne College (1891), at Hickory; Shaw University (1865), at Raleigh; and Wake Forest University (1834), at Winston-Salem.

Monument to Wilbur and Orville Wright, the aeronautical pioneers, near Kill Devil Hills, N.C. State of North Carolina

INDEX TO MAP OF NORTH CAROLINA

Cities and Towns

Abbottsburg H 5
Aberdeen G 4
Acme J 6
Ahoskie L 2
Alamance F 2
Alarka D 8
Albemarle ⊙ E 4
Alexander Mills B 4
Alliance M 4
Altamahaw G 2
Andrews C 9
Angier H 4
Ansonville E 4
Apex H 3
Archdale F 3
Arlington D 2
Asheboro ⊙ F 3
Asheville ⊙ E 8
Atlantic N 5
Aulander L 2
Aurora M 4
Avondale B 4
Ayden L 4
Badin E 4
Bailey J 3
Bakersville ⊙ B 7
Balfour F 8
Banner Elk C 7
Bannertown D 1
Barker Heights E 9
Bat Cave F 8
Battleboro K 2
Bayboro ⊙ M 4
Bear Creek G 3
Beaufort ⊙ M 5
Beech Creek C 6
Belhaven M 3
Bellwood B 4
Belmont D 4
Belville J 6
Benson J 4
Bessemer City C 4
Beta D 8
Bethel L 3
Beulaville K 5
Biltmore Forest F 8
Biscoe F 4
Black Creek K 3
Black Mountain F 8
Bladenboro H 5
Blowing Rock C 7
Boger City C 4
Boiling Springs B 4
Bolton J 6
Boone ⊙ D 6
Boonville D 2
Brevard ⊙ E 9
Bridgeton M 4
Broadway G 4
Brookford C 3
Browns Summit F 2
Bryson City ⊙ D 8
Buies Creek H 4
Bullock H 2
Burgaw ⊙ J 5
Burlington F 2
Burnsville ⊙ B 7
Butner H 2
Buxton P 4
Bynum G 3
Calabash H 7
Calypso J 4
Camden ⊙ N 2
Candler E 8
Candor F 4
Canton E 8
Cape Carteret M 5
Carolina Beach K 6
Carrboro G 3
Carthage ⊙ F 4

⊙ County seat

Cary H 3
Castle Hayne K 6
Caswell Beach J 7
Catawba C 3
Catharine Lake K 5
Cedar Falls F 3
Chadbourn H 6
Chadwick Acres L 6
Chapel Hill G 3
Charlotte ⊙ D 4
Cherokee D 8
Cherryville C 4
China Grove D 3
Chocowinity L 4
Claremont C 3
Clarkton H 6
Clayton J 3
Clemmons E 2
Cleveland D 3
Cliffside B 4
Climax F 3
Clinton ⊙ J 5
Clyde E 8
Coats H 4
Coinjock N 2
Coleridge F 3
Columbia ⊙ N 3
Columbus ⊙ F 9
Concord ⊙ D 4
Connellys Springs B 3
Conover C 3
Conway L 2
Cooleemee D 3
Cornelius D 4
Cove City L 4
Cramerton C 4
Creedmoor H 2
Creswell N 3
Crossnore C 7
Cruso E 8
Cullowhee D 8
Cumberland H 5
Currituck ⊙ O 2
Dallas C 4
Danbury ⊙ E 2
Davidson D 4
Davis M 5
Delco J 6
Denton E 3
Dobson ⊙ D 2
Dortches K 2
Dover L 4
Drexel B 3
Dunn H 4
Durham ⊙ H 2
Dysartsville G 8
Eagle Springs F 4
East Arcadia J 6
East Bend D 2
East Flat Rock F 9
East Laurinburg G 5
East Marion B 3
East Spencer E 3
Eden F 1
Edenton ⊙ M 2
Edgemount B 2
Efland G 2
Elizabeth City ⊙ N 2
Elizabethtown ⊙ H 5
Elkin D 2
Elk Park A 2
Ellerbe F 4
Elm City K 3
Elmwood D 3
Elon College G 2
Enfield K 2
Engelhard O 3
Enka E 8
Erwin H 4
Etowah E 8
Fair Bluff H 6
Fairfield N 3
Fairmont G 6
Fairview E 8
Faison J 4
Faith E 3
Fallston C 4
Farmville K 3
Fayetteville ⊙ H 4
Flat Rock F 9
Fletcher E 8
Forest City B 4
Fountain K 3
Four Oaks H 4
Foxfire F 4
Franklin ⊙ C 9
Franklinton J 2
Franklinville F 3
Freeland J 6
Fremont J 3
Fuquay-Varina H 3
Garland J 5
Garner H 3
Gaston K 1
Gastonia ⊙ C 4
Gatesville ⊙ M 2
Gibson F 5
Gibsonville F 2
Glen Alpine B 3
Glen Raven G 2
Goldsboro ⊙ K 4
Graham ⊙ G 2
Granite Falls C 3
Granite Quarry D 3
Grantsboro M 4
Green Mountain B 7
Greensboro ⊙ F 2
Greenville ⊙ L 3
Grifton L 4
Grover C 4
Halifax ⊙ K 2
Hamilton L 3
Hamlet F 5
Harkers Island M 5
Harrisburg D 4
Hatteras O 4
Havelock L 5
Haw River G 2
Hayesville ⊙ C 9
Hays C 2
Haywood G 3
Hazelwood D 8
Henderson ⊙ J 2
Hendersonville ⊙ F 8
Henrietta B 4
Hertford ⊙ N 2
Hickory C 3
Hiddenite C 3
Highlands D 9
High Point E 3
High Shoals C 4
Hildebran B 3
Hillsborough ⊙ G 2
Hobgood L 2
Hobucken N 4
Hoffman F 4
Hollister K 2
Holly Springs H 3
Hookerton K 4
Hope Mills H 5
Hot Springs E 7
Hubert L 5
Hudson C 3
Huntersville D 4
Icard C 3
Indian Beach M 5
Jackson ⊙ L 2
Jacksonville ⊙ K 5
James City M 4
Jamestown F 3
Jamesville M 3
Jason K 4
Jefferson ⊙ E 6
Jonesville D 2
Kannapolis D 4
Kenansville ⊙ K 5
Kenly J 3
Kernersville E 2
Kill Devil Hills O 3
King E 2
Kings Mountain C 4
Kinston ⊙ K 4
Kittrell H 2
Kitty Hawk O 2
Knightdale J 3
Knotts Island O 2
Kure Beach K 7
La Grange K 4
Lake Lure A 4
Lake Toxaway E 9
Lakeview G 4
Lake Waccamaw J 6
Landis D 3
Laurel Hill F 5
Laurel Park E 8
Laurinburg ⊙ F 5
Lawndale B 4
Lawrence K 2
Leland J 6
Lenoir ⊙ C 3
Lexington ⊙ E 3
Liberty F 3
Lilesville F 5
Lillington ⊙ H 4
Lincolnton ⊙ C 4
Littleton K 2
Long Beach J 7
Longview C 3
Longwood H 7
Longwood Park F 5
Louisburg ⊙ J 2
Lowell C 4
Lowgap D 1
Lowland N 4
Lucama J 3
Lumberton ⊙ G 5
Lynn F 9
McCain G 4
Macclesfield K 3
Madison E 2
Magnolia K 5
Maiden C 3
Mamers G 4
Manteo ⊙ O 3
Marble C 9
Marion ⊙ A 3
Marshall ⊙ E 8
Marshallberg N 5
Mars Hill E 7
Marshville E 4
Matthews D 4
Maury K 4
Maxton G 5
Mayodan F 2
Maysville L 5
Mebane G 2
Merrimon M 5
Mesic M 4
Middlesex J 3
Midland E 4
Midway Park K 5
Minnesott Beach M 5
Mint Hill D 4
Misenheimer E 4
Mocksville ⊙ D 3
Moncure G 3
Monroe ⊙ E 5
Mooresville D 3
Morehead City M 5
Morganton ⊙ B 3
Morven E 5
Mount Airy D 1
Mount Gilead F 4
Mount Holly D 4
Mount Mourne D 3
Mount Olive K 4
Mount Pleasant E 4
Murfreesboro M 2
Murphy ⊙ C 9
Nags Head O 3
Nashville ⊙ K 3
Navassa K 6

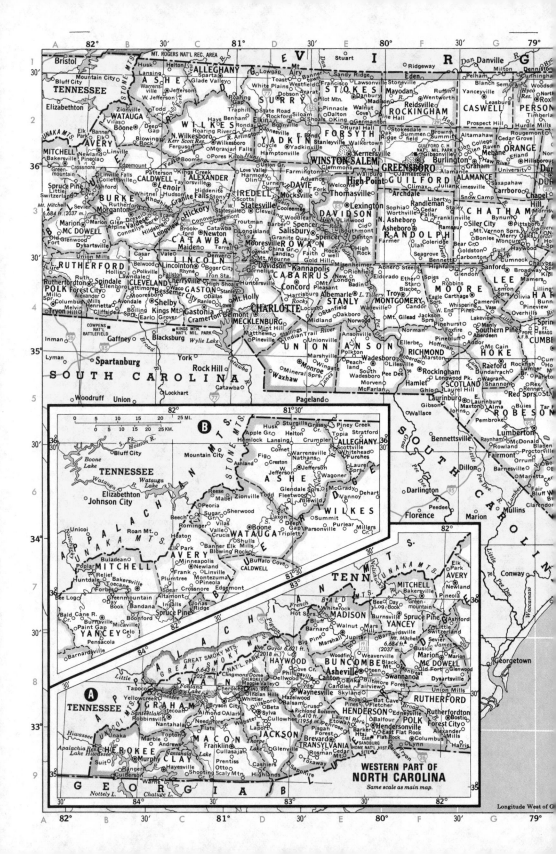

WESTERN PART OF
NORTH CAROLINA

Same scale as main map.

Longitude West of G

Index to Map of North Carolina

Neuse ☉ . . . . .H 3
New Bern ☉ . . . . .L 4
Newland ☉ . . . . .C 7
Newport . . . . .M 5
New River . . . . .K 5
Newton ☉ . . . . .C 3
Newton Grove . . . . .J 4
Norlina . . . . .J 2
North Asheboro . . . . . .F 3
North Harlowe . . . . . . .M 5
North Roxboro . . . . . . .G 2
North Wilkesboro . . . . .C 2
Norwood . . . . .E 4
Oakboro . . . . .E 4
Oak City. . . . . .L 3
Oak Ridge . . . . .F 2
Ocracoke . . . . .O 4
Old Fort . . . . .A 3
Oriental . . . . .M 4
Oteen . . . . .E 8
Oxford ☉ . . . . .H 2
Parkton . . . . .H 5
Parkwood . . . . .H 3
Peachland . . . . .E 5
Pembroke . . . . .G 5
Penrose . . . . .E 8
Phillipsville . . . . .D 8
Pikeville . . . . .J 4
Pilot Mountain . . . . .D 2
Pinebluff . . . . .F 4
Pine Hall . . . . .F 2
Pinehurst . . . . .F 4
Pine Knoll Shores . . . . .M 5
Pine Level . . . . .J 4
Pineola . . . . .C 7
Pinetops . . . . .K 3
Pineville . . . . .D 4
Piney Creek. . . . . .E 5
Pink Hill . . . . .K 4
Pinnacle . . . . .E 2
Pisgah Forest . . . . .E 9
Pittsboro ☉ . . . . .G 3
Plymouth ☉ . . . . .M 3
Polkton . . . . .E 4
Pollocksville . . . . .L 5
Poplar Branch . . . . .O 2
Princeton . . . . .J 4
Princeville . . . . .L 3
Raeford ☉ . . . . .G 5
Raleigh (cap.) ☉ . . . . . .H 3
Ramseur . . . . .F 3
Randleman . . . . .F 3
Ranger. . . . . .B 9
Ranlo . . . . .C 4
Raynham . . . . .G 5
Red Springs . . . . .G 5
Reidsville . . . . .F 2
Rennert . . . . .G 5
Rex . . . . .H 5
Rhodhiss . . . . .B 3
Richlands . . . . .K 5
Rich Square . . . . .L 2
Ridgeway . . . . .J 2
Riegelwood . . . . .J 6
Roanoke Rapids . . . . . . .K 2
Roaring Gap . . . . .D 2
Roaring River . . . . .C 2
Robbins . . . . .F 4
Robbinsville ☉ . . . . .C 8
Robersonville . . . . .L 3
Rockingham ☉ . . . . .F 5
Rockwell . . . . .E 3
Rocky Mount. . . . . .K 3
Rocky Point. . . . . .K 6
Rolesville . . . . .J 3
Ronda . . . . .D 2
Roper . . . . .M 3
Roseboro . . . . .J 5
Rose Hill . . . . .J 5
Rosman . . . . .E 9
Rowland . . . . .G 5
Roxboro ☉ . . . . .H 2

Royal Cotton Mills . . . .H 2
Royal Pines. . . . . .E 8
Ruffin . . . . .F 2
Rural Hall . . . . .E 2
Rutherford College. . . .B 3
Rutherfordton ☉ . . . . . .A 4
Saint Pauls . . . . .H 5
Salemburg . . . . .J 4
Salisbury ☉ . . . . .D 3
Saluda . . . . .F 9
Sandy Ridge . . . . .E 1
Sanford ☉ . . . . .G 4
Saxapahaw . . . . .G 3
Scaly Mountain. . . . . . . .D 9
Scotland Neck. . . . . .L 2
Seaboard . . . . .K 1
Sealevel. . . . . .N 5
Selma . . . . .J 3
Shallotte . . . . .J 7
Sharpsburg . . . . .K 3
Shelby ☉ . . . . .C 4
Siler City . . . . .G 3
Skyland . . . . .E 8
Smithfield ☉ . . . . .J 3
Sneads Ferry . . . . .L 5
Snow Hill ☉ . . . . .K 4
Sophia . . . . .F 3
Soul City . . . . .J 2
Southern Pines. . . . . . . .G 4
South Goldsboro. . . . . . .J 4
South Mills . . . . .N 2
Southmont. . . . . .E 3
Southport ☉ . . . . .J 7
South Weldon . . . . .K 2
Sparta ☉ . . . . .C 1
Spencer . . . . .D 3
Spindale . . . . .B 4
Spring Hope . . . . .J 3
Spring Lake . . . . .H 4
Spruce Pine . . . . .C 7
Stacy . . . . .N 5
Stallings . . . . .D 4
Stanfield . . . . .E 4
Stanley . . . . .C 4
Stanleyville . . . . .E 2
Stantonsburg . . . . .K 3
Star . . . . .F 4
State Road . . . . .D 2
Statesville ☉ . . . . .D 3
Stedman . . . . .H 4
Stokesdale. . . . . .F 2
Stoneville . . . . .F 2
Stony Point . . . . .C 3
Summerfield . . . . .F 2
Swannanoa . . . . .F 8
Swanquarter ☉ . . . . . . .N 4
Swansboro . . . . .L 5
Sylva ☉ . . . . .D 8
Tabor City . . . . .H 6
Tarboro ☉ . . . . .K 3
Taylorsville ☉ . . . . .C 3
Thomasville . . . . .E 3
Toast . . . . .D 2
Trenton ☉ . . . . .L 4
Trent Woods . . . . .L 4
Troutman . . . . .D 3
Troy ☉ . . . . .F 4
Tryon . . . . .A 4
Ulah . . . . .F 3
Union Mills . . . . .B 3
Valdese . . . . .B 3
Vanceboro . . . . .L 4
Vass. . . . . .G 4
Wadesboro ☉ . . . . .E 5
Wagram . . . . .G 5
Wake Forest . . . . .H 3
Walkertown . . . . .E 2
Wallace . . . . .J 5
Walnut Cove . . . . .E 2
Walnut Creek . . . . .K 4
Wanchese . . . . .O 3
Warrensville . . . . .B 2
Warrenton ☉ . . . . .J 2
Warsaw . . . . .J 4

Washington ☉ . . . . . . .M 3
Washington Park . . . . . .M 3
Waxhaw. . . . . .D 5
Waynesville ☉ . . . . .E 8
Weaverville . . . . .E 8
Welcome . . . . .E 3
Weldon . . . . .K 2
Wendell . . . . .J 3
Wentworth ☉ . . . . .F 2
West End . . . . .F 4
Westfield . . . . .D 2
West Jefferson . . . . .D 6
West Statesville . . . . . . .C 3
Whitakers . . . . .K 2
Whiteville ☉ . . . . .H 6
Whitnel . . . . .B 3
Wilkesboro ☉ . . . . .C 2
Williamsboro . . . . .H 2
Williamston ☉ . . . . .M 3
Wilmington ☉ . . . . .J 6
Wilson ☉ . . . . .K 3
Windsor ☉ . . . . .L 2
Winfall . . . . .N 2
Wingate . . . . .E 5
Winston-Salem ☉ . . . . .E 2
Winterville . . . . .L 3
Winton ☉ . . . . .L 2
Wise . . . . .J 2
Woodfin . . . . .E 8
Woodland . . . . .L 2
Woodleaf . . . . .D 3
Wrightsville Beach . . . . .K 6
Yadkinville ☉ . . . . .D 2
Yanceyville ☉ . . . . .G 2
Youngsville . . . . .J 2
Zebulon . . . . .J 3

Other Features

Albemarle (sound) . . . . .N 2
Alligator (lake) . . . . .N 3
Alligator (river) . . . . .N 3
Angola (swamp) . . . . . . .K 5
Apalachia (res.) . . . . . . .B 9
Appalachian (mts.) . . . . .E 7
Ashe (island) . . . . .L 6
Bald (mts.). . . . . .E 7
B. Everett Jordan
  (lake) . . . . .H 3
Black (river) . . . . .J 5
Blue Ridge (mts.) . . . . . .C 2
Bodie (island) . . . . .O 2
Bragg, Fort . . . . .H 4
Broad (river) . . . . .B 4
Buggs Island (lake) . . . .H 1
Cape Fear (river) . . . . . .H 5
Cape Hatteras Nat'l
  Seashore . . . . .O 4
Cape Lookout Nat'l
  Seashore . . . . .N 5
Carl Sandburg Home
  Nat'l Hist. Site. . . . . . .E 9
Catawba (river) . . . . .D 5
Catfish (lake) . . . . .L 5
Chatuge (lake) . . . . .C 9
Cherokee Ind. Res. . . . .D 8
Cherry Point Marine
  Air Sta. . . . . .M 5
Chowan (river) . . . . .M 2
Clingmans Dome (mt.) . .D 8
Contentnea (creek). . . . .J 3
Core (banks) . . . . .N 5
Core (sound). . . . . .N 5
Corncake (inlet) . . . . . . .K 7
Croatan (sound) . . . . . . .O 3
Currituck (sound) . . . . . .O 2
Dan (river) . . . . .G 1
Deep (river) . . . . .F 3
Drum (inlet) . . . . .N 5
Fear (cape) . . . . .K 7
Fishing (creek) . . . . .K 2
Fontana (lake). . . . . .C 8
Fort Bragg. . . . . .H 4

Fort Raleigh Nat'l Hist.
  Site. . . . . .O 3
French Broad (river). . . .E 7
Gaston (lake) . . . . .K 1
Great (lake) . . . . .L 5
Great Dismal (swamp) . .N 1
Great Smoky (mts.) . . . .C 8
Great Smoky Mts.
  Nat'l Park. . . . . .C 8
Green (swamp) . . . . .J 6
Guilford Courthouse
  Nat'l Mil. Park . . . . . . .F 2
Guyot (mt.) . . . . .D 8
Hatteras (cape). . . . . . . .P 4
Hatteras (inlet) . . . . .O 4
Hatteras (island) . . . . . .P 4
Haw (river) . . . . .F 2
High Rock (lake) . . . . . . .E 3
Hiwassee (lake). . . . . . . .B 9
Hiwassee (river). . . . . . . .B 9
Holly Shelter (swamp) . .K 6
Hunting (river) . . . . .D 2
Hyco (res.) . . . . .G 2
James (lake) . . . . .F 8
Lanes (creek) . . . . .E 5
Lejeune, Camp . . . . .L 5
Little (river) . . . . .J 3
Little (river) . . . . .G 4
Little Pee Dee (river) . . .G 6
Little Tennessee
  (river) . . . . .C 8
Long (lake) . . . . .L 5
Lookout (cape). . . . . . . .M 5
Lumber (river) . . . . .G 6
Mattamuskeet (lake) . . .N 3
Meherrin (river) . . . . . . .L 1
Mitchell (mt.) . . . . .A 3
Moores Creek Nat'l
  Battlefield . . . . .J 6
Nantahala (lake) . . . . . .C 9
Neuse (river). . . . . .M 5
New (river) . . . . .K 5
New River (inlet). . . . . . .L 6
Nolichucky (river). . . . . .A 7
Norman (lake). . . . . .D 3
North East Cape Fear
  (river) . . . . .K 4
Ocracoke (island). . . . . .O 4
Onslow (bay). . . . . .L 6
Oregon (inlet) . . . . .P 3
Pamlico (river) . . . . .M 4
Pamlico (sound) . . . . . . .N 4
Pee Dee (river) . . . . .E 4
Phelps (lake). . . . . .N 3
Pigeon (river) . . . . .D 7
Pope AFB . . . . .G 4
Portsmouth (island) . . . .O 5
Pungo (lake) . . . . .N 3
Pungo (river) . . . . .M 4
Raleigh (bay) . . . . .N 5
Richland Balsam (mt.) . .E 8
Roanoke (island) . . . . . .O 3
Roanoke (river). . . . . . . .L 2
Rocky (river) . . . . .D 4
Santeetlah (lake). . . . . . .C 8
Scott, W. Kerr (res.) . . . .C 2
Six Run (creek) . . . . . . .J 4
Smith (island) . . . . .K 7
South (river) . . . . .H 5
South Yadkin (river). . . .D 3
Stone (mts.) . . . . .D 6
Tar (river) . . . . .K 3
Thorpe (lake) . . . . .D 9
Tillery (lake) . . . . .E 4
Trent (river). . . . . .L 4
Unaka (mts.) . . . . .B 7
Unicoi (mts.) . . . . .B 9
Waccamaw (lake) . . . . . .J 6
Waccamaw (river) . . . . . .G 7
Watauga (river) . . . . .B 6
Whiteoak (swamp) . . . . .L 5
Wright Brothers Nat'l
  Mem. . . . . .O 2
Yadkin (river) . . . . .E 3

☉ County seat

The historic State Capitol at Raleigh, N.C.
State of North Carolina

Cultural Institutions. North Carolina has a number of notable cultural institutions. One of the leading museums is the North Carolina Museum of Art, at Raleigh, with a large collection of European and American art. The University of North Carolina maintains art museums at Chapel Hill (the Ackland Art Museum) and at Greensboro (Weatherspoon Art Gallery). Exhibits on North Carolina history can be found in the Greensboro Historical Museum and in the North Carolina Museum of History at Raleigh. Other museums in the state include the Country Doctor Museum, at Bailey; the Charlotte Nature Museum; the High Point Historical Society Museum; and the Catawba Museum of Anthropology, at Salisbury.

The first public library was founded in the state about 1700. Today, the main research libraries are at Duke University and the University of North Carolina at Chapel Hill. Large public libraries are in Charlotte and Greenville. The state library is in Raleigh.

The North Carolina Symphony Orchestra, based in Raleigh, has a national reputation. Other musical institutions include the National Opera Association, in Raleigh; the Charlotte Opera Association; and the Transylvania Music Camp (a summer school for musicians), at Brev-

ard. The American Dance Festival, based in Durham, is a noted summer festival of modern dance. Historical dramas are presented outdoors each summer on Roanoke Island, at Boone, and at Cherokee. The Playmakers Repertory Company is a noted theatrical group that makes its home in Chapel Hill.

Historical Sites. Historical landmarks include Fort Raleigh National Historic Site, on Roanoke Island, encompassing the first English settlement (1585) in North America; Moores Creek National Battlefield, near Currie, the site in 1776 of an important patriot victory in the American Revolution; Guilford Courthouse National Military Park, near Greensboro, where American forces defeated the British in 1781; and Bentonville Battleground State Historic Site, near Smithfield, including the location of a Union victory in 1865 during the American Civil War. Also of note are Wright Brothers National Memorial, near Kitty Hawk, where Wilbur and Orville Wright in 1903 made the first sustained flight in a heavier-than-air machine; Carl Sandburg Home National Historic Site, at Flat Rock, including the farm home of the poet and biographer; and the childhood home of the writer Thomas Wolfe, in Asheville.

Sports and Recreation. Offshore and freshwater fishing, swimming, hiking, and hunting are popular outdoor activities in North Carolina, which also is noted for its many fine golf courses. Major automobile racetracks are at Charlotte and at Rockingham. Great Smoky Mountains National Park is a favorite recreation area.

Communications. In the early 1980s, North Carolina had 215 AM and 89 FM commercial radio stations and 19 commercial television stations. In the same period it had 55 daily newspapers, with a total daily circulation of about 1.4 million. The first radiobroadcaster to go on the air in the state was WBT, at Charlotte, in 1922; the first television stations, WBTV, Charlotte, and WFMY Greensboro, began operations in 1949; and the first newspaper, the *North Carolina Gazette,* was initially published in New Bern in 1751. Influential newspapers in the early 1980s included the *Charlotte Observer,* the *Greensboro Daily News,* the *Winston-Salem Journal,* and the *News & Observer,* issued in Raleigh.

GOVERNMENT AND POLITICS

North Carolina is governed under a constitution adopted in 1970; previous constitutions had been adopted in 1776 and 1868. Amendments to the constitution may be proposed by the state legislature or by a constitutional convention. To become effective, an amendment must be approved by a majority of persons voting on the issue in an election.

Executive. The chief executive of North Carolina is a governor, who is elected to a 4-year term and may serve a maximum of two terms. The lieutenant governor, also elected for four years, succeeds the governor on the latter's death, removal from office, or incapacity to serve. Other major state officials, all elected to 4-year terms, are the attorney general, auditor, secretary of state, superintendent of public instruction, and treasurer and the commissioners of agriculture, labor, and insurance.

Legislature. North Carolina's legislature, called the General Assembly, consists of a 50-member Senate and a 120-member House of Representatives. All legislators are elected to 2-year terms. The lieutenant governor presides over the Senate, and the House elects a Speaker as its presiding officer.

Judiciary. The court of last resort in North Carolina is the supreme court, made up of a chief justice and six associate justices, all of whom are popularly elected to 8-year terms. The intermediate appellate court of the state is the court of appeals, with 12 judges, and the major trial court is the superior court, with 66 judges. The state also has district courts. The appellate justices and

most superior court judges are popularly elected to 8-year terms, and district judges are elected to 4-year terms.

Local Government. North Carolina's 100 counties are governed by popularly elected boards of commissioners. Other elected county officials include the sheriff, treasurer, accountant, and attorney. The state has about 470 municipalities; most larger cities use the council-manager form of government.

National Representation. North Carolina elects 2 senators and 11 representatives to the U.S. congress. The state has 13 electoral votes in presidential elections.

Politics. From the 1870s until the 1960s the Democratic party dominated all levels of North Carolina politics. The Republican party gained strength in the state during the 1960s, and although Democrats continue to win most local elections, the two parties are fiercely competitive in statewide contests. Jesse A. Helms (1921–   ), first elected to the U.S. Senate from North Carolina in 1972, was an influential conservative voice within the Republican party in the early 1980s, when he chaired the Senate Committee on Agriculture, Nutrition, and Forestry.

A fishing village of Ocracoke Island on the Outer Banks of North Carolina.   State of North Carolina

In a typical tobacco harvest, such as this one in Bakersville, N.C., the ripe leaves of the tobacco plants are stripped from the stalks, hung on sticks, and then cured. North Carolina is the nation's leading producer of tobacco.   Clyde H. Smith–Peter Arnold, Inc.

ECONOMY

The economy of North Carolina was dominated by farming until the 1920s, when such manufacturing industries as the production of textiles, furniture, and tobacco products began to provide the bulk of the state's annual income. In the early 1980s manufacturing was the leading economic activity, but farming, forestry, and tourism also were important sectors of the state economy. In addition, a growing number of research and development concerns were being established in North Carolina, notably in facilities such as Research Triangle Park, near Raleigh. Handicrafts, such as baskets and pottery, were important products of the Blue Ridge region in the W part of the state.

Agriculture. Farming is an important segment of the economy of North Carolina. Annual farm income in the early 1980s was about $3.6 billion; about 60% was derived from the sale of crops, and the remainder came from sales of livestock and livestock products. The state has some 93,000 farms, which have an average size of 51 ha (126 acres). Overall, the leading agricultural commodities are tobacco, broiler chickens, corn, hogs, soybeans, and dairy products. North Carolina typically leads the nation in annual tobacco and sweet-potato production and it ranks third in peanut production; these commodities are mostly grown in the Atlantic Coastal Plain region. North Carolina's yearly broiler chicken output usually ranks fourth in the U.S.; a large proportion is raised in the Piedmont Plateau region. Among the state's other major crops are wheat, beans, tomatoes, hay, apples, and peaches; additional livestock and livestock products include beef cattle, hogs, turkeys, and chicken eggs.

Forestry and Fishing. North Carolina's extensive forests are the source of a large annual harvest of timber, which usually is fairly evenly divided between hardwoods and softwoods. The primary uses of the timber are for paper and furniture production and in housing construction.

NORTH CAROLINA

DATE OF STATEHOOD: November 21, 1789; 12th state

CAPITAL:	Raleigh
MOTTO:	*Esse quam videri* (To be, rather than to seem)
NICKNAME:	Tar Heel State
STATE SONG:	"The Old North State" (words by William Gaston; music by Mrs. E. E. Randolph)
STATE TREE:	Pine
STATE FLOWER:	Flowering dogwood
STATE BIRD:	Cardinal
POPULATION (1980):	5,881,813; 10th among the states
AREA:	136,412 sq km (52,669 sq mi); 28th largest state; includes 9909 sq km (3826 sq mi) of inland water
COASTLINE:	484 km (301 mi)
HIGHEST POINT:	Mt. Mitchell, 2037 m (6684 ft)
LOWEST POINT:	Sea level, at the Atlantic coast
ELECTORAL VOTES:	13
U.S. CONGRESS:	2 senators, 11 representatives

POPULATION OF NORTH CAROLINA SINCE 1790

Year of Census	Population	Classified As Urban
1790	394,000	0%
1820	639,000	2%
1850	869,000	2%
1880	1,400,000	4%
1900	1,894,000	10%
1920	2,559,000	19%
1940	3,572,000	27%
1960	4,556,000	40%
1970	5,084,000	46%
1980	5,882,000	48%

POPULATION OF TEN LARGEST CITIES

	1980 Census	1970 Census
Charlotte	314,447	241,420
Greensboro	155,642	144,076
Raleigh	150,255	122,830
Winston-Salem	131,855	133,683
Durham	100,831	95,438
High Point	63,380	63,229
Fayetteville	59,507	53,510
Asheville	53,583	57,820
Gastonia	47,333	47,322
Wilmington	44,000	46,169

CLIMATE

	ASHEVILLE	WILMINGTON
Average January temperature range	−2.8° to 8.9° C (27° to 48° F)	2.2° to 13.9° C (36° to 57° F)
Average July temperature range	17.2° to 28.9° C (63° to 84° F)	22.2° to 31.7° C (72° to 89° F)
Average annual temperature	13.3° C (56° F)	17.8° C (64° F)
Average annual precipitation	1143 mm (45 in)	1372 mm (54 in)
Average annual snowfall	457 mm (18 in)	51 mm (2 in)
Mean number of days per year with appreciable precipitation	130	116
Average daily relative humidity	75%	71%
Mean number of clear days per year	102	114

NATURAL REGIONS OF NORTH CAROLINA

PRINCIPAL PRODUCTS OF NORTH CAROLINA

ECONOMY

State budget. . . . . revenue $6.2 billion
expenditure $5.7 billion
State personal income tax, per capita $178
Personal income, per capita $7819
Assets, commercial banks (82) . . . . $23.5 billion
Labor force (civilian) 2,783,000
    Employed in services   24%
    Employed in manufacturing   30%
    Employed in wholesale and retail trade 18%
    Employed in government   16%

	Quantity Produced	Value
FARM PRODUCTS.		**$3.6 billion**
Crops		**$2.2 billion**
Tobacco.	347,000 metric tons	$1.1 billion
Corn	3.3 million metric tons	$379 million
Soybeans	971,000 metric tons	$280 million
Peanuts	132,000 metric tons	$66 million
Vegetables . . .	223,000 metric tons	$47 million
Wheat.	286,000 metric tons	$39 million
Hay	538,000 metric tons	$37 million
Livestock and Livestock Products		**$1.4 billion**
Chickens	771,000 metric tons	$424 million
Hogs.	386,000 metric tons	$319 million
Milk.	709,000 metric tons	$231 million
Eggs.	3.2 billion	$174 million
Turkeys	180,000 metric tons	$158 million
MINERALS		**$361 million**
Stone	31.2 million metric tons	$125 million
Sand, gravel. .	7.3 million metric tons	$24 million
Feldspar	463,000 metric tons	$16 million
FISHING.	**161,570 metric tons**	**$68.8 million**

	Labor and Proprietors' Income
FORESTRY	**$13.7 million**
MANUFACTURING	**$12.0 billion**
Textile mill products.	$3.0 billion
Electric and electronic equipment.	$996 million
Furniture and fixtures.	$996 million
Nonelectric machinery	$931 million
Chemicals and allied products	$780 million
Food and kindred products	$653 million
Tobacco manufactures.	$629 million
Lumber and wood products.	$480 million
Fabricated metal products	$474 million

OTHER . . . . **$20.8 billion**
Services. . . . . $4.9 billion
Government and government
   enterprises. . . . . $6.2 billion
Transportation and public utilities. . . . . $2.5 billion
Finance, insurance, and real estate . . . $1.6 billion
Wholesale trade . . . . $2.2 billion
Retail trade . . . . $3.4 billion

ANNUAL PRODUCTION OF GOODS BY SECTOR

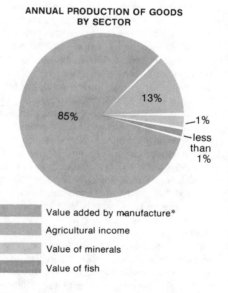

85%   13%   —1%   —less than 1%

   Value added by manufacture*
   Agricultural income
   Value of minerals
   Value of fish

* The value added by an industry is a measure of the value created in its products, not counting such production costs as raw materials and power.

Sources: U.S. government publications

The annual catch of North Carolina's important fishing industry totals about 161,570 metric tons and has a value of some $68.8 million. The most important types of fish, in order of weight of catch, are industrial fish (especially menhaden), edible shellfish (especially shrimp), and edible finfish (especially flounder). Shrimp is the single most important part of the catch.

Mining. The yearly value of North Carolina's relatively small mineral output was about $361 million in the early 1980s. The principal minerals were stone, phosphate rock, lithium, sand and gravel, and cement. The state usually leads the U.S. in the production of feldspar, lithium, mica, and olivine. Additional minerals produced include asbestos, kaolin and other clay, talc, and gemstones.

Manufacturing. In the early 1980s North Carolina's manufacturing industries together employed some 833,900 workers and accounted for 85% of the yearly value of goods produced in the state. The leading categories of manufactures included textiles, tobacco products, chemicals and pharmaceuticals, furniture, apparel, and electrical and electronic equipment. North Carolina is the leading textile-producing state in the U.S. Output of such textile items as cotton yarn, nylon and polyester fiber, and denim fabric is concentrated in the Piedmont Pleateau region, especially in Gaston, Cabarrus, Guilford, and Mecklenburg counties. The state also leads the nation in manufacturing tobacco products and furniture. Cigarette production is concentrated in Durham, Raleigh, and Winston-Salem, and furniture making is centered in such Piedmont Plateau communities as High Point, Hickory, and Thomasville. Other major manufactures of North Carolina include nonelectrical machinery; processed food; bricks and other construction materials; and paper, plastic, and rubber goods.

Tourism. North Carolina's natural environment, which includes ocean beaches as well as forested mountains, attracts large numbers of tourists each year. Great Smoky Mountains National Park, located partly in Tennessee, usually receives more visitors annually than any other national park in the U.S. The scenic Blue Ridge Parkway, also a unit of the National Park Service, is an automobile route built along the crest of the Blue Ridge Mts. Attractions in the coastal area of North Carolina include two national seashores, Cape Hatteras, in the Outer Banks, and Cape Lookout, on the mainland. A major privately owned tourist attraction in the state is Carowinds Theme Park, a large amusement park located at the border with South Carolina, near Charlotte. Many visitors are lured by North Carolina's splendid golf courses, such as those at Pinehurst and Southern Pines, and by the state's historical sites. North Carolina maintains 40 state parks and recreation areas.

Transportation. North Carolina has a comprehensive transportation system. The state has about 149,700 km (about 93,020 mi) of roads, including 1231 km (765 mi) of Interstate Highways. It also has some 5755 km (some 3575 mi) of operated railroad track, with Greensboro and Raleigh as major rail hubs. A section of the Atlantic Intracoastal Waterway, an important shipping route, is along the coast of North Carolina; the state's main seaports are Morehead City, Southport, and Wilmington. The busiest of North Carolina's 286 airports serve Charlotte, the Greensboro-High Point and Raleigh-Durham areas, and Winston-Salem.

Energy. In the early 1980s North Carolina's installed electricity-generating capacity was 15.6 million kw, and its yearly electricity production totaled 72.1 billion kwh. About 84% of the electricity was generated in facilities burning coal; hydroelectric installations and nuclear power plants each accounted for about 7.5%.   J.D.Lo.

HISTORY

On July 4, 1584, two English explorers, commissioned by Sir Walter Raleigh, dropped anchor off the coast of the region comprising present-day North Carolina. Although the region was inhabited by hostile Indians, they reported favorably on it, and as a result a colonizing expedition set out from Plymouth the following year. On Aug. 17, 1585, a colony was established on Roanoke Island, but it was abandoned a year later. On July 22, 1587, another group commissioned by Raleigh landed on the island. The 121 settlers were led by John White (fl. 1585–93), whose granddaughter, Virginia Dare, born on Aug. 18, 1587, was the first child of English parents born in America. White went back to England for supplies and returned in 1590 to find that the colony had completely vanished (see CROATAN). In 1629 the land south of Virginia, which was called Carolina, was granted to Sir Robert Heath by Charles I, king of England, but Heath failed to make use of the land, and in 1663 Charles II granted the Carolina territory to eight proprietors. The proprietors divided the grant into North and South Carolina and established a Fundamental Constitution, a system of government drawn up by the English philosopher John Locke. The constitution provided for four houses of parliament and three orders of nobility; it was never put fully in operation and was finally abandoned in 1693.

The proprietary period of the colony, which

lasted from 1663 to 1729, was turbulent, because of the independence of the settlers, who occasionally drove out a governor whom they regarded as obnoxious. Indian troubles also beset the colony, but in 1713 the Tuscarora, after having massacred many settlers, were defeated and expelled from the Carolinas. The Carolinas did not prove a financial success to most of the proprietors, and in 1728 seven of them sold their grants to the Crown. In 1744 the eighth proprietor exchanged his grant for a smaller strip of land in North Carolina. The colonists continued to rebel against the authorities, who were now royal governors, and from 1765 to 1771 the Regulators (q.v.), a group of colonists who refused to pay taxes, were in a state of rebellion against royal authority.

The Years After Independence. The first provincial congress met in 1774 and sent delegates to the First Continental Congress. According to tradition, in May 1775 the so-called Mecklenburg Declaration of Independence of the citizens of Mecklenburg Co. was enacted, which declared that the royal commissions of the colonies were null and void and advocated the establishment of an independent government. Few historians, however, believe that the Mecklenburg Declaration is authentic. On April 12, 1776, North Carolina became the first colony to instruct its delegates in Congress to vote for independence. The first constitution of the state was adopted on Dec. 18, 1776. North Carolina soldiers took part in many of the important battles of the American Revolution, and in 1776 and 1781 the state was invaded by the British. Delegates were sent to the Constitutional Convention in 1787, but they refused to ratify the instrument in 1788 on the grounds that the central government was too strong. The state did not vote in the first presidential election. After the adoption of the Bill of Rights, North Carolina ratified the U.S. Constitution on Nov. 19, 1789.

The period between the ratification of the Constitution and the American Civil War was marked by internal dissension over representation in the state government between the eastern and western counties and by the migration of many North Carolina settlers to western territories. In February 1861 the state opposed secession from the Union; but when Abraham Lincoln issued a call for troops in order to coerce the seceding states, sentiment in North Carolina changed, and on May 20, 1861, the state passed an ordinance of secession. During the Civil War, North Carolina provided the Confederacy with more than 120,000 troops, lost more soldiers than any other Southern state, and during the last year of the war, furnished the Confederate army with food. In 1867, during the period of Reconstruction, the civil authority was superseded by the military. The constitution of 1868 established black suffrage, and in the same year the Ku Klux Klan began functioning in the state. The federal government withdrew its military forces from the state in 1868.

The 20th Century. During the first half century, North Carolina's economy centered on its traditional tobacco and textile industries. World War II produced a shift to more diversified industrial development that accelerated in the postwar years. Today, although the state remains the nation's leading tobacco producer, the industry faces an uncertain future, while imports have inflicted losses on textile mills. Nearly half the population lives and works in urban areas, and demands for expanded public and social services have increased. Strict conservation laws protect the state's unique coastal regions from industrial encroachment.

For further information on this topic, see the Bibliography in volume 28, section 1185.

NORTH CAROLINA, UNIVERSITY OF, state-controlled institution of higher learning, chartered in 1789, and opened for instruction in Chapel Hill, N.C., in 1795. Since 1963, besides the main campus at Chapel Hill, the university has maintained divisions at Greensboro, Raleigh, Charlotte, Asheville, and Wilmington. In addition, ten state-supported institutions were merged with the university in 1971; the merger resulted in a statewide system of 16 constitutent institutions, administered in Chapel Hill.

Of the larger divisions, North Carolina State University at Raleigh, founded as a land-grant college in 1888, offers a full range of degree programs in agriculture and forestry, in addition to courses in engineering, education, and the sciences. The University of North Carolina at Chapel Hill offers degree programs at all levels in the arts, sciences, and professions.

NORTH CASCADES NATIONAL PARK, N Washington, established in 1968. The park encompasses a region of spectacular alpine scenery, with glaciers, mountain lakes, and deep canyons characteristic of the rugged Cascade Range. Lush forests occupy the steep-walled valleys, and the wildlife includes cougar, black and grizzly bear, wolverine, moose, and marten. The park is divided into two units by the Ross Lake National Recreation Area. The N unit is centered on the Picket Range and includes Mt. Shuksan (2755 m/ 9038 ft). The S unit contains the Eldorado Peaks and Mt. Logan (2768 m/9080 ft). Area, 2042.8 sq km (788.7 sq mi).

NORTH CHARLESTON, city, Charleston and Berkeley counties, SE South Carolina, an industrial suburb N of Charleston (from which its name is derived); inc. 1972. Paper, chemicals, and safety products are manufactured here. Pop. (1970) 21,211; (1980) 62,534.

NORTH CHICAGO, manufacturing city, Lake Co., NE Illinois, on Lake Michigan, near Waukegan; inc. 1909. Major products include pharmaceuticals, metal goods, building materials, and machinery. The Great Lakes Naval Training Center is nearby. A 1937 sit-down strike at a steel plant here led to a 1939 U.S. Supreme Court decision ruling such strikes illegal. Pop. (1970) 47,275; (1980) 38,774.

NORTH DAKOTA, one of the West North Central states of the U.S., bounded on the N by the Canadian provinces of Saskatchewan and Manitoba, on the E by Minnesota, on the S by South Dakota, and on the W by Montana. The Red River of the North forms most of the E boundary.

North Dakota entered the Union on Nov. 2, 1889, as the 39th state. Possessing fertile soils and extensive grazing lands, North Dakota has tradi-

tionally been an agricultural state. By the early 1980s, although mining and manufacturing had grown in importance, the state economy remained dominated by agriculture. The name of the state is derived from a Sioux Indian term. North Dakota is called the Flickertail State—a reference to the indigenous flickertail ground squirrel.

LAND AND RESOURCES

North Dakota, with an area of 183,117 sq km (70,702 sq mi), is the 17th largest state in the U.S.; 5.3% of the land area is owned by the federal government. The state is roughly rectangular in shape, and its extreme dimensions are about 340 km (about 210 mi) from N to S and about 580 km (about 360 mi) from E to W. Elevations range from 229 m (750 ft) along the Red River of the North in the NE corner of the state to 1069 m (3506 ft) atop White Butte in the Badlands of the SW. The mean elevation is 579 m (1900 ft).

Physical Geography. The E part of North Dakota lies in the Western Great Lakes Lowland region. This is an area of plains containing many glacial features such as moraines and flat plains that

The beautifully rugged Badlands of the Little Missouri River drainage area in southwestern North Dakota.
North Dakota State Game and Fish Dept.

The expansive grasslands of western North Dakota once provided grazing for huge herds of buffalo and antelope. Today, although most large animals have disappeared, antelope still roam free.   Ed Bry–North Dakota Game and Fish Department

were formerly the beds of glacial lakes. The bed of the ancient Lake Agassiz, along the E border, contains the state's richest soils. Scattered marshes and small lakes are found throughout the Western Great Lakes Lowland. On the W border of the lowlands is an escarpment, a steep slope 90 to 180 m (about 300 to 600 ft) high known as the Missouri Coteau. To the W of this escarpment lies the Great Plains, known in North Dakota as the Missouri Plateau. The topography of this region is varied. Many flat-topped buttes stand as high as about 180 m (about 600 ft) above the plains, and a strip of Badlands, which are spectacular formations produced by the erosion of soft sedimentary rocks, is found in the SW.

Rivers and Lakes. Western North Dakota is drained by the Missouri R. and its tributaries, which include the Little Missouri, Knife, Heart, and Cannonball rivers. The E plains are drained by the north-flowing Red River of the North and its tributaries—the Pembina, Forest, Goose, Maple, Sheyenne, and Wild Rice rivers. The N central part of the state is drained by the Souris R., and the SE part by the James R., a tributary of the Missouri R. Numerous small natural lakes are in the glaciated part of the state; the largest of these is Devils Lake. The largest body of water in the state is Lake Sakakawea, formed behind Garrison Dam on the Missouri R.

Climate. North Dakota has a continental climate, marked by long harsh winters and short hot summers. Humidity is usually low in summer, mitigating the heat. The average annual temperature ranges from 6.1° C (43° F) in the SW to 2.2° C (36° F) in the NW. The recorded temperature has ranged from −51.1° C (−60° F) in 1936 to 49.4° C (121° F) also in 1936. The average annual precipitation decreases from 559 mm (22 in) in the SE to 356 mm (14 in) in the SW. About three-fourths of the precipitation is received during the warm months. Winters are relatively dry; the average annual snowfall is approximately 815 mm (about 32 in).

Plants and Animals. Before the land was plowed, most of North Dakota was grassland. Tall grasses, mostly bluestem, dominated the E prairies, and short grasses, such as grama, needle, and wheat grass, were found in the W. Forests cover barely 1% of the state's land area. Trees are confined to the river valleys and the adjacent valley walls, where oak, ash, cottonwood, and aspen are the most common species. In the W small stands of red cedar occur in the Badlands. Wild flowers are numerous in the prairie lands.

Formerly, great herds of bison grazed the prairies. Today pronghorn antelope are found in the W, and deer are present in all areas of the state. A variety of small mammals occur, including

INDEX TO MAP OF NORTH DAKOTA

Cities and Towns

Abercrombie ....H 3
Adams ....F 1
Alexander ....A 2
Alfred ....F 3
Amidon ⊙ ....A 3
Anamoose ....D 2
Aneta ....G 2
Arthur ....G 2
Ashley ⊙ ....E 3
Beach ⊙ ....A 3
Belcourt ....E 1
Belfield ....A 3
Berthold ....C 1
Beulah ....C 2
Binford ....F 2
Bisbee ....E 1
Bismarck ⊙ (cap.)...D 3
Bottineau ⊙ ....D 1
Bowbells ⊙ ....B 1
Bowman ⊙ ....A 3
Buxton ....G 2
Cando ⊙ ....E 1
Carrington ⊙ ....F 2
Carson ....C 3
Casselton ....G 3
Cavalier ⊙ ....G 1
Center ⊙ ....C 2
Cogswell ....G 3
Columbus ....B 1
Cooperstown ⊙ ......F 2
Crosby ⊙ ....A 1
Crystal ....G 1
Devils Lake ⊙ ......F 1
Dickinson ⊙ ....B 3
Drake ....D 2
Drayton ....G 1
Dunn Center ....B 2
Dunseith ....D 1
Edgeley ....F 3
Edinburg ....G 1
Edmore ....F 1
Elgin ....C 3
Ellendale ⊙ ....F 3
Emerado ....G 2
Enderlin ....G 3
Esmond ....E 1
Fairmount ....H 3
Fargo ⊙ ....H 3
Fessenden ⊙ ....E 2
Finley ⊙ ....G 2
Flasher ....C 3
Flaxton ....B 1
Fordville ....G 1
Forman ⊙ ....G 3
Fort Totten ....E 2
Fort Yates ⊙ ....D 3
Garrison ....C 2
Glasston ....G 1
Glenburn ....C 1
Glen Ullin ....C 3
Goldenvalley ....B 2
Goodrich ....D 2
Grafton ⊙ ....G 1
Grand Forks ⊙ ......H 2

Granville ....D 1
Grenora ....A 1
Gwinner ....G 3
Halliday ....B 2
Hankinson ....H 3
Hannaford ....F 2
Hannah ....F 1
Harvey ....E 2
Hatton ....G 2
Hazelton ....D 3
Hazen ....C 2
Hebron ....C 3
Hettinger ⊙ ....B 3
Hillsboro ⊙ ....G 2
Hoople ....G 1
Hope ....G 2
Hunter ....G 2
Jamestown ⊙ ....F 3
Kenmare ....B 1
Kensal ....F 2
Killdeer ....B 2
Kindred ....G 3
Kulm ....F 3
Lakota ⊙ ....F 1
LaMoure ⊙ ....F 3
Langdon ⊙ ....F 1
Lankin ....F 1
Lansford ....C 1
Larimore ....G 2
Leeds ....E 1
Lehr ....E 3
Lidgerwood ....G 3
Lignite ....B 1
Linton ⊙ ....D 3
Lisbon ⊙ ....G 3
Litchville ....F 3
McClusky ⊙ ....D 2
McVille ....F 2
Maddock ....E 2
Mandan ⊙ ....C 3
Manning ⊙ ....B 2
Manvel ....G 1
Marion ....F 3
Marmarth ....A 3
Max ....C 2
Mayville ....G 2
Medina ....E 3
Medora ⊙ ....A 3
Michigan ....F 1
Milnor ....G 3
Minnewaukan ⊙ ......E 1
Minot ⊙ ....C 1
Minto ....G 1
Mohall ⊙ ....C 1
Mott ⊙ ....B 3
Napoleon ⊙ ....E 3
New England ....B 3
New Leipzig ....B 3
New Rockford ⊙ .....F 2
New Salem ....C 3
New Town ....B 1
Noonan ....A 1
Northwood ....G 2
Oakes ....F 3
Oberon ....E 2
Osnabrock ....F 1

Page ....G 2
Park River ....G 1
Parshall ....B 2
Pembina ....G 1
Petersburg ....F 2
Plaza ....C 1
Portland ....G 2
Powers Lake ....B 1
Ray ....A 1
Reeder ....B 3
Regent ....B 3
Rhame ....A 3
Richardton ....B 3
Riverdale ....C 2
Rocklake ....E 1
Rolette ....E 1
Rolla ⊙ ....E 1
Rugby ⊙ ....E 1
Rutland ....G 3
Saint John ....E 1
Saint Thomas ....G 1
Sawyer ....C 1
Scranton ....A 3
Selfridge ....C 3
Sherwood ....C 1
Sheyenne ....E 2
Solen ....D 3
Stanley ⊙ ....B 1
Stanton ⊙ ....C 2
Steele ⊙ ....E 3
Strasburg ....D 3
Streeter ....E 3
Surrey ....C 1
Tappen ....E 3
Tioga ....B 1
Tolna ....F 2
Tower City ....G 3
Towner ⊙ ....D 1
Turtle Lake ....D 2
Tuttle ....E 2
Underwood ....D 2
Upham ....D 1
Valley City ⊙ ......G 3
Velva ....D 1
Wahpeton ⊙ ....H 3
Walhalla ....G 1
Washburn ⊙ ....D 2
Watford City ⊙ .....A 2
Westhope ....C 1
Wildrose ....A 1
Williston ⊙ ....A 1
Willow City ....D 1
Wilton ....D 2
Wimbledon ....F 2
Wing ....D 2
Wishek ....E 3
Wyndmere ....H 3
Zap ....C 2
Zeeland ....E 4

Other Features

Ashtabula (lake)....G 2
Audubon (lake)......C 2
Badlands (reg.).....A 3

Beaver (creek) .....A 2
Beaver (creek) .....E 3
Cannonball (river) ..C 3
Cedar (creek) ......B 3
Clark Buttes (mt.)...C 3
Coteau du Missouri
  (plains) ....C 2
Cut Bank (creek) ...C 1
Darling (lake) .....C 1
Des Lacs (river) ...C 1
Devils (lake) ......F 1
Fort Berthold Ind. Res..B 2
Fort Totten Ind. Res....F 2
Fort Union Trading
  Post Nat'l Hist. Site..A 1
Garrison (dam) .....C 2
Goose (river) ......G 2
Grand Forks AFB ....G 2
Heart (river) ......B 3
Horsehead (lake) ...E 2
International Peace
  Garden ....E 1
James (river) ......F 3
Jamestown (res.) ...F 2
Killdeer (mts.) ....B 2
Knife River Indian
  Villages Nat'l Hist.
  Site ....C 2
Little Missouri (river) ..A 2
Long (lake) ....D 3
Maple (river) ......G 3
Minot AFB ....C 1
Missouri (river) ...D 2
North Fork (Grand)
  (river) ....B 4
Oahe (lake) ....D 3
Park (river) ....G 1
Pembina (river) ....F 1
Pipestem (river) ...E 2
Red River of the North
  (river) ....G 1
Sakakawea (lake) ...C 2
Sentinel Butte (mt.) ..A 3
Sheyenne (river) ...G 3
Souris (river) .....D 1
Standing Rock Ind.
  Res. ....C 3
Sweetwater (lake) ..F 1
Theodore Roosevelt
  Nat'l Park (Elkhorn
  Ranch) ....A 2
Theodore Roosevelt
  Nat'l Park (North
  Unit) ....A 2
Theodore Roosevelt
  Nat'l Park (South
  Unit) ....A 3
Tschida (lake) .....B 3
Turtle Mt. Indian Res...D 1
White Butte (mt.) ..A 3
Wild Rice (river) ..G 3
Yellowstone (river) ..A 2

⊙ County seat

bobcat, lynx, badger, beaver, mink, raccoon, and rabbit. Prairie dog towns, which are extensive underground communities, are found in the Badlands. Birdlife is diverse, especially in summer, when vast numbers of waterfowl breed in the state's lakes and marshes. Bass, pike, perch, carp, and catfish inhabit the state's streams and rivers.
Mineral Resources. North Dakota has great deposits of petroleum, which are found in the Williston Basin in the W part of the state. The state has some of the largest reserves of lignite in the nation, concentrated mostly in the W. Sand and gravel are mined throughout the state. Other mineral resources include natural gas and clay.

W.E.Ak.

POPULATION

According to the 1980 census, North Dakota had 652,717 inhabitants, an increase of 5.7% over 1970. The average population density was 3.6 people per sq km (9.2 per sq mi), one of the lowest in the country. Most of the population was concentrated in the metropolitan areas of the state's four largest cities. Whites made up 95.8% of the population and blacks 0.4%. Additional population groups included some 20,119 American Indians and 1979 persons of Asian or

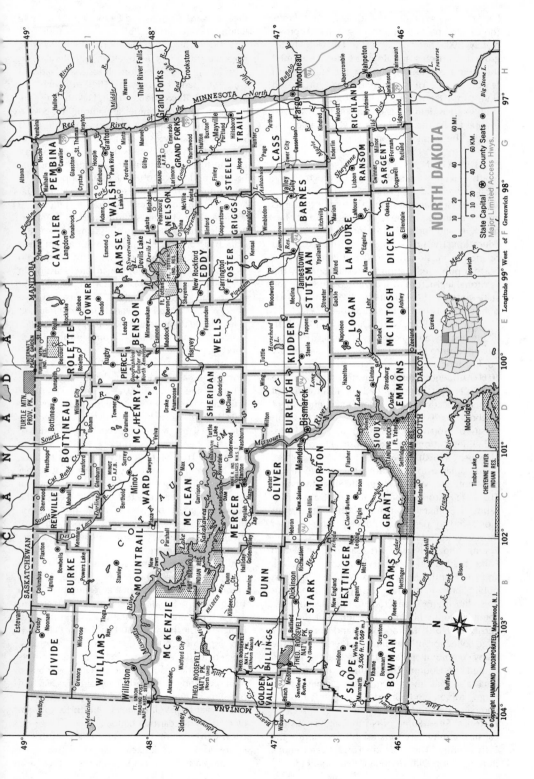

NORTH DAKOTA

State Capital ⊕   ⊛ County Seats
Major Limited Access Hwys.

0   10 20   40   60 MI.

0   20   40   60 KM.

E   Longitude 99° West of F Greenwich 98°   G   97°   H

179

Pacific Islands origin; the Ojibwa and Sioux (qq.v.) are the largest Indian groups. Approximately 3900 persons were of Hispanic background. Lutherans and Roman Catholics formed the largest religious groups in the state. North Dakota is one of the nation's least urbanized states; in 1980 about 49% of all state residents lived in areas defined as urban and the rest lived in rural areas. The biggest cities were Fargo; Bismarck, the capital; Grand Forks; Minot, and Jamestown.

EDUCATION AND CULTURAL ACTIVITY

North Dakota's cultural life owes much to the local Indian and immigrant Scandinavian, Russian, and German traditions. Cultural institutions are concentrated in the larger cities of Fargo, Bismarck, Grand Forks, and Minot.

Education. The first school in North Dakota was opened by missionaries in 1818 at Pembina. Support for public education was established by the territorial legislature in 1862, and by the time the state entered the Union in 1889, almost 1400 public schools had been established.

In the early 1980s, North Dakota had 719 public elementary and secondary schools, with a total annual enrollment of about 76,800 elementary pupils and 40,100 secondary students. Some 10,660 students attended private schools. In the same period, the state had 16 institutions of higher education, with a combined enrollment of about 34,070. The largest university is the University of North Dakota (1884), at Grand Forks. Other institutions include North Dakota State University (1890), at Fargo; Jamestown College (1883), at Jamestown; Minot State College (1913), at Minot; and Mary College (1955), at Bismarck. The State Historical Society of North Dakota Museum at Bismarck contains exhibits on the region's Indian past and pioneer history. Other museums include the Buffalo Trails Museum, in Epping; the University Art Galleries, in Grand Forks; the Makoti Threshers Museum, in Makoti; and the Frontier Museum, in Williston. The first public library in the state was opened by a women's club in 1897, and today North Dakota has some 70 public libraries. The library of the University of North Dakota, at Grand Forks, has a large collection of Scandinavian literature. Of the many community theater groups, the best known is the Little Country Theater in Fargo. North Dakota also has three symphony orchestras—at Fargo, Minot, and Grand Forks—and a ballet company at Grand Forks.

Historical Sites. Some of North Dakota's historical sites are military forts established during the 19th century. They include Forts Abercrombie, Buford, Clark, Dilts, Mandan, Pembina, Ransom,

Rice, Seward, Totten, and Union. Other notable landmarks are Sitting Bull's Grave Historic Site (the burial place of the Sioux chief), Writing Rock Historic Park (a boulder with Indian inscriptions), and Theodore Roosevelt National Park with part of Roosevelt's Elkhorn Ranch.

Sports and Recreation. North Dakota's fishing and hunting opportunities are among the best in the nation; especially abundant are game birds such as duck, grouse, pheasant, and goose. In June and July rodeos are held in many towns. During the long winters, ice skating, skiing, ice hockey, and snowmobile races are popular.

Communications. In the early 1980s, North Dakota had 28 commercial AM radio stations, 10 commercial FM radio stations, and 13 commercial television stations. In the same period, the state had 10 daily newspapers, with a combined daily circulation of some 195,600. The first radio station, WDAY in Fargo, began broadcasting in 1922, and the first television station, KCJB in Minot, began operation in 1953. The first newspaper, *Frontier Scout,* appeared in Fort Union in 1864. The leading newspapers today are the *Bismarck Tribune,* the *Fargo Forum,* and the *Grand Forks Herald.*

GOVERNMENT AND POLITICS

North Dakota is governed under its original constitution, adopted in 1889, as amended. A constitutional amendment may be proposed by the state legislature or by an initiative. To become effective, it must be approved by a majority of voters in a general election.

Executive. The chief executive of North Dakota, the governor, is popularly elected to a 4-year term and may serve an unlimited number of terms. Other state elected officials include the lieutenant governor (who succeeds the governor upon the latter's death, removal from office, or incapacity to serve), attorney general, secretary of state, and treasurer.

Legislature. The bicameral Legislative Assembly of North Dakota consists of a Senate, with 50 members, and a House of Representatives, with 100 members. Senators are popularly elected to 4-year terms and representatives to 2-year terms.

Judiciary. The highest court in North Dakota is the Supreme Court, which has five members, elected to 10-year terms. The major trial courts are the district courts, which have a combined total of 26 judges elected to 6-year terms. Each of the state's county courts has one judge elected to a 4-year term. All judges in North Dakota are elected on nonpartisan ballots.

Local Government. In the early 1980s North Dakota had 53 counties, each of which was governed by a board of commissioners. Other local

North Dakota is typified by vast stretches of land, beautiful vistas, and enormous farms, such as this one engaged in a harvest of soybeans. Alvis Upitis–Shostal Associates

officials, also elected to 4-year terms, include the sheriff, clerk, and treasurer. The state has more than 360 municipalities and approximately 1360 townships.

National Representation. North Dakota sends two senators and one representative to the U.S. Congress and had three electoral votes in presidential elections.

Politics. In national, state, and local politics, North Dakota has traditionally been dominated by the Republican party. In the 1960s and '70s, however, the Democrats made substantial gains in statewide contests. In presidential voting since 1940, North Dakota has usually favored the Republican candidate.

ECONOMY

Since its settlement by non-Indians in the mid-19th century, North Dakota has had an economy dominated by agriculture, primarily the growing of wheat and other grains. Mineral production became increasingly important after 1951, with the tapping of the state's large petroleum reserves. Manufacturing, government (including

military installations), and tourism have also grown to give the state a more diversified economic base.

Agriculture. Farming accounts for 72% of the annual value of goods produced in North Dakota. The state has some 40,000 farms, which average 422 ha (1043 acres) in size. Crops account for about two-thirds of North Dakota's yearly farm income. Wheat, barley, sugar beets, hay, and sunflowers are leading crops. Wheat is grown in all areas, but is especially important in the N. Other crops include potatoes, rye, and flax. North Dakota leads the nation in the production of durum and other spring wheat, as well as barley, flax, and sunflowers. Irrigation agriculture is increasing in importance, especially in the semiarid W along the Missouri R.

Livestock accounts for about one-third of the annual farm income. Beef cattle are most important and are raised primarily in the W; hogs, dairy cattle, and sheep are raised in the SE.

Mining. The mining industry accounts for about 11% of the yearly value of goods produced in

NORTH DAKOTA

NORTH DAKOTA

DATE OF STATEHOOD: November 2, 1889; 39th state

CAPITAL:	Bismarck
MOTTO:	Liberty and union, now and forever, one and inseparable
NICKNAMES:	Flickertail State; Sioux State
STATE SONG:	"North Dakota Hymn" (words by James W. Foley; music by C. S. Putnam)
STATE TREE:	American elm
STATE FLOWER:	Prairie rose
STATE BIRD:	Meadowlark
POPULATION (1980):	652,717; 46th among the states
AREA:	183,117 sq km (70,702 sq mi); 17th largest state; includes 3633 sq km (1403 sq mi) of inland water
HIGHEST POINT:	White Butte, 1069 m (3506 ft)
LOWEST POINT:	229 m (750 ft), along the Red River
ELECTORAL VOTES:	3
U.S. CONGRESS:	2 senators; 1 representative

POPULATION OF NORTH DAKOTA SINCE 1870

Year of Census	Population	Classified As Urban
1870	2,400	0%
1880	37,000	7%
1890	191,000	6%
1900	319,000	7%
1920	647,000	14%
1940	642,000	21%
1960	632,000	35%
1970	618,000	44%
1980	653,000	49%

POPULATION OF TEN LARGEST CITIES

	1980 Census	1970 Census
Fargo	61,383	53,365
Bismarck	44,485	34,703
Grand Forks	43,765	39,008
Minot	32,843	32,290
Jamestown	16,280	15,385
Dickinson	15,924	12,405
Mandan	15,513	11,093
Williston	13,336	11,280
West Fargo	10,099	5,161
Wahpeton	9,064	7,076

CLIMATE

CLIMATE	FARGO	BISMARCK
Average January temperature range	−20° to −9.4° C (−4° to 15° F)	−19.4° to −7.2° C (−3° to 19° F)
Average July temperature range	15° to 28.3° C (59° to 83° F)	13.9° to 28.9° C (57° to 84° F)
Average annual temperature	5° C (41° F)	5° C (41° F)
Average annual precipitation	508 mm (20 in)	406 mm (16 in)
Average annual snowfall	889 mm (35 in)	965 mm (38 in)
Mean number of days per year with appreciable precipitation	100	96
Average daily relative humidity	72%	68%
Mean number of clear days per year	87	94

NATURAL REGIONS OF NORTH DAKOTA

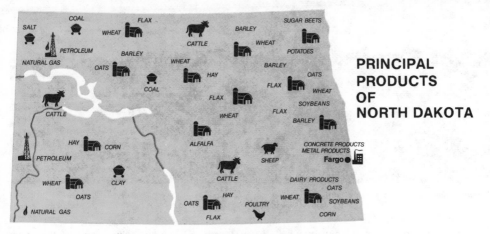

PRINCIPAL PRODUCTS OF NORTH DAKOTA

ECONOMY

State budget. . . . . revenue $1.0 billion
expenditure $910 million
State personal income tax, per capita $75
Personal income, per capita $8747
Assets, commercial banks (172) . . . . $4.2 billion
Labor force (civilian) 290,500
    Employed in services   28%
    Employed in wholesale and retail trade   22%
    Employed in government   17%
    Employed in manufacturing   6%

	Quantity Produced	Value
FARM PRODUCTS		**$2.4 billion**
Crops		**$1.6 billion**
Wheat	4.9 million metric tons	$822 million
Sunflowers	1.0 million metric tons	$241 million
Hay	2.3 million metric tons	$189 million
Barley	10.5 million metric tons	$130 million
Dry beans	122,000 metric tons	$66 million
Livestock and Livestock Products		**$781 million**
Cattle	372,000 metric tons	$519 million
Milk	395,000 metric tons	$107 million
Hogs	44,000 metric tons	$35 million
Sheep	6600 metric tons	$7 million
MINERALS		**$1.3 billion**
Petroleum	40 million barrels	$605 million
Coal†	15.4 million metric tons	$594 million
Natural gas	1.4 billion cu m	$50 million
Sand, gravel	5.0 million metric tons	$15 million

† Value estimated from govt. indications

FISHING . . . . 330 metric tons $111,000

                  Labor and Proprietors' Income

FORESTRY $405,000

MANUFACTURING . . . . $262 million
    Nonelectric machinery . . . . $74 million
    Food and kindred products . . . . $62 million
    Printing and publishing . . . . $28 million
    Stone, clay, and glass products . . . . $17 million
    Petroleum and coal products . . . . $13 million
    Fabricated metal products . . . . $13 million
    Transportation equipment . . . . $12 million
    Motor vehicles and equipment . . . . $8 million

OTHER . . . . **$2.9 billion**
Services . . . . $631 million
Government and government
  enterprises . . . . $782 million
Transportation and public utilities . . . . . . $403 million
Finance, insurance, and real estate . . . . $215 million
Wholesale trade . . . . $397 million
Retail trade . . . . $440 million

ANNUAL PRODUCTION OF GOODS BY SECTOR

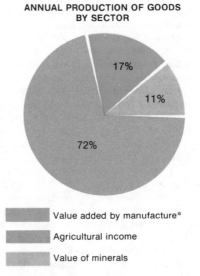

Value added by manufacture*

Agricultural income

Value of minerals

* The value added by an industry is a measure of the
value created in its products, not counting such production costs as raw materials and power.

Sources: U.S. government publications

Baling alfalfa on a North Dakota farm.
U.S. Bureau of Reclamation

North Dakota. Petroleum makes up about half of the value of the state's mineral output and is found primarily in the W. Lignite, the second most important mineral, comes from strip mines, primarily in the W central part of the state. Natural gas is produced in the SW and the NW. Other mineral products include sand and gravel, clays, lime, and salt.

Manufacturing. Enterprises engaged in manufacturing account for about 17% of the yearly value of goods produced in North Dakota and employ some 17,300 workers. The manufacturing of non-electrical machinery, particularly farm equipment, is the state's largest industry, in which more than one-fourth of the manufacturing labor force is employed. This is followed closely in importance by the manufacturing of food products and the printing and publishing industries. Among the principal food products are flour, cereals, butter, cheese, and sugar (processed from sugar beets). Other important manufactures are fabricated metals and stone, clay, and glass products. North Dakota also has several oil refineries. Although manufacturing has grown in importance, North Dakota still has one of the smallest manufacturing outputs of any state.

Tourism. Each year several million visitors produce in excess of $350 million for the North Dakota economy. Tourism has been growing rapidly in the state, and the industry provides some 16,200 jobs. About 1 million persons visit Theodore Roosevelt National Park. The state also maintains a system of 21 park and recreation areas, including Fort Lincoln State Park, near Mandan.

Transportation. A network of about 171,400 km (about 106,500 mi) of federal, state, and local roads serves all parts of North Dakota. This figure includes 920 km (572 mi) of Interstate Highways that cross the state from E to W and from N to S

along the E border, linking most of the major cities. The railroad network remains relatively dense, with a total of about 8050 km (about 5000 mi) of operated track in the state.

North Dakota has some 365 airports. The busiest airport in the state is at Fargo; the airport serving Bismarck and Mandan is the second most important.

Energy. The electricity-generating plants in North Dakota have a total capacity of about 3.4 million kw and produce about 15.8 billion kwh of electricity per year. The state has abundant and diverse energy resources, including coal, petroleum, natural gas, and waterpower resources. Some 55% of the generated electric power is sold and exported to neighboring states. About 85% of the electricity is thermally generated, with coal by far the most important fuel. Almost all the remainder is generated by the hydroelectric power project located at Garrison Dam on the Missouri R.   E.P.H.

HISTORY

Mound Builders settled along the rivers of the eastern two-thirds of present-day North Dakota about AD 1500. Beginning about 1700, the east was occupied by the Chippewa and the Yanktonais Sioux. Farther west the Teton branch of the Sioux nation roamed the plains. Along the Missouri River, the sedentary Mandan, Arikara, and Hidatsa, with their distinctive earth lodges and agriculture, contrasted sharply with the Sioux, who followed the buffalo.

Exploration and Settlement. The first European known to have been in the area was the French-Canadian explorer Pierre Gaultier de Varennes, sieur de La Vérendrye, who visited a Mandan village near what is now Bismarck in 1738. In the ensuing period, fur traders from his posts in Canada dealt with the Indians on the Red River as far south as Grand Forks. In the 1790s the Canadian

North West Co. and Hudson's Bay Co. built trading posts on the Red River in the northeast corner of the state.

North Dakota became a U.S. possession as part of the Louisiana Purchase of 1803, but its boundary with Canada was not agreed on until 1818. White settlement began in 1812, when people from the Selkirk Settlement at Winnipeg, Canada, founded a colony at Pembina. A community of Indians and métis (persons of mixed Indian and white ancestry) grew up around the fur-trading posts. Métis staffed the trains of carts carrying furs and merchandise between Winnipeg and Saint Paul, Minn. After 1859 steamboats on the river sped such goods between the two cities.

The Dakota Territory, which included North and South Dakota, as well as Wyoming and Montana, was created in 1861. When warfare broke out between the Sioux and white settlers in neighboring Minnesota the following year, many Indians sought refuge in the Dakota Territory, but most were eventually confined to the area west of the Missouri River.

Statehood. In the 1870s railroad links with St. Paul brought settlers from the East, among them many Norwegian and German immigrants. The bonanza farm craze of 1875-90 attracted so many settlers that the state of North Dakota was created in 1889. Despite hard times, population grew. The Republican party, dominated by the political boss Alexander McKenzie, (1850-1922), controlled the state government until 1906.

Continuing economic setbacks to farmers brought the Socialist-oriented Nonpartisan League (NPL) to power in 1917. It created the state-owned mill and elevator complex and the Bank of North Dakota, but was driven from office in 1921. In the 1920s prices for farm crops dropped, and many banks failed. During the Great Depression of the 1930s many people left the state; the economy was saved only by federal intervention. Prosperity returned during World War II and continued into the 1960s. The energy crisis of the 1970s led to a boom in oil and coal development in the western counties. The one-party Republican character of politics altered somewhat after 1960, when the Democratic-NPL party began a 20-year tenure of the governor's office. In 1980 the population was smaller than it had been in 1930.   R.P.W.

For further information on this topic, see the Bibliography in volume 28, section 1211.

NORTHEAST BOUNDARY DISPUTE, long-standing dispute between the U.S. and Great Britain concerning the northeastern boundary line with eastern Canada. It arose, like the Northwest Boundary Dispute, from the vagueness of the line laid down in Article II of the Treaty of Paris (1783). By this article the line was to run from the northwestern corner of Nova Scotia, northward from the source of the Saint Croix River to the dividing range of the Québec Highlands and then to the northwestern head of the Connecticut River down the Connecticut River to the 45th parallel and west along that parallel to the Saint Lawrence River. It was difficult to state exactly where the dividing line of the highlands lay, although it was clear that Great Britain wished that those highlands should form a buttress to the fortifications of Québec. This part of the boundary caused the most trouble. The location of the northwestern head of the Connecticut led to much dispute. Jay's Treaty (q.v.) settled what was meant by the St. Croix line, but neither the boundary terms in the Treaty of Ghent (1814) nor the decision (1831) of William I, king of the Netherlands, made the lines clear. The king had been chosen to arbitrate the dispute but recommended a solution unacceptable to the U.S. The quarrel over the islands in Passamaquoddy Bay was easily settled (1817), and the U.S. obtained Mosse, Frederick, and Dudley islands. The Aroostook War (1838-39), a bloodless controversy between New Brunswick and Maine, made both the U.S. and British governments wish for a definite boundary (*see* AROOSTOOK). Accordingly, Alexander Baring, 1st Baron Ashburton (1774-1848), was sent by Great Britain to Washington as a special minister, and after talks of an informal character with Secretary of State Daniel Webster, he arrived at a satisfactory solution, known as the Webster-Ashburton Treaty (1842). Great Britain secured the highlands and a circuitous route between Québec and Halifax; the U.S. secured seven-twelfths of the disputed territory and the right to carry timber down the Saint John River. In lieu of territory lost by Maine and Massachusetts, the U.S. gained Rouses Point on Lake Champlain.

NORTHEAST PASSAGE, water route that extends from the North Sea of Europe, along the Arctic coast of Asia, and through the Bering Sea to the Pacific Ocean. The British began the quest for the Northeast Passage in 1553 with an expedition commanded by the navigator Sir Hugh Willoughby (d. 1554), who sighted Novaya Zemlya and reached Lapland, where he died. During 1878-79 the Swedish explorer Adolf Erik Nordenskjöld became the first to traverse the passage by rounding Cape Chelyuskin and reaching Yokohama, Japan.

NORTHERN EXPEDITION, military campaign launched by Chiang Kai-shek in 1926 against the warlords in northern China, with the aim of unifying the country under the Kuomintang (q.v.). The campaign began in July, when the National Revolutionary Army, under Chiang's command, began its march into central China. Supplied with Soviet matériel and immeasurably aided by Communist cadres, who mobilized peasants and workers, Chiang succeeded in gaining control of most of central China by March 1927. At that time, however, fearing they were becoming too powerful and having just married into the capitalist Soong family, Chiang split with the Communists and ordered their elimination. Thus delayed while he consolidated his position, the Northern Expedition was completed with the capture of Peking in 1928. The Communists, scattered by Chiang's forces, later regrouped in Jiangxi (Kiangsi) Province, from where they started their Long March (q.v.) in 1934.

NORTHERN IRELAND, integral part of the United Kingdom of Great Britain and Northern Ireland, situated in the NE portion of the island of Ireland. Northern Ireland is bounded on the N and NE by the North Channel, on the SE by the Irish Sea, and on the S and W by the Republic of Ireland. It includes Rathlin Island in the North Channel and several smaller offshore islands. Northern Ireland is also known as Ulster, because it comprises six of the nine counties that constituted the former province of Ulster. The total area of Northern Ireland is 14,148 sq km (5463 sq mi).

LAND AND RESOURCES

Northern Ireland has an extreme N to S extension of about 135 km (about 85 mi) and an extreme E to W extension of about 175 km (about 110 mi). The shoreline is characterized by numerous irregularities and is about 530 km (about 330 mi) long. The major indentations are Lough Foyle in the N and Belfast, Strangford, and Carlingford loughs in the E. A striking feature of the N coast is the Giant's Causeway (q.v.), a rock formation consisting of thousands of closely placed, polygonal pillars of black basalt.

The country consists mainly of a low, flat plain in the approximate center of which is Lough Neagh (about 390 sq km/about 150 sq mi), the largest lake in the British Isles. Other important lakes are Lough Erne and Upper Lough Erne. Apart from several isolated elevations, three major areas of considerable height are the Sperrin Mts. in the NW, the Antrim Plateau along the NE coast, and the Mourne Mts. in the SE. The highest point in the country is Slieve Donard (852 m/2796 ft), a peak in the Mourne Mts.

The chief rivers are the Foyle R., which forms part of the NW boundary and flows into Lough Foyle at Londonderry, and the Upper Bann and Lower Bann rivers. The former rises in the Mourne Mts. and empties into Lough Neagh; the latter flows out of Lough Neagh to the North Channel. Among the many other rivers are the Main, Blackwater, Lagan, Erne, and Bush. Because of the generally flat terrain, drainage is poor, and the areas of marshland are extensive.

Climate. The climate of Northern Ireland is mild and damp throughout the year. The prevailing westerly winds from the Gulf Stream are largely responsible for the lack of extreme summer heat

The Wishing Arch in county Antrim is one example of the many coves and inlets of Northern Ireland's coastline.
UPI

Thatched cottages are a common sight in Northern Ireland.
UPI

and winter cold. The average annual temperature is approximately 10° C (50° F); temperatures average about 14.4° C (about 58° F) in July and about 4.4° C (about 40° F) in January. Rainfall is distributed evenly during the year. The annual precipitation frequently exceeds 1016 mm (40 in) in the N and is about 760 mm (about 30 in) in the S. The level of humidity is high.

Natural Resources. The most valuable natural resources of Northern Ireland are its fertile soil and rich pasturelands. Natural waterpower is abundant. The chief minerals are basalt, limestone, sand and gravel, granite, chalk, clay, and shale; bauxite, iron ore, and coal also are found in small amounts. Peat is important as a fuel.

Plants and Animals. In general, the plants and animals of Northern Ireland are similar to those of the island as a whole. The only distinctive plant is a species of wild orchid, *Spiranthes stricta,* found in the valleys of the Upper and Lower Bann rivers. Distinctive species of animal life include the pollan, a freshwater variety of whitefish found in Lough Neagh and Lough Erne.

POPULATION

The majority of the people are of Scottish or English ancestry and are known commonly as the Scotch-Irish. The remainder of the population is Irish, principally native to Ulster.

English is the sole official language. Unlike the Republic of Ireland, Northern Ireland does not encourage the use of the Gaelic language.

Population Characteristics. The population of Northern Ireland (1980 est.) was 1,547,300. The population is almost equally divided between urban and rural dwellers. The overall density was 109 persons per sq km (283 per sq mi). The population is unevenly distributed, however, with greater concentrations in the E half.

The capital and largest city of Northern Ireland is Belfast (pop., 1980 est., 345,800), which is surrounded by such substantial and growing industries as shipbuilding and the manufacture of textiles. The country's other major city is Londonderry (91,200).

Political Divisions. Northern Ireland is divided into 26 districts. Each district is governed by an elected council.

Religion. The population of Northern Ireland is predominantly Protestant. The largest single denomination, however, is the Roman Catholic (about 31% of the country's total population). The largest Protestant denominations are the Presbyterian, the Church of Ireland, and the Methodist. Unlike England, Northern Ireland has no established, or state, church. The Church of Ireland (see IRELAND, CHURCH OF), at one time a branch of the Church of England, was dissociated from it in 1871. Much conflict between Northern Ireland's Roman Catholics and Protestants occurred in the 1970s and early '80s. (See History below.)

Education. Education in Northern Ireland is free and compulsory for children between the ages of 5 and 15. The educational system is essentially similar to that of England. In the early 1980s Northern Ireland had about 1125 primary

Royal Ave. stretches through the heart of Belfast, capital of Northern Ireland. Belfast is the focus of political and religious strife between Great Britain and Northern Ireland.
UPI

schools, annually attended by approximately 199,550 pupils and staffed by more than 8300 teachers. Secondary schools numbered about 260 and were attended by about 164,200 students taught by 10,400 instructors. The country has two universities: Queen's University of Belfast, founded as Queen's College in 1845, and the New University of Ulster (1965), in Coleraine. The total annual university enrollment in the early 1980s was about 7800. Two colleges, the Belfast College of Technology (1901) and the Union Theological College (1978), are in Belfast; the Ulster Polytechnic (1971) is in Newtownabbey.

Culture. Originally, Northern Ireland was culturally indistinguishable from the remainder of Ireland. With the waves of colonization from England and especially Scotland during the 17th century, however, the N section (known as Ulster) evolved its own cultural identity. Religion constitutes the most significant difference between life in Northern Ireland and in the Repub-

lic of Ireland. In addition, Northern Ireland is considerably more urbanized and industrialized than the Republic of Ireland.

Northern Ireland shares the early cultural glories of all Ireland. To Ulster belongs one of the two great cycles of Irish myths that contain the exploits of Cú Chulainn and the tragic story of Deirdre. Despite a thriving theatrical movement in Belfast and much literary activity, no Northern Irish writer has approached the achievements of the writers of the Irish literary revival.

Major museums in Northern Ireland include the Ulster Museum, in Belfast, which houses a collection of Irish antiquities, and the Ulster Folk and Transport Museum, in Hollywood.

ECONOMY

In general, the economy of Northern Ireland is based on agriculture and manufacturing and is closely related to that of Great Britain as a whole. In 1980-81 the country had an estimated budget that included revenue and expenditure balanced at about $4 billion.

Agriculture. Small farms predominate in Northern Ireland, and production generally includes both crops and livestock. Livestock on farms in the early 1980s numbered approximately 1.5 million cattle, 1.1 million sheep, 691,400 pigs, and 11.2 million chickens. The leading crops in the country were potatoes, barley, hay, oats, turnips, apples, and pears.

Forestry and Fishing. Northern Ireland is sparsely forested, but the state afforestation program has made considerable progress, and in the early 1980s about 60,000 cu m (about 2.1 million cu ft) of timber were felled annually. The fish catch in 1980 was about 13,600 metric tons. Saltwater fishing is centered on the E coast, principally off Newcastle; the most important species caught include whiting, herring, and scallops. Freshwater fisheries operate in Lough Neagh, Lough Erne, and Upper Lough Erne; the species caught include salmon, trout, eel, and pollan.

Mining and Manufacturing. Mining and quarrying are relatively unimportant economic activities in Northern Ireland. They employed only about 2100 workers in 1980. The chief minerals are basalt, sand and gravel, peat, chalk, limestone, and granite.

Manufacturing is the largest single source of the total national product. In 1979 the industrial output of Northern Ireland was valued at about $1.9 billion. Manufacturing and construction accounted for more than one-third of the total work force.

Traditionally, the leading industries of Northern Ireland have been the manufacture of textiles and clothing. Linen is the most important textile manufactured; cotton cloth and fabrics woven of synthetic fibers rank next in importance. Shipbuilding and the manufacture of aircraft also are major industries; big shipyards are in Belfast. Other manufactures include textile machinery, electrical and electronic equipment, processed food, liquor, tobacco products, and chemicals.

External Trade. About 80% of Northern Ireland's external trade is with Great Britain, and the currency of Great Britain is the legal tender of Northern Ireland. A large portion of the exports to Great Britain is transshipped to other countries, however. Northern Ireland exports linen goods, textiles, clothing, machinery, and food, notably meat, potatoes, and dairy products. Imports consist chiefly of raw materials and metals, fuel, produce, and an assortment of manufactured goods.

Transportation and Communications. Northern Ireland has about 23,415 km (about 14,550 mi) of roads, including 108 km (67 mi) of motorway. The Northern Ireland Railways Co. provided passenger service on 338 km (210 mi) of railroad track. Daily steamship and airline services connect Belfast with the rest of the United Kingdom.

Northern Ireland has three daily newspapers, the *Belfast Telegraph,* the *Irish News and Belfast Morning News,* and the *News Letter.* In the early 1980s the dailies, published in Belfast, had a combined daily circulation of about 265,000.

Labor. The system of labor relations in Northern Ireland is based on the same principles as that of Great Britain. A major proportion of trade unionists in Northern Ireland are members of trade unions with headquarters in Great Britain.

A picturesque sight in rural Ireland, an itinerant knife grinder on his two-wheeled donkey cart. UPI

NORTHERN IRELAND

GOVERNMENT

Northern Ireland, an integral part of Great Britain, sends 12 members to the British House of Commons. In 1979 the Redistribution of Seats Act recommended that this number be increased to 17. The Government of Ireland Act, which was passed by the British Parliament in 1920 and was modified by several subsequent agreements between Northern Ireland and Great Britain, is the basic constitutional document of the country. The act gave Northern Ireland local autonomy; the government of Great Britain retained control over defense, foreign policy, currency, tariffs, and communications. In 1972, however, because of religious strife, direct rule was reimposed. It was relinquished in 1974 and that same year reimposed under the terms of the Northern Ireland Act. Following this act, the head of the Northern Ireland government became the secretary of state for Northern Ireland. The secretary of state and the secretary's ministers are directly responsible to the British Parliament. Before 1972 Northern Ireland had a governor, who served as the official head of state, and its own bicameral Parliament.

Local Government. Northern Ireland is divided into 26 districts for the purposes of local government. Each district is run by a council responsible for a variety of administrative functions.

Political Parties. Northern Ireland's major political organization, the Ulster Unionist party, governed Northern Ireland from 1921 to 1972. Other important political parties include the Social Democratic and Labour party, the Democratic Unionist party, and the Alliance party.

Judiciary. The highest court is the Supreme Court of Judicature of Northern Ireland, which consists of the High Court, the Court of Appeal, and the Crown Court. Lower courts include county courts with criminal and civil jurisdiction and magistrates' courts for minor offenses.

HISTORY

For the history of Ireland before 1920, see IRELAND: *History.* In 1920, when Ireland was granted home rule, six counties of the province of Ulster, northermost of the four Irish provinces, were given the opportunity to separate politically from the rest of the island and preserve a close relation with Great Britain. Under the Government of Ireland Act of 1920, the six counties became a separate political division, with its own constitution. The Irish Free State (later Eire, and now the Republic of Ireland) did not accept the separation as permanent, but Northern Ireland consistently refused to consider a reunion. The boundary between the two was fixed permanently in 1925.

Northern Ireland, as an integral part of the United Kingdom, participated in World War II, supplying military personnel and producing ships, aircraft, and cloth for military uniforms. The ports of Belfast and Londonderry were of strategic importance to Allied shipping. Belfast was damaged considerably by air raids.

Northern Ireland After World War II. In 1949, when Eire withdrew completely from the Commonwealth of Nations, the partition of Ireland became a major consideration in both divisions. In the 1949 elections in Northern Ireland, the Nationalist party, which supported union with the Republic of Ireland, was decisively defeated by the Ulster Unionist party. On May 17 the British Parliament passed a bill retaining Northern Ireland as a part of the United Kingdom until the local Parliament decided otherwise.

Persistent economic difficulties through the postwar years led to the formation, in 1955, of a Northern Ireland Development Council, which met with considerable success. By the mid-1960s some 230 new firms had been founded and another 200 considerably expanded.

Irregulars of the outlawed Irish Republican Army (IRA) initiated, in December 1955, a campaign of terrorism on behalf of the union of Northern Ireland with the Republic of Ireland, bombing British military installations in county Fermanagh. Acts of terrorism continued through 1957 and 1958, although gradually becoming less frequent in the early 1960s. The government of the republic condemned terrorism as a means of achieving unification, and in 1962 the IRA announced that it had abandoned the campaign.

Growing Violence. By the late 1960s, however, religious division and violence had again increased in Northern Ireland, particularly in Belfast. In 1968, Roman Catholics, long discontented over what they felt to be discrimination in employment, housing, and parliamentary representation, organized a civil rights movement. Moderate Protestants recognized a need for governmental reform, but a right-wing faction of the ruling Ulster Unionist party called for the resignation of the centrist prime minister, James D. Chichester-Clark, later Baron Moyola (1923-), for failing to deal stringently with the Roman Catholic opposition, which had frequently erupted into riots. In early 1971 he was succeeded as prime minister by the former minister of development Brian Faulkner (1921-77).

After a sharp escalation of violence the British abolished the Northern Ireland Parliament in early 1972 and reimposed direct rule. In March 1973, in a referendum largely boycotted by Roman Catholics, the voters of Northern Ireland

British troops face Irish rioters as news reaches the Roman Catholics of Belfast of the death of Bobby Sands, the first IRA hunger striker, in May 1981. A month earlier, Sands had been elected a member of the British Parliament. Wide World Photos

once again chose to retain ties with Great Britain rather than join the republic. A 15-member Northern Ireland executive, made up of both Protestants and Roman Catholics, took office at the beginning of 1974. This intercommunal government was opposed by extremist Protestants, who in mid-1974 spearheaded a general strike. The work stoppage resulted in widespread disruption, and in May, Great Britain again imposed direct rule. Violence increased in the following years. Two Belfast women, Mairead Corrigan (1944–) and Betty Williams (1943–), were jointly awarded the Nobel Peace Prize for 1976 for working to reconcile Northern Ireland's religious communities. Their work, however, was futile. Violence continued, and attempts to bring the two factions together were fruitless. The so-called Provisional Wing of the IRA maintained a steady terrorist pressure. In August 1979 it murdered Lord Mountbatten of Burma and on the same day ambushed a party of British soldiers, killing 18 of them. Lord Mountbatten's murder was roundly condemned, and by 1981 the IRA was employing a new tactic to revive sympathy: a

hunger strike by detained members. Several young IRA members thus starved themselves to death in 1981, each death setting off a new round of violence. The division between the Northern Irish communities meanwhile remained as sharp as ever, with no solution in sight.

For further information on this topic, see the Bibliography in volume 28, section 931.

NORTHERN LIGHTS. *See* AURORA.

NORTHERN MARIANA ISLANDS, COMMONWEALTH OF THE, island group, in the Pacific Ocean, part of Micronesia, E of the Philippines and S of Japan. The approximately 16 coral and volcanic islands, including all of the Mariana Islands except Guam, comprise an area of 477 sq km (184 sq mi). The principal islands are Saipan (122 sq km/47 sq mi), Tinian (101 sq km/39 sq mi), and Rota (83 sq km/32 sq mi). The economy is based on agriculture, some light manufacturing and tourism. Major exports include vegetables, beef, and pork. The island of Saipan contains the seat of government, a busy seaport, and an international airport.

The Marianas were discovered in 1521 by Ferdinand Magellan, a Portuguese explorer sailing for Spain. The islands, known as the Ladrones Islands (Thieves Islands), were not colonized until 1668, when Spanish Jesuit settlers arrived and claimed them for Spain. They renamed the islands for Mariana of Austria (1634–96), then regent of Spain. In 1898, Guam was ceded by Spain to the U.S., and the following year Germany purchased the rest of the island group. After World War I the German, or northern, Marianas were placed under Japanese control as a League of Nations mandate. The islands were captured by the U.S. during World War II, and in 1947 were made part of the U.S.-administered UN Trust Territory of the Pacific Islands. In 1975 the inhabitants of the northern Marianas voted to become a U.S. commonwealth, and in 1978 the islands became internally self-governing. Full status as a U.S. commonwealth was dependent on UN approval, which was being sought in the early 1980s. Pop. (1980) 16,862.

NORTHERN TERRITORY, territory, N Australia, bounded on the N by the Timor Sea, the Arafura Sea, and the Gulf of Carpentaria; on the E by Queensland; on the S by South Australia; and on the W by Western Australia. The territory consists mainly of low tablelands with altitudes of less than 610 m (2000 ft). The N coast is a lowland area, Mt. Zeil (1510 m/4955 ft), in the Macdonnell Ranges at the S part of the territory, is the highest peak. The climate is tropical. Precipitation, which occurs mainly between November and April, ranges from 1524 mm (60 in) annually along the coast to about 254 mm (about 10 in) in the interior. The marsupial, alligator, snake, water buffalo, and tropical bird are common. The most important forms of vegetation are grasses, mangroves, and eucalyptus trees. Darwin is the capital, largest city, and principal port. Area 1,346,200 sq km (519,771 sq mi); pop. (1981 est.) 125,900.

Cattle raising is a primary economic activity. The territory is rich in minerals, with gold, silver, copper, uranium oxide, and manganese ore produced in significant quantities. Despite the lack of water and the presence of numerous insect pests in the territory, the government has made successful efforts to develop farming in the interior. Peanuts are the chief commercial crop.

The territorial government is headed by an administrator appointed by the central government of Australia and aided by a legislative assembly of 19 elected members. The Northern Territory was given increased autonomy in 1978–79.

NORTH GERMAN CONFEDERATION (Ger. *Norddeutscher Bund*), union of independent German states north of the Main River, formed in 1867 under the leadership of Prussia on the initiative of the Prussian foreign minister, Otto von Bismarck. Prussia had defeated Austria in the Seven Weeks' War of 1866. It next moved to establish a confederation of north German states under Prussian leadership. The North German Confederation replaced the Germanic Confederation, a union of 39 German states under Austrian leadership that had been established (1815) by the Congress of Vienna at the end of the Napoleonic Wars. Twenty-two German states adhered to the North German Confederation. According to the agreement, each retained its own government but submitted its military forces to the control of the confederation; the commander in chief of the combined armies was the king of Prussia. A legislative body was created; its president was the king of Prussia, but the duties of the office were performed by a chancellor, who was responsible only to the king.

Alliances were entered into between the North German Confederation and the important states to the south of the Main, namely, the kingdom of Bavaria, the Grand Duchy of Baden, and the kingdom of Württemberg, under which these states agreed to place their military forces under command of the king of Prussia in case of war against the confederation. The North German Confederation was an important step toward the unification of Germany, finally achieved in 1871 at the end of the Franco-Prussian War. After their victory in this war, the states of the North German Confederation and all the remaining states of Germany (except Austria) were combined to form the German Empire. The constitution of the confederation was adopted with slight modification as the constitution of the empire.

NORTHGLENN, city, Adams Co., central Colorado, near the confluence of Clear Creek and the South Platte R.; inc. 1969. Primarily a residential suburb of Denver, Northglenn is situated in the vicinity of the Rocky Mountain Arsenal and Stapleton International Airport. The area was mostly farmland until 1960, when the community began rapid development. Pop. (1970) 27,785; (1980) 29,847.

NORTH HAVEN, town, New Haven Co., S Connecticut, on the Quinnipiac R., a residential and industrial suburb N of New Haven (whence its name); settled about 1650, separated from New Haven and inc. 1786. Manufactures include aerospace equipment, machinery, and chemicals. A junior college is here. Pop. (1970) 22,194; (1980) 22,080.

NORTH HIGHLANDS, urban community, Sacramento Co., N central California, near the American R. It is primarily a residential suburb of Sacramento. McClellan Air Force Base is nearby. Pop. (1970) 31,854; (1980) 37,825.

NORTH ISLAND. *See* NEW ZEALAND.

NORTH KOREA. *See* KOREA, NORTH.

NORTH LAS VEGAS, city, Clark Co., SE Nevada; inc. 1946. It is primarily a residential suburb of Las Vegas and has some manufacturing industries. Tourism and Nellis Air Force Base are important to the city's economy. Lake Mead National Recreation Area is in the vicinity. The community was settled in the early 1920s and was originally given the name Vegas Verde; it received the name North Las Vegas in 1932. Pop. (1970) 46,067; (1980) 42,739.

NORTH LITTLE ROCK, city, Pulaski Co., central Arkansas, on the Arkansas R., N of Little Rock (whence its name); inc. 1904. It is a residential, manufacturing, and railroad center; local products include cosmetics, chemicals, textiles, processed food, and metal goods. The city is the seat of a junior college and the site of Burns Park, one of the largest municipal parks in the U.S. The community, once part of Little Rock, was formerly known as Argenta. Its present name was permanently adopted in 1917. Pop. (1970) 60,040; (1980) 64,288.

NORTHMEN. *See* VIKINGS.

NORTH MIAMI, city, Dade Co., SE Florida, on Biscayne Bay, near Miami; inc. as a city 1952. It is a tourist center and has motion picture studios. The community, incorporated as the town of Miami Shores in 1926, was renamed North Miami five years later. It grew rapidly after World War II, especially after the Keystone Point area on the bay was developed. Pop. (1970) 34,767; (1980) 42,566.

NORTH MIAMI BEACH, city, Dade Co., SE Florida, on the Atlantic Ocean and the Oleta R., N of Miami Beach; inc. 1931. It is primarily residential and has some resort facilities. The community, settled in 1898, was known as Fulford before the present name was adopted in 1931. Its main growth began in the late 1940s. Pop. (1970) 30,544; (1980) 36,553.

NORTH OLMSTED, city, Cuyahoga Co., NE Ohio; inc. as a city 1950. It is primarily a residential suburb of Cleveland and has some industrial firms. The community, settled in 1815 as Kingston, was renamed about 1829 for Aaron Olmstead, a Connecticut merchant who in the early 19th century had purchased the section of the old Western Reserve on which the settlement was established. The area remained chiefly agricultural until the 1950s, when the city began a period of rapid growth. Pop. (1970) 34,861; (1980) 36,486.

NORTH PLATTE, city, seat of Lincoln Co., central Nebraska, at the confluence of the North Platte and South Platte rivers; settled 1866, inc. 1873. It is a railroad center situated in an agricultural area; one of the largest railroad classification yards of the U.S. is here. Manufactures include packed meat and flour. North Platte is the site of a community college; the Lincoln County Historical Society Museum, exhibiting pioneer items; and the annual Nebraskaland Days celebration, featuring a rodeo. Scouts Rest Ranch, once the home of Buffalo Bill, and Lake Maloney are nearby. Pop. (1970) 19,447; (1980) 24,509.

NORTH PLATTE, river, formed by several headstreams that rise in the Rocky Mts. in N Colorado. It flows N into Wyoming, where it bends to flow SE across Wyoming and Nebraska, where it joins the South Platte R. Its total length is 995 km (618 mi). Numerous dams and reservoirs on the river are part of an irrigation, flood control, and hydroelectric scheme.

NORTH POLE, point at the N end of the earth's axis. The geographic North Pole is situated in the central Arctic Ocean in a region covered by drifting pack ice. It was first reached in 1909 by the U.S. explorer Robert E. Peary. The North Pole is located at a considerable distance from the magnetic pole (q.v.) to which a compass needle points.

NORTH RHINE-WESTPHALIA, state, W West Germany, bounded on the N and NE by the state of Lower Saxony, on the E by the state of Hesse, on the S by the state of Rhineland-Palatinate, and on the W by Belgium and the Netherlands. Düsseldorf is the capital. Other important cities are Essen, Cologne, Dortmund, and Bonn, the federal capital. The NW part of the state is a lowland, which rises in the NE into the hilly Teutoburger Wald. The E, S, and W parts are rolling uplands, which in the W reach an elevation of 800 m (2625 ft). The uplands are cut by a series of valleys, of which the Rhine, Ruhr, and Möhne are the most important. The Rhine, Ems, and Weser rivers, the main rivers in the state, flow in a S to N direction.

North Rhine-Westphalia is the most industrialized and most populous state in West Germany. Coal mining, coke production, pig-iron production, and steelmaking, the chief industries, are centered in the Ruhr Valley, which has some of the largest reserves of bituminous coal in W Europe. Other industries include the manufacture of textiles, chemicals, and machinery. The state also produces about one-third of the electricity of West Germany. Extensive agricultural areas are found throughout the state. The Rhineland is known for its wine production. Cereals, pota-

Although badly polluted, the Rhine is still a river of legend. The picture shows the castle Gutenfels, one of many overlooking the famous stream. German Information Center

toes, and beets are grown throughout Westphalia. Dairy farming and cattle and hog raising are also important. Because of the well-known cathedrals and castles along the Rhine R., tourism is a major industry.

Under the 1950 constitution, the state is governed by a cabinet, headed by a minister-president. The cabinet is responsible to the popularly elected diet. The state is divided into six administrative districts.

The Rhine area was the homeland of numerous German tribes who successively fought the Celts and other German peoples, the Romans, and the Franks. Merovingian and Carolingian rulers used the Rhineland as a base for penetrating Germany from the 6th to the 9th century. After the breakup of the Carolingian dynasty, a number of separate bishoprics and duchies emerged. These small states fell prey to their stronger neighbors: France moved into Lorraine in the 16th century and into Alsace in the 17th century; also in the 17th century Brandenburg gained a foothold in Westphalia and gained Cleves and Mark. Although Louis XIV, king of France, was not able to extend his control, the French Revolution and the Napoleonic Wars helped to consolidate many of the small states. The left bank of the Rhine was ceded to France in 1801. Further changes came with the creation of the Confeder-

ation of the Rhine in 1806 and the kingdom of Westphalia in 1807. Although the Congress of Vienna (1814–15) undid much of this partition, France, Prussia, and Bavaria gained new areas. Prussia acquired Westphalia between 1815 and 1817 and annexed various Rhineland areas following the Seven Years' War.

After World War I, Allied forces occupied the Ruhr and other parts of the Rhineland. In 1930 the last Allied troops left the Rhineland, and in 1936 German troops reoccupied the area. During World War II, the Ruhr area was heavily bombed. In 1946 the state was created out of Westphalia and the N part of the Rhine province; Lippe was added in 1947.

Area, 34,069 sq km (13,154 sq mi); pop. (1980 est.) 17,040,700.

NORTH RICHLAND HILLS, city, Tarrant Co., N Texas, near Lake Grapevine. It is a suburb of Fort Worth and experienced large-scale development during the 1970s. Pop. (1970) 16,514; (1980) 30,592.

NORTH SEA (Lat. *Mare Germanicum*), arm of the Atlantic Ocean, between the E coast of Great Britain and the continent of Europe. The Strait of Dover, with the English Channel, forms the S link with the Atlantic. The greatest width of the North Sea is about 645 km (about 400 mi), its greatest length about 965 km (about 600 mi), and its area about 575,000 sq km (about 222,000 sq mi). A number of rivers flow into the S part of the North Sea; the most important of these are the Elbe, Weser, Ems, Rhine (which is joined at its mouth by the Meuse), and Scheldt (or Schelde) on the Continent and the Thames and Humber in Great Britain. The sea reaches its greatest depth off the coast of Norway. The shallow Dogger Bank occupies the S central part of the sea. The tides of the North Sea are very irregular, because two tidal waves enter it, one from the N and one from the S.

Rain and fog occur at all seasons, and the violent NW storms blowing toward the shoals on the SE coast make navigation dangerous, especially along the coast of the peninsula of Jutland. North Sea fisheries provide support for inhabitants of the surrounding countries. Beginning in the late 1970s, much petroleum was produced from the sea floor. By means of the Nord-Ostsee Kanal, ships enter the Baltic Sea without making the longer passage N around Jutland.

NORTH STAR or **POLE STAR,** conspicuous star in the northern hemisphere, located closest to the point toward which the axis of the earth is directed, thus roughly marking the location of the north celestial pole. A pole star has been used by navigators throughout recorded history for charting navigation routes and is still used for determining true azimuth and astronomic latitude. The positions of the celestial poles change as the earth's axis moves with the earth's precessional motion (see ECLIPTIC), and as the north celestial pole assumes different positions relative to the constellations, different stars become the North Star.

During the past 5000 years the line of direction of the North Pole has moved from the star Thuban, or alpha (α) Draconis, in the constellation Draco, to within one degree of the bright star Polaris, also known as alpha (α) Ursae Minoris, in the constellation Ursa Minor (Little Dipper), which is now the North Star. Polaris is a binary star of second magnitude, and is located at a distance of about 300 light-years from the earth. It is easy to locate in the sky because the two stars opposite the handle in the bowl of the dipper in the constellation Ursa Major (Big Dipper), which are called the Pointers, point directly toward the star Polaris. See BIG DIPPER; CONSTELLATION; LITTLE DIPPER.

In the year 7500 the brightest star in the constellation Cepheus, α (alpha) Cephei, will mark the pole, and in the year 15,000 the star Vega, in the constellation Lyra, will be the North Star. About 9000 years after that, Polaris will again become the North Star.

NORTH TONAWANDA, city, Niagara Co., W New York, on the Niagara R. at the W terminus of the New York State Barge Canal System; inc. as a city 1897. It forms a manufacturing and distribution center and shares a harbor with the adjoining city of Tonawanda. Diversified products here include chemicals, paint, plastic, metal, paper, and wood items. The area was settled in the early 19th century. The name Tonawanda is derived from an Iroquois term meaning "swift running water." Pop. (1970) 36,012; (1980) 35,760.

NORTHUMBERLAND, county, extreme NE England; Newcastle upon Tyne, in the adjacent metropolitan county of Tyne and Wear, serves as the administrative center. Northumberland comprises a coastal plain on the E along the North Sea and an upland area of hills and moors in the W. The Cheviot Hills extend along the Scottish border in the N. Agriculture and livestock raising are the chief occupations. In Northumberland are remains of Hadrian's Wall, constructed by the Romans in the 2d century AD. In the 7th century the region formed part of the Anglo-Saxon kingdom of Northumbria. Until the union of England with Scotland (1603), the county suffered repeatedly from border wars. Area, 5032 sq km (1943 sq mi); pop. (1981) 299,905.

NORTHUMBERLAND, John Dudley, Duke of (c. 1502–53), English courtier and military commander. His father, Edmund Dudley (c. 1462–1510), a lawyer involved in tax extortion under King Henry VII, was executed upon the accession of King Henry VIII. Dudley's mother remarried, and his stepfather gained him favor at court. He was made governor of Calais in 1538 and warden of the Scottish marches in 1542, the year he was elevated to the peerage as Viscount Lisle. He was created earl of Warwick in 1546. Upon the accession of King Edward VI, a minor, in 1547, Dudley became joint regent and lord chamberlain of England. After subduing a Scottish rebellion in 1547, he embarked on a struggle for power with the Seymour family, headed by Edward Seymour. Dudley was created duke of Northumberland in 1550 and two years later disposed of his rival, Seymour, by having him tried and executed on false charges. Subsequently, he conspired to gain the succession to the English throne for his heirs by marrying his son, Guildford (d. 1554), to Lady Jane Grey. His resistance to the accession of Queen Mary I led to his execution in 1553.

NORTHUMBRIA, kingdom in Anglo-Saxon England, formed in the early 7th century, probably by King Ethelfrith (d. 616), out of the two earlier kingdoms of Bernicia and Deira. Northumbria included all England north of the Humber River and part of the Scottish Lowlands. It became the strongest kingdom in England under King Edwin, and under King Oswald (605?–42), English martyr and saint, it was the champion of Christianity against the pagan Anglo-Saxon kingdom of Mercia. The separate existence of this kingdom was brought to an end by Egbert, king of Wessex, and the first Saxon king recognized as sovereign of all England, in 827. The name survives in the modern county of Northumberland.

NORTH VANCOUVER, city, S British Columbia, Canada, on Burrard Inlet of the Strait of Georgia opposite Vancouver (to which it is connected by bridges); inc. as a city 1907. It is a shipping and tourist center with some manufacturing industries, including the production of boats, chemicals, and wood items. A junior college is here. The community, settled about 1863, was named Moodyville in 1872 and was given its present name in 1907. Pop. (1976) 31,934; (1981) 33,952.

NORTH VIETNAM. See VIETNAM.

NORTHWEST BOUNDARY DISPUTE, controversy between the U.S. and Great Britain concerning the boundary between the U.S. and the British colony of Canada. The dispute originated because the Treaty of Paris of 1783 established the boundary as a line extending west from the northwestern point of Lake of the Woods to the Mississippi River. The treaty negotiators used Mitchell's Map of North America to set the boundary; the map, however, depicted the northern source of the Mississippi about 245 km (about 152 mi) north of its actual location. Great Britain and the U.S. disputed the boundary from 1792 until the Convention of 1818 was accepted, setting the boundary at the 49th parallel, about 245 km (about 152 mi) north of the Mississippi source. The agreement extended the northern boundary westward to the Rocky Mountains.

The U.S. proposed to continue the line to the Pacific Ocean as a means of dividing the Oregon country between the two claimants. The offer was rejected by Great Britain, which claimed it would give the Columbia River to the U.S. The U.S. agreed that the two powers would occupy the Oregon territory jointly for ten years. During the administration of President John Tyler, the British offered to accept the 49th parallel as far west as the Columbia River and from there to follow the Columbia River to the Pacific. The government of the U.S., however, declined. In the U.S., popular opposition by those who wanted to extend U.S. territory north to 54°40′ N gave rise to the slogan "Fifty-four forty, or fight." The Democratic party, and its national platform of 1844, asserted the right of the U.S. to the whole of Oregon. The dispute was settled by the Oregon Treaty in 1846: The boundary line was established at the 49th parallel to the middle of the channel that separates Vancouver Island from the continent, extending south through the channel and the Strait of Juan de Fuca to the Pacific Ocean. Navigation of the channel and straits was to remain free and open to both the U.S. and the British.

See also PARIS, TREATY OF; WASHINGTON, TREATY OF.

NORTHWESTERN UNIVERSITY, privately controlled institution of higher learning, in Chicago and Evanston, Ill., chartered in 1851, and opened for instruction four years later; women were first admitted in 1869. Eight divisions of the university are located in Evanston, a suburb of Chicago, on a campus stretching along the shore of Lake Michigan. They include the college of arts and sciences (founded 1855), the school of speech (1878), the school of music (1895), the graduate school of management (1908), the graduate school (1910), the Medill School of Journalism (1921), the school of education (1926), and the technological institute (1939, formerly the school of engineering). The remaining schools, located on the Chicago campus, are the school of medicine (1859), the school of law (1859), the school of dentistry (1891), and the evening divisions (1932). The degrees of bachelor, master, and doctor are granted. The university has connections with the Garrett Theological Seminary and the Seabury-Western Seminary, both in Evanston.

NORTH-WEST FRONTIER PROVINCE, province, NW Pakistan. The region is between Afghanistan and the Indus R. In 1849, following the Second Sikh War, the British seized control of the region, most of which was formed into frontier districts, and attached it for administrative purposes to the Punjab. In 1901 a British commission confined the new North-West Frontier Province mainly to the N of the Gumal R. In 1947, after the termination of British control over India, the province became a division of newly independent Pakistan. From 1955 to 1970 it was part of the consolidated province of West Pakistan. Its capital is Peshawar. Pop. (1981 prelim.) 10,885,000.

NORTHWEST PASSAGE, route for ships between the Atlantic Ocean and the Pacific Ocean via the marine waterways of N Canada and the coastal waters off N Alaska. Efforts to discover a navigable sea route from Europe to China and India by way of the ice-clogged waters of arctic North America began in the 1490s with the voyages of John Cabot. He was unsuccessful, as were many later attempts. The ill-fated expedition (1845–48) of Sir John Franklin unknowingly came close to finding a route. Franklin's ships disappeared, and during attempts to find them the existence of a

Northwest Passage was proved (1850–54). Finally, in 1903–06, Roald Amundsen made the first transit of the passage. In 1969 a U.S. icebreaking oil tanker, the *Manhattan,* became the first large vessel to negotiate the passage.

NORTHWEST REBELLIONS, insurrections (1869–70 and 1885) by French-speaking frontierspeople, particularly the métis (people of mixed French and Indian extraction), against Canadian federal authority. The first one was triggered in the Red and Assiniboine river valleys in 1869, when the Hudson's Bay Co. transferred its territorial rights to Canada. The métis, fearing for their hunters' way of life as land seekers rushed in, prevented the federally appointed governor from establishing his authority and set up their own provisional government at Fort Garry (now Winnipeg) under their leader, Louis Riel. A British-Canadian force ended this insurrection in the spring of 1870 without armed resistance. Shortly afterward the province of Manitoba was established.

As Manitoba subsequently filled with English-speaking settlers, the métis moved farther west, settling around Battleford, Sask. When the Canadian government inevitably extended its control into this area in 1884, the métis again saw their land and way of life threatened by newcomers. They recalled Riel from the U.S., where he had previously fled, and he again proclaimed his own government. In March 1885 the métis defeated a detachment of North West Mounted Police sent to restrain them, and some Indian tribes then joined the rebellion. Greatly alarmed, the Canadian government rushed a large force to the area, and the rebellion was crushed in May. Louis Riel was subsequently found guilty of treason and hanged, an act that gravely affected relations between the French and English in Canada.

NORTHWEST TERRITORIES, administrative region of Canada, encompassing all the country N of lat 60° N, except Yukon Territory and the northernmost parts of Québec Province and Newfoundland. It is bounded on the N by the Arctic Ocean; on the NE by Baffin Bay; on the E by Baffin Bay, Davis Strait, and Hudson Bay; on the S by the provinces of Manitoba, Saskatchewan, Alberta, and British Columbia; and on the W by Yukon Territory. The region comprises an extensive mainland, a complex of thousands of islands (usually called the Arctic Islands) extending from the mainland N to within about 800 km (about 500 mi) of the North Pole, and the islands of Hudson, James, and Ungava bays.

The Northwest Territories was acquired by Canada in 1870, and its present boundaries were drawn in 1912. A vast, sparsely settled region, the Northwest Territories was formerly important mainly as a fur-trapping region. Since the 1950s, however, it has become increasingly significant for its mineral production.

LAND AND RESOURCES

The Northwest Territories, with an area of 3,379,684 sq km (1,304,903 sq mi), covers more than one-third of Canada; more than 99% of the land area is owned by the federal government. The area is approximately evenly divided between the continental mainland and the Arctic Islands, 18 of which are larger than Canada's smallest province (Prince Edward Island). The largest of these are Baffin Island, Ellesmere Island, and Victoria Island (qq.v.). The region's extreme dimensions are about 2700 km (about 1680 mi) from N to S and about 2900 km (about 1800 mi) from E to W. Elevations range from sea level to 2762 m (9062 ft) atop Mt. Sir James MacBrien, near the Yukon border. Barbeau Peak (2616 m/8584 ft) on N Ellesmere Island is the highest point in the Arctic Islands. The total length of coastline (including islands) is about 161,740 km (about 100,500 mi).

Physical Geography. The Northwest Territories encompasses a great variety of surface features.

A scenic view of Pangnirtung Fjord. One of the many picturesque inlets on Baffin Island, the fjord extends from Cumberland Sound, in the eastern part of the island. Located on the fjord is Baffin's most sizable trading post, Pangnirtung. The name means "place of the caribou stag" in the language of the Inuit (Eskimo).
Photo Researchers, Inc.

The gold-mining city of Yellowknife, on Great Slave Lake, is the capital of the Northwest Territories.

Shostal Associates

The hilly and rocky Canadian Shield (q.v.) makes up the E two-thirds of the mainland region. It is bordered on the W by a N extension of the low-lying Interior Plains of North America. Farther W this region gives way to the Western Mountain System, a rugged area with peaks averaging about 1524 m (about 5000 ft) in elevation. The Arctic Islands are mountainous in the E, averaging about 1830 to 2135 m (about 6000 to 7000 ft) in elevation and containing spectacular ice caps. To the W the islands include extensive lowlands. The islands of the NW are characterized by plateaus and hills. Successive glaciations have stripped soil from most areas of the Northwest Territories, and where soil does exist, poor drainage and permanently frozen subsoil (permafrost) generally make it poor. Only in a few places in the S Interior Plains do soils offer any agricultural potential.

Rivers and Lakes. The Canadian Shield is dotted with countless lakes, remnants of the ice sheets that once covered the area. At the W edge of the shield region are two of the largest lakes of North America: Great Bear Lake and Great Slave Lake (qq.v.). These two lakes and most of the W mainland drain N to the Arctic Ocean by the great Mackenzie R. By far the region's most important river, the Mackenzie flows NW and empties through an extensive delta into Mackenzie

Bay. To the E the Coppermine and Back rivers, both of which drain to the Arctic, form other major river systems. The Thelon R. is the most important of those flowing E to Hudson Bay.

Climate. The climate ranges from subarctic to arctic. Long and very cold winters occur in all places; the mean January temperature is below −28.9° C (−20° F), and −51.1° C (−60° F) is often recorded. The lowest temperatures usually occur in the Mackenzie Valley rather than the Arctic Islands, where the climate is moderated by the surrounding waters. Summers in the Arctic Islands and along the continental coast are relatively cool (July average, 4.4° C/40° F) in contrast to the warm temperatures of the Mackenzie Valley and much of the mainland (July average, 15.6° C/60° F). The recorded temperature in the territories has ranged from −57.2° C (−71° F), in 1917, to 39.4° C (103° F), in 1941. The sea is ice-covered much of the year and, in the extreme NW, for the entire year. The low temperatures and the ice-sealed waters contribute to the low annual precipitation, which averages 305 mm (12 in) on the mainland. In the Arctic Islands, annual precipitation decreases from 406 mm (16 in) in the SE to only 51 mm (2 in) in the N and NW. At least half the precipitation occurs as snow.

Plants and Animals. The tree line extends diagonally across the Northwest Territories from the mouth of the Mackenzie SE to Hudson Bay just S of the Manitoba border. Much of the area S of this line is treeless, however, because of surface rock in the E and high elevation in the W. Consequently, only about 9% of the total area is forested. Spruce, pine, birch, and larch are the dominant trees, and the best stands are found along the Mackenzie R. and its S tributaries. North of the tree line and at higher elevations is arctic tundra, consisting of low shrubs and grasses.

In the forested areas, typical animals include caribou, moose, grizzly and black bear, wolf, lynx, beaver, marten, and muskrat. A herd of wood bison is established at Wood Buffalo National Park, which straddles the Alberta border. In the tundra are caribou, musk-ox, polar bear, and Arctic fox. Seal, walrus, and narwhal are important sea mammals. Whales, formerly abundant in Arctic waters, have been reduced by hunting to a population dominated by the relatively small beluga whale. Large numbers of migratory birds nest and raise their young during the short arctic summer, flying S in autumn. Freshwater fish include lake trout, whitefish, pickeral, northern pike, arctic char, and grayling.

Mineral Resources. The Northwest Territories is rich in mineral resources. These include gold, found in the vicinity of Yellowknife on the N shore of Great Slave Lake, silver and uranium to the N, lead and zinc on the S shore of Great Bear Lake and in the Arctic Islands, tungsten in the SW, and iron ore on N Baffin Island. Petroleum and natural gas occur in the Mackenzie Valley.

W.C.W.

POPULATION

According to the 1981 census, the Northwest Territories had 45,741 inhabitants, an increase of 31.4% over 1971. The overall population density in 1981 was only about 1 person for every 74 sq km (about 1 per 29 sq mi). The population of the territory is comparatively diverse, and includes approximately 12,000 Inuit (Eskimo), 2800 American Indians, as well as a small number of métis (persons of mixed Indian and white ancestry). English was the mother tongue of about 54% of

POPULATION OF NORTHWEST TERRITORIES SINCE 1911

Year of Census	Population	Percentage of Total Can. Pop.
1911	6,507	0.1%
1931	9,316	0.1%
1951	16,004	0.1%
1961	22,998	0.1%
1971	34,807	0.2%
1981	45,741	0.2%

POPULATION OF SIX LARGEST COMMUNITIES

	1981 Census	1971 Census
Yellowknife	9483	6122
Inuvik	3147	2669
Hay River	2863	2406
Frobisher Bay	2333	2050
Fort Smith	2298	—
Pine Point	1861	1217

the population; slightly less than 3% had French as their mother tongue. Some 50% of all the inhabitants of the Northwest Territories lived in areas defined as urban, and the rest lived in rural areas. The largest communities were Yellowknife, the capital; Inuvik; Fort Smith; Hay River; and Frobisher Bay.

EDUCATION AND CULTURAL ACTIVITY

The Northwest Territories has made great strides during the past few decades to provide for a unified educational system; the establishment of cultural facilities, however, has not been pursued with equal speed.

Education. Missionaries to the Northwest Territories supplied all the educational facilities until the 1950s, when the Canadian government accepted responsibility for the education of the territories' dispersed population. In 1969 the territorial department of education was created, and in the early 1980s the Northwest Territories had about 71 public elementary and secondary schools with a combined annual enrollment of 12,600 students. Because of the great distances separating small settlements, many of the newer schools were built as centralized residential educational facilities. The Northwest Territories has no institutions of higher education.

Cultural Institutions. Because the population in the territories is small and widely distributed, cultural facilities and activities are severely limited. Two museums of note do exist, however: the Museum of the North, with exhibits relating to the region's history and culture, in Yellowknife; and the Northern Life Museum and National Exhibition Center, also with displays pertaining to regional history and the Indian and Inuit (Eskimo) cultures, in Fort Smith.

Sports and Recreation. Fishing, hunting, and boating are the most popular sports in the Northwest Territories, a land filled with lakes and rivers. Three national parks—Auyuittuq, Nahanni, and Wood Buffalo—provide additional recreational activities such as camping, hiking, and swimming.

Communications. In the early 1980s, the Northwest Territories had 29 radiobroadcasting sta-

INDEX TO MAP OF NORTHWEST TERRITORIES

Cities and Towns

Aklavik . . . . .B 3
Alert . . . . .E 1
Arctic Bay . . . . .D 2
Baker Lake . . . . .D 3
Broughton Island . . . . .E 3
Cambridge Bay . . . . . . .C 3
Cape Dorset . . . . .E 3
Chesterfield Inlet . . . . .D 3
Clyde . . . . .E 2
Coppermine . . . . .C 3
Coral Harbour . . . . .D 3
Eskimo Point . . . . .D 3
Eureka . . . . .D 1
Fort Franklin . . . . .B 3
Fort Good Hope . . . . . .B 3
Fort Liard . . . . .B 3
Fort McPherson . . . . . .B 3
Fort Norman . . . . .B 3
Fort Providence . . . . . .C 3
Fort Resolution . . . . . . .C 3
Fort Simpson . . . . .B 3
Fort Smith . . . . .C 3
Frobisher Bay . . . . .E 3
Gjoa Haven . . . . .D 3
Grise Fiord . . . . .D 2
Hay River . . . . .C 3
Holman Island . . . . .C 2
Igloolik . . . . .D 3
Inuvik . . . . .B 3
Isachsen . . . . .C 2
Lac la Martre . . . . .C 3
Lake Harbour . . . . .E 3
Mould Bay . . . . .B 2
Norman Wells . . . . .B 3
Pangnirtung . . . . .E 3
Paulatuk . . . . .B 3
Pelly Bay . . . . .D 3
Pine Point . . . . .C 3
Pond Inlet . . . . .E 2
Port Burwell . . . . .E 3
Port Radium . . . . .C 3
Rae-Edzo . . . . .C 3

Rankin Inlet . . . . .D 3
Repulse Bay . . . . .D 3
Resolute Bay . . . . .D 2
Sachs Harbour . . . . . . .B 2
Snowdrift . . . . .C 3
Spence Bay . . . . .D 3
Tuktoyaktuk . . . . .B 2
Whale Cove . . . . .D 3
Wrigley . . . . .B 3
Yellowknife (cap.) . . . . .C 3

Other Features

Akpatok (island) . . . . . .E 3
Amadjuak (lake) . . . . . .E 3
Amund Ringnes
    (island) . . . . .D 2
Amundsen (gulf) . . . . . .B 2
Auyuittuq Nat'l Park . . .E 3
Axel Heiberg (island) . . .D 1
Back (river) . . . . .C 3
Baffin (bay) . . . . .E 2
Baffin (region) . . . . .D 2
Baffin (island) . . . . .E 3
Banks (island) . . . . .B 2
Barbeau (peak) . . . . . . .D 1
Barrow (strait) . . . . .D 2
Bathurst (cape) . . . . . . .B 2
Bathurst (island) . . . . . .D 2
Beaufort (sea) . . . . .B 2
Boothia (gulf) . . . . .D 3
Boothia (pen.) . . . . .D 2
Borden (island) . . . . . . .C 2
Borden (pen.) . . . . .D 2
Brodeur (pen.) . . . . .D 2
Bylot (island) . . . . .E 2
Chantrey (inlet) . . . . . . .D 3
Coats (island) . . . . .D 3
Columbia (cape) . . . . . .E 1
Contwoyto (lake) . . . . .C 3
Cornwall (island) . . . . . .D 2
Cornwallis (island) . . . .D 2
Coronation (gulf) . . . . . .C 3

Cumberland (pen.) . . . . .E 3
Cumberland (sound) . . .E 3
Davis (strait) . . . . .F 3
Devon (island) . . . . .D 2
Dubawnt (lake) . . . . . . .C 3
Dyer (cape) . . . . .E 3
Ellef Ringnes (island). . .C 2
Ellesmere (island) . . . . .D 2
Fort Smith (region) . . . .C 3
Foxe (basin) . . . . .D 3
Foxe (chan.) . . . . .D 3
Foxe (pen.) . . . . .E 3
Frobisher (bay) . . . . . . .E 3
Garry (lake) . . . . .C 3
Great Bear (lake) . . . . . .B 3
Great Slave (lake) . . . . .C 3
Hall (pen.) . . . . .E 3
Hazen (lake) . . . . .E 1
Hazen (strait) . . . . .C 2
Home (bay) . . . . .E 3
Hudson (bay) . . . . .D 3
Hudson (strait) . . . . .E 3
Inuvik (region) . . . . .B 2
Jones (sound) . . . . .D 2
Kane (basin) . . . . .E 2
Kasba (lake) . . . . .C 3
Keewatin (region) . . . . .D 3
Kennedy (chan.) . . . . . . .E 1
King William (island) . . .D 3
Kitikmeot (region) . . . . .C 2
La Marte (lake) . . . . . . .C 3
Lancaster (sound) . . . . .D 2
Lands End (cape) . . . . . .B 2
Liard (river) . . . . .B 4
M'Clintock (chan.) . . . . .C 2
M'Clure (strait) . . . . .C 2
Mackenzie (bay) . . . . . . .B 3
Mackenzie (mts.) . . . . . .B 3
Mackenzie (river) . . . . . .B 3
Mackenzie King
    (island) . . . . .C 2
Macmillan (pass) . . . . . .B 3
Mansel (island) . . . . . . .D 3
Melville (island) . . . . . . .C 2

Melville (pen.) . . . . .D 3
Nahanni Nat'l Park . . . .B 3
Nansen (sound) . . . . . . .D 1
Nares (strait) . . . . .E 2
Nettilling (lake) . . . . . . .E 3
Nonacho (lake) . . . . . . .C 3
Nottingham (island) . . .E 3
Nueltin (lake) . . . . .D 3
Ottawa (islands) . . . . . .D 4
Padloping (island) . . . . .E 3
Parry (chan.) . . . . .C 2
Parry (islands) . . . . .C 2
Prince Charles (island). .E 3
Prince of Wales
    (island) . . . . .D 2
Prince Regent (inlet) . . .D 2
Queen Elizabeth
    (islands) . . . . .C 1
Queen Maud (gulf) . . . .C 3
Resolution (island) . . . . .E 3
Roes Welcome
    (sound) . . . . .D 3
Sir James MacBrien
    (mt.) . . . . .B 3
Slave (river) . . . . .C 3
Smith (sound) . . . . .E 2
Somerset (island) . . . . .D 2
Southampton (island). . .D 3
Stallworthy (cape) . . . . .D 1
Stefansson (island) . . . .C 2
Sverdrup (islands) . . . . .C 2
Thelon (river) . . . . .C 3
Ungava (bay) . . . . .E 4
Victoria (island) . . . . . . .C 2
Victoria (strait) . . . . .C 3
Viscount Melville
    (sound) . . . . .C 2
Wager (bay) . . . . .D 3
Wholdaia (lake) . . . . . . .C 3
Wollaston (pen.) . . . . . .C 3
Wood Buffalo Nat'l
    Park . . . . .C 3
Yathkyed (lake) . . . . . . .D 3

tions, as well as about 30 television transmitters. There was no daily newspaper.

GOVERNMENT

The federal government exerts considerable influence over the government of the Northwest Territories.

Executive. The chief executive of the Northwest Territories is a commissioner, who operates under instructions periodically given by the Canadian governor-general in council or by the minister of Indian affairs and northern development. The commissioner, who is appointed by the federal government, presides over the Legislative Assembly and a council composed of a deputy commissioner and five other members.

Legislature. The unicameral Northwest Territories Legislative Council contains 22 seats, including those of the executive council. Members of the legislature are popularly elected to serve 4-year terms.

Judiciary. The Northwest Territories' highest court, the supreme court, is presided over by one judge located in Yellowknife. Below this is the court of appeal, composed of the chief justice of Alberta, justices of the court of appeal of Alberta, and judges of the supreme court of the North-

west Territories and the territorial court of the Yukon Territory. All judges are appointed by the Canadian governor-general in council.

Local Government. In the early 1980s the Northwest Territories had five administrative regions—Fort Smith, Inuvik, Baffin, Keewatin, and Kitikmeot (Central Arctic). It also sometimes is divided into the districts of Franklin, Keewatin, and Mackenzie. Incorporated municipalities included 1 city, 5 towns, 1 village, and 20 hamlets.

National Representation. The Northwest Territories is represented in the Canadian Parliament by one senator appointed by the Canadian governor-general in council and by two members of the House of Commons popularly elected to terms of up to five years.

ECONOMY

Since World War II minerals have displaced furs as the major economic resources of the Northwest Territories. Mining and, to a lesser degree, tourism, commercial fishing, and transportation and service activities now provide the region's economic base. Trapping, although still carried on by some Indians and Inuit, is of declining importance. For many Inuit, handicraft work, such as soapstone carving, is now more important.

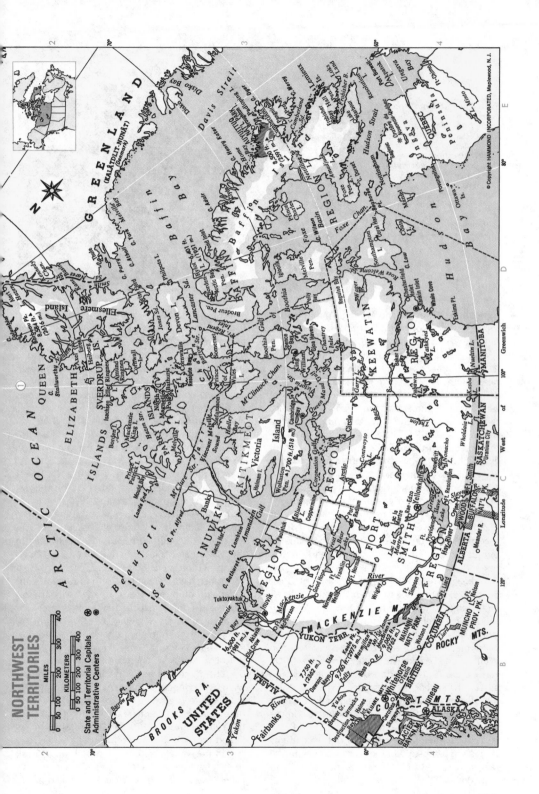

NORTHWEST TERRITORIES

MILES
0 50 100 200 300 400

KILOMETERS
0 50 100 200 300 400

⊛ State and Territorial Capitals
⊕ Administrative Centers

GREENLAND
(KALẤDLIT-NUNẤT)
(Denmark)

ARCTIC OCEAN

QUEEN ELIZABETH ISLANDS

SVERDRUP IS.

PARRY ISLANDS

Ellesmere Island

Baffin Bay

Davis Strait

Disko Bay

QUEBEC

Ungava Peninsula

KEEWATIN REGION

HUDSON BAY

MANITOBA

SASKATCHEWAN

ALBERTA

KITIKMEOT

INUVIK REGION

FORT SMITH REGION

MACKENZIE MTS.

YUKON TERR.

BRITISH COLUMBIA

ROCKY MTS.

BROOKS RA.

UNITED STATES

ALASKA

Beaufort Sea

Victoria Island

Banks Island

Whitehorse

Yellowknife

Fairbanks

Juneau

© Copyright HAMMOND INCORPORATED, Maplewood, N.J.

201

Two Inuit (Eskimo) hunters pose with the tools of their trade, rifles and a harpoon, on Baffin Island. Inuit are among the ablest hunters in the world, wresting a livelihood from as stern an environment as has been faced by any human group. The seal, whale, walrus, and other animals they take provide them not only with food and clothing but with many other necessities.
Photo Researchers, Inc.

Agriculture, Forestry, and Fishing. Arable land is found in the S Northwest Territories. Agriculture, however, is of negligible importance because it is economically unprofitable in the harsh physical environment. A small number of reindeer are raised in the N Mackenzie Valley. Forestry is only of limited importance, with timber cut for local use. Extensive forest tracts in the Slave and Liard river valleys in the SW may be significant for the future growth of forestry. Fishing is also not a major sector of the region's economy. Lake trout and whitefish are caught commercially in Great Slave Lake and other lakes.

Mining and Manufacturing. Mining accounts for nearly 98% of the yearly value of goods produced in the Northwest Territories. Production is mainly from seven mines: lead and zinc (which together make up more than half the value of mineral production) from Pine Point and a newly opened mine near Arctic Bay on the NW Baffin Island, silver from mines in the vicinity of Great Bear Lake, gold from two mines in the Yellowknife area, and tungsten from the Western Mountain System. Uranium prospecting is active W of Hudson Bay.

Petroleum has been extracted near Norman Wells in the Mackenzie Valley since the 1920s. Natural gas is also produced at this field as well as at others near the S border. Exploration for petroleum and gas is being undertaken in the Mackenzie delta, offshore in Beaufort Sea, in the NW Arctic Islands, and in S Davis Strait off Baffin Island. The manufacturing sector of the economy is small and mostly limited to the processing of raw materials. An oil refinery is located at Norman Wells.

Tourism. Because of its great size and relative isolation, the Northwest Territories has a small tourist industry; in the early 1980s some 35,000 tourists visited the territories annually. Despite the greater effort and expense for the traveler, the region is drawing increasing numbers of tourists, who enjoy its special attractions such as excellent sport fishing, unspoiled wilderness areas, and unique arctic landscapes. Two national parks were established within the territories in 1972: Nahanni in the SW and Auyuittuq on E Baffin Island.

Transportation. The waterways of the Northwest Territories provided transportation for the region's early fur trade. Since the 1920s, air transportation has become dominant throughout the area, including the Arctic Islands. In addition, roads and one railroad have been constructed in the Mackenzie Valley, where the best developed transportation services are found. The Northwest Territories has 1790 km (1112 mi) of federal, territorial, and municipal roads. Linkage with the Alberta and continental road systems is provided by the Mackenzie Highway, which extends 127 km (79 mi) N from the Alberta border to Hay River and 435 km (270 mi) down the Mackenzie R. to Fort Simpson. The Liard Highway, now under construction from Fort Simpson southeastward, will connect with the Alaska Highway. The Yellowknife Highway (346 km/215 mi) branches off beyond Hay River to reach the territorial capital, Yellowknife. In 1979 the Dempster Highway linked Inuvik in the Mackenzie delta with Dawson in the Yukon; about 250 km (about 155 mi) of its length are in the territories. The Great Slave Lake Railway, 208 km (129 mi) of which are in

NORTHWEST TERRITORIES

JOINED THE CANADIAN CONFEDERATION:
July 15, 1870

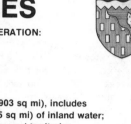

CAPITAL:	Yellowknife
FLORAL EMBLEM:	Mountain avens
POPULATION (1981):	45,741
AREA:	3,379,684 sq km (1,304,903 sq mi), includes 133,294 sq km (51,465 sq mi) of inland water; largest of the provinces and territories
COASTLINE:	161,765 km (100,516 mi)
HIGHEST POINT:	Mt. Sir James MacBrien, 2762 m (9062 ft)
LOWEST POINT:	Sea level, along the Arctic Ocean
PRINCIPAL RIVERS:	Mackenzie, Back, Thelon, Coppermine
PRINCIPAL LAKES:	Great Bear, Great Slave, Dubawnt, Baker
CANADIAN PARLIAMENT:	1 member of the Senate; 2 members of the House of Commons

PRINCIPAL PRODUCTS OF NORTHWEST TERRITORIES

ECONOMY

Province budget. . . . . revenue $315 million
expenditure $317 million
Provincial gross domestic product
(with Yukon Territory). . . . . $923 million
Personal income, per capita (with Yukon
Territory). $10,231

	Quantity Produced	Value
MINERALS		**$391 million**
Zinc	895,000 metric tons	$179 million
Gold	3000 kg.	$63 million
Lead	53,000 metric tons	$58 million
Natural gas . .	430 million cu m	$41 million
Silver	46,000 kg	$36 million
Petroleum. . . .	1.1 million barrels	$12 million
FISHING.	**1700 metric tons**	**$2 million**
FURS	**273,000 pelts**	**$5 million**

Value of Shipments

MANUFACTURING (with Yukon Territory)   **$26 million**

CLIMATE

	HAY RIVER	CLYDE
Mean January temperature range.	−25.5° C (−14° F)	−26.9° C (−16° F)
Mean July temperature range.	15.6° C (60° F)	4.6° C (40° F)
Average annual temperature . .	−4.4° C (24° F)	−11.1° C (12° F)
Average annual precipitation	340 mm (13 in)	206 mm (8 in)
Average annual snowfall	1651 mm (65 in)	1529 mm (60 in)
Average number of days per year with appreciable precipitation.	109	94
Average dates of freezing temperatures (0° C/32° F or less):		
Last in spring	June 6	July 13
First in autumn.	Sept. 11	July 18

ARCTIC ISLAND PLATEAUS & HILLS

EASTERN MOUNTAINS

INTERIOR PLAINS

ARCTIC LOWLANDS

WESTERN MOUNTAIN SYSTEM

CANADIAN SHIELD

Mackenzie R.

NATURAL REGIONS OF NORTHWEST TERRITORIES

the Northwest Territories, is the only railroad. It is linked to the Canadian national railroad system and parallels the Mackenzie Highway N from Alberta, to terminate at Hay River and at the Pine Point mine to the E.

Settlements on the Arctic coast and in the Arctic Islands receive most supplies in a summer supply visit by ships from the S, which are often escorted by icebreakers. From the base port of Hay River, tugs and barges operate along the Mackenzie R. and on Great Slave Lake. Tuktoyaktuk, the N terminus of this service, is the most important Arctic Ocean harbor in Canada. The river, however, is ice-free only three or four months a year. Scheduled airline transportation extends as far N as Resolute in the N central Arctic Islands. Major airports in the Northwest Territories provide flights to Edmonton, Winnipeg, and Montréal. An E-W service also links Frobisher Bay on Baffin Island to Yellowknife and to Whitehorse in the Yukon. Yellowknife is the busiest airport; other important airports are located at Inuvik, Frobisher Bay, and Resolute. From these points, smaller "bush planes" provide charter service to all parts of the territories. By the mid-1980s most communities in the Northwest Territories with populations of more than 100 will have improved airports and aviation support services.

Energy. The electricity-generating plants in the Northwest Territories have a total capacity of 164,000 kw and produce about 384 million kwh of electricity each year. Slightly more than two-thirds of the electricity is produced by hydroelectric plants; the remainder is diesel generated. Major hydroelectric plants are located on the Snare R. N of Yellowknife and on the Taltson R. N of Fort Smith. Major diesel-electric plants are located at Inuvik, Yellowknife, and Frobisher Bay. Most isolated communities have small diesel plants. W.C.W.

HISTORY

From the year 1000 to 1350 Europeans from Greenland and Iceland probably made many landfalls on the eastern shores of the Canadian arctic zone, and it is believed that the Scottish-born explorer Sir Henry Sinclair, earl of Orkney (d. 1400?), landed on Baffin Island in 1398. The first official explorer of the region was the English navigator Sir Martin Frobisher, who claimed Baffin Island for England in 1577. Henry Hudson, John Davis, William Baffin, Luke Foxe (1586-1635), Thomas James (1593?-1635?), and numerous other English explorers traversed the area of Hudson Bay and many of the northern islands from 1610 to 1632, in search of the Northwest Passage between Europe and the Orient. In 1670

the Hudson's Bay Co. was given a fur-trading charter by the government of England for the entire Hudson Bay drainage area, then known as Rupert's Land. One of the company's employees, the Canadian explorer Henry Kelsey (1670?-1729?), was the first white man to penetrate into the interior of the continent from Hudson Bay.

The Hudson's Bay Co. and its rival, the North West Co., were responsible for much of the exploration in the region during the 18th century. Peter Pond (1740-1807), an American explorer in the employ of the North West Co., mapped (1768-88) the region of Great Slave Lake. Sir Alexander Mackenzie, a Scottish explorer working for the same company, discovered and canoed down the Mackenzie River to the Arctic Ocean in 1789. Later he headed west and crossed the mountains, becoming the first white man to reach the Pacific Ocean by land. The British explorer Samuel Hearne (1745-92) of the Hudson's Bay Co. traveled (1770-71) overland from Fort Churchill (in what is now Manitoba) to the mouth of the Coppermine River on the Arctic Ocean.

The search for the Northwest Passage was continued during the 19th century. Many explorers in the employ of the Hudson's Bay Co. and also many official expeditions sponsored by the British government explored (1800-59) most of the Arctic region. The noted British navigator Sir John Franklin explored more than 3200 km (more than 2000 mi) of the Arctic coast, and he was lost with his crew while seeking the passage in 1845. The remains of Franklin's ship and crew were not found until 1859; in that interval, about 40 search vessels brought back detailed descriptions of Arctic waters.

From British to Canadian Sovereignty. In 1870, Rupert's Land and the North-Western Territory were transferred to Canada by the British government. All the islands in the North American arctic zone that had been claimed by Britain were transferred to Canada in 1880. Portions of this vast region were used to form the province of Manitoba in 1870; the district of Keewatin in 1876; the districts of Franklin and Mackenzie in 1895; and the Yukon Territory in 1898. The provinces of Alberta and Saskatchewan were formed from the remaining area in 1905, and the newly defined Northwest Territories emerged. In 1912 the boundaries of Manitoba, Ontario, and Québec were extended northward to Hudson Bay and Hudson Strait, and the present boundaries of the three districts of the Northwest Territories were established in 1920.

20th-Century Development. Oil was discovered at Norman Wells in 1920, and during World War ll oil production was increased greatly under the Canol project, which was sponsored jointly by the U.S. and Canada. Pitchblende and silver were discovered in 1930 on the eastern shore of Great Bear Lake, and the radium and uranium from this area helped make Canada one of the principal world sources of fissionable material. In the Yellowknife area, on the northern shore of Great Slave Lake, gold was discovered in 1933 and is still one of the top four minerals in the territories. The most important mineral development occurred at Pine Point, on the south shore of Great Slave Lake. Large deposits of high-grade lead and zinc ores are being exploited and have increased enormously the value of mineral production of the Northwest Territories.

Since the mid-1960s the Northwest Territories has experienced a great increase in education facilities and public health and welfare programs, as well as resources development. With the transfer of the seat of government from Ottawa to Yellowknife and the increase in political autonomy, provincial status is expected to evolve more rapidly.

A network of radar warning stations, maintained jointly by the U.S. and Canada, extends in part across the Arctic Archipelago and its adjacent waters. The network, which is known popularly as the Distant Early Warning (DEW) line, is designed to give ample warning in the event of enemy attack.

The strong demand for petroleum, crude oil, and natural gas, as well as the lack of major new discoveries in the Western provinces, prompted exploration along the Canadian frontier in the early 1970s. Major oil and gas discoveries in the Mackenzie River delta near Tuktoyaktuk and on Ellef Ringnes, Melville, and several other islands in the Arctic have created much optimism about the future potential of this area as a source of petroleum.

In early 1973 the Canadian government announced the start of an all-weather highway to run from the Alberta-Northwest Territories border to Tuktoyaktuk on the Arctic Ocean, east of the mouth of the Mackenzie River. The road would facilitate oil and natural-gas exploration in the region. A Canadian-U.S. accord of April 20, 1977, permitting construction of the Alcan natural-gas pipeline from Prudhoe Bay, Alaska, through the Yukon Territory to the lower U.S., was a victory for environmentalists and natives of the Northwest Territories. They had influenced the defeat of an alternative route, along the Mackenzie River. Rev. by P.R.

For further information on this topic, see the Bibliography in volume 28, section 1117.

NORTHWEST TERRITORY, in American history, region that constitutes the present states of Ohio, Indiana, Illinois, Michigan, Wisconsin, and the eastern part of Minnesota, a total area of about 688,621 sq km (about 265,878 sq mi). The area was ceded by Great Britain to the U.S. in 1783. On the basis of their early charters, Virginia, New York, Massachusetts, and Connecticut claimed the greater part of it. The other states refused to recognize these claims and insisted that the territory should belong to the country as a whole. New York ceded its claims in 1781; Virginia, in 1784; Massachusetts, in 1785; and Connecticut, in 1786. All of these colonies, however, reserved for special purposes certain lands from the cession. Virginia retained in southern Ohio a considerable area known as the Virginia Military district, and Connecticut retained about 1,315,230 ha (3,250,000 acres), known as the Western Reserve, in northern Ohio.

On March 1, 1784, Thomas Jefferson, then a member of the Continental Congress, reported to Congress a temporary plan of government, but no plan was accepted until the Northwest Ordinance of 1787. The ordinance provided for the formation of not less than three, nor more than five, states. It defined the boundaries of these states, forbade slavery in the territory, and set at 60,000 free inhabitants the population requirement for statehood there. In October 1787, Gen. Arthur St. Clair (1736–1818) was appointed the first governor of the territory. In July 1800, the western part of the territory was constituted into the District of Indiana; in January 1805, Michigan Territory was created; in February 1809, the Illinois Territory was organized; and in April 1836, part of Michigan Territory was organized into the Territory of Wisconsin.

NORTH YORK, city, part of the Municipality of Metropolitan Toronto, S Ontario, Canada, on the Humber R.; inc. as a city 1979. It is a residential and industrial city. Black Creek Pioneer Village, with approximately 30 buildings depicting the development of a Canadian farm community from the 1790s to the 1860s, is here. The township of North York was established in 1922 and was designated a borough in 1967. Pop. (1976) 558,398; (1981) 559,521.

NORTH YORKSHIRE, county, N England; Northallerton is the administrative center. North Yorkshire comprises two separate upland areas; the Pennine Chain in the W and the Cleveland Hills and Yorkshire Moors (much of which is included in North York Moors National Park) in the E. Between the upland areas is the lowland Vale of York. Primarily agricultural, the county produces dairy items and grains. A major coalfield is worked near Selby. York is the chief commercial center. North Yorkshire was created in 1974 with the merger of parts of the former North, East, and West Ridings of Yorkshire (*see* YORKSHIRE). Area, 8309 sq km (3208 sq mi); pop. (1981) 666,610.

NORTON, Charles Eliot (1827–1908), American writer, editor, and educator, who, in his popular lectures, interpreted European culture to generations of Harvard University students. From 1873 to 1897 he was a professor of art history at Harvard. One of his most famous works is a translation of Dante's *Divine Comedy* (1891–92); he also wrote travel sketches of Italy, and studies of ancient art and medieval church architecture and edited the works of several contemporary literary figures. As editor, along with James Russell Lowell, of the *North American Review,* and a founder of the magazine the *Nation,* Norton exerted great influence on 19th-century American fiction.

NORWALK, city, Los Angeles Co., SW California, on the San Gabriel R.; inc. as a city 1957. It is a residential and industrial community located near Los Angeles. A junior college is here, and Pio Pico State Historic Park is nearby. The settlement, established in 1868 as Corvallis, was renamed in the 1870s for Norwalk, Conn. The railroad reached here in 1875, and the community subsequently prospered as a shipping center for the surrounding agricultural and lumbering area. Pop. (1970) 90,164; (1980) 85,286.

NORWALK, city, Fairfield Co., SW Connecticut, on Long Island Sound, at the mouth of the Norwalk R.; inc. as a city 1893. It is a research and manufacturing center. Scientific instruments, electronic systems, electrical devices, clothing, and marine equipment are produced, and a community college, a technical college, and numerous historic structures are here. Founded in 1651, the community had by the mid-18th century developed small trades and a hatting industry. In 1779 during the American Revolution, the town was burned by the British. In the early 19th century, Norwalk was a thriving port; it was reached by railroad in 1848. The city's name is derived either from "north walk" (a trail N from the seashore) or from the Indian name "Naromake." Pop. (1970) 79,288; (1980) 77,767.

NORWAY (Nor. *Norge*), constitutional monarchy of N Europe, occupying the W and N portions of the Scandinavian Peninsula. It is bounded on the N by the Barents Sea, on the NE by Finland and the USSR, on the E by Sweden, on the S by Skagerrak and the North Sea, and on the W by the Atlantic Ocean. With its many indentations and offshore islands, the Norwegian coastline totals some 21,200 km (about 13,200 mi) in length. A naturally protected passageway is located between the screen of offshore islands, known locally as the skerry guard, and the mainland. The country's name, meaning "northern way," reflects the importance of this coastal water route in linking the many small fjord and valley communities that are otherwise separated by rugged mountains. Norway has an area of 324,219 sq km (125,182 sq mi).

The overseas territories of Norway include Svalbard (q.v.), an archipelago in the Arctic Ocean; Jan Mayen (q.v.), a volcanic island NE of Iceland, and Bouvet Island, an uninhabited island in the South Atlantic Ocean. Norway also claims Peter I Island, off Antarctica, and the portion of the Antarctic continent, lying between long 20° W and 45° E, known as Queen Maud Land.

LAND AND RESOURCES

Norway is an extremely mountainous land, nearly one-third of which lies N of the Arctic Circle. Its coastline is, in proportion to its area, longer than that of any major country in the world. Both of these geographical facts have been especially significant in the historical development of the nation.

Physiographic Regions. Since ancient times the Norwegian people have recognized four main regions in their land: Vestlandet (West Country), Østlandet (East Country), Trøndelag (Trondheim region), and Nord Norge (North Norway). More recently, a fifth region, Sørlandet (South Country), has been recognized.

The broad bulge that constitutes the S part of Norway contains the highest parts of the Scandinavian mountain system. These mountains, which trend in a generally SW to NE direction, separate the West Country from the East Country. The mountains are a complex system of sharp and rounded peaks, called *fjell,* and high plateaus, called *vidder.* The ranges include the Dovrefjell in the N, and the Jotunheimen ("realm of the giants") in the central region. This latter range contains Glittertinden, at 2472 m (8110 ft), the highest peak in Scandinavia. In the S is the Hardangervidda, a vast mountain plateau averaging about 1000 m (about 3300 ft) in elevation. The West Country is characterized by the steep descent of the mountains to the sea. During the Ice Age, glaciers cut deeply into former river valleys, creating a spectacular fjord landscape. One of the largest, Sognafjorden, is 160 km (100 mi) long, and, in places, its rock walls rise abruptly from the sea to heights of 1000 m (3281 ft) or more. Three lowland areas contain most of the West Country's population and agriculture: the S coast of Boknafjord, the lower parts of Hardangerfjord, and the coastal islands. These islands are formed by the *strandflat,* a rock shelf lying in

The midnight sun. The northern areas of Norway, within the Arctic Circle, experience periods of continuous daylight during the summer.

Norwegian Information Service

The Geirangerfjord. Numerous fjords, or steep-sided narrow inlets, indent the long Norwegian coastline.
Björn Bölstad–Peter Arnold

some places just above—in others, just below—the level of the sea.

The East Country comprises the more gradual E slopes of the mountains. This is a land of valleys and rolling hills. The lower parts of the valleys, particularly around the Oslofjord, contain some of Norway's best agricultural land. The East and West countries are connected by a number of valleys, the most important being Hallingdal. The South Country comprises the extreme S tip of Norway, the focus of which is the city of Kristiansand. It is characterized by particularly pleasant summer weather.

The Trøndelag, located N of the highest mountains, resembles the East Country, with a landscape of valleys that cut through hills and converge on fjords. The focus of this region is the broad Trondheimsfjord, which is sheltered from the sea by peninsulas and islands. A great deal of agricultural land is located around this body of water.

North Norway is a vast region of fjords and mountains. Most of the population is settled on the *strandflat* coast and islands. The archipelago of the Lofoten and Vesterålen islands, Norway's major coastal island groups, is formed by the glaciated tops of an ancient volcanic mountain range, now partially submerged. In the northernmost part of this region the fjords face the cold waters of the Arctic Ocean. From the fjord heads the land rises to the vast Finnmarksvidde, a bleak mountain plateau. This region contains some of the largest glaciers in Europe.

Rivers and Lakes. The Glåma (Glomma) in the SE is the longest river of Norway. With its tributaries it drains about one-eighth of the country's area. Rivers flowing in a SW direction along the steep W slope are generally short and have many rapids and falls. Those flowing SE, along the gentle E slope, are generally longer. Norway has many thousands of glacial lakes, the largest of which is Lake Mjøsa in the SE.

Climate. The warm waters of the North Atlantic Drift (an extension of the Gulf Stream) flow along the Atlantic coast of Norway and have a pronounced moderating effect on the climate. A maritime climate prevails over most of the coastal islands and lowlands. Winters are mild and summers are normally cool. At Bergen the mean January temperature is 1.7° C (35° F), and the mean July temperature is 14.2° C (57.5° F). Moisture is plentiful the year round. The average annual precipitation on the coast is about 1778 mm (about 70 in). In the interior, a more continental climate prevails; winters are colder, and summers are warmer. At Oslo the January mean temperature is −3.5° C (25.7° F) and the July mean is 17.5° C (63.5° F). Precipitation is generally less here than on the coast, averaging less than 1016 mm (less than 40 in) annually. In the highlands of North Norway the climate is subarctic. The coastal areas of this region, however, have a moderate maritime climate and most ports, even in the far N, are ice-free in winter.

Vegetation and Animal Life. Forests cover slightly more than one-fifth of Norway's land area. Deciduous forests are found in the coastal districts of S and SW Norway. The principal species here are oak, ash, hazel, elm, maple, and linden. In favored locations birch, yew, and evergreen holly may be found. To the E and N the forests have increasing numbers of conifers. Thick boreal coniferous forests are found in coastal regions and in the valleys of E and central Norway. These forests are dominated by Scotch pine and Norway spruce, but also contain birch, alder, aspen, and mountain ash. Wildberries, such as blueberries, cranberries, and cloudberries, grow in most woodland areas. In the far N and at high elevations are tundra regions. The tundra is a treeless heath, with vegetation consisting mainly of hardy dwarf shrubs and wild flowers.

Reindeer, polar fox, polar hare, wolf, wolverine, and lemming are common in the N and in the higher mountain areas. Elk, deer, fox, otter, and marten are found in the S and SE. Both freshwater and saltwater fish abound. Salmon, trout, grayling, perch, and pike are common in the streams and lakes. Herring, cod, halibut, mackerel, and other species inhabit coastal waters.

Mineral Resources. Norway's principal mineral resources are petroleum and natural gas, which are extracted from the vast reserves located along the continental shelf of the North Sea. Other mineral resources include modest amounts of iron ore, copper, zinc, and coal.

POPULATION

The population of Norway is ethnically homogeneous. Apart from several thousand Lapps (*Sa-mer*) and people of Finnish origin in North Norway, the country has no significant minority groups.

Population Characteristics. The population of Norway (1981 est.) is about 4,092,340. Norway has the lowest population density in continental Europe, with 13 persons per sq km (33 per sq mi). The population is growing very slowly, with an annual rate of increase of only 0.4% during 1975–79. Life expectancy in Norway is among the highest in the world. About half the country's population lives in the SE, and more than three-quarters of all Norwegians live within 16 km (10 mi) of the sea. Nearly 70% of Norway's population is urban.

Principal Cities. Oslo is the national capital and the principal port and industrial center. It is also the largest city, with an estimated population of about 452,023 in 1981. Bergen, the cultural center of W Norway and the second largest city, has a population of about 207,799. Other important cities are the commercial center of Trondheim (134,976) and the port of Stavanger (90,687).

Language. *See* NORWEGIAN LANGUAGE.

Religion. Some 98% of the population belongs to the Evangelical Lutheran Church of Norway. The church is supported by the state, and the clergy is nominated by the king. Complete religious freedom is guaranteed, however, and other churches, mostly Protestant and Roman Catholic, have a total membership of about 150,000. Religious preferences tend to be nominal; a 1977 survey showed that only 16% of all Norwegian adults had attended church six times or more in that year.

EDUCATION AND CULTURAL ACTIVITY

The Norwegian people take a strong interest in their cultural heritage. For its relatively small population, the country has produced a disproportionately large number of internationally renowned artists.

Education. Compulsory education was established in Norway by the Primary School Act of 1827. Changes made since the 1960s have reduced regional disparities and increased access for all social groups to the educational system.

Education is free and compulsory in most municipalities for children between the ages of 7 and 16. Norway has almost no illiteracy. For their primary education, children attend a 6-year lower school and a 3-year upper school. Three years of secondary school is then available. In the early 1980s Norway had about 3520 primary schools with a combined annual enrollment of 591,300 students and some 1000 secondary and vocational schools with a combined enrollment of about 183,660 students.

A section of the harbor at Bergen, Norway's principal
shipping center and second largest city.
Susan McCartney–Photo Researchers, Inc.

Norway has four universities and several colleges of university standing, all of which are administered by the state. These institutions have a
combined yearly enrollment of about 41,000 students. The principal university is the University
of Oslo (1811); the others are located at Bergen,
Tromsø, and Trondheim. Teacher-training
schools and other colleges have a total of about
33,000 students.

Cultural Life. Norway has preserved a rich folk
culture that retains elements from the Viking age
(see VIKING ART). Norwegians today have a great
interest in preserving folk art and music. The collection of folk music is supported by the government. Modern Norwegian culture has evolved
from the great flowering of the arts that occurred
in the 19th century under the influence of national romanticism. Early expressions of a truly
Norwegian style were produced by the painter
Johan Christian Dahl (1788–1857) and the composer Edvard Grieg. Other important artists

include the composer Christian Sinding (1856–
1941), the painter Edvard Munch, and the sculptor Gustav Vigeland (1869–1943), whose sculpture park near Oslo has gained international
attention. See NORWEGIAN LITERATURE.

Cultural Institutions. Oslo is the undisputed cultural center of Norway. Bergen, Trondheim, and
Stavanger are important regional centers. The
country's largest art museum is the National Gallery in Oslo. Natural history museums are located
in Oslo, Stavanger, Bergen, Trondheim, and
Tromsø. Many other museums display artifacts of
regional and national culture; the most notable
of these is the Norwegian Folk Museum in Oslo.
The municipal library system in Norway, begun
in the early 20th century, is patterned after the
U.S. model. In addition, the state maintains specialized libraries, the largest of which is the Oslo
University Library (1815), which serves as the national library. Also important is the National Archives in Oslo.

Performing-arts organizations include the National Theater and the national ballet and opera, all in Oslo; and the National Stage, in Bergen. The Oslo Philharmonic is the principal orchestra; other permanent orchestras are in Bergen and Trondheim. Since 1953 Bergen has held an international music festival each year.

Communications. Radio and television broadcasting in Norway are under government administration, but management is generally free of government intervention. In the early 1980s the country registered more than 1.3 million radio licenses and 1.2 million television licenses. In the same period about 1.7 million telephones were in use. Some 72 daily newspapers are published in Norway. Nearly 4000 books were published in 1979, giving Norway one of the highest per capita publishing rates in the world.

GOVERNMENT

Norway is a constitutional, hereditary monarchy. The constitution was enacted on May 17, 1814. Although this document has been amended many times, the principal features remain unchanged.

Executive. Executive power is vested in the king. The king's powers, however, are nominal, and administrative duties are carried out by the cabinet of ministers, which is headed by the prime minister. The king makes all governmental appointments on the recommendation of the party in power.

Legislative. Legislative authority is vested in the parliament, called the Storting. It consists of 155 members popularly elected every four years, and it may not be dissolved by the executive. The Storting elects one-quarter of its members to make up an upper house, the *Lagting;* the remainder constitute the lower house, the *Odelsting.*

Judiciary. Norway's highest court is the supreme court, or *Høyesterett,* consisting of a president and 17 judges. Below this are five (regional) courts of appeal, which hear both civil and criminal cases. In addition, conciliation courts handle civil suits, and district and town courts hear criminal cases. Except in the case of conciliation courts, whose board members are locally elected, all judges are appointed by the king.

Local Government. Norway is divided into 19 counties (*fylker*). The counties are divided into rural and urban municipalities, each of which has a governing council, elected every four years.

Political Parties. The Labor party is the strongest party and governed almost continuously from 1935 to 1981, when a Conservative-led coalition government was formed. The Labor program calls for a planned economy and the nationalization of major industries. The other major parties are the Conservative party, which advocates free enterprise; the Center party, which favors the decentralization of decision making in Norway; the Christian Democratic party, which advocates a democratic policy based on Christian principles; and the Liberal party, which represents a wide range of popular movements. Minority parties include the Socialist Left party, the Progress party, and the Norwegian Communist party.

Social Welfare. Health insurance is mandatory for all inhabitants, with the state, the employer, and the individual all contributing to the health fund. All medical care is free. In the late 1970s Norway had 1 doctor for every 567 inhabitants. A compulsory National Pension Scheme that was put into effect in 1967 provides old-age, disability, rehabilitation, widow, widower, and other benefits.

Defense. The king is commander in chief of the armed forces, which in the early 1980s totaled some 37,000 men in the army, navy, and air force. A 12- to 15-month military term is compulsory for all male citizens when they reach the age of 19. A home guard, with a strength of about 85,000, serves local areas. The defense of Norway is also bound up with the North Atlantic Treaty Organization, which the country joined in 1949.

ECONOMY

Although the Norwegian economy is based on free enterprise, the government exercises a considerable amount of supervision and control. The country's large merchant fleet remains of great importance to the economy. The 20th century has been a period of great industrial expansion for Norway, based primarily on extensive and inexpensive waterpower resources, but also aided by better use of other resources. The country has one of the highest standards of living in the world; the gross national product (GNP) per capita jumped from about $2500 in 1964 to about $13,600 in 1980. National budget estimates for the early 1980s showed about $17.3 billion in revenue and $18.1 billion in expenditure.

Labor. In 1980 Norway had a total employed labor force of 1.9 million, which was distributed among the various economic sectors as follows: agriculture, forestry, and fishing, 8.4%; mining and manufacturing, 21%; construction and utilities, 8.7%; services, 31.6%; commerce and finance, 17.6%; and transportation, 8.9%. Labor is highly organized. The Norwegian Federation of Trade Unions comprises 36 national unions and has a total of about 680,000 members.

Agriculture. Agriculture accounts for 3.5% of the annual Norwegian GNP. Because of the mountainous terrain and limited agricultural soils, less

INDEX TO MAP OF NORWAY

Counties

Akershus . . . . .C 3
Aust-Agder . . . . .B 4
Buskerud . . . . .C 3
Finnmark . . . . .G 1
Hedmark . . . . .C 3
Hordaland . . . . .B 3
Møre og Romsdal . . . .B 3
Nordland . . . . .D 2
Nord-Trøndelag . . . . . .D 2
Oppland . . . . .C 3
Oslo . . . . .B 2
Østfold . . . . .B 2
Rogaland . . . . .B 4
Sogn og Fjordane . . . . .B 3
Sør-Trøndelag . . . . . . .C 3
Telemark . . . . .C 4
Troms . . . . .E 1
Vest-Agder . . . . .B 4
Vestfold . . . . .B 2

Cities and Towns

Afjord . . . . .C 3
Ål . . . . .C 3
Ålesund . . . . .B 3
Ålgard . . . . .B 4
Alta . . . . .F 1
Alvdal . . . . .C 3
Åmli . . . . .C 4
Åndalsnes . . . . .C 3
Årdalstangen . . . . .C 3
Arendal . . . . .C 4
Årnes . . . . .C 3
Askim . . . . .B 2
Åskvoll . . . . .B 3
Aurland . . . . .B 3
Balestrand . . . . .B 3
Bamble . . . . .C 4
Banak . . . . .G 1
Barentsburg . . . . .A 1
Berg . . . . .E 1
Bergen . . . . .B 3
Berkål . . . . .C 3
Berlevåg . . . . .H 1
Bodø . . . . .D 2
Borge . . . . .D 1
Borre . . . . .B 2
Bråte . . . . .C 4
Brønnøysund . . . . .C 2
Bygland . . . . .C 4
Dale . . . . .B 3
Davik . . . . .B 3
Dombas . . . . .C 3
Dovre . . . . .C 3
Drammen . . . . .A 2
Drøbak . . . . .B 2
Egersund . . . . .B 4
Eidfjord . . . . .B 3
Eidsfoss . . . . .A 2
Eidsvoll . . . . .C 3
Eigersund . . . . .B 4
Eina . . . . .C 3
Elverum . . . . .C 3
Fagernes . . . . .C 3
Farsund . . . . .B 4
Flekkefjord . . . . .B 4
Flora . . . . .B 3
Fredrikstad . . . . .B 2
Gamvik . . . . .H 1
Geilo . . . . .C 3
Geiranger . . . . .B 3
Gjøvik . . . . .C 3
Glomfjord . . . . .D 2
Gol . . . . .C 3
Gran . . . . .C 3
Grimstad . . . . .C 4
Grong . . . . .D 2
Gulen . . . . .B 3
Halden . . . . .C 4
Haltdalen . . . . .C 3
Hamar . . . . .C 3
Hammerfest . . . . .F 1
Harstad . . . . .E 1

Hasvik . . . . .F 1
Hauge . . . . .B 4
Haugesund . . . . .B 4
Hemnes . . . . .D 2
Hermansverk . . . . .B 3
Hølen . . . . .B 2
Holmestrand . . . . .A 2
Holmsbu . . . . .B 2
Honningsvåg . . . . .G 1
Horten . . . . .B 2
Inset . . . . .C 3
Jostedal . . . . .B 3
Karasjok . . . . .G 1
Kautokeino . . . . .F 1
Kirkenes . . . . .H 1
Kistrand . . . . .G 1
Kjeller . . . . .B 2
Kongsberg . . . . .C 4
Kongsvinger . . . . .D 3
Kopervik . . . . .B 4
Koppang . . . . .C 3
Kornsjø . . . . .C 4
Kragerø . . . . .C 4
Kristiansand . . . . .C 4
Kristiansund . . . . .B 3
Kvinnherad . . . . .B 3
Kviteseid . . . . .C 4
Lærdal . . . . .B 3
Lakselv . . . . .G 1
Larvik . . . . .A 2
Lavik . . . . .B 3
Løbesby . . . . .G 1
Lenvik . . . . .E 1
Lesja . . . . .C 3
Levanger . . . . .C 3
Lillehammer . . . . .C 3
Lillesand . . . . .C 4
Lillestrøm . . . . .B 2
Lødingen . . . . .D 1
Loen . . . . .B 3
Løkken . . . . .C 3
Lom . . . . .C 3
Longyearbyen . . . . .B 1
Lysaker . . . . .B 2
Mael . . . . .C 3
Mandal . . . . .B 4
Meråker . . . . .C 3
Mo . . . . .D 2
Moi . . . . .B 4
Molde . . . . .B 3
Mosjøen . . . . .D 2
Moskenesøy . . . . .D 2
Moss . . . . .B 2
Mysen . . . . .C 4
Namsos . . . . .C 2
Narvik . . . . .E 1
Naustdal . . . . .B 3
Nesttun . . . . .B 3
Nittedal . . . . .B 2
Nordli . . . . .D 2
Nøtterøy . . . . .B 2
Notodden . . . . .C 4
Ny-Ålesund . . . . .A 1
Odda . . . . .B 3
Olden . . . . .B 3
Oppdal . . . . .C 3
Orkanger . . . . .C 3
Oslo (cap.) . . . . .B 2
Otta . . . . .C 3
Otterøy . . . . .B 3
Øvre Sirdal . . . . .B 4
Polmak . . . . .H 1
Porsgrunn . . . . .C 4
Rakkestad . . . . .C 4
Rena . . . . .C 3
Ringebu . . . . .C 3
Ringerike . . . . .A 2
Risør . . . . .C 4
Rjukan . . . . .C 4
Roa . . . . .C 3
Roan . . . . .C 2
Røldal . . . . .B 4
Røros . . . . .C 3
Ryggebyen . . . . .B 2
Saetermoen . . . . .E 1
Sand . . . . .B 4

Sandane . . . . .B 3
Sandefjord . . . . .A 2
Sandnes . . . . .B 4
Sandvika . . . . .A 2
Sarpsborg . . . . .B 2
Selje . . . . .B 3
Singsås . . . . .C 3
Skåneviksjøen . . . . . . .B 4
Ski . . . . .B 2
Skien . . . . .C 4
Skjåk . . . . .C 3
Skreia . . . . .C 3
Skudeneshavn . . . . . . .B 4
Smelror . . . . .H 1
Snåsa . . . . .D 2
Solund . . . . .B 3
Son . . . . .B 2
Stalheim . . . . .B 3
Stavanger . . . . .B 4
Stavern . . . . .A 2
Steinkjer . . . . .C 2
Stor-Elvdal . . . . .C 3
Støren . . . . .C 3
Storøya . . . . .B 1
Sulitjelma . . . . .E 2
Sunndalsøra . . . . .C 3
Svanvik . . . . .H 1
Sveagruva . . . . .B 1
Svelvik . . . . .B 2
Svolvaer . . . . .D 1
Talvik . . . . .F 1
Tana . . . . .H 1
Terråk . . . . .D 2
Tønsberg . . . . .B 2
Treungen . . . . .C 4
Tromsø . . . . .E 1
Trondheim . . . . .C 3
Trysil . . . . .D 3
Tvedestrand . . . . .C 4
Tynset . . . . .C 3
Tysnes . . . . .B 3
Ullensvang . . . . .B 3
Ulvik . . . . .B 3
Vadsø . . . . .H 1
Valle . . . . .B 4
Vanylven . . . . .B 3
Vardø . . . . .H 1
Vigrestad . . . . .B 4
Vik . . . . .B 3
Volda . . . . .B 3
Voss . . . . .B 3

Other Features

Alst (fjord) . . . . .C 2
Alsten (island) . . . . .D 2
Alta (river) . . . . .F 1
Altevatn (lake) . . . . .E 1
Andfjorden (fjord) . . . . .E 1
Andøy (island) . . . . . . .D 1
Arnøya (island) . . . . . . .F 1
Bardu (river) . . . . .E 1
Barentsøya (island) . . .B 1
Bellsund (bay) . . . . .A 1
Bjørna (fjord) . . . . .B 3
Bjørnøya (island) . . . . .B 2
Boknafjord (fjord) . . . . .B 4
Bremanger (island) . . . .B 3
Dønna (island) . . . . . . .D 2
Dovrefjell (hills) . . . . . . .C 3
Edgeøya (island) . . . . . .B 1
Femundsjø (lake) . . . . .C 3
Folda (Nordland)
(fjord) . . . . .D 2
Folda (Nord-
Trøndelag) (fjord) . . .C 2
Frohavet (bay) . . . . .C 3
Frøya (island) . . . . .C 3
Glåma (river) . . . . .C 3
Glittertinden (mt.) . . . . .C 3
Hadsel (fjord) . . . . .D 1
Hardanger (fjord) . . . . . .B 4
Hardangervidda (plat.) .B 3
Hinlopenstreten
(strait) . . . . .A 1

Hinnøya (island) . . . . . .E 1
Hitra (island) . . . . .C 3
Hopen (island) . . . . . . .B 1
Hornsund (bay) . . . . . . .A 1
Hortens (fjord) . . . . .C 2
Is (fjord) . . . . .A 1
Jostedalsbreen
(glacier) . . . . .B 3
Kjølen (mts.) . . . . .D 2
Kobbfjorden (fjord) . . . .G 1
Kong Karls Land
(island) . . . . .B 1
Kongs (fjord) . . . . .A 1
Kvaenangen (fjord) . . . .F 1
Kvaløy (island) . . . . . . .E 1
Kvaløya (island) . . . . . .G 1
Lågen (river) . . . . .C 3
Lakse (fjord) . . . . .G 1
Langøya (island) . . . . . .D 1
Leka (island) . . . . .C 2
Lindesnes (prom.) . . . . .B 4
Lista (pen.) . . . . .B 4
Lofoten (islands) . . . . . .D 1
Lopphavet (bay) . . . . . .F 1
Magerøya (island) . . . . .G 1
Mohn (cape) . . . . .B 1
Namsen (river) . . . . . . .D 2
Nord (fjord) . . . . .B 3
Nordaustlandet
(island) . . . . .B 1
Nordkapp (North)
(cape) . . . . .A 1
Nordkinn (headland) . . .H 1
Nordkinn (pen.) . . . . . . .G 1
North (cape) . . . . .G 1
Norwegian (sea) . . . . . .C 2
Ofot (fjord) . . . . .E 1
Oslo (fjord) . . . . .B 2
Otra (river) . . . . .B 4
Pasvik (river) . . . . .H 1
Platen (cape) . . . . .B 1
Porsangen (fjord) . . . . .G 1
Prins Karls Forland
(island) . . . . .A 1
Rana (fjord) . . . . .D 2
Rana (river) . . . . .D 2
Rauma (river) . . . . .C 3
Reisa (river) . . . . .F 1
Ringvassøy (island) . . . .E 1
Romsdals (fjord) . . . . . .B 3
Røsvatn (lake) . . . . .D 2
Salt (fjord) . . . . .D 2
Salt (river) . . . . .D 2
Seiland (island) . . . . . . .F 1
Senja (island) . . . . .E 1
Skagerrak (strait) . . . . .C 4
Smøla (island) . . . . .B 3
Snåsavatn (lake) . . . . . .D 2
Sognafjorden (fjord) . . .B 3
Sørkapp (cape) . . . . . . .A 1
Spitsbergen (island) . . .A 1
Steinneset (cape) . . . . .B 1
Stor (fjord) . . . . .B 1
Sulitjelma (mt.) . . . . .E 2
Svalbard (arch.) . . . . . . .A 2
Tana (fjord) . . . . .H 1
Tana (river) . . . . .G 1
Tjuv (fjord) . . . . .B 1
Tokke (river) . . . . .C 4
Trondheims (fjord) . . . . .C 3
Trysil (river) . . . . .D 3
Tunnsjøen (lake) . . . . . .D 2
Tyrifjord (lake) . . . . .A 2
Vaerøy (island) . . . . . . .D 2
Vagåvatn (lake) . . . . . . .C 3
Vannøy (island) . . . . . . .E 1
Varanger (fjord) . . . . . . .H 1
Varangerhalvøya
(pen.) . . . . .H 1
Vega (fjord) . . . . .C 2
Vega (island) . . . . .C 2
Vest (fjord) . . . . .D 2
Vesterålen (islands) . . .D 1
Vestvågøya (island) . . .D 2
Vikna (island) . . . . .C 2

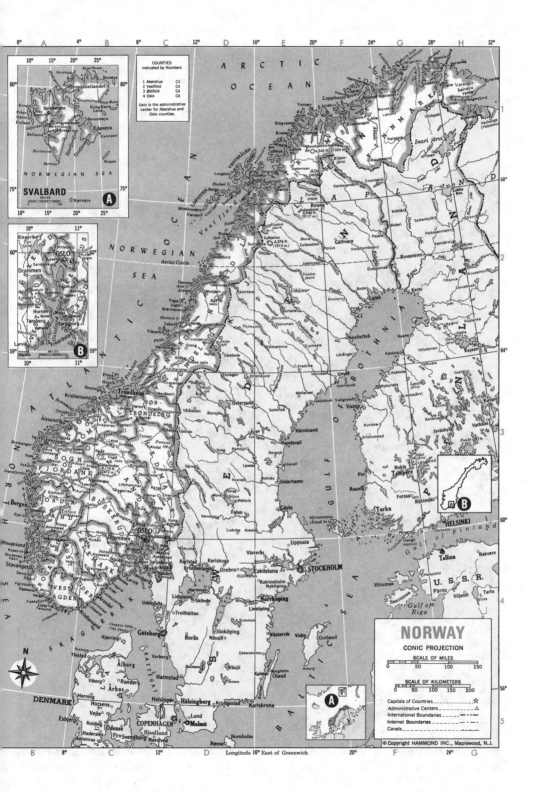

NORWAY

CONIC PROJECTION

© Copyright HAMMOND INC., Maplewood, N.J.

Farmers harvesting grain in the Morgedal Valley. Although only a minute fraction of Norway's terrain is suitable for agriculture, it is one of the country's important industries.

J. L. Stage–Photo Researchers, Inc.

214

than 3% of the total land area is cultivated. Grains are grown in the East Country and the Trøndelag. The West Country and North Norway specialize in livestock raising and dairy farming. The leading crops (with their 1980 production in metric tons) are barley (670,000), potatoes (568,000), oats (400,000), and wheat (65,000). In the same period the country had nearly 2 million sheep, 976,000 cattle, and 666,000 hogs. Norway is self-sufficient in many agricultural products, but grains, fruits, and vegetables must be imported.

Forestry. The Norwegian forestry industry accounts for about 1% of the yearly GNP, and forest products make up some 6% of all yearly exports. Forestry is concentrated in the East and South countries, where 60% of the productive forestland is located. Most forestland is owned by private individuals; state ownership is important only in North Norway. In 1980 timber production totaled about 9.1 million cu m (about 321 million cu ft), more than 90% of which was softwood.

Fishing. The fishing industry produces slightly less than 1% of the yearly GNP. Nonetheless, Norway ranks as one of the leading fishing nations in the world, accounting for nearly 5% of the world's total catch. The large motorized fishing fleet has expanded its catch area to the banks of Newfoundland. The total yearly marine catch in the early 1980s was about 2.4 million metric tons. Cod makes up about one-third the value of the fish catch. Other important species are capelin, pollack, haddock, mackerel, and herring. Fish farming, mainly of salmon and sea trout, is of increasing importance.

Mining. Before offshore drilling for petroleum began in the 1970s, mining was relatively unimportant in Norway. This sector now accounts for 9.6% of the annual GNP, of which more than 95% is derived from crude oil and natural-gas production. Petroleum production began on a trial basis in 1971. In 1974 a pipeline was completed to carry crude oil to Teesside, England. By the early 1980s, the annual crude petroleum production was more than 24 million metric tons; natural-gas production was 25.1 billion cu m (886 billion cu ft). Natural gas is piped to both Scotland and West Germany. Other mineral products included iron ore (3.8 million metric tons), copper (26,000), zinc (79,000), and coal (284,000). The largest iron mines are located at Sydvaranger near the Soviet border. All the coal is mined in Svalbard.

Manufacturing. Enterprises engaged in manufacturing account for 17.6% of the yearly GNP of Norway. The electrochemical and electrometal-lurgical industries form the most important sector of manufacturing. These industries need an abundance of inexpensive electrical power, which Norway can supply. Although all raw materials for the country's aluminum industry must be imported, Norway possesses some 6% of the world aluminum refining capacity. It is also an important producer of ferroalloys.

Norway has traditionally been a major shipbuilding nation, and in the mid-1970s between 3 and 4% of the world's new tonnage was produced here. Shipbuilding declined dramatically in the late 1970s, however, as the industry encountered financial problems; many shipyards have since shifted some of their capacity to the production of equipment for the oil and gas fields. Other major manufactures include machinery, pulp and paper products, textiles, and confections. The country has several petroleum refineries and a major integrated iron and steel plant at Mo, near the Arctic Circle.

Energy. In the late 1970s Norway obtained 59% of its total energy requirements from electricity, 34% from petroleum, and 7% from solid fuel and natural gas. In the early 1980s the annual electricity production was about 84 billion kwh, nearly all of which was generated by waterpower stations. Norway is the world's seventh largest producer of hydroelectricity.

Transportation. Building roads and railroads is difficult and expensive because of Norway's rugged terrain, and in much of the country water traffic is still important. Norway is served by a road network of about 81,700 km (about 50,765 mi), nearly one-third of which is main roads. The road network is most dense in the East Country. Railroads are state operated and have a total length of 4241 km (2635 mi), more than half of which is electrified. Coastal shipping, of both passengers and freight, is especially important in the West Country, the Trøndelag, and North Norway. The coastal towns of Bergen (in the SW) and Kirkenes (near the Soviet border) are linked by daily boat service. Oslo is the country's principal port. The Norwegian merchant marine, with 2753 vessels, is one of the largest in the world. It is an important source of earnings and helps to redress the usual unfavorable balance of trade. Domestic air service is also well developed. The country has 38 airports.

Currency and Banking. The basic monetary unit of Norway is the krone (6.1 kroner equal U.S.$1; 1982). The krone is divided into 100 øre. The central bank is the Bank of Norway (est. 1816), which is the sole bank of issue. Norway also has some 352 savings banks and 27 commercial banks.

Foreign Trade. The composition and direction of Norwegian export trade changed dramatically in the 1970s with the development of North Sea petroleum and natural-gas reserves. Norway is now Europe's largest exporter of these two products, which together account for about half of the country's total annual exports. Other major exports include machinery, ships, aluminum, chemicals, pulp and paper products, and food products. Imports include machinery and transport equipment, petroleum products, chemicals, foodstuffs, and ores. In the early 1980s annual exports were valued at about $18 billion and imports at $15.6 billion. The three most important trading partners were Great Britain (which takes about two-fifths of all exports), Sweden, and West Germany. Other important trading nations include Denmark, the U.S., and Finland.   J.G.R.

HISTORY

According to archaeological research, Norway was inhabited as early as 14,000 years ago by a hunting people with a paleolithic culture derived from western and central Europe. Later, colonies of farming people from Denmark and Sweden were established in the region. These settlers spoke a Germanic language that became the mother tongue of the later Scandinavian languages. The new arrivals settled around the large lakes and along the coasts. Mountains and fjords formed natural barriers around the various settlements, which, remote from each other and almost inaccessible by land, became independent, each recognizing only the authority of its chief. In time social life in the separate settlements came to be headed by an aristocracy and, eventually, by petty kings. By the time of the first historical records of Scandinavia, about the 8th century AD, some 29 small kingdoms existed in Norway.

The Viking Period. Inevitably, the kings turned their attention to the sea, the easiest way of communication with the outside world. Ships of war were built and sent on raiding expeditions, initiating the era of the Vikings (q.v.). The northern sea rovers were traders, colonizers, and explorers as well as plunderers. During the 9th century they established settlements in Ireland, Britain, and Iceland and in the Orkney, Faeroe, and Shetland islands. About a century later Greenland was settled from Iceland. Bands of the northern Vikings penetrated Russia, and their fleets visited Rome and Constantinople. Everywhere they became famous as great warriors, and in some cases they settled in foreign countries, notably in France, where Vikings became the ancestors of the Normans of Normandy. Their complicated religious mythology, in which brave

A stave church of timber, typical of Norwegian church architecture of the Middle Ages. Norwegian Information Service

deeds in battle were extolled and warriors killed in combat were admitted to Valhalla, or heaven, symbolized the Viking way of life.

In the 9th century the first successful attempt to form a united Norwegian kingdom was made by King Harold the Fairhaired of Vestfold, a country in the southeast. Succeeding to the throne of his kingdom as a child in 860, he managed to establish his supremacy over all Norway shortly before 900. Norway's unification was short-lived; at Harold's death in 933 his sons divided Norway, with Eric Bloodaxe (d. 954) as overking. Dissensions and wars among the heirs disrupted the temporary unity. Moreover, many of the petty rulers refused to surrender their independence and warred continually against the descendants of Harold. In addition to the domestic struggles, both Denmark and Sweden were attempting to acquire Norwegian territory.

Christianity Introduced. In 995 Olaf I, a great-grandson of Harold I, became king. Before his accession Olaf had lived in England, where he had been converted to Christianity. He ascended the throne with the firm purpose of forcing Christianity on Norway and was partially successful. Five years after his accession he quarreled with King Sweyn I of Denmark; in the naval battle of Svold (probably in Øresund), Olaf was defeated by the combined Danish and Swedish fleets, supported by disaffected Norwegian chiefs. Olaf was killed in the battle, and Norway was divided by the coalition. After a short period of disorder the country was reunited by Olaf II, who drove out the foreigners and made himself king of Norway in 1015. He continued the religious work of his predecessor, using the sword against all who refused to be baptized. By about 1025 Olaf was more powerful than any previous Norwegian king had been. He aroused the enmity of the powerful nobles, who, together with Canute II, king of England and Denmark, in 1028 drove Olaf into exile in Russia. Two years later Olaf returned and was killed in battle.

Native Kings. On the death of Canute in 1035, Olaf's son, Magnus I, was called from Russia by partisans of his father. He became king and then united Denmark and Norway under his rule. For the next three centuries a succession of native kings ruled Norway. Although internal confusion and wars between rival claimants to the throne disrupted the country intermittently, Norway began to emerge as a united nation, enjoying a comparative prosperity brought by its great trading fleets. The Norwegians had become strongly Christian, and a powerful clergy was one of the strongest influences in the kingdom. In 1046 Magnus made his uncle Harold Hårdråde coruler. At the death of Magnus one year later, Harold became king as Harold III; he was killed while participating in the invasion of England in 1066. The last king of the line of Harold III was Sigurd I (c. 1090–1130), whose rule lasted from 1103 until his death.

Dynastic conflict followed the death of Sigurd. Of the many later kings, the most notable was Sverre (1152?–1202), king from 1184 to 1202. A statesman of great ability, Sverre built a strong monarchy and considerably weakened the power of the clergy and the great nobles. Under Håkon IV (r. 1217–63) Norway reached the apex of its medieval prosperity and political and cultural power. Iceland was added to the kingdom in 1262, and royal authority was greatly increased by Håkon and his son, Magnus VI; the landed aristocracy was virtually crushed by Håkon V (1270–1319). After that the old noble families gradually declined, and for the most part the Norwegian people became a nation of peasants. Commercial activity was usurped by the increasingly powerful Hanseatic League. The death of Håkon V in 1319, without male heirs, gave the throne to King Magnus II of Sweden, the three-year-old son of Håkon's daughter. In 1343 Magnus was succeeded by his son, Håkon VI (1339–80), and in 1380 the latter's son, Olaf II (1370–87), king of Denmark, became king of Norway as Olaf IV. The young king exercised only nominal rule, the power being in the hands of his mother, Margaret I. When he died, he was succeeded by his mother as ruler of Norway and Denmark and, in 1389, of Sweden also. To obtain German support against the dukes of Mecklenburg, who claimed the Swedish throne, Margaret had her grandnephew, Eric of Pomerania (1382–1459), elected nominal ruler as Eric VII.

Ruins of a church in Hamar, in eastern Norway; dating from 1150, the structure was burned in 1567 when the Swedes destroyed the city.
Norwegian Information Service

Union with Denmark and Sweden. By the Union of Kalmar in 1397, the three kingdoms were made a single administrative unit. Norwegian prosperity and culture declined steadily after the union. Moreover, the plague, called the Black Death, had swept Norway in the 14th century, decimating the population. Sweden and Denmark were larger and wealthier than Norway, which the kings, for the most part, neglected. During the subsequent four centuries Norway remained stagnant under the arbitrary rule of Danish officials.

The Napoleonic Wars at the beginning of the 19th century finally occasioned the end of the union. After the defeat of Napoleon in 1814, Denmark, an ally of France, was compelled to sign the Treaty of Kiel, ceding Norway to Sweden. The Norwegians, however, disavowed the treaty. They declared themselves an independent kingdom, drew up a liberal constitution, and offered the Crown to the Danish crown prince Christian Frederick. The Norwegian move was disapproved by the European powers, and, at the head of an army, Marshal Jean Bernadotte, later King Charles XIV John, persuaded Norway to accept the Treaty of Kiel. In return for this acceptance, Norway was allowed to retain the newly promulgated constitution. By the Act of Union of 1815, Norway was given its own army, navy, customs, and legislature and permitted full liberty and autonomy within its own boundaries.

Second Union with Sweden. After 1814, the Norwegian Storting, or legislature, was chiefly occupied with stabilizing and improving the financial condition of Norway and in implementing and guarding its newly won self-government. Despite the bitter opposition of Charles XIV John, an autocratic monarch, the Norwegian legislature passed a law in 1821 abolishing the Danish-created peerage, a vestige of the onerous Danish rule. The Storting held that the true Norwegian nobility were the peasant descendants of the medieval barons. Norwegian nationalism increased, and the movement for independence was headed by the Peasant party, preeminent in the Storting. During the postunion period, the Storting complained that Swedish treatment of Norway was not consistent with the spirit of the Act of Union and with the status of Norway as a coequal state. At length, in 1839, Charles XIV John appointed a joint committee of Swedes and Norwegians to revise the wording of the Act of Union. Charles died in 1844, before the committee submitted its report. Charles's son, Oscar I, admitted the justice of many Norwegian claims and made himself popular by granting Norway a national flag for its navy, although the flag bore the symbol of union with Sweden.

Gloomy Olso residents watch in silence as German reinforcements march into the Norwegian capital in May 1940, a month after the Nazi occupation. Wide World Photos

Ascendant nationalism. The liberal movement in Norwegian politics, accompanying the surge of nationalism, became more pronounced after the revolutions of 1848 in the major countries of Europe. Political nationalism was bolstered by intellectual and cultural nationalism. Norwegian folktales and folk songs were collected and arranged and became extremely popular. Norwegian dictionaries, histories, and grammars were compiled. The literary renaissance included such writers as Henrik Ibsen, Björnstjerne Björnson, Jonas Lie (1833–1908), and Alexander Kielland (1849–1906).

Struggle for freedom. As a national policy, the Norwegians maintained their refusal to permit closer relations with Sweden than those provided by the Act of Union. When, in 1860, Sweden began to propose revisions in the act designed to give the ruling country additional powers, the two greatest Norwegian political parties, the Lawyers party and the Peasant party, combined to form the liberal Venstre ("Left") party and blocked the revisions. Another significant controversy between the two countries was occasioned by renewed Swedish attempts at constitutional revision, including establishment of the royal right to dissolve the Storting. Led by Johan Sverdrup (1816–92), president of the Storting, the Norwegian legislature engaged in a long struggle with King Oscar II. Oscar was forced to yield in 1884. Norwegian policy then centered on demands for a separate consular service and a Norwegian flag for the merchant marine without the symbol of union. The flag was approved by Sweden in 1898, but Sweden balked at the demand for a consular service. In 1905, after protracted negotiations, the Norwegian ministry then in office resigned and subsequently refused Oscar's request that they withdraw their resignations. As a result the Storting declared that Oscar was no longer ruler of Norway and proclaimed the country an independent kingdom. In a plebiscite in August 1905 the Norwegian people voted overwhelmingly for separation from Sweden. The Swedish Riksdag ratified the separation in October. A month later Prince Carl of Denmark accepted the Norwegian crown as Håkon VII.

Independence. The Norwegian government, dominated by ministers with liberal politics, became one of the most advanced in Europe in matters of social legislation, education, and political liberties. In 1907 Norwegian women became the first in Europe to be given voting rights. Unemployment insurance benefits, old-age pensions, and liberal laws concerning divorce and illegitimacy made Norway famous for its advanced social policies.

After the beginning of World War I in 1914 the sovereigns of Sweden, Norway, and Denmark agreed to maintain the neutrality of the Scandinavian countries and to cooperate for their mutual interest. The policy of neutrality and friendship thus established continued to be joint policy after the war. The world economic depression that began in 1929 affected Norway considerably because of its dependence on commerce. The Labor party was elected to power in 1935 and continued the policies of moderation and political liberalism that had dominated Norwegian politics since 1905.

World War II. Norway maintained its traditional neutrality when World War II began in 1939. Despite sympathy for Finland during the Russo-Finnish phase of the conflict, Norway rejected an Anglo-French demand for transit of troops to aid Finland. German maritime warfare along the Norwegian coast, however, made neutrality increasingly difficult. On April 8, 1940, Great Britain and France announced that they had mined Norwegian territorial waters to prevent their use by German supply ships. The next day German forces invaded Norway.

Assisted by the Nasjonal Samling (National Union) party and disloyal Norwegian army officers, the Germans attacked all important ports. Vidkun Quisling, head of the Nasjonal Samling, proclaimed himself head of the Norwegian government. King Håkon and his cabinet, after an unsuccessful attempt at resistance, withdrew to Great Britain in June. For five years thereafter, London was the seat of the Norwegian government-in-exile. Political leaders in Norway refused to cooperate in any way with Josef Terboven (1898–1945), the German commissioner. In September Terboven dissolved all political parties except the Nasjonal Samling, set up a so-called National Council composed of the party members and other German sympathizers, and announced the abolition of the monarchy and the Storting. These and other still more repressive measures of the Germans and their puppet government, headed by Quisling, were met with mass resistance by the Norwegian people.

Quisling proclaimed martial law in September 1941 because of large-scale sabotage and espionage on behalf of the Allies. The leaders of the Resistance in Norway cooperated closely with the government-in-exile in London, preparing for eventual liberation. The German forces in Norway finally surrendered on May 8, 1945, and King Håkon returned to Norway in June. To punish traitors, the death penalty, abolished in 1876, was restored. Terboven and some leading German sympathizers committed suicide; Quisling, along

These traditionally dressed Lapp women were arrested in early 1981 for occupying Prime Minister Brundtland's office for 24 hours shortly after she assumed her post. The women were protesting the government's decision to develop a northern stream.   UPI

with some 25 other Norwegians, was tried and executed for treason.

Labor governments. The government-in-exile resigned after temporary order was established. In the general elections of October 1945, the Labor party won a majority of votes, and a labor cabinet was headed by Einar Gerhardsen (1897–   ). The party remained in power for the next 20 years. Under its stewardship, Norway became a charter member of the UN in 1945, participated in the European Recovery Program in 1947, and joined the North Atlantic Treaty Organization (NATO) in 1949. The NATO membership, by which the country abandoned its traditional neutrality, was tacitly approved by the Norwegian people in the elections of October 1949.

The Norwegian economy came out of the war badly damaged, both by ruthless German exploitation and by domestic sabotage. Reconstruction, however, began at once, directed by the Labor government, which soon took over the planning of the entire economy, reinforcing the country's position in international markets and redistributing the national wealth along more egalitarian lines. Within three years, the Norwegian gross national product had reached its prewar level. This development was accompanied by new social legislation that greatly increased the welfare of the citizens. A chronic

trade deficit during the 1950s was partly alleviated by large loans from the World Bank. In 1960 Norway became one of the founding members of the European Free Trade Association (EFTA).

Political Shifts. The parliamentary elections held in September 1961 resulted in the failure of the Labor party for the first time since World War II to win a majority of seats, although it kept its place as the leading party. Gerhardsen, who had been prime minister since the end of the war, except for an interval in 1951–55, was designated once again to head the cabinet. In 1965 the Labor party was defeated in general elections, ending a 30-year rule. King Olaf V, who had succeeded Håkon VII on the latter's death in 1957, then asked Per Borten (1913–   ), leader of the Center party, to form a government. He headed a coalition of nonsocialist parties. Economic policies, however, did not markedly change.

In 1970 Norway applied for membership in the European Economic Community, or EEC (now the European Community), a move that gave rise to increasing dissension within the government. Early in the following year Borten resigned after charges were made that he had divulged confidential information. Trygve Bratteli (1910–84) of the Labor party then formed a minority government that campaigned strongly for EEC membership. In a referendum in 1972, however, the voters vetoed the government's recommendation. As a result, it resigned and was succeeded by a centrist coalition headed by Lars Korvald (1916-   ) of the Christian People's party. In May 1973 Norway signed a free-trade agreement with the EEC. Labor suffered considerable losses in the 1973 elections, but Bratteli again was able to form a minority government.

Bratteli resigned in January 1976, but the party remained in power until the elections of September 1981, when the nonsocialist parties gained a comfortable majority in the Storting and formed a coalition government headed by Kåre Willoch (1928-   ) of the Conservative party. A broader coalition government, again headed by Willoch, was formed in 1983.

The country's economic prospects brightened considerably in the late 1960s, when oil and gas deposits were discovered in the Norwegian sector of the North Sea; exploitation by a state company began in the '70s. Despite devastating mishaps in 1977 and, especially, in 1980, when more than 120 people perished, oil from the North Sea fields accounted for some 30 percent of the country's annual export earnings in the early 1980s.

For further information on this topic, see the Bibliography in volume 28, sections 843, 987.

NORWEGIAN ELKHOUND, breed of sporting or hunting dog that originated in Norway over 6000 years ago. The breed is noted for its ability to hunt big game, including bear and elk as well as lynx and raccoon. Today, its principal use in Norway is to hunt elk; it is also frequently employed

Norwegian elkhound   Walter Chandoha

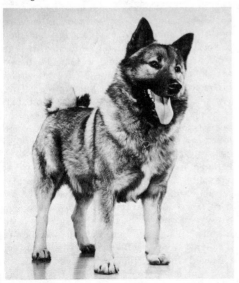

as a draft animal. The dog is greatly valued in Norway and in other countries as a pet of unusual intelligence, friendliness, and loyalty. The Norwegian Elkhound is a medium-sized dog, with a short, compact, strongly built body. The male is about 51 cm (about 20 in) high at the shoulder, the female about 46 cm (about 18 in); the dog weighs about 20 kg (about 45 lb). It has a short head; pointed ears; brown eyes; a powerful neck; a broad and deep chest; straight legs; a thick, fairly smooth coat, gray in color; and a short, curled tail that is carried high.

NORWEGIAN LANGUAGE, language of the people of Norway. It belongs to the West Scandinavian branch of the Germanic languages (q.v.), a subfamily of the Indo-European languages (q.v.).

Like the other Scandinavian languages, Norwegian is derived from an ancient common Scandinavian language, which can be traced through runic inscriptions to the 3d century AD. Because of significant dialectal changes during the Viking age (c. 800-1050), Old Norse (or Old Norwegian), a language from which the modern tongue is derived, came into being and was spread by Norwegian migration to Iceland and other areas in the North Atlantic. The Latin alphabet, replacing runic signs, was introduced with Christianity, and a distinct Norwegian written language evolved in the 11th century. Subsequently, Norwegian was influenced by Danish, Low German, and Swedish. The Danish influence became dominant during the more than 400 years between 1380 and 1814, during which Norway was united with Denmark under the Danish crown.

The Danish language, introduced to Norway by government officials, spread after the Reformation through books printed in Denmark and became, in the 16th century, the written language of Norway, being generally spoken by the educated classes, especially in the cities. The Norwegian dialects continued in use in the country districts and among the working and middle classes of the towns. During the 19th century, the spoken Danish developed into a language called Dano-Norwegian, which was heavily Danish in structure and vocabulary, but with native Norwegian pronunciation and some native grammatical influences. Later termed *riksmål*, it became the official language of Norway. Dano-Norwegian is the language of such literary figures as the poet and dramatist Henrik Ibsen.

Subsequently, however, a strong nationalistic and romantic movement awakened a desire for a language people felt was their own. In response to this desire, the linguist Ivar Aasen (1813-96) began, in the middle of the 19th century, the construction of a new national literary language, the *landsmål* ("country speech"), based on Norwegian dialects and free of Danicisms. This endeavor won public support, and the landsmal, further developed, became an important secondary language.

Under pressure of the landsmal movement, the riksmal went through a series of significant reforms (1907, 1917, and 1938) emphasizing strictly Norwegian speech and spelling. The names of the two languages were officially changed: The riksmal became the *bokmål* ("book language") and the landsmal, the *nynorsk* ("New Norse"). The two languages have equal validity in law, and both must be taught in the schools. The bokmal, still the leading language, is strongest in eastern Norway, the nynorsk in western Norway. Changes continue to occur in both languages. J.N.

NORWEGIAN LITERATURE, literature of the Norwegian people, dating from about AD 800 to the present. This literature may be grouped into three periods. In the first period (c. 800–c. 1400), Norway largely shared its literature with Iceland; in the second (c. 1400–1814), it generally shared its literature with Denmark; in the third (1814 to the present), Norway developed an independent literature.

Norwegian-Icelandic Period (c. 800–c. 1400). The Old Norse (early Norwegian and Icelandic) literature is essentially a product of the Viking age. The deeds, beliefs, history, and lore of the Norwegian Vikings who settled Iceland at the end of the 9th century found expression in poems, tales, and legends. These are transmitted orally but not written down until the 13th century, chiefly in Icelandic manuscripts. *See* ICELANDIC LITERATURE.

The oldest literature extant is the group of poems called the *Poetic Edda*. These famous poems tell the tales of Norse and Germanic gods and human heroes. Another type of poetry more complex and metaphorical, known as the skaldic poetry, was composed for oral presentation by skalds (bards or court poets). The earliest known skald was a Norwegian, Bragi Boddason, who lived in the first half of the 9th century. When skaldic poetry ceased in Norway, it continued in Iceland. A somewhat later development of Old Norse literature is the saga, a prose epic or narrative. The sagas were told by the Icelanders but were not concerned solely with Icelandic events. Thus, the renowned *Heimskringla* by Snorri Sturluson is a 13th-century history of Norwegian kings. In general, the sagas are built on and carry forward Norwegian traditions.

In the 13th century the religious and courtly literature of continental Europe reached Norway through translations and adaptations of homilies, legends of saints, and tales of such heroes as Arthur, Charlemagne, and Theodoric. Of prime importance as a Norwegian literary creation was "The King's Mirror," a didactic treatise in verse on manners and morals. Ballads also entered the literary tradition in the 13th century; they had flourished in Norway centuries before they were put in writing.

Norwegian-Danish Period (c. 1400–1814). At the end of the 13th century, Norway entered into a union with Denmark that lasted more than 400 years. The flowering of Old Norse literature had come to an end, and for two centuries little literary writing was done in Norway. After the Reformation literary activity slowly resumed, with a simultaneous growth of Danish influence. Books printed in Copenhagen made their way to Norway, which had no printing press until 1643. When Danish became the official language in Norway, it was adopted by Norwegian writers. The influence of humanism was discernible in the writings of Absalon Pederssøn Beyer (1528-75) and Peder Claussøn Friis (1545-1614) in the 16th century. Friis's translation of Snorri's *Heimskringla* stirred patriotic feelings. In the 17th century, the clergyman Petter Dass wrote "The Trumpet of Nordland," a long topographical poem describing northern Norway.

During the 18th century Norway contributed significantly to the common literature of the twin kingdoms. The leading writer was Ludvig Holberg, who was born in Norway and retained many of his Norwegian characteristics, although he did his life work in Denmark. Having traveled widely in Europe, he brought to the Nordic countries impulses from French rationalism and English deism. Holberg wrote important historical works, satirical poems, and moralistic essays, but he became most famous for his comedies, classical plays that are still performed in both Norway and Denmark. Among Holberg's successors, Johan Herman Wessel (1742-85), known for his tragicomedy *Kiaerlighed uden strømper* (Love Without Stockings, 1772), was the most outstanding. Other writers of the period were the poets Christian Braunman Tullin (1728-65) and Johan Nordahl Brun (1745-1816) and the critical essayist Claus Fasting (1746-91).

Period of Independence (1814 to the present). As a result of the Napoleonic Wars, Norway became separated from Denmark and united with Sweden, with qualified independence. Although Norway did not break all its cultural ties with Denmark, a strong movement for the creation of a national Norwegian literature arose. It was encouraged by the romantic movement, then dominant in Europe, and led by the poet and dramatist Henrik Arnold Wergeland. As an editor and educator who fought the Danish tradition, he is considered the founder of Norwegian literary culture. His opponent, the poet Johan Sebastian Welhaven (1807-73), became a spokesman for the continuation of Danish culture.

Nationalism and romanticism led to the discovery of the oral popular literature, exemplified in the collection of folktales gathered by the poets Peter Christian Asbjørnsen (1812-85) and Jørgen Moe (1813-82). The linguist Ivar Aasen (1813-96) began the study of Norwegian dialects, and the poet and journalist Aasmund Olafsson Vinje (1818-70) proved that the country speech was well suited for poetry. The glories of early Norwegian history were extolled by the historian Peter Andreas Munch (1810-63). The novelist Camilla Collett (1813-95), on the other hand, foreshadowed literary realism in *Amtmandens døttre* (The Governor's Daughters, 1854-55).

A new generation of writers, headed by the great dramatist Henrik Ibsen and the writer, theater director, and political leader Björnstjerne Björnson, reflected nationalism and romanticism in their early works but later turned to realism and social criticism. Ibsen probed human aspirations and limitations in historical, poetical, realistic, and symbolic plays, gaining world fame with such masterpieces as *Brand* (1866), *Peer Gynt* (1867), *A Doll's House* (1879), and *The Master Builder* (1892). Björnson, a public-spirited reformer and a writer of boundless vitality, gave expression to a philosophy of growth in stories, novels, plays, and poems.

Björnstjerne Björnson   Norwegian Embassy Information Service

Other outstanding representatives of Norwegian realism were Jonas Lie (1833-1908), a novelist whose style ultimately took an impressionistic turn, and Alexander Kielland (1849-1906), whose novels and short stories display debonair wit. Naturalistic pessimism characterizes the novels of Armalie Skram (1846-1905), and changing intellectual and spiritual views were voiced in novels by Arne Garborg.

In the 1890s a neoromantic movement began. Lyric poetry came to the forefront, exemplified in the works of Nils Collett Vogt (1864-1937), Vilhelm Krag (1871-1933), and, especially, Sigbjørn Obstfelder (1866-1900). Artistic individualism and satire prevail in the plays of Gunnar Heiberg (1857-1929). In short stories and novels Hans Kinck (1865-1926) stressed the interplay of the individual, race, nature, and society. The outstanding writer of the period was Knut Hamsun, an individualist of exceptional sensibility, who was drawn by the subconscious and irrational.

The peaceful dissolution of the union of Norway with Sweden in 1905 inaugurated a period of rapid progress. New important writers emerged, most of them following a resurgent realism marked by a concern with social problems. Olav Duun (1876-1939) reached his zenith with *Juvikfolke* (The People of Juvik, 1918-23), a series of novels of rural life. Johan Bojer wrote novels on the new industrial morality. Johan Falkberget

Henrik Ibsen   Norwegian Embassy Information Service

(1879–1967) depicted mining life and was praised for his epic work *Christianus Sextus*. The greatest fame, however, came to Sigrid Undset, whose trilogy *Kristin Lavransdatter* (1920–22; trans. 1923–27), for which she received (1928) the Nobel Prize, made medieval Norway come alive through characters drawn with modern psychological insight. Among outstanding poets of the period were Herman Wildenvey (1886–1959), Olaf Bull (1883–1933), Olav Aukrust (1883–1929), and Olav Nygard (1884–1924).

The new generation of writers active between the two world wars was much affected by ideological conflicts and international tensions. The tone was set by the poet Arnulf Øverland (1889–1968), the satiric novelist Sigurd Hoel (1890–1960), and the dramatist Helge Krog (1889–1962). Internationally known Tarjei Vesaas (1897–1970) wrote regional novels and short stories with a strong psychological undercurrent; his poetry, breaking with traditional patterns, shows a lyric concern for nature. The Danish-born Aksel

Sigrid Undset   Norweigian Embassy Information Service

Knut Hamsun   Norwegian Embassy Information Service

Sandemose (1899–1965) was recognized for his searching psychological novels. Nordahl Grieg (1902–43), a novelist, dramatist, and poet, reflected the fluctuating moods of the interwar period. Like Øverland he wrote poems against the German occupation during World War II.

After the war ended, its origins and meaning, and especially the theme of the psychology of traitors, were vigorously explored in many novels, by such writers as Odd Bang-Hansen (1908–) and Kåre Holt (1917–). Such themes gradually evolved into general social criticism—as in the work of the novelist and poet Jens Ingvald Bjørneboe (1920–76)—but fiction style remained largely traditional. A large body of poetry was written in the postwar period; among the more experimental poets were, besides Tarjei Vesaas, Halldis Moreu Vesaas (1907–), Paal Brekke (1923–), Peter R. Holm (1931–), and Stein Mehren (1935–).

For further information on this topic, see the Bibliography in volume 28, section 843.

NORWICH, industrial city, New London Co., SE Connecticut, located where the Yantic and Shetucket rivers join to form the Thames R.; inc. as a city 1784. Major manufactures include textiles, clothing, metal and paper goods, leather items, and electronic equipment. Norwich is the site of the Slater Memorial Museum, with a diverse collection including paintings and sculpture, and the Leffingwell Inn (begun 1675), which houses a historical museum. The settlement, established in 1659, grew as a shipbuilding and shipping center during the 18th century. It is the birthplace of the American Revolution general Benedict Arnold. In 1952 the town and the city of Norwich were consolidated. Pop. (1970) 41,739; (1980) 38,074.

NORWICH, city, administrative center of Norfolk, E England, on the Wensum R. Norwich is a university and cathedral city with manufactures that include footwear, silk, electrical equipment, and mustard. Educational institutions here include the University of East Anglia (1961), the Norwich School of Art (1846), and a grammar school dating from the mid-16th century. Principal among the city's many notable ecclesiastical structures is the cathedral, begun in 1096, that is almost wholly Norman in style. Norwich was founded in Saxon times and received its first charter in 1158. Flemish immigrants introduced the wool-weaving industry in the 14th century, and the town remained a prosperous textile center until the late 18th century. Pop. (1981) 122,270.

NORWICH TERRIER, breed of small terrier popular in Great Britain in the last two decades of the 19th century and introduced into the U.S. about 1920. The dog is useful for hunting rabbits and other small game and is popular as a pet. The Norwich terrier is 25 to 30 cm (10 to 12 in) high at the withers and weighs 4.5 to 5 kg (10 to 12 lb). It has dark, bright eyes; a strong jaw; a short, strong neck; short and powerful legs; and a medium-sized tail. The hair of the coat is hard and wiry,

usually red in color, but sometimes either black and tan or grizzle. The dog is a hardy, active little animal and is noted for its loyalty.

NORWOOD, town, Norfolk Co., E Massachusetts, on the Neponset R., near Boston; inc. 1872. It is a residential, commercial, and manufacturing center. Major products include electronic and photographic equipment, metal goods, scientific instruments, and printed materials. The community, settled in 1678, was known by the 1730s as the South Parish of Dedham. In 1872 Norwood was established as an independent town. Pop. (1970) 30,815; (1980) 29,711.

NORWOOD, city, Hamilton Co., SW Ohio; inc. 1903. It is a residential and industrial community surrounded by Cincinnati. Products include motor vehicles, machinery, footwear, printed materials, metal and rubber goods, playing cards, and aerospace equipment. The Athenaeum of Ohio (1829), a college, is here. The community, settled in 1804 and named Sharpsburg in 1809, was incorporated as a village under its present name in 1888. Pop. (1970) 30,420; (1980) 26,342.

NOSE, organ of smell (q.v.), and also part of the apparatus of respiration and voice (see VOICE AND SPEECH). Considered anatomically, it may be divided into an external part—the visible projection portion, to which the term nose is popularly restricted—and an internal part, consisting of two chief cavities, or nasal fossae, separated from each other by a vertical septum, and subdivided by spongy or turbinated bones projecting from the outer wall into three passages, or meatuses,

Structure of External Nose

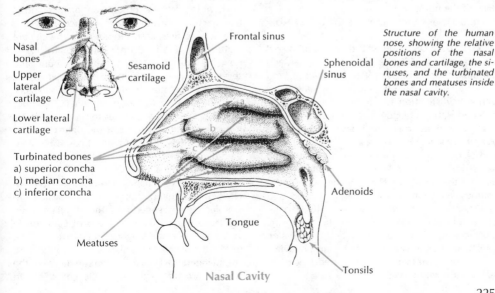

Structure of the human nose, showing the relative positions of the nasal bones and cartilage, the sinuses, and the turbinated bones and meatuses inside the nasal cavity.

with which various sinuses in the ethmoid, sphenoid, frontal, and superior maxillary bones communicate by narrow apertures.

The margins of the nostrils are usually lined with a number of stiff hairs (vibrissae) that project across the openings and serve to arrest the passage of foreign substances, such as dust and small insects, which might otherwise be drawn up with the current of air intended for respiration. The skeleton, or framework, of the nose is partly composed of the bones forming the top and sides of the bridge, and partly of cartilages. On either side are an upper lateral and a lower lateral cartilage, to the latter of which are attached three or four small cartilaginous plates, termed sesamoid cartilages. The cartilage of the septum separates the nostrils and, in association posteriorly with the perpendicular plate of the ethmoid and with the vomer, forms a complete partition between the right and left nasal fossae.

The nasal fossae, which constitute the internal part of the nose, are lofty and of considerable depth. They open in front through the nostrils and behind end in a vertical slit on either side of the upper pharynx, above the soft palate (q.v.), and near the orifices of the Eustachian tubes, leading to the tympanic cavity of the ear (q.v.).

The mucous membrane lining the nose varies in its structure in different parts of the organ. In the olfactory region the mucous membrane is very thick and colored by a brown pigment. The olfactory nerve, or nerve of smell, terminates in the nasal cavity in several small branches; these ramify in the soft mucous membrane and end in tiny varicose fibers that in turn terminate in elongated epithelial cells projecting into the free surface of the nose.

For diseases of the nose, see COLD, COMMON; RHINITIS.

NOSTRADAMUS, assumed Latin name of Michel de Nostredame (1503–66), French physician and astrologer, born in Saint Remi, Provence, and educated at Avignon and Montpellier. He achieved distinction for his treatment of those stricken with the plague during outbreaks of the disease in southern France. He was also called to Aix and Lyon in 1545 during a plague epidemic in those cities. Nostradamus subsequently attracted widespread attention by his claim that he could predict the future, and in 1555 he published a famous collection of prophecies, in rhymed quatrains, called *Centuries.* Catherine de Médicis, queen of France, invited him to court to cast the horoscopes of her sons, and upon the accession of Charles IX, he was appointed court physician. The name Nostradamus is now used to denote any person who professes to be a seer.

NOTATION, in science or art, any system of marks or symbols used to represent entities, processes, facts, or relationships in an abbreviated or nonverbal form. (*See,* for example, CHEMICAL REACTION; MUSICAL NOTATION.) In the arts, notation is also used in choreography (*see* DANCE NOTATION) and in plotting camera or acting movement. Special symbolic vocabularies are also useful with certain games, such as chess; for diagrammatic offensive or defensive study by teams in many sports; and for military strategy. Shorthand, too, is a form of notation.

For the history of mathematical notation, *see* NUMERALS. *See also* MATHEMATICS.

NOTRE DAME, UNIVERSITY OF, Roman Catholic institution of higher education, founded in 1842 by the Congregation of Holy Cross and governed by a predominantly lay board of trustees. The university is in Notre Dame, a suburb of South Bend, Ind. The university includes colleges of arts and letters, law, science, engineering, and business administration, and a graduate school. The degrees of bachelor, master, and doctor are conferred. In 1967 a new curriculum was organized leading to the degree of master in business administration. The Laetare Medal, granted to American Catholic laypersons for beneficent human endeavor, was inaugurated by the university in 1883. The university libraries house more than 1 million bound volumes. The art gallery has a wide range of works, including a Dr. Thomas Dooley memorial collection.

NOTTINGHAM, city, administrative center of Nottinghamshire, central England, on the Trent R. It is a transportation center located in a coalmining region. For centuries Nottingham has been noted for the production of lace; other manufactures include pharmaceuticals, tobacco products, textiles, and computers. In the city are Nottingham Castle (11th cent., rebuilt 1670s), now housing an art gallery and museum, and several theaters. Nottingham is the seat of the University of Nottingham (1948) and a polytechnic college. An early Saxon settlement, Nottingham was taken by the Danes in the 9th century. It was granted a charter and the right to hold a market in 1155. In 1642 Charles I raised his standard here, marking the start of the English Revolution. Pop. (1981) 271,080.

NOTTINGHAM, Charles Howard, 1st Earl of (1536–1624), English statesman and naval commander. He succeeded his father, William Howard (1510?–73) as Baron Howard of Effington in 1573 and was made knight of the Garter in 1574. In 1585 he became lord high admiral and in 1588 commanded the English fleet in the defeat of the Spanish Armada. With Robert Devereux, 2d earl of Essex, he commanded the English naval expedition that in 1596 sank the Spanish fleet and sacked the city of Cádiz. Howard was created earl of Nottingham in 1597. In 1601 he took a leading part in suppressing the rebellion of Essex against Queen Elizabeth I. He served on many royal commissions, including those for the trial of Mary, queen of Scots, in 1586, for the trial of Essex in 1601, for the union of England and Scotland in 1604, and for the trial of the conspirators in the Gunpowder Plot in 1606.

NOTTINGHAMSHIRE, county, central England; Nottingham is the administrative center. Nottinghamshire comprises lowlands in the E and an upland area in the W. Sherwood Forest, a hilly and largely deforested area, occupies much of the W portion of the county. Agricultural activities include dairying and the growing of grains, fruit, and vegetables. Manufactures include hosiery, lace, clothing, bicycles, and machinery. In Anglo-Saxon times the region was part of the kingdom of Mercia. Area, 2164 sq km (836 sq mi); pop. (1981) 982,631.

NOUADHIBOU, formerly PORT-ÉTIENNE, town, NW Mauritania, administrative center of Dakhlet-Nouadhibou Region, on the Atlantic Ocean. It is a fishing and fish-processing center. The nearby seaport of Point-Central in 1963 became the shipping center for iron ore produced in the interior around Fdérick. Pop. (est.) 22,000.

NOUAKCHOTT, city, capital of Mauritania, near the Atlantic Ocean, in the W part of the country. It is Mauritania's main administrative and economic center and is served by an international airport and a nearby seaport. The National School of Administration (1966), the National Institute of Advanced Islamic Studies (1961), the National Library, and the National Archives are here. The community grew after being selected as the site of the national capital in 1957, three years before Mauritania achieved full independence. Pop. (1977 est.) 135,000.

NOUMÉA, also Numea, town, capital of the French overseas territory of New Caledonia, in the SW Pacific Ocean. It is located on the protected harbor in the SW part of New Caledonia island and is the territory's chief port and principal administrative and economic center. Nickel-ore mining and refining and tourism are important to the town's economic base. The National Conservatory of Arts and Crafts (1971) and the Bernheim Library are here. Nouméa was annexed by France in 1853 and was a French penal colony from 1864 to 1897. The town developed rapidly after it became the site of a U.S. air base during World War II. Pop. (1982) 60,112.

NOUN. *See* PARTS OF SPEECH.

NOVA IGUAÇU, formerly MAXAMBAMBA, city, SE Brazil, in Rio de Janeiro State, in the Sarapuí R. valley. It is a suburb of the city of Rio de Janeiro that benefits from its location near the main highway and rail routes connecting Rio de Janeiro and São Paulo. Diversified industries range from processing of citrus and other local agricultural products to the manufactures of chemicals, pharmaceuticals, and machinery. Its population increased considerably in the 1970s. Pop. (1980 prelim.) 491,802.

NOVALIS, pseudonym of FRIEDRICH LEOPOLD, FREIHERR VON HARDENBURG (1772–1801), German poet, who was a founder of the romantic movement. Novalis was born into a noble family in Oberwiederstedt, Saxony. Educated in law, science, and philosophy at the universities of Jena, Leipzig, and Wittenberg, he became a civil servant but devoted most of his energies to writing. He is noted for his lyric poetry and prose, characterized by deep religious mysticism. Novalis's best-known work is *Hymns to the Night* (1800; trans. 1889), which expresses his grief and desolation over the death of his fiancée. His *Sacred Songs* (1799; trans. 1956) had great influence on other writers. His best work is usually considered the unfinished novel *Heinrich von Ofterdingen* (1802; trans. 1842), whose dreamy tone and poetic imagination make it a masterpiece of German romanticism. Novalis also wrote essays expressing a romantic nostalgia for the supposed unity of medieval Christian Europe.

NOVARA, city, N Italy, capital of Novara Province, in Piedmont Region. It is an agricultural marketing center, principally for rice. Industries include publishing and the manufacture of metal products, chemicals, and toys. Novara was founded by Ligurians and became a Roman colony. A free town during the Middle Ages, it later came under the control of the duchy of Milan and then passed to the house of Savoy in 1734. In 1849 the Austrians were victorious here over the Piedmontese under Charles Albert. Pop. (1981 est.) 102,039.

NOVA SCOTIA, one of the Maritime provinces of Canada, bordered on the N by the Bay of Fundy, the province of New Brunswick, Northumberland Strait, and the Gulf of Saint Lawrence and on the E, S, and W by the Atlantic Ocean. Nova Scotia consists primarily of a mainland section, linked to New Brunswick by the Isthmus of Chignecto, and Cape Breton Island, separated from the mainland by the Strait of Canso.

Nova Scotia is sometimes known as the Land of Evangeline, a reference to the American poet Henry Wadsworth Longfellow's *Evangeline* (1847), about the expulsion of the French-speak-

Sunrise over the harbor of Halifax, the capital of Nova Scotia and the principal Atlantic seaport of Canada.

ing Acadians from the area in 1755. On July 1, 1867, Nova Scotia became one of the founding members of the Canadian Confederation. The province's name, which is Latin for New Scotland, was first applied to the region in the 1620s by settlers from Scotland.

LAND AND RESOURCES

Nova Scotia, with an area of 55,491 sq km (21,425 sq mi), is the smallest Canadian province or territory except for Prince Edward Island; about 3% of its land area is owned by the federal government. The province has an extreme length of about 600 km (about 375 mi) and an extreme breadth of about 160 km (about 100 mi); almost 5% of its area consists of inland water surface. Elevations range from sea level, along the coast, to 532 m (1747 ft), in Cape Breton Highlands National Park. The coastline of Nova Scotia is about 7580 km (about 4710 mi) long. Sable Island is situated about 160 km (about 100 mi) offshore in the Atlantic.

Physical Geography. Nova Scotia can be divided into four major geographical regions—the Atlantic Uplands, the Nova Scotia Highlands, the Annapolis Lowland, and the Maritime Plain. The Atlantic Uplands, which occupy most of the S part of the province, are made up of ancient resistant rocks largely overlain by rocky glacial deposits. The Nova Scotia Highlands are composed of three separate areas of uplands. The W section includes North Mt., a long ridge of traprock along the Bay of Fundy; the central section takes in the Cobequid Mts., which rise to 367 m (1204 ft) atop Nuttby Mt.; and the E section contains the Cape Breton Highlands, with the province's highest point. The Annapolis Lowland, in the W, is a small area with considerable fertile soil. Nova Scotia's fourth region, the Maritime Plain, occupies a small region fronting on Northumberland Strait. The plain is characterized by a low, undulating landscape and substantial areas of fertile soil.

Rivers and Lakes. Most of Nova Scotia's rivers radiate outward in the Atlantic Uplands and the Nova Scotia Highlands. The rivers, which generally are short and narrow, include the Saint Mary's (the province's longest at 95 km/59 mi), Mersey, Shubenacadie, La Have, and Mira. The Annapolis R. flows parallel to the NW coast. The province contains hundreds of lakes, the largest being Bras d'Or Lake, a saltwater lake in the center of Cape Breton Island. The biggest bodies of fresh water are Lakes Rossignol and Ainslie and Kejimkujik and Grand lakes. The Bay of Fundy and some of its arms, including Minas Basin and Cobequid and Chignecto bays, are noted for their great tidal ranges.

A fishing boat in the waters off Nova Scotia. Fishing is the leading industry of the easternmost Maritime province of Canada.   Canadian Consulate

Climate. The sea moderates the climate of Nova Scotia, which has mild winters compared to the interior of Canada and slightly cooler summers than many other areas in the S part of the nation. Halifax, which is fairly typical of the province, has a mean January temperature of $-3.2°$ C (26.2° F) and a mean July temperature of 18.3° C (65° F) and annually receives some 1320 mm (some 52 in) of precipitation, including about 210 mm (about 8.3 in) of snow. The recorded temperature of Nova Scotia has ranged from $-41.1°$ C ($-42°$ F), in 1920 at Upper Stewiacke, to 38.3° C (101° F), in 1935 at Collegeville. Fog is common along the S coast of the province in spring and early summer.

Plants and Animals. Forest covers about three-quarters of the land area of Nova Scotia. Much of the forest is made up of mixed hardwoods and softwoods and includes birch, maple, oak, balsam fir, hemlock, red spruce, and white pine. Softwoods such as balsam fir and spruce predominate in most of Cape Breton Island and in coastal regions in other parts of the province. Nova Scotia is known for its large number of wild flowers, notably aster, goldenrod, lily, violet, and wild rose.

Nova Scotia's large animals include many white-tailed deer and some moose and black bear. The province also has large numbers of beaver, chipmunk, mink, muskrat, rabbit, red fox, and squirrel. Inland streams contain salmon and

INDEX TO MAP OF NOVA SCOTIA

Cities and Towns

Advocate Harbour .....C 2
Aldershot.........C 2
Amherst............C 2
Annapolis Royal......B 3
Antigonish...........E 2
Arichat...............G 2
Aylesford...........C 2
Baddeck............G 1
Barrington Passage ...B 4
Bear River..........B 3
Belle Côte..........F 1
Berwick.............C 2
Bible Hill...........D 2
Bridgetown..........B 3
Bridgewater.........C 3
Brookfield..........D 2
Brooklyn............C 3
Canning.............C 2
Canso...............G 2
Cape North..........G 1
Chester.............C 3
Chéticamp..........F 1
Church Point........B 3
Clark's Harbour ......B 4
Clementsport........B 3
Dartmouth..........D 3
Debert..............D 2
Digby...............B 3
Dominion............H 1
Donkin..............H 1
Ecum Secum.........E 2
Elmsdale...........D 3
Enfield.............D 3
Englishtown ....G 1
Florence............G 1
Gabarus............G 2
Glace Bay..........H 1
Goldboro...........F 2
Grand-Étang........G 1
Guysborough........F 2
Halifax (cap.)......D 3
Hantsport..........C 2
Herring Cove.......D 3
Hopewell...........E 2
Ingonish...........G 1
Ingonish Beach ......G 1
Inverness..........F 1
Joggins............C 2
Judique............F 2
Kentville...........C 2
Kingston...........C 3
Lakeside...........D 3

Lawrencetown ....B 3
Lawrencetown ....D 3
Liverpool...........C 3
Lockeport..........B 4
Londonderry........D 2
Louisbourg.........G 2
Louisdale..........G 2
Lower West Pubnico ...A 4
Lunenburg..........C 3
Mabou..............F 1
Maccan.............C 2
Mahone Bay........C 3
Margaree Centre .....G 1
Margaree Forks.......F 1
Meteghan...........A 3
Middle Musquodoboit..E 2
Middleton..........B 3
Milford Station......D 2
Milton.............C 3
Mira Road..........G 1
Moser River.........E 3
Mulgrave...........F 2
Musquodoboit
  Harbour.........D 3
New Germany.......C 3
New Glasgow.......E 2
New Waterford......G 1
Nictaux............C 3
Noel...............D 2
North Sydney.......G 1
Oxford.............D 2
Parrsboro..........C 2
Petit-de-Grat.......G 2
Petit-Étang.........F 1
Pictou.............E 2
Port Hawkesbury......F 2
Port Hood..........F 1
Port Mouton........B 4
Prospect...........D 3
Pugwash...........D 2
Reserve Mines ....G 1
River Hébert........C 2
River John..........D 2
Riverport..........C 3
Sackville..........D 3
Saint Peters........G 2
Salmon River.......D 2
Saulnierville.........A 3
Scotchtown.........G 1
Sheet Harbour ......E 3
Shelburne..........B 4
Sherbrooke.........E 2
Ship Harbour ......E 3
Shubenacadie.......D 2

Springhill.............D 2
Stellarton.............E 2
Stewiacke.............D 2
Sydney ....G 1
Sydney Mines.........G 1
Tatamagouche ....D 2
Terence Bay ....D 3
Thorburn.............E 2
Three Mile Plains .....C 3
Timberlea.............D 3
Trenton ....E 2
Truro.................D 2
Tusket................B 4
Upper Stewiacke.......E 2
Waverley ....D 3
Wedgeport ....A 4
Western Shore ....C 3
West Pubnico ....B 4
Westville ....E 2
Weymouth ....B 3
Windsor..............C 2
Wolfville..............C 2
Yarmouth ....A 4

Other Features

Ainslie (lake).........F 1
Amet (sound) ....D 2
Andrew (island) ......G 2
Annapolis (river).......B 3
Aspy (bay)............G 1
Boularderie (island)....G 1
Bras d'Or (lake).......G 2
Breton (cape)..........H 2
Brier (island)..........A 3
Canso (strait).........F 2
Cape Breton (island)...G 1
Cape Breton
  Highlands Nat'l Park..G 1
Cape Sable (island) ....B 4
Carleton (river).........B 4
Chedabucto (bay)......F 2
Chignecto (bay) ....C 2
Chignecto (cape).......B 2
Cobequid (bay)........D 2
Country (harbor).......F 2
Digby Neck (pen.).....A 3
Fisher (lake) ....B 3
Fort Anne Nat'l Hist.
  Park ....B 3
Fortress of
  Louisbourg Nat'l
  Hist. Park..........H 2

Fundy (bay)...........B 2
Gabarus (bay)........G 2
Gaspereau (lake)......C 3
George (cape).........F 2
Georges (bay).........F 2
Grand Pré Nat'l Hist.
  Park ....C 2
Great Pubnico (lake) ..B 4
Haute (island).........B 2
Jordan (bay)..........B 4
Kejimkujik (lake)......B 3
Kejimkujik Nat'l Park ..B 3
La Have (island).......C 3
La Have (river)........C 3
Liverpool (bay).........C 3
Long (island)..........A 3
McNutt (island).......B 4
Madame (island)......G 2
Mahone (bay).........C 3
Medway (river).......B 3
Mersey (river).........B 3
Minas (basin).........C 2
Minas (chan.).........C 2
Mira (bay).............H 1
Mira (river)...........G 2
Molega (lake).........C 3
Mouton (island) ......C 4
North (cape)..........G 1
Northumberland
  (strait) ....D 1
Nuttby (mt.)..........D 2
Panuke (lake).........C 3
Pictou (island)........E 2
Ponhook (lake)........C 3
Port Royal Nat'l Hist.
  Park ....B 3
Roseway (river).......B 3
Rossignol (lake).......B 3
Sable (cape)..........B 4
Sable (island).........H 4
Saint Ann's (bay).....G 1
Saint Lawrence (gulf)..E 1
Saint Margarets (bay)..D 3
Saint Marys (bay)......A 3
Saint Paul (island)....G 1
Scatarie (island)......H 1
Sherbrooke (lake)......C 3
Shubenacadie (lake) ..D 3
Split (cape)...........C 2
Tancook (island).......C 3
Tor (bay).............F 2
Verte (bay)...........D 1
West (point)..........G 4

trout; lobster, scallop, cod, haddock, herring, striped bass, and swordfish inhabit coastal marine waters.

Mineral Resources. Nova Scotia contains large deposits of coal, gypsum, and salt. Among the province's other mineral deposits are barite, clay, copper, peat, sand and gravel, stone, and zinc. Some petroleum and natural gas have been found under the Atlantic near Nova Scotia.

W.F.S.

POPULATION

According to the 1981 census, Nova Scotia had 847,442 inhabitants, an increase of 7.4% over 1971. In 1981 the overall population density was 15 persons per sq km (40 per sq mi). English was the native language of some 93% of the people; about 5% had French as their first language. More than 5500 American Indians lived in Nova Scotia, about three-fourths on reserves. The churches with the largest membership in the province

were the Roman Catholic church, the United Church of Canada, and the Anglican Church of Canada. About 56% of all Nova Scotians lived in areas defined as urban, and the rest lived in rural areas. Halifax was the biggest city and capital of the province; other major communities were Dartmouth, Sydney, Glace Bay, and Truro.

EDUCATION AND CULTURAL ACTIVITY

Nova Scotia has a number of notable educational and cultural institutions. Its scenic landscape offers a wide variety of opportunities for outdoor sports and recreation.

Education. Nova Scotia's first education act, in 1766, provided for public schools, but not until 1811 did nondenominational, free public education begin here. In the early 1980s there were 610 public elementary and secondary schools with a combined annual enrollment of approximately 190,500 students. In the same period the province's institutions of higher education enrolled

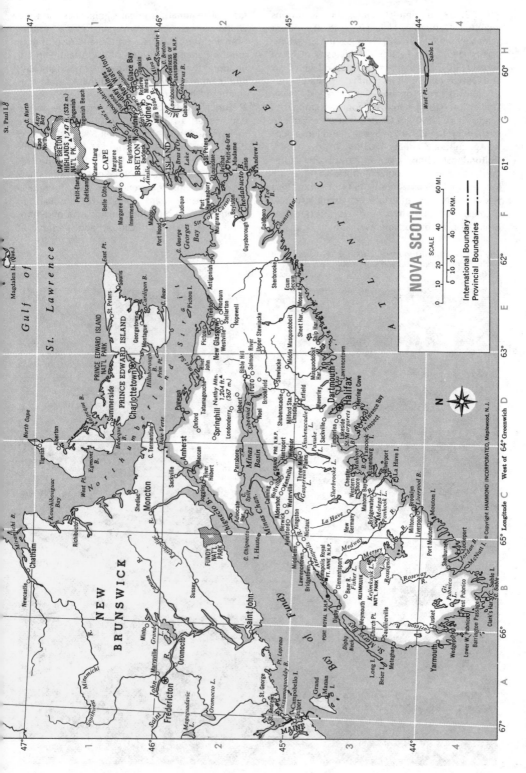

NOVA SCOTIA

SCALE

International Boundary
Provincial Boundaries

© Copyright HAMMOND INCORPORATED, Maplewood, N.J.

65° Longitude C   West of 64° Greenwich D   63°

NEW BRUNSWICK

Gulf of St. Lawrence

Magdalen Is. (Que.)

St. Paul I.

Cape North

CAPE BRETON HIGHLANDS NAT'L PK. 1,747 ft. (532 m.)

PRINCE EDWARD ISLAND

PRINCE EDWARD ISLAND NAT'L PARK

Charlottetown

Summerside

Amherst

FUNDY NAT'L PARK

Fredericton

Saint John

Moncton

MAINE

CAPE BRETON ISLAND

Sydney

Halifax

Dartmouth

Yarmouth

ATLANTIC OCEAN

231

about 21,000 full-time students. The institutions included Dalhousie University (1818), Mount Saint Vincent University (1925), Saint Mary's University (1802), the Technical University of Nova Scotia (1907), and the Nova Scotia College of Art and Design (1887), all in Halifax; Acadia University (1838), in Wolfville; Saint Francis Xavier University (1853), in Antigonish; Université Sainte-Anne (1890), in Church Point; the College of Cape Breton (1954), in Sydney; and Nova Scotia Agricultural College (1905), in Truro.

Cultural Institutions. Many of Nova Scotia's foremost museums and other cultural facilities are located in Halifax. Among them are the Nova Scotia Museum, with exhibits covering historical themes; the Public Archives of Nova Scotia, featuring displays of documents, paintings, and arti-

facts of regional historical significance; and the Dalhousie Arts Centre, which includes an auditorium and the Dalhousie Art Gallery. Also of note are the Fisheries Museum of the Atlantic, in Lunenburg; the Desbrisay Museum, in Bridgewater, with historical collections; and the Acadian Museum, in Chéticamp.

Historical Sites. Nova Scotia has preserved or reconstructed a number of historical sites. These include Alexander Graham Bell National Historic Park, in Baddeck, with exhibits relating to Bell's inventions while he lived here; Fort Anne National Historic Park, in Annapolis Royal, including the remains of a French fort built from 1695 to 1708; Fort Edward National Historic Park, in Windsor, containing the remains of a mid-18th-century earthen fortification; and Fortress of

The Fortress of Louisbourg on Cape Breton Island, built by the French about 1713 and extensively restored in the 1960s. Canadian Consulate

Halifax Citadel, one of numerous historic forts in Halifax, which at one time was a strongly fortified British garrison town. Canadian Consulate

Louisbourg National Historic Park, near Louisbourg, including a partial reconstruction of a large French fort (built 1720–45; destroyed by the English, 1760). Grand Pré National Historic Park, near Grand Pré, encompasses the site of a former Acadian village; York Redoubt National Historic Site includes a defense battery (begun 1790s) guarding Halifax Harbour; and Halifax Citadel National Historic Park, in Halifax, contains a massive 19th-century stone fortress. Also of interest is Sherbrooke Village Restoration, in the Sherbrooke area, a restoration of a lumbering and mining community of the 1860s.

Sports and Recreation. Nova Scotia's several national and provincial parks, its lengthy shoreline, and its rivers and lakes offer ideal conditions for boating, swimming, fishing, hiking, camping, and hunting. Golf, tennis, skiing, and ice hockey are also popular sports in the province.

Communications. In the early 1980s Nova Scotia had 28 radiobroadcasting stations and 4 originating television stations. The first radio station in the province, CHNS in Halifax, began operation in 1922. CJCB-TV in Sydney, Nova Scotia's first commercial television station, went on the air in 1954. The *Halifax Gazette,* the first newspaper published in Canada, was initially printed in Halifax in 1752. In the early 1980s Nova Scotia had seven daily newspapers with a total daily circulation of about 192,000. Influential newspapers included the *Mail-Star* of Halifax and the *Cape Breton Post* of Sydney.

GOVERNMENT AND POLITICS

Nova Scotia has a parliamentary form of government.

Executive. The nominal chief executive of Nova Scotia is a lieutenant governor appointed by the Canadian governor-general in council to a term of five years. The lieutenant governor, representing the British sovereign, holds a position that is largely honorary. The premier, who is responsible to the provincial legislature, is the actual head of government and presides over the executive council, or cabinet, which also includes the attorney general, minister of finance, minister of education, and about 15 other officials.

Legislature. The unicameral Nova Scotia Legislative Assembly is made up of 52 members, each popularly elected to a term of up to five years. The lieutenant governor, on the advice of the premier, may call for an election before the 5-year term has been completed.

Judiciary. Nova Scotia's highest tribunal, the supreme court, is composed of an appeal division with seven justices and a trial division with 10 justices. Supreme court justices are appointed by the Canadian governor-general in council and serve until the age of 75.

Local Government. Nova Scotia is divided into 18 counties, which together are subdivided into 24 rural municipalities. Within the municipalities are a total of 3 incorporated cities and 39 incorporated towns, most of which are governed by a mayor and council.

National Representation. Nova Scotia is represented in the Canadian Parliament by 10 senators appointed by the Canadian governor-general in council and by 11 members of the House of Commons popularly elected to terms of up to five years.

Politics. Since Nova Scotia became a province in 1867, the Liberal party has been most successful in obtaining control of the provincial government. From 1956 to 1970, however, the Progressive Conservative party held a majority in the Legislative Assembly, and it regained this position in 1978.

ECONOMY

In the 19th century Nova Scotia was known as a trading, shipbuilding, and fishing area. During the 20th century the province's economy was expanded and diversified, in part through the establishment of war-related industries in the two world wars. In the early 1980s manufacturing was the leading economic activity, but farming, fishing, and mining also were important.

Agriculture. Only about 4% of the land area of Nova Scotia is used for agriculture, with some of the best farmland located on the Isthmus of

NOVA SCOTIA

JOINED THE CANADIAN CONFEDERATION:
July 1, 1867; one of the four original provinces

CAPITAL:	Halifax
MOTTO:	*Munit haec et altera vincit* (One defends and the other conquers)
FLORAL EMBLEM:	Trailing arbutus (Mayflower)
POPULATION (1981):	847,442
AREA:	55,491 sq km (21,425 sq mi), includes 2650 sq km (1023 sq mi) of inland waters; 11th largest among the provinces and territories
COASTLINE:	7578 km (4709 mi)
HIGHEST POINT:	532 m (1745 ft), on Cape Breton
LOWEST POINT:	Sea level, along the Atlantic Ocean
PRINCIPAL RIVERS:	Mersey, Saint Mary's, La Have, Annapolis
PRINCIPAL LAKES:	Bras d'Or, Rossignol, Ainslie, Kejimkujik
CANADIAN PARLIAMENT:	10 members of the Senate; 11 members of the House of Commons

POPULATION OF NOVA SCOTIA SINCE 1851

Year of Census	Population	Percentage of Total Can. Pop.
1851	276,854	11.4%
1871	387,800	10.5%
1891	450,396	9.3%
1901	459,574	8.6%
1921	523,837	6.0%
1931	512,846	4.9%
1951	642,584	4.6%
1961	737,007	4.0%
1971	788,960	3.7%
1981	847,442	3.5%

POPULATION OF TEN LARGEST COMMUNITIES

	1981 Census	1971 Census
Halifax	114,594	122,035
Dartmouth	62,277	64,770
Sydney	29,444	33,230
Glace Bay	21,466	22,440
Truro	12,552	13,047
New Glasgow	10,464	10,849
Amherst	9,684	9,966
New Waterford	8,808	9,579
Sydney Mines	8,501	8,991
North Sydney	7,820	8,604
Yarmouth	7,475	8,516

CLIMATE

CLIMATE	HALIFAX	SYDNEY
Average January temperature range	−8.3° to 0° C (17° to 32° F)	−9.4° to −1.1° C (15° to 30° F)
Average July temperature range	13.3° to 23.3° C (56° to 74° F)	12.8° to 23.9° C (55° to 75° F)
Average annual temperature	6.1° C (43° F)	6.1° C (43° F)
Average annual precipitation	1319 mm (52 in)	1341 mm (53 in)
Average annual snowfall	2108 mm (83 in)	2880 mm (113 in)
Average number of days per year with appreciable precipitation	152	179
Average dates of freezing temperatures (0° C/32° F or less):		
Last in spring	May 1	May 23
First in autumn	Nov. 1	Oct. 16

NATURAL REGIONS OF NOVA SCOTIA

NOVA SCOTIA HIGHLANDS

MARITIME PLAIN

ANNAPOLIS LOWLAND

ATLANTIC UPLANDS

PRINCIPAL PRODUCTS OF NOVA SCOTIA

ECONOMY

Sources: Canadian Government Publications
(All figures are in Canadian dollars)

Province budget. . . . . revenue $1.6 billion
expenditure $1.6 billion
Provincial gross domestic product . . . . $6.4 billion
Personal income, per capita $7845
Labor force (civilian) 368,000
   Employed in agriculture   2%
   Employed in manufacturing   14%
   Employed in services   30%

	Quantity Produced	Value
FARM PRODUCTS		**$196 million**
Crops		**$36 million**
Fruits	55,000 metric tons	$14 million
Floriculture and nursery products		$9 million
Vegetables . . .	19,000 metric tons	$5 million
Potatoes	37,000 metric tons	$4 million
Livestock and Livestock Products		**$160 million**
Dairy prod. . . .	88,000 kiloliters	$56 million
Cattle	46,000	$51 million
Hogs	194,400	$22 million
Poultry	15,000 metric tons	$22 million
MINERALS		**$263 million**
Coal	2.7 million metric tons	$131 million
Salt	1.0 million metric tons	$28 million
Sand, gravel. .	11.5 million metric tons	$28 million
Gypsum	4.8 million metric tons	$26 million
FISHING	436,800 metric tons	**$232 million**
FORESTRY		**$100 million**

Value of Shipments

MANUFACTURING . . . . **$3.5 billion**
  Petroleum and coal products . . . . $858 million
  Food and beverage products. . . . . $859 million
  Paper and allied products . . . . $378 million
  Wood products . . . . $96 million
  Fabricated metal products . . . . $91 million
  Textiles . . . . $76 million
  Printing and publishing . . . . $64 million
  Electrical products . . . . $62 million
  Nonmetallic mineral products . . . . $56 million

Wages and Salaries
OTHER . . . . **$4.7 billion**
  Service-producing industries. . . . . $2.7 billion
  Community, business, and personal
    service industries . . . . $1.0 billion
  Transportation, communications, and
    other utilities . . . . $410 million
  Public administration . . . . $515 million

ANNUAL PRODUCTION OF GOODS BY SECTOR

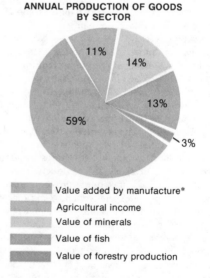

  Value added by manufacture*
  Agricultural income
  Value of minerals
  Value of fish
  Value of forestry production

* The value added by an industry is a measure of the value created in its products, not counting such production costs as raw materials and power.

Chignecto (connecting the province with New Brunswick) and in the Annapolis Lowland. The province has about 3440 farms, which have an average size of some 90 ha (some 220 acres). Annual cash receipts from sales of crops and livestock and livestock products totaled about Can. $196 million in the early 1980s, with livestock and livestock products accounting for about four-fifths of the income. The leading farm commodities are dairy products, beef cattle, poultry, hogs, eggs, fruit (especially apples grown in the Annapolis Lowland), potatoes and other vegetables, hay, barley, and wheat.

Forestry. Nova Scotia has a substantial forestry industry, with about 4.2 million cu m (about 148 million cu ft) of wood harvested per year. Most of the wood is used for making paper, and the rest is chiefly sawed into lumber. In addition, many trees are cut for use as Christmas trees.

Fishing. Nova Scotia and British Columbia have the largest fishing industries in Canada. In Nova Scotia the yearly fish catch in the early 1980s was worth about Can.$231.6 million, with most of the income derived from sales of shellfish, especially scallop and lobster. Next in value was cod, with herring not far behind. Haddock, pollack, and redfish also were important. Leading fishing ports include Digby, Liverpool, Lunenburg, Shelburne, and Yarmouth.

Mining. Coal, the most important material mined in Nova Scotia, had a total yearly value in the early 1980s of about Can.$131 million, some 7% of the Canadian total. The main coal mines are on Cape Breton Island. Approximately two-thirds of the gypsum mined annually in Canada is produced in the province. Other important mineral products of Nova Scotia include salt, sand and gravel, clay, peat, lead, zinc, and barite.

Manufacturing. By far the leading sector of the Nova Scotia economy is manufacturing, which in the early 1980s employed some 41,000 persons. The yearly value of shipments was about Can.$3.5 billion. Major manufactures include processed food (notably fish products), paper and paper items, transportation equipment (especially ships, aerospace supplies, and motor vehicles), iron and steel, refined petroleum, textiles, printed materials, and electrical and electronic equipment. Halifax and the Sydney area are important manufacturing centers.

Tourism. Each year Nova Scotia attracts large numbers of tourists, many of whom are lured by the province's lovely scenery (especially on Cape Breton Island) and its many opportunities for outdoor-recreation activities. Popular areas include Cape Breton Highlands and Kejimkujik national parks, several national historic parks and

At Halifax, the capital of Nova Scotia, the picturesque North West Arm, an inlet of the Atlantic Ocean, affords a snug natural harbor for small craft.
Canadian Government Travel Bureau

sites, and 12 provincial parks. Many people also visit Halifax.

Transportation. Most coastal areas of Nova Scotia are well served by transportation facilities, but many places in the interior have poor transport connections. The province has some 25,350 km (some 15,750 mi) of roads, about half of which are paved. The Trans-Canada Highway ranges from the New Brunswick border, near Amherst, to Sydney Mines, on Cape Breton Island, by way of the Canso Causeway (completed 1955) between the island and the mainland. Nova Scotia is also served by about 1970 km (about 1225 mi) of operated railroad track. Halifax is a major seaport with modern facilities for handling containerized shipping. Ferries link the province with New Brunswick, Newfoundland, Prince Edward Island, and Maine. Nova Scotia's busiest airports are those at Halifax and Sydney.

Energy. The province's installed electricity-generating capacity is about 1.7 million kw (approximately 2.3% of the total Canadian capacity), but it annually produces only about 6.1 billion kwh, or some 1.8% of the country's total electricity. Hydroelectrical facilities represent about one-fifth of the capacity, with the balance largely accounted for by thermal installations burning refined petroleum or coal.   A.H.

HISTORY

The area now known as Nova Scotia was originally inhabited by tribes of Abnaki and Micmac Indians. The Venetian explorer John Cabot, sailing under the English flag, may have reached Cape Breton Island in 1497.

Colonial Period. The first settlers of the area were the French, who called it Acadie (Acadia) and founded Port Royal in 1605. Acadia included present-day New Brunswick, Nova Scotia, and Prince Edward Island. The English, rivals of the French in Europe and the New World, refused to recognize French claims to Acadia, which they called Nova Scotia (New Scotland) and granted to the Scottish poet and courtier Sir William Alexander in 1621.

This act initiated nearly a century of Anglo-French conflict, resolved by the British capture of Port Royal (now Annapolis Royal) in 1710 and the French cession of mainland Acadia to the British by the Peace of Utrecht in 1713. Thus, the bulk of the Roman Catholic French-Acadians came under Protestant British rule. In order to overawe their new subjects, the British founded the town of Halifax as naval base and capital in 1749. Distrusting the Acadians' loyalty in the French and Indian War, however, in 1755 the British deported them. This ruthless action was described by the American poet Henry Wadsworth Longfellow in *Evangeline* (1847). The British replaced the Acadians with settlers from New England and, later, from Scotland and northern England. In 1758 the British conquered the French fortress of Louisbourg on Cape Breton, which was joined to Nova Scotia and ceded to them in 1763.

During the American Revolution, the British colony of Nova Scotia became a refuge for thousands of Americans loyal to Britain, including many blacks. In 1784 the new colony of New Brunswick was carved out of mainland Nova Scotia to accommodate these United Empire Loyalists. Cape Breton also became separate. The remaining Nova Scotians, augmented by some returned Acadians and many Scots and Irish immigrants, lived by fishing, lumbering, shipbuilding, and trade. Some attained great wealth as privateers during the Napoleonic Wars and the War of 1812.

After prolonged political struggle, Britain granted Nova Scotia (which included Cape Breton after 1820) local autonomy, or responsible

government, in 1848. Economic uncertainty and political unease at the time of the American Civil War stimulated some interest in associating with the other British North American provinces, but many tradition-minded Nova Scotians distrusted the Canadians of Ontario and Québec. In 1867, without consulting the electorate, the Nova Scotia government took its reluctant people into the Canadian Confederation.

Post-Confederation Period. Although joining the union failed to arrest Nova Scotia's economic decline, it resulted in rail connections to the west and a federal tariff that encouraged local manufacturing. An iron and steel industry developed in Pictou Co. and on Cape Breton, near extensive coal mines. Agricultural areas found export markets, especially for apples. From the end of World War I through the depression of the 1930s, Nova Scotia suffered industrial decline and accompanying unemployment and labor unrest. Thousands migrated to central and western Canada or immigrated to the U.S. The Maritime Rights movement of the 1920s, protesting Nova Scotia's unfavorable economic position in relation to the rest of Canada, accomplished little.

After a revival of shipbuilding in World War II, Nova Scotian industry faced problems of obsolete equipment, heavy freight costs, and dwindling resources. Local government attempts to reverse the trend through investment and diversification were disappointing. The economy was particularly hard hit by the increase in oil prices after 1973. The federal government is trying to remedy the situation by developing offshore oil and gas resources, subsidizing freight rates, and implementing an equalization program that gives Nova Scotia a greater share of federal aid. R.B.W.

For further information on this topic, see the Bibliography in volume 28, section 1116.

NOVA AND SUPERNOVA (Lat. *novus*, "new"), in astronomy, names of two kinds of explosive events that take place in some stars. A nova is a star (q.v.) that suddenly increases greatly in brightness and then slowly fades, but may continue to exist for some time. A supernova exhibits the same pattern of behavior, but the causative explosion destroys or profoundly alters the star. Supernovas are much rarer than novas, which are observed fairly frequently in photographs of the sky.

Novas. Before the era of modern astronomy, a star that appeared suddenly where none had been seen before was called a nova, or "new star." This is a misnomer, as the stars involved had existed long before they became visible to the naked eye. Astronomers estimate that perhaps about a dozen novas occur in the Milky

Way (q.v.), or Galaxy, each year, but most of them are too distant to be seen or are obscured by interstellar matter. Indeed, novas are often more easily observed in other, nearby galaxies rather than in the earth's. Novas are named according to the year of their occurrence and the constellation—that is, the region of the sky—in which they appear. Typically, a nova flares up to several thousand times its original brightness in a matter of days or hours. It next enters a transition stage, during which it may fade and grow bright again; the pattern varies greatly among novas. The star then fades gradually to or near its original level of brightness. In some cases it may become a nova again; the so-called white dwarfs, in particular, flare repeatedly, although their brightness variations are minor.

In a sense, therefore, novas may be considered variable stars, but only because of their stage of development: Far from being new, novas are stars in a late stage of evolution. They apparently behave as they do because their outer layers have built up an excess of helium through nuclear reactions and expand too rapidly to be contained. The star explosively emits a small fraction of its mass as a shell of gas—the cause of the increase in brightness—and then settles down. Such a star is thought often to be the smaller member of a binary (two-star) system, subject to a continuous infall of matter from the larger star. This is perhaps always the case with dwarf novas, which erupt repeatedly at regular intervals of a few to hundreds of days.

Novas in general show a relationship between their maximum brightness and the time they take to fade a certain number of magnitudes. By means of measurements of nearer novas of known distance and magnitude, astronomers can use novas in other galaxies as indicators of the distance to those galaxies.

Supernovas. A supernova explosion is far more spectacular and destructive than a nova and much rarer. Such events may occur no more than once every few years in the Galaxy; and despite their increase in brilliance by a factor of billions, only a few are ever observable to the naked eye. Only three of these have been positively identified in recorded history, the best known of which is the one that occurred in AD 1054 and is now known as the Crab nebula. Supernovas, like novas, are more often seen in other galaxies.

The mechanisms that produce supernovas are less certain, particularly in the case of stars approximately as massive as the earth's sun, an average star. Stars that are more massive, however, are thought sometimes to explode in the late stages of their evolution as a result of gravita-

tional collapse, when the pressure created by nuclear processes within the star is no longer able to withstand the weight of the star's outlying layers. Little may remain after the explosion except the expanding shell of gases. The Crab nebula, however, is an example of a supernova that has left behind a pulsar, or rapidly rotating neutron star. Supernovas are significant contributors to the interstellar material from which new stars are formed.

NOVATIAN (c. 200–c. 258), Roman theologian, who became the second antipope (from 251). A leader among the Roman clergy, Novatian espoused the doctrine of Montanism (q.v.). His acceptance of that belief developed into the Novatian Schism. St. Cornelius, who favored a lenient attitude toward those Christians who lapsed into idolatry, was elected pope in 251, and Novatian established himself as antipope. The Novatianists became heretical when they sought to deny penance to all persons who had sinned, and, in 251, they were excommunicated by Cornelius. The Novatianists established their own church, which endured until they were formally reunited with the Catholic church by the Council of Nicaea in 325. Novatian himself is thought to have been martyred during the persecutions of the Roman emperor Valerian.

Novatian was the first Roman theologian to write in Latin. Two of his nine known treatises have survived: *On the Trinity* and *On Jewish Foods.*

NOVATO, city, Marin Co., W California, near San Francisco; inc. 1960. It is primarily a residential center and has book-distribution facilities and a plant producing communications equipment. Hamilton Air Force Base (dedicated 1935) and a junior college are here, and Point Reyes National Seashore is nearby. The city's name is derived from Rancho de Novato, a Mexican land grant (1838) that included part of the site of the modern city and probably was named for a Chokeche Indian leader. Large apple orchards were developed here in the 1860s, and the community was platted in 1888. Its main growth dates from the 1950s. Pop. (1970) 31,006; (1980) 43,916.

NOVAYA ZEMLYA, archipelago, northwestern USSR, part of the Russian SFSR, in the Arctic Ocean. It comprises two large islands, separated by a narrow strait, Matochkin Shar, and many small islands located N of the Arctic Circle. The archipelago separates the Barents Sea on the W from the Kara Sea on the E. It is about 965 km (about 600 mi) long and from 56 to 145 km (35 to 90 mi) wide. Novaya Zemlya was discovered as early as the 10th century. In 1594 the Dutch navigator Willem Barents explored the archipelago.

NOVEL, fictional prose narrative in which characters and situations are depicted within the framework of a plot. It constitutes the third stage in the development of imaginative fiction, following the epic and the romance, which it largely absorbed but never quite displaced. The word *novel* (Lat. *novellus,* diminutive of *novus,* "new") appears to have been applied during the early Renaissance to any new story. The term *novella* was applied by the Italian writer Giovanni Boccaccio to the short, anecdotal prose narratives in his *Decameron.* When his tales were translated, the term *novel* itself passed into the English language.

Origins of the Novel. Fiction narratives in prose were composed throughout the ancient world, and to these the term *novel* has been indiscriminately applied. Many tales that subsequently became part of the European literary tradition originated in Egypt. In India the novel probably can be said to have a precursor in the *Daśakumā-racarita* (Tales of Ten Princes), a prose romance by Dandin, a Sanskrit writer of the late 6th century AD. In Japan was written what many scholars regard as the first real novel, *The Tale of Genji* (11th cent.; trans. 1935), by Baroness Murasaki Shikibu. What are often now called novels had a considerable vogue among the Greeks in the early centuries of the Christian era. Worthy of mention are the *Æthiopica* by Heliodorus of Emesa, Syria; the *Ephesiaca* by Xenophon of Ephesus; and *Daphnis and Chloë,* the most exquisite of the pastoral romances, generally attributed to Longus. The chief examples of "novels" written in Latin are the *Metamorphoses* or *The Golden Ass* by Lucius Apuleius and the *Satyricon,* which is generally considered the work of Gaius Petronius Arbiter.

The long narrative verse tale, the equally voluminous prose romance, and the Old French *fabliau* (q.v.) flourished in Europe during the Middle Ages, contributing to the development of the novel. Advances in realism were made in Spain during the 16th century with the so-called picaresque, or rogue, story, in which the protagonist is a merry vagabond who goes through a series of realistic and exciting adventures. Examples are the anonymous *Lazarillo de Tormes* (1554) and Mateo Alemán's *Guzman de Alfarache* (1559–1604). Between 1605 and 1612 the Spanish writer Miguel de Cervantes published what is considered the first great novel of the Western world, *Don Quixote de la Mancha.* It recounted the adventures of a country gentleman driven mad by reading chivalric romances, which he accepted as factual. Thus, the first great novel introduced the overriding moral purpose of the form—to teach individual human beings what is possible to specific men and women living in specific societies. A further advance in psychological realism was made by the Comtesse de la Fayette in *La princess de Clèves* (1678). In *The Pilgrim's Progress* (1678–84), John Bunyan's observations of the way of the world and its characters are of such brilliance that what was basically a religious allegory can be regarded as a realistic novel.

18th Century: The Rise of the Novel. As the novel became increasingly popular during the 18th century, writers examined society with greater depth and breadth. They wrote revealingly about people living within, or escaping from, the pressures of society. Criticism was implicit of characters attempting to ignore society and its conventions, and of society for failing to satisfy human aspirations.

The English masters. Five men of the 18th century—Daniel Defoe, Samuel Richardson, Henry Fielding, Tobias Smollett, and Laurence Sterne—wrote the first classic English novels and set high standards and models for later work in the form. In *Pamela* (1740) and *Clarissa* (1747–48), written in the form of letters exchanged between lovers, friends, and kinsmen, Richardson brought to a traditional theme of the older romances—a young woman's defense of her chastity—a psychological realism still unsurpassed. Fielding, in *Joseph Andrews* (1742), *Tom Jones* (1749), and *Amelia* (1751), depicted contemporary life and morals with a generosity combined with great classical learning, enabling him to write what he called "comic epic." Smollett's *Roderick Random* (1748) followed a picaresque hero against a vivid panorama of lower-class society. *The Expedition of Humphry Clinker* (1771), also by Smollett, was gentler in its social criticism, but the comedy is merciless in its depiction of human foibles and vanities. Between 1760 and 1767 Sterne turned the novel inside out with his comic masterpiece *The Life and Opinions of Tristram Shandy,* in which the hero, who is the narrator, is not born until halfway through the book. Sterne had no real successors until James Joyce and Virginia Woolf, who investigated the relations between life on the one hand and literature and language on the other.

Development of genres. Many categories of the novel became recognizable in the 18th century, although they were rarely self-contained or mutually exclusive. One was the didactic novel, in which theories of education and politics were expressed. Most famous was the French philosopher Jean Jacques Rousseau's *Émile; ou, Traité de l'éducation* (1762). An English didactic novel was *Caleb Williams* (1794), by the political philosopher William Godwin; this work may also be seen as an example of the Gothic novel, in which the element of horror is created by the use of apparitions, supernatural manifestations, chains, dungeons, tombs, and nature in its more terrifying aspects. The first Gothic novel was Horace Walpole's *The Castle of Otranto* (1764). Later examples are Ann Radcliffe's *The Mysteries of Udolpho* (1794), Matthew Lewis's *The Monk* (1796), and Mary Wollstonecraft Shelley's *Frankenstein* (1818). Charles Brockden Brown's *Wieland; or, The Transformation* (1798) was the first American Gothic novel. The Gothic strain has been potent in fiction ever since.

One of the most enduring genres in the English novel—uncommon in American fiction—is the comedy of manners, which is concerned with the clash, mirrored in speech and behavior, between characters formed by particular cultural and social conditions. Perhaps the first writer in the genre was Fanny Burney (*Evelina,* 1778; *Cecilia,* 1782), but the great exemplar was Jane Austen (*Pride and Prejudice,* 1813; *Emma,* 1816). Her abiding theme is ostensibly that of young women securing, or not securing, husbands; her underlying serious concern is with the attainment of self-knowledge. Such are Austen's wit, irony, and psychological perception, allied with her strict sense of correct social behavior, that she is the unchallenged genius of the genre.

19th Century: Development of the Modern Novel. Dates for the first appearance of the modern novel must be arbitrary, but two French novelists, Stendhal and Honoré de Balzac, were certainly formative influences.

France. The protagonists of Stendhal's *Le rouge et le noir* (The Red and the Black, 1830) and *La chartreuse de Parme* (The Charterhouse of Parma, 1839) represented a new kind of hero, the "outsider" at odds with society, fired by new opportunities made possible by the Napoleonic regime; Stendhal is the master psychologist of love, ambition, and the thirst for power. Similarly, Balzac made himself the historian of the France of his time in *La comédie humaine* (1831–48), a sequence of 47 volumes that portrayed a society marked by ruthless ambition and exploitation of technology and finance.

The next generation of French novelists displayed a keen interest in the novel as an art form and as a medium for the quasi-scientific study of society. Gustave Flaubert's aim in *Madame Bovary* (1857) and *L'education sentimentale* (1869) was to write about ordinary life with the classical sense of form and precision with which epics were written. He believed that novelists should have toward their subjects the objectivity of the scientist. In art, Flaubert taught, treatment was all; nothing was good or bad but that art made it so. Flaubert's admiration for the scientist was echoed by Émile Zola, who, conceiving the novel as equivalent to a laboratory experiment using real people, analyzed the effects of heredity and environment on a French family in *Les Rougon-Macquart* (1871 onward), a series of 20 novels. He seized on the findings of the scientists with a romantic's fervor.

England. A prominent characteristic of the modern novel, as well as the modern spirit, has been a strong sense of the past. The English novel early in the 19th century was dominated by Sir Walter Scott, whose Waverley novels (1814–28) are the product of a passion for history. Throughout the 19th century the historical novel was the most reputable form of fiction. In England, Charles Dickens, William Makepeace Thackeray, Anthony Trollope, and George Eliot all attempted to write such novels; Thackeray's *Henry Esmond* (1852) was in some ways the most successful. Novelists abroad who came under Scott's influence included, in Italy, Alessandro Manzoni, with *I promessi sposi* (The Betrothed, 1825–27); in France, Balzac, Victor Hugo, and Alexandre Dumas *père;* in Germany, Gustav Freytag; and in the U.S., James Fenimore Cooper.

Another preoccupation of modern English novelists has been the critique of society, using the techniques of dialogue, characterization, and description developed in the 18th-century classics. Dickens achieved his criticisms of Victorian society not so much by means of realism as by the prolific invention of comic characters and situations presented sometimes affectionately, sometimes in fierce contempt, but always with the utmost intensity. Vision of life and structure of novel alike are sustained by such pervasive metaphors as entombment, imprisonment, and rebirth. The greatest imaginative English writer since Shakespeare, Dickens gave his novels the sweep of poetic dramas. His contemporaries—Thackeray (*Vanity Fair,* 1847–48), Eliot (*Middlemarch,* 1871–72), and Trollope (*Barchester Towers,* 1857)—appear almost conventional by comparison, although they produced remarkably detailed panoramas and pointed analyses of English life at crucial moments in the century. Eliot, a writer of great erudition, did considerably more. Her characters contend seriously with life's options; they are thinking beings.

Some Victorians sought refuge from the evils of city and town life in the rural, the pastoral, and the poetic. Emily Brontë's *Wuthering Heights* (1847) was an impassioned drama of the conflict of opposed ways of being that could be symbolized by winter gales and summer sunshine, but for all its lyric intensity the novel was most skillfully constructed and documented. Her sister Charlotte's *Jane Eyre* (1847) astonishes still as the revelation of the mind of a young woman of intellectual and spiritual ardor who knows her worth and demands equality with the man she loves. Poetry makes its appearance in the novels of George Meredith—*The Ordeal of Richard Feverel* (1859) and *The Egoist* (1879)—always to express a character's state of mind at a specific moment. It was also a feature of Thomas Hardy's novels. In *Tess of the D'Urbervilles* (1891) and *Jude the Obscure* (1895) Hardy set down the tragedy of 19th-century humanity, which he saw as that of the best human impulses defeated by the forces of malevolent fate.

The U.S. The early American novelists William Gilmore Simms and Nathaniel Hawthorne claimed that their fictions were not novels but romances; according to Hawthorne, conditions of life in America rendered anything like the English novel impossible. The American novel still often tends to the romance and to be allegorical, even mythic. Hawthorne's *The Scarlet Letter* (1850) subtly explores the nature of sin and the Puritan conscience. By an extension of Hawthorne's symbolic method, Herman Melville wrote *Moby Dick* (1851), his great poetic drama of the pursuit of the ultimate, in the guise of a whaling story.

In his masterpiece of comic irony, *The Adventures of Huckleberry Finn* (1884), Mark Twain exposed the viciousness of a self-complacent society. The book also showed how expressive native American speech could be and thus helped to found a uniquely American literary style. This style was taken a step further by Stephen Crane in *The Red Badge of Courage* (1895).

American novelists, although less sure of their grasp of social dynamics than the English Victorians, did not ignore the great changes occurring in the social structure during the Gilded Age. Mark Twain's friend William Dean Howells examined the newly rich seeking social respectability in *The Rise of Silas Lapham* (1885). Bitter indictments of social abuses were written by Edward Bellamy (*Looking Backward*, 1888), Frank Norris (*McTeague*, 1899; *The Octopus*, 1901), and Theodore Dreiser (*Sister Carrie*, 1900).

The American expatriate Henry James looked to Europe and showed himself to be Flaubert's successor. Taking as a main theme the exploitation of innocence by experience, usually in the form of European exploitation of Americans, as in *The Portrait of a Lady* (1881) and *The Wings of the Dove* (1902), he made his novels what can

almost be called artifacts, so great was his concern for form and shape. His approach to fiction was essentially aesthetic; he sought to give it the intensity of great poetry or painting.

Russia. In Russia, the novel became a weapon against despotic censorship and a vehicle for the expression of ethical and philosophical ideas. Nikolay Gogol attacked serfdom and satirized provincial character types in *Dead Souls* (1842). Fyodor Dostoyevsky, a self-professed disciple of Gogol's, argued that "human nature is defined by its extremes" and became a great psychologist of the desperate, the abnormal, and the outcast. His *Crime and Punishment* (1866), *The Idiot* (1868), *The Possessed* (1871–72), and *The Brothers Karamazov* (1879–80) had a deep, worldwide influence on literature and thought.

The most Westernized of 19th-century Russian novelists, Ivan Turgenev, described in delicate impressionistic style the lives of people of goodwill frustrated by czardom in such novels as *Fathers and Sons* (1862) and *Virgin Soil* (1877). Leo Tolstoy was unrivaled, in novels such as *War and Peace* (1865–69) and *Anna Karenina* (1875–77), in the representation of the life of instinct and domestic affections; but he wrote in ceaseless quest of a deeper meaning to life than that given by the instincts and domestic affections alone.

The 20th Century: Exploration and Experimentation. The psychological and philosophical themes of the later 19th-century novelists were brought to a peak of development by three great early 20th-century figures: Marcel Proust, a Frenchman; Thomas Mann, a German; and James Joyce, an Irishman. Proust, in *Remembrance of Things Past* (1913–27), undertook one of the most ambitious of all literary efforts. In this series of novels Proust minutely analyzed the nature of memory and obsessive love in the context of a complex and changing society. Symbolic representations of the problems of modern Europe were combined with psychological insight and a masterly range of cultural understanding in Mann's novels (*Buddenbrooks*, 1901; *The Magic Mountain*, 1924). Joyce's *Ulysses* (1922) is based on the *Odyssey* of Homer, but the action takes place during a single day in modern Dublin. At times the mental lives of the characters are revealed by the technical device known as "stream of consciousness," by which the unceasing flux of thoughts and associations, conscious and otherwise, is rendered. *Ulysses*, a work of enormous learning, is a comic masterpiece that carried realism further than it had hitherto been taken. These three novelists thus took the novel to what are still felt to be limits: Proust, in social analysis and exhaustive personal reminiscence; Mann, in broad cultural and philosophical concern; and Joyce, in psychological realism and technical experimentation.

Other European novelists of this century joined Mann in depicting their characters as advocates or embodiments of philosophical ideas. Among modern philosopher-novelists were Hermann Hesse (*Steppenwolf*, 1927) and the French writers André Gide (*The Pastoral Symphony*, 1919; *The Counterfeiters*, 1926), François Mauriac (*Vipers' Tangle*, 1932), André Malraux (*Man's Fate*, 1933), Jean-Paul Sarte (*Nausea*, 1938), and Albert Camus (*The Plague*, 1947). Later French novelists, in what came to be known as the "new novel," portrayed characters primarily through their relationship to external objects. The best known of these was Alain Robbe-Grillet (*Jealousy*, 1957).

The Austrian writer Franz Kafka's haunting, dreamlike narratives (*The Trial*, 1925; *The Castle*, 1926) mark him, like his heroes, as a man apart. The French-writing Irishman Samuel Beckett (*Molloy*, 1951; *Malone Dies*, 1951) resembles Kafka in his parables of human futility and Joyce in his love of word play.

In Russia, Tolstoy's influence on later writers was reinforced by Marxist aesthetics. Maksim Gorki (*The Mother*, 1907), Mikhail Sholokhov (*And Quiet Flows the Don*, 1934), and Boris Pasternak (*Doctor Zhivago*, 1956) continued to deal with the interrelationships of personal problems and political events. The Russian émigré Vladimir Nabokov (*Lolita*, 1955; *Pale Fire*, 1962), who wrote in German and in English, spurned the moral and philosophical concerns of Tolstoy for an aestheticism suggestive of Proust.

England. "The historian of fine consciences" was what Joseph Conrad called Henry James, and so was Conrad himself. He was the novelist of extreme situations, of man striving to be loyal to an ideal conception of himself, as in *Lord Jim* (1900). A naturalized British subject, born in Poland, Conrad was a sailor for 20 years, and these experiences gave him the material for much of his work; he celebrated the life of the sea and the exotic East with an eloquence unsurpassed. In his great novel, *Nostromo* (1904), he turned an imaginary South American country—prey to the forces of nationalism, conservatism, liberalism, imperialism, and commercial exploitation—into a microcosm of the modern world.

Conrad showed the futility of all human action. He was philosophically and temperamentally at odds with his English contemporaries, H. G. Wells and Arnold Bennett. Bennett's *The Old Wives' Tale* (1908) and the *Clayhanger* trilogy (1910–15) showed the effects of environ-

ment—the industrial English Midlands—on his characters; Wells, a man bristling with ideas, preached in novels of immense liveliness and comic invention (*Tono-Bungay*, 1909) the gospel of education and scientific progress.

By 1914, among progressive thinkers, faith in the social sciences had been displaced, at least temporarily, by psychoanalysis and the light it threw on the irrational in human behavior. Proof of Sigmund Freud's theory of the Oedipus complex (thought to be the key to the nature of sexual relations) seemed offered by D. H. Lawrence's novel *Sons and Lovers* (1913). Written with great lyrical intensity, it tells of a young man's growing up in a coal-mining community. In *The Rainbow* (1915), *Women in Love* (1920), and *Lady Chatterley's Lover* (1928), Lawrence explored the nature of female sexuality.

Stream of consciousness was used in ways more delicate and cerebral than Joyce by Virginia Woolf in *Mrs. Dalloway* (1925), *To the Lighthouse* (1927), and *The Waves* (1931). E. M. Forster (*Howards End*, 1910; *A Passage to India*, 1924) rendered in ironical comedy and delicate symbolism the clash between classes and races.

The novel in England since the death of Joyce has been criticized for lack of comic inventiveness. Nonetheless, Evelyn Waugh (*Decline and Fall*, 1928; *A Handful of Dust*, 1934), Joyce Cary (*The Horse's Mouth*, 1944), Kingsley Amis (*Lucky Jim*, 1954), and Iris Murdoch (*A Severed Head*, 1961; *Nuns and Soldiers*, 1981) have all contributed to the tradition of English comic writing.

A most brilliant storyteller, much influenced by cinema, Graham Greene (*The Power and the Glory*, 1940; *The End of the Affair*, 1951; *The Quiet American*, 1955) gained worldwide readership for his novels of sinners pursued by a loving God.

A feature of recent years has been the many novel-sequences whose authors assessed their life experience in records of lives much like their own. Particularly noteworthy were C. P. Snow's *Strangers and Brothers* (11 vol., 1940–70); Anthony Powell's *A Dance to the Music of Time* (12 vol., 1951–75); Doris Lessing's five novels published as *Children of Violence* (1952–69); and Paul Scott's four novels on the end of British rule in India, published as *The Raj Quartet* (1978).

The U.S. American authors early in the 20th century depicted society with a view to reform or revolution. They focused on specific injustices, as did Upton Sinclair (*The Jungle*, 1906), or on the corrupting effects of capitalist society, as did Sinclair Lewis (*Main Street*, 1920; *Babbitt*, 1922), Theodore Dreiser (*An American Tragedy*, 1925), John Dos Passos (*U.S.A.*, collected in 1938),

James T. Farrell (*Studs Lonigan: A Trilogy*, 1935), John Steinbeck (*The Grapes of Wrath*, 1939), and Richard Wright (*Native Son*, 1940).

More subjective, and showing a more original use of language, are the novels of F. Scott Fitzgerald (*The Great Gatsby*, 1925; *Tender Is the Night*, 1934), Ernest Hemingway (*The Sun Also Rises*, 1926; *A Farewell to Arms*, 1929; *For Whom the Bell Tolls*, 1940), Thomas Wolfe (*Look Homeward, Angel*, 1929), and Nathanael West (*The Day of the Locust*, 1939). Fitzgerald's *The Great Gatsby* takes on an extra dimension in that Gatsby transcends the individual and personifies the American dream at one moment in history. The myth-making propensities of American novelists are evident in William Faulkner's works, particularly in *Light in August* (1932) and *Absalom, Absalom!* (1936). Other writers portrayed the decaying South with a perceptive eye for the eccentricities and depths of human character: Katherine Anne Porter (*Noon Wine*, 1937), Robert Penn Warren (*All the King's Men*, 1946), William Styron (*Lie Down in Darkness*, 1951), and Eudora Welty (*The Ponder Heart*, 1954).

After World War II works of great power were published by a group of American-Jewish writers who brought to American fiction a strain from 19th-century Russian fiction: Norman Mailer (*The Naked and the Dead*, 1948), Saul Bellow (*The Adventures of Augie March*, 1953), Bernard Malamud (*The Assistant*, 1957), Joseph Heller (1923– ; *Catch-22*, 1961), Philip Roth (*Goodbye, Columbus*, 1959), and Isaac Bashevis Singer, who won the Nobel Prize in 1978 for his novels and short stories. Among significant American novelists today are John Updike (the three *Rabbit* novels, 1960–81), James Baldwin (*Go Tell It on the Mountain*, 1953; *Tell Me How Long the Train's Been Gone*, 1968), and Joyce Carol Oates (1938–), a prolific writer of poetry and criticism as well as novels (*Garden of Earthly Delights*, 1967; *Wonderland*, 1971; *A Bloodsmoor Romance*, 1982).

See also articles on the literature of the various nations of the world, such as AMERICAN LITERATURE.   W.A.

For further information on this topic, see the Bibliography in volume 28, section 823.

NOVEMBER, 11th month of the Gregorian calendar, having 30 days. Among the Romans it was the ninth month of a year composed of 10 months. November consisted of 29 days until Julius Caesar gave it 31 days in his calendar.

NOVENA, in Roman Catholic practice, nine days of public or private prayer. The custom of extending a devotion nine days is of Roman origin: The *parentalia novendialia* was a nine-day observance celebrated by the ancient Romans in honor of deceased family members. The custom was adopted for Christian usage during the 17th century, although its prototype is sometimes seen in the period of prayer spent by the disciples of Jesus prior to the descent of the Holy Spirit (see Acts 1–2). Private novenas are frequently made in honor of the Virgin Mary. Perhaps the best-known liturgical novena is in honor of the Holy Spirit, celebrated as a preparation for Pentecost Sunday. Although the practice can appear superstitious, it is considered a legitimate devotional aid to extended prayer.

NOVERRE, Jean Georges (1727–1810), French choreographer, whose efforts to reform ballet led to his comparison with his friend, the German composer and opera reformer Christoph Willibald Gluck. Born in Paris, Noverre studied under the noted French dancer Louis Dupré (1697–1774) and was influenced by the French dance reformer Marie Sallé (1707–56). He later studied mime under the English actor David Garrick. Noverre made his debut as a dancer in 1743 and in 1754 became ballet master at the Paris Opéra-Comique. Finding little support in France for his theories, which included discarding traditional masks and subordinating virtuosity to dramatic requirements, he worked in various German cities. In 1755 Garrick invited him to London to revive his first ballet. *Les fêtes Chinoises* (Chinese Festival, 1749). In 1760 he became ballet master in Stuttgart (now in West Germany), where he produced his famous ballet *Médée et Jason* (1763). Under the patronage of his former student Queen Marie Antoinette of France, he obtained a long-desired position as director of the Paris Opéra in 1776. During the French Revolution he taught in England. His most influential writings are his *Lettres sur la danse* (1760).

NOVGOROD, city, capital of Novgorod Oblast, Russian SFSR, in W European USSR, on the Volkhov R., near Lake Ilmen. The city is the commercial center for a rich farm region, and industries here produce fertilizer, processed food, furniture, and china. Novgorod retains examples of early Russian architecture, including the Kremlin and the Hagia Sophia (Cathedral of the Holy Wisdom; both 11th cent.).

One of the oldest Russian cities, Novgorod was founded as early as the 5th or 6th century. In 862 Rurik, founder of the Russian monarchy, became prince of Novgorod. In 1136 the city achieved independence from Kiev and, with a democratic form of government, became the capital of sovereign Great Novgorod. In the 13th and 14th centuries, Novgorod flourished as a trade outpost of the Hanseatic League and was a major cultural center. It repulsed Tatar invasions in the late 13th century. In 1478 the city was annexed by its rival, Moscow, under Ivan III. The city declined as a trading center after the establishment of nearby Saint Petersburg (now Leningrad) in 1703. During the German occupation (1941–44) of World War II, the city was severely damaged. Pop. (1980 est.) 192,000.

NOVI SAD, city, N Yugoslavia, capital of Vojvodina Autonomous Province, on the Danube R., near Belgrade. It is the commercial center of an important agricultural area. Industries include the manufacturing of electrochemical equipment, industrial porcelain, candy, and agricultural machinery. Novi Sad also has factories engaged in the manufacture of electrical equipment, textiles, chemicals, and pottery. Founded in 1670, the city was the cultural center of the Serbian people in the 18th and 19th centuries. It was incorporated into Yugoslavia in 1918. Pop. (est.) 213,900.

NOVOCAINE. See PROCAINE.

NOVOKUZNETSK, formerly STALINSK, city, Russian SFSR, in S Siberian USSR. A major industrial center in the mineral-rich Kuznetsk Basin, the city is at the head of navigation of the Tom R. and is served by several rail lines. Manufactures include iron and steel, chemicals, aluminum, and coke. The city was founded in 1617 as Kuznetsk around a Russian fortress. In 1932 an iron and steel works was completed nearby, and the new industrial sector was united with the older settlement and named Stalinsk. The city was renamed Novokuznetsk in 1961. Pop. (1980 est.) 545,000.

NOVOSIBIRSK, formerly NOVONIKOLAYEVSK, city, capital of Novosibirsk Oblast, Russian SFSR, in S Siberian USSR. Located on the Ob R., Novosibirsk is the largest city and one of the chief industrial centers of Siberia. Manufactures include mining equipment, turbines, textiles, chemicals, and heavy machine tools. It is the seat of a university and a scientific research center and has opera and ballet companies. The city, founded in 1893 as a stop on the new Trans-Siberian Railroad, received its present name in 1925. During World War II many industries were moved to Novosibirsk from the combat areas of European USSR. Pop. (1980 est.) 1,328,000.

NOYES, John Humphrey (1811–86), American social reformer, founder of the Oneida Community, born in Brattleboro, Vt., and educated at Dartmouth College and Yale Divinity School. In 1833 he was licensed as a Congregational minister but the following year lost his license because of his "perfectionist" doctrine that attributed a dual sexual nature to God and taught that no one was bound by any moral code be-

cause Jesus Christ saved the human race from sin. Noyes experimented with communal living, establishing the Perfectionist Community in Putney, Vt., in the late 1830s. In 1846 public condemnation of his tenet of "complex marriage," the practice of free sexual sharing within a community, forced him to disband his community; two years later he reestablished it in Oneida, N.Y. Faced with adultery charges, Noyes fled to Canada in 1880. He wrote a number of religious treatises, including *Bible Communism* (1848) and *Scientific Propagation* (c. 1873).

NU, U (1907–), first prime minister (1948–58 and 1960–62) of independent Burma. He was born in Wakema and educated at Rangoon University. As a member of the Thakin movement (*see* BURMA) and president of the student union, he took part, along with Aung San and Ne Win, in staging the student strike of 1936. During the Japanese occupation in World War II, Nu served as foreign minister in the Japanese-backed government of Ba Maw (1897–1977). In 1947, when Aung San was assassinated, Nu assumed leadership of the nationalist movement and negotiated the independence agreement with the British. He became prime minister the following year. As such he held the country together during the turbulent postindependence years and was widely respected abroad for his contributions to the Nonaligned Nations. He failed, however, to provide effective administrative leadership at home, and in 1958 he stepped down temporarily for Ne Win's army government. Voted in again in 1960, he was finally removed by Ne Win's coup in 1962. After that U Nu was long exiled, but he was allowed to return to Burma in 1980.

NUBIA, region, NE Africa, roughly occupying both sides of the Nile R. valley between Aswan, Egypt, and Khartoum, Sudan. The area of the region in NE Sudan is called the Nubian Desert. In ancient times Nubia was called Cush and ruled by Egypt for some 1800 years. In the 8th century BC the Nubians achieved independence and subjugated Egypt. After maintaining some degree of independence for more than 2000 years, Nubia was conquered by the Arabs in the 14th century and by Egypt in 1820. In the late 19th century the region was controlled by the Muslim revolutionary leader known as the Mahdi.

NUCLEAR CHEMISTRY, the study of atomic nuclei, especially of radioactive nuclei, and their reactions with neutrons and other nuclei (*see* ATOM AND ATOMIC THEORY).

Nuclide Decay. Atomic nuclei consist of positively charged protons and neutral, or uncharged, neutrons (*see* NEUTRON; PROTON). The number of protons in a nucleus is also the atomic number,

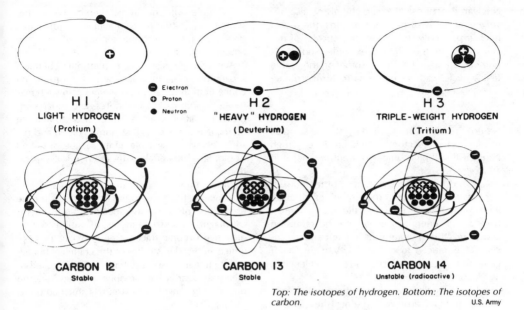

H 1 LIGHT HYDROGEN (Protium)	● Electron ⊕ Proton ● Neutron

H 2
"HEAVY" HYDROGEN
(Deuterium)

H 3
TRIPLE-WEIGHT HYDROGEN
(Tritium)

CARBON 12
Stable

CARBON 13
Stable

CARBON 14
Unstable (radioactive)

Top: The isotopes of hydrogen. Bottom: The isotopes of carbon.   U.S. Army

which defines the chemical element. All nuclei, for example, with 11 protons are nuclei of sodium (Na) atoms (see ELEMENTS, CHEMICAL). An element can have various isotopes the nuclei of which have differing numbers of neutrons (see ISOTOPE). For example, stable sodium nuclei contain 12 neutrons, whereas those with 13 are radioactive. These isotopes are notated as $^{23}_{11}Na_{12}$ and $^{24}_{11}Na_{13}$, where the left-hand subscript indicates the atomic number and the right-hand, the number of neutrons. The superscript represents the total number of nucleons, or neutrons and protons. Any species of nucleus designated by certain atomic and neutron numbers is called a nuclide.

Radioactive nuclides are unstable: They undergo spontaneous transformation into nuclides of other elements, releasing energy in the process (see RADIOACTIVITY). These transformations include alpha (α) decay (the emission of a helium nucleus, $^4_2He^{2+}$), and beta (β) decay or positron (β^+) decay. In β decay a neutron is transformed into a proton with the simultaneous emission of a high-energy electron. In β^+ decay a nuclear proton converts into a neutron with the emission of a high-energy positron (see ELEMENTARY PARTICLES). For example, ^{24}Na undergoes β decay to form the next higher element, magnesium:

$$^{24}_{11}Na_{13} \rightarrow {}^{24}_{12}Mg_{12} + \beta + \gamma \text{ rays}$$

Gamma (γ) radiation, like light, is electromagnetic radiation (q.v.), but by virtue of their much higher frequency, γ rays are enormously more powerful. When α or β decay occurs, the resulting nucleus is often left in an excited (higher energy) state. Gamma rays are emitted as the nucleus drops to a lower energy state. See also ELECTRON; POSITRON.

Any characterization of radioactive nuclide decay must include a determination of the half-life of the nuclide, that is, the time it takes for half of a sample to decay. The half-life of ^{24}Na, for example, is 15 hours. Nuclear chemists also determine the types and energies of radiation emitted by the nuclide.

Early Experiments. Radioactivity was discovered in uranium salts by the French physicist Henri Becquerel in 1896. In 1898 the French scientists Marie and Pierre Curie discovered the naturally occurring radioactive elements polonium ($_{84}Po$) and radium ($_{88}Ra$). During the 1930s, Irène and Frédérick Joliot-Curie made the first artificial radioactive nuclides by bombarding boron ($_5B$) and aluminum ($_{13}Al$) with α particles to form radioactive isotopes of nitrogen ($_7N$) and phosphorus ($_{15}P$). Naturally occurring isotopes of these elements are stable.

The German nuclear chemists Otto Hahn and Fritz Strassmann (1902–) discovered nuclear fission in 1938. When uranium is irradiated with neutrons, some uranium nuclei split into two nuclei of about half the atomic number of uranium. Fission releases enormous energy and is used in nuclear fission weapons and reactors (see NUCLEAR ENERGY).

Nuclear Reactions. Nuclear chemistry also involves the study of nuclear reactions: the use of nuclear projectiles to convert one species of nucleus into another. If, for example, sodium is bombarded with neutrons, some of the stable $^{23}_{11}Na_{12}$ nuclei capture neutrons to form radioactive $^{24}_{11}Na_{13}$ nuclei:

$$^{23}_{11}Na_{12} + ^{1}_{0}n_{1} \rightarrow ^{24}_{11}Na_{13}$$

Neutron reactions are studied by placing samples inside nuclear reactors, which produce a high neutron flux (high number of neutrons per unit area).

Nuclei can also react with each other, but being positively charged, they repel each other with great force. The projectile nucleus must have a high energy to overcome the repulsion and to react with target nuclei. High-energy nuclei are produced in cyclotrons, Van de Graaff generators, or other electronuclear accelerators. *See* Particle Accelerators.

A typical nuclear reaction is the one that was used to produce artificially the next heavier element above uranium ($_{92}U$), the heaviest element that occurs in nature (*see* Periodic Law). Neptunium ($_{93}Np$) was made by bombarding uranium (mostly $^{238}_{92}U$) with deuterons (nuclei of the heavy hydrogen isotope, $^{2}_{1}H_{1}$) to knock out two neutrons, forming $^{238}_{93}Np$:

$$^{238}_{92}U_{146} + ^{2}_{1}H_{1} \rightarrow ^{238}_{93}Np_{145} + 2\,^{1}_{0}n_{1}$$

Radiochemical Analysis. Alpha particles, most of which are emitted by elements with atomic numbers above 83, have discrete energies characteristic of the emitting nuclide. Thus, α emitters can be identified by measuring the energies of the α particles. The samples being measured must be very thin, as α particles lose energy rapidly on passing through material. Gamma rays also have discrete energies characteristic of the decaying nuclide, so γ-ray energies can also be used to identify nuclides. Because γ rays can pass through considerable material without losing energy, samples need not be thin. Beta-particle (and positron) energy spectra are not useful for identifying nuclides; they are spread over all energies up to a maximum for each β emitter. *See* Particle Detectors.

Nuclear-chemical techniques are frequently used to analyze materials for trace elements—elements that occur in minute amounts. The technique used is called activation analysis. A sample is irradiated with nuclear projectiles, usually neutrons, to convert stable nuclides into radioactive ones, which are then measured with nuclear radiation detectors. For example, any sodium in a sample can be detected by irradiating the sample with neutrons, thereby converting some of the stable $^{23}_{11}Na_{12}$ nuclei into radioactive ^{24}Na and measuring the amount of ^{24}Na by counting the β particles and v rays emitted.

Activation analysis can (without chemical separation) measure nanogram (4×10^{-11} oz) concentrations of about 35 elements in such materials as soil, rocks, meteorites, and lunar samples. Activiation analysis can be used to analyze biological samples, such as human blood and tissue; however, fewer elements can be observed in biological materials without chemical separations.

Other important applications of nuclear chemistry include the development of methods for the production of radioactive species used for medical diagnoses and treatments, as well as for radioactive isotopic tracers (see Isotopic Tracer), which are used in studies of the chemical behavior of elements. Isotopic tracers are also used to measure wear in automobile engines, and in other studies involving extremely small amounts of material.

See also articles on the chemical elements mentioned above.   G.E.G.

NUCLEAR ENERGY, energy released during the splitting or fusing of atomic nuclei. The energy of any system, whether physical, chemical, or nuclear, is manifested by its ability to do work or to release heat or radiation. The total energy in a system is always conserved, but it can be transferred to another system or changed in form.

Until about 1800 the principal fuel was wood, its energy derived from solar energy stored in plants during their lifetimes. Since the Industrial Revolution, people have depended on fossil fuels—coal and petroleum—also derived ultimately from solar energy stored over geological time spans. When a fossil fuel such as coal is burned, atoms of hydrogen and carbon in the coal combine with oxygen atoms in air; water and carbon dioxide are produced and heat is released, equivalent to about 3.6 kwh per lb or about 10 eV per atom of carbon. This amount of energy is typical of chemical reactions resulting from changes in the electronic structure of the atoms. A part of the energy released as heat keeps the adjacent fuel hot enough to keep the reaction going.

The Nuclear Atom. The atom consists of a small, massive, positively charged core (nucleus) surrounded by electrons (see Atom and Atomic Theory). The nucleus, containing most of the mass of the atom, is itself composed of neutrons and protons bound together by very strong nuclear forces, much greater than the electrical forces that bind the electrons to the nucleus. The mass number A of a nucleus is the number of nucleons, or neutrons and protons, it contains; the atomic number Z is the number of positively charged protons. A specific nucleus is designated as $^A_Z X$. The expression $^{235}_{92}$U, for example, represents uranium-235. *See* ISOTOPE.

The binding energy of a nucleus is a measure of how tightly its neutrons and protons are held together by the nuclear forces. The binding energy per nucleon, the energy required to remove one neutron or proton from a nucleus, is a function of the mass number A. The curve of binding energy implies that if two light nuclei near the left end of the curve coalesce to form a heavier nucleus, or if a heavy nucleus at the far right splits into two lighter ones, more tightly bound nuclei result, and energy will be released.

Nuclear energy can be released by the fusion of two light nuclei, for example, when two heavy hydrogen nuclei, deuterons ($^2_1$H), combine, in the reaction

$$^2_1 H + {}^2_1 H \rightarrow {}^3_1 He + {}^1_0 n + 3.2\ \text{MeV} \quad (1)$$

producing a helium-3 atom, a free neutron ($^1_0$n), and 3.2 MeV, or 5.1×10^{-13} J (1.2×10^{-13} cal). Nuclear energy is also released when the fission of a heavy nucleus such as $^{235}_{92}$U is induced by the absorption of a neutron.

$$^1_0 n + {}^{235}_{92} U \rightarrow {}^{140}_{55} Cs + {}^{93}_{37} Rb + \\ 3\,{}^1_0 n + 200\ \text{MeV} \quad (2)$$

producing cesium-140, rubidium-93, three neutrons, and 200 MeV, or 3.2×10^{-11} J (7.7×10^{-12} cal). The energy per nuclear reaction is measured in millions of electron volts. A fission reaction releases 10 million times as much energy as is released in a typical chemical reaction. *See* NUCLEAR CHEMISTRY.

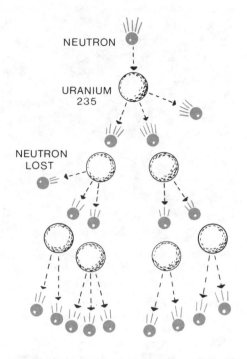

Neutrons released by fission of one atom produce additional fissions, causing a self-sustaining chain reaction.
U.S. Atomic Energy Commission

Nuclear Energy from Fission. The two key characteristics of nuclear fission important for the practical release of nuclear energy are both evident in equation (2). First, the energy per fission is very large. In practical units, the fission of 1 lb (0.454 kg) of uranium-235 releases 8.5 million kwh as heat. Second, the fission process initiated by the absorption of one neutron in uranium-235

Differences in hydrogen atoms. All hydrogen isotopes have one electron and one neutron; deuterium also contains a neutron; tritium has a second neutron, making it radioactive.
Oak Ridge Institute of Nuclear Studies

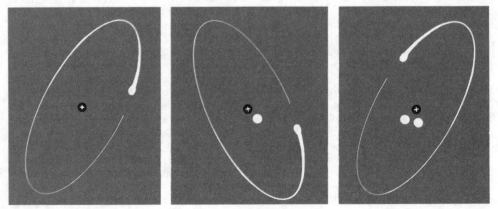

The world's first nuclear reactor, at the University of Chicago, produced thermal power of about 200 W. Today, reactors produce more than a million thermal kilowatts.
Argonne National Laboratory

releases about 2.5 neutrons, on the average, from the split nuclei. The occurrence of a chain reaction is therefore possible.

Naturally occurring uranium contains only 0.71 percent uranium-235; the remainder is the non-fissile isotope uranium-238. A mass of natural uranium by itself, no matter how large, cannot sustain a chain reaction because only the uranium-235 is easily fissionable. The probability that a fission neutron with an initial energy of about 1 MeV will induce fission is rather low, but can be increased by a factor of hundreds when the neutron is slowed down through a series of elastic collisions with light nuclei such as hydrogen, deuterium, or carbon. This fact is the basis for the design of practical energy-producing fission reactors.

In December 1942 at the University of Chicago, the Italian physicist Enrico Fermi succeeded in producing the first nuclear chain reaction. This was done with an arrangement of natural uranium lumps distributed within a large stack of pure graphite, a form of carbon. In Fermi's "pile," or nuclear reactor, the graphite moderator served to slow the neutrons.

NUCLEAR POWER REACTORS

The first large-scale nuclear reactors were built in 1944 at Hanford, Wash., for the production of nuclear weapons material. The fuel was natural uranium metal; the moderator, graphite. Plutonium was produced in these plants by neutron absorption in uranium-238; the power produced was not used.

Light and Heavy Water Reactors. A variety of reactor types, characterized by the type of fuel, moderator, and coolant used, have been built throughout the world since then for the production of electric power. In the U.S., with few exceptions, power reactors use nuclear fuel in the form of uranium oxide isotopically enriched to about 3 percent uranium-235. The moderator and coolant are highly purified ordinary water. A reactor of this type is called a light water reactor (LWR).

In the pressurized water reactor (PWR), a version of the LWR system, the water coolant operates at a pressure of about 150 atm. It is pumped through the reactor core, where it is heated to about 325° C (about 620° F). The superheated water then passes through a steam generator where steam is produced to drive one or more turbine-generator systems. The reactor pressure vessel is about 15 m (about 49 ft) high and 5 m (about 16.4 ft) in diameter, with walls 25 cm (about 10 in) thick. The core houses some 82 metric tons of uranium oxide contained in thin corrosion-resistant tubes, clustered into fuel bundles.

In the boiling water reactor (BWR), a second type of LWR, the water coolant is permitted to boil within the core, by operating at somewhat lower pressure. The steam produced directly in the reactor pressure vessel is used to drive the turbine. No external steam generator is required.

The power level of an operating reactor is monitored by a variety of thermal, flow, and nuclear instruments. Power output is controlled by inserting or removing from the core a group of neutron-absorbing control rods. The position of these rods determines the power level at which

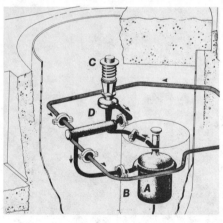

The molten-salt reactor (top) is a complex system designed for low-cost electric power production of nuclear fission. The simplified line drawing (above) shows (A) reactor vessel, where the fuel (highly radioactive fluoride salts of uranium, lithium, beryllium, and zirconium) is circulated at 649° C (1200° F) to produce 10,000 kw in heat by fission; (B) thermal shield; (C) fuel pump; (D) heat exchanger, where the heat is removed for power production. Controlled thermonuclear fusion has been achieved experimentally with the use of complex devices such as the DCX-2 system (right), developed at the Oak Ridge National Laboratory. The DCX-2 is capable of creating a dense plasma of heavy hydrogen at temperatures of more than 100,000,000° C (212,000,000° F). Oak Ridge National Laboratory

the chain reaction is just self-sustaining. Another set of absorber rods, the safety rods, can be driven rapidly into the core to terminate the chain reaction in the event of any abnormal system behavior.

During operation, and even after shutdown, a large 1000-megawatt (Mw) power reactor contains billions of curies of radioactivity. Radiation emitted from the reactor during operation and from the fission products after shutdown is absorbed in thick concrete shields around the reactor and primary coolant system. Other safety features include emergency core cooling systems to prevent core overheating in the event of malfunction of the main coolant systems, a large steel and concrete containment building to retain any radioactive elements that might escape from the reactor in the event of a leak, and spray cooling systems to ensure the integrity of the containment building in the event of a pressure rise within it.

More than 100 LWR plants were operating or being built in the U.S. in the early 1980s, with comparable numbers in other countries. In 1980 about 12 percent of the electric energy generated in the U.S. came from such nuclear power plants.

In the initial period of nuclear power development in the early 1950s, enriched uranium was available only in the U.S. and the USSR. The nuclear power programs in Canada, France, and Great Britain therefore centered about natural uranium reactors, in which ordinary water cannot be used as the moderator because it absorbs too many neutrons. In response to this limitation, Canadian engineers developed a reactor cooled and moderated by deuterium oxide (D_2O), or heavy water. The ten-reactor CANDU system has operated satisfactorily, and similar plants have been built in India, Argentina, and elsewhere.

In Great Britain and France the first full-scale power reactors were fueled with natural uranium metal rods, graphite-moderated, and cooled with carbon dioxide gas under pressure. These initial designs have been superseded in Great Britain by a system that uses enriched uranium fuel. In France the initial reactor type chosen was dropped in favor of the PWR of U.S. design when enriched uranium became available from French

The second nuclear-powered aircraft carrier of the U.S. Navy, the 95,000-ton USS Nimitz, joined the Atlantic Fleet in 1975. The world's largest warship can operate for 13 years without refueling.   U.S. Navy

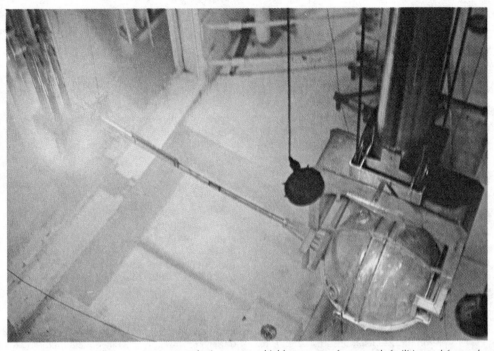

In neutron physics, reactor shields necessary for research facilities and for nuclear power applications, for instance, in nuclear submarines, are tested in experiments such as the manganese salt bath. The reactor is seen glowing at the left in the picture; the sphere to the right contains fissionable materials such as uranium-233 and uranium-238 and the salt solution.   Oak Ridge National Laboratory

isotope-enrichment plants. The USSR has a large nuclear power program, using both graphite-moderated and PWR systems.

Propulsion Reactors. Nuclear power plants similar to the PWR are used for the propulsion plants of large surface naval vessels such as the aircraft carrier USS *Nimitz*. The basic technology of the PWR system was first developed in the U.S. naval reactor program directed by Adm. Hyman G. Rickover. Reactors for submarine propulsion are generally physically smaller and use more highly enriched uranium to permit a compact core. The U.S., Great Britain, the USSR, and France all have nuclear-powered submarines with such power plants.

Three experimental seagoing nuclear cargo ships were operated for limited periods by the U.S., Germany, and Japan. Although they were technically successful, economic conditions and restrictive port regulations brought an end to these projects. The USSR built the first nuclear-powered icebreaker, the *Lenin*, which has operated successfully in clearing Arctic sea-lanes.

Research Reactors. A variety of small nuclear reactors have been built in many countries for use in education and training, research, and the pro-duction of radioactive isotopes for industry, agriculture, and medicine (*see* ISOTOPIC TRACER). These reactors generally operate at power levels near 1 Mw, except at major national nuclear development centers.

A widely used type is called the swimming pool reactor. The core is partially or fully enriched uranium-235 contained in aluminum alloy plates, immersed in a large pool of water that serves as both coolant and moderator. The neutrons produced in the reactor are absorbed by appropriate materials to produce radioisotopes, or they are allowed to leave the reactor in special beam tubes for experimental purposes.

Breeder Reactors. Uranium, the natural resource on which nuclear power is based, occurs in scattered deposits throughout the world. Its total supply is not fully known and may be limited unless very low concentration sources such as granites and shale were to be used. Conservatively estimated U.S. resources of uranium having an acceptable cost lie in the range of 2 to 5 million metric tons. The lower amount could support an LWR nuclear power system providing about 30 percent of U.S. electric power for only about 50 years. The principal reason for this relatively brief life span of the LWR nuclear power system is its very low efficiency in the use of uranium: Only approximately 1 perent of the energy content of the uranium is made available in this system.

The key feature of a breeder reactor is that it produces more fuel than it consumes. It does this by promoting the absorption of excess neutrons in a fertile material such as uranium-238. Several breeder reactor systems are technically feasible. In one type, thorium is the fertile material. It is transmuted by neutron absorption in a reactor into uranium-233, a fissionable isotope of uranium similar to the naturally occurring uranium-235. The breeder system that has received the greatest worldwide attention uses uranium-238 as the fertile material. When uranium-238 absorbs neutrons in the reactor, it is transmuted to a new fissionable material, plutonium, through a nuclear process called β (beta) decay. The sequence of nuclear reactions is

$$^{238}_{92}U + ^{1}_{0}n \rightarrow ^{239}_{92}U \xrightarrow[\beta]{} ^{239}_{93}Np \xrightarrow[\beta]{} ^{239}_{94}Pu \quad (3)$$

In beta decay a nuclear neutron decays into a proton and a beta particle (q.v.).

When plutonium-239 itself absorbs a neutron, fission can occur, and on the average about 2.8 neutrons are released. In an operating reactor, one of these neutrons is needed to cause the next fission and keep the chain reaction going. On the average about 0.5 neutron is uselessly lost by absorption in the reactor structure or coolant. The remaining 1.3 neutrons can be absorbed in uranium-238 to produce more plutonium via the reactions in equation (3).

The breeder system that has had the greatest development effort is called the liquid metal fast breeder reactor (LMFBR). In order to maximize the production of plutonium-239, the velocity of the neutrons causing fission must remain fast—at or near their initial release energy. Any moderating materials that might slow the neutrons must be excluded from the reactor. For this reason water cannot be used as the coolant. A molten metal, liquid sodium, is the preferred coolant liquid. Sodium has very good heat transfer properties, melts at about 100° C (about 212° F), and does not boil until about 900° C (about 1650° F). Its main drawbacks are its chemical reactivity with air and water and the high level of radioactivity induced in it in the reactor.

Development of the LMFBR system began in the U.S. before 1950, with the construction of the first experimental breeder reactor, EBR-1. Subsequently, numerous other experimental plants were built in the U.S., Great Britain, the USSR, France, Germany, and Japan. These have served to prepare the way for large plants for electric power production.

In one design of a large LMFBR power plant, the core of the reactor consists of thousands of thin stainless steel tubes containing mixed uranium and plutonium oxide fuel: about 15 to 20 percent plutonium-239, the remainder uranium. Surrounding the core is a region called the breeder blanket, which contains similar rods filled only with uranium oxide. The entire core and blanket assembly measures about 3 m (about 10 ft) high by about 5 m (about 16.4 ft) in diameter and is supported in a large vessel containing molten sodium that leaves the reactor at about 500° C (about 930° F). This vessel also contains the pumps and heat exchangers that aid in removing heat from the core. Steam is produced in a second sodium loop, separated from the radioactive reactor coolant loop by the intermediate heat exchangers in the reactor vessel. As in the LWRs, the entire nuclear reactor system is housed in a large steel and concrete containment building.

The first large-scale plant of this type for the generation of electricity, called Super-Phenix, is under construction in France. An intermediate-scale plant, the BN-600 was built in the USSR on the shore of the Caspian Sea for the production of power and the desalination of water. The British have a large 250-Mw prototype in operation in Scotland.

The LMFBR produces about 20 percent more fuel than it consumes. In a large power reactor enough excess new fuel is produced over 20 years to permit the loading of another similar reactor. In the LMFBR system about 75 percent of the energy content of natural uranium is made available, in contrast to the 1 percent in the LWR.

NUCLEAR FUELS AND WASTES

The hazardous fuels used in nuclear reactors present handling problems throughout the course of their use. This is particularly true of the spent fuels, which must be stored or disposed of in some way.

The Nuclear Fuel Cycle. Any electric power generating plant is only one part of a total energy cycle. The nuclear fuel cycle includes many steps. In the U.S., uranium is mined and the ore concentrated at scattered mines in the western states. The concentrated ore is shipped to a conversion plant, where its chemical form is changed to uranium hexafluoride gas, UF_6, the feed material for an isotope enrichment plant. In the latter facility, natural uranium containing 0.7 percent uranium-235 is separated into two streams, one enriched to about 3 percent uranium-235, the other a depleted stream—the

This photograph of the experimental breeder-reactor room at the Argonne National Laboratory, in Argonne, Ill., shows the circular reactor itself housed in a large tank of liquid sodium located beneath the center structure. The remote-controlled equipment located at the left is used by scientists to both load and unload the reactor from a safe distance.
Argonne National Laboratory

tails—containing most of the original uranium, now at a concentration of about 0.3 percent uranium-235. The tails stream is stored and the enriched product sent to a fuel fabrication plant. There the enriched UF_6 gas is converted to uranium oxide powder, then into ceramic pellets that are loaded into corrosion-resistant fuel rods. These are assembled into fuel elements and are shipped to the reactor power plant.

A typical 1000-Mw pressurized water reactor has about 200 fuel elements, one-third of which are replaced each year because of the depletion of the uranium-235 and the buildup of fission products that absorb neutrons. At the end of its life in the reactor, the fuel is tremendously radioactive because of the fission products it contains

and hence is still producing a considerable amount of energy. The discharged fuel is placed in water storage pools at the reactor site for a year or more.

At the end of the cooling period the spent fuel elements are shipped in heavily shielded casks either to permanent storage facilities, or to a chemical reprocessing plant where the unused uranium and the plutonium-239 produced in the reactor are recovered and the radioactive wastes concentrated. (In the early 1980s neither such facility was yet available in the U.S. for power plant fuel, and temporary storage was used.)

The spent fuel still contains almost all the original uranium-238, about one-third of the uranium-235, and some of the plutonium-239 produced in the reactor. In cases where the spent fuel is sent to permanent storage, none of this potential energy content is used. In cases where the fuel is reprocessed, the uranium is recycled through the diffusion plant, and the recovered plutonium-239 may be used in place of some uranium-235 in new fuel elements.

The low use of uranium in the LWR system is evident from these fuel cycles. In the open cycle, most of the feed uranium ends up in the tails stream and waste storage. Even in the closed cycle, where the uranium-235 and plutonium-239 are recovered and reused, only about 1 percent of the total uranium energy potential is used.

The fuel cycle for the LMFBR must be a closed one, because the plutonium bred in the reactor is recycled for use in new fuel. The feed to the fuel element fabrication plant consists of recycled uranium-238, depleted uranium from the isotope separation plant stockpile, and part of the recovered plutonium-239. No additional uranium needs to be mined, as the existing tails stockpile could support many breeder reactors for centuries. Because the breeder produces more pluto-

This cardiac pacemaker is powered by a minute thermo-electric generator, fueled by plutonium-238. Because of this fuel, the pacemaker requires surgical replacement only about once every ten years. National Institutes of Health

nium-239 than it requires for its own refueling, about 20 percent of the recovered plutonium is stored for later use in starting up new breeders. Because new fuel is bred from the uranium-238, instead of using only the natural uranium-235 content, about 75 percent of the potential energy of uranium is made available with the breeder cycle.

The final step in any of the fuel cycles is the long-term storage of the highly radioactive wastes, which remain biologically hazardous for thousands of years. Several technologies appear satisfactory for the safe storage of wastes, but no large-scale facilities have been built to demonstrate the process. In the open LWR fuel cycle, the fuel elements would be stored in shielded, guarded repositories for later final disposition. In the closed cycles the concentrated wastes would be converted to very stable compounds, fixed in ceramics or glass, encapsulated in stainless steel canisters, and buried far underground in very stable geological formations.

Nuclear Safety. Public concern about the acceptability of nuclear power from fission arises from two basic features of the system. The first is the high level of radioactivity (q.v.) present at various stages of the nuclear cycle. The second is the fact that the nuclear fuels uranium-235 and plutonium-239 are the materials from which nuclear weapons are made. *See* NUCLEAR WEAPONS; RADIOACTIVE FALLOUT.

U.S. President Dwight D. Eisenhower announced the U.S. Atoms for Peace program in 1953. It was perceived as offering a future of cheap plentiful energy. The utility industry hoped that nuclear power would replace increasingly scarce fossil fuels and lower the cost of electricity. Groups concerned with conserving natural resources foresaw a reduction in air pol-

The spectacular heat glow, caused by the radioactive decay of a pellet of curium-242, depicts a powerful isotopic power source. As in the case of other transuranium elements, curium undergoes fission spontaneously and is an important heat source, providing small packets of power for long periods of time.
Oak Ridge National Laboratory

lution and strip mining. The public in general looked favorably on this new energy source, seeing the program as a realization of hopes for the transition of nuclear power from wartime to peaceful uses. Nevertheless, after this initial euphoria, reservations about nuclear energy grew as greater scrutiny was given to issues of nuclear safety and weapons proliferation. In the U.S. and other countries many groups oppose nuclear power, and the regulatory process has become complex. Sweden, for example, intends to limit its program to about ten reactors. Austria has terminated its program. On the other hand, Great Britain, France, Germany, and Japan are proceeding vigorously.

Radiological hazards. Radioactive materials emit penetrating, ionizing radiation that can injure living tissues. The commonly used unit of exposure is the roentgen equivalent in man, or rem. Each person in the U.S. is exposed to about 0.15 rem per year due to natural background radiation sources. An exposure to an individual of 500 rem is likely to be fatal. A large population exposed to low levels of radiation will experience about one additional cancer for each 10,000 rem total exposure and a similar level of genetic injury. *See* RADIATION EFFECTS, BIOLOGICAL.

Radiological hazards can arise in most steps of the nuclear fuel cycle. Radioactive radon gas is a common air pollutant in underground uranium mines. During the World War II period of the nuclear program, the level to which miners were exposed may have been excessive, but conditions have improved as a result of better instrumentation, improved ventilation systems, and more stringent regulations. The mining and ore-milling operations leave large amounts of waste material, still containing small concentrations of uranium, on the ground. These wastes must be retained in waterproof basins and covered with a thick layer of soil to prevent their indiscriminate release into the biosphere.

Uranium enrichment and fuel fabrication plants contain large quantities of 3 percent uranium-235 in the form of a corrosive gas, uranium hexafluoride, UF_6. The radiological hazard, however, is low, and the usual care taken with a valuable material posing a typical chemical hazard suffices to ensure safety.

Reactor safety systems. The safety of the power reactor itself has received the greatest attention. In an operating reactor, the fuel elements contain by far the largest fraction of the total radioactive inventory. A number of barriers prevent fission products from leaking into the biosphere during normal operation. The fuel is clad in corrosion-resistant tubing. The heavy steel walls of the primary coolant system of the PWR form a second barrier. The water coolant itself absorbs some of the biologically important radioactive isotopes such as iodine. The steel and concrete building is a third barrier.

During the operation of a power reactor, some radioactive effluents are inevitably released. The total exposure to people living nearby is usually only a few percent of the natural background radiation. Major concerns arise, however, from radioactive releases caused by accidents in which fuel damage occurs and safety devices fail. The major danger to the integrity of the fuel is a loss-of-coolant accident in which the fuel is damaged or even melts. Fission products are released into the coolant, and if the coolant system is breached, fission products enter the reactor building.

Reactor systems rely on elaborate instrumentation to monitor their condition and to control the safety systems used to shut down the reactor under abnormal circumstances. Backup safety systems that inject boron into the coolant itself to further assure shutdown are part of the PWR design. Light water reactor plants operate at high coolant pressure. In the event of a large pipe break, much of the coolant would flash into steam and core cooling could be lost. To prevent a total loss of core cooling, reactors are provided with emergency core cooling systems that begin to operate automatically on the loss of primary coolant pressure. In the event of a steam leak into the containment building from a broken primary coolant line, spray coolers are actuated to condense the steam and prevent a hazardous pressure rise in the building.

In safety analyses of plants of this type, the probability of an accident producing severe core damage is estimated to be about 1 in 20,000 per reactor-year. Despite the many safety features described above, however, an accident did occur in 1979 at the Three Mile Island PWR near Harrisburg, Pa. A maintenance error and a defective valve led to a loss-of-coolant accident. The reactor itself was shut down by its safety system when the accident began, and the emergency core cooling system began operating as required a short time into the accident. Through a misunderstanding about the actual state of the system, however, the operators turned off the emergency cooling. Severe core damage occurred, and a substantial fraction of the volatile fission products in the core was released to the containment building. A small amount of radioactive gas escaped from the building; the resulting total human exposure was about 5000 rem. Individual levels, however, were low: Statistically, no more

Construction workers at the Brown's Ferry Nuclear Power Plant near Athens, Ala., install the pressure vessel for one of the reactors. Designed to be the world's largest nuclear generating station, it was closed down temporarily after a fire in March 1975 ignited electric cable insulation and threatened to destroy the plant. Some of the reactor safety systems were damaged, but no radiation escaped. Tennessee Valley Authority

than one person is likely to contract cancer during the next 25 years due to this accident. The financial damage to the utility was very large, $1 billion or more, and the psychological stress on the public, especially those people who live in the area near the nuclear power plant, was in some instances severe.

The official investigation of the accident named operational error and inadequate control room design, rather than simple equipment failure, as the principal causes of the accident. The importance of comprehensive operator training,

management philosophy about safety, and improved regulatory practices was emphasized in the final report.

Fuel reprocessing and waste management. The fuel reprocessing step poses a combination of radiological hazards. One is the accidental release of fission products if a leak should occur in chemical equipment or the cells and building housing it. Another may be the routine release of low levels of inert radioactive gases such as xenon and krypton. The technology needed to ensure safe operation of a chemical reprocessing plant appears feasible, but no plant is yet licensed in the U.S.

Of major concern in chemical reprocessing is the separation of plutonium-239, a weapons material. The hazards of its surreptitious diversion, or intentional but hidden production for weapons purposes, can best be controlled by political rather than technical means. Improved security measures at sensitive points in the fuel cycle and expanded international inspection by the International Atomic Energy Agency (IAEA) offer the best prospects for controlling the hazards of plutonium diversion.

The last step in the nuclear fuel cycle, waste management, remains one of the most controversial. The principal issue here is not so much the present danger as the danger to generations far in the future. Many nuclear wastes remain radioactive for thousands of years, beyond the span of any human institution. The technology for packaging the wastes so that they pose no current hazard is relatively straightforward. The difficulty lies both in being adequately confident that future generations are well protected and in making the political decision on how and where to proceed with waste storage. Permanent but potentially retrievable storage in deep stable geological formations seems the best solution. It is safe for the present and seems likely to be a good long-term solution, and yet leaves the option of using better methods if any become available in the future.

NUCLEAR FUSION

The release of nuclear energy can occur at the low end of the binding energy curve of Fig. 1 through the coalescence of two light nuclei into a heavier one. The energy radiated by stars like the sun arises from such fusion reactions deep in

The amount of energy required to remove a single proton or neutron from an atomic nucleus varies with the weight of the nucleus. The graph of this relationship is called the curve of binding energy.

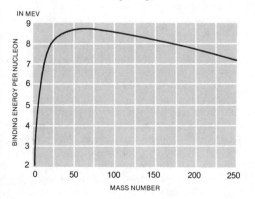

their interiors. At the enormous pressure and at temperatures above 15 million ° C (27 million ° F) existing there, hydrogen nuclei combine according to equation (1) and give rise to most of the energy released by the sun.

Nuclear fusion was first achieved on earth in the early 1930s by bombarding a target containing deuterium, the mass-2 isotope of hydrogen, with high-energy deuterons in a cyclotron (*see* PARTICLE ACCELERATORS). To accelerate the deuteron beam a great deal of energy is required, most of which appeared as heat in the target. As a result, no net useful energy was produced. In the 1950s the first large-scale but uncontrolled release of fusion energy was demonstrated in the tests of thermonuclear weapons by the U.S., the USSR, Great Britain, and France. This was such a brief and uncontrolled release that it could not be used for the production of electric power.

In the fission reactions discussed earlier, the neutron, which has no electric charge, can easily approach and react with a fissionable nucleus, for example, uranium-235. In the typical fusion reaction, however, the reacting nuclei both have a positive electric charge, and the natural repulsion between them, called Coulomb repulsion, must be overcome before they can join. This occurs when the temperature of the reacting gas is sufficiently high—50 to 100 million ° C (90 to 180 million ° F). In a gas of the heavy hydrogen isotopes deuterium and tritium at such temperature, the fusion reaction

$$\begin{aligned} {}_1^2\text{H} + {}_1^3\text{H} &\rightarrow {}_2^4\text{He} + 3.6 \text{ MeV} + \\ &{}_0^1\text{n} + 14 \text{ MeV} \end{aligned} \quad (4)$$

occurs, releasing about 17.6 MeV per fusion event. The energy appears first as kinetic energy of the helium-4 nucleus and the neutron, but is soon transformed into heat in the gas and surrounding materials.

If the density of the gas is sufficient—and at these temperatures the density need be only 10^{-5} atm, or almost a vacuum—the energetic helium-4 nucleus can transfer its energy to the surrounding hydrogen gas, thereby maintaining the high temperature and allowing subsequent fusion reactions, or a fusion chain reaction, to take place. Under these conditions, "nuclear ignition" is said to have occurred.

The basic problems in attaining useful nuclear fusion conditions are (1) to heat the gas to these very high temperatures, and (2) to confine a sufficient quantity of the reacting nuclei for a long enough time to permit the release of more energy than is needed to heat and confine the gas. A subsequent major problem is the capture of this energy and its conversion to electricity.

This experimental apparatus, known as the Elmo Bumpy Torus (EBT) fusion device, represents one line of development in the continuing effort to design a nuclear reactor that will harness the power of nuclear fusion.
Union Carbide Corp.'s Nuclear Division–Oak Ridge National Laboratory

At temperatures of even 100,000° C (180,000° F), all the hydrogen atoms are fully ionized. The gas consists of an electrically neutral assemblage of positively charged nuclei and negatively charged free electrons. This state of matter is called a plasma (q.v.).

A plasma hot enough for fusion cannot be contained by ordinary materials. The plasma would cool very rapidly, and the vessel walls would be destroyed by the temperatures present. However, since the plasma consists of charged nuclei and electrons, which move in tight spirals around strong magnetic field lines, the plasma can be contained in a properly shaped magnetic field region without reacting with material walls.

In any useful fusion device, the energy output must exceed the energy required to confine and heat the plasma. This condition can be met when the product of confinement time τ and plasma density n exceeds about 10^{14}. The relationship $\tau n \geq 10^{14}$ is called the Lawson criterion.

Numerous schemes for the magnetic confinement of plasma have been tried since 1950 in the U.S., the USSR, Great Britain, Japan, and elsewhere. Thermonuclear reactions have been observed, but the Lawson number rarely exceeded

10^{12}. One device, however—the tokamak, originally suggested in the USSR by Igor Tamm and Andrey Sakharov—began to give encouraging results in the early 1960s.

The confinement chamber of a tokamak has the shape of a torus, with a minor diameter of about 1 m (about 3.3 ft) and a major diameter of about 3 m (about 9.8 ft). A toroidal magnetic field of about 50,000 G is established inside this chamber by large electromagnets. A longitudinal current of several million amperes is induced in the plasma by the transformer coils that link the torus. The resulting magnetic field lines, spirals in the torus, stably confine the plasma.

Based on the successful operation of small tokamaks at several laboratories, two large devices were built in the early 1980s, one at Princeton University in the U.S. and one in the USSR. In the tokamak, high plasma temperature naturally results from resistive heating by the very large toroidal current, and additional heating by neutral beam injection in the new large machines should result in "ignition" conditions.

Another possible route to fusion energy is that of inertial confinement. In this concept, the fuel—tritium or deuterium—is contained within a tiny pellet that is then bombarded on several sides by a pulsed laser beam. This causes an implosion of the pellet, setting off a thermonuclear reaction that ignites the fuel. Several laboratories in the U.S. and elsewhere are currently pursuing this possibility.

Progress in fusion research has been promising, but the development of practical systems for breeding tritium and the conversion of fusion energy to electric power has barely begun. The research is expensive, as well; in fact, in 1984 President Ronald Reagan drastically reduced funding for such research, which may force the U.S. to pursue nuclear fusion projects more in conjunction with Japanese and European efforts than in competition with them.

If fusion energy does become practical, it offers the following advantages: (1) a limitless source of fuel, deuterium from the ocean; (2) no possibility of a reactor accident, as the amount of fuel in the system is very small; and (3) waste products much less radioactive and simpler to handle than those from fission systems.   S.Si.

For further information on this topic, see the Bibliography in volume 28, section 537.

NUCLEAR MAGNETIC RESONANCE *or* **NMR,** technique developed in the 1950s by the Swiss-born U.S. physicist Felix Bloch (1905–83) for the spectroscopic analysis of substances. In the early 1980s, NMR also became a diagnostic tool for obtaining more precise images of tissues within the human body than are possible with CAT scans or ultrasonics (*see* RADIOLOGY). In NMR, a substance is placed in a strong magnetic field that affects the spin of the atomic nuclei of certain isotopes of common elements. A radio wave passed through the substance then reorients these nuclei. When the wave is turned off, the nuclei release a pulse of energy that provides data on the molecular structure of the substance and that can be transformed into an image by computer techniques. In its medical applications, NMR is now more commonly referred to as magnetic resonance imaging (MRI), to avoid the negative connotations of the word "nuclear." NMR does not, in fact, involve radioactivity and ionizing radiation.

NUCLEAR PHYSICS. *See* ATOM AND ATOMIC THEORY; ELEMENTARY PARTICLES; NUCLEAR ENERGY; PHYSICS; QUANTUM THEORY.

NUCLEAR REGULATORY COMMISSION (NRC), independent agency of the U.S. government established to regulate civilian nuclear activities. The Energy Reorganization Act of 1974 abolished the Atomic Energy Commission (AEC) and transferred its regulatory responsibilities to the NRC, with headquarters in Bethesda, Md. All develop-

mental activities were merged into a new Energy Research and Development Administration, which in 1977 became part of the Department of Energy. The NRC's programs are designed to protect public health and safety, preserve environmental quality, protect nuclear materials from theft or diversion and nuclear facilities from sabotage, and assure conformity with U.S. anti-trust laws. These programs include standards and regulations, safety reviews and licensing actions, technical studies, inspections and enforcement, and safety research.

A major responsibility of the NRC is regulating the use of nuclear energy to generate electricity in nuclear power reactor plants. This activity also involves regulation of most of the nuclear-fuel cycle, from the milling of uranium ores through their chemical conversion, fabrication into fuel elements, use in reactors, reprocessing, and transportation to final storage and disposal of the radioactive wastes. Outside the fuel cycle, the NRC regulates a wide variety of radioactive material uses in industry, commerce, agriculture, medicine, and education.

NUCLEAR WEAPONS, explosive devices, designed to release nuclear energy (q.v.) on a large scale, used primarily in military applications. The first atomic bomb (or A-bomb), which was tested on July 16, 1945, at Alamogordo, N.Mex., represented a completely new type of artificial explosive. All explosives (q.v.) prior to that time derived their power from the rapid burning or decomposition of some chemical compound. Such chemical processes release only the energy of the outermost electrons in the atom. *See* ATOM AND ATOMIC THEORY.

Nuclear explosives, on the other hand, involve energy sources within the core, or nucleus (q.v.), of the atom. The first A-bomb gained its power from the splitting, or fission, of all the atomic nuclei in several kilograms of plutonium (q.v.). A sphere about the size of a baseball produced an explosion equal to 20,000 tons of TNT.

Subsequently, other types of bomb were developed to tap the energy of light elements, such as hydrogen. In these bombs the source of energy is the fusion process, in which nuclei of the isotopes (*see* ISOTOPE) of hydrogen combine to form a heavier helium nucleus (see Thermonuclear, or Fusion, Weapons below).

Weapons research since 1945 has resulted in the production of bombs that range in power from a fraction of a kiloton (1000 tons of TNT equivalent) to many megatons (1 million tons of TNT equivalent). Furthermore, the physical size of the bomb has been drastically reduced, permitting the development of nuclear artillery shells and small missiles that can be fired from portable launchers in the field. Although nuclear bombs were originally developed as strategic weapons to be carried by large bombers, nuclear weapons are now available for a variety of both strategic and tactical applications. Not only can they be delivered by different types of aircraft, but rockets and guided missiles of many sizes can now carry nuclear warheads and can be launched from the ground, the air, or underwater. Large rockets can carry multiple warheads for delivery to separate targets.

Fission Weapons. Three areas of investigation were important in the development of fission weapons.

Energy liberation in fission. In 1905 Albert Einstein published his special theory of relativity (q.v.). According to this theory, the relation between mass and energy is expressed by the equation $E = mc^2$, which states that a given mass (m) is associated with an amount of energy (E) equal to this mass multiplied by the square of the speed of light (c). A very small amount of matter is equivalent to a vast amount of energy. For example, 1 kg (2.2 lb) of matter converted completely into energy would be equivalent to that of 22 megatons of TNT.

In 1939, as a result of experiments by the German chemists Otto Hahn and Fritz Strassmann (1902–), who split the uranium atom into two roughly equal parts by bombardment with neutrons (*see* NEUTRON), the Austrian physicist Lise Meitner, with her nephew, the British physicist Otto Robert Frisch (1904–79), explained the process of nuclear fission, which placed the release of atomic energy within reach.

The chain reaction. When the uranium or other suitable nucleus fissions, it breaks up into a pair of nuclear fragments and releases energy. At the same time, the nucleus emits very quickly a number of fast neutrons, the same type of particle that initiated the fission of the uranium nucleus. This makes it possible to achieve a self-sustaining series of nuclear fissions; the neutrons that are emitted in fission produce a chain reaction, with continuous release of energy.

The light isotope of uranium, uranium-235, is easily split by the fission neutrons and, upon fission, emits an average of about 2.5 neutrons. One neutron per generation of nuclear fissions is necessary to sustain the chain reactions. Others may be lost by escape from the mass of chain-reacting material, or they may be absorbed in impurities or in the heavy uranium isotope, uranium-238, if it is present. Any substance capable of sustaining a fission chain reaction is known as a fissile material.

Critical mass. A small sphere of pure fissile material, such as uranium-235, about the size of a golf ball, would not sustain a chain reaction. Too many neutrons escape through the surface area, which is relatively large compared with its volume, and thus are lost to the chain reaction. In a mass of uranium-235 about the size of a baseball, however, the number of neutrons lost through the surface is compensated for by the neutrons generated in additional fissions taking place within the sphere. The minimum amount of fissile material (of a given shape) required to maintain the chain reaction is known as the critical mass. Increasing the size of the sphere produces a supercritical assembly, in which the successive generations of fissions increase very rapidly, leading to a possible explosion as a result of the extremely rapid release of a large amount of energy. In an atomic bomb, therefore, a mass of fissile material greater than the critical size must be assembled instantaneously and held together for about a millionth of a second to permit the chain reaction to propagate before the bomb explodes. A heavy material, called a tamper, surrounds the fissile mass and prevents its premature disruption. The tamper also reduces the number of neutrons that escape.

If every atom in 0.5 kg (1.1 lb) of uranium were to split, the energy produced would equal the explosive power of 9.9 kilotons of TNT. In this hypothetical case, the efficiency of the process would be 100 percent. In the first A-bomb tests, this kind of efficiency was not approached. Moreover, a 0.5-kg (1.1-lb) mass is too small for a critical assembly.

Detonation of atomic bombs. Various systems have been devised to detonate the atomic bomb. The simplest system is the gun-type weapon, in which a projectile made of fissile material is fired at a target of the same material so that the two weld together into a supercritical assembly. The atomic bomb exploded by the U.S. over Hiroshima, Japan, on Aug. 6, 1945, was a gun-type weapon. It had the energy equivalent of about 20 kilotons of TNT.

A more complex method, known as implosion, is utilized in a spherically shaped weapon. The outer part of the sphere consists of a layer of closely fitted and specially shaped devices, called lenses, consisting of high explosive and designed to concentrate the blast toward the center of the bomb. Each segment of the high explosive is equipped with a detonator, which in turn is wired to all other segments. An electrical impulse explodes all the chunks of high explosive simultaneously, resulting in a detonation wave that converges toward the core of the weapon.

At the core is a sphere of fissile material, which is compressed by the powerful, inwardly directed pressure, or implosion. The density of the metal is increased, and a supercritical assembly is produced. The Alamogordo test bomb, as well as the one dropped by the U.S. on Nagasaki, Japan, on Aug. 9, 1945, were of the implosion type. Each was equivalent to about 20 kilotons of TNT.

Regardless of the method used to attain a supercritical assembly, the chain reaction proceeds for about a millionth of a second; during this process vast amounts of heat energy are liberated. The extremely fast release of a very large amount of energy in a relatively small volume causes the temperature to rise to tens of millions of degrees. The resulting rapid expansion and vaporization of the bomb material causes a powerful explosion to occur.

Production of Fissile Material. Much experimentation was necessary to make the production of fissile material practical.

Separation of uranium isotopes. The fissile uranium-235 isotope accounts for only 0.7 percent of natural uranium; the remainder is composed of the heavier uranium-238. No chemical methods suffice to separate uranium-235 from ordinary uranium, because both uranium isotopes are chemically identical. A number of techniques were devised to separate the two, all of which depend in principle on the slight difference in weight between the two types of uranium atoms.

A huge gaseous-diffusion plant was built during World War II in Oak Ridge, Tenn. This plant was enlarged after the war, and two similar plants were built near Paducah, Ky., and Ports-

mouth, Ohio. The feed material for this type of plant consists of extremely corrosive uranium hexafluoride gas, UF_6. The gas is pumped against barriers that have many millions of tiny holes, through which the lighter molecules, which contain uranium-235 atoms, diffuse at a slightly greater rate than the heavier molecules, containing uranium-238 (*see* DIFFUSION). After the gas has been cycled through thousands of barriers, known as stages, it is highly enriched in the lighter isotope of uranium. The final product is weapon-grade uranium containing more than 90 percent uranium-235.

Producing plutonium. Although the heavy uranium isotope uranium-238 will not sustain a chain reaction, it can be converted into a fissile material by bombarding it with neutrons and transforming it into a new species of element. When the uranium-238 atom captures a neutron in its nucleus, it is transformed into the heavier isotope uranium-239. This nuclear species quickly disintegrates to form neptunium-239, an isotope of element 93 (*see* NEPTUNIUM). Another disintegration transmutes this isotope into an isotope of element 94, called plutonium-239. Plutonium-239, like uranium-235, undergoes fission after the absorption of a neutron and can be used as a bomb material. Producing plutonium-239 in large quantities requires an intense source of neutrons; the source is provided by the controlled chain reaction in a nuclear reactor. *See* NUCLEAR CHEMISTRY.

During World War II nuclear reactors were designed to provide neutrons to produce plutonium. The U.S. Atomic Energy Commission established reactors in Hanford, Wash., and near Aiken, S.C., capable of manufacturing large quantities of plutonium each year.

Thermonuclear, or Fusion, Weapons. Even before the first atomic bomb was developed, scientists realized that a type of nuclear reaction different from the fission process was theoretically possible as a source of nuclear energy. Instead of using the energy released as a result of a chain reaction in fissile material, nuclear weapons could utilize the energy liberated in the fusion of light elements. This process is the opposite of fission, since it involves the fusing together of the nuclei of isotopes of light atoms such as hydrogen. It is for this reason that the weapons based on nuclear-fusion reactions are often called hydrogen bombs, or H-bombs. Of the three isotopes of hydrogen the two heaviest species, deuterium and tritium (qq.v.), combine most readily to form helium. Although the energy release in the fusion process is less per nuclear reaction than in fission, 0.5 kg (1.1 lb) of the lighter material contains many more atoms; thus, energy liberated from 0.5 kg (1.1 lb) of hydrogen-isotope fuel is equivalent to that of about 29 kilotons of TNT, or almost three times as much as from uranium. This estimate, however, is based on complete fusion of all hydrogen atoms. Fusion reactions occur only at temperatures of several millions of degrees, the rate increasing enormously with increasing temperature; such reactions consequently are known as thermonuclear (heat-induced) reactions. Strictly speaking, the term *thermonuclear* implies that the nuclei have a range (or distribution) of energies characteristic of the temperature. This plays an important role in making rapid fusion reactions possible by an increase in temperature.

Following the explosion of the first atomic bomb in New Mexico, the test site shows a shallow crater surrounded by an area of devastation 1460 m (4800 ft) in diameter. UPI

Development of the hydrogen bomb was impossible before the perfection of A-bombs, for only the latter could yield that tremendous heat necessary to achieve fusion of hydrogen atoms. Atomic scientists regarded the A-bomb as the trigger of the projected thermonuclear device.

Thermonuclear tests. Following developmental tests in the spring of 1951 at the U.S. Eniwetok Proving Grounds in the Marshall Islands during Operation Greenhouse, a full-scale, successful experiment was conducted on Nov. 1, 1952, with a fusion-type device. This test, called Mike, which was part of Operation Ivy, produced an explosion with power equivalent to several million tons of TNT (that is, several megatons). The Soviet Union detonated a thermonuclear weapon in the megaton range in August 1953. On March 1, 1954, the U.S. exploded a fusion bomb with a power of 15 megatons. It created a glowing fireball, more than 4.8 km (more than 3 mi) in diameter, and a huge mushroom cloud, which quickly rose into the stratosphere.

The March 1954 explosion led to worldwide recognition of the nature of radioactive fallout (q.v.). The fallout of radioactive debris from the huge bomb cloud also revealed much about the nature of the thermonuclear bomb. Had the bomb been a weapon consisting of an A-bomb trigger and a core of hydrogen isotopes, the only persistent radioactivity from the explosion would have been the result of the fission debris from the trigger and from the radioactivity induced by neutrons in coral and seawater. Some of the radioactive debris, however, fell on the *Lucky Dragon,* a Japanese vessel engaged in tuna fishing about 160 km (about 100 mi) from the test site. This radioactive dust was later analyzed by Japanese scientists. The results demonstrated that the bomb that dusted the *Lucky Dragon* with fallout was more than just an H-bomb.

Fission-Fusion-Fission Bomb. The thermonuclear bomb exploded in 1954 was a three-stage weapon. The first stage consisted of a big A-bomb, which acted as a trigger. The second stage was the H-bomb phase resulting from the fusion of deuterium and tritium within the bomb. In the process helium and high-energy neutrons were formed. The third stage resulted from the impact of these high-speed neutrons on the outer jacket of the bomb, which consisted of natural uranium, or uranium-238. No chain reaction was produced, but the fusion neutrons had sufficient energy to cause fission of the uranium nuclei and thus added to the explosive yield and also to the radioactivity of the bomb residues.

Effects of Nuclear Weapons. The effects of nuclear weapons were carefully observed.

Blast effects. As is the case with explosions caused by conventional weapons, most of the damage to buildings and other structures from a nuclear explosion results, directly or indirectly, from the effects of blast. The very rapid expansion of the bomb materials produces a high-pressure pulse, or shock wave, that moves rapidly outward from the exploding bomb. In air, this shock wave is called a blast wave because it is equivalent to and is accompanied by powerful winds of much greater than hurricane force. Damage is caused both by the high excess (or overpressure) of air at the front of the blast wave and by the extremely strong winds that persist after the wave front has passed. The degree of blast damage suffered on the ground depends on the TNT equivalent of the explosion; the altitude at which the bomb is exploded, referred to as the height of burst; and the distance of the structure from ground zero, that is, the point directly under the bomb. For the 20-kiloton A-bombs detonated over Japan, the height of burst was about 550 m (about 1800 ft), because it was estimated that this height would produce a maximum area of damage. If the TNT equivalent had been larger, a greater height of burst would have been chosen.

Assuming a height of burst that will maximize the damage area, a 10-kiloton bomb will cause severe damage to wood-frame houses, such as are common in the U.S., to a distance of more than 1.6 km (more than 1 mi) from ground zero, and moderate damage as far as 2.4 km (1.5 mi). (A severely damaged house probably would be beyond repair.) The damage radius increases with the power of the bomb, approximately in proportion to its cube root. If exploded at the optimum height, therefore, a 10-megaton weapon, which is 1000 times as powerful as a 10-kiloton weapon, will increase the distance tenfold, that is, out to 17.7 km (11 mi) for severe damage and 24 km (15 mi) for moderate damage of a frame house.

Thermal effects. The very high temperatures attained in a nuclear explosion result in the formation of an extremely hot incandescent mass of gas called a fireball. For a 10-kiloton explosion in the air, the fireball will attain a maximum diameter of about 300 m (about 1000 ft); for a 10-megaton weapon the fireball may be 4.8 km (3 mi) across. A flash of thermal (or heat) radiation is emitted from the fireball and spreads out over a large area, but with steadily decreasing intensity. The amount of heat energy received a certain distance from the nuclear explosion depends on the power of the weapon and the state of the atmosphere. If the visibility is poor or

A mushroom cloud forms after a tactical nuclear-weapon explosion at a Nevada test site in 1951. A partial nuclear-test ban was signed by the U.S., the USSR, and Great Britain in 1963.   Shostal Associates

the explosion takes place above clouds, the effectiveness of the heat flash is decreased. The thermal radiation falling on exposed skin can cause what are called flash burns. A 10-kiloton explosion in the air can produce moderate (second-degree) flash burns, which require some medical attention, as far as 2.4 km (1.5 mi) from ground zero; for a 10-megaton bomb, the corresponding distance would be more than 32 km (more than 20 mi). Milder burns of bare skin would be experienced even farther out. Most ordinary clothing provides protection from the heat radiation, as does almost any opaque object. Flash burns occur only when the bare skin is di-

rectly exposed, or if the clothing is too thin to absorb the thermal radiation.

The heat radiation can initiate fires in dry, flammable materials, for example, paper and some fabrics, and such fires may spread if conditions are suitable. The evidence from the A-bomb explosions over Japan indicates that many fires, especially in the area near ground zero, originated from secondary causes, such as electrical short circuits, broken gas lines, and upset furnaces and boilers in industrial plants. The blast damage produced debris that helped to maintain the fires and denied access to fire-fighting equipment. Thus, much of the fire damage in

Japan was a secondary effect of the blast wave.

Under some conditions, such as existed at Hiroshima but not at Nagasaki, many individual fires can combine to produce a fire storm similar to those that accompany some large forest fires. The heat of the fire causes a strong updraft, which produces strong winds drawn in toward the center of the burning area. These winds fan the flame and convert the area into a holocaust in which everything flammable is destroyed. Inasmuch as the flames are drawn inward, however, the area over which such a fire spreads may be limited.

Penetrating radiation. Besides heat and blast, the exploding nuclear bomb has a unique effect—it releases penetrating nuclear radiation, which is quite different from thermal (or heat) radiation (see RADIOACTIVITY). When absorbed by the body, nuclear radiation can cause serious injury. For an explosion high in the air, the injury range for these radiations is less than for blast and fire damage or flash burns. In Japan, however, many individuals who were protected from blast and burns succumbed later to radiation injury.

Nuclear radiation from an explosion may be divided into two categories, namely, prompt radiation and residual radiation. The prompt radiation consists of an instantaneous burst of neutrons and gamma rays, which travel over an area of several square miles. Gamma rays are identical in effect to X rays (see X RAY). Both neutrons and gamma rays have the ability to penetrate solid matter, so that substantial thicknesses of shielding materials are required.

The residual nuclear radiation, generally known as fallout, can be a hazard over very large areas that are completely free from other effects of a nuclear explosion. In bombs that gain their energy from fission of uranium-235 or plutonium-239, two radioactive nuclei are produced for every fissile nucleus split. These fission products account for the persistent radioactivity in bomb debris, because many of the atoms have half-lives measured in days, months, or years.

Two distinct categories of fallout, namely, early and delayed, are known. If a nuclear explosion occurs near the surface, earth or water is taken up into a mushroom-shaped cloud and becomes contaminated with the radioactive weapon residues. The contaminated material begins to descend within a few minutes and may continue for about 24 hours, covering an area of thousands of square miles downwind from the explosion. This constitutes the early fallout, which is an immediate hazard to human beings. No early fallout is associated with high-altitude explosions. If a nuclear bomb is exploded well above the ground, the radioactive residues rise to a great height in the mushroom cloud and descend gradually over a large area.

Human experience with radioactive fallout has been minimal. The principal known case histories have been derived from the accidental exposure of natives and fishermen to the fallout from the 15-megaton explosion that occurred on March 1, 1954. The nature of radioactivity, however, and the immense areas contaminable by a single bomb undoubtedly make radioactive fallout potentially one of the most lethal effects of nuclear weapons.

Climatic effects. Besides the blast and radiation damage from individual bombs, a large-scale nuclear exchange between nations could conceivably have a catastrophic global effect on climate. This possibility, proposed in a paper published by an international group of scientists in December 1983, has come to be known as the "nuclear winter" theory. According to these scientists, the explosion of no more than one-half of the warheads now in existence in the U.S. and the Soviet Union would throw enormous quantities of dust and smoke into the atmosphere. The amount could be sufficient to block off sunlight for several months, particularly in the northern hemisphere, destroying plant life and creating a subfreezing climate until the dust dispersed. The ozone layer might also be affected, permitting further damage as a result of the sun's ultraviolet radiation. Were the results sufficiently prolonged, they could spell the virtual end of human civilization.

The nuclear winter theory has since become the subject of enormous controversy. It found support, however, in a study released one year later by the U.S. National Research Council, and other groups have undertaken similar research. Its implications for the acceptability of nuclear warfare as a strategic concept are now widely recognized.

Clean H-bombs. On the average, about 50 percent of the power of an H-bomb results from thermonuclear-fusion reactions and the other 50 percent from fission that occurs in the A-bomb trigger and in the uranium jacket. A clean H-bomb is defined as one in which a significantly smaller proportion than 50 percent of the energy arises from fusion. Because fusion does not produce any radioactive products directly, the fallout from a clean weapon is less than that from a normal or average H-bomb of the same total power. If an H-bomb were made with no uranium jacket but with a fission trigger, it would be relatively clean. Perhaps as little as 5 percent of the total explosive force might result from fission; the weapon would thus be 95 percent clean. An H-bomb with no uranium jacket and no fission trigger, if it could be realized, might be regarded as 100 percent clean. This would be the so-called neutron bomb. Although no radioactive fission products would result, the large number of neutrons released in the thermonuclear reactions would induce radioactivity in materials, especially earth and water, in the vicinity of the explosion. The neutrons could also cause radiation injury to exposed individuals. Blast and heat effects attendant on the explosion of a neutron bomb would undoubtedly be significant. See also ARMS CONTROL, INTERNATIONAL; GUIDED MISSILES; WARFARE. S.G.

For further information on this topic, see the Bibliography in volume 28, sections 195, 555–56.

NUCLEIC ACIDS, extremely complex molecules produced by living cells and viruses. Their name comes from their initial isolation from the nuclei of living cells. Certain nucleic acids, however, are found not in the cell nucleus but in cell cytoplasm. Nucleic acids have at least two functions: to pass on hereditary characteristics from one generation to the next, and to trigger the manufacture of specific proteins. How nucleic acids accomplish these functions is the object of some of the most intense and promising research currently carried on. The nucleic acids are the fundamental substances of living things, believed by researchers to have been first formed about 3 billion years ago, when the most elementary forms of life began on earth. The origin of the so-called genetic code they carry has been accepted by researchers as being very close in time to the origin of life itself (see EVOLUTION; GENETICS). Biochemists have succeeded in deciphering the code, that is, determining how the sequence of nucleic acids dictates the structure of proteins.

The two classes of nucleic acids are the deoxyribonucleic acids (DNA) and the ribonucleic acids (RNA). The backbones of both DNA and RNA molecules are shaped like helical strands. Their molecular weights (see MOLECULE) are in the millions. To the backbones are connected a great number of smaller molecules (side groups) of four different types (see AMINO ACIDS). The sequence of these molecules on the strand determines the code of the particular nucleic acid. This code, in turn, signals the cell how to reproduce either a duplicate of itself or the proteins it requires for survival.

All living cells contain the genetic material DNA. The cells of bacteria may have but one strand of DNA, but such a strand contains all the information needed by the cell in order to reproduce an identical offspring. The cells of mammals contain scores of DNA strands grouped together in chromosomes. In short, the structure of a DNA molecule or combination of DNA molecules determines the shape, form, and function of the offspring. Some viruses, called retroviruses, contain only RNA rather than DNA, but viruses in themselves are generally not considered true living organisms (see VIRUS).

The pioneering research that revealed the general structure of DNA was performed by Francis Crick, James Dewey Watson, and Maurice Wilkins. Wilkins obtained an X-ray diffraction picture of the DNA molecule in 1951. Using this picture, Crick and Watson were able to construct a model of the DNA molecule that was completed in 1953. For their work, these scientists received the 1962 Nobel Prize in physiology or medicine. Arthur Kornberg synthesized DNA from "off-the-shelf" substances, for which he was awarded with Severo Ochoa the 1959 Nobel Prize in physiology or medicine. The DNA that he synthesized, although structurally similar to natural DNA, was not biologically active. In 1967, however, Kornberg and a team of researchers at Stanford University succeeded in producing biologically active DNA from relatively simple chemicals.

Certain kinds of RNA have a slightly different function from that of DNA. They take part in the

Maurice H. F. Wilkins studies a model of a DNA molecular structure. Wilkins won a Nobel Prize for discoveries concerning the molecular structure of nucleic acids.   UPI

actual synthesis of the proteins a cell produces. This is of particular interest to virologists because many viruses reproduce by "forcing" the host cells to manufacture more viruses. The virus injects its own RNA into the host cell, and the host cell obeys the code of the invading RNA rather than that of its own. Thus the cell produces proteins that are, in fact, viruses instead of the proteins required for cell function. The host cell is destroyed, and the newly formed viruses are free to inject their RNA molecules into other host cells.

The structure of two types of RNA and their function in protein production have been determined, one type by a team of Cornell University and U.S. Department of Agriculture investigators led by Robert W. Holley of Cornell, and the other type by James T. Madison (1933–   ) and George A. Everett (1924–   ) of the Department of Agriculture. Important research into the interpretation of the genetic code and its role in protein synthesis was also performed by the Indian-born American chemist Har Gobind Khorana at the University of Wisconsin Enzyme Institute and the American biochemist Marshall W. Nirenberg of the National Heart Institute. In 1970 Khorana achieved the first complete synthesis of a gene and repeated his feat in 1973. Since then one type of RNA has been synthesized. Also, in the early 1980s, a team of biologists at the National Jewish Hospital in Denver, Colo., proved that in some cases RNA can function as a true catalyst (q.v.). *See also* HEREDITY.   S.Z.L.

For further information on this topic, see the Bibliography in volume 28, section 444.

NUCLEUS, in atomic structure, the positively charged central mass of an atom about which the orbital electrons revolve. The nucleus is composed of nucleons, that is, protons and neutrons, and its mass accounts for nearly the entire mass of the atom. *See* ELEMENTARY PARTICLES; NEUTRON; PROTON.

NUCLEUS, in biology. *See* CELL: *Structure and Function.*

NUDISM, worldwide movement that advocates the manner and cult of life in the nude. Specifically, nudism is practiced for the physical benefit derived from exposure of the body to healthful qualities of sunlight and fresh air; in a wider sense, however, it is a philosophy and a way of life. The proponents of nudism maintain that clothing should be abandoned when not absolutely necessitated by the rigors of the weather, as it serves to focus erotic attention on the body, thereby exciting an unhealthy sexual prurience. The shame customarily associated with nakedness in modern civilized society results, according to nudists, from centuries of cultural conditioning against complete exposure of the body in public. Nudism, by correcting in its practitioners this false sense of shame, enhances their self-assurance and furnishes them with a new appreciation of the essential beauty and dignity of the human body. Critics attack the nudist philosophy as being indecent and the publications put out by the movement as obscene.

Archaeological evidence indicates that nudism, in the form of sunbathing, was practiced in antiquity by the Babylonians, Assyrians, Greeks, and Romans. In modern times the rise of nudism is identified with the *Nacktkultur* ("Culture of Nakedness") movement in Germany. The advocates of this movement emphasized its value in relation to preventive hygiene, claiming for their practices a highly tonic effect on both body and mind. With the advent of National Socialism in Germany, however, the movement declined as a result of strong government restrictions. Nudist societies are maintained in most European countries and are particularly prevalent in Norway, Sweden, and Finland. In the U.S., the first organized nudist movement was the American League of Physical Culture established in 1929. Since World War II, interest in nudism has made some advances in the U.S. and Canada. Currently the American Sunbathing Association, with headquarters at Orlando, Fla., represents many clubs that are located throughout the U.S.; the Canadian Sunbathing Association has headquarters in London, Ont.

NUESTRA SEÑORA DE LA ASUNCIÓN. *See* ASUNCIÓN.

NUEVA SAN SALVADOR, formerly SANTA TECLA, city, central El Salvador, capital of La Libertad Department, at the S foot of San Salvador volcano, near San Salvador. Situated on the Pan-American Highway, the city is in an area of coffee plantations and livestock farms, and many large estates are located here. Local industries manufacture leather products, soap, and candles. The city was founded as Nueva Ciudad de San Salvador in 1854 after San Salvador, the capital, had been destroyed by an earthquake; it served as capital of the republic from 1855 to 1859 and became departmental capital in 1865. Pop. (est.) 35,100.

NUEVO LAREDO, city, NE Mexico, in Tamaulipas State, on the Rio Grande, opposite Laredo, Tex. Connected to Laredo by the International Bridge and by rail, it is a major port of entry and a tourist center, as well as a market for cattle, cotton, grains, and sugarcane raised in the area. Industries include textile and flour milling, cotton ginning, fruit canning, sawmilling, coffee and vegetable-oil processing, and printing. The city was founded in the mid-1700s and was considered a part of Laredo until 1848, when the E bank of the river was ceded to the U.S. Pop. (1979 est.) 223,606.

NUFFIELD RADIO ASTRONOMY LABORATORIES. See JODRELL BANK EXPERIMENTAL STATION.

NUKUALOFA, capital and largest town of Tonga, on the N coast of Tongatapu Island, in the S Pacific Ocean. It is the island's chief port and principal economic, administrative, and tourist center. Copra, vanilla, and bananas are exported. Petroleum deposits were discovered offshore in the 1970s. The red-roofed Royal Palace (1865–67), on the waterfront, is a major landmark. In 1643 the Dutch navigator Abel Janszoon Tasman landed here. Pop. (est.) 18,400.

NULLIFICATION, in the history of American political theory, the alleged right of a state to suspend operation of a federal law within its boundaries. The right of nullification was asserted on the basis of a belief that states are the ultimate sources of sovereignty, and that the federal government is simply a league of freely associated states, the authority of which the state is free to recognize or ignore in accordance with its best interests. This belief stemmed from the beginning of the republic, when the states, jealous of their sovereignty and fearful of tyranny, agreed to yield certain of their powers to the U.S., as specifically set forth in the U.S. Constitution only after the looser Articles of Confederation had proved ineffective. The principle of nullification was supported by many of the founders. In 1798 and 1799, the Kentucky and Virginia resolutions, drafted by James Madison and Thomas Jefferson, respectively, affirmed the validity of nullification and warned against federal usurpation of state sovereignty. The New England states nullified an unpopular embargo in 1809–10, and 15 years later Georgia nullified federal laws relating to American Indians.

As the development of industry and more intensive settlement linked the different parts of the country more closely together, nullification was opposed by advocates of the primacy of the federal government. One of the foremost of these, U.S. Senator Daniel Webster, in his most famous speech before the U.S. Senate, warned Senator Robert Young Hayne of South Carolina in 1830 that nullification would cause the Union to fall apart and that the American flag, "stained with the blood of fratricidal war," would wave over "the dismembered fragments of our once glorious empire." Soon after, in 1832, South Carolina called a state convention that declared "null, void, and no law" the high protective tariff of that year. President Andrew Jackson threatened to send troops to enforce the tariff in the port of Charleston. Senator John C. Calhoun of South Carolina, one of the leading advocates of nullification, joined with Senator Henry Clay of Virginia to reconcile the claims of South Carolina with those of the federal government. As a result, a compromise tariff was passed, the South Carolina convention repealed the ordinance of nullification, and both sides of the controversy claimed a victory.

A final resolution of the question of nullification was thus postponed until 1861, when South Carolina, followed by other southern states, seceded from the Union and precipitated the Civil War. Although at the cost of the "blood of fratricidal war" predicted by Webster, this great conflict confirmed the primacy of the federal government in the authority granted it by the Constitution, and no subsequent attempts have been made by any states to nullify federal laws. Nevertheless, the question of distribution of powers between the states and the federal government remains a live issue. The current proponents of states' rights, still principally from the South, expound a point of view that, in opposing extensions of federal power, has descended lineally from the original nullification theories of Jefferson and Calhoun.

NUMAZU, city and port, Japan, in Shizuoka Prefecture, S Honshu Island, at the mouth of the Kano R., on Suruga Bay, near the city of Shizuoka. It is an important road hub and a rail junction on the Tokaido Line; connections are made here for the Izu Peninsula resort towns and for Mt. Fuji. The city is a market center in an area of sericulture and agricultural production. Silk, fish, and vegetables are traded here. Manufactures include machinery and textiles. Numazu is an old settlement; a castle existed here from 1479 to 1868. Seaside resorts, including the emperor's villa, lie E and S of the city. Numazu Park is a scenic spot on the bay. Numazu became a city in 1923. Pop. (1980 prelim.) 203,699.

NUMBER, word or symbol used to designate quantities or, by extension, entities having quantitylike properties.

Rational Numbers. The simplest numbers are the natural numbers, 1, 2, 3, . . . , used in counting; they are also called the whole numbers, positive integers, or positive rational integers. The natural numbers are closed with respect to addition and multiplication; that is, the sum and product of two natural numbers are always natural numbers. Because the quotient of two natural numbers, however, is not always a natural number, it is convenient to introduce the positive fractions to represent the quotient of any two natural numbers. The natural number n is identified with the fraction $n/1$. Furthermore, because the difference of two positive fractions is not always a positive fraction, it is expeditious to introduce the negative fractions (including the negative integers) and the number zero (0). The positive and negative integers and fractions, and the number 0, comprise the rational number system.

The sum, difference, product, or quotient of two rational numbers is always a rational number. Division of any number by zero, however, is not allowed (see ZERO). It can be shown that every rational number can be represented as a repeating or periodic decimal, that is, as a number in the decimal notation, which after a certain point consists of the infinite repetition of a finite block of digits. Conversely, every repeating decimal represents a rational number. Thus, $617/50$ $= 12.34000\ldots$, and $2317/990 = 2.34040\ldots$. The first expression is usually written as 12.34, omitting the inifinite repetition of the block consisting of the single digit 0. The second expression is frequently written as $2.3\overline{40}$ or $2.3\underline{40}$ or 2.340 to indicate that the block of two digits, 4 and 0, is repeated infinitely. The first type of expression is called a finite or terminating decimal, and the second type of expression is called an infinite periodic or repeating decimal (the term *infinite* is frequently omitted).

Irrational Numbers. The development of geometry indicated the need for more numbers; the length of the diagonal of a square with sides one unit long cannot be expressed as a rational number. Similarly, the ratio of the circumference to the diameter of a circle is not a rational number. These and other needs led to the introduction of the irrational numbers. A decimal expansion that is neither of the two types described above represents an irrational number. For example, $\sqrt{2} =$ $1.4142135623\ldots$ and $\pi = 3.1415926535\ldots$ are irrational numbers, and their decimal expansions are necessarily nonterminating and nonperiodic. The totality of the rational and irrational numbers makes up the so-called real number system. *See also* NUMERALS.

Imaginary Numbers. The product of a real number multiplied by itself is 0 or positive; the equation $x^2 = -1$ has no solutions in the real number system. If such a solution is desired, new numbers must be invented. Let $i = \sqrt{-1}$ be a new number representing a solution of the preceding equation. All numbers of the form $a + bi$, in which a and b are real numbers, belong to the complex number system. If b is not 0, the complex number is called an imaginary number; if b is not 0 but a is 0, the complex number is called

a pure imaginary; if b is 0, the complex number is a real number.

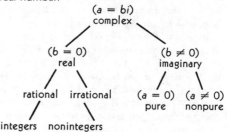

Imaginary numbers (the term must not be used in a literal sense but in the technical sense just described) are extremely useful in the theory of alternating currents and many other branches of physics and natural science.

The relationships of the various types of numbers are illustrated in the so-called number family tree. See accompanying diagram.

Complex Numbers. In 1799 the German mathematician Karl Friedrich Gauss proved that every algebraic equation of degree n having the form $x^n + a_1x^{n-1} + \ldots + a_{n-1}k_{sx} + a_n = 0$ in which $a_1, a_2 \ldots, a_n$ are arbitrary complex numbers, is satisfied by at least one complex root (see EQUATIONS, THEORY OF).

Whereas real numbers represent points on a line, complex numbers can be placed in correspondence with the points on a plane. To represent the complex number $a + bi$ geometrically, the x-axis is used as the axis of the real number a, and the y-axis serves as the axis of the pure imaginary bi; the complex number, therefore, corresponds to the point P with the rectangular coordinates a and b (see GEOMETRY). The line, or vector (q.v.), joining the origin with the point P (a,b) is the diagonal of a rectangle with the sides a and bi. If the complex number $a + bi$ is multiplied by -1, the vector OP is rotated through 180°, and the point P falls in the third quadrant; a rotation of 90°, therefore, represents multiplication of the complex number by i, as $-1 = 1^{-2}$, and $i(a + bi)$ represents a point in the second quadrant if $a + bi$ represents a point in the first.

Mystical and magical qualities have been ascribed to numbers both in antiquity and in modern times. The pseudoscience of numerology attempts to interpret the occult by means of the symbolism of numbers, which is based on the Pythagorean doctrine that all things are numbers and consist of geometrical figures in various patterns. See PYTHAGORAS.   J.Si.

For further information on this topic, see the Bibliography in volume 28, section 368.

NUMBERS, fourth book of the Old Testament, so named because the opening chapters concern the census, or numbering, of the Israelite tribes. The English title is derived from the title of the book in the Vulgate, Numeri (Lat., "Numbers"). Numeri is in turn a translation of the title of the book in the Greek-language version called the Septuagint. The Jews, who have named each of the five books constituting the Pentateuch after the first word or first significant word of the Hebrew text, refer to Numbers as Be-Midbar (Heb., "In the Wilderness"). The book continues the account of the origins and early history of the Jewish people begun in the books of Genesis and Exodus.

"In the Wilderness" is by far a more appropriate title than "Numbers," because the book is concerned chiefly with the desert wanderings of the Israelites under the leadership of Moses. It records the events from their final days at Mount Sinai until their arrival, nearly 40 years later, at the plains of Moab, close to the Promised Land of Canaan. The book may be divided into three sections: (1) the final days at Mount Sinai (1:1-10:10); (2) a period of approximately 38 years of wandering in the desert south of the Promised Land (10:11-20:13 or, as some scholars prefer, 10:11-21:13); and (3) the final approach to the border of Canaan from the east.

The first section almost exclusively concerns statistical and legal matters. The second section begins with an account of the Israelites' departure from Sinai. It relates, among other stories, that of the sedition of Aaron and Miriam, the brother and sister of Moses (chap. 12); and that of the sending out of Israelite spies into Canaan, their conflicting reports, and the Israelites' condemnation to 40 years in the wilderness (chap. 13-14). Chapter 17 tells of the miraculous budding of Aaron's rod, a sign that the priestly tribe of Levites was divinely appointed.

The third section of Numbers tells of the Israelites' unsuccessful attempt to enter Canaan through the land of Edom, and of Aaron's death (20:14-29); relates the selection of the Hebrew leader Joshua as successor to Moses (27:12-23); and tells (chap. 32) of the distribution of land east of the Jordan River to the tribes of Gad and Reuben. A résumé of the stages of Israel's journey from Egypt to the border of Canaan (33:1-49) is followed by a description of the ideal boundaries of Canaan. The book closes with provisions for the apportionment of the land, the establishment of Levitical cities and cities of refuge for murderers, and rules for marriage to keep the lands of Israel intact (chap. 34-36). Notable throughout is the emphasis on matters of interest to the priests of Israel, indicating the probable main source of the subject matter of the Book of Numbers, the so-called P source, dating from about the 6th century BC.

For a discussion of the documentary hypothesis, *see* BIBLE.

NUMBER SYSTEMS, in mathematics, various notational systems that have been or are being used to represent the abstract quantities called numbers. A number system is defined by the base it uses, the base being the number of different symbols required by the system to represent any of the infinite series of numbers. Thus, the decimal system in universal use today (except for computer application) requires ten different symbols, or digits, to represent numbers and is therefore a base-10 system.

Throughout history, many different number systems have been used; in fact, any whole number greater than 1 can be used as a base. Some cultures have used systems based on the numbers 3, 4, or 5. The Babylonians used the sexagesimal system, based on the number 60, and the Romans used (for some purposes) the duodecimal system, based on the number 12. The Mayans used the vigesimal system, based on the number 20. The binary system, based on the number 2, was used by some tribes and, together with the system based on 8, is used today in computer systems. For historical background, *see* NUMERALS.

Place Values. Except for computer work, the universally adopted system of mathematical notation today is the decimal system, which, as stated, is a base-10 system. As in other number systems, the position of a symbol in a base-10 number denotes the value of that symbol in terms of exponential values of the base. That is, in the decimal system, the quantity represented by any of the ten symbols used—0, 1, 2, 3, 4, 5, 6, 7, 8, and 9—depends on its position in the number. Thus, the number 3,098,323 is an abbreviation for $(3 \times 10^6) + (0 \times 10^5) + (9 \times 10^4) + (8 \times 10^3) + (3 \times 10^2) + (2 \times 10^1) + (3 \times 10^0,$ or $3 \times 1)$. The first "3" (reading from right to left) represents 3 units; the second "3," 300 units; and the third "3," 3 million units. In this system the zero (q.v.) plays a double role; it represents naught, and it also serves to indicate the multiples of the base 10: 100, 1000, 10,000, and so on. It is also used to indicate fractions of integers: 1/10 is written as 0.1, 1/100 as 0.01, 1/1000 as 0.001, and so on.

Two digits—0, 1—suffice to represent a number in the binary system; 6 digits—0, 1, 2, 3, 4, 5—are needed to represent a number in the sexagesimal system; and 12 digits—0, 1, 2, 3, 4, 5, 6, 7, 8, 9, t (ten), e (eleven)—are needed to represent a number in the duodecimal system. The number

30155 in the sexagesimal system is the number $(3 \times 6^4) + (0 \times 6^3) + (1 \times 6^2) + (5 \times 6^1) + (5 \times 6^0) = 3959$ in the decimal system; the number 2et in the duodecimal system is the number $(2 \times 12^2) + (11 \times 12^1) + (10 \times 12^0) = 430$ in the decimal system

To write a given base-10 number n as a base-b number, divide (in the decimal system) n by b, divide the quotient by b, the new quotient by b, and so on until the quotient 0 is obtained. The successive remainders are the digits in the base-b expression for n. For example, to express 3959 (base 10) in the base 6, one writes

```
6 ) 3959
  )  659  5
  )  109  5
  )   18  1
  )    3  0
  )    0  3
```

from which, as above, $3959_{10} = 30155_6$. (The base is frequently written in this way as a subscript of the number.) The larger the base, the more symbols are required, but fewer digits are needed to express a given number. The number 12 is convenient as a base because it is exactly divisible by 2, 3, 4, and 6; for this reason, some mathematicians have advocated adoption of base 12 in place of the base 10.

Binary System. The binary system plays an important role in computer technology. The first 20 numbers in the binary notation are 1, 10, 11, 100, 101, 110, 111, 1000, 1001, 1010, 1011, 1100, 1101, 1110, 1111, 10000, 10001, 10010, 10011, 10100. The zero here also has the role of place marker, as in the decimal system. Any decimal number can be expressed in the binary system by the sum of different powers of two. For example, starting from the right, 10101101 represents $(1 \times 2^0) + (0 \times 2^1) + (1 \times 2^2) + (1 \times 2^3) + (0 \times 2^4) + (1 \times 2^5) + (0 \times 2^6) + (1 \times 2^7) = 173$. This example can be used for the conversion of binary numbers into decimal numbers. For the conversion of decimal numbers to binary numbers, the same principle can be used, but the other way around. Thus, to convert, the highest power of two that does not exceed the given number is sought first, and a 1 is placed in the corresponding position in the binary number. For example, the highest power of two in the decimal number 519 is $2^9 = 512$. Thus, a 1 can be inserted as the 10th digit, counted from the right: 1000000000. In the remainder, $519 - 512 = 7$, the highest power of 2 is $2^2 = 4$, so the third zero from the right can be replaced by a 1: 1000000100. The next remainder, 3, consists of the sum of two powers of 2: 2^1 + 2^0, so the first and second zeros from the right are replaced by 1: $519_{10} = 1000000111_2$.

Arithmetic operations in the binary system are extremely simple. The basic rules are: $1 + 1 = 10$, and $1 \times 1 = 1$. Zero plays its usual role: $1 \times 0 = 0$, and $1 + 0 = 1$. Addition, subtraction, and multiplication are done in a fashion similar to that of the decimal system:

```
  100101        1011010          101
+ 110101      - 110101       ×  1001
 1011010        100101          101
                               000
                              000
                              101
                            101101
```

Because only two digits (or bits) are involved, the binary system is used in computers, since any binary number can be represented by, for example, the positions of a series of on-off switches. The "on" position corresponds to a 1, and the "off" position to a 0. Instead of switches, magnetized dots on a magnetic tape or disk also can be used to represent binary numbers: a magnetized dot stands for the digit 1, and the absence of a magnetized dot is the digit 0. Flip-flops—electronic devices that can only carry two distinct voltages at their outputs and that can be switched from one state to the other state by an impulse—can also be used to represent binary numbers; the two voltages correspond to the two digits. Logic circuits in computers (see COMPUTER; ELECTRONICS) carry out the different arithmetic operations of binary numbers; the conversion of decimal numbers to binary numbers for processing, and of binary numbers to decimal numbers for the readout, is done electronically.

For further information on this topic, see the Bibliography in volume 28, section 368.

NUMBER THEORY, branch of mathematics that deals with the properties and relationships of numbers (see NUMBER). According to this broad definition, the theory of numbers includes most of mathematics, particularly mathematical analysis. Generally, however, the theory of numbers is confined to the study of integers, or occasionally to some other set of numbers having properties similar to the set of all integers, that is, whole numbers as opposed to fractions.

Nature of Integers. If a, b, c are integers such that $a = bc$, a is called a multiple of b or of c, and b or c is called a divisor or factor of a. If c is not ± 1, b is called a proper divisor of a. Even integers, which include 0, are multiples of 2, for example, $-4, 0, 2, 10$; an odd integer is an integer that is not even, for example, -5, 1, 3, 9. A perfect number is a positive integer that is equal to the sum of all its positive, proper divisors; for example, 6, which equals $1 + 2 + 3$, and 28, which equals $1 + 2 + 4 + 7 + 14$, are perfect numbers. A positive number that is not perfect is imperfect and is deficient or abundant according to whether the sum of its positive, proper divisors is smaller or larger than the number itself. Thus, 9, with proper divisors 1, 3, is deficient; 12, with proper divisors 1, 2, 3, 4, 6, is abundant.

Primes. Much of the theory of numbers is devoted to the study of primes. A number p, ($p \neq \pm 1$) is a prime if its only divisors are ± 1, $\pm p$. A number a is composite, if $a = bc$, in which neither b nor c is ± 1. The first ten positive primes are 2, 3, 5, 7, 11, 13, 17, 19, 23, 29; the first ten positive composite numbers are 4, 6, 8, 9, 10, 12, 14, 15, 16, 18. A composite number can be factored into a product of primes in only one way, apart from the order of the factors; thus, 9 $= 3 \times 3$; $10 = 2 \times 5$; $12 = 2 \times 2 \times 3$.

The ninth book of the *Elements* by the Greek mathematician Euclid contains the proof of the proposition that the number of primes is infinite, that is, no largest prime exists. The proof is remarkably simple: let p be a prime and $q = 1 \times 2 \times 3 \times \ldots \times p + 1$, that is, one more than the product of all the integers from 1 through p. The integer q is larger than p and is not divisible by any integer from 2 through p, inclusive. Any one of its positive divisors, other than 1, and any one of its prime divisors, therefore, must be larger than p. It follows that there must be a prime larger than p.

Although the number of primes is infinite, the primes become relatively scarce as one proceeds further and further out into the number system. Indeed, the number of primes between 1 and n, for very large values of n, is approximately n divided by the natural logarithm of n. Twenty-five percent of the numbers between 1 and 100, 17 percent of the numbers between 1 and 1000, and 7 percent of the numbers between 1 and 1,000,000 are primes.

Two primes that differ by 2 (for example, 5, 7; 17, 19; 101, 103) are called twin primes. It is not known whether the number of twin primes is infinite. Another conjecture is that every even number greater than 2 can be expressed as the sum of two primes; thus, $4 = 2 + 2$; $6 = 3 + 3$; $8 = 3 + 5$; $10 = 5 + 5$; $20 = 3 + 17$; $100 = 3 + 97$; however, a general proof is still lacking.

The greatest common divisor of two integers a and b is the largest positive integer that divides both a and b exactly. Euclid gave a method for finding this figure for two integers. If the greatest common divisor of two integers is 1, the two numbers are said to be relatively prime, or one integer is said to be prime to the other. If p, q, $\ldots$, u are the distinct prime divisors of a positive integer n, the number of positive integers not exceeding and prime to n is given by the formula

$$\phi(n) = n \left(1 - \frac{1}{p}\right)\left(1 - \frac{1}{q}\right) \ldots \left(1 - \frac{1}{u}\right)$$

If a, b, m are integers (m, positive) such that $a - b$ is a multiple of m, then a is congruent to b with respect to the modulus m, which is written

$$a \equiv b \ (\text{mod } m)$$

This expression itself is called a congruence; congruences behave in many resepcts like equations. The theory of congruences is very important in number theory; for example, congruence theory can be used to solve problems known as Chinese remainders. An illustrative problem of this type is: Find the first two positive integers having the remainders 2, 3, 2, when divided by 3, 5, 7, respectively. The answer, 23 and 128, was given by the Chinese mathematician Sun-Tsŭ in the 1st century AD. J.Si.

For further information on this topic, see the Bibliography in volume 28, section 368.

NUMERALS, signs or symbols for graphic representation of numbers. The earliest forms of number notation were simply groups of straight lines, either vertical or horizontal, each line corresponding to the number 1. Such a system is inconvenient when dealing with large numbers, and as early as 3400 BC in Egypt and 3000 BC in Mesopotamia a special symbol was adopted for the number 10. The addition of this second number symbol made it possible to express the number 11 with 2 instead of 11 individual symbols and the number 99 with 18 instead of 99 individual symbols. Later numeral systems introduced extra symbols for a number between 1 and 10, usually either 4 or 5, and additional symbols for numbers greater than 10. In Babylonian cuneiform notation the numeral used for 1 was also used for 60 and for powers of 60; the value of the numeral was indicated by its context. This was a logical arrangement from the mathematical point of view because $60° = 1$, $60^1 = 60$, and $60^2 = 3600$. The Egyptian hieroglyphic system used special symbols for 10, 100, 1000, and 10,000.

The ancient Greeks had two parallel systems of numerals. The earlier of these was based on the initial letters of the names of numbers: The number 5 was indicated by the letter pi; 10 by the letter delta; 100 by the antique form of the letter H; 1000 by the letter chi; and 10,000 by the letter mu. The later system, which was first introduced

NUMERALS AND NUMBERS

Arabic	Roman	Name
0		zero, naught
1	I	one
2	II	two
3	III	three
4	IIII or IV	four
5	V	five
6	VI	six
7	VII	seven
8	VIII	eight
9	VIIII or IX	nine
10	X	ten
11	XI	eleven
12	XII	twelve
13	XIII	thirteen
14	XIIII or XIV	fourteen
15	XV	fifteen
16	XVI	sixteen
17	XVII	seventeen
18	XVIII	eighteen
19	XVIIII or XIX	nineteen
20	XX	twenty
21	XXI	twenty-one
22	XXII	twenty-two
23	XXIII	twenty-three
24	XXIIII or XXIV	twenty-four
25	XXV	twenty-five
30	XXX	thirty
31	XXXI	thirty-one
32	XXXII	thirty-two
40	XL or XXXX	forty
50	L	fifty
60	LX	sixty
70	LXX	seventy
80	LXXX	eighty
90	LXXXX or XC	ninety
100	C	one hundred
200	CC	two hundred
300	CCC	three hundred
400	CCCC or CD	four hundred
500	D	five hundred
600	DC	six hundred
1000	M	one thousand
2000	MM	two thousand
3000	MMM	three thousand
10,000	$\overline{X}$	ten thousand
20,000	$\overline{XX}$	twenty thousand
100,000	$\overline{C}$	one hundred thousand
1,000,000	$\overline{M}$	one million
1,000,000,000	M	one billion (U.S. and France) one thousand million (Great Britain and Germany)
1,000,000,000,000	$\overline{\overline{M}}$	one trillion (U.S. and France) one billion (Great Britain and Germany)

about the 3d century BC, employed all the letters of the Greek alphabet plus three letters borrowed from the Phoenician as number symbols. The first nine letters of the alphabet were used for the numbers 1 to 9, the second nine letters for the decades from 10 to 90, and the last nine letters for the hundreds from 100 to 900. Thousands were indicated by placing a bar to the left of the appropriate numeral, and tens of thousands by placing the appropriate letter over the letter *M*. The late Greek system had the advantage that large numbers could be expressed with a minimum of symbols, but it had the disadvantage of requiring the user to memorize a total of 27 symbols.

Roman Numerals. The system of number symbols created by the Romans had the merit of expressing all numbers from 1 to 1,000,000 with a total of seven symbols: I for 1, V for 5, X for 10, L for 50, C for 100, D for 500, M for 1000, $\overline{M}$ for 1,000,000. (A small bar placed over the numeral multiplies the numeral by 1000.) Thus, theoretically, it is possible, by using an infinite number of bars, to express the numbers from 1 to infinity. In practice, however, one bar is usually used; two are rarely used, and more than two are almost never used. Roman numerals are still used today, more than 2000 years after their introduction. The Roman system had one drawback, however, in that it was not suitable for rapid written calculations.

Arabic Numerals. The common system of number notation in use in most parts of the world today is the Arabic system. This system was first developed by the Hindus and was in use in India in the 3d century BC. At that time the numerals 1, 4, and 6 were written in substantially the same form used today. The Hindu numeral system was probably introduced into the Arab world about the 7th or 8th century AD. The first recorded use of the system in Europe was in 976.

The important innovation in the Arabic system was the use of positional notation, in which individual number symbols assume different values according to their position in the written numeral. Positional notation is made possible by the use of a symbol for zero. The symbol 0 makes it possible to differentiate between 11, 101, and 1001 without the use of additional symbols, and all numbers can be expressed in terms of ten symbols, the numerals from 1 to 9 plus 0. Positional notation also greatly simplifies all forms of written numerical calculation.

For further information on this topic, see the Bibliography in volume 28, section 368.

NUMEROLOGY. *See* NUMBER.

NUMIDIA, ancient Roman name for that part of northern Africa roughly equivalent to modern Algeria. Numidia was inhabited by two tribes noted for their horsemanship. In the Second Punic War (218–201 BC) between Carthage and Rome the western tribe of Numidians supported Hannibal, the leader of Carthage. Masinissa (238?–149 BC), king of the eastern Numidians, joined the Romans. With the victory of Rome, all Numidia was united under Masinissa's rule. The most famous of his successors were Jugurtha and

The square is Nuremberg's marketplace, providing almost everything from fresh fruits and vegetables to flowers. UPI

Juba I (d. 46 BC). After the victory of Julius Caesar over Juba in the African war, Numidia became (46 BC) a Roman province called Africa Nova. In 30 BC the Roman emperor Augustus restored the western part of Numidia to Juba II (d. AD 19), and five years later the eastern part was united with Africa Vetus to form the province of Africa. Under Emperor Septimius Severus (r. 193–211), Numidia once more became a separate province. The country was conquered by the Vandals in the 5th century and the Arabs in the 8th century; it remained under Arab control until the French conquest of Algeria in the 19th century.

NUMISMATICS. *See* COINS AND COIN COLLECTING.

NUN, member of a religious order for women, living in a convent under vows of poverty, chastity, and obedience. Female monasticism occurs notably in Roman Catholicism, although it is not limited to that church or to Christianity. In Roman Catholicism the orders vary in the stipulations of the vows, some being permanent and others only for fixed periods of time. The orders vary somewhat in dress, purpose, and rule, but all follow generally the same basic principles. The nuns are devoted to a purely contemplative life or to a life of charity, including teaching and nursing. The heads of convents are variously called abbesses, prioresses, and mothers superior, and a nun is generally addressed as "Sister."

NÚÑEZ CABEZA DE VACA, Álvar. *See* CABEZA DE VACA, ÁLVAR NÚÑEZ.

NUREMBERG (Ger. *Nürnberg*), city, S West Germany, in Bavaria, on the Pegnitz R., near Fürth. It is a commercial and industrial center, served by railroads and the Ludwig Canal, which connects the Danube and Main rivers. The city is widely known for its toys and spiced bread (*Lebkuchen*); other products include motor vehicles, electrical and electronic equipment, office machinery, textiles, and precision instruments. Among the city's points of interest are the Gothic Saint Sebald's Church (mainly 13th cent.), a castle (begun 11th cent.), the German National Museum, a museum of transportation, the house (now a museum) where the artist Albrecht Dürer lived, and extensive parts of the old city walls (chiefly 15th cent.). A section of the University of Erlangen-Nuremberg is here.

First mentioned in 1050, Nuremberg was made a free imperial city in 1219. It subsequently became known for its manufactures, especially woodenware. During the 15th and 16th centuries the city was a great center of commerce and culture; among the artists who worked here then were the sculptor Veit Stoss, the bronze caster Peter Fischer, the painter and woodcarver Michael Wolgemut, and Dürer. Also active here at the time were the meistersinger, members of guilds formed to cultivate music and poetry; they included the poet and dramatist Hans Sachs. In 1806 Nuremberg passed to Bavaria, and in 1835 the city became a terminus of the first German railroad. From 1933 to 1938 annual conventions of the National Socialist German Workers (or Nazi) party were held here; at the 1935 meeting the Nuremberg Laws, depriving German Jews of many civil rights, were promulgated. As a major center for producing military equipment, the city was badly damaged by Allied bombardments during World War II. After the war Nuremberg was (1945-46) a site of trials of suspected German war criminals; the trials were conducted by an international tribunal of Allied jurists. Pop. (1980 est.) 483,900.

NUREMBERG TRIALS. *See* War Crimes Trials.
NUREYEV, Rudolf Hametovich (1938-), Soviet-born ballet dancer and choreographer, the most virtuosic and charismatic male dancer of his generation. Born in Irkutsk, he danced professionally from the age of 15, studied at the Leningrad Ballet School (1955-58), and in 1958 became soloist with the Kirov Ballet in Leningrad. In 1961, in Paris on tour with the Kirov Ballet, he defected to the West. In 1962 he became associated with the Royal Ballet of London, making the first of many appearances with the British ballerina Margot Fonteyn. He also danced with the American Ballet Theatre, the Martha Graham Company, and other companies. He reconstructed and recast the choreography of *Swan Lake* (film, 1966) *Don Quixote* (film, 1973) and other ballets of the 19th-century Russian choreographer Marius Petipa, and was the subject of the film *I Am a Dancer* (1972). His autobiography, *Nureyev,* was published in 1962. An Austrian citizen since 1982, he became artistic director of the Paris Opera Ballet in 1983.

NURSERY RHYMES, simple verses, often accompanied by a simple tune, used for the entertainment and education of small children. Most nursery rhymes have been handed down from one generation to another. Among the oldest are those related to telling time, counting, or learning the alphabet. The rhyme beginning "Thirty days hath September," for example, has its origins in a medieval French poem. The origins of many others, however, such as "Humpty-Dumpty" or "Ladybug, Ladybug, Fly Away Home," are open to conjecture; some theorists think that a number of seemingly naive nursery rhymes have concealed political or topical significance. Like popular songs or ballads, some nursery rhymes have an appeal due to their music as well as their words; "London Bridge Is Falling Down" probably comes from an old English dance tune. New additions to the old favorites occur from time to time. "Twinkle, Twinkle, Little Star" by the English writers Ann Taylor (1782-1866) and Jane Taylor (1783-1824) was published in 1806; its familiar music is a setting by Mozart

of an old French tune. "Mary Had a Little Lamb" is an 1830 composition by the American author Josepha Buell Hale (1788-1879).

Collections of nursery rhymes began to appear in the 18th century. *Tommy Thumb's Pretty Song Book* (2 vol., 1744) included "Little Tom Tucker," "Sing a Song of Sixpence," and "Who Killed Cock Robin?" *Mother Goose's Melody,* various editions of which were published in the 1780s, has become the most famous collection. "Jack and Jill," "Hush-a-bye Baby," and "Hickory-Dickory Dock" are among the 51 selections it contains. *See* Children's *Literature*

NURSERY SCHOOL AND DAY NURSERY. *See* Preschool Education.

NURSING, in general, the process of caring for, or nurturing, another individual. More specifically, nursing refers to the functions and duties carried out by persons who have had formal education and training in caring for other people. Two major categories of nurses exist: practical and professional. Practical nurses usually have one year of classroom and hospital training in a vocational or technical school. Upon graduation, they must pass licensing examinations in the state in which they intend to practice. They are then entitled to use the initials LPN (licensed practical nurse) or LVN (licensed vocational nurse) after their names. These nurses practice primarily in hospitals or nursing homes under the supervision of professional nurses. Professional nurses, who also have administrative responsibilities, practice in hospitals and a variety of other health settings, including clinics, doctors' offices, industry, public health agencies, and schools—and, most recently, in their own private practices.

Functions and Duties. Many of the varied duties of a nurse are technical in nature, ranging from taking blood pressure to managing complex life-support systems in intensive care units. In addition, however, a nurse must be a teacher, counselor, and manager, concerned with promoting and maintaining the health of their patients, as well as caring for them when they are ill.

A nurse has both dependent and independent functions. The former are those that must be carried out under the orders of a licensed physician or dentist, including such duties as administering medications and changing dressings on wounds. Independent functions are those that nurses carry out based on their own professional judgment. Such duties include bathing patients, positioning them to prevent joint deformities, teaching people how best to care for themselves, and providing nutritional counseling. In the U.S., a nurse's functions are controlled by the nurse practice act of the state involved.

Nurses shown at the National Institutes of Health, Bethesda, Md., attend a clinic on radiation.
World Health Organization

With the explosion of technical knowledge in the field of health care since World War II, nurses have also begun to specialize in particular areas of nursing care. These include medical-surgical, maternal-newborn, psychiatric, pediatric, and community-health nursing. Within each of these areas are opportunities for further specialization. In addition, a new and expanded role for nurses was developed in the 1960s—that of the nurse practitioner. These nurses function within the same general areas of specialization, but their duties have been expanded beyond those usually performed by nurses. Nurse practitioners perform physical examinations, make diagnoses based on the data they gather, provide nursing services to their patients, and refer them to physicians when necessary. They also provide health education and counseling to patients and their families. Such nurses include pediatric, geriatric, and family nurse practitioners and nurse-midwives. Many of these nurses have opened private practices or have joined the practice of a physician, and many have master's degrees.

Nursing Education. Formal nursing education in the U.S. had its antecedents in Europe and England. One of the first formal training programs

for nurses was begun in 1836 in Kaiserwerth, Germany, by Pastor Theodor Fliedner (1800–64) for the Order of Deaconesses. Other religious orders were also providing formalized nurses' training in Europe at that time, but Fliedner's school is noteworthy for having given the British nursing reformer Florence Nightingale her formal training. Her experience at Kaiserwerth gave her the impetus to organize nursing care on the battlefields of the Crimean War and, later, to establish a nurse training program at Saint Thomas's Hospital in London. In the late 1800s training schools patterned after this model were established in the U.S.

Originally, nurses received little or no classroom preparation; most of their training came from an apprenticeship. All programs were directed by hospitals, and nursing students provided low-cost service to the institutions; upon graduation, most of them worked as private-duty nurses. Hospital-based programs still exist today and are known as diploma schools of nursing. They now provide a sound educational background for nursing practice, but the diploma they grant is not an academic degree, and credits awarded by the hospital are not transferable to colleges or universities. Most diploma schools, however, are affiliated with a college, where their nursing students can take courses for academic credit. Their major focus is to prepare nurses to give direct bedside care in hospitals and nursing homes, and graduates are eligible to take the licensing exam in the state in which they wish to practice. Upon passing, they are allowed to use the initials RN (registered nurse) after their names.

Many diploma schools closed after 1965, when the American Nurses' Association (ANA) published a position paper stating that all nurses should be educated in institutions of higher learning. The paper also stated that nursing should be practiced on two levels: that of the professional (by nurses who have baccalaureate or higher degrees); and that of the technical (by nurses who have associate degrees). The asso-

ciate degree nursing program, a new type of nursing education that strongly emphasized technical skills, had been introduced into U.S. educational programs in 1952. The graduate of this program functions as a bedside nurse and does not have the qualifications to assume administrative responsibilities.

Based on ANA recommendations, a professional nurse must have a baccalaureate or higher degree. The 4-year program leading to the baccalaureate usually includes two years of nursing courses with classes in community-health nursing and leadership and management skills. Emphasis is placed on the role of the nurse as a health teacher and advocate for patients. Graduates of both the associate and baccalaureate programs take state licensing exams and may then use the initials RN after their names.

Master's and doctoral degrees in nursing usu-

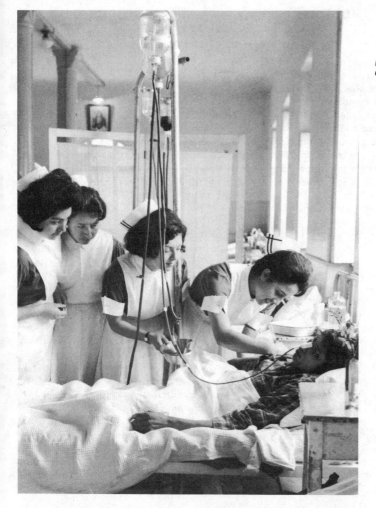

Nurses caring for a patient at Quito Hospital, Ecuador.
World Health Organization

ally require the applicant to be a graduate of an accredited baccalaureate program in nursing. The emphasis of these programs is primarily on research, advanced clinical practice, and the preparation of nursing educators and administrators.

Organizations. The ANA is the professional organization for nurses in the U.S. It is made up of state and local organizations, and its major purposes are to promote high standards of nursing care, to improve the quality and availability of health care, and to foster the professional development of nurses.

Another organization supporting the profession is the National League for Nursing (NLN); its membership includes nurses, persons from other health professions, and interested laypersons. One major function of the NLN is the accreditation of educational programs in nursing. It also offers testing and consultation services.

The International Council of Nurses is a worldwide organization established as a federation of national nursing organizations. The ANA represents the U.S. in this council. In addition to the above organizations, a variety of professional groups focus on clinical specialties.

History of Nursing. In earlier centuries, nursing care was usually provided by volunteers who had little or no training—most commonly men and women of various religious orders. During the Crusades, for example, some military orders of knights also provided nursing care, most notably the Knights Hospitalers. By the end of the 18th century nurses were functioning in hospitals, but they were commonly persons who had been imprisoned for drunkenness or who could not find work elsewhere—probably because hospitals in those days were dirty and pestilent and were considered unsuitable environments for "proper" young women.

Modern nursing may be said to have begun in the mid-19th century with the advent of the Nightingale schools for training nurses. In the U.S., the Spanish-American War and, later, World War I established the need for more nurses in both military and civilian life. As a result, nursing schools increased their enrollments, and several new experimental programs were developed. In 1920 a study funded by the Rockefeller Foundation and known as the Goldmark Report recommended that schools of nursing be independent of hospitals and that students no longer be exploited as cheap labor. As a result, several university schools of nursing were opened. In 1934 a study by the Committee on the Grading of Nursing Schools suggested a decrease in the supply of nurses and an increase in the quality of educational programs.

A group of students in nursing and midwifery at a health center in Libreville, Gabon. World Health Organization

During the depression of the 1930s, large numbers of nurses were unemployed, and the number of schools declined. World War II, however, brought about another increased demand. The Cadet Nurse Corps, begun in 1943, subsidized nursing education for thousands of young people who agreed to engage in nursing for the duration of the war. In 1948 a study by Esther Lucile Brown (1898–   ), called Nursing for the Future, recommended that all schools of nursing be affiliated with colleges and universities and that accreditation should be provided for nursing programs; the 1964 Nurse Training Act provided government funding for nursing education. Since the end of World War II, technological advances in medicine and health have required nurses to become acquainted with the functioning of sophisticated equipment, to learn about an increasing number of medications, and to design nursing care appropriate for patients in the health care delivery system. E.P.C.

For further information on this topic, see the Bibliography in volume 28, section 491.

NUT, term commonly and loosely applied to any dry, hard-shelled fruit or seed having a rind that can be easily separated from the internal, edible kernel. In botanical terminology, the term nut is restricted to a one-seeded fruit that has developed from a compound ovary, that has external walls hardened to a woody consistency, and that is indehiscent, which means that it does not split open to release its seed. Such so-called true nuts may be edible or inedible; common examples are acorns, beechnuts, chestnuts, and hazelnuts. Examples of fruits or seeds that are incorrectly and popularly termed nuts include almonds and walnuts, which are drupes with the fleshy outer layer removed; peanuts, which are seeds contained in pods; and horse chestnuts and Brazil nuts, which are seeds contained in capsules.

NUTCRACKER, common name for any bird in the genus *Nucifraga,* of the crow family, found in the coniferous forests of the colder regions of the northern hemisphere. The birds are so called because of their long, heavy bills, which they use to crack nuts. They also eat insects and the eggs and young of other birds. The best-known species are the European nutcracker, *N. caryocatactes,* about 33.8 cm (about 13.5 in) long and Clark's nutcracker, *N. columbiana,* about 31.2 cm (about 12.5 in) long, found in western North America. Clark's nutcracker, which is light gray in general body color, with black and white wings and tail, inhabits high mountains just below the timberline. It is noted for its unusual flying habits, often dropping from a high peak with its wings closed and plummeting a few hundred meters before suddenly opening them in flight.

NUTHATCH, common name for any of 15 species of passerine birds that constitute the subfamily Sittinae, of the family Sittidae, and are widely distributed in the northern hemisphere. The birds, which rarely exceed 14 cm (5.5 in) in length, are bluish-gray in general body color. They have long, straight, sturdy bills, long wings, and short tails. Nuthatches are noted for their curious arboreal habits. Obtaining their sole support from their powerful feet and long claws, they often move about head downward on the vertical surface of a tree trunk, digging into crevices in the bark for adult insects, larvae, or eggs. The birds also feed on grain and nuts, breaking them by pecking at the hard outer coatings with their bills. Nuthatches have a characteristic high-pitched, nasal cry. They nest in natural crevices or in nesting holes in trees abandoned by other birds, especially woodpeckers. The nest is lined with pieces of bark, rabbit hair, grass, and feathers. Usually four to ten creamy-white eggs, speckled with brown, gray, or purple, are deposited in a clutch.

The four North American species are all contained within the genus *Sitta.* The most common species, *S. carolinensis,* the white-breasted nuthatch, is found throughout the U.S. east of the Rocky Mountains and is abundant in winter as well as summer. It is about 14 cm (about 5.5 in) long and is grayish-blue above and white below, with patches of brown on the lower abdomen. The adult male is characterized by a black crown. The pygmy nuthatch, *S. pygmaea,* of the western U.S., is about 10 cm (about 4 in) long.

NUTLEY, town, Essex Co., NE New Jersey, on the Passaic R., a residential community near Newark; inc. 1902. Pharmaceuticals and dyes are manufactured. The town was settled in the 1680s; in the late 19th century, writers and artists established a colony here. Pop. (1970) 31,913; (1980) 28,998.

NUTMEG, common name applied to evergreen shrubs and trees of the family Myristicaceae, especially to plants of the genus *Myristica.* The family, which is a member of the order Magnoliales (*see* MAGNOLIA), comprises about 8 genera and 100 species. The nutmeg is native to the Moluccas in Indonesia; it has also been widely cultivated in southern Asia, the West Indies, and Brazil for its seeds, which yield various spices, and for its timber. Plants in the family are dioecious, with inconspicuous flowers. The fruit is a yellow drupe having a diameter of about 5 cm (about 2 in), popularly called the nutmeg apple, which splits into two equal halves, thereby revealing the seed surrounded by a fleshy outer coating. In plants of the genus *Myristica,* which contains about 80 species, this seed is dried to form the culinary spice popularly known as nutmeg; the fleshy coating is peeled off and also dried, to form the spice known as mace. The

Nutmeg, Myristica

commonest nutmeg tree is *M. fragrans,* which grows to a height of about 15 m (50 ft).

NUTRIA. *See* COYPU.

NUTRITION, HUMAN, science that deals with nutrients and other food substances, and with how the body assimilates them. The extremely complex processes that nutrients undergo in the body—how they affect one another, how they are broken down and released as energy, and how they are transported and used to rebuild countless specialized tissues and sustain the overall health of the individual—are understood only approximately. Nevertheless, important nutrition decisions need to be made for the health of individuals, of groups such as the very young and the aged, and of entire populations suffering from malnutrition.

Essential Nutrients. Nutrients are classified into five major groups: proteins (*see* PROTEIN), carbohydrates (*see* CARBOHYDRATE), fats (*see* FATS AND OILS), vitamins (*see* VITAMIN), and minerals. These groups comprise between 45 and 50 substances that scientists have established, mostly through experiments with animals, as essential for maintaining normal growth and health. Besides water and oxygen, they include about eight amino acids from proteins, four fat-soluble and ten water-soluble vitamins, about ten minerals, and three electrolytes. Although carbohydrates are needed for the body's energy, they are not considered absolutely essential, because protein can be converted for this purpose.

Energy. The body uses energy to carry on vital activities and to maintain itself at a constant temperature. By using a calorimeter, scientists have been able to establish the energy amounts of the body's fuels—carbohydrates, fats, and protein. About 4 cal each are yielded by 1 g (0.035 oz) of pure carbohydrate and 1 g of pure protein; 1 g of pure fat yields about 9 cal. (A kilogram calorie, used in nutrition, is defined as the heat energy needed to raise the temperature of 1 kg of water from 14.5° to 15.5° C.) Carbohydrates are the most abundant foods in the world, and fats are the most concentrated and easily stored fuel. If the body exhausts its available carbohydrates and fats, it can use proteins directly from the diet or break down its own protein tissue to make fuel. Alcohol is also a source of energy and yields 7 cal. per g. Alcohol cannot be oxidized by the body cells but must be processed by the liver into fat, which is then stored by the liver or in the adipose tissue.

Functions of Nutrients. The functions of the various categories of nutrients are described below.

Proteins. The primary function of protein is to build body tissue and to synthesize enzymes,

some hormones such as insulin that regulate communication among organs and cells, and other complex substances that govern body processes. Animal and plant proteins are not used in the form in which they are ingested but are broken down by digestive enzymes (proteases) into nitrogen-containing amino acids. Proteases disrupt the peptide bonds by which the ingested amino acids are linked, so that they can be absorbed through the intestine into the blood and recombined into the particular tissue needed.

Proteins are usually readily available from both animal and plant sources. Of the 20 amino acids that make up protein, 8 are considered essential; that is, because the body cannot synthesize them, they must be supplied ready-made in foods. If these essential amino acids are not all present at the same time and in specific proportions, the other amino acids, in whole or in part, cannot be used for metabolizing human protein. Therefore, a diet containing these essential amino acids is very important for sustaining growth and health. When any of the essential amino acids is lacking, the remaining ones are converted into energy-yielding compounds, and their nitrogen excreted. When an excess of protein is eaten, which is often the case with heavy meat diets in the U.S., the extra protein is similarly broken down into energy-yielding compounds. Because protein is far scarcer than carbohydrates and yields the same 4 cal/g, the eating of meat beyond the tissue-building demands of the body becomes an inefficient way to procure energy. Foods from animal sources contain complete proteins because they include all the essential amino acids. In most diets, a combination of plant and animal protein is recommended: 0.8 g/kg of body weight is considered a safe daily allowance for normal adults.

During and after illness or infection, the body requires increased amounts of protein to rebuild its tissues. Children also require more protein than do adults for growth, and children weaned on low-protein cereal paps suffer from retarded growth and greater susceptibility to diseases. This in turn brings on protein-calorie malnutrition (q.v.), or kwashiorkor, characterized by loss of body fat and wasting of muscle. In poverty-stricken countries, this syndrome claims up to 50 percent of children before they reach the age of five.

Minerals. Inorganic mineral nutrients are required in the structural composition of hard and soft body tissues; they also participate in such processes as the action of enzyme systems, the contraction of muscles, nerve reactions, and the clotting of blood (*see* BLOOD: *Coagulation;* NERvous System). These mineral nutrients, all of which must be supplied in the diet, are of two classes: the so-called major elements such as calcium, sodium, potassium, magnesium, iron, and iodine; and trace elements such as copper, cobalt, manganese, selenium, and molybdenum.

Calcium is needed for developing the bones and maintaining their rigidity. It also contributes in forming intracellular cement and the cell membranes and in regulating nervous excitability and muscular contraction. About 90 percent of calcium is stored in bone, where it can be reabsorbed by blood and tissue. Milk and milk products are the chief source of calcium.

Phosphorus, also present in many foods and especially in milk, combines with calcium in the bones and teeth. It plays an important role in energy metabolism of the cells, affecting carbohydrates, lipids, and proteins.

Magnesium, which is present in most foods, is essential for human metabolism and is important for maintaining the electrical potential in nerve and muscle cells. A deficiency in magnesium among malnourished persons, especially alcoholics, leads to tremors and convulsions.

Sodium, which is present in small and usually sufficient quantities in most natural foods, is found in liberal amounts in salted prepared and cooked foods. It is present in extracellular fluid, which it plays a role in regulating. Too much sodium causes edema, an overaccumulation of extracellular fluid. Evidence now exists that excess dietary salt largely contributes to high blood pressure.

Iron is needed to form hemoglobin, which is the pigment in red blood cells responsible for transporting oxygen, but the mineral is not readily absorbed by the digestive system. It exists in sufficient amounts in men, but women of menstrual age, who need nearly twice as much iron because of blood loss, often have deficiencies and must take in absorbable iron.

Iodine is needed to synthesize hormones of the thyroid gland. Without it, the gland swells, causing goiter, a condition that was prevalent before the use of iodized salt in the 1930s, especially in parts of the midwestern U.S., where iodine was lacking in drinking water.

Trace elements are other inorganic substances that appear in the body in minute amounts and are essential for good health. Little is known about the exact ways they function in the body, and most knowledge about them comes from how their absence, especially in animals, affects health. Trace elements appear in sufficient amounts in most foods.

Among the more important trace elements is copper, which is present in many enzymes and in copper-containing proteins found in the blood, brain, and liver. Copper deficiency is associated with the failure to use iron in the formation of hemoglobin. Zinc is also important in forming enzymes. Deficiency in zinc is believed to impair growth and, in severe cases, to cause dwarfism. Fluorine, which is retained especially in the teeth and bones, has been found necessary for growth in animals. Fluorides, a category of fluorine compounds, are important for protecting against demineralization of bone. The fluoridation of water supplies has proved an effective measure against tooth decay, reducing it by as much as 40 percent. Other trace elements include chromium, molybdenum, and selenium.

Vitamins. Vitamins are organic compounds that mainly function in enzyme systems to enhance the metabolism of proteins, carbohydrates, and fats. Without these minute substances, the breakdown and assimilation of foods could not take place. In addition, certain vitamins participate in the formation of blood cells, hormones, nervous system chemicals, and genetic materials. Vitamins are classified into two groups, the fat-soluble and the water-soluble vitamins. Fat-soluble vitamins include vitamins A, D, E, and K. The water-soluble vitamins include vitamin C and the B-vitamin complex.

Fat-soluble vitamins are usually absorbed with foods that contain fat. They are broken down by bile (see Liver), and the emulsified molecules pass through the lymphatics and veins to be distributed through the arterial system. Excess amounts are stored in the body's fat and in the liver and kidneys. Because fat-soluble vitamins can be stored, they do not have to be consumed every day.

Vitamin A affects the well-being of the epithelial tissues, such as the epidermis of the skin and the lining of the mouth and digestive and respiratory tracts. Deficiencies in vitamin A lead to bacterial invasion of these areas. An early symptom of vitamin A deficiency is night blindness, a difficulty in adapting to darkness. Sources of vitamin A are animal liver, whole milk, egg yolks, yellow-orange vegetables such as carrots and yams, and spinach.

Vitamin D increases the absorption of calcium and phosphorus and helps bone mineralization. It is produced by the body when the body is exposed to ultraviolet light; in sun-poor countries, children once suffered from rickets (q.v.) as a result of vitamin D deficiency. Vitamin D is available in only a few foods, especially fatty fishes, eggs, liver, and butter, but is now readily obtained in vitamin D fortified milk.

Vitamin E is an essential nutrient for many vertebrate animals, but its role in the human body has not been established. It has been popularly advocated for a great variety of afflictions, but no clear evidence exists that it alleviates any specific disease. Vitamin E is found in seed oils and wheat germ.

Vitamin K is necessary for the coagulation of blood. It assists in forming the enzyme prothrombin, which, in turn, is needed to produce fibrin for blood clots. Vitamin K is produced in sufficient quantities in the intestine by bacteria, but is also provided by leafy green vegetables such as spinach and kale, egg yolk, and many other foods.

The water-soluble vitamins, C and B complex, cannot be stored and therefore need to be consumed daily to replenish the body's needs. Vitamin C, or ascorbic acid, is important in the synthesis and maintenance of connective tissue. It prevents scurvy (q.v.), which attacks the gums, skin, and mucous membranes, and its main source is citrus fruits.

The most important B-complex vitamins are thiamine (B_1), riboflavin (B_2), nicotinic acid or niacin (B_3), pyridoxine (B_6), pantothenic acid, lecithin, choline, inositol, para-aminobenzoic acid (PABA), folic acid, and cyanocobalamin (B_{12}). These vitamins serve a wide range of important metabolic functions and prevent such afflictions as beriberi and pellagra (qq.v.). They are found mostly in yeast and liver.

Carbohydrates. Carbohydrates are the most abundant and least expensive foods and are the body's main source of energy. In countries where animals are scarce as food, carbohydrates make up the major portion of the diet. Without them, the body must rely on fats and protein for energy. Carbohydrates burn more efficiently than fats or proteins and put less stress on the body when oxidized. When fat is burned, it leaves large amounts of toxic metabolites in the blood, thus burdening the kidneys. When protein is converted to energy, not only is the body deprived of its amino acids for replacing tissues, but also the kidneys are burdened with eliminating excess nitrogen.

The two kinds of carbohydrates are starches, which are found mainly in the grains, the legumes, and the tubers, and sugars, which are found in plants and fruits. Carbohydrates are used by the cells in the form of glucose (q.v.), the body's main fuel. After absorption from the small intestine, glucose is processed in the liver, which stores some as glycogen, a starchlike substance, and passes the rest into the bloodstream. In combination with fatty acids, glucose forms triglycerides, which are fat compounds that can be easily broken down into combustible ketones. Glucose and triglycerides are carried by the bloodstream to the muscles and organs to be oxidized, and excess quantities are stored as fat in the adipose and other tissues, to be retrieved and burned at times of low carbohydrate intake.

The carbohydrates containing the most nutrients are the complex carbohydrates, such as unrefined grains, tubers, vegetables, and fruit, which also provide protein, vitamins, minerals, and fats. A less beneficial source is foods made from refined sugar, such as candy and soft drinks, which are high in calories but low in nutrients and fill the body with what nutritionists call empty calories.

Fats. Although scarcer than carbohydrates, fats produce more than twice as much energy. Being a compact fuel, fat is efficiently stored in the body for later use when carbohydrates are in short supply. Animals obviously need stored fat to tide them over dry or cold seasons, as do humans during times of scarce food supply. In industrial nations such as the U.S., however, with the continuous availability of foods and with machines replacing human labor, the accumulation of body fat has become a serious health concern.

In a way similar to that in which protein is broken down by digestive enzymes into amino acids to form the body's proteins, dietary fats are broken down into fatty acids that pass into the blood to form the body's own triglycerides. The fatty acids that contain as many hydrogen atoms as possible on the carbon chain are called saturated fatty acids and are derived mostly from animal sources. Unsaturated fatty acids are those having some of the hydrogen atoms missing; this group includes monounsaturated fatty acids, which have a single pair of hydrogens missing, and polyunsaturated fatty acids, which have more than one pair missing. Polyunsaturated fats are found mostly in seed oils. Saturated fats in the bloodstream have been found to raise the level of cholesterol (q.v.), and polyunsaturated fat tends to lower it. Saturated fats generally are solid at room temperature; polyunsaturated fats are liquid.

Food Types. Foods can be roughly classified into breads and cereals; pulses, or legumes; tubers, or starchy roots; vegetables and fruits; meat, fish, and eggs; milk and milk products; fats and oils; and sugars, preserves, and syrups.

Breads and cereals include wheat, rice, maize, and millet. They are high in starches and are easily procured sources of calories. Although protein is not abundant in whole cereals, the large quantity that is commonly consumed often supplies significant amounts, which, however, must be supplemented with other protein foods to supply all the essential amino acids. White wheat flour and polished rice are low in nutrients, but, as whole grains containing the germ and outer seed layer, wheat and rice supply the body with needed fiber; the B vitamins thiamine, niacin, and riboflavin; and the minerals zinc, copper, manganese, and molybdenum.

Pulses, or legumes, include the peas and beans and other such vegetables. They are high in starch and contain proteins with some of the amino acids that are often lacking in cereals. The combination of the two, particularly beans and rice, has served as an adequate source of protein, especially in protein-scarce tropical countries.

Tubers, or starchy roots, include potatoes, cassava, taro, and yams. Besides being a good calorie source, these foods, especially potatoes, contain enough nutrients to sustain adults for long periods.

Vegetables and fruits are a direct source of many minerals and vitamins lacking in cereal diets, especially vitamin C from citrus fruits and vitamin A from the carotene of leafy vegetables and carrots. Sodium, cobalt, chloride, copper, magnesium, manganese, phosphorus, and potassium are present in vegetables. The mostly indigestible cellulose of vegetables supplies the roughage needed to pass food through the digestive tract. Many of the more fragile, water-soluble vitamins exist in vegetables and fruit and can be easily destroyed by overcooking.

Meat, fish, and eggs supply all the essential amino acids that the body needs to assemble its own proteins. Meats usually contain about 20 percent protein, 20 percent fat, and 60 percent water. Organ meats are rich sources of vitamins and minerals. All fish are high in protein, and the oils of some are rich in vitamins D and A. Egg white is the most concentrated form of protein.

Milk and milk products include whole milk, cheese, yogurt, and ice cream, all of which are well known for their abundant protein, phosphorus, and especially calcium. Milk is also rich in vitamins but contains no iron and, if pasteurized, no vitamin C. Although milk is essential for children, for adults too much can cause unsaturated fatty acids to build in the blood system.

Fats and oils include butter, lard, suet, and vegetable oils. They are all high in calories, but, apart from butter and such vegetable oils as red palm oil, they contain few nutrients.

Sugars, preserves, and syrups are heavily consumed in more affluent countries, where they make up a large portion of the carbohydrate intake of individuals. Americans eat their own weight in sugar every year. Honey and maple syrup are composed of over 75 percent sugar and contain few nutrients. Sugar causes tooth decay, probably more from its continuous use than from the amount consumed.

Dietary Guidelines. The Food and Nutrition Board of the National Research Council, National Academy of Sciences, has set dietary standards called Recommended Dietary Allowances (RDA). These describe the daily amounts of energy, protein, minerals, and fat-soluble and water-soluble vitamins needed by normal healthy males and females from infancy to old age. A male, for example, 23 to 50 years old and weighing 70 kg (154 lb) has an RDA of 56 g of protein, 45 mg of ascorbic acid, and 10 mg of iron. A female 23 to 50 years old and weighing 58 kg (128 lb) has an RDA of 46 g of protein, 45 mg of ascorbic acid, and 18 mg of iron. As the U.S. diet is rapidly changing from fresh-produce foods to packaged and prepared foods, importance is increasingly placed on the need for individuals to understand—especially through nutritional labeling—whether a product meets RDA levels.

Numerous nutrition experts of the U.S. Departments of Agriculture and of Health and Human Services have voiced concern that Americans generally eat too much food and, specifically,

An African fisherman dries his catch before smoke-curing it. Drying is one of the earliest methods of food preservation.   United Nations

too much fat, cholesterol, sugar, and salt. The fat intake of Americans has risen from 32 to 42 percent of the total diet since 1900. Pointing to the incidence of obesity, diabetes, heart attacks, high blood pressure, and tooth decay, the Senate Select Committee on Nutrition and Human Needs suggested that Americans should eat 30 percent fewer calories from fats, 45 percent fewer calories from refined sugars, and 70 percent more calories from complex carbohydrates and naturally occurring sugars, and that they should reduce cholesterol intake by one-half and salt intake by two-thirds.

As for individual dietary guidelines, scientists in the federal government's food and health services recommended that a person should eat a variety of foods; maintain ideal weight; avoid too much fat, saturated fat, and cholesterol; eat foods with adequate starch and fiber; avoid too much sugar; avoid too much sodium; and drink alcohol in moderation, if at all.

The science of nutrition is still far from solving many fundamental questions about how foods affect certain individuals. Why some people can discontinue eating at a certain point and why others eat obsessively, for example, is still a mystery. Researchers have recently found that shortly after ingestion, foods influence the release of important brain chemicals and that carbohydrate foods, in particular, trigger the release of serotonin, which, in turn, suppresses the desire for carbohydrates. Such a mechanism may have evolved to prevent people from glutting themselves on carbohydrates and failing to procure harder-to-find protein. Until recent times, carbohydrate foods were far more accessible than protein. Serotonin is believed to work in complex relationships with insulin and several amino acids, especially tryptophan, all of which participate in monitoring the appetite for various food types. In this same area of research, nutrition experts are trying to unravel the relationship between diabetes and obesity and the role that sweets play for people with these afflictions.

For further information on this topic, see the Bibliography in volume 28, section 608.

NUX VOMICA, name given to the seed of *Strychnos nux-vomica,* a tree native to the Coromandel Coast of India, Sri Lanka, and other parts of Southeast Asia. The seeds contain two alkaloids closely related to each other that act as powerful poisons on the animal body, causing violent tetanic convulsions and death.

These alkaloids are named strychnine and brucine. *See* STRYCHNOS.

NYASA, LAKE. *See* MALAWI, LAKE.
NYASALAND. *See* MALAWI.

NYERERE, Julius Kambarage (1922–), first president of Tanzania (1962–). The son of a minor chief in Butiama in what was then British-ruled Tanganyika, Nyerere was educated as a teacher but entered politics in 1954 and founded the Tanganyika African National Union (TANU); he became the colony's chief minister when TANU won the elections of 1960. Nyerere continued as prime minister when Tanganyika became independent in 1961, but resigned early in 1962 to concentrate on restructuring TANU for its postindependence role. Elections in 1962 brought him back as president of a republic. In 1964, following a revolution on the Arab-dominated island of Zanzibar and a mutiny in his army, Nyerere formed a union of the two countries, with himself as president. His government has emphasized *ujamaa* ("familyhood"), a unique form of rural socialism, and aiding the liberation of white-dominated countries in southern Africa.

NYÍREGYHÁZA, town, NE Hungary, seat of Szabolcs-Szatmár Co. It is a popular tourist and health resort and the economic and transportation center for a prosperous agricultural region. The Jósa András Museum, containing a collection of archaeological and ethnological items, is here. Rebuilt on the ruins of an older settlement destroyed during the Ottoman Turkish occupation of Hungary, the community developed in the 18th century as the center for the reclaimed Nyírség swamp region. Manufacturing industries were built up after World War II. Pop. (1981 est.) 110,636.

NYLON, term applied to a synthetic resin widely used for textile fibers, characterized by great strength, toughness, and elasticity, and processed also in the form of bristles and molded articles. Nylon was developed in the 1930s by scientists of Eleuthère Irénée du Pont de Nemours, headed by the American chemist Wallace Hume Carothers (1896–1937). It is usually made by polymerizing adipic acid and hexamethylenediamine, an amine derivative (*see* POLYMER). Adipic acid is derived from phenol; hexamethylenediamine is made by treating adipic acid catalytically with ammonia and hydrogenating the product (*see* HYDROGENATION). Nylon is insoluble in water and in ordinary organic solvents; it dissolves in phenol, cresol, and formic acid, and melts at 263° C (505° F).

In making textile fibers, small chips of the nylon polymer, which is obtained as a tough, ivory-like material, are melted and forced through holes in a metal disk called a spinneret. The filaments are congealed by a blast of air and are then drawn to about four times their original lengths. The diameter of the filaments is con-

NYLON PRODUCTION

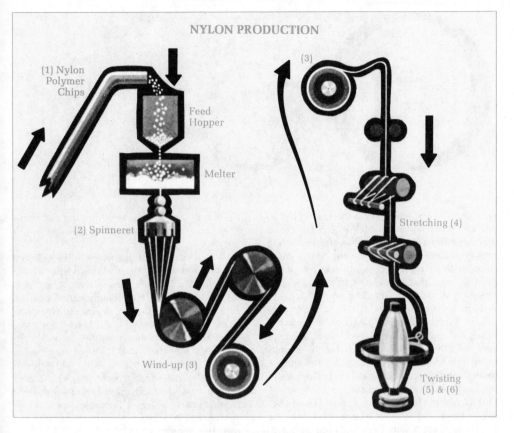

(1) Nylon Polymer Chips

Feed Hopper

Melter

(2) Spinneret

(3)

Stretching (4)

Wind-up (3)

Twisting (5) & (6)

Production of nylon: (1) Nylon polymer chips flow to a feed hopper and are melted; (2) Melted chips are pumped into a spinneret and extruded to form continuous solid monofilaments; (3) Filaments are taken up on a bobbin; (4) Nylon is stretched; (5 and 6) Assembled continuous filaments are twisted into yarn and wound onto bobbins.
Man-Made Fiber Producers Assn., Inc.

trolled by changing the rate at which the molten nylon is pumped into the spinneret and the rate at which the filaments are drawn away. Filaments much finer than those of ordinary textile fibers can be made from nylon. Nylon fibers have the appearance and luster of silk; their tensile strength is higher than that of wool, silk, rayon, or cotton. Dyes are applied either to the molten mass of nylon or to the yarn or finished fabric. Acetate rayon dyes are usually used for nylon.

Nylons made from acids and amines other than adipic acid and hexamethylenediamine have somewhat different properties but resemble generally the nylon described above.

Nylon is used in the manufacture of fabrics for such articles as hosiery, night garments, underwear, blouses, shirts, and raincoats. Nylon fabrics are water-resistant; they dry quickly when laundered and usually require no ironing. Nylon fibers are also used for parachutes, insect screen-ing, medical sutures, strings for tennis rackets, brush bristles, rope, and fishing nets and line. Molded nylon is also used for many articles, including insulating material, combs, dishware, and machinery parts.

NYMPHS, in Greek and Roman mythology, lesser divinities or spirits of nature, dwelling in groves and fountains, forests, meadows, streams, and the sea. They are usually described as young and beautiful maidens, fond of music and dancing. The nymphs were distinguished according to the various parts of nature they represented, and included the Oceanids, or daughters of Oceanus, the ocean that flows around the earth; the Nereids, or daughters of the sea god Nereus, nymphs of the Mediterranean Sea; the Potameides, river nymphs; the Naiads, nymphs of springs and freshwater streams; the Oreads, nymphs of mountains and grottoes; and the Dryads, nymphs of the forests.

O, 15th letter and 4th vowel in the English alphabet and other alphabets of Western Europe. It was originally a Phoenician character that stood for a guttural breathing sound. The Greeks adopted this sign to represent *omicron*, or the short *o*, and added a separate sign for the long *o*, *omega*. A single letter, standing for both sounds, was incorporated into the Latin alphabet. In English the letter *o* represents a long sound, as in the words *old* and *bone*; and a short sound, as in *hot* and *golf*. The letter also stands for the sounds heard in *shorn, wolf, son,* and *do*. The long *o* sound is indicated by a variety of spellings, as in the words *sew, dough,* and *foe*.

OAHU, island, Honolulu Co., central Hawaii, between Kauai and Molokai islands; known as the Gathering Place. Oahu is about 64 km (about 40 mi) long and 42 km (26 mi) wide. The island is the commercial center of Hawaii and is important to U.S. defenses in the Pacific. Pearl Harbor naval base is situated here. The chief agricultural industries are the growing and processing of pineapples and sugarcane; tourism also is very important to the economy. Among the many popular beaches is the renowned Waikiki, backed by the famous Diamond Head, an extinct volcano. The largest community, Honolulu, is the state capital. Area, 1526 sq km (589 sq mi); pop. (1980 est.) 762,000.

OAK, common name of the genus *Quercus*, comprising a large group of hardwood trees that are widespread in the North Temperate Zone. The oak genus contains about 450 species and is a member of the Fagaceae family, the only family in the beech (q.v.) order, Fagales. Oaks are distinguished from the other ten or so genera in the beech order by various technical characteristics of their minute, clustered flowers, but they are easily recognized by their distinctive fruit, the acorn. The related tan oak, genus *Lithocarpus*, one species of which occurs in the coastal ranges of California and Oregon, also produces an acorn, but it is distinguished from the oak genus by its upright rather than hanging male flower clusters.

About 60 species of oak occur in the U.S. and Canada, and about 150 additional species are found in Mexico. They grow in a variety of habitats, from seacoasts to high mountain slopes and from wet lowlands to high, dry mesas. Flowering occurs in the spring, usually before the new leaves appear, and large quantities of pollen are often shed into the wind. The trees may be deciduous (losing their leaves in the fall) or evergreen. Most eastern U.S. species are deciduous— the live oak, *Q. virginiana*, of the southeastern coastal plain being a notable exception— whereas the West has both many evergreen and many deciduous species.

Oaks produce durable, tough wood and are important lumber trees. The wood is used in cabinetry and barrel making and as flooring and veneers. Corks are made from the thick, spongy bark of the cork oak, *Q. suber*, which occurs in the Mediterranean region. Several species yield tannins, which are used in the leather-tanning industry, and others yield dyes from their bark. Oaks are of some horticultural importance, but because most are slow growing, they are more often planted in public parks and gardens than in private lawns. Scarlet oak, *Q. coccinea*, willow oak, *Q. phellos*, and pin oak, *Q. palustris*, however, are moderate to fast-growing species that are well suited to both purposes.   M.R.C.

OAK FOREST, city, Cook Co., NE Illinois, a residential community S of Chicago. The city, named for its oak trees, is the site of a large hospital specializing in rehabilitation. Pop. (1970) 19,271; (1980) 26,096.

OAKLAND, city, seat of Alameda Co., W California, on the E shore of San Francisco Bay, adjacent to Berkeley; inc. as a city 1854. The hub of a large metropolitan area that extends E to the San Joaquin Valley, the city is a major deepwater ship-

White oak, Quercus alba. The Wye Oak, near Wye Mills, Md., is believed to be one of the largest white oaks in the U.S. It is approximately 29 m (95 ft) high, with a branch spread of 50 m (165 ft).
Maryland Department of Information

ping point with an excellent natural harbor and great containerized-cargo-handling facilities. It is linked with San Francisco by the long San Francisco-Oakland Bay Bridge (1936) and is served by a major international airport and the Bay Area Rapid Transit system. Oakland also is an important manufacturing center; products include primary and fabricated metal, machinery, engines, glass containers, and processed food.

A U.S. Army base and a large U.S. naval supply center are here, as are Mills College (1852), Holy Names College (1868), California College of Arts and Crafts (1907), and junior colleges. The city is the site of the Oakland Museum, with art, history, and natural science exhibits; Patti McClain's Museum of Vintage Fashion; Chabot Observatory; a zoo; and many parks. It supports a symphony orchestra, ballet companies, and theatrical groups. Lake Merritt, a large body of salt water bordered by a park, is in the center of the city. The Oakland/Alameda County Coliseum Com-

plex here is the home of major league sports teams. Other tourist attractions in Oakland include Jack London Square, a picturesque waterfront region where the writer lived; the Morcom Amphitheater of Roses; and Dunsmuir House and Gardens.

A Spanish grant for the area now including Oakland was issued to Don Luis Maria Peralta in 1820. In 1852 Moses Chase leased a tract from Peralta's sons and platted the community, which was named for a grove of oak trees on the site. The city became a terminus of the first transcontinental railroad in 1869 and developed as a major railhead after 1880. Its growth as a shipping center accelerated during World War II. Pop. (1970) 361,561; (1980) 339,337.

OAK LAWN, village, Cook Co., NE Illinois, on Stony Creek; inc. 1909. It is a residential suburb of Chicago with some industry, including the manufacture of metal and paper products and machine tools. The Palos Hills Forest Preserve and Lake Calumet are nearby. Oak Lawn grew rapidly in the 1960s. Pop. (1970) 60,305; (1980) 60,590.

OAKLEY, Annie (1860–1926), professional name of PHOEBE ANNE OAKLEY MOSEE, American markswoman and performer, born in a pioneer log cabin in Darke Co., Ohio. Associated with Buffalo Bill's Wild West Show from 1885 to 1902, she was the sensation of America and Europe because of her almost uncanny accuracy with a rifle, a weapon she began to use at the age of six to help provide food for her family. As a young woman she was one of the best-known professional game hunters in the country. Performing with a rifle, she could hit a playing card thrown into the air a dozen times before it finally touched the ground.

OAK PARK, village, Cook Co., NE Illinois, adjoining Chicago on the W; inc. 1902. Oak Park, primarily a residential community, is the birthplace and childhood home of the novelist Ernest Hemingway. The architect Frank Lloyd Wright also lived here (1890–1910), and more than 20 of the village's structures were designed by him. Oak Park was settled in the 1830s and named for a ridge of oak trees that defined its original boundary. Its population expanded rapidly following the Chicago fire in 1871. Pop. (1970) 62,511; (1980) 54,887.

OAK PARK, city, Oakland Co., SE Michigan; inc. 1945. It is a suburb of Detroit with some industry, including the manufacture of motor-vehicle parts, tools and dies, canvas products, electronic equipment, and machinery. Pop. (1970) 36,762; (1980) 31,537.

OAK RIDGE, city, Anderson and Roane counties, central Tennessee, on Black Oak Ridge (hence its name), near Knoxville; inc. 1959. It is a leading center for research and production in the field of nuclear energy. Major facilities include Oak Ridge National Laboratory, Oak Ridge Y-12 Plant, and Oak Ridge Gaseous Diffusion Plant. Electronic equipment and scientific instruments are other important manufactures. In the city are Oak Ridge Associated Universities (1946), a research and educational center run jointly by some 40 southern universities and colleges; the American Museum of Science and Energy; and a large arboretum. The community, originally called Clinton Engineer Works, was founded in 1942 by the U.S. government as part of the secret Manhattan Project to develop an atomic bomb. Its population reached a peak of more than 75,000 by the end of World War II. During 1955–59 ownership of the community of Oak Ridge passed to its residents. Pop. (1970) 28,319; (1980) 27,662.

OAKVILLE, industrial town, Regional Municipality of Halton, SE Ontario, Canada, a port on Lake Ontario at the mouth of Oakville Creek; inc. 1857. Major manufactures include railroad equipment, motor vehicles, refined petroleum, electrical lamps, chemicals, pharmaceuticals, machinery, and containers. The community, settled in the 1820s, grew as a shipbuilding and shipping center. In 1962 Oakville was amalgamated with Trafalgar township, thereby significantly increasing the area of the community. Pop. (1976) 68,950; (1981) 75,773.

OATES, Titus (1649–1705), English conspirator, the principal informer in the so-called Popish plot in England, born in Oakham, and educated at the University of Cambridge. Taking advantage of the public's hostility toward Roman Catholics, in 1678 Oates gave the authorities details of a fictitious plot by Roman Catholics to murder the Protestant monarch Charles II. Oates swore that the plan was to replace Charles with his Roman Catholic brother, James, duke of York.

As a result of the perjured testimony of Oates and his followers about 35 people lost their lives between 1678 and 1681, while Oates himself for a time received a large pension and lived in Whitehall Palace. A reaction set in against Oates and in 1684 he was imprisoned. In 1685, with the accession of the duke of York as King James II, Oates was found guilty of perjury and sentenced to life imprisonment. After James was deposed by the Glorious Revolution in 1688, Oates was freed by the new king, William III.

OATH, sworn statement, affirmation, or pledge, usually based upon religious principles and often used in legal matters. In a court of law, for example, every witness must swear or affirm that the testimony he or she gives is the truth. Another example is the oath taken by a public official, such as the president or vice-president of the U.S., when that official assumes office. The taking of an oath generally implies some legal or moral sanction for failing to carry out one's sworn pledge; a trial witness, for instance, may be charged with the crime of perjury for lying while under oath.

The oath has its origins in religious customs, and some form of binding oath can be found in every culture. Oaths are administered upon entering such varied institutions as military service, secret societies, religious orders, and marriage bonds.

OATS, common name for the seeds or grains of plants belonging to the genus *Avena,* and for the plants themselves. The genus, a member of the family Gramineae (*see* GRASSES); contains about 50 species that grow widely in the cooler temperate regions of the world. Several are cultivated for their grain, which is used as feed for cattle and horses and also for human consumption as a cereal. The green plants are often used for hay, silage, and pasture, and the dried straw is a popular bedding for livestock.

Oats are important rotation crops on livestock and grain farms in the northern U.S., Canada, and northern and eastern Europe.

Oats are normally sown in early spring and harvested in mid- to late summer. In the southern U.S. and in the southern regions of Europe, oats may be sown in the fall. The most widely planted species is the common oat (*A. sativa*). Other important species include the cultivated red oat (*A. byzantina*), the wild red oat (*A. sterilis*), and the side oat (*A. orientalis*). The wild oat (*A. fatua*) is a common and often costly weed that grows in the cooler, drier regions of North America, Europe, and Asia. Cultivated oats were derived from wild oats, probably *A. fatua,* by farmers in the Middle East and Europe about 4500 years ago.

Oat grains as harvested consist of highly digestible groat (seed) held within an indigestible hull. Compared with other grains, whole (unhulled) oats produce feeds that are high in protein (12 percent), fat (5 percent), and fiber (12 to 14 percent) and low in carbohydrates (about 64 percent). Research efforts have focused on developing oat varieties with improved yields, higher protein and energy content, and stronger resistance to rust, to virus diseases, and to attacks by insects.

As cereals and porridges, which are derived from roasted grains, oats are high in protein and are particularly good sources of thiamine, or vitamin B_1 (*see* VITAMIN). In recent years the use of oats has been extended to ready-to-eat breakfast cereals and a wide variety of processed foods. Oat flour contains antioxidants that retard rancidity in fat-containing foods; it is an ingredient of such products as peanut butter, margarine, chocolate, and doughnut flours and is a preservative inner coating for the paper bags used to package salted nuts, coffee, and potato chips. Oat flour also serves as a fat stabilizer in ice cream and other dairy products. The most important industrial product from oats is furfural, a chemical derived from oat hulls and used as a solvent in various refining industries.

The USSR, the U.S., and Canada are the world's largest producers of oats, in that order. World production in the early 1980s was about 50 million metric tons annually; 20 percent of this total was produced in the U.S.

See also CROP FARMING. W.D.P.

OB, river, Siberian USSR, rising in SW Siberia, on the N slopes of the Altai Mts., near the border with Mongolia. The Ob, about 3700 km (about 2300 mi) long, flows generally NW where it receives its chief tributary, the Irtysh R., turns to the N, and empties into the Gulf of Ob, an arm of the Arctic Ocean. The river drains an area of more than 2,590,000 sq km (more than 1 million sq mi). An important water route for the region, the Ob is used principally to transport lumber and grain, although navigation is impeded by ice in winter. A few industrial cities and a hydroelectric plant have been built on the banks of the river near its source. The combined Ob-Irtysh system, the longest river system of Asia, is about 5568 km (about 3460 mi) long.

OBADIAH, shortest book of the Old Testament, consisting of only one chapter of 21 verses. It is one of 12 short prophetic books known, primarily because of their brevity, as the Minor Prophets. Tradition attributes it to the 6th-century BC Hebrew prophet Obadiah, but many modern scholars question the unity of the book and ascribe it to more than one author, one of whom may have been Obadiah. It is generally agreed that the book dates from postexilic times; verses 11–14 most probably refer to the fall of Jerusalem in 586 BC. Many dates have been suggested, however, for other passages, some of them as early as the 9th century and others as late as the 4th century BC.

The first part of Obadiah (1–14) foretells the fall of Judah's traditional enemy, Edom. The specific grievance against Edom expressed in the book doubtless was provoked by the hostility of the Edomites at the time of the capture of Jerusalem. Apparently, the Edomites assisted in the destruction of the city and in the capture of Israelite refugees. The remainder of the book (15–21) is eschatological in nature. A "day of the Lord" (15) is prophesied, at which time, in addition to Edom, the neighboring nations will be punished for their behavior toward Israel. Thereafter, Israel will possess all of Palestine and "the kingdom shall be the Lord's" (21).

OBELISK, four-sided tapering shaft terminating in a pyramid or conical top. In ancient Egypt, pairs of these monoliths, each hewn from a single piece of red granite and set on a cubical base, often flanked temple entrances and were associated with sun worship. The pointed tops were frequently sheathed in brass or gold; sculptured dedicatory or commemorative hieroglyphs about the Egyptian pharaohs usually ran down the sides of the shaft. Obelisks were produced throughout ancient Egyptian history, the dwarf specimens generally dating from the earliest and latest peri-

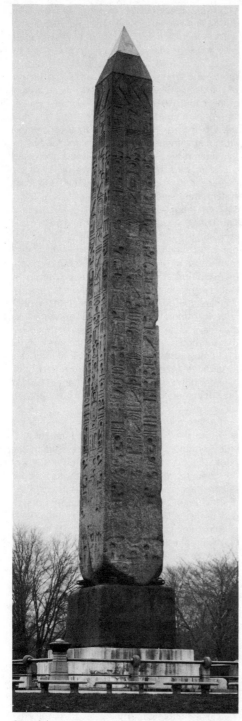

One of the two Egyptian obelisks (15th cent. BC) popularly called Cleopatra's Needles is now in Central Park, New York City. The other is in London.

Metropolitan Museum of Art

ods, and the giant specimens from the Middle Kingdom.

The obelisk form is still used in monuments and decorations and as an architectural adjunct. It was a popular feature in baroque and neoclassical tombs and has been used everywhere in the Western world as an ornamental element in parks, gardens, and cemeteries. It has often been added to fountains, balustrades, and gables. The Bunker Hill Monument in Boston, and the Washington Monument in Washington, D.C., are built in the shape of obelisks; as opposed to the traditional obelisk, which is carved from a single piece of solid rock, these monuments are masonry towers constructed of many stone blocks.

OBERAMMERGAU, town, S West Germany, in Bavaria, on the Ammer R. Situated in the Bavarian Alps, Oberammergau is a popular tourist resort and noted wood-carving center. The famous Passion Play, which originated in 1634, is performed here. It was first presented by the inhabitants in gratitude for the end of a plague epidemic. Except for the years 1870, 1920, and 1940, the play has been presented every tenth year since 1680 in keeping a vow made by the 17th-century townspeople. The day-long performances, attended by thousands, are held in the open air. Pop. (1977 est.) 4876.

OBERHAUSEN, city, W West Germany, in North Rhine-Westphalia, near the Rhine R. It is a manufacturing center and rail junction situated in the Ruhr industrial district. Products include iron and steel, chemicals, metal goods, glass items, and machinery. Oberhausen received a charter in 1874. Pop. (1980 est.) 229,300.

OBERLIN COLLEGE, privately controlled nondenominational institution of higher learning, in Oberlin, Ohio, founded in 1833, and known as Oberlin Collegiate Institute until 1850, when its present name was adopted. Oberlin was the first coeducational college in the U.S. Two years after its founding the college admitted students "without respect to color," becoming the first U.S. college to do so; before the American Civil War it was known as a center for antislavery activities. Charles Grandison Finney (1792–1875), professor of theology and president of Oberlin from 1851 to 1866, first promulgated at the college his doctrine of evangelical Calvinism known as Oberlin Theology.

Divisions include the College of Arts and Sciences and the Conservatory of Music. The degrees granted are the bachelor of arts in liberal arts and sciences and the master of arts in some departments. The conservatory grants the degrees of bachelor of music and bachelor of fine arts in music and the graduate degrees of master

The prayer after the Last Supper, from the famous Oberammergau Passion play. The drama depicts the suffering, death, and resurrection of Christ.   Lufthansa-German Airlines

of music in teaching, music theater, music education, and conducting.

OBESITY, body condition characterized by storage of excessive amounts of fat in adipose tissue beneath the skin and within other organs, including muscles. All mammals store body fat; in normal women 25 percent, and in normal men 15 percent, of body weight is stored as fat.

Deposition of fat, which has twice the potential energy of carbohydrate or protein, is a way of storing energy for times of future need. Storage of greatly increased amounts of fat, however, is associated with impairment of health. Data from insurance company records show that persons who are 30 percent or more overweight run measurably increased risks of disease, notably diabetes, cardiovascular and gallbladder disease, and arthritis, and often encounter complications in surgery.

Obesity is only rarely caused by disturbances of the endocrine system (q.v.). It is not inherited, nor do fat babies necessarily grow up to be fat adults. Obesity is a result of taking in more energy in food than one uses in activity. Scientists have found that both obese and normal-weight people go on eating binges, but people of normal weight reduce their intake afterward to compensate, whereas obese people do not. Besides excess eating, obesity can also be caused by reduced activity, and this often occurs in persons who are sedentary or bedridden.

Many approaches to weight loss have been tried in obese people, with only limited success. Diet pills, containing the stimulant drug dextroamphetamine or one of its derivatives, became popular in the 1950s, but the Food and Drug Administration issued a series of warnings to physicians that they did not work and could be habit-forming, and their use declined. Many complex diets have been promoted for weight loss, but no scientific evidence exists that they are effective for grossly obese people. One form of diet developed to provide nourishment for hospitalized people, the liquid protein diet, was marketed commercially until 1979, when it was found that several people had died while using this mixture as a sole source of nutrition. The mixture upset the natural balance of sodium and potassium in the body, leading to impaired heart function.

Surgical procedures used to aid weight loss include intestinal bypass and gastric bypass. In the former operation a length of intestine is removed to reduce absorption of nutrients. This operation has been largely abandoned because it produced severe side effects, such as liver damage and chronic diarrhea, and caused several deaths. In the gastric bypass procedure most of the stomach is closed off with surgical staples. Only a small pouch remains to receive food, thereby greatly reducing the person's eating capacity.

Since obesity is thought to result from abnormal eating habits, many people believed that behavior modification would be an effective

291

treatment. In this therapy people are taught to eat only at certain times of the day or in certain places, to eat slowly, and to keep a written record of all they eat. Only about 15 percent of people treated this way, however, lose a significant amount of weight and do not gain it back in the following year. *See also* NUTRITION, HUMAN.

OBOE, double-reed wind instrument with a wood body and narrow conical bore. It was invented by the French musicians Jean Hotteterre (d. about 1678) and Michel Philidor (d. about 1659), who modified the louder shawm (the prevailing double-reed instrument) for indoor use. Their oboe, called *hautbois* (Fr. "high, or loud, wood"), as was the shawm, had a narrower bore than the shawm's, a body in three sections instead of one, and a smaller reed grasped near its tip by the player's lips (on a shawm the mouth encloses the entire reed, the lips resting on a wooden disk at the base of the reed). By 1700 most orchestras included a pair of oboes. Early oboes had seven finger holes and two keys; by the 1700s, four-keyed models were also in use. In the 1800s additional keys were added, reaching 15 or more, and the bore and sound holes were redesigned. Oboes of the French school (played in most countries today) have a very narrow bore and a penetrating, focused sound. Those of the German school (played principally in Vienna and the USSR) have a wider bore and a more easily blending sound. The range of the modern oboe extends two and one-half octaves upward from the B below middle C. Composers of solo works for the oboe include George Frideric Handel, Robert Schumann, and Carl Nielsen.

The English horn (*cor anglais*) is an alto oboe, a fifth lower in pitch, and is probably identical with the *oboe da caccia* ("hunting oboe") used by Johann Sebastian Bach. The *oboe d'amore* (invented about 1720, revived occasionally) is pitched a third below the oboe. The heckelphone (invented 1904) is an improved baritone oboe, pitched an octave below the oboe. The term *oboe* also refers generically to any double-reed instrument, such as European folk shawms (for example, the Balkan *zurla*), the ancient Greek *aulos*, the Indian *nagasuaram*, and the Japanese *hichiriki*.

OBOTE, (Apollo) Milton (1925–), prime minister (1962–66) and president (1966–71, 1980–) of Uganda. Born in Lango, the son of a chief, Obote was a labor organizer in Kenya before returning to Uganda in 1957 to serve in the legislative council under the British. He was the founder (1960) of the Uganda People's Congress and at its head led his country to independence in 1962. Declaring Uganda a unitary republic instead of a federal one, he assumed the presidency in 1966 and subsequently attempted to form a one-party state, but he was ousted in 1971 by Maj. Gen. Idi Amin and went into exile in Tanzania. After Amin's overthrow in 1979, Obote returned to his homeland and, following elections in 1980, was restored to the presidency.

OBREGÓN, Álvaro (1880–1928), Mexican soldier and president (1920–24), born near Alamos, Sonora State. In 1912 he organized a force of about 400 Indians. As commander of this force he entered the service of Francisco Madero, president of Mexico, and crushed a revolt. After the death of Madero in 1913, Obregón supported Venustiano Carranza as the nation's new leader. During the ensuing two years, Obregón helped defeat the various rebel forces led by Carranza's rival Victoriano Huerta, and by the popular revolutionaries Francisco Villa, better known as Pancho Villa, and Emiliano Zapata; in a battle against Villa, Obregón lost his right arm. On the election of Carranza to the presidency in 1915, Obregón was appointed commander in chief of the Mexican army. In 1920 he led a successful revolt against Carranza and soon afterward was elected president. He instituted a number of labor, agrarian, and educational reforms, and in 1923 he secured the formal recognition of his government by the U.S. Between 1924 and 1928 he was politically inactive. He was reelected president in 1928 but was assassinated before he could take office.

A music student rehearses a composition for oboe.
Editorial Photocolor Archives

OBSCENITY, act, utterances, or items (primarily publications and films) deemed contrary to public standards of sexual morality. Obscene items are often called pornography (q.v.). Because public standards vary, any definition of obscenity is relative to the time and place in which it is formulated. Obscenity has not, in fact, always been considered a public concern. In England, for example, until the early 1700s publishing sexually indecent material was not an offense.

The U.S. has had obscenity laws since 1842. These laws have at times been stringent and their enforcement vigorous. To liberal thinkers, such laws were controversial and even misguided (by contemporary standards), as in the suppression of the Irish novelist James Joyce's literary masterpiece *Ulysses* until 1933. In the 1950s the U.S. Supreme Court relaxed prohibitions on the sale, distribution, and possession of obscene materials. In 1973, however, it reversed its more liberal direction, and assigned the determination of what was obscene to the states, making "contemporary community standards" the key. In practice these standards vary substantially from one community to another.

OBSERVATORY, building or series of buildings specially constructed for use in making astronomical observations. Modern observatories customarily house telescopes, although the term is also sometimes applied to buildings used for observing magnetic or meteorological phenomena. The earliest known astronomical observatories were built by the Chinese and the Babylonians about 2300 BC. These observatories were probably little more than high platforms giving an unobstructed view of the sky. About 300 BC the most famous observatory of classical times was built in Alexandria, Egypt. It was probably equipped with instruments, such as the astrolabe (q.v.), by which the celestial latitude and longitude of a star or planet could be measured. The Alexandria observatory existed for approximately 500 years.

After the beginning of the Christian era, the Arabs established a number of observatories at Damascus, and Baghdad and at Mokatta near Cairo in Egypt. The last named was built about AD 1000. The first observatory in Europe was set up in Nuremberg (now in West Germany) in 1471. A century later, a large and well-equipped observatory was built by the Danish astronomer Tycho Brahe on the island of Ven. Brahe's observatory, in which he lived and worked from 1576 to 1596, was equipped with a large quadrant used in making accurate measurements of the altitudes of celestial bodies. The observations Brahe made were used by the German astrono-

mer Johannes Kepler in developing his theory of the solar system.

After the invention of the telescope about 1609, a number of new observatories were built in various European cities. Among the most famous were the French National Observatory at Paris, established in 1667, and the British Royal Observatory, often called the Greenwich Observatory (q.v.), founded in 1675. Both are still in existence. The first observatory to be constructed in the U.S. was built at Chapel Hill, N.C., in 1831. The Naval Observatory (q.v.) at Washington, D.C., was established in 1842. Other famous U.S. observatories are the Lick Observatory (q.v.), the Mount Wilson Observatory, the Palomar Observatory (see HALE OBSERVATORIES), and the Yerkes Observatory (q.v.).

Many observatories are situated on tops of mountains, where the best conditions for observation are found. Examples are the Pic du Midi Observatory in the Pyrenees and the Kitt Peak National Observatory (q.v.) near Tucson, Ariz.

Classification of Observatories. Astronomical observatories are classified into several types. Government observatories are usually occupied with continuous observation of the stars and planets for the preparation of navigational tables and the determination of standard times (see NAVIGATION). Observatories connected with educational institutions are used chiefly for training students in the techniques of astronomical observation. Certain university observatories and other observatories not connected with institutions are dedicated to purely observational problems such as the discovery of comets and the discovery and measurement of variable stars. Many of the larger observatories are entirely devoted to the problems of astrophysics (q.v.). In addition, some observatories have separate instruments that are used to study solar phenomena; a few observatories make only solar observations.

In the 1950s a new type of observatory was established for the study of radio emanations from the sun and stars. Research in this field, called radio astronomy (q.v.), is conducted with instruments known as radio telescopes.

A number of amateur astronomers build their own observatories in or near their homes. Such observatories usually contain telescopes and other equipment constructed by the owners. These observatories supplement the work of professional observatories by making measurements of variable stars, meteors, and comets, which are too numerous to be constantly watched by professional astronomers.

High-Altitude and Orbital Observatories. A relatively new field of astronomical technology is

The Palomar Observatory in southern California, with its 200-in (508-cm) Hale reflecting telescope, photographed by moonlight. The telescope was the largest in the world until the 1970s.

concerned with study of the universe from a point high above the earth, using equipment carried by balloons, rockets, and orbiting observatories. Carrying telescopes, cameras, and instruments for spectral analysis, these vehicles provide a means of studying the stars and planets free of distortion from the atmosphere.

The first space observatory, the satellite *Cosmos 215,* was launched by the Soviet Union in March 1968. Equipped with eight telescopes for

studying ultraviolet radiation from outer space and one for X rays, it had limited success in its six-week life. In December 1968 the U.S. launched the *Orbiting Astronomical Observatory* (*OAO 2*), a satellite equipped with spectrometers designed to study ultraviolet radiation from young stars and to photograph planets and interstellar matter. In the early 1970s several high-level observatories were launched. *Skylab,* a U.S. orbiting observatory occupied by three crews for a total of 171 days in 1973–74, was equipped with six telescopes for solar observation. In 1986 the space shuttle (*see* SPACE EXPLORATION) is slated to carry the space telescope, a 96-in. (244-cm) reflector, into orbit.

For further information on this topic, see the Bibliography in volume 28, section 377.

OBSIDIAN, dark, semitranslucent natural glass produced when molten igneous rock (magma) pushes its way up to the earth's surface and cools so rapidly that its constituent ions do not have time to crystallize. The composition of this glassy volcanic rock varies considerably, from that of a light-colored rhyolite (q.v.) to that of a dark basalt (q.v.). Because it is easy to shape by flaking, obsidian was prized by primitive humans, who used it to make weapons and tools.

OBSTETRICS, branch of medicine concerning the management of pregnancy, labor, and the period immediately following childbirth. It involves the psychological and social aspects of childbearing, as well as the biomedical. Obstetricians strive to ensure that every pregnancy results in a healthy mother and baby.

Obstetrics has not always been so broadly defined. Until recently, it involved only the mechanics of childbirth, and early practitioners did not have medical training. As early as 1303, the term *midwife* was used for women who assisted in home deliveries, and eventually the term *midwifery* evolved in reference to their practice. In modern Great Britain the terms *midwifery* and *obstetrics* are used interchangeably, but in the U.S. they are not.

Improvements in the practice of obstetrics can be measured by the decline in maternal and infant death rates. Historically these rates have been extremely high. In the past few decades, however, increasing attention has been paid to nutrition and hygiene. Medical care has also improved due to the discovery of antibiotics, which combat infection, the use of blood transfusions to treat hemorrhage, and the development of surgical techniques needed in childbirths threatening the life of either the mother or child. In addition, a trend developed toward hospital rather than home deliveries, along with a general upgrading in the skills and training of physicians specializing in pregnancy and childbirth.

Medical improvements have thus dramatically reduced the number of women and infants who die as a result of childbirth. In 1935 in the U.S., for example, 12,544 women died as a result of giving birth, whereas in 1979 this number was reduced to 270. The number of infants who are stillborn or who die during the first 28 days following birth has also dropped. In 1950 in the

U.S., 141,117 infants died in the first 28 days of life, but in 1979 only 45,000 infants were stillborn or died in the first weeks of life. Not all these deaths were preventable, because birth defects (q.v.) are a major cause of infant death.

Obstetrics is closely related to other medical specialties, particularly gynecology (q.v.). The two specialties are often regarded as the same; gynecology, however, is concerned with the female reproductive organs in the nonpregnant state, whereas obstetrics treats the pregnant state.　　　　　　　　　　　　　　M.R.

OCALA, city, seat of Marion Co., N central Florida. It is a processing and shipping center of an area producing citrus fruit, vegetables, livestock, timber, phosphates, limestone, and fuller's earth. Manufactures include mobile homes, forest products, fertilizer, and processed food. A junior college and a horse research center are here, and many thoroughbred horse farms are in the area. Ocala National Forest, Silver Springs, and other tourist attractions are nearby. The name of the community, platted in 1846, is derived from a Timucua Indian word of unknown meaning. Pop. (1970) 22,583; (1980) 37,170.

OCARINA, small, egg-shaped flute with a protruding whistle mouthpiece and usually ten finger holes. The ocarina is a globular flute, a flute type found in many cultures. The modern ocarina originated in Italy in the early 19th century. It gained great popularity among street players and was made in families from soprano to bass for ensemble playing. Made of hollow metal, earthenware, or plastic, it produces a muted, flutey tone. In the U.S. it is colloquially called a "sweet potato."

O'CASEY, Sean (1880–1964), Irish dramatist, whose plays deal realistically with Dublin slum life and the Irish struggle for independence. He was an important figure in the Irish literary revival of the early 20th century.

O'Casey was born in Dublin on March 30, 1880. As a young man living in the slums, he worked as an unskilled laborer. He became active in the Irish labor movement and in the nationalist struggle against British rule, but disillusioned with the middle-class leadership of the nationalists, he did not take part in the Easter Rebellion (q.v.) and turned to the theater as a means of social and political protest. O'Casey's plays, often drawn from episodes in his own life, are characterized by a lyrical prose style; tense and compelling dramatic situations; and a rich sense of irony and wit. At the same time, they evince a deep feeling for the tragedy of ordinary lives and a hatred of political and religious oppression.

OCCASIONALISM

Many of O'Casey's plays were first produced at Dublin's noted Abbey Theatre (q.v.). Although recognized early in his career as one of Ireland's important dramatists, O'Casey left Ireland and moved to England in 1926, because of the bad reception his plays encountered. An Abbey Theatre audience, enraged by his truthful depiction of the Irish people in *The Plough and the Stars* (1926), incited a riot. Among his other plays are *The Shadow of a Gunman* (1923) and *Juno and the Paycock* (1924).

In addition to the straightforward realistic manner employed in these powerful and effective dramas, O'Casey experimented successfully with expressionism and symbolism in *The Silver Tassie* (1928), *Red Roses for Me* (1942), and *Cock-a-Doodle Dandy* (1949).

O'Casey's six-volume autobiography appeared from 1939 to 1954; in it he discussed, in subjective, stream-of-consciousness style, his personal life and his experience in the theater. O'Casey died in Torquay, England, on Sept. 18, 1964.

OCCASIONALISM, term employed to designate the philosophical system devised by the followers of the 17th-century French philosopher René Descartes, who, in attempting to explain the interrelationship between mind and body, concluded that God is the only cause. The occasionalists began with the assumption that certain actions or modifications of the body are preceded, accompanied, or followed by changes in the mind. This assumed relationship presents no difficulty to the popular conception of mind and body, according to which each entity is supposed to act directly on the other; these philosophers, however, asserting that cause and effect must be similar, could not conceive the possibility of any direct mutual interaction between substances as dissimilar as mind and body.

According to the occasionalists, the action of the mind is not, and cannot be, the cause of the corresponding action of the body. Whenever any action of the mind takes place, God directly produces in connection with that action, and by reason of it, a corresponding action of the body; the converse process is likewise true. This theory did not solve the problem, for if the mind cannot act on the body (matter), then God, conceived as mind, cannot act on matter. Conversely, if God is conceived as other than mind, then he cannot act on mind. A proposed solution to this problem was furnished by exponents of radical empiricism such as the American philosopher and psychologist William James. This theory disposed of the dualism of the occasionalists by denying the fundamental difference between mind and matter.

Sean O'Casey   UPI

OCCULTISM (Lat. *occulere,* "to hide"), belief in hidden or mysterious powers not explained by known scientific principles of nature, and the attempt to bring these powers within human control by scientific methods. The medieval concept of occult properties included only those properties that may be revealed by experimentation. The alchemists, astrologers, seers, and others who practiced this "science" of experimentation were a small group, usually in conflict with orthodox theology. Consequently, their work was considered mysterious, and the term *occultism* gradually came to denote the study of supernatural forces. Nevertheless, all the so-called natural sciences stemmed from occultism, and early scientists were frequently called magicians and sorcerers because of the mystery attributed to their investigations by most of their contemporaries.

Modern occultism is generally considered to have begun with the concept of animal magnetism, first developed by the Austrian physician Franz Anton Mesmer in the late 18th century. Mesmer believed that certain individuals possess occult powers, comparable to the powers of the magnet, that can be used to invoke the supernatural. In the mid-19th century occultism took the form of spiritualism, a belief that the spirits of the dead may manifest themselves through the agency of living persons called mediums. After the turn of the century occultism included

296

serious investigations of forms of extrasensory perception (ESP) such as mental telepathy. Although still not within the usual area of scientific research, these are considered by some valid natural phenomena explicable by accepted scientific methods.

OCCUPATIONAL AND ENVIRONMENTAL DISEASES,

illnesses caused by exposure to disease-causing agents in the environment, as opposed to illnesses related primarily to an individual's genetic makeup or to immunological malfunctions. In everyday use, the term *environmental disease* is confined to noninfectious diseases and to diseases caused largely by exposures beyond the immediate control of the individual; the latter restriction eliminates diseases related to personal habits such as smoking or to the use or abuse of medications or drugs such as alcohol. Occupational disease, a major category of environmental disease, refers to illness resulting from job-related exposures.

Historically, awareness of environmental diseases began with the recognition of occupational illnesses, because exposures are usually more intense in work settings than in the general environment and therefore can more readily produce overt illnesses. Examples include silicosis, a lung disease of pottery workers exposed to silica dust in clay; scrotal skin cancer in chimney sweeps exposed to soot; neurological disease in potters exposed to lead glazes; and bone disease in workers exposed to phosphorus in the manufacture of matches. Many such diseases first gained public attention during the Industrial Revolution in the 19th century.

Causes. Environmental diseases are caused by chemical agents, radiation, and physical hazards. The effects of exposure, in both natural and work settings, are greatly influenced by the exposure routes: primarily air pollution and water pollution (qq.v.), contaminated food, and direct contact with toxins. Synergistic effects—two or more toxic exposures acting together—are also important, as illustrated by the greatly increased risk of lung cancer in asbestos workers who smoke cigarettes. The potential interaction of multiple hazardous chemicals at toxic waste dumps poses a current public health problem that is of unknown dimensions.

Chemicals. Industrial society has introduced or increased human exposure to thousands of chemicals in the environment. Examples are inorganic materials such as lead, mercury, arsenic, cadmium, and asbestos and organic substances such as polychlorinated biphenyls (PCBs), vinyl chloride, and the pesticide DDT (q.v.). Of particular concern is the delayed potential for these chemicals to produce cancer, as in the cases of lung cancer and mesothelioma caused by asbestos, liver cancer caused by vinyl chloride, and leukemia caused by benzene. Minamata disease, caused by food contaminated with mercury, and Yusho disease, from food contaminated with chlorinated furans, are examples of acute toxic illnesses occurring in nonoccupational settings.

The full toxic potential of most environmental chemicals has not been completely tested. Extent and frequency of illness are related to dose of toxin, in degrees depending on the toxin. For chronic or delayed effects such as cancer or adverse reproductive effects, however, no "safe" dose threshold may exist below which disease is not produced. Thus, the cancer-producing potential of ubiquitous environmental contaminants such as DDT or the PCBs remains undefined.

Radiation. Ionizing and nonionizing radiation can produce both acute and chronic health effects, depending on dose levels. The effects of nonionizing radiation at lower dose levels, however, are uncertain at present. Ionizing radiation at high doses causes both acute disease and delayed effects such as cancer. Victims include workers exposed to various occupational use of X rays or radioactive materials. Although the disease-producing potential of ionizing radiation at

The Mad Hatter of Alice in Wonderland had a grim background of occupational disease. In the 19th century, felt-hat makers often exhibited effects of chronic mercury poisoning through exposure to mercury salts during the manufacturing process.

An emergency crew caps a ruptured tank of corrosive acid that had been spewing toxic fumes, forcing evacuation of the neighborhood. Spills of industrial poisons are among the worst health hazards of modern society.   Wide World Photos

low doses also is uncertain, an increase in chromosome damage has been observed in workers in nuclear shipyards. *See* RADIATION EFFECTS, BIOLOGICAL.

Physical hazards. Major physical hazards include traumatic injuries and noise. Trauma arising from unsafe environments accounts for a large proportion of preventable human illness, and noise in the work place is responsible for the most prevalent occupational impairment: hearing loss or permanent deafness.

Forms of Environmental Disease. Environmental diseases can affect any organ system of the body. How the diseases are expressed depends on how the particular environmental agent enters the body, how it is metabolized, and by what route it

is excreted. The skin, lungs, liver, kidneys, and nervous system are commonly affected by different agents in different settings. Of particular concern is the capacity of many environmental agents to cause various cancers, birth defects or abortions (through fetal exposure), and mutations in germ cells, the last-named raising possibilities of environmentally caused genetic diseases in later generations.

Environmental illnesses can be mild or severe and can range from transient to chronic, depending on the doses of toxin received. Some diseases occur abruptly after a toxic exposure, whereas the time of onset of other diseases varies after exposure. Environmentally induced cancers, for example, commonly involve latency periods of

A stream polluted by dumping of toxic chemicals is viewed by a resident of the community. Local outbreaks of environmental diseases as the result of such long-term and frequently unsuspected pollutions have gained much public attention in recent years, as people become more concerned about environmental problems.
Wide World Photos

15 to 30 or more years. Those illnesses that occur directly after a distinct toxic exposure usually are easily identified as being environmentally or occupationally caused. If the exposure is not clear-cut or illness is delayed, however, the cause is difficult to identify, as clinical features alone are usually nonspecific. In addition, many different causes, environmental or otherwise, may produce identical illnesses. In such instances, epidemiological studies of exposed populations can help relate exposures to the illnesses they cause.

Occurrence. Total frequencies of environmental illness are difficult to measure because of the reasons just described. When causes can be identified, however, scientists observe that frequencies of occurrence of a particular illness vary directly with the severity and extent of exposure. Particularly frequent in the work place are skin lesions from many different causes and pulmonary diseases related to the inhalation of various dusts (for example, silicosis, asbestosis, and brown lung disease). Environmental agents can also cause biological effects without overt clinical illness (for example, chromosome damage from irradiation). The health significance of such subclinical changes is not yet clear.

Agencies and Laws. The regulation of work-place practices and of potential environmental pollution has evolved as the use of chemicals and human exposure to potential toxins have grown more widespread and complex in modern society. In the U.S. numerous laws are directed at protecting occupational and environmental health. Most were passed since 1960, including the Occupational Safety and Health Act (OSHA) of 1970 and the Resource Conservation and Recovery Act of 1979. Means for the rapid cleanup of toxic waste dumps were provided in the Comprehensive Environmental Response, Compensation, and Liability Act of 1980.

Federal agencies responsible for enforcing such environmental and occupational health laws consist principally of the Environmental Protection Agency (q.v.) and the Occupational Safety and Health Administration within the Department of Labor. The Food and Drug Administration (q.v.), within the Department of Health and Human Services (HHS), and the Department of Agriculture have regulatory responsibility for preventing the contamination of food supplies. Federal field investigations of potential environmental and occupational hazards are handled through the Center for Environmental Health and the National Institute for Occupational Safety and Health, which are components of the Centers for Disease Control, within HHS. General environmental health research and toxicological

testing are directed through the National Institutes of Health and the National Toxicology Program, also within HHS. Comparable regulations and agencies at state and local levels, working with their federal counterparts, play a crucial role as well.

International coordination of environmental and occupational control activities in many countries is guided through the World Health Organization (q.v.). In the developing parts of the world, such activities are of critical importance as modern industrialization proceeds in the face of poverty and growing populations.

Current Research. Current trends in research in this field focus on the relation of low-dose exposures to human health, the influence of environmental toxins on both male and female reproductive functions, and the potential health implications of subclinical indications of biological damage (for example, genetic or chromosomal damage). In such research, increased emphasis is being placed on delayed or long-term health effects and on a wide range of potential synergistic interactions between environments and hosts.   C.W.H.

For further information on this topic, see the Bibliography in volume 28, sections 508, 623.

OCCUPATIONAL SAFETY AND HEALTH ADMINISTRATION (OSHA), agency of the U.S. Department of Labor established by an act of Congress in 1970. Its main responsibilities are to provide for occupational safety by reducing hazards in the workplace and enforcing mandatory job safety standards and to implement and improve health programs for workers. OSHA regulations and standards apply to most private businesses in the U.S.

From its beginnings, OSHA has been a controversial agency that has drawn much criticism from both business and labor groups. Businesses have charged that the agency's regulations are difficult to understand and often unreasonably rigid; that penalties are unfair, paperwork is excessive, and the cost of compliance is burdensome to small companies. Labor, on the other hand, has called OSHA's enforcement procedures weak and complained that the agency has failed to reduce occupational hazards. Since 1977 the agency has made an effort to concentrate on dangerous industries and to eliminate out-of-date regulations. Meanwhile, the powers of OSHA are being challenged by some businesses in the courts.

The agency, directed by the assistant secretary for occupational safety and health, is headquartered in Washington, D.C. It has ten regional offices located throughout the U.S.

OCCUPATIONAL THERAPY, paramedical treatment involving planned activity administered by an occupational therapist under the direction of a physician. Its purpose is to promote the recovery of persons stricken with mental illness or physical disability, sometimes following accidents. Originally regarded as a way of filling the time of convalescent patients, it has now become a program of work specifically selected for its physical, mental, and vocational value.

The therapist's work is based on the physician's statement of the patient's diagnosis, prognosis, personality, and physical and emotional limitations, as well as the objectives sought. Often, the therapist engages in a form of vocational rehabilitation (see REHABILITATION, VOCATIONAL) in choosing activities that will teach new basic skills of daily living to those who never acquired them or who have lost them, as in the case of amputees or those otherwise recently crippled. Additionally, in dealing with patients who have never been employed, who have held jobs requiring no skills, or who must change their type of work because of their acquired disability, the therapist may also engage in prevocational testing and guidance.

The trained therapist is versed in such activities as gardening, weaving, hand industries, music, various types of recreation and education, creative handicrafts such as clay modeling and leather tooling, and manual arts. After determining the patient's willingness to involve him- or herself in a given field, the therapist will employ one or more of these activities to create the desired result in a variety of ways. Whether dealing with the physically or emotionally ill, the chronic patient, normal adults, the aged, or children, the therapist works in two areas: the functional and the psychological or psychiatric.

Functional Therapy. Functional therapy operates within the limits of the patient's physical tolerance to develop or reestablish nervous and muscular coordination, to extend the motion of joints, and to strengthen muscles. Functional therapy is especially important for those who have lost the use of a limb through amputation and must be taught to use artificial members. It is also important for those who have suffered attacks of arthritis, cerebral palsy, poliomyelitis, or neurological disabilities. Although such therapy may not restore total function, even a degree of restoration will often help the patient to be able to work again.

Psychological and Psychiatric Therapy. The services of a psychologist are of value to the ill or disabled patient whose attitude is one of depression that leads the patient to regard him- or herself as useless. Such therapy, in providing mental stimulus and exercise, can do much to restore a normal outlook and prepare the way for retraining in a skill within the patient's limited capacity. The psychiatrist is called upon to deal with cases of more severe depression where a patient's outlook cannot be improved by routine psychological therapy, where the patient cannot adjust to hospital life, where the disability seems overwhelming, and where the patient's condition is such that he or she must be followed, supported, and reassured when beginning to engage in some form of productive work (see PSYCHOTHERAPY). Such therapy can also serve in diagnosis by observation of the patient's reaction to a normal work situation, which may suggest additional forms of treatment that may move the patient farther along the road to recovery.

OCEAN CITY, town, Worcester Co., SE Maryland, on a barrier island in the Atlantic Ocean; inc. 1876. It is a popular summer beach resort with deep-sea fishing facilities. Assateague Island National Seashore is just S. The town was laid out as a resort in 1872. Pop. (1970) 1493; (1980) 4946.

OCEAN CITY, city, Cape May Co., SE New Jersey; inc. 1897. It is a summer resort and yachting center situated on an island between the Atlantic Ocean and Great Egg Harbor Inlet. The Ocean City Historical Museum is here. The settlement was established by Methodist ministers in 1879. Pop. (1970) 10,575; (1980) 13,949.

OCEANIA, name sometimes used to designate the division of the globe comprising all the islands in the Pacific Ocean. The subdivisions of Oceania are Melanesia, Micronesia, and Polynesia, which are grouped together in accordance with the physical and cultural characteristics of the inhabitants, and the Malay Archipelago. Australia and New Zealand are occasionally included.

For further information on this topic, see the Bibliography in volume 28, sections 674, 1250.

OCEANIA, FRENCH. See FRENCH POLYNESIA.

OCEANIAN ART AND ARCHITECTURE, the arts, artifacts, and buildings of Oceania, which consists of a major island, New Guinea (comprising the Indonesian province of Irian Jaya and the independent state of Papua New Guinea), and three large groups of smaller islands. East of New Guinea is Melanesia, which includes the Admiralty Islands, New Britain, New Ireland, the Solomon Islands, the New Hebrides, and New Caledonia; northward are the islands known collectively as Micronesia; and eastward again, spread across the central Pacific Ocean, are the Polynesian groups of islands.

The visual arts are known to have been practiced with great vigor by all the indigenous peoples of Oceania during the 200 years in which the Western world has been in contact with them. Presumably the same was true before this and throughout prehistory, but little evidence has survived, as the materials used—wood, ochres, shell, feathers, and clay—are short-lived in tropical conditions. Before contact was made with the West, the Oceanic cultures were Neolithic; metalworking techniques were never discovered, and the universal material for tools was stone, supplemented by bone and shell. Nevertheless, Oceania is enormously rich in the arts of sculpture, painting, and architecture, as well as in such highly refined crafts as pottery, weaving, and matting and in the ephemeral art of self-adornment.

New Guinea. New Guinea, with one-third the land area of Oceania and the largest population of all the Oceaniaon islands, presents an impressive number of art styles. A broad distinction may be drawn between the styles of the highlands in the central cordillera of mountains and those of the lowlands to the south and north, along with the northern coastal range of mountains.

Art of the highlands. The central highlands in Papua New Guinea is the home of perhaps the most colorful self-decoration in the world, in the form of feather headdresses and face paint. In the eastern highlands, self-decoration diminishes, but painted bark-cloth constructions are attached to dancers' backs and carried in ceremonies. Masking traditions are slight, and architecture is unambitious.

Art of the lowlands. Of the lowlands areas, only that around the Geelvink Bay in north Irian Jaya shows any direct influence from Indonesia: Canoe prows and many domestic objects are decorated with relief or openwork designs of scrolls. Scrolls are also incorporated in the small wood figures (*korwar*), which are thought to be containers of supernatural power.

Eastward of Geelvink Bay, the Humboldt Bay-Lake Sentani area is notable for figure sculpture of monumental simplicity. Human images also form part of large-scale architectural sculpture, for the huge pyramidal ceremonial houses, and as elements of jetties. Bark-cloth paintings show both disciplined arrangements of scrolls and free groupings of animals, fish, birds, and plants.

On the south coast of New Guinea, two major style areas are that of the related Mimika and Asmat tribal groups and that of the Marind-anim west of them. The Mimika and Asmat carve canoes with elaborate prows, large poles surmounted with groups of figures and openwork flanges at the upper end, and larger-than-life-size figures carved in the round. Marind-anim art is of a completely different order, carvings being merely components of great constructed costumes symbolizing the creator spirits and used in pageants celebrating them. Totally transitory in nature, these costumes are amalgamations of colored seeds, plants, feathers, and carvings made into brilliant theatrical properties. Architecture has reached no level of great interest.

Farther east, around the vast Gulf of Papua in southern Papua New Guinea, mask-making and wood carving are major activities. The Kerewa make long-snouted masks of basketry, and the Purari and Elema make huge constructions of bark cloth on cane frames, based on two forms, a flat ellipse and a cone. A unique type of mask is produced in the small Torres Strait islands, in the form of animal and human representations constructed from plates of turtle shell.

Wood sculpture is produced in great quantities and varying styles. Three-dimensional sculpture is of greater importance in the west and includes notable human figures from the Kiwai Islanders and the Gogodala. Carvings of the Kerewa, Purari, and Elema are generally two-dimensional reliefs of humans or spirits on ovate boards.

Art of the Sepik Basin. Across the central ranges of New Guinea lies the basin of the Sepik River and its tributaries, bordered on the north by coastal mountains and the littoral. The area is justly famous as the home of a profusion of art styles that cannot easily be formulated in a brief account. Major stylistic areas are the west, including the upper Sepik River; the area south of the Sepik; the middle and lower course of the river; and the area between it and the coast. In the west, a variety of bark and bark-cloth masks with painted designs are made, ranging in size from little more than caps to cones 6 m (20 ft) high. Otherwise, the main works are shields. Their carved or painted designs are simple and geometric, with only a few crude representational elements. A great number of local styles are found along the river and coast, as well as in the intermediate area; almost every object made, whether secular or religious, is carved and painted. Figure sculpture (often over-life-size), hanging hooks, slit gongs, shields, drums, and ceremonial seats are some of the more important works. In general, human and animal forms are seminaturalistic; the most notable variants are the famous masks with greatly lengthened noses. Architecture is on a grand scale. For example, the men's ceremonial houses of the Iatmul have towering steeples at either end and are also repositories of architectural sculpture; those of the

Abelam have single huge gables entirely covered in vivid bark paintings.

On the east coast, Astrolabe Bay is a center of some large figure sculpture and some particularly massive and imposing wooden masks. Masks in barkcloth or wood are made in the Huon Gulf area farther to the south, where the inhabitants of the Tami Islands also carve exquisite bowls for export.

Off the extreme southeast tip of New Guinea are the archipelagoes collectively known as the Massim area. A highly curvilinear style is practiced here, especially for several types of elaborate canoe prow decorations.

An Abelam men's ceremonial house, from the Middle Sepik River area of New Guinea. Typical is its high triangular facade, the upper portion of which is covered by sheets of bark decorated with stylized faces and geometric patterns. Malcolm Kirk–Peter Arnold, Inc.

Melanesia. The art of the Admiralty Islands is almost entirely secular, being the work of specialists among the Manus people and intended for trade to other groups. The items include beds, slit gongs, bowls, weapons, and house ladders, all of which often incorporate human and crocodile figures. These articles are predominantly red, with small geometric patterning in black and white.

New Ireland has three main stylistic areas: The northwest is the home of the *malanggan* style; in a central plateau the main works are the *uli* figures; the southwest is mainly notable for small chalk figures similar to those of northern New Britain. *Malanggan* is a collective name for both a series of mortuary rites and the carving and masks made for them. These carvings are among the most fantastic of all Oceania, usually consisting of a central figure or figures around which a virtual cage of bars and struts incorporates yet other human, bird, and fish images. *Uli*, by contrast, are massive, single hermaphroditic figures, also commemorative in purpose.

Southwest New Ireland figures and some crescentic carved canoe prows are akin to those made across the strait between New Ireland and northern New Britain by the Tolai people. The stone figures made in this area are associated with the Iniet society, as are large openwork wooden figures and dance wands. Another powerful society, the Dukduk, use conical masks with stylized faces in black and white.

Masks in bark cloth and other impermanent materials figure largely in the art of other New Britain tribes, notably the mountain-dwelling Baining, whose works include figures in bark cloth up to 12 m (40 ft) high. The masks of the Sulka are constructed of pith strips, often capped with brilliantly polychromed umbrellalike disks. Wooden masks, as well as those of the conical bark-cloth form, are found only in the small Witu Islands off the west coast and among the Kilenge of the southeast end of the island. In the carvings from Buka and Bougainville, the most northerly of the Solomon Islands, a standard conventionalized human figure in low relief is used consistently. The only masks from the area, in bark cloth, are also made here. The art of the central Solomons is highly distinctive because of the predominance of black coloration and the use of shell, especially mother-of-pearl inlay. The most famous carvings of the area are the small figures of protective spirits (*nguzu nguzu*) that were originally attached to the towering prows of war canoes. In the southeast islands, a prominent theme is the grouping of birds and fish, as on the bowls used in ceremonials of communion with

Typical of the central Solomon Islands are wood sculptures, painted black and decorated with bands of inlaid mother-of-pearl, such as this late 19th-century canoe prow ornament.
Metropolitan Museum of Art–

the gods thought to control these creatures. Houses used to shelter the canoes have posts carved with large figures of divinities.

Much of the art of Vanuatu is associated with grade societies, by ascent through which many men gain prestige. Masks and commemorative figures accompany the rituals of each grade. Figures are often of wood, but less permanent materials are also used, especially the fibrous core of the tree fern, and compounds of spider web and vegetable matter on bamboo armatures.

The fernwood figures of the Banks Islands are attenuated and unpainted, but in the rest of the island group a vivid range of colors is lavishly applied. A dramatic range of gestures characterizes the figures and masks of the Mbotgote of southern Malekula, where a certain grotesque approach to naturalism is found in body proportions. Figures from North Malekula and the offshore islands have exaggerated heads with enormous noses and disk-shaped eyes.

In New Caledonia the visual arts are limited to a narrow range of sculpture; figures and masks are made only at the northwest end of the island. The masks are particularly impressive, with exposed teeth and disproportionately large hooked noses; the wooden carvings are crowned with bulbous wigs of human hair and further decked with black feather costumes. Elsewhere on the island, sculpture is used for architectural decoration; elaborate finials are made for the conical ceremonial houses, which also have massive lintels and doorjambs carved with human faces and geometric patterns.

Micronesia. The Micronesian area, lying north of New Guinea, consists of a number of archipelagoes of tiny islands. Sculpture is relatively scarce. In the Carolines group of the western part of Micronesia, the large men's houses of the Palau Islands are decorated with painted gables and female figures. In the Mortlock Islands similar houses have large gable masks. Small rain charms, prow ornaments, and shell-inlaid bowls are among the few other Micronesian carved objects extant. Notable crafts are pottery and weaving on simple looms (also found in the Santa Cruz Islands). Eastern Micronesian sculpture includes figures from Nukuoro, a few of which are over-life-size, and from the Gilbert Islands. All of these show considerable influence from Polynesian sources.

Polynesia. The art of Polynesia, with some justice, is often said to be more homogeneous than that of the rest of Oceania. Throughout much of this island group, human representations are simplified and have smooth unornamented integuments. Surface decoration largely consists of small-scale geometric patterns, some of them based on radical stylization of the human body. The most significant architectural form is the *marae*, a sacred enclosure and platform constructed of stone. Artistry is of a high order, a finely wrought degree of finish being sought and prized. This is a function of the social order, which throughout Polynesia is rigidly hierarchical, consisting of hereditary classes of rulers, priestly experts, workers, and, in the past, slaves.

Only small numbers of figure sculptures appear to have been produced by the western Polynesian island groups of Samoa, the Fijis, and the Tongas. A number of small ivory figures from Tonga show a mastery of both compact and massive form. Weapons and headrests from all three groups are varied and extremely elegant and are often inlaid with small ivory elements. Bowls in human and animal form are frequently used as oil containers in Fijian ritual. Basketry, a notably Polynesian craft, reached an extremely high level in Tonga, as did matting in Samoa. Bark cloth is made in enormous quantities for ceremonial occasions and is painted or stamped with designs.

Central Polynesia, including the Cook, Austral,

The apex of a Maori meeting-house facade, from New Zealand. Its distinctive features include the characteristic Maori head, with its shell-inlaid eyes, wide figure-eight mouth, and protruding tongue.
W. E. Ruth—Bruce Coleman, Inc.

Society, and Gambier island groups, is rich in sculpture, especially figures of deities. The most naturalistic are several from Mangareva in the Gambier Islands. Elsewhere figures tend to be squat with hypertrophied heads, as on Aitutaki and Raratonga in the Cook Islands, in the Society Islands, and in the Austral Islands. Certain divine symbols are unexpectedly bizarre: The Raratonga staff gods are essentially poles with large stylized heads at one end and a row of almost abstract figures along the shaft, which terminates in a phallus. On Mangaia, Mitiaro, and other islands the staff gods take the form of clublike objects with longitudinal ridges consisting of great numbers of abstract figures. Perhaps the most spectacular achievements of this Polynesian tendency to abstraction are the tall standing drums from the Austral Islands, with their many registers of reduced figures.

In the Marquesas Islands, figures are covered with geometric patterns. This convention is actually an extension of the Marquesan custom of tattooing the entire body. The figure sculpture is similar to that of central Polynesia, except that the eyes are depicted as large circles. Such figures also occur on ivory earplugs and the remarkable shell and tortoiseshell diadems. As in the Austral Islands, some large figures are carved in stone.

The most important stone sculpture of Oceania, however, was carried out on Easter Island, where a large number of colossi were carved from the soft rock of the island's central volcanic crater. Wood carving was limited to small figures and other objects. The male figures are well known for their curious state of emaciation; effigies of lizard- and bird-headed men also were made. Dance staffs of exceptionally graceful form are abstractions of human heads and torsos.

The largest surviving wooden sculptures of Oceania are huge temple images produced in the Hawaiian Islands. While displaying many of the Polynesian conventions, the Hawaiian sculptures have an especially dynamic aggressiveness, partly achieved by distorting the human face. Smaller works, such as bowls, spear rests, and drums, also incorporate human images. The magnificence and ambition that pervade Hawaiian art are seen in the lavish use of brilliant feathers. These were applied in bold designs to netting, forming the huge crescentic cloaks and capes of nobles. Feathers were also used on basketry helmets and large images of the gods.

The Maori, living in New Zealand, are perhaps the best known of the Polynesian artists. Theirs is a rich, multilayered art in which frequently distorted human figures are shown covered with a web of curvilinear designs, placed (in the case of relief sculptures) against a background of additional designs. Communal meetinghouses, rectangular structures with pitched roofs, and food-storage buildings were provided with a wealth of carved lintels, posts, beams, wall panels, and facades. The great war canoes have carvings at prow and stern. Boxes for prized feather ornaments are completely decorated, as are weapons and many domestic objects. Nephrite was used for certain types of clubs, adze blades, and the famous pendants called *hei tiki.*

See also COSTUME; MASK; TATTOOING; WOOD CARVING. For additional information on the geography and languages of islands and nations mentioned, see individual articles.   D.Ne.

For further information on this topic, see the Bibliography in volume 28, section 674.

OCEAN AND OCEANOGRAPHY, great body of salt water comprising all the oceans and seas that cover nearly three-fourths of the surface of the earth, and the scientific study of the physical, chemical, and biological aspects of the so-called world ocean. The major goals of oceanography are to understand the geologic and geochemical processes involved in the evolution and alteration of the ocean and its basin, to evaluate the interaction of the ocean and the atmosphere so that greater knowlege of climatic variations can be attained, and to describe how the biological productivity in the sea is controlled.

Ocean Basin Structure. The world ocean covers 71 percent of the earth's surface, or about 361 million sq km (140 million sq mi). Its average depth is 5000 m (16,000 ft), and its total volume is about 1,347,000,000 cu km (322,300,000 cu mi). The three major subdivisions of the world ocean are the Atlantic Ocean, the Pacific Ocean, and the Indian Ocean (qq.v.), which are conventionally bounded by the continental masses (*see* CONTINENT) or by ocean ridges or currents; they merge below 40° S lat in the Antarctic Circumpolar Current, or West Wind Drift, where they are then often referred to as the Antarctic Ocean. In the north polar region the nearly circular Arctic Ocean, almost landlocked except between Greenland and Europe, is considered by some part of the Atlantic and by others a fourth ocean subdivision. From the shorelines of the continents a submerged part of the continental mass, called the continental shelf, extends seaward an average distance of 75 km (43 mi); it varies in width from nearly zero to 1500 km (930 mi). The shelf gives way abruptly at a depth of about 200 m (660 ft) to a steeper zone known as the continental slope, which descends about 3500 m (12,000 ft). The continental rise, a gradually sloping zone of sediment that is considered part of the ocean bottom, extends about 600 km (370 mi) from the base of the continental slope to the flat abyssal plains of the deep-ocean floor. In the central parts of the oceans are the mid-ocean ridges, which are extensive mountain chains with inner troughs that are heavily intersected by cracks, called fracture zones. The ridges are sections of a continuous system that winds for 60,000 km (40,000 mi) through all the oceans. The Mid-Atlantic Ridge extends from the Norwegian Sea through the volcanic islands of Iceland and the Azores to the South Atlantic, where it is equidistant from the African and South American coasts. The ridge continues into the Indian Ocean, with a branch that reaches into the Gulf of Aden and the Red Sea, then passes between Australia and Antarctica and into the eastern South Pacific. The East Pacific Rise extends north to the Gulf of California; Easter Island and the Galápagos are volcanic islands that are part of this submarine mountain chain. The ridge system seems to merge into the continents in several areas, such as the Red Sea and the Gulf of California, and such areas are regions of great geologic activity, characterized by volcanoes, or earthquakes and faults, such as the San Andreas fault in southern California (see EARTHQUAKE; FAULT; VOLCANO).

The midocean ridges play a key role in plate tectonics (movements in the earth's crust), for it is from "hot spots," or plumes, in these formations that molten rock upwells from the earth's mantle and spreads laterally on both sides, adding new material to the earth's rigid crustal plates. The plates are moving apart, currently at the rate of 1 to 10 cm (0.39 to 3.9 in) a year and are being forced against adjacent plates. From the Mid-Atlantic Ridge, the continents, which rest on the plates and which once were joined, have moved away from one another. In the Pacific Ocean, plates are also moving apart from the East Pacific Rise, but the bordering plates are overlapping them and forcing them under at the edges. At these places, along almost the entire rim of the Pacific, deep trenches are formed as crust is subducted and returned to the mantle. The Pacific trenches commonly reach depths of more than 7 km (4.3 mi); the deepest known point, in the Mariana Trench east of the Philippines, is about 10.9 km (6.8 mi). Trench areas, or subduction zones, are characterized by volcanic and seismic activity, indicative of the motions and stresses of the earth's crustal plates (see PLATE TECTONICS; SEISMOLOGY).

The structure and topography of the ocean floor are studied through the use of sonar (q.v.) and seismic techniques. Depths are found by measuring the time for a sound wave to travel from the surface of the ocean to bottom, and to return (see SOUNDING). Often several returns are recorded, indicating several layers of sediment below the surface of the ocean floor. More extensive studies of the structure beneath the ocean floor are carried out by one ship firing an explosive in the water, and another recording the reception of sound waves on sensitive instruments. Some of the waves travel directly to the second ship; others travel to the ocean floor, are refracted within the layers of sediment, and then travel to the ship. The strength of the explosive and the distance between the ships determine the amount of detail of the subbottom structure that is made available. In this way the thickness of the sediments can be determined.

Composition of Sediment. The ocean floor is covered by an average of 0.5 km (0.3 mi) of sediment, but the thickness varies up to about 7 km (4.3 mi) in the Argentine Basin in the South Atlantic. Some regions, particularly the central parts of the midocean ridges where new crust is formed, have little, if any, sediment on them. The sediments are studied by dredging and by taking core samples. From 1968 to 1983, the Deep Sea Drilling Project, conducted by the National Science Foundation's research ship *Glomar Challenger,* obtained sedimentary columns from the ocean floor in many places; the foundation's new program, called the Ocean Drilling Program, will make use of a more advanced ship named *SEDCO/BP* (see DEEP-SEA EXPLORATION; MINING). These sediments are found to consist of rock particles and organic remains; the compositions depend on depth, distance from continents, and local variants such as submarine volcanoes or high biological productivity. Clay minerals, which are formed by the weathering of continental rocks and carried out to sea by rivers and wind, are usually abundant in the deep sea. Thick deposits of such detrital material are often

Opposite page: The relief map of the North Atlantic Ocean floor shows in detail a portion of the Mid-Atlantic Ridge, which is 19,000 km (12,000 mi) long. At a point on the ridge southwest of the Azores, volcanic rock has been found rising up through the earth's crust, a discovery that gives evidence of the plate-tectonic theory of continent formation and movement. (See diagram under PLATE TECTONICS.) The map from which the detail presented here is derived is based on bathymetric studies by Bruce C. Heezen and Marie Tharp of the Lamont-Doherty Geological Observatory. The numbers on the map, when accompanied by a • and –, show depth in feet below sea level; when accompanied by a • alone, they show height above sea level; when inside parentheses, they indicate height above the 4877-m (16,000-ft) average depth of the abyssal plains. ©1973. National Geographic Society

NATIONAL GEOGRAPHIC SOCIETY

-462
(15538)

MID-OCEAN CANYON

ISLAND OF
NEWFOUNDLAND

PE
ETON
AND

-42
MIQUELON
ISLANDS   GRAND BANKS
-330   OF
NEWFOUNDLAND

-168 · FLEMISH
CAP

·-14760

-15420

LAURENTIAN
CONE

·-15900

-15300

BISCAY ABYSSAL PLAIN

-15420 ·

-1540C

-4500
(11500)

R
I
F
T

V
A
L
L
E
Y

Pico
615
(236/5)

AZORES

-17280

·-17700

·-1668

GOHM ABYSSAL PLAIN

-17400 ·

CORNER
SEAMOUNTS

OCEANOGRAPHER FRACTURE ZONE

R
I
D
G
E

-870

AMPERE   ·-132
SEAMOUNT   (15868)

·-12000

-9341 ·

-18300

M
I
D
-
A
T
L
A
N
T
I
C

-12000

-960
(15040)

-17820

6106 · MADEIRA
ISLANDS

-15000 ·

-13200

-1470
(14530)

·-12600

CANARY   · 12198
ISLANDS   (28198)

-12844 ·

·-6978
(9022)

·-18624

·-16200

·-17753

·-17060

·-13500

CAPE VERDE ISLANDS

KRYLOV   ·-4260
SEAMOUNT

9281
(25281)

· Dakar

GAMBIA ABYSSAL PLAIN

·-15748

·-15994

-4035

DEMERARA

·-8333

ABYSSAL

SIERRA
LEONE
RISE

AMAZON CONE

PLAIN

·-16404

S
OUTH

CONTINENTAL SHELF

·-262

ST. PETER · 64
AND ST. PAUL ROCKS (606/)

ROMANCHE FRACTURE ZONE

AMERICA

CEARA ABYSSAL
PLAIN

·-1680

·-25800

Amazon

1053 · FERNANDO
DE NORONHA

found near mouths of rivers and on continental shelves; fine particles of clay are spread through the ocean and accumulate slowly on the deep-ocean floor. Also accumulating in the sediments of many regions are the hard remains of small organisms such as the calcium carbonate shells of foraminifera (q.v.), and the siliceous shells of marine protozoans, examples of which are radiolaria and diatomaceous algae (*see* DIATOM; PROTOZOA).

Dating Techniques. Vast quantities of microscopic plants and animals live close to the ocean's surface. When they die, their shell remains drift down to the ocean floor and accumulate in thick layers of sediment. When studied in sedimentary core samples, which can represent many millions of years of deposits, they provide a detailed and continuous history of the earth's environmental changes. The record is particularly informative for the most recent 2 million to 5 million years, during which major fluctuations in global climate have occurred. Successive ice ages can be traced by the relative scarcity or abundance of the shells of warm-water and cold-water diatoms in various layers of a sedimentary core, as the organisms migrated to more hospitable habitats with fluctuations in the sea-surface temperature. Geochemical records of these same fluctuations are revealed by determining the ratios of two isotopes of oxygen, oxygen-16 and oxygen-18, in the shells of foraminifera. The ratio of the two isotopes is proportional to the temperature of the water in which the organism grew; hence, a temperature record is preserved when each organism dies and its shell drifts to the ocean floor. The records of climatic fluctuation found in ocean-floor sediments are much more continuous than similar records on land; they also lend themselves to worldwide correlation. The absolute ages of climatic changes can be determined by correlating the evidence of temperature changes with radioactive-dating techniques (*see* CHRONOLOGY; DATING METHODS; RADIOACTIVITY). Thorium-230 dating is applicable to samples younger than 300,000 years, potassium-argon dating to samples in the range of 75,000 years, and carbon-14 dating to samples younger than 40,000 years. Several other radioactive dating techniques are available for samples of very recent age. A geophysical method of dating is also commonly used; it relies on determining the magnetic orientations of sediment particles, since it is now known that the earth's magnetic field has reversed its orientation several times in the past few million years (*see* GEOPHYSICS). Such dating techniques have shown that the ocean basins are no older than 200 million years.

Oceanographers lowering a coring apparatus from the side of a research vessel. The apparatus is designed to take samples of the ocean bottom.
Lamont Geographical Observatory, Columbia University

Composition of Seawater. Seawater is a dilute solution of several salts, and the salinity of seawater is expressed in terms of total dissolved salts in parts per thousand parts of water. Salinity varies from nearly zero in continental waters to about 44 parts per 1000 in the Red Sea, which is a region of high evaporation. In the main ocean, salinity averages about 35 parts per 1000, varying between 34 and 36 parts per 1000. The major cations, or positive ions, present, and their approximate abundance per 1000 parts of water are as follows: sodium, 10.5; magnesium, 1.3; calcium, 0.4; and potassium, 0.4 parts. The major anions, or negative ions, are chloride, 19 parts per 1000, and sulfate, 2.6 parts. These ions constitute the major portion of the dissolved species in seawater, with bromide ions, bicarbonate, silica, various trace elements, and inorganic and organic nutrients making up the remainder. The ratios of the major ions vary little throughout the ocean, and only their total concentration changes. The major nutrients, although not abundant in comparison with the major ions, are extremely important in the biological productivity of the sea. Trace metals are of specific importance for cer-

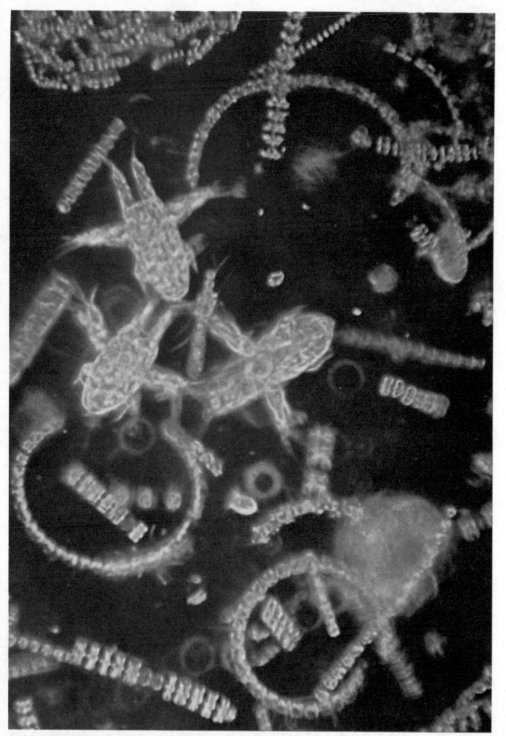

A photomicrograph study of a drop of seawater reveals the variety of microscopic animal and plant life called plankton. Algae, bacteria, and diatoms that make up the plankton are found drifting in the oceans of the world. A liter of seawater may contain more than 1 million such organisms.

Dr. Roman Vishniac

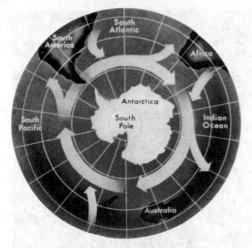

Diagram showing how the Antarctic gyre (current wheel) links all the oceans together. Scholastic Magazines, Inc.

tain organisms, but carbon, nitrogen, phosphorus, and oxygen are almost universally important to marine life. Carbon is found mainly as bicarbonate, HCO_3^-; nitrogen as nitrate, NO_3^-; and phosphorus as phosphate, $PO_4^{\equiv}$.

Temperature. The temperature of surface ocean water ranges from 26° C (79° F) in tropical waters to −1.4° C (29.5° F), the freezing point of seawater, in polar regions. Surface temperatures generally decrease with increasing latitude, with seasonal variations far less extreme than on land. In the upper 100 m (330 ft) of the sea, the water is almost as warm as at the surface. From 100 m to approximately 1000 m (3300 ft), the temperature drops rapidly to about 5° C (41° F), and be-

low this it drops gradually about another 4° to barely above freezing. The region of rapid change is known as the thermocline.

Ocean Currents. The surface currents of the ocean are characterized by large gyres, or currents that are kept in motion by prevailing winds, but the direction of which is altered by the rotation of the earth (*see* CORIOLIS FORCE). The best known of these currents is probably the Gulf Stream (q.v.) in the North Atlantic; the Kuroshio (q.v.) in the North Pacific is a similar current, and both serve to warm the climates of the eastern edges of the two oceans. In regions where the prevailing winds blow offshore, such as the west coast of Mexico and the coast of Peru and Chile, surface waters move away from the continents and they are replaced by colder, deeper water, a process known as upwelling, from as much as 300 m (1000 ft) down. This deep water is rich in nutrients, and these regions have high biological productivity and provide excellent fishing. Deep water is rich in nutrients because decomposition of organic matter exceeds production in deeper water; plant growth occurs only where photosynthetic organisms have access to light (*see* PHOTOSYNTHESIS). When organisms die, their remains sink and are oxidized and consumed in the deeper water, thus returning the valuable nutrients to the cycle. The regions of high productivity are generally regions of strong vertical mixing in the upper regions of the ocean. In addition to the western edges of the continents, the entire region around Antarctica is one of high productivity because the surface water there sinks after being chilled, causing deeper water to replace it.

Although the surface circulation of the ocean

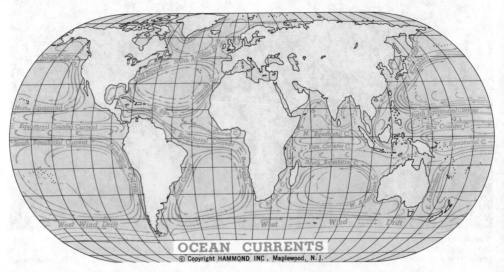

OCEAN CURRENTS
© Copyright HAMMOND INC., Maplewood, N.J.

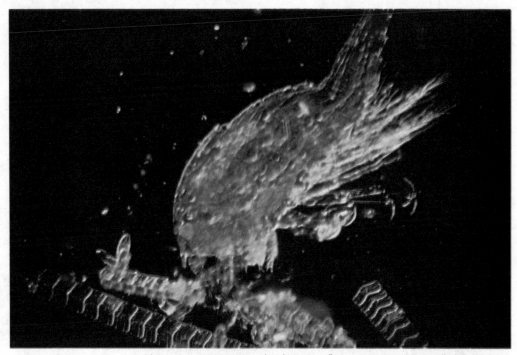

The marine crustacean seen breaking apart floating microorganisms, called diatoms, is found in all the oceans of the world.   Dr. Roman Vishniac

is a function of winds and the rotation of the earth, the deeper circulation in the oceans is a function of density differences between adjacent water masses and is known as thermohaline circulation. Salinity and temperature determine density, and any process that changes the salinity or temperature affects the density. Evaporation increases the salinity, hence the density, and causes the water to become heavier than the water around it, so it will sink. Cooling of seawater also increases its density. Because ice discriminates against sea salts, partial freezing increases the salinity of the remaining cold water, forming a mass of very dense water. This process is occurring in the Weddell Sea, off Antarctica, and is responsible for forming a large part of the deep water of the oceans. Water sinks in the Weddell Sea to form what is known as the Antarctic Bottom water, which flows gradually northward into the Atlantic and eastward into the Indian and Pacific oceans. In the North Atlantic, saline water cools and sinks to a moderate level to form the North Atlantic Deep water, which flows slowly southward; this water mass is less dense than the Antarctic Bottom water, and hence flows at less depth. Whereas speeds of surface currents can reach as high as 250 cm/sec, or 5.5 mph, a maximum for the Gulf Stream, speeds of deep currents vary from 2 to 10 cm/sec or less. Once a water mass sinks below the surface, it loses contact with the atmosphere, and can no longer exchange gases with it. Oxygen, dissolved in the water, is used up in the oxidization of dead organic matter, and it is slowly depleted as the water mass remains below the surface. Thus, the oxygen content gives the oceanographer a qualitative idea of the "age" of the water mass, that is, the time it has been away from the surface. Radioactive carbon-14 is produced in the atmosphere and enters the ocean in the form of carbon dioxide gas, which equilibrates, or keeps in balance, with the bicarbonate ion of seawater. Carbon-14 has a half-life of about 5700 years and decays with time; so its activity in a deep-water mass is largely a measure of the time since that water mass was at the surface.

The general pattern of deep-ocean circulation that is apparent from these measurements is that the deep-water masses formed in the North Atlantic and off Antarctica mix and flow together through the Indian and Pacific oceans, and that the oldest water found is in the deep North Pacific, which has an age of up to 1500 years.

Resources. The oceans are being looked to as a major source of food for the future. High productivity characterizes certain regions in the

The sargassum fish is a small, beautifully shaped and colored fish of the genus Histrio.
It follows masses of the brown algae, genus Sargassum, *floating in the open sea, as in
the Sargasso Sea in the North Atlantic.*   Dr. Roman Vishniac

oceans, but larger regions of low productivity also exist. Production is the amount of organic matter fixed, or changed into stable compounds, by photosynthetic organisms in a given unit of time. Estimates of the yearly world ocean production of organic matter, fixed from inorganic carbon and nutrients, amount to about 130 billion metric tons. This process begins with phytoplankton, which are photosynthetic plants that turn carbon into organic matter with the aid of sunlight; zooplankton and fish feed on phytoplankton, and each member of this part of the food web (q.v.) has its own predator (*see* PLANKTON). Most of this organic matter is recycled and reused, so that the standing crop of organic material is only a small fraction of this annual total. The harvestable amount of organic matter is a function of technology, tastes, needs, and the ability of the system to sustain this harvest. Presently, yearly harvests amount to about 52.5 million metric tons of fish, 1.5 million metric tons of large whales, and about 700,000 metric tons of seaweed. Estimates of the maximum harvestable amounts on a sustained-yield basis amount to about 150 million to 200 million metric tons per year. Thus, predictions are that the sea can yield only about three to four times the present amount of organic food resources. The decline of

the whaling industry in recent years is a strong case against rapid and unwise exploitation of oceanic food resources (*see* WHALING). Food from the sea will be a good source of protein, but cannot meet the total world demand for calories in the future. The present yield of about 60 million tons per year supplies about 60 trillion kilocalories, or about 2 percent of the calories needed by the present world population. These 60 million tons yield about 12 million tons of protein, which is nearly 30 percent of the needs of the world at the present time.

The mineral resources of the sea have only recently begun to be known. The sea is so enormous that the supply of several valuable metals is abundant, but it is difficult to extract these materials. The sea is estimated, for example, to contain 10 billion tons of gold; yet the concentration of the metal is so low that it is impossible to recover this resource. Today the major minerals being obtained from seawater are magnesium, bromine, and sodium chloride, or common salt. The ocean floor yields sand, gravel, and oyster shells for construction purposes, and small quantities of diamonds are found in some submarine gravel bars. Phosphorite is a phosphorous mineral known to be available on the seafloor, which has potential use as an agricultural fertilizer.

Much interest has been expressed recently in manganese nodules, which are spherical concretions on the seafloor containing about 20 percent manganese, 10 percent iron, 0.3 percent copper, 0.3 percent nickel, and 0.3 percent cobalt. These are all valuable minerals that have not been obtained yet to any great extent from the seafloor.

Offshore oil and gas wells at present supply about 17 percent of the world petroleum production. Most of these wells are in the shallow waters of the continental shelves, but deep-sea drilling techniques are expected to discover petroleum on the outer continental margins. Many geologic structures under the seafloor are reservoirs for petroleum and also contain significant sulfur deposits; this mineral is now being extracted from some of these deposits.

Pollution. The sea is expected to yield still larger quantities of valuable resources in the future. At present the water itself is being utilized on a small scale through desalination, and as humans have become more dependent on the resources of the sea, the concern for preserving the integrity of the ocean has grown. The contaminative effect of increasing technological development and industrialization has already been known to disrupt and destroy the fragile coastal ecology by indiscriminate discharge of industrial and municipal waste products into the sea. The pollution of the marine environment by petroleum and chemical spillage, and sewage disposal into the oceans or into the streams leading into them, have helped focus world attention on the need for controlled use of resources and planned disposal of waste products. Other pollution concerns are the effects of insecticides and pesticides on marine fish and birds, increasing levels of lead in the surface waters, and the disposal of hot water from power plants into the sea with untoward effects on marine life.

See also CONSERVATION; WATER POLLUTION.
J.F.W. & E.B.S.

For further information on this topic, see the Bibliography in volume 28, section 424.

OCEAN PERCH, a marine fish, *Sebastes marinus,* often called rosefish, found in temperate waters on both sides of the Atlantic at depths of 90 to 185 m (300 to 600 ft). The body is compressed and the head has ridges and spines, two on the gill cover and five on a bony plate covering the cheek from the eye to the gill cover. The body is red. The ocean perch grows to a length of 92 cm (36 in). It is viviparous, and one female bears as many as 20,000 young. Once considered a trash fish, within the last 50 years it has become a valuable commercial fish sold in the form of frozen fillets and fish cakes.

OCEANSIDE, city, San Diego Co., SW California, on the Pacific Ocean (whence its name); inc. 1888. It is a beach resort and a trade center for a rich farm area producing limes, avocados, and tomatoes. Manufactures include electrical and electronic equipment, boats, and clothing. Nearby Camp Pendleton, a large U.S. Marine Corps base, is important to the economy. A community college is here, and Mission San Luis Rey (1798, restored) is close by. The community grew as a tourist and farm center after the arrival of the railroad in 1883. Pop. (1970) 40,494; (1980) 76,698.

OCEANSIDE, unincorporated community, in the town of Hempstead, Nassau Co., SE New York, on the S shore of Long Island. It is a residential suburb of New York City and a summer resort and contains some industry. Pop. (1970) 35,372; (1980) 33,639.

OCEANUS, in Greek mythology, one of the Titans, the son of Uranus and Gaea. With his wife, the Titan Tethys, he ruled over Ocean, a great river encircling the earth, which was believed to be a flat circle. The nymphs of this great river, the Oceanids, were their daughters, and the gods of all the streams on earth were their sons. In later legends, when Zeus, chief of the Olympian gods, and his brothers, Poseidon and Hades, overthrew the Titans and assumed their power, Poseidon and his wife, Amphitrite, succeeded Oceanus and Tethys as rulers of the waters.

OCELOT, medium-sized mammal, *Felis pardalis,* of the cat family (q.v.), Felidae, found from Texas to Peru. The ocelot, which somewhat resembles the domestic cat in form, attains a length of about 91 cm (about 36 in). The back of the animal is tinted with olive-tan or chestnut and is marked with black stripes and spots. The belly is usually white, marked with black. Ocelots are good climbers and hunt in forests at night for their food, which consists of birds and small mammals. Two kittens are normally produced in a litter. The animals have been hunted nearly to extinction for their pelts.

OCHOA, Severo (1905–), Spanish-American biochemist, who was the first to synthesize a nucleic acid, the substance that exists in all living cells and controls heredity. Ochoa was born in Luarca, Spain, and educated at the University of Madrid. After graduate work in Glasgow, Berlin, and Heidelberg, he taught at the universities of Madrid, Heidelberg, and Oxford. In 1940 he settled in the U.S., becoming a citizen in 1956. Ochoa joined the faculty of the College of Medicine of New York University in 1942; in 1954 he was named chairman of the department of biochemistry. Ochoa shared the 1959 Nobel Prize in physiology or medicine with the American biochemist Arthur Kornberg; Ochoa was honored for research on ribonucleic acid (RNA), Kornberg for research on deoxyribonucleic acid (DNA). Ochoa had synthesized RNA in 1955.

OCHS, Adolph Simon (1858–1935), American newspaper publisher, born in Cincinnati, Ohio, and educated in the primary schools of Knoxville, Tenn. He was a newsboy and printer's apprentice (1869–73), a compositor (1873–77), and in 1877 became a staff member of the *Chattanooga Dispatch* and then its editor in chief. The following year he became publisher of the *Chattanooga Times,* which he made one of the outstanding newspapers of the South. In 1896 Ochs gained control of the then bankrupt *New York Times.* As its publisher he followed a policy of thorough, nonpartisan, and unsensational coverage of news, in contrast to the yellow journalism prevailing at the time, and by his journalistic method he developed the *New York Times* into one of the leading newspapers in the world. He also was responsible for introducing rotogravure printing of newspaper photographs to journalism. From 1902 to 1912 he was the owner of the *Philadelphia Times* and the *Philadelphia Public Ledger;* he consolidated the two newspapers, retaining the latter name. He was a member of the executive committee and a director of the Associated Press news agency from 1900 until his death.

OCKEGHEM, Johannes (c. 1420–96), Flemish composer, the most important composer of his generation in the Netherlands school that dominated Renaissance music. Possibly a pupil of the eminent Netherlands-school composer Gilles Binchois (c. 1400–60), Ockeghem served as composer and choirmaster to three French kings: Charles VII, Louis XI, and Charles VIII. At his death, a *Déploration* (lament) was composed by his pupil (according to tradition), the French composer Josquin Desprez, and a lament by the philosopher Erasmus was set to music by the French composer Johannes Lupi (c. 1506–39). Ockeghem's masses, motets, and chansons (secular part-songs) show great skill at counterpoint based on melodic imitation.

OCKHAM or OCCAM, William of (c. 1285–1349?), known as Doctor Invincibilis (Lat., "unconquerable doctor") and Venerabilis Inceptor (Lat., "worthy initiator"), English philosopher and Scholastic theologian, who is considered the greatest exponent of the nominalist school, the leading rival of the Thomist and Scotist schools. See NOMINALISM; SCHOLASTICISM.

Ockham was born in Surrey, England. He entered the Franciscan order and studied and taught at the University of Oxford from 1309 to

1319. Denounced by Pope John XXII for dangerous teachings, he was held in house detention for four years (1324–28) at the papal palace in Avignon, France, while the orthodoxy of his writings was examined. Siding with the Franciscan general against the pope in a dispute over Franciscan poverty, Ockham fled to Munich in 1328 to seek the protection of Louis IV, Holy Roman emperor, who had rejected papal authority over political matters. Excommunicated by the pope, Ockham wrote against the papacy and defended the emperor until the latter's death in 1347. The philosopher died in Munich, apparently of the plague, while seeking reconciliation with Pope Clement VI.

Ockham won fame as a rigorous logician who used logic to show that many beliefs of Christian philosophers (for example, that God is one, omnipotent, creator of all things; and that the human soul is immortal) could not be proved by philosophical or natural reason but only by divine revelation. His name is applied to the principle of economy in formal logic, known as Ockham's razor, which states that entities are not to be multiplied without necessity.   W.N.C.

OCMULGEE NATIONAL MONUMENT, central Georgia, near Macon, established in 1934. The monument preserves some of the most important remains of the Mound Builders in the southeastern U.S. Within the area are remains of many centuries of Indian occupation, representing settlements of successive tribes of Indians believed to have lived here as early as 8000 BC. Remains of earthwork fortifications are here, as well as burial and ceremonial mounds. The monument has a museum containing Indian artifacts. Area, 2.8 sq km (1.1 sq mi).

O'CONNELL, Daniel (1775–1847), called The Liberator, leader of the fight to win political rights for the Irish Roman Catholics in the early 19th century.

O'Connell was born on Aug. 6, 1775, near Cahirciveen, county Kerry, and educated in France. He returned to Ireland, studied law, and was admitted to the bar in Dublin in 1798. During the next two decades he was active in the movement to repeal British laws that barred Roman Catholics from Parliament. In 1823 he organized the Catholic Association, which played an important role in the passage of the Catholic Emancipation Act six years later. O'Connell entered the British House of Commons for county Clare in 1829, retaining his seat until his death. O'Connell often allied himself with the Whig party in Parliament. He became lord mayor of Dublin in 1841.

As head of the Catholic Association he received a large yearly income from voluntary con-

O'Connor's work, essentially two novels and two volumes of short stories, has been described as an unlikely mixture of southern Gothic, prophecy, and evangelistic Roman Catholicism. The novels are *Wise Blood* (1952) and *The Violent Bear It Away* (1960); the short-story collections are *A Good Man Is Hard to Find* (1955) and *Everything that Rises Must Converge* (posthumous, 1965). O'Connor is frequently compared to the American novelist William Faulkner for her portrayal of southern character and milieu and to the Austrian writer Franz Kafka for her preoccupation with the grotesque. A basic theme of her work is the individual's vain attempt to escape the grace of God.

O'CONNOR, Sandra Day (1930–), American jurist, born in El Paso, Tex., on March 26, 1930, and educated at Stanford University. O'Connor first entered public office as an assistant attorney general in Arizona (1965-69); she later served as a state senator (1969-74) and a superior court judge (1974-79). In 1979 she was appointed to the Arizona Court of Appeals. President Ronald Reagan nominated O'Connor as an associate justice of the U.S. Supreme Court in July 1981. After confirmation by the U.S. Senate, she was sworn in on September 25, thus making her the first woman to attain this position.

O'CONNOR, Thomas Power, called Tay Pay (1848-1929), Irish journalist and nationalist leader, born in Athlone, county Westmeath, and educated at Queen's College, Galway. While working as a free-lance newspaperman, O'Connor wrote *Life of Lord Beaconsfield* (1876), an acrid biography of the British statesman Benjamin Disraeli, 1st earl of Beaconsfield. In 1880 he was elected to the British Parliament and there supported the nationalist leader Charles Stewart Parnell. O'Connor's long, unbroken tenure in Parliament secured him the popular title Father of the House of Commons. He became president of the Irish Nationalist League in 1883 and made the first of several tours to the U.S. in 1881 to raise funds for support of the nationalist movement. O'Connor founded several radical Irish newspapers, including the *Star and the Sun,* and a literary publication, *T.P.'s Weekly* (1902). He wrote many articles, short stories, and two longer works, *The Parnell Movement* (1886) and *Memoirs of an Old Parliamentarian* (1929).

OCTAVE. *See* INTERVAL.

OCTAVIA (d. 11 BC), Roman matron, daughter of the Roman general Gaius Octavius (d. 59 BC), grandniece of Julius Caesar, and sister of Octavian, who became emperor as Augustus. Octavia was distinguished for her beauty and her virtue. In 40 BC on the death of her first husband, the

Daniel O'Connell   New York Public Library Picture Collection

tributions by the Irish people, who supported him in a series of demonstrations in favor of Irish home rule. After one of these demonstrations, in 1843, he was arrested and convicted of seditious conspiracy but the conviction was subsequently reversed by the House of Lords, and he resumed his career. At this time a great famine descended on Ireland, and younger members of O'Connell's party began to advocate revolutionary doctrines that he had always opposed. Their arguments in favor of violent opposition to British rule led to an open split in Irish ranks in 1846. O'Connell, distressed by this disaffection among the Irish and in ill health, moved to Genoa, Italy, where he died on May 15, 1847.

O'CONNOR, (Mary) Flannery (1925-64), American writer, whose novels and short stories focusing on humanity's spiritual deformity and flight from redemption earned her a unique place in 20th-century American fiction.

Born in Savannah, Ga., on March 25, 1925, O'Connor was educated at the Georgia State College for Women and the State University of Iowa. Most of her life was spent in Milledgeville, Ga., where she raised peacocks and wrote. She died Aug. 3, 1964, of lupus, a disease that had crippled her for the last ten years of her life.

consul Gaius Claudius Marcellus, she consented to marry Octavian's rival Mark Antony to make secure the reconciliation between him and her brother. When Antony deserted her for the Egyptian queen Cleopatra, Octavia remained loyal to her husband, even abiding him with reinforcements on occasion. Octavian was indignant at the treatment she received and wished her to leave her husband's house. When war broke out between Octavian and Antony in 32, the latter crowned his insults by sending Octavia a notice of divorce. When Mark Antony died in Egypt after being defeated by Octavian in 30, Octavia brought up not only her own children but also Antony's children by his first wife, Fulvia (d. 40 BC), and by Cleopatra. Octavia herself had five children: two daughters by Antony, and a son and two daughters by her first husband. Her son, Marcus Claudius Marcellus (42–23 BC), was adopted by Augustus and apparently intended to succeed the latter as emperor, but died at the age of 20. Among the descendants of two of Octavia's daughters, Antonia Major (fl. 1st cent. AD) and Antonia Minor (36 BC–AD 37), were three rulers of the Roman Empire: the emperors Claudius I, Nero, and Caligula.

OCTAVIA (c. AD 40–62), Roman empress, the daughter of the Roman emperor Claudius I and his third wife Valeria Messalina (d. AD 48). In 52 Octavia married her cousin Nero, who later deserted her at the request of his mistress Poppaea Sabina (d. AD 65). Through the jealousy of Poppaea, whom Nero married in 62, a charge of adultery was brought against Octavia; she was sent to the island of Pandataria (now Ventotene) and there executed. She is the heroine of a contemporary tragedy erroneously attributed to the Roman philosopher Seneca.

OCTAVIAN. *See* AUGUSTUS.

OCTOBER, tenth month of the Gregorian calendar, containing 31 days. October was the eighth month of the ancient Roman calendar as evidenced by the name October (Lat. *octo*, "eight"). Columbus Day occurs on October 12 and is observed as a holiday in most states and territories of the U.S. Halloween occurs on October 31 and is observed in the U.S. and other countries with masquerading, bonfires, and games.

OCTOPUS, carnivorous marine mollusk (q.v.) of the genus *Octopus*, order Octopoda, class Cephalopoda (*see* CEPHALOPOD), found worldwide in tropical and warm temperate waters. It is characterized by a soft body with a well-developed brain and by eight arms bearing two rows of suckers each. As in the vertebrates, the two large, complex eyes of the octopus are cameralike in structure, and their vision is acute. The animals

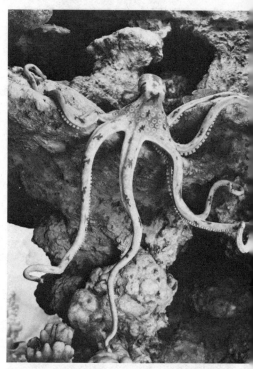

Octopus of the family Octopodidae. Sucker disks are on the underside of its tentacles. American Museum of Natural History

can change the color and texture of their skin rapidly. Much of their life is spent in hiding, and many species—such as the common octopus, *O. vulgaris,* which can grow to about 1 m (about 3 ft) long—choose a natural hole among rocks or in a pile of rubble. A small species, however, such as the pygmy octopus, *O. joubini,* which is about 2 cm (about 5 in) long, may prefer an empty clamshell having both valves still connected by a ligament; settling into one half, it pulls the shell shut with its suckers.

When an octopus emerges to find food such as crustaceans and bivalve mollusks, it often lures its victim by wiggling the tip of an arm like a worm; or it glides near and pounces on a crab, sinking its beak into the shell and injecting a poison that kills; the poison of a very few species is dangerous to humans. Octopuses are preyed upon in turn by a number of fishes, including the moray eel. When an octopus is attacked, it draws water into its mantle cavity and expels it with great force through a funnel. The result is a jet-propelled exit, usually behind a cloud of "ink," a dark substance the octopus ejects for defense. The ink of some species seems to have a paralyzing effect on the sensory organs of the predator.

A male interested in mating approaches a female just close enough to stretch out a modified arm, the hectocotylus, and caress the female. This arm has a deep groove between the two rows of suckers and ends in a spoonlike tip. After a period of love play the male inserts its arm under the mantle of the female, and the spermatophores travel down the groove on the hectocotylus to the female's oviduct. Soon after mating, the female begins to lay eggs, each enclosed in a transparent capsule, in its lair, producing about 150,000 in two weeks. The female guards them for the next 50 days, jetting water to aerate and clean them. The young of such species as the white-spotted octopus, *O. macropus,* are only about 3 mm (about 0.12 in) long. They float to the surface and become part of the plankton for about a month, then sink and begin their normal life on the bottom. Octopuses generally stay in one area as adults, but those species with planktonic larvae are found all over the world because the currents and tides move them.

ODA NOBUNAGA (1534-82), Japanese feudal lord, who started the unification of the country, then torn by local wars. Working from a modest family base in the province of Owari, he gradually gained control of the whole region and occupied (1568) the capital city of Kyoto. Five years later he drove out the last Ashikaga shogun. He went on to destroy the temporal power of the Buddhist sects and monasteries and, as a counterbalance to their influence, encouraged Christian missionaries. By 1580 he had extended his authority over all of central Japan. Before he could realize his goal of winning control of the whole country, however, he was assassinated by one of his vassals.

ODD FELLOWS, INDEPENDENT ORDER OF, secret fraternal benefit society, organized in England in the 18th century and introduced into the U.S. in 1819 (*see* FRATERNAL ORDERS). The order maintains homes for the aged, the poor, and widows and orphans; provides its members with financial aid in cases of sickness or death; and gives educational benefits to high school graduates. National headquarters is in Arlington, Va.

ODE, dignified and elaborately structured lyric poem praising and glorifying an individual, commemorating an event, or describing nature intellectually rather than emotionally. Odes were originally songs performed to the accompaniment of a musical instrument.

Classical Odes. Among the ancient Greeks, odes fell into two broad categories, choral odes and those to be sung by one person. The single-voice ode was cultivated by Sappho, Alcaeus, Anacreon, and others. The choral ode, which is patterned after the movements of the chorus in Greek drama, has a three-part stanza structure: the strophe, the antistrophe, and the epode, marking a turn from one intellectual position to another and then a recounting of the entire ode subject. The strophe and antistrophe have the same metrical scheme; the epode has a different structure.

Pindar is considered the greatest lyric poet of Greece; extant portions of his work include 45 victory odes commemorating, among other festivals, the Olympian Games. Roman poets such as Horace and Catullus imitated the single-voice Greek odes of Alcaeus and Sappho,with their simpler structure and more personal style than the Pindaric odes; but they wrote them to be declaimed rather than to be sung.

Modern Odes. The modern form of the ode dates from the Renaissance; like the Latin ode it is pure poetry, not intended for musical accompaniment. The French poet Pierre de Ronsard wrote odes both in the Pindaric and the Horatian style. The earliest English odes include the "Epithalamion" and the "Prothalamion," or marriage hymns, by the 16th-century poet Edmund Spenser. Among other English writers of odes, in the 17th century, were Ben Jonson and Andrew Marvell, who wrote in the Horatian mode, and John Milton, whose ode "On the Morning of Christ's Nativity" follows Pindaric form. Milton's contemporary, Abraham Cowley, failed to understand the strophe-antistrophe-epode divisions of the classical Pindaric and Horatian ode, but he impressed his own conception of the ode as a lofty and tempestuous composition on later English and American literature. As a result, the ode in English is usually a succession of stanzas in lines of varying length and meter. A rebirth of the ode occurred during the 18th century. The English writers John Dryden and Alexander Pope both wrote odes commemorating St. Cecilia, patron of sacred music, Dryden's work being intended for a musical setting. The Englishman William Collins, one of the greatest lyric poets of the age, wrote exquisite nature odes—for example, "To Evening." During the romantic period in England Percy Bysshe Shelley wrote "Ode to the West Wind" and John Keats produced his great odes, including "Ode on a Grecian Urn."

The popularity of the ode form waned during Victorian times, but interest in the 20th century revived with works such as "Ode on the Confederate Dead" by the American writer Allen Tate and a variety of ode lyrics by the English poet W. H. Auden.

ODENSE, city and port, S central Denmark, capital of Fyn Co., on the island of Fyn. Odense is a major commercial and transportation center, linked by a deepwater canal with Odense Fjord. Principal manufactures include machinery, metal products, motor vehicles, glass, processed foods, and textiles. The city, which dates from the early 10th century, contains the Cathedral of Saint Canute, built in the 13th century, the best example of Gothic architecture in Denmark. The Church of Our Lady was constructed in the 12th century. Odense is the birthplace of the Danish writer Hans Christian Andersen. Pop. (1981 est.) 169,183.

ODER, also Odra, river, Europe, an important transportation artery. It rises near Olomouc, Czechoslovakia, and flows generally NE into Poland, where it is the second longest river. The Oder continues generally N past Racibórz, Opole, Wrocław, and Kostrzyn into the Baltic Sea at Szczecin. The river is 906 km (563 mi) long and navigable from Racibórz. The Oder is connected by canal with the Spree, Havel, and Elbe rivers in East Germany.

Before World War II the Oder flowed through German territory; with the defeat of Germany in 1945 a provisional German-Polish border was set along a line formed by the Oder and Neisse rivers. The government of West Germany delayed recognizing the new border and the subsequent loss of about 103,600 sq km (about 40,000 sq mi) of land until 1970.

ODESSA, city, seat of Ector Co., W Texas; inc. 1927. It is a commercial and manufacturing center situated in the Permian Basin, a major petroleum- and livestock-producing area. Principal products include oil-drilling equipment, petrochemicals, and plastic items. In the city are the University of Texas of the Permian Basin (1969); a junior college; the Globe of the Great Southwest, a reproduction of the Shakespearean Globe Theatre in England; and the Presidential Museum, containing items associated with U.S. presidents. The Odessa Crater, one of the largest meteor craters in the U.S., is nearby. The community, established in 1881 as a railroad stop, is probably named for Odessa in the USSR. The settlement grew rapidly after the discovery in the 1920s of great oil deposits in the area. Pop. (1970) 78,380; (1980) 90,027.

ODESSA, city, capital of Odessa Oblast, Ukrainian SSR, in SW European USSR. Located on the Black Sea, the city is one of the chief trade and fishing ports of the USSR, its harbor kept open in winter by icebreakers. It also is a major manufacturing, railroad, and cultural center and, with its mild climate, a popular resort. Products of the city include refined petroleum, processed food, plastics, pharmaceuticals, and clothing. Institutes of higher learning here include a university, polytechnic and medical schools, a marine academy, and a music conservatory. The city also has several museums and theaters and an opera house.

The site of the city may have been occupied by an ancient Greek colony, and Crimean Tatars traded here in the 14th century. Odessa itself was founded in 1794 as a Russian naval fortress on territory annexed (1792) from Turkey. By the early 19th century the Russian settlement had become an important grain-exporting port. During the Crimean War (1853–56), Odessa was bombarded by combined French and British naval forces. In 1905 the city was the site of a workers' uprising, supported by the crew of the Russian battleship *Potëmkin*. Odessa suffered heavy damage during World War II, when it was occupied (1941–44) by German and Romanian forces; many civilians were killed by the occupying powers. Pop. (1980 est.) 1,057,000.

ODETS, Clifford (1906–63), American playwright, born in Philadelphia, and reared in New York City. He left school at the age of 15 to become an actor. In 1931 he was a founder of the Group Theatre in New York City. Most of his plays were produced by the Group Theatre, including *Waiting for Lefty* (1935), a one-act play that established his fame, *Awake and Sing* (1935), and *Till the Day I Die* (1935). After the unsuccessful production of his *Paradise Lost* (1935), Odets went to Hollywood, where he wrote the motion picture scenario of *The General Died at Dawn* (1936). Returning to New York City, he wrote more plays for the Group Theatre, including

Clifford Odets

Golden Boy (1937), *Silent Partner* (1938), *Rocket to the Moon* (1938), *Night Music* (1940), and *Clash by Night* (1941), all concerned with the frustration of individual potential by economic insecurity and the materialistic ideals of middle-class society. Odets subsequently spent several years in Hollywood and wrote many motion picture scenarios, including *None but the Lonely Heart* (1943) and *The Story on Page One* (1959). He also wrote the plays *The Big Knife* (1949) and *The Country Girl* (1950).

ODIN (O.N. *Odhinn*, A.S. *Woden*, O.H.G. *Wōdan*, *Woutan*), in Norse mythology, king of the gods. His two black ravens, Huginn ("Thought") and Muninn ("Memory"), flew forth daily to gather tidings of all that was being done throughout the world. As god of war, Odin held court in Valhalla, where all brave warriors went after death in battle. His greatest treasures were his eight-foot steed, Sleipner, his spear, Gunger, and his ring, Draupner. Odin was also the god of wisdom, poetry, and magic, and he sacrificed an eye for the privilege of drinking from Mimir, the fountain of wisdom. Odin's three wives were earth goddesses, and his eldest son was Thor, the god of Thunder.

ODYSSEUS, in Greek legend, a Greek hero, ruler of the island of Ithaca and one of the leaders of the Greek army during the Trojan War. Homer's *Odyssey* recounts Odysseus's adventures and ultimate return home ten years after the fall of Troy. Initially, Odysseus was mentioned as the son of Laertes, king of Ithaca, although in later tradition Sisyphus, king of Corinth, was considered his real father, his mother having later married Laertes. At first Odysseus refused to accompany the Greeks to Troy, feigning madness by sowing his fields with salt, but the Greeks placed his son Telemachus in front of the plow, and Odysseus was compelled to admit his ruse and join the invading army. Throughout the *Iliad* of Homer, he is portrayed as a brave, sagacious, cunning warrior, and he is awarded the famous armor of the Greek warrior Achilles on the latter's death. Odysseus was responsible for bringing the Greek heroes Neoptolemus and Philoctetes to Troy for the final stage of the conflict. In the *Odyssey* it is said that he proposed the strategem of the Trojan Horse, the means by which Troy was conquered.

In the works of later classical writers, particularly those of the Greek poet Pindar, the Greek playwright Euripides, and the Roman poet Vergil, Odysseus is characterized as a cowardly and scheming politician. In Latin his name is rendered as Ulysses.

ODYSSEY. *See* HOMER.

OECOLAMPADIUS, Johannes (1482-1531), German scholar and preacher who led the Reformation (q.v.) in Basel, Switzerland. Originally named Johannes Hursgen, he was born at Weinsberg, in Bavaria. Trained in classical languages, he Grecized his last name and moved to Basel in 1515 to assist the Dutch humanist scholar Desiderius Erasmus in preparing his Greek New Testament. After two years (1518-20) as a preacher at Augsburg, Germany, Oecolampadius entered a Bridgettine monastery. His discovery of the work of Martin Luther and his increasing discontent with the Roman Catholic doctrine of transubstantiation (q.v.) prompted him to leave in 1522. Returning to Basel, he became a professor of theology and preached at Saint Martin's Church. Thereafter, he was an ardent supporter of the Reformation. At the Marburg Colloquy (1529), Oecolampadius espoused the view of the Swiss reformer Huldreich Zwingli, who taught that the Eucharist was merely symbolic of the body and blood of Christ.

OEDIPUS, in Greek mythology, king of Thebes, the son of Laius and Jocasta, king and queen of Thebes. Laius was warned by an oracle that he would be killed by his own son. Determined to avert his fate, he bound together the feet of his newborn child and left him to die on a lonely mountain. The infant was rescued by a shepherd, however, and given to Polybus, king of Corinth, who named the child Oedipus ("Swollen-foot") and raised him as his own son. The boy did not know that he was adopted, and when an oracle proclaimed that he would kill his father, he left Corinth. In the course of his wanderings he met and killed Laius, believing that the king and his followers were a band of robbers, and thus unwittingly fulfilled the prophecy.

Lonely and homeless, Oedipus arrived at Thebes, which was beset by a dreadful monster called the Sphinx. The frightful creature frequented the roads to the city, killing and devouring all travelers who could not answer the riddle that she put to them. When Oedipus successfully solved her riddle, the Sphinx killed herself. Believing that King Laius had been slain by unknown robbers, and grateful to Oedipus for ridding them of the Sphinx, the Thebans rewarded Oedipus by making him their king and giving him Queen Jocasta as his wife. For many years the couple lived in happiness, now knowing that they were really mother and son.

Then a terrible plague descended on the land, and the oracle proclaimed that Laius's murderer must be punished. Oedipus soon discovered that he had unknowingly killed his father. In grief and despair at her incestuous life, Jocasta killed herself, and when Oedipus realized that she was dead and that their children were accursed, he put out his eyes and resigned the throne. He lived in Thebes for several years, but was finally banished. Accompanied by his daughter Antigone, he wandered for many years. He finally arrived at Colonus, a shrine near Athens sacred to the powerful goddesses called the Eumenides. At this shrine for supplicants Oedipus died, after the god Apollo had promised him that the place of his death would remain sacred and would bring great benefit to the city of Athens, which had given shelter to the wanderer.

OEDIPUS COMPLEX. See PSYCHOANALYSIS.

OEHLENSCHLÄGER, Adam Gottlob (1779–1850), Danish poet and dramatist, who was the leader of the romantic movement in Danish literature. He was born in Copenhagen. His poetry and dramatic works were influenced by those of the romantic movement in Germany and by the Old Norse sagas. His first published volume of verse was *Digte* (Poems, 1803). He traveled throughout Europe from 1805 to 1809, returning to Denmark to become professor of aesthetics at the University of Copenhagen. Most of his plays are based on Scandinavian history or Norse mythology. They include the lyric drama *Sanct-Hansaften-Spil* (St. John's Eve Play, 1803) and the historical tragedies *Hakon Jarl* (Earl Hakon, 1807), *Baldur hin Gode* (Baldur the Good, 1808), and *Axel and Valborg* (1809; trans. 1851). Other important works are the tragedy *Correggio* (1811; trans. 1846) and the fantasy in verse *Aladdin of the Wonderful Lamp* (1820; trans. 1857).

OERSTED, Hans Christian (1777–1851), Danish physicist and chemist, born in Rudköbing, and educated at the University of Copenhagen. He was appointed professor of physics at the University of Copenhagen in 1806. In 1819 he discovered that a magnetic needle is deflected at right angles to a wire carrying an electric current, thus initiating the study of electromagnetism. In 1825 Oersted became the first to isolate the element aluminum. His *Manual of Mechanical Physics* appeared in 1844.

O'FAOLÁIN, Seán (1900–), Irish fiction writer, essayist, and biographer. O'Faoláin's experiences as an active participant in the Irish nationalist conflict influenced the short-story collection *Midsummer Night Madness* (1932) and the novel *A Nest of Simple Folk* (1933). His critical writing concerns such matters as censorship by the Irish church and the cultural and social problems faced by the Irish people, past and present. He also published biographies of the Irish statesmen Daniel O'Connell and Eamon De Valera and in 1949 wrote *The Irish,* a study of the national temperament. Until the 1930s he taught in the U.S., England, and Ireland.

OFFALY, county, Republic of Ireland, in Leinster Province, situated in the central plain of the republic, and bounded on the W by the Shannon R. Peat is produced; hops, barley, potatoes, and turnips are grown; and livestock is raised. Manufacturing establishments include textile mills, distilleries, and shoe factories. Most of the county is level; the Bog of Allen covers the SE, and the Slieve Bloom Mts. rise to 518 m (1700 ft) in the SW. The county town is Tullamore, and the width of the county is crossed by the Grand Canal. Danish raths, or hill fortresses, and remains of ancient churches and monasteries are among the points of interest. The county was part of the kingdom of Offaly in ancient Ireland. It became county King's in 1568 and was renamed in 1921. Area, 1997 sq km (771 sq mi); pop. (1979) 57,183.

OFFENBACH, full name Offenbach am Main, city, central West Germany, in Hesse, on the Main R., near Frankfurt. The city is known for the manufacture of leather goods; other products include chemicals and machinery. A Renaissance palace (16th cent.) is here. Offenbach was first mentioned in the 10th century; it passed to Hesse-Darmstadt in 1816. Pop. (1980 est.) 111,200.

OFFENBACH, Jacques (1819–80), French composer, whose operettas are considered masterpieces of satire. Born in Cologne, Germany, he studied at the Paris Conservatoire and in 1837 became a cellist at the Paris Opéra-Comique, where his first operetta, the one-act *Pepito,* was performed (1853). In 1849 he became conductor at the Théâtre Français. Subsequently he managed the Bouffes-Parisiens Theater (1855–61) and the Théâtre de la Gaité (1873–75). By 1875 he had composed 90 operettas, many of them to librettos by the French writer Ludovic Halévy (1834–1908). Of Offenbach's works, the most often performed today are *Orpheus in the Underworld* (1858), *La Périchole* (1868), and his masterpiece, the grand opera *Tales of Hoffmann* (1880, premiered posthumously, 1881), which contains the popular "Barcarolle." Offenbach's musical style is prevailingly witty and light.

OFFICE MACHINES, equipment designed to increase the productivity of clerical and professional workers in performing routine or repetitive tasks. Since 1900, commercial, governmental, and service organizations have increasingly utilized equipment to simplify, standardize, and systematize work steps. Office machines in use by the mid-1960s include typewriters, dictation equipment, tabulating machines, sorters, adding machines, document conveyors, microfilm equipment, copiers, and teletype machines. Because the percentage of the work force employed in offices has grown, the productivity made possible by office machines has become increasingly indispensable to economic growth. As a result, office automation has received considerable attention from systems analysts and other members of the business community since the mid-1970s. Some older office machines have been redesigned and a number of new devices developed. Unlike earlier equipment, which was primarily mechanical, these newer devices contain electronic components that improve reliability, lower cost, and significantly increase versatility and productivity. These machines can be categorized by the tasks that they perform or aid. Office machines can prepare and reproduce office documents; perform financial and statistical calculations; record, store, and process information; and expedite the handling of mail and other communications.

Document Preparation. Office documents usually consist of handwritten or mechanically or electronically produced records containing numeric and alphabetic information in graphic or electronically coded form.

Typewriters. The typewriter has been in use since the 19th century. Today, manual typewriters have been replaced in many offices by electric models. Although the first manual and electric typewriters contained key bars on which individual type slugs were mounted, many electric models now feature a spherical metal element on which type characters are embossed. As individual keys are pressed, the element rotates, tilts, and strikes the ribbon to print the appropriate characters. These typing elements can be easily removed and replaced, enabling one machine to produce documents in different type styles. Some typewriters also employ a special combination of ribbons that allows the typist to remove incorrect characters from the paper. The newest typewriters, sometimes called intelligent typewriters, feature electronic components that can automatically center headings, align decimal points in numerical tables, and store frequently used words and phrases for automatic printing.

Word-processing technology has further simplified the preparation of typewritten documents. As introduced in the mid-1970s, the term *word processing* encompasses two groups of office machines: dictation equipment and automatic typewriters and text-editing machines.

Dictation machines. Dictation equipment creates a voice recording for subsequent transcription by a typist. A dictation system consists of two components: a microphone and recorder that capture spoken words electronically on a magnetic tape cassette or some other magnetizable medium and a transcriber, or playback device, with a speaker that converts the recorded signal to audible sounds (*see* SOUND RECORDING AND REPRODUCTION). The typical recorder is a desk-top device that accepts an audio cassette with a capacity of up to 120 minutes; the playback element makes possible the review of previously recorded material. When dictation is completed, a typist inserts the tape cassette into a separate transcriber for playback. Portable recorders, com-

Modern electronic typewriters mark a great advance over the familiar electric and manual typewriters of the past. This machine provides disk storage of the typed text; the stored material can easily be modified, and the typing is displayed to the operator for automated changes before it is committed to the paper. Olivetti

patible with desk-top transcribers, can be used away from the office. Some large offices employ central recording and playback equipment that can be linked through the office telephone system. These central units can record many hours of voice communications. Typists with earphones can transcribe from the central playback unit while new material is being dictated on the recording unit.

Text-editing equipment. Automatic typewriters and other text-editing systems, often called word processors, speed repetitive typing, error correction, the typing of revised drafts, and related tasks. These tasks are accomplished by recording typed characters in an encoded, or machine-readable, form on a magnetizable medium for subsequent use. The earliest word processors were typewriterlike devices that printed characters on paper and simultaneously recorded equivalent information on tape or cards coated with magnetizable ferric (iron) oxide. Corrections or revisions of the encoded text could be made electronically on the tape or card, eliminating the need to retype the entire document. When all changes had been made, the recorded and edited text would be automatically played back through the typewriter to produce the desired final version of a document.

Newer word processors employ a keyboard and a video-display unit, a televisionlike device, for the initial recording and display of typed text. Changes can be made in the displayed text by retyping incorrect characters or by adding, deleting, or rearranging portions of text. The final displayed text is then recorded on a magnetizable disk or other medium, and it may be transmitted to an attached printer to produce a paper document. Subsequent revisions can be made by recalling the recorded text to the display screen and typing the required modifications.

The simplest video-display word processors are self-contained systems designed for use by a single typist. These systems are actually microcomputers programmed to perform word-processing tasks (see COMPUTER). More versatile word-processing systems employ preprogrammed minicomputers that can be used simultaneously by several operators, each working at a separate keyboard and video-display unit. These multioperator systems provide more extensive magnetic storage and one or more printers that are shared by the various operators.

Document Reproduction. Office machines for the full-size reproduction of documents can be divided into two groups: copiers designed to make one or several reproductions and duplicators designed to make many copies.

Electrostatic copying. Most copiers, and many duplicators, are electrostatic devices in which document images are created out of electrical charges to which powdered ink particles are applied. In the xerographic variant of the electrostatic process, a mirror image of the page to be copied is induced electrostatically onto a metal cylinder and then transferred to an ordinary sheet of paper (see XEROGRAPHY). Less expensive machines that are designed for low-volume output produce copy on paper coated with a developer. Copier speeds range from a few pages per minute to more than one page per second. Advanced devices are equipped with automatic feeders, automatic sorters, and other timesaving attachments. Some machines can copy both sides of a document automatically, make modest reductions of large documents, and reproduce colored documents.

Other techniques. Although some duplicators employ electrostatic technology, others employ offset lithography (q.v.), in which a specially prepared master is used to produce multiple copies. Some small offset presses are used in offices, but most are located in independent printing establishments, or in central printing departments of large organizations, where they are operated by trained personnel. Other, once common copying and duplicating processes retain a very limited role in the contemporary office. In spirit duplication, a paper master bearing images formed from a carbon dye is moistened with an alcohol solution, dissolving some of the dye, which can then be deposited on a piece of paper. This process is repeated rapidly to print multiple copies.

In mimeography, a stencillike master is created by typing or otherwise removing an ink-impervious coating from a fibrous tissue. The master is mounted on a cylinder that forces ink through the stencil onto paper (see PRINTING TECHNIQUES). Thermographic duplication, which uses heat-sensitive copy paper, is rarely found in modern business offices. The diazo process, which uses an ammonia-sensitive paper, continues to be used in engineering and architectural offices to reproduce drawings.

In order to reduce storage requirements and to simplify the handling and retrieval of documents, microfilm equipment is widely used to produce miniature reproductions of documents, which can then be magnified for display on microfilm, microcard, or microfiche readers. Paper enlargements can be made using reader-printers that can both display the images and print them.

Computing Equipment. Various types of counting and calculating machines have been used to handle financial, statistical, and other numerical data in offices. Today, the electronic calculator, which is the least expensive of such devices, has virtually replaced older mechanical adding machines. A prominent part of the electronic calculator is a keyboard used to initiate operations ranging from simple arithmetic to complicated mathematical functions. Calculators designed for statisticians, scientists, and engineers are often programmed to perform a predetermined sequence of numerical operations automatically, thereby simplifying complex, repetitive calculations. Calculators provide answers either in an electronic display or by printing onto a strip of paper.

Computers. During the 1950s and '60s, financial and other numerical record-keeping tasks were performed by bookkeeping machines, billing machines, tabulating equipment, and other types of electromechanical accounting devices. Since the 1970s, such machines have been largely replaced by electronic computers. During the early '70s, computers serving a large organization were typically located in a central facility accessible to the organization's various offices. Office personnel either prepared and packaged data for submission to a central keypunch department, or they keypunched the data themselves. These data were then combined and prepared for processing by the computing center staff, and the results returned to the office as paper printouts. This form of computing is still used in offices.

In the mid-1970s, computing systems were developed that allow video display and printing terminals to be linked electronically to remote computers. The results of the computing process are then returned to the office almost immediately. These so-called time-sharing arrangements, in which two or more offices share the use of a central computer, remain an important type of computer use.

Minicomputers and microcomputers. Time sharing has been increasingly supplemented by the use of relatively small, self-contained computers in separate offices. The earliest of these devices, called minicomputers, entered general business use in the mid-1970s and are now used widely. They enable an organization to decentralize its computing resources by placing computers under the direct control of the users rather than under centralized staff, who are sometimes perceived to be unresponsive to user needs. Because of their increasing versatility and decreasing cost, many minicomputers now offer data processing choices and capacities approaching those of some larger computers and greatly exceeding those of comparably priced computers manufactured just a few years ago.

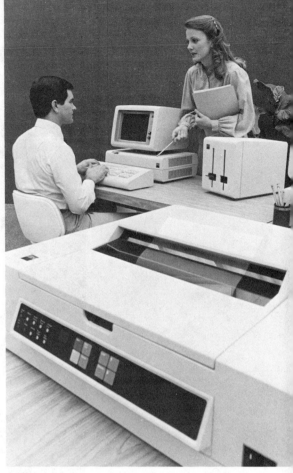

Small business computers such as this contain information storage units and can combine data processing and word processing functions.   IBM Corp.

The so-called microcomputer has further extended the concept of computer decentralization. As the name suggests, microcomputers are generally smaller and less versatile than minicomputers; also, microcomputers are designed to be operated by one or merely a few office workers, whereas minicomputers might serve an entire department within an organization. The rapidly growing popularity and decreasing price of microcomputers have promoted the marketing of programs that enable office workers to automate various record-keeping, billing, planning, and related operations. A variant form of microcomputer, which is known as an intelligent terminal, is both a self-contained, programmable computing device and a terminal that can be linked to remote computers.

Electronic Mail. Office workers often use various electronic devices to transmit recorded information from one site to another. Such devices employ telephone lines, microwave links, satellites,

Facsimile transceivers are a form of electronic mailing system, in which print fed into the machine is converted into electric impulses, sent to a receiving site in that form, and then reconstructed to produce a facsimile.　　3M Company

or other communications equipment to transmit and receive information. Historically, telegraphy, radiotelegraphy, and electronic mail have had as one of their primary uses the rapid transmission of urgent messages.

In facsimile transmission (q.v.), one of the oldest forms of electronic mail technology, the pattern of dark and light areas on textual or graphic matter is converted into a series of electrical impulses. At the receiving site, the incoming signal is reconstructed to produce a facsimile of the transmitted information. The process takes from 6 minutes to less than 1 minute, depending on the type of equipment. Special types of facsimile equipment can transmit microfilm images to remote locations for reconstruction as microfilm or paper copies. Telex, a system of direct-dial teleprinter exchange, and Teletypewriter Exchange (TWX) are, likewise, older, well-established examples of electronic mail technologies. TWX is customarily used for electronic communications

within North America, whereas Telex is widely used for international message transmission. In either case, a message is entered at a typewriter-like terminal for transmission over a network of telegraphic lines to a designated compatible receiver that prints the message onto paper. An operator need not be present at the receiver. Some word processors can also prepare messages for transmission to TWX terminals, Telex terminals, or other word processors.

Computer-based electronic message systems are an alternative to telephonic communications or conventional interoffice memoranda. Such systems allow a user to type a message at a terminal for transmission to a designated recipient. The computer stores the message until the recipient is ready to view it. At that time, the message may be displayed on the terminal screen, printed onto paper, relayed electronically to a third person, or retained inside the computer for future reference. With a variant form of computer-based message system, called computer teleconferencing, messages can be exchanged among three or more persons.

Integrated Office Systems. In the early and mid-1980s manufacturers of advanced electronic office machines began marketing equipment that could perform more than one of the functions described in preceding portions of this article. Such devices, which further expedite the processing and communication of information, consist of computers equipped with programs that enable office workers at a given terminal to perform word processing, order copies of documents, perform calculations, update stored records, and transmit messages to other workers. Some of these devices can also communicate electronically with computers at other sites by means of telephone, microwave, or satellite links.

Other Devices. Electronic devices represent the dominant form of office automation. Although a variety of mechanical devices remain in use, the newest models contain some electronic components. These devices include mail-handling equipment (postage-metering machines, scales, letter-opening machines, folding and inserting machines); automatic addressing equipment; audio paging systems; paper cutters, binders, and staplers; time-recording machines; and coin-sorting, counting, wrapping, and related money-handling equipment.   W.Sa.

OFFICE OF PRICE ADMINISTRATION (OPA), agency of the U.S. government in World War II, created by a presidential order issued in April 1941. This agency was charged with forestalling inflation by stabilizing rents and prices and by preventing speculation, hoarding, profiteering, and price manipulation. Subsequently, the powers of the OPA were expanded by several congressional enactments to include the rationing of scarce commodities to consumers and the determination of maximum prices for goods and residential rents. The OPA was notably successful during World War II. After the conclusion of hostilities in 1945, price controls were abolished. The OPA was disbanded in 1947.

OFFSET PRINTING. *See* PRINTING TECHNIQUES.

O'FLAHERTY, Liam (1896–1984), Irish novelist, born in the Arran Islands, county Galway, and educated at University College, Dublin. He was a leading Irish novelist of the early 20th century. His works are characterized by realism and powerful drama. Among O'Flaherty's books are *Thy Neighbor's Wife* (1924), *The Informer* (1925, subsequently made into a motion picture of the same name), *Mr. Gilhooley* (1926), *Land* (1946), *Two Lovely Beasts and Other Stories* (1950), *In-*

surrection (1951), and *The Stories of Liam O'Flaherty* (1956).

OGADEN, arid upland region, SE Ethiopia, in Harar Province, bordered on the N and E by Somalia. Ogaden is sparsely settled; the population is primarily Somali, a Muslim people engaged in nomadic herding. The region was occupied by Ethiopia in 1891 and in 1936 was incorporated in the colony of Italian Somaliland. It came under British military occupation in 1941 and was returned to Ethiopia in 1948. Since the 1960s Somalia has disputed Ethiopia's claim to the region. Repeated border fighting led to a brief occupation (1977–78) of the area by Somalia.

OGASAWARA-GUNTO. *See* BONIN ISLANDS.

OGBOMOSHO, city, SW Nigeria, in Oyo State. One of Nigeria's major cities, it is a commercial and manufacturing center situated in an agricultural region producing cotton and tobacco. Manufactures include textiles, footwear, rubber goods, and processed food. A large mosque and portions of a 17th-century city wall are landmarks. Ogbomosho was founded by the Yoruba in the 17th century and grew rapidly as a refugee center for Yoruba during the Fulani invasions of the early 19th century. Pop. (est.) 432,000.

OGDEN, city, seat of Weber Co., N Utah, at the confluence of the Ogden and Weber rivers, near Salt Lake City; inc. 1851. It is an industrial and railroad center. Major manufactures of the area include processed food, clothing, aerospace equipment, metal products, and building materials. Construction, tourism, Hill Air Force Base, and the Ogden Defense Depot are also important to the city's economy. Ogden is the site of Weber State College (1889); the Ogden Tabernacle and Temple; the Pioneer Hall Museum and Miles Goodyear Cabin, featuring artifacts from the pioneer days; and Eccles Community Arts Center, exhibiting works by local artists. The Great Salt Lake and the Snow Basin Winter Sports Area on Mt. Ogden are nearby. A group of Mormons settled here in 1847. The community was laid out in 1850 by the Mormon leader Brigham Young and named for the Canadian fur trader and explorer Peter Skene Ogden. Pop. (1970) 69,478; (1980) 64,407.

OGDEN, Peter Skene (1794–1854), Canadian fur trader and explorer, who lived in the western U.S., including the coastal region of Oregon, northern California, and the Snake River area. As a fur trader for the Hudson's Bay Co., he was led to new territory in dealing with the Indians west of the Rockies. Ogden made the first approach to the Sierra Nevadas from the east, discovering Carson and Owens lakes in 1829. In 1847 Ogden rescued the survivors of the Marcus Whitman

OGDENSBURG

massacre, in which the members of the missionary's family and 12 members of his group were slain by Cayuse Indians. Ogden, Utah, is named in his honor.

OGDENSBURG, city, St. Lawrence Co., N New York, a port at the confluence of the Saint Lawrence and Oswegatchie rivers, opposite Prescott, Ont.; inc. as a city 1868. Dairy items, electrical parts, and hardware are produced in the city. Located here are a junior college and a museum housing a major collection of works by the frontier artist Frederic Remington. The site was settled (1749) by the French as a fortress and Indian mission. The city is named for Samuel Ogden, who purchased the land in 1792. In August 1940 it was the site of the Ogdensburg Declaration, in which President Franklin D. Roosevelt and Canadian Prime Minister William Mackenzie King announced the establishment of the Permanent Joint Board on Defense. Pop. (1970) 14,554; (1980) 12,375.

James Edward Oglethorpe

OGLETHORPE, James Edward (1696–1785), British philanthropist and colonist, born in London, and educated at the University of Oxford. He was elected to the House of Commons in 1722 and subsequently became interested in prison reform, particularly in alleviating the condition of those imprisoned for debt. He formulated a plan for the resettlement of debtors in America and in 1732 was granted a royal charter for the purpose of realizing this plan. With a band of 116 emigrants, Oglethorpe landed at the present site of Charleston, S.C., early in 1733, and on Feb. 12,

1733, he founded the colony of Savannah, in what is now the state of Georgia. He acted as administrator of the colony for ten years and in 1742 defeated a Spanish force that had invaded the colony from Florida. In 1743 Oglethorpe returned to England, where he was commissioned a general in 1765. In his later years he associated with the literary circle led by the British critic Samuel Johnson.

O'HARA, John (1905–70), prolific American writer of novels and short stories. Believing that all good fiction is good social history, O'Hara set many of his novels and short stories in realistically described but fictionally named Pennsylvania towns. His dominant themes are class conflict, status, and sexual mores. O'Hara's ability to create characters and his ear for dialogue are shown in *Appointment in Samarra* (1934), his acclaimed first novel; *Butterfield 8* (1935), a story of New York City life; *A Rage to Live* (1949); *Ten North Frederick* (1955), which won the National Book Award; *From the Terrace* (1958); and *The Lockwood Concern* (1965).

A gifted short-story writer, O'Hara began writing for *The New Yorker* in 1928; during his lifetime he sold 225 stories to the magazine, more than any other writer. His first collection, *The Doctor's Son and Other Stories* (1935), was followed by 12 more, one of which—*Pal Joey* (1940)—was made into a successful Broadway musical.

O'HIGGINS, Bernardo (1778–1842), Chilean leader, who helped win independence for his country and served as its first chief executive. Born in Chillán, O'Higgins was an illegitimate son of Ambrosio O'Higgins (1720?–1801), an Irish-born Spanish governor of Chile and viceroy of Peru. After spending several years studying in England and Spain, O'Higgins returned to Chile in 1802. He took part in the nationalist revolution against Spain in 1810 and in 1813 was made commander of the patriot army under the revolutionary leader José Miguel Carrera (1786–1821). Defeated by royalist troops at Rancagua in 1814, O'Higgins fled across the Andes with most of his followers. There he joined the Argentine revolutionist José de San Martín, with whom he returned to defeat the Spanish at Chacabuco in February 1817. He was made supreme director of Chile in the same month, and he proclaimed Chilean independence in 1818. Ruling as a virtual dictator, O'Higgins tried to liberalize Chilean society, but alienated the Roman Catholic clergy by his toleration of Protestants, and angered aristocratic landowners by trying to abolish laws that protected their estates. Deposed in 1823, he spent the rest of his life in exile in Peru.

The skyline of Cincinnati, including Riverfront Stadium. Cincinnati is Ohio's third largest city after Cleveland and Columbus, and is its principal port on the Ohio River.
Mike Fink–Ohio Office of Travel and Tourism

OHIO, one of the East North Central states of the U.S., bordered on the N by Michigan and Ontario, Canada; on the E by Pennsylvania and West Virginia; on the S by West Virginia and Kentucky; and on the W by Indiana. Lake Erie forms most of the N boundary, and the Ohio R. forms much of the E and all of the S boundaries.

Ohio entered the Union on March 1, 1803, as the 17th state. It has been a major manufacturing state since the 19th century and in the early 1980s was especially associated with the production of transportation equipment, iron and steel, and rubber items. The state also has a large farming industry. Presidents Ulysses S. Grant, Rutherford B. Hayes, James A. Garfield, Benjamin Harrison, William McKinley, William Howard Taft, and Warren G. Harding were born in Ohio. The state's name is taken from the Ohio R., the name of which is derived from an Iroquoian Indian term for "fine, or good, river." Ohio is known as the Buckeye State.

LAND AND RESOURCES

Ohio, with an area of 107,044 sq km (41,330 sq mi), is the 35th largest state of the U.S.; 1.3% of the land area is owned by the federal government. Ohio is roughly square in shape; its extreme dimensions are about 360 km (about 225 mi) from E to W and about 350 km (about 215 mi) from N to S. Elevations range from 132 m (433 ft), along the Ohio R. in the SW, to 472 m (1550 ft), atop Campbell Hill in the W central part of the state. The approximate mean elevation is 259 m (850 ft). Ohio's shoreline along Lake Erie is about 500 km (about 310 mi) long.

Physical Geography. The physical landscape of Ohio is composed of four distinct regions. In the N is a part of the Eastern Great Lakes Lowland, an area of relatively flat topography with few steep-sided valleys. The soils are generally low in lime content and have to be drained before they are suitable for agriculture. Most of the W half of Ohio is made up of a section of the Till Plains, which is generally composed of a gently undulating landscape formed by glacially deposited material. The soils of this region are mainly gray-brown and acidic. In the S portion of the state is a small part of the Interior Low Plateaus. The landscape here is hilly, with bluffs along the rivers. The soils are chiefly gray-brown and red-yellow. Almost all of the E half of the state forms part of the Appalachian Plateau region. Generally hilly, with steep valley sides and narrow valley bottoms, it makes up the most rugged section of Ohio. The N part of the Appalachian Plateau region was somewhat smoothed by glaciation and has soils of glacial till. The S portion, unaffected by glaciers, is more rugged. Soils of the area are generally thin and not very fertile.

Rivers and Lakes. Drainage in the N third of Ohio flows into Lake Erie through such rivers as the Maumee, Sandusky, Vermilion, and Cuyahoga. Most of the remainder of the state is drained S toward the Ohio R., the major tributaries of which include the Great Miami, Scioto, Hocking, and Muskingum rivers. A small area in the W drains into the Wabash R. system of Indiana. Two notable flood-control programs are the Miami Conservancy District along the Great Miami R. and the Muskingum Conservancy District along the Muskingum R. Besides a portion of Lake Erie, Ohio has many lakes, most of which are comparatively small. Some of the bigger bodies of water—including the largest, Grand Lake, in the W—were formed by dams on rivers. The artificial lakes are concentrated in the Appalachian Plateau region.

Climate. Ohio has two main climate regions. The S portion of the state has a humid subtropical climate, with a frost-free season of 180 to 240 days; the N section has a humid continental climate, with a frost-free season of 120 to 180 days. Precipitation is fairly evenly distributed over the course of a year, with somewhat higher monthly totals in the spring. Snowfall is generally heaviest in the NE. Except for heavy thunderstorms and a few localized tornadoes each year, Ohio is usually not struck by damaging storms. As examples of the state's climate, Cincinnati, in the SW, has an average annual temperature of about 12.8° C (about 55° F) and receives some 1020 mm (about 40 in) of precipitation per year; Columbus, in the center, has a mean annual temperature of 10.8° C (51.5° F) and receives some 940 mm (about 37 in) of moisture each year; and Cleveland, in the NE, has an average annual temperature of 10° C (50° F) and gets about 889 mm (about 35 in) of precipitation per year. The recorded temperature in Ohio has ranged from −39.4° C (−39° F), in 1899 at Milligan, to 45° C (113° F), in 1897 at Thurman and in 1934 near Gallipolis.

Plants and Animals. Forests cover nearly one-quarter of Ohio and are made up principally of hardwoods. Maple and beech are dominant in the N, and oak and hickory are most common in the S. About 95% of the commercial timberland is privately owned. Other abundant plants include black-eyed Susan, buttercup, chamomile, dandelion, honeysuckle, Queen Anne's lace, and sunflower.

White-tailed deer, wild turkey, and beaver are common in much of Ohio. Other mammals found throughout the state include rabbit, squirrel, opossum, coyote, fox, raccoon, and skunk. Endangered mammals include the bobcat and otter, found in SE Ohio. Ducks live in many parts of the state as do hawks, grouse, pheasant, owls, cardinals, kingfishers, larks, and woodpeckers. Endangered bird species include the sharp-shinned hawk and the bald eagle. Among the reptiles of Ohio are snapping and box turtles, liz-

Although Ohio is primarily a manufacturing state, agriculture plays a significant part in its economy. Most of its farms, as with this dairy farm, are relatively small in size.
The Ohio Farmer

INDEX TO MAP OF OHIO

Communities

Community	Ref
Aberdeen	C 8
Ada	C 4
Addyston	B 9
Adena	C 4
Akron ⊙	G 3
Alger	C 4
Alliance	H 4
Amberley	C 9
Amherst	F 3
Andover	J 2
Ansonia	A 5
Antwerp	A 3
Arcanum	A 6
Archbold	B 2
Arlington	C 4
Arlington Heights	C 9
Ashland ⊙	F 4
Ashley	E 5
Ashtabula	J 2
Ashville	E 6
Athens ⊙	F 7
Attica	E 3
Atwater	H 3
Aurora	H 2
Austinburg	J 2
Austintown	J 3
Avon	F 3
Avon Lake	F 2
Ayersville	B 3
Bainbridge	D 7
Ballville	D 3
Baltimore	E 6
Barberton	G 3
Barnesville	H 6
Barton	J 5
Batavia ⊙	B 7
Bay Village	G 9
Beach City	G 4
Beachwood	J 9
Beavercreek	C 6
Bedford	H 9
Bedford Heights	J 9
Bellaire	J 5
Bellbrook	C 6
Belle Center	C 5
Bellefontaine ⊙	C 5
Bellevue	E 3
Bellville	E 4
Beloit	G 7
Belpre	G 10
Berea	J 4
Bergholz	J 4
Bethel	B 8
Bethesda	H 5
Beverly	G 6
Bexley	E 6
Blanchester	B 7
Blue Ash	C 9
Bluffton	C 4
Boardman	J 3
Bolivar	G 4
Botkins	B 5
Bowling Green ⊙	C 3
Bradford	B 5
Bradner	C 3
Bratenahl	H 9
Brecksville	H 10
Bremen	F 6
Brewster	G 4
Bridgeport	J 5
Bridgetown	B 9
Brilliant	J 5
Brimfield	H 3
Bristolville	J 3
Broadview Heights	H 10
Brookfield	J 3
Brooklyn	H 9
Brooklyn Heights	H 9
Brook Park	G 9
Brookside	J 5
Brookville	A 6
Brunswick	G 3
Bryan ⊙	A 3
Buckeye Lake	F 6
Bucyrus ⊙	E 4
Burlington	F 9
Burton	H 3
Butler	F 4
Byesville	G 6
Cadiz ⊙	H 5
Calcutta	J 4
Caldwell ⊙	G 6
Cambridge ⊙	G 5
Camden	A 6
Campbell	J 3
Canal Fulton	G 4
Canal Winchester	E 6
Canfield	J 3
Canton ⊙	G 4
Cardington ⊙	E 5
Carey	D 4
Carrollton ⊙	H 4
Castalia	E 3
Cedarville	C 6
Celina ⊙	A 4
Centerburg	E 5
Centerville	B 6
Chagrin Falls	H 2
Chardon ⊙	H 2
Chauncey	F 7
Chesapeake	E 9
Chesterland	H 2
Cheviot ⊙	B 9
Chillicothe ⊙	E 7
Cincinnati ⊙	B 9
Circleville ⊙	D 6
Cleveland ⊙	H 9
Cleveland Heights	H 9
Cleves	B 9
Clinton	G 4
Clyde	E 3
Coal Grove	E 9
Coldwater	A 5
Columbiana	J 4
Columbus (cap.) ⊙	E 6
Columbus Grove	B 4
Continental	B 3
Convoy	A 4
Cortland	J 3
Coshocton ⊙	G 5
Covedale	B 10
Covington	B 5
Craig Beach	H 3
Crestline	E 4
Creston	F 4
Cridersville	B 4
Crooksville	F 6
Crystal Lakes	C 6
Cuyahoga Falls	G 3
Dalton	G 4
Danville	F 5
Dayton ⊙	B 6
Deer Park ⊙	C 9
Defiance ⊙	B 3
Degraff	C 5
Delaware ⊙	D 5
Delphos	B 4
Delta	B 2
Dennison	H 5
Deshler	C 3
Devola	H 7
Dillonvale	J 5
Dover	G 4
Doylestown	G 4
Dresden	G 5
Dunkirk	C 4
East Canton	H 4
East Cleveland	H 9
Eastlake	J 8
East Liverpool	J 4
East Palestine	J 4
East Sparta	H 4
Eaton ⊙	A 6
Eaton Estates	G 3
Edgerton	A 2
Edgewood	J 2
Elida	B 4
Elmore	D 3
Elmwood Place	B 9
Elyria ⊙	F 3
Englewood	B 6
Enon	C 6
Euclid	C 9
Evendale	C 9
Fairborn	C 6
Fairfax	C 9
Fairfield	A 7
Fairlawn	G 3
Fairport Harbor	H 2
Fairview Park	G 9
Fayette	B 2
Findlay ⊙	C 3
Flushing	J 5
Forest	C 4
Forest Park	B 9
Forestville	C 10
Fort McKinley	B 6
Fort Recovery	A 5
Fort Shawnee	B 4
Fostoria	D 3
Frankfort	D 7
Franklin	B 6
Franklin Furnace	E 8
Frazeysburg	F 5
Fredericktown	F 5
Fremont ⊙	D 3
Gahanna	E 6
Galion	E 4
Gallipolis ⊙	F 8
Gambier	F 5
Garfield Heights	J 9
Garrettsville	H 3
Gates Mills	C 5
Geneva	J 2
Genoa	D 2
Georgetown ⊙	C 8
Germantown	B 6
Gibsonburg	D 3
Girard	J 3
Glendale	C 9
Glouster	F 6
Gnadenhutten	G 5
Golf Manor	C 9
Goshen	C 4
Grafton	F 3
Grandview Heights	E 6
Granville	E 5
Greenfield	D 7
Greenhills	B 9
Greensburg	G 4
Green Springs	D 3
Greentown	G 4
Greenville ⊙	A 5
Greenwich	E 3
Groesbeck	B 9
Grove City	D 6
Groveport	E 6
Hamden	F 7
Hamilton ⊙	A 7
Harrison	A 9
Hartville	H 4
Heath	F 5
Hebron	E 6
Hicksville	A 3
Highland Heights	D 5
Hilliard	D 6
Hillsboro ⊙	C 7
Hiram	H 3
Holgate	B 2
Holland	C 3
Hopedale	J 5
Huber Heights	B 6
Hubbard	J 3
Hudson	H 3
Huron	E 3
Independence	H 9
Indian Hill	C 9
Ironton ⊙	E 8
Jackson ⊙	D 7
Jacksonburg	B 6
Jackson Center	B 5
Jamestown	C 6
Jefferson ⊙	J 2
Jeffersonville	D 6
Jewett	H 5
Johnstown	E 5
Kent	H 3
Kenton ⊙	C 4
Kettering	B 6
Kingston	E 7
Kingsville	J 2
Kirtland	H 2
Lagrange	F 3
Lakemore	H 3
Lakeview	C 4
Lakewood	G 9
Lancaster ⊙	E 6
Lansing	J 5
Leavittsburg	J 3
Lebanon ⊙	B 7
Leesburg	C 7
Leetonia	J 4
Leipsic	C 3
Lewisburg	A 6
Lexington	E 4
Liberty Center	B 3
Lima ⊙	B 4
Lincoln Heights	C 9
Lisbon ⊙	J 4
Lockland	C 9
Lodi	F 3
Logan ⊙	F 6
London ⊙	D 6
Lorain	F 2
Lordstown	J 3
Loudonville	F 4
Louisville	H 4
Loveland	D 9
Lowellville	J 3
Luckey	D 3
Lynchburg	C 7
Lyndhurst ⊙	J 9
McArthur ⊙	F 7
McComb	C 3
McConnelsville ⊙	G 6
McDonald	J 3
Macedonia	J 10
Mack	B 9
Madeira	C 9
Madison	H 2
Magnolia	H 4
Malta ⊙	G 6
Malvern	H 4
Manchester	C 8
Mansfield ⊙	F 4
Mantua	H 3
Maple Heights	H 9
Maria Stein	A 5
Mariemont	C 9
Marietta ⊙	G 7
Marion ⊙	D 4
Martins Ferry	J 5
Marysville ⊙	D 5
Mason	B 7
Massillon	H 4
Masury	J 3
Maumee	C 2
Mayfield	J 9
Mayfield Heights	J 9
Mechanicsburg	C 5
Medina ⊙	G 3
Mentor	H 2
Mentor-on-the-Lake	H 2
Miamisburg	B 6
Middleburg Heights	G 10
Middlefield	H 3
Middleport	F 7
Middletown	A 6
Midland	C 7
Milan	E 3
Milford	D 9
Millersburg ⊙	F 4
Minerva	H 4
Minerva Park	E 5
Mingo Junction	J 5
Minster	B 5
Mogadore	H 3
Monroe	B 7
Monroeville	E 3
Montgomery	C 9
Montpelier	A 2
Moraine	B 6
Moreland Hills	J 9

⊙ County seat

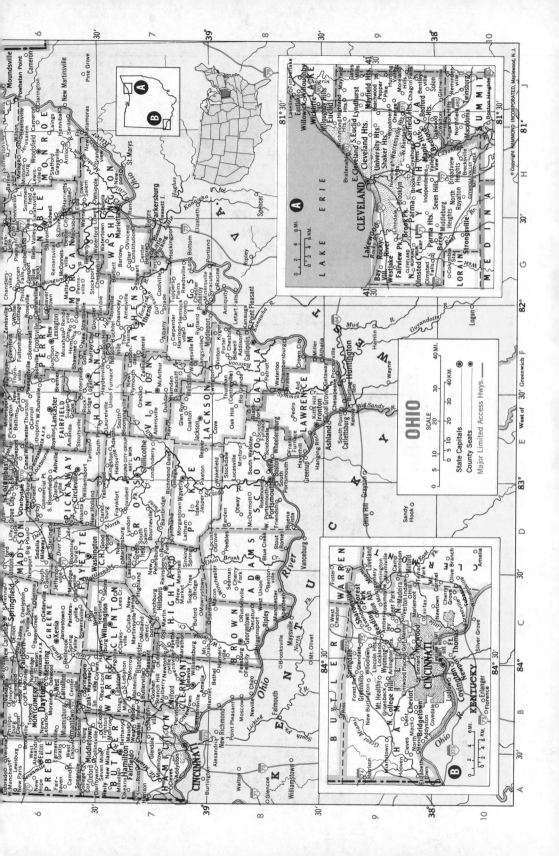

OHIO

SCALE

0 5 10 20 30 40 MI.
0 5 10 20 30 40 KM.

✳ State Capitals
⊛ County Seats
━━━ Major Limited Access Hwys.

© Copyright HAMMOND INCORPORATED, Maplewood, N.J.

A

CLEVELAND

LAKE ERIE

B

CINCINNATI

Index to Map of Ohio

Morrow B7
Mount Gilead ☉ E4
Mount Healthy B9
Mount Orab C7
Mount Sterling D6
Mount Vernon ☉ E5
Munroe Falls H3
Napoleon B3
Navarre H4
Neffs J5
Nelsonville F7
Nevada D4
Newark ☉ F5
New Boston E8
New Bremen B5
Newburgh Heights H9
New Carlisle C6
Newcomerstown G5
New Concord G6
New Lebanon B6
New Lexington ☉ F6
New London F3
New Madison A6
New Matamoras H6
New Miami A7
New Middletown J3
New Paris A6
New Philadelphia ☉ G5
Newport H7
New Richmond B8
New Straitsville F6
Newton Falls J3
New Washington E4
Niles C3
North Baltimore C3
North Canton H4
North College Hill B9
Northfield J10
North Hampton C6
North Industry H4
North Kingsville J2
North Olmsted G9
North Randall H9
Northridge B6
North Ridgeville F3
North Royalton H10
Northwood D2
North Zanesville G6

Norton D5
Norwalk ☉ E3
Norwood B9
Oak Harbor D2
Oak Hill E8
Oakwood B6
Oakwood H9
Oberlin F3
Obetz E6
Olmsted Falls G9
Ontario E4
Orange J9
Oregon D2
Orrville F4
Orwell J3
Ottawa ☉ C2
Ottawa Hills C2
Ottoville B4
Oxford A6
Painesville ☉ H2
Parma H9
Parma Heights H9
Pataskala E6
Paulding ☉ A3
Payne A3
Peebles D8
Pemberville D3
Pepper Pike J9
Perry H2
Perrysburg D2
Piketon D7
Pioneer B2
Piqua B5
Plain City D5
Plains, The F7
Pleasant Hill B5
Plymouth E4
Poland J3
Pomeroy ☉ F7
Port Clinton ☉ E2
Portsmouth ☉ D8
Powhatan Point J6
Prospect D5
Radnor D5
Randolph H3
Ravenna ☉ H3
Reading B9
Reno Beach D2
Reynoldsburg E6
Richfield G3
Richmond Heights J9

Richwood D5
Ripley C8
Rittman G4
Rockford A4
Rocky River G10
Rosemont D8
Roseville F6
Ross B9
Rossford C2
Rossmoyne B9
Russells Point C5
Sabina C7
Sagamore Hills J10
Saint Bernard B9
Saint Clairsville ☉ J5
Saint Henry A5
Saint Marys B4
Saint Paris C5
Salem J4
Salineville J4
Sandusky ☉ E3
Scio H5
Sebring H4
Seven Hills H9
Seville G3
Shadyside J5
Shaker Heights H9
Sharonville C9
Sheffield F3
Sheffield Lake F3
Shelby E4
Shreve G4
Sidney ☉ B5
Silver Lake H3
Silverton C9
Smithfield J5
Smithville G4
Solon J9
Somerset ☉ F6
Somerville A7
South Amherst F3
South Euclid H9
South Lebanon B7
South Point E9
South Russell J9
South Zanesville G6
Spencerville B4
Springboro B6
Springdale ☉ B9
Springfield ☉ C6
Steubenville ☉ J5

Stow H3
Strasburg G4
Streetsboro H3
Strongsville G10
Struthers J3
Stryker B3
Sugarcreek G5
Sunbury E5
Swanton C2
Sycamore D4
Sylvania C2
Tallmadge H3
Terrace Park B9
Thurston E6
Tiffin ☉ D3
Tiltonsville J5
Tipp City B6
Toledo ☉ D2
Toronto J5
Trenton B7
Trotwood B6
Troy ☉ B5
Uhrichsville H5
Union B6
Union City A5
University Heights H9
Upper Arlington D6
Upper Sandusky ☉ D4
Urbana ☉ C5
Utica F5
Vandalia B6
Van Wert ☉ A4
Vermilion F3
Versailles A5
Vienna J3
Walbridge C2
Walton Hills J9
Wapakoneta ☉ B4
Warren ☉ J3
Warrensville Heights H9
Washington Court
  House ☉ D6
Waterville C3
Wauseon ☉ B2
Waverly ☉ D7
Waynesburg H4
Waynesville C5
Wellington F3
Wellston F7

Wellsville J4
West Alexandria A6
West Carrollton B6
Westerville D5
Westfield Center G3
West Jefferson D6
West Lafayette G5
Westlake G9
West Liberty C5
West Milton B6
Weston C3
West Portsmouth D8
West Salem F4
West Union ☉ C8
West Unity B2
Wheelersburg E8
Whitehall E6
Whitehouse C2
Wickliffe J8
Willard D3
Williamsburg B7
Willoughby J8
Willoughby Hills J8
Willowick J8
Wilmington ☉ C7
Windham H3
Wintersville J5
Woodlawn C9
Woodsfield ☉ H6
Woodville D3
Wooster ☉ G4
Worthington E5
Wyoming C9
Xenia ☉ C6
Yellow Springs C6
Yorkville J5
Youngstown ☉ J3
Zanesville ☉ G6

Other Features

Auglaize (river) B4
Black (river) F3
Blanchard (river) C4
Blennerhassett
  (island) G7
Buckeye (lake) F6
Campbell (hill) C5
Chagrin (river) J8
Cuyahoga (river) H10

Cuyahoga Valley Nat'l
  Rec. Area H10
Deer Creek (lake) D6
Delaware (lake) D5
Erie (lake) E5
Grand (river) H2
Great Miami (river) A7
Hocking (river) F7
Huron (river) E3
Indian (lake) C5
James A. Garfield
  Nat'l Hist. Site G2
Kelleys (island) E2
Kokosing (river) E5
Little Miami (river) C9
Little Muskingum
  (river) H6
Loramie (lake) B5
Mad (river) C6
Maumee (bay) D2
Maumee (river) A3
Middle Bass (island) E2
Mohican (river) F4
Mound City Group
  Nat'l Mon. E7
Muskingum (river) G6
Ohio (river) B8
Olentangy (river) D4
Perry's Victory and
  International Peace
  Memorial E2
Portage (river) D3
Pymatuning (res.) J2
Rickenbacker AFB E6
Rocky (river) G9
Rocky Fork (lake) D7
Saint Joseph (river) A3
Saint Marys (lake) A4
Sandusky (bay) E3
Sandusky (river) D3
Scioto (river) D8
South Bass (island) E2
Stillwater (river) B5
Tiffin (river) B3
Tuscarawas (river) H5
Vermilion (river) F3
Wabash (river) A5
William H. Taft Nat'l
  Hist. Site C10
Wright-Patterson AFB B6

☉ County seat

332

Aerial view of Columbus, capital of Ohio and the state's second largest city. Flowing through the urban center is the Scioto River.

City of Columbus

ards, brown snake, milk snake, copperhead, and timber rattlesnake. The state's fish include bass, sunfish, perch, trout, pike, and catfish.

Mineral Resources. Ohio contains significant deposits of a variety of minerals. Lime is found mainly in the NW, coal and clay occur in the E, petroleum and natural-gas deposits are in the NE and several other areas, gypsum and salt are situated near Lake Erie, and sand and gravel are found throughout the state. Je.E.Gr.

POPULATION

According to the 1980 census, Ohio had 10,797,- 624 inhabitants, an increase of 1.3% over 1970. The average population density was 101 people per sq km (261 per sq mi). Whites made up 88.9% of the population and blacks 10%; additional population groups included some 13,105 persons of Asian Indian origin, 11,986 American Indians, 9911 persons of Chinese ancestry, 7435 persons of Filipino background, 7257 persons of Korean extraction, and 5479 persons of Japanese descent. Approximately 119,880 persons were of Hispanic background. Roman Catholics formed the largest single religious group; other major religious groups included Lutherans, Methodists, and Presbyterians. In 1980 about 73% of all Ohio's residents lived in areas defined as urban, and the rest lived in rural areas. The state's biggest cities were Cleveland; Columbus, the capital; Cincinnati; Toledo; Akron; and Dayton.

EDUCATION AND CULTURAL ACTIVITY

Ohio is served by a comprehensive educational system and also has numerous cultural institutions, including well-known museums and musical organizations.

Education. Ohio's first school was opened in 1773 by Moravian missionaries near present-day New Philadelphia. The statewide public school system had its beginnings in a law of 1825 requiring counties to raise tax money to finance schools. The first public high schools were established about 1850. In the early 1980s Ohio had 3958 public elementary and secondary schools. Annual public school enrollment totaled about 1,312,400 in the elementary schools and about 645,028 in the high schools. In addition, some 268,800 students attended private schools each year. In the same period Ohio had 135 institutions of higher education, with a combined yearly enrollment of about 489,150 students. Among the most notable of these institutions were the University of Akron (1870); Antioch University, at Yellow Springs; Bowling Green State University (1910); Case Western Reserve University, at Cleveland; the University of Cincinnati (1819); the University of Dayton (1850); Denison University (1831), at Granville; Hiram College (1850); John Carroll University (1886), at Cleveland; Kent State University (1910); Kenyon College (1824), at Gambier; Miami University

(1809), at Oxford; Oberlin College; Ohio State University, at Columbus; Ohio University (1804), at Athens; the University of Toledo (1872); Wilberforce University (1856); the College of Wooster (1866); and Youngstown State University (1908).

Cultural Institutions. Ohio's cultural institutions are primarily located in the larger cities. Leading museums include the Akron Art Institute; the Cincinnati Art Museum; the Cincinnati Museum of Natural History; the Taft Museum, at Cincinnati, famous for its collections of European and Asian art; the Cleveland Museum of Art; the Cleveland Museum of Natural History; the Western Reserve Historical Society and Frederick C. Crawford Auto-Aviation Museum, at Cleveland; the Columbus Museum of Art; the Ohio Historical Center, at Columbus; the Dayton Art Institute; the Toledo Museum of Art; and the U.S. Air Force Museum, near Dayton. Also of interest are the Cy Young Museum, at Newcomerstown, containing baseball memorabilia; and the Pro Football Hall of Fame, at Canton. Cincinnati and Cleveland have major public library systems, and Ohio State University maintains important research collections. The Cleveland Orchestra is one of the leading orchestras of the U.S.; other Ohio cities supporting orchestras include Akron, Canton, Cincinnati, Columbus, Dayton, Toledo, and Youngstown. Opera companies are located in Cincinnati, Dayton, Cleveland, Columbus, and Toledo. Major theatrical organizations in Ohio include the Great Lakes Shakespeare Festival, at Lakewood; Karamu House and Theater, at Cleveland; the Cleveland Playhouse; and the Cincinnati Playhouse in the Park.

Historical Sites. Indian mounds, pioneer strongholds, and the burial places of several U.S. presidents are among Ohio's historical sites. Mound City Group National Monument, near Chillicothe, includes 23 burial mounds of the Hopewell Indians dating from about 200 BC to AD 500. The Great Serpent Mound, near Peebles, has a snakelike shape. Schoenbrunn Village State Memorial, near New Philadelphia, contains a reconstruction of Ohio's first non-Indian community, established by Moravian missionaries in 1772. The birthplace and boyhood home of President Taft, at Cincinnati, is preserved as a national historic site. Also of historical interest is the burial place of President Hayes, at Fremont; of President Garfield, at Cleveland; of President McKinley, at Canton; and of President Harding, at Marion. Perry's Victory and International Peace Memorial, at Put-in Bay, on South Bass Island, commemorates a great U.S. naval victory during the War of 1812.

Sports and Recreation. Hunting, fishing, swimming, and boating are popular in Ohio. Ski areas are at Boston Mills, Brandywine, Bellefontaine, Mansfield, and elsewhere. Cuyahoga Valley National Recreation Area encompasses part of the Cuyahoga R. valley between Cleveland and Akron. Ohio has several major league professional sports teams, including the Cleveland Indians and the Cincinnati Reds (baseball), the Cleveland Browns and the Cincinnati Bengals (football), and the Cleveland Cavaliers (basketball). Famous golf courses are located in the Akron and Columbus areas. Ohio State University is noted for the excellence of its sports teams.

Communications. Ohio has a comprehensive communications system. Ohio's first radio station, WHK in Cleveland, began operations in 1922, and the state's first television station, WEWS-TV in Cleveland, started broadcasting in 1947. In the early 1980s the state had 124 AM and 130 FM commercial radio stations and 25 commercial television stations. The first newspaper in Ohio, the *Centinel of the North-Western Territory*, went to press at Cincinnati in 1793. In the early 1980s the state had 95 daily newspapers, which had a combined daily circulation of about 3,290,000. Among the leading dailies are the *Akron Beacon Journal;* the *Cincinnati Enquirer;* the *Cincinnati Post;* the *Plain Dealer,* published in Cleveland; the *Columbus Citizen-Journal;* the *Columbus Dispatch;* the *Dayton Daily News;* and the *Blade,* issued in Toledo.

GOVERNMENT AND POLITICS

Ohio is governed under a constitution adopted in 1851, as amended; a previous constitution had been adopted in 1802. An amendment to the constitution may be proposed by the state legislature, a voters' initiative, or a constitutional convention. To become effective, an amendment must be approved by a majority of persons voting on the issue in a general election.

Executive. Ohio's chief executive is a governor, who is popularly elected to a 4-year term and is eligible to serve an unlimited number of terms but not more than two in succession. Other elected state officials are the lieutenant governor (who succeeds to the governorship in case of a vacancy), the secretary of state, the attorney general, the auditor, and the treasurer.

Legislature. The Ohio legislature, called the General Assembly, consists of a 33-member Senate and a 99-member House of Representatives. Senators are popularly elected to 4-year terms, and representatives to 2-year terms.

Judiciary. The Ohio supreme court, the state's highest tribunal, consists of a chief justice and six associate justices. Its members are popularly

The Arcade is a popular location in downtown Cleveland's busy shopping district. Built between 1888 and 1890, it is of special architectural interest as well. Ohio Office of Travel and Tourism

elected to 6-year terms. The state's intermediate appellate courts are courts of appeal, which have a total of 52 judges, popularly elected to 6-year terms. The major trial courts are the 88 courts of common pleas (one in each county), which together have 321 judges, all popularly elected to 6-year terms. Other judicial bodies include county courts, municipal courts (in larger cities), probate courts, and juvenile courts.

Local Government. Ohio is divided into 88 counties, each of which is governed by a popularly elected three-member board of commissioners. All incorporated places with 5000 or more inhabitants are classified as cities under Ohio law; smaller incorporated communities are designated as villages. The state does not have a legal entity called a town. The mayor-council form of government is most common in Ohio's approximately 200 cities.

National Representation. Ohio is represented in the U.S. Congress by 2 senators and 21 representatives. It has 23 electoral votes in presidential elections.

Politics. Although Democrats outnumber Republicans by a significant margin among registered voters in Ohio, most national and state races are closely fought, with the Republicans holding an edge in the presidential elections since 1900.

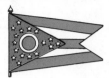

OHIO

DATE OF STATEHOOD: March 1, 1803; 17th state

CAPITAL: Columbus
MOTTO: With God, all things are possible
NICKNAME: Buckeye State
STATE SONG: "Beautiful Ohio" (words by Ballard MacDonald; music by Mary Earl)

STATE TREE: Buckeye
STATE FLOWER: Scarlet carnation
STATE BIRD: Cardinal
POPULATION (1980): 10,797,624; 6th among the states
AREA: 107,044 sq km (41,330 sq mi); 35th largest state; includes 842 sq km (325 sq mi) of inland water
HIGHEST POINT: Campbell Hill, 472 m (1550 ft)
LOWEST POINT: 132 m (433 ft), along the Ohio River
ELECTORAL VOTES: 23
U.S. CONGRESS: 2 senators; 21 representatives

POPULATION OF OHIO SINCE 1800

Year of Census	Population	Classified As Urban
1800	45,000	0%
1820	581,000	2%
1850	1,980,000	12%
1880	3,198,000	32%
1900	4,158,000	48%
1920	5,759,000	64%
1940	6,908,000	67%
1960	9,706,000	73%
1970	10,657,000	75%
1980	10,798,000	73%

POPULATION OF TEN LARGEST CITIES

	1980 Census	1970 Census
Cleveland	573,822	750,879
Columbus	565,032	540,025
Cincinnati	385,457	453,514
Toledo	354,635	383,062
Akron	237,177	275,425
Dayton	203,371	243,023
Youngstown	115,436	140,909
Canton	93,077	110,053
Parma	92,548	100,216
Lorain	75,416	78,185

CLIMATE

	CLEVELAND	DAYTON
Average January temperature range	−6.7° to 0.6° C (20° to 33° F)	−6.7° to 2.2° C (20° to 36° F)
Average July temperature range	16.1° to 27.8° C (61° to 82° F)	17.8° to 29.4° C (64° to 85° F)
Average annual temperature	10° C (50° F)	11.1° C (52° F)
Average annual precipitation	889 mm (35 in)	864 mm (34 in)
Average annual snowfall	1321 mm (52 in)	686 mm (27 in)
Mean number of days per year with appreciable precipitation	155	134
Average daily relative humidity	71%	70%
Mean number of clear days per year	70	80

EASTERN GREAT LAKES LOWLAND

APPALACHIAN

TILL PLAINS

PLATEAU

Ohio R.

INTERIOR LOW PLATEAUS

NATURAL REGIONS OF OHIO

PRINCIPAL PRODUCTS OF OHIO

ECONOMY

Stage budget . . . . revenue $12.2 billion
expenditure $11.4 billion
State personal income tax, per capita $81
Personal income, per capita $9462
Assets, commercial banks (407) . . . . $52.9 billion
Labor force (civilian) 4,988,600
    Employed in services   25%
    Employed in manufacturing   27%
    Employed in wholesale and retail trade 19%

	Quantity Produced	Value
FARM PRODUCTS		**$3.8 billion**
Crops		**$2.5 billion**
Corn	14.0 million metric tons	$1.1 billion
Soybeans	3.7 million metric tons	$1.0 billion
Wheat	1.8 million metric tons	$275 million
Vegetables	417,000 metric tons	$57 million
Livestock and Livestock Products		**$1.3 billion**
Milk	1.9 million metric tons	$562 million
Cattle	270,000 metric tons	$340 million
Hogs	315,000 metric tons	$262 million
Eggs	2.3 billion	$95 million
MINERALS		**$2.5 billion**
Coal	36.8 million metric tons	$1.2 billion
Petroleum	13 million barrels	$469 million
Natural gas	3.9 billion cu m	$275 million
Stone	38.0 million metric tons	$130 million
FISHING	**4760 metric tons**	**$3.4 million**

	Labor and Proprietors' Income
FORESTRY	**$4.5 million**
MANUFACTURING	**$29.1 billion**
Nonelectric machinery	$4.8 billion
Primary metals	$4.2 billion
Fabricated metal products	$3.5 billion
Motor vehicles and equipment	$2.8 billion
Electric and electronic equipment	$2.2 billion
Rubber and plastics products	$2.0 billion
Chemicals and allied products	$1.7 billion
Food and kindred products	$1.4 billion
Stone, clay, and glass products	$1.4 billion
Transportation equipment	$1.3 billion
OTHER	**$42.6 billion**
Services	$12.1 billion
Government and government enterprises	$9.4 billion
Transportation and public utilities	$5.5 billion
Finance, insurance, and real estate	$3.5 billion
Wholesale trade	$4.8 billion
Retail trade	$7.3 billion

ANNUAL PRODUCTION OF GOODS BY SECTOR

6%

3%

91%

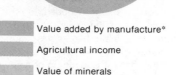

Value added by manufacture*

Agricultural income

Value of minerals

* The value added by an industry is a measure of the value created in its products, not counting such production costs as raw materials and power.

Sources: U.S. government publications

Notable Ohio political figures include Robert A. Taft, a Republican who represented the state in the U.S. Senate from 1939 until his death in 1953, and former astronaut John H. Glenn, Jr., also a native Ohioan, who won election as a U.S. senator in 1974 and was reelected in 1980.

ECONOMY

Ohio was a leading farming state in the mid-19th century. Shortly thereafter manufacturing became the main economic activity in the state, although agriculture remained important. The development of factories was aided by the ready availability of such basic industrial raw materials as coal and iron ore, by an extensive transportation system, and by proximity to major markets. In the early 1980s Ohio was particularly noted for the manufacture of transportation equipment, farm machinery, rubber products, and iron and steel.

Agriculture. Ohio's farm income in 1980 was about $3.8 billion, 12th highest among the U.S. states. About two-thirds of the income was derived from the sale of crops, and the rest came from sales of livestock and livestock products. The state contains about 94,000 farms, which have a relatively small average size of 70 ha (173 acres). The most valuable commodities of Ohio, which is situated in the E part of the productive Corn Belt, are corn, soybeans, dairy goods, and beef cattle; the state is among the leading producers of soybeans and corn. Other important crops include hay, wheat, oats, tomatoes, potatoes, cucumbers, sugar beets, tobacco, apples, peaches, cherries, and grapes. Additional major livestock and livestock products of Ohio are hogs, sheep, wool, turkeys, broiler chickens, and chicken eggs. Farms are located throughout the state. Fruit growing is concentrated in the Eastern Great Lakes Lowland, which, along with the Ohio R. valley, also is noted for vegetable production. Sugarcreek, in the E, and Van Wert, in the W, are important cheese-producing centers. Maple syrup is produced in the NE part of the state.

Forestry and Fishing. Although considerable portions of S and E Ohio are wooded, forestry is an unimportant part of the state's economy. Ohio contributes a negligible share of the nation's output of forest products. Almost 90% of the state's annual timber harvest is made up of hardwoods. Two-thirds of the output is used for lumber and about one-eighth for pulp and paper. Ohio has a long shoreline on Lake Erie, but the lake's water quality has deteriorated so badly in the 20th century as a result of the admixture of industrial and urban waste that the fish population has declined substantially. The state's yearly fish catch

in the early 1980s was valued at only about $3.4 million.

Mining. Ohio has no metallic mineral deposits of any consequence, but it is rich in other industrial raw materials, such as sand for glassmaking, clay for ceramics and pottery making, limestone for making cement and fertilizer, and salt. The SE third of Ohio is underlaid by major bituminous coal seams, which are part of the Appalachian Field. Coal is the principal product of the state's mining industry, and the next most valuable mineral products are natural gas, produced primarily from fields in central and E Ohio, and petroleum, recovered chiefly in the NW and central parts of the state. Other mineral products include gravel, abrasive stone, and gypsum.

Manufacturing. Ohio is among the leading manufacturing states in the U.S. In the early 1980s its manufactures employed some 1.4 million workers. The chief categories of products made in Ohio are transportation equipment (especially motor vehicles, motor-vehicle parts, and aerospace items), nonelectrical machinery (notably farm machinery, machine tools, and office machines), and primary metal (particularly iron and steel). Ohio also produces a wide variety of other fabricated items such as metal, rubber, and plastic goods; electrical and electronic equipment; glass; chemicals; construction materials; sporting goods; printed materials; textiles and clothing; soap and toiletries; refined petroleum; and processed food. No fewer than 12 areas in Ohio are of national stature as manufacturing centers. Easily the most important of these is the Cleveland area, where motor vehicles, iron and steel, and machinery lead the roster of manufactures. Next come Cincinnati, a city important for machine tools and soap, and Dayton, which is well known as a producer of cash registers, motor-vehicle parts, and aircraft and refrigeration equipment. Among the state's other major manufacturing centers are Columbus (fabricated metals and machinery), Akron (machinery), Toledo (glass products and weight scales), Canton (steel), Youngstown (steel), and Lorain-Elyria (ships, steel, and air brakes).

Tourism. Ohio enjoys a substantial tourist business. Many tourist activities center around Lake Erie and the numerous inland lakes. Attractions on the Lake Erie shoreline are concentrated in the Sandusky vicinity on the Marblehead Peninsula and at Cedar Point, and offshore islands also are popular vacation spots. Many tourists visit the homes of the several U.S. presidents born here. The Ohio Caverns, near West Liberty, are a popular destination. Professional sports events and museums and other cultural institutions draw

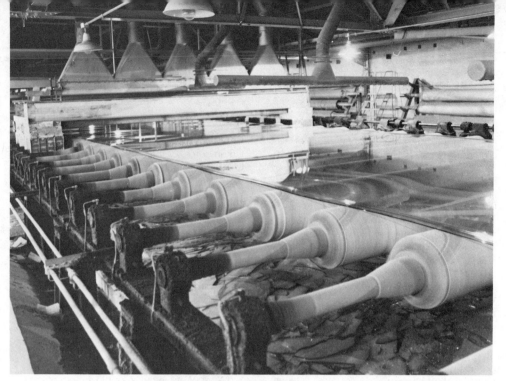

Still warm from the annealing oven, a continuous ribbon of glass moves toward the final manufacturing stages at a Toledo glass plant. Ohio has some of the largest glass manufacturers in the nation.   Libbey-Owens-Ford Co.

visitors to Cincinnati and Cleveland. Ohio maintains 68 state parks and recreation areas.

Transportation. Ohio is located astride a main corridor for E-W land travel in the U.S. and is served by a dense network of transportation facilities. The state has about 178,800 km (about 111,100 mi) of roads, including 2470 km (1535 mi) of Interstate Highways. Ohio is also served by some 11,630 km (7225 mi) of operated railroad track. Much freight is shipped on the Ohio R. and by way of such major Lake Erie ports as Toledo, Cleveland, Ashtabula, and Conneaut. Ships can reach the Atlantic Ocean from Ohio via the Great Lakes-Saint Lawrence Seaway system, and the Gulf of Mexico can be reached via the Ohio and Mississippi rivers. Ohio has 674 airports, the busiest of which is Hopkins International Airport, serving Cleveland. Lima, which is an important petroleum-refining center, is a major junction point in the system of oil pipelines that connect Ohio with Oklahoma and Louisiana.

Energy. Ohio is both a massive producer and consumer of electricity. Its power plants have an installed capacity of 27.4 million kw, and in 1980 they produced 110.2 billion kwh of electricity, the fourth highest total among the U.S. states. About 97% of Ohio's electricity is produced in facilities burning coal, and most of the rest is generated in nuclear power plants.   E.H.W.

HISTORY

The first European to explore the territory of present-day Ohio was probably the French explorer Robert Cavalier, sieur de La Salle, who claimed to have discovered and ascended the Ohio River in 1669. When, in 1682, La Salle claimed the entire valley of the Mississippi River for France, the region between the Great Lakes (to Lake Erie) and the Ohio River was considered a French possession. French claims were not acknowledged by contiguous British colonies, particularly Virginia, which claimed all the territory north of the Ohio River and west of the Mississippi. After about 1730, traders from Pennsylvania and Virginia entered the area, and in 1749 the British government awarded a royal grant to the Ohio Co. (q.v.), organized by Virginia planters and London merchants, to settle and trade in the valley of the Ohio. The French governor of Canada, the marquis de la Galissonière, in the same year sent an officer, Pierre de Bienville (1693–1759), to bury lead markers in the name of France along the riverbanks. Settlements established by the Ohio Co. inevitably caused French resentment, and in 1754 clashes between the French and their Indian allies and the British precipitated the French and Indian War. By the terms of the Treaty of Paris in 1763, the victorious British acquired undisputed title to the territory. The Indian allies of

339

France, however, refused to acknowledge British supremacy; they revolted in 1763 in the so-called Conspiracy of Pontiac. The Indian war was ended by treaty in 1765.

Conflicting Claims. In 1774, Great Britain made the territory part of Canada. Resentment of the American colonies at the annexation of land claimed by them was one of the causes of the American Revolution. During the war, the American frontier leader George Rogers Clark invaded and held the region from 1779 to 1783. In the latter year Great Britain ceded its rights to the area, known as the Northwest Territory, to the U.S. By 1786 all the states had ceded their separate claims in the Northwest Territory to the federal government, except Connecticut, which retained its claim to the Western Reserve until 1800, and Virginia, which retained its claim to the Virginia Military District, between the Little Miami and Scioto rivers, until 1852. The U.S. Congress in 1785 enacted the Land Ordinance, establishing conditions for sale of land in the territory, and in 1787 passed the Northwest Ordinance, providing for administration of the territory. The Ohio Co. of Associates was organized in 1786 by veteran officers and soldiers to facilitate land sales.

Early Settlement. The first authorized permanent settlement was founded in 1788 at Marietta, the building of which was supervised by the American Revolution officer and pioneer Rufus Putnam (1738–1824), one of the founders of the Ohio Co. of Associates. Cincinnati was established in 1789, and in 1798 Cleveland was founded in the Western Reserve. Indians, alarmed at the increasing number of settlers, rose in a series of frontier wars; in 1795 the Indians, defeated by American forces, ceded the rights to most of present-day Ohio. Territorial government, under a federal governor, was instituted in 1799. Ohio was separated from the remainder of the Northwest Territory in 1800, and in 1803 it became the first state of the territory to be admitted to the Union. The state capital was first established at Chillicothe, and, after several moves, it was fixed at Columbus in 1816.

Ohio became continually more prosperous and populous after achieving statehood; its population, about 45,400 in 1800, increased to more than 230,700 by 1810. The invention of the steamboat made Cincinnati a great river port; and the completion of the Erie Canal from Lake Erie to the Hudson River in 1825 and of the Ohio and Erie Canal from Portsmouth to Cleveland in 1835 gave the state a shipping route to the Atlantic Ocean, inaugurating an era of prosperity. During this period the Mormons under Joseph Smith

came to Kirtland, and until 1838 Ohio was the center of Mormonism.

The state was strongly antislavery from its inception, and its cities became famous stops on the Underground Railroad for escaping slaves. During the American Civil War Ohio furnished large contributions of money and troops to the Union forces. Although no major battles were fought in Ohio, in 1863 Morgan's Raid, a series of attacks by Confederate troops under Gen. John H. Morgan (1825–64), caused severe damage in southern Ohio.

After the Civil War. Manufacturing gradually replaced agriculture as the leading Ohio industry, and Ohio politics became dominated by the industrialists, notably Marcus Hanna. Political corruption was notorious until the 1890s, when Ohio citizens demanded reform measures. In 1912 an amendment to the state constitution provided for initiative and referendum and recall. Another amendment authorized flood-control measures in southern Ohio, where floods often devastated the river valleys.

Ohio's accelerated industrial development after World War I led to the rapid growth of several major cities. Their prosperity was drastically reversed in the 1930s, when the Great Depression forced factory closings and left thousands of workers jobless. During World War II, with production of military supplies, the economy began to recover. By mid-century Ohio had become a center for space research and atomic energy projects. Industrial expansion was furthered in the 1960s by the Saint Lawrence Seaway, which opened the ports of Ohio's Lake Erie to international trade.

In the wake of this new, dynamic growth the state was faced with the problem of industrial pollution on the one hand and, on the other, demands for improved social services—most notably the provision of adequate public school education. In the 1970s and '80s Ohio made vigorous efforts to meet these challenges.

For further information on this topic, see the Bibliography in volume 28, section 1199.

OHIO, river, E central U.S., formed by the confluence of the Allegheny and Monongahela rivers at Pittsburgh, Pa. It is 1579 km (981 mi) long and a principal tributary of the Mississippi R. The Ohio flows NW out of Pittsburgh and then gradually SW, forming the boundaries between Ohio and West Virginia, Ohio and Kentucky, Indiana and Kentucky, and Illinois and Kentucky; it joins the Mississippi R. at Cairo, Ill. The chief tributaries of the Ohio include the Tennessee, Wabash, and Kentucky rivers. Among the cities on the Ohio are Cincinnati, Ohio; Evansville, Ind.; Wheeling,

A view of the Ohio River from the Indiana shoreline.
Standard Oil Co. (N.J.)

W.Va.; and Louisville, Ky. The Ohio R. is navigable throughout its course.

OHIO COMPANY, name of two companies organized in the 18th century for the colonization of the Ohio country. The first company was organized in 1749. The British government granted the company 500,000 acres (about 200,000 ha) of land around the forks of the Ohio River. The colonizing efforts of the company were seen by the French as a challenge to their claim on the region, and the rivalry helped to cause the French and Indian War. In 1770 the Ohio Co. merged with the Vandalia Co.

The second company, the Ohio Co. of Associates, was formed in 1786. In 1787 a large tract of land was purchased, and in the following year the city of Marietta was founded by colonists sent out by the company.

OHIO STATE UNIVERSITY, state-assisted land-grant institution of higher learning, in Columbus, Ohio, with regional campuses in Lima, Mansfield, Marion, and Newark, and the Agricultural Technical Institute at Wooster. The university was chartered in 1870 and opened in 1873; until 1878 it was called Ohio Agricultural and Mechanical College. The divisions of the university include the colleges of the arts, biological sciences, humanities, mathematics and physical sciences, and social and behavioral sciences; the colleges of administrative science, agriculture and home economics, dentistry, education, engineering, law, medicine, optometry, pharmacy, veterinary medicine, and the graduate school

and university college. The schools of allied medical professions, architecture, home economics, journalism, music, natural resources, nursing, social work, and health, physical education, and recreation are affiliated with the appropriate colleges. The degrees of associate, bachelor, master, doctor, and professional degrees are granted.

OHM. *See* ELECTRICAL UNITS.

OHM, Georg Simon (1787-1854), German physicist, best known for his research on electrical currents. He was born in Erlangen and educated at the University of Erlangen. From 1833 to 1849 he was director of the Polytechnic Institute of Nuremberg, and from 1852 until his death he was professor of experimental physics at the University of Munich. His formulation of the relationship between current, electromotive force, and resistance, known as Ohm's law, is the basic law of current flow. The unit of electrical resistance was named the ohm in his honor. *See* ELECTRIC CIRCUIT.

OHM'S LAW. *See* ELECTRIC CIRCUIT.

OHRID, LAKE, lake, about 340 sq km (about 130 sq mi) in area, straddling the mountainous border between SW Yugoslavia and E Albania. The deepest lake of the Balkan Peninsula, it is drained to the N by the Drin R. Underground springs feed the lake, which is also connected by underground channels to nearby Lake Prespa. Its picturesque setting and good beaches, as well as the medieval ruins on its shores, make Lake Ohrid a resort center.

OIL. *See* ESSENTIAL OILS; FATS AND OILS; PETROLEUM.

OILBIRD, also guacharo, *Steatornis,* only surviving species of a bird family, Steatornithidae, in the goatsucker order Caprimulgiformes. The oilbird is found in colonies in deep caverns in northern South America and Trinidad, and is especially abundant near Cumana, Venezuela. Young oilbirds are valued as food and for their fat, which is extracted and used as a butter substitute. The oilbird resembles the goatsucker but has a stronger beak and eats palm nuts rather than insects. It is about 30 cm (about 12 in) long. The mottled plumage is reddish brown and gray, barred with black and dotted with white. The oilbird emerges from its cave at night to seek its food, avoiding obstacles by echolocation rather than by using its weak eyes.

OIL PAINTING, art of applying oil-based colors to a surface to create a picture or other design. Oil painting developed in Europe in the late Middle Ages. It quickly found wide acceptance because—in contrast to older wax- and water-based media, such as encaustic, fresco, tempera, and watercolor—it is easier to work with and permits a greater variety of effects. Oil paint dries relatively slowly with little change in color. Tones are therefore easy to match, blend, or grade, and corrections are easy to make. The painter is not limited to linear brushstrokes but may apply paint in glazes, washes, blobs, trickles, spray, or thick impasto. Without being restricted to a prearranged design, the painter can freely change and improvise. Rich effects can be obtained with color and chiaroscuro (shading).

Materials and Technique. Most artists today use commercial materials but some prefer to make their own in the traditional way. Oil paint consists of pigment ground in oil that dries on exposure to air. The pigments, or colored powders, must be lightproof, insoluble, and chemically inert. The oil is usually linseed but may be poppy or walnut. Sometimes varnish is added to the mixture, which is then ground. The stiff, creamy paste that results is packaged in flexible tubes.

The painting surface consists of a support, either a wood or composition panel, or more frequently, linen, cotton, or jute canvas stretched on a frame or glued to a board. The support is covered with a ground, a thin coating of gesso or other gypsum and glue, or size. The ground makes the support less absorbant and provides an even painting surface that is neither too rough nor too smooth. The ground may be white but is often given a toning coat of gray, tan, or pink.

Traditionally, oil painting proceeds in stages. First the design may be sketched on the ground in pencil, charcoal, or paint diluted with turpentine. Then broad areas of color are filled in with thin paint. They are successively refined and corrected in thicker paint to which oil and varnish are added. The paint is usually applied with brushes made from stiff hog bristle, although softer brushes of badger or sable hair may be used. Paint may also be applied with a flexible, wide-bladed painting or palette knife, or the fingers. The process may require only a few sessions or extend over months or even years.

Once the painting has thoroughly dried, at least a year after completion it is varnished to protect it from dirt and to enrich the color. Because all varnishes eventually darken, the varnish used should be removable and eventually replaced.

History. Oil painting was traditionally thought to have been invented by the Flemish painter Jan van Eyck in the early 15th century, but it is now known to have existed earlier. Van Eyck explored the medium within the linear conventions of tempera, making a detailed drawing on a gesso-covered panel and then building up layers of transparent oil glazes. His technique was brought to Italy by the Venetian painter Antonello da Messina and was fully exploited by Renaissance painters. The Venetians took the further step of painting on canvas, which provided a much larger surface and could be rolled up for shipping. They developed a freer style based on a rough monochrome underpainting in tempera with added oil glazes. Dutch painters such as Rembrandt and Frans Hals and the Spanish Painter Diego Velázquez experimented with broad brush strokes and impasto. Academic painters of the 18th and 19th centuries did under-painting in black and gray oil and then repainted in color. The range of their colors was limited, however, and many have faded. All work was done in the studio.

In the 19th century, developments in chemistry produced new and brilliant pigments. The invention of collapsible tin tubes, replacing the old bladders, meant that artists could work out-of-doors directly from nature. Chemical additives to keep paint fresh made possible greater use of impasto. Underpainting virtually disappeared. French impressionists applied masses of small dots of bright color directly to the canvas. With the development of nonobjective painting in the 20th century, painters experimented with new techniques. They built up texture with sand, ashes, or plaster, stained canvases, and worked with commercial house paints and spray paints. They combined paint with photography and printed materials in collage. The versatility of oil paint has made it one of the most expressive media of the 20th-century artist.

For further information on this topic, see the Bibliography in volume 28, sections 712–13.

OISE, river, rising in the Ardennes region of S Belgium. It flows generally SW through the French departments of Nord, Aisne, Oise, and Val d'Oise, and Yvelines and enters the Seine R. near Pontoise. It is 299 km (186 mi) long. In World War I French troops were heavily attacked on the Oise and the last great German effort was made in this area.

OISTRAKH, David Fyodorovich (1908–74), Soviet violinist, known for his phenomenal technique and powerful tone. Born and trained in Odessa, he taught at the Moscow Conservatory, where his son, the violinist Igor Oistrakh (1931–) was one of his students. Oistrakh was strongly committed to new music, discussing violin technique with the Soviet composer Sergey Prokofiev and performing works composed for him by such Soviet composers as Aram Khachaturian and Dmitry Shostakovich. In 1958 Oistrakh began a parallel career as a conductor.

OITA, city and port, Japan, capital of Oita Prefecture, NE Kyushu Island, on Beppu Bay. It is a manufacturing center noted for livestock and raw silk. From the 13th century Oita was the seat of the Otomo daimyos, the most powerful of the Kyushu lords. It was at Oita, formerly called Funai, that the Portuguese navigator Fernão Mendes Pinto (c. 1514–83) landed in 1543 and introduced firearms to the Japanese. The Jesuits established a mission at Oita soon after. Pop. (1980 prelim.) 360,484.

OJIBWA or **CHIPPEWA,** largest and most important North American Indian tribe of the Algonquian linguistic family. They inhabited an extensive territory reaching into southern Canada between Lake Huron and the Turtle Mountains in North Dakota. According to Ojibwa tradition, the tribe originally emigrated from the region of the Saint Lawrence River in the east, in company with the related Ottawa and Potawatomi. The three tribes separated at what is now Mackinaw City, Mich., the Ojibwa spreading westward along both shores of Lake Superior, while the two other tribes went southward. The Ojibwa tribe was scattered over a vast area. It comprised a large number of bands divided into permanent clans said to have numbered more than 20. Originally, the clans were divided into five phratries, or groups, from which the 20 developed. One of the clans claimed the hereditary chieftainship of the entire tribe; another claimed precedence in the councils of war.

The economy of the Ojibwa was based chiefly on hunting, fishing, farming, and the gathering of wild fruits and seeds, particularly the abundant wild rice of the lake region; they also made sugar from maple syrup. Their houses were built on pole frames in wigwam shape and were usually covered with birchbark. Birchbark sheets were also used for keeping simple pictographic records of tribal affairs. Ojibwa mythology was elaborate; the chief religious and superstitious rites centered around the Medewiwin, or grand medicine society.

Although the Ojibwa were one of the largest Indian tribes north of Mexico, they did not have extensive relations with the early European explorers and settlers. They became known to Europeans in the mid-17th century, when they were confined within a narrow area along the shore of Lake Superior by the hostile incursions of the Sioux and Fox. They acquired firearms from the French about 1690, drove off their enemies, and subsequently greatly expanded their territory. The Ojibwa supported the French against the English in the various wars fought in North America—namely, King William's War, Queen Anne's War, King George's War, and the French and Indian War. In the American Revolution and the War of 1812, they sided with the British against the Americans. In 1815 they joined with the other belligerent tribes in signing a treaty of peace with the U.S. government. Under the terms of subsequent treaties, they sold the greater part of their former territories. At the present time the Ojibwa live on reservations in Michigan, Minnesota, Wisconsin, North Dakota, and Montana.

OKA, river, European USSR, in the Russian SFSR. It rises S of Orël and flows 1477 km (918 mi) N and NE through highly populated agricultural and industrial areas, to Gorkiy, where it joins the Volga R., of which it is the chief W affluent.

OKAYAMA, city of Japan, capital of Okayama Prefecture, SW Honshu Island, a port on the Asahi R., near the Inland Sea. It is an important commercial and manufacturing center; products include stoneware, machinery, textiles, chemicals, and rubber goods. In the city are a 16th-century castle and Koraku-en Park, a noted public garden laid out in 1786. Okayama University (1949) also is here. The main growth of Okayama as an industrial center began in the late 19th century. Pop. (1980 prelim.) 545,737.

OKAZAKI, city, Japan, in Aichi Prefecture, S Honshu Island, on the Yahagi R., near Nagoya. A road junction on the Tokaido rail line, it is also the center of a cotton-spinning and weaving industry. In Okazaki Park is the feudal castle that was the birthplace of Iyeyasu (1542–1616), founder of the Tokugawa shogunate. Pop. (1980 est.) 262,370.

OKEECHOBEE, LAKE, lake, S Florida, on the N edge of the Everglades. The third largest freshwater lake wholly within the U.S., Okeechobee is about 56 km (about 35 mi) long and 48 km (30 mi) wide and has an area of about 1813 sq km (about 700 sq mi).

O'KEEFFE, Georgia (1887–   ), American abstract painter, famous for the purity and lucidity of her still-life compositions. O'Keeffe was born in Sun Prairie, Wis., and studied at the Art Institute of Chicago and the Art Students League of New York. She taught art in Texas from 1913 to 1918. In 1916 the American photographer and art gallery director Alfred Stieglitz (whom she married in 1924) became interested in her abstract drawings and exhibited them at "291," his gallery in New York City; her work was shown annually in Stieglitz's galleries until his death in 1946.

O'Keeffe, who moved to New Mexico in 1949, is best known for her large paintings of desert flowers and scenery, in which single blossoms or objects such as a cow's skull, bones, or rocks are presented as if in close-up. Although O'Keeffe handles her subject matter representationally, the starkly linear quality, the thin, clear coloring, and the boldly patterned composition produce abstract designs. A number of O'Keeffe's works have a surrealistic effect, the flower paintings in particular—such as *Black Iris* (1926, Metropolitan Museum of Art, New York City)—having sexual connotations.

In the 1960s, inspired by a series of airplane flights, O'Keeffe introduced motifs of sky and clouds, as seen from the air, into her paintings. One of her largest works is the 7.3-m (24-ft) wide mural *Sky above Clouds* (1965, collection of the artist). O'Keeffe's paintings hang in museums and private collections throughout the U.S.

For further information on this person, see the section Biographies in the Bibliography in volume 28.

OKEFENOKEE SWAMP, large swamp, SE Georgia and NE Florida. It is drained by the Saint Marys and Suwannee rivers. It is made up of islands, lakes, brush vines, and cypress forests and contains a great variety of animals, birds, and fish. Okefenokee Swamp is about 72 km (45 mi) long and covers an area of about 1709 sq km (660 sq mi), much of it lies within the Okefenokee National Wildlife Refuge.

OKEGHEM, Johannes. *See* OCKEGHEM, JOHANNES.

O'KELLY, Sean Thomas (1882–1966), Irish journalist and political leader, second president of Éire (now the Republic of Ireland), born and educated in Dublin. He was a frequent contributor to Irish and American newspapers on the subject of Irish politics, and to disseminate his views on Irish independence he founded and edited in Dublin the newspaper *The Nation*. For many years O'Kelly was vice-president of the Fianna Fáil, or Republican party, and he was one of the founders of the Sinn Fein. O'Kelly was elected a deputy to the first Dáil Éireann, the parliament of Ireland in 1919, when he also became an envoy to France and Italy. From 1924 to 1926 O'Kelly was his country's envoy to the U.S. He was minister of finance from 1939 until 1945, when he was elected president of Éire. O'Kelly was re-elected in 1952 and served until 1959.

OKHOTSK, SEA OF, NW arm of the Pacific Ocean. Covering an area of approximately 1,528,100 sq km (about 590,000 sq mi), it is bounded on the E by Kamchatka Peninsula, on the SE by the Kuril Islands and the Japanese island of Hokkaido, and on the W by the island of Sakhalin and the Far Eastern coast of the USSR. The sea, which is rich in marine life, freezes over during the winter months and is frequently fogbound.

OKINAWA, island, SW Japan, lying between the East China Sea on the W and the North Pacific Ocean on the E. With an area of 1176 sq km (454 sq mi), it is the largest of the Ryukyu Islands (q.v.). The terrain of the N two-thirds of the island is mountainous and forested. The S third is hilly, rolling country and contains most of the population. The island's climate is hot and humid and typhoons frequently strike in summer. The principal economic activities are agriculture,

Cow's Skull: Red, White, and Blue *(1931), an oil painting by Georgia O'Keeffe.*
Metropolitan Museum of Art–Alfred Stieglitz Collection

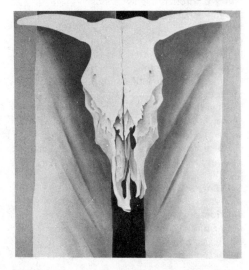

fishing, lumbering, food processing, and the manufacture of textiles and pottery. U.S. military bases and tourism are also important to the economy. Naha is the largest city and major port.

Until the 14th century Okinawa was an independent kingdom. Between the 14th and 19th centuries the island paid tribute to China, and Okinawa was annexed by Japan in 1879. On April 1, 1945, during World War II, U.S. forces landed on the W coast of Okinawa, thus beginning the last great amphibious operation of the war, and one of the most bitter of the Pacific campaigns. After 82 days of fighting, organized Japanese resistance ceased, and Okinawa airfields were quickly reconstructed and used by the U.S. Air Force. Okinawa remained under U.S. control from 1945 to 1972, when it was returned to Japan.

OKLAHOMA, one of the West South Central states of the U.S., bounded on the N by Colorado and Kansas, on the E by Missouri and Arkansas, on the S by Texas, and on the W by Texas and New Mexico. The Red R. forms much of the S boundary.

Oklahoma is called the Sooner State, a reference to the settlers who were here before the federal government officially opened the land to settlement. It was admitted to the Union on Nov. 16, 1907, as the 46th state. Oklahoma's economy has traditionally been dominated by agriculture and mining, but by the early 1980s manufacturing had grown to become the single largest economic sector. The name of the state is derived from two Choctaw Indian words meaning "red people" and was originally proposed by a Choctaw chief in the 1860s.

LAND AND RESOURCES

Oklahoma, with an area of 181,185 sq km (69,956 sq mi), is the 18th largest state in the U.S.; 3.6% of the land area is owned by the federal government. The state is roughly rectangular in shape with a narrow protruding section, the Panhandle, in the NW; its extreme dimensions are about 370 km (about 230 mi) from N to S and about 750 km (about 466 mi) from E to W. Elevations range from 87 m (287 ft) along the Little R. in the SE corner of the state to 1516 m (4973 ft) atop Black Mesa in the extreme NW. The approximate mean elevation is 396 m (1300 ft).

Physical Geography. Oklahoma encompasses a diversity of landscapes. In the W, confined almost entirely to the Panhandle, is the Great Plains region. Although generally level, this region rises some 914 m (about 3000 ft) in elevation from E to W. The central two-thirds of the state is occupied by the Osage Plains. This is a gently rolling region, interrupted only by the Wichita and Arbuckle mountains in the S and the

Gypsum Hills in the W. Much of this region is underlain with sandstone and shale, which has formed a reddish soil of moderate fertility. In the NE corner of the state is the Ozark Plateau. In contrast to the plains, this is a hilly region. Streams have cut deep valleys in the limestone formations of the plateau and have formed steep bluffs at the junction of the plateau and plains. To the S of the Ozark Plateau is the Arkansas Valley, a region that incorporates the valley of the Arkansas R. and the surrounding plains. This region has fertile soils and is one of the state's most important agricultural areas. The Ouachita Mts., to the S, constitute the most rugged region of Oklahoma. The mountains are primarily sandstone ridges, separated by narrow valleys. In the SE corner of the state, lying along the Red R., is the West Gulf Coastal Plain, a relatively flat area with fertile, sandy soils.

Rivers and Lakes. Oklahoma is divided into two major drainage systems. The N and W two-thirds of the state are drained by the Arkansas R. and its tributaries, including the Cimarron, Neosho, North Canadian, and Canadian rivers. The S part of the state is drained by the Red R. and its principal tributary, the Washita R. The natural lakes of Oklahoma are small; numerous federal and state dam-building projects have, however, created more than 200 artificial lakes, some of which are extensive. Among the largest are Lake Eufala in the SE; Lake Texoma on the Texas-Oklahoma border; and in the NE, Lake O' The Cherokees, and Ologah, Keystone, and Gibson lakes.

Climate. The climate of Oklahoma is diverse, changing from a humid subtropical regime in the SE to a semiarid continental climate in the W. Daily and seasonal extremes of temperature are characteristic. Summers are hot throughout the state; winters are frequently mild but severe weather does occur, often without warning. The average annual temperature ranges from 13.9° C (57° F) in the W to 18.9° C (66° F) in the SE. The recorded temperature has ranged from −32.8° C (−27° F) in 1905 to 48.9° C (120° F) in 1936.

The annual precipitation decreases from a maximum of more than 1270 mm (more than 50 in) in the SE to only 381 mm (15 in) in the Panhandle. Rainfall is heaviest in late spring and early summer. Powerful storms occur with relative frequency; Oklahoma has more tornadoes per unit area than any region in the U.S.

Plants and Animals. Forests cover only about 19% of the total land area of Oklahoma; about half this area is of commercial value. The forests are located almost entirely in the relatively moist E half of the state. The southern pine is the principal commercial tree and is found primarily in the

SE. Commercially valuable hardwoods include walnut, pecan, hickory, elm, ash, and oak. The W half of Oklahoma is a grassland containing a scattering of drought-resistant trees, such as juniper, blackjack, post oak, redbud, and cottonwood. In the extreme W and in the Panhandle, trees are confined to the banks of watercourses.

Deer, otter, raccoon, mink, and squirrel inhabit the forested regions. Rabbit, gopher, prairie dog, and coyote are common in the grasslands. Birdlife is abundant in virtually all sections of the state. Among the most common species are the meadowlark, mockingbird, scissortail, robin, blue jay, cardinal, crow, and sparrow. The Great Salt Plains in the N part of the state constitutes a major wildlife refuge for ducks.

Mineral Resources. Oklahoma is rich in mineral resources, particularly the energy minerals of petroleum, natural gas, and coal. Petroleum and natural gas are found in all sections of the state, but most coal is concentrated in the NE and the Arkansas Valley. The state also has significant deposits of high-grade granite, as well as gypsum, salt, and helium.   J.F.R.

POPULATION
According to the 1980 census, Oklahoma had 3,025,290 inhabitants, an increase of 18.2% over 1970. The average population density was 17 people per sq km (43 per sq mi); most of the population was concentrated in the E half of the

state. Whites made up 85.9% of the population and blacks 6.8%. Oklahoma has the nation's second largest population of American Indians, totaling some 169,297 individuals, or about 5.6% of the population. Among the largest of the state's many Indian groups are the Cherokee, Chickasaw, Choctaw, Creek, and Seminole (qq.v.). Additional population groups included 4671 persons of Vietnamese origin, 2879 persons of Asian Indian background, 2698 persons of Korean extraction, and 2461 persons of Chinese ancestry. Approximately 57,400 persons were of Hispanic background. Southern Baptists formed the largest single religious group in the state. In 1980 about 67% of all Oklahomans lived in areas defined as urban, and the rest lived in rural areas. The state's two biggest cities were Oklahoma City (the capital) and Tulsa. The next largest cities—Lawton, Norman, and Enid—were considerably smaller.

EDUCATION AND CULTURAL ACTIVITY
Because Oklahoma is a relatively sparsely populated state, many of its educational and cultural institutions are concentrated in its major cities, particularly in Oklahoma City and Tulsa.

Education. The first schools established in the territory were founded in the 1820s by missionaries. Support for a public school system was provided by a legislative act of 1906 that was confirmed by the constitution of 1907. In the

View of the Wichita Mts., in southwestern Oklahoma.
Oklahoma Planning and Resources Board

Aerial view of downtown Tulsa, Okla. The nearby Port of Catoosa on the Arkansas River makes the city one of the major U.S. inland deepwater ports, facilitating shipping between the Gulf of Mexico and the Great Lakes.   Tulsa Chamber of Commerce

early 1980s Oklahoma had 1895 public elementary and secondary schools with a combined annual enrollment of about 398,900 elementary pupils and 178,900 secondary students. About 16,300 students attended private schools. In the same period Oklahoma had 45 institutions of higher education, with a total enrollment of about 160,300 students. Among these schools were the University of Oklahoma, in Norman; Oklahoma State University (1890), in Stillwater; Central State University (1890), in Edmond; Southwestern Oklahoma State University (1901), in Weatherford; Phillips University (1906), in Enid; the University of Tulsa (1894) and Oral Roberts University (1965), in Tulsa; Oklahoma City University (1901); Saint Gregory's College (1875), in Shawnee; and the University of Science and Arts of Oklahoma (1908), in Chickasha.

Cultural Institutions. Many of the state's museums exhibit collections of historical material on the American Indian and the western pioneer. Included among these are the Thomas Gilcrease Institute of American History and Art and the Philbrook Art Center, both in Tulsa; the Oklahoma Historical Society Museum and the Oklahoma Art Center, both in Oklahoma City; and the Cherokee National Historical Society museum, in Tahlequah. The University of Oklahoma

at the Norman campus includes the University of Oklahoma Museum of Art, featuring objects and paintings from Europe and the Orient, and the Stovall Museum of Science and History. Of interest also are the Tom Mix Museum, in Dewey, and the National Cowboy Hall of Fame and Western Heritage Center, in Oklahoma City.

Historical Sites. The heritage of the Old West is commemorated in a number of Oklahoma's historic sites, including Indian City U.S.A., a recreation of villages typical of the Plains Indians, near Anadarko; the Fort Sill Military Reservation and National Historic Landmark, built in 1869, near Lawton; the Pawnee Bill Ranch, near Pawnee; and the Old Creek Indian Council House, in Okmulgee. Other points of interest include the Will Rogers Memorial, near Claremore, and the Home of Sequoyah, commemorating the creator of the Cherokee alphabet, near Sallisaw.

Sports and Recreation. Oklahoma's lakes, ponds, and rivers provide ample recreational opportunities for swimming, fishing, and boating. In addition, ideal conditions for hiking, climbing, and camping are found at such places as Chickasaw National Recreation Area, Lake Texoma Recreation Area, the Wichita Mountains Wildlife Refuge, and the Salt Plains National Wildlife Refuge. Hunting and horseback riding are also popular.

347

INDEX TO MAP OF OKLAHOMA

Cities and Towns

Ada ⊙ ... E 3
Afton ... F 1
Alex ... D 3
Allen ... E 3
Altus ⊙ ... B 3
Alva ⊙ ... C 1
Anadarko ⊙ ... C 2
Antlers ⊙ ... F 3
Apache ... C 3
Arapaho ⊙ ... C 2
Ardmore ⊙ ... E 3
Arkoma ... G 2
Arnett ⊙ ... B 1
Atoka ⊙ ... E 3
Barnsdall ... E 1
Bartlesville ⊙ ... E 1
Beaver ⊙ ... A 1, C 4
Beggs ... E 2
Bethany ... D 2
Billings ... D 1
Binger ... C 2
Blackwell ... D 1
Blair ... B 3
Blanchard ... D 2
Boise City ⊙ ... A 4
Boley ... E 2
Boswell ... F 3
Boynton ... F 2
Bristow ... E 2
Broken Arrow ... F 1
Broken Bow ... G 3
Buffalo ⊙ ... B 1
Burns Flat ... B 2
Cache ... C 3
Caddo ... E 3
Calera ... E 4
Canton ... C 1
Carmen ... C 1
Carnegie ... C 2
Catoosa ... F 1
Cement ... C 3
Chandler ⊙ ... E 2
Checotah ... F 2
Chelsea ... F 1
Cherokee ⊙ ... C 1
Cheyenne ⊙ ... B 2
Chickasha ⊙ ... D 2
Chilocco ... D 1
Chouteau ... F 2

Claremore ⊙ ... F 1
Clayton ... F 3
Cleveland ... E 1
Clinton ... B 2
Coalgate ⊙ ... E 3
Colbert ... E 4
Collinsville ... B 3
Comanche ... C 2
Copan ... E 1
Cordell ⊙ ... C 2
Covington ... D 1
Coweta ... F 2
Crescent ... D 2
Cushing ... E 2
Cyril ... C 3
Davenport ... E 2
Davis ... D 3
Depew ... E 2
Dewar ... F 2
Dewey ... E 1
Dill City ... B 2
Drumright ... E 2
Duncan ⊙ ... D 3
Durant ⊙ ... E 3
Eldorado ... B 3
Elk City ... B 2
Elmore City ... D 3
El Reno ⊙ ... D 2
Enid ⊙ ... D 1
Erick ... B 2
Eufaula ... F 2
Fairfax ... E 1
Fairland ... F 1
Fairview ⊙ ... C 1
Fletcher ... C 3
Forgan ... A 1, C 4
Fort Gibson ... F 2
Frederick ⊙ ... C 3
Garber ... D 1
Geary ... C 2
Goodwell ... B 4
Grandfield ... C 3
Granite ... B 3
Grove ⊙ ... G 1
Guthrie ⊙ ... D 2
Guymon ⊙ ... B 4
Hammon ... B 2
Hartshorne ... F 3
Haskell ... F 2

Healdton ... D 3
Heavener ... G 3
Helena ... C 1
Hennessey ... D 1
Henryetta ... E 2
Hinton ... C 2
Hobart ⊙ ... B 2
Holdenville ⊙ ... E 2
Hollis ⊙ ... B 3
Hominy ... E 1
Hooker ... B 4
Hugo ⊙ ... F 3
Hydro ... C 2
Idabel ⊙ ... G 3
Inola ... F 1
Jay ⊙ ... G 1
Jenks ... F 2
Keota ... G 2
Keyes ... A 4
Kingfisher ⊙ ... D 2
Kiowa ... F 3
Konawa ... E 3
Krebs ... F 2
Lamont ... D 1
Laverne ... A 1, C 4
Lawton ⊙ ... C 3
Lexington ... D 2
Lindsay ... D 3
McAlester ⊙ ... F 2
McCurtain ... G 2
McLoud ... D 2
Madill ⊙ ... E 3
Mangum ⊙ ... B 2
Marietta ⊙ ... E 1
Marlow ... D 3
Maud ... E 2
Maysville ... D 3
Medford ⊙ ... D 1
Medicine Park ... C 3
Meeker ... E 2
Miami ⊙ ... G 1
Midwest City ... D 2
Minco ... D 2
Moore ... D 2
Mooreland ... B 1
Morris ... F 2
Mounds ... E 2
Mountain View ... C 2
Muldrow ... G 2
Muskogee ⊙ ... F 2
Newkirk ⊙ ... D 1

Noble ... D 2
Norman ⊙ ... D 2
Nowata ⊙ ... F 1
Oilton ... E 1
Okarche ... D 2
Okeene ... C 1
Okemah ⊙ ... E 2
Oklahoma City (cap.) ⊙ ... D 2
Okmulgee ⊙ ... E 2
Owasso ... F 1
Panama ... G 2
Pauls Valley ⊙ ... D 3
Pawhuska ⊙ ... E 1
Pawnee ⊙ ... E 1
Perkins ... E 2
Perry ⊙ ... D 1
Picher ... G 1
Ponca City ... D 1
Pond Creek ⊙ ... D 1
Porum ... F 2
Poteau ⊙ ... G 2
Prague ... E 2
Pryor ⊙ ... F 1
Purcell ⊙ ... D 3
Quinton ... F 2
Ramona ... E 1
Ringling ... D 3
Roff ... D 3
Rush Springs ... D 3
Ryan ... D 3
Salina ... F 1
Sallisaw ⊙ ... G 2
Sand Springs ... E 1
Sapulpa ⊙ ... E 2
Savanna ... F 2
Sayre ⊙ ... B 1
Selling ... C 1
Seminole ... E 2
Sentinel ... B 2
Shattuck ... B 1
Shawnee ⊙ ... E 2
Shidler ... E 1
Skiatook ... E 1
Snyder ... C 3
Spiro ... G 2
Stigler ⊙ ... F 2
Stillwater ⊙ ... D 2
Stilwell ⊙ ... G 2
Stonewall ... E 3
Stratford ... D 3

Stroud ... E 2
Sulphur ⊙ ... D 3
Tahlequah ⊙ ... G 1
Talihina ... F 3
Taloga ⊙ ... B 1
Tecumseh ... E 2
Temple ... C 3
Terral ... D 4
Texhoma ... B 4
Thomas ... C 2
Tipton ... B 3
Tishomingo ⊙ ... E 3
Tonkawa ... D 1
Tulsa ⊙ ... F 1
Tuttle ... D 2
Velma ... D 3
Vian ... G 2
Vici ... B 1
Vinita ⊙ ... F 1
Wagoner ⊙ ... F 2
Walters ⊙ ... C 3
Warner ... F 2
Watonga ⊙ ... C 2
Waukomis ... D 1
Waurika ⊙ ... D 3
Waynoka ... C 1
Weatherford ... C 2
Weleetka ... E 2
Wellston ... E 2
Westville ... G 1
Wetumka ... E 2
Wewoka ⊙ ... E 2
Wilburton ⊙ ... F 3
Wilson ... D 3
Wister ... G 3
Woodward ⊙ ... B 1
Wright City ... F 3
Wynnewood ... D 3
Wynona ... E 1
Yale ... E 1

Other Features

Altus (res.) ... B 3
Altus AFB ... B 3
Arkansas (river) ... C 3
Atoka (res.) ... F 3
Black Mesa (mt.) ... A 4
Boston (mts.) ... G 2
Broken Bow (lake) ... G 3

Canadian (river) ... D 3
Canton (lake) ... C 1
Cherokees (lake) ... G 1
Chickasaw Nat'l Rec. Area ... E 3
Cimarron (river) ... C 1
Eufaula (lake) ... F 2
Fort Cobb (res.) ... C 2
Fort Gibson (lake) ... C 3
Fort Sill ... B 1
Fort Supply (lake) ... B 2
Great Salt Plains (lake) ... C 1
Hudson (lake) ... F 1
Hugo (lake) ... F 3
Hulah (lake) ... E 1
Illinois (river) ... G 1
Kaw (lake) ... D 1
Keystone (lake) ... E 1
Kiamichi (river) ... F 3
Lake O' The Cherokees (lake) ... G 1
Little (river) ... G 3
Murray (lake) ... D 3
Neosho (river) ... F 1
North Canadian (river) ... C 2
North Fork Red (river) ... A 2
Oologah (lake) ... F 1
Osage Indian Res. ... E 1
Ouachita (mts.) ... F 3
Ozark (plat.) ... G 1
Prairie Dog Town Fork (river) ... A 3
Red (river) ... E 4
Robert S. Kerr (res.) ... F 2
Salt Fork, Arkansas (river) ... D 1
Tenkiller Ferry (lake) ... G 2
Texoma (lake) ... E 3
Tinker AFB ... D 2
Tom Steed (res.) ... C 3
Vance AFB ... C 1
Washita (river) ... D 3
Waurika (lake) ... C 3
Wichita (mts.) ... C 3
Wister (lake) ... G 3
Wolf (creek) ... A 1

⊙ County seat

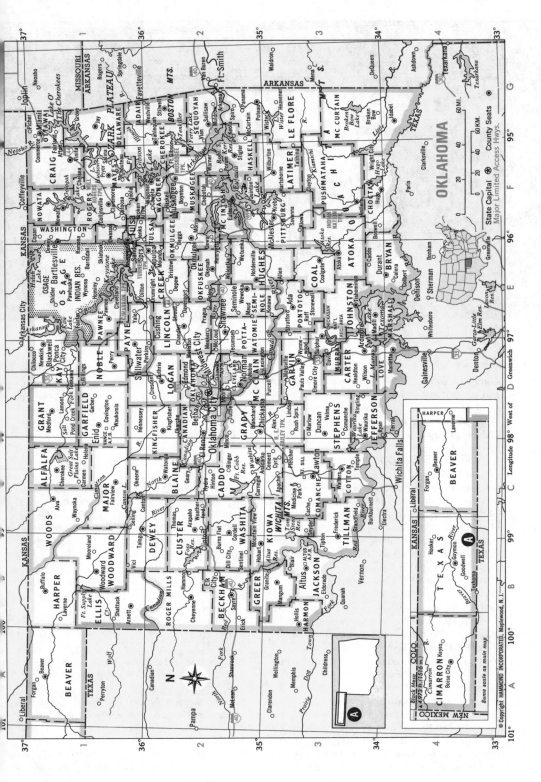

349

Rodeos are a regular occurrence in Oklahoma, a state in which many traditions of the Old West are faithfully maintained. Shostal Associates

Communications. In the early 1980s Oklahoma had 67 AM and 53 FM commercial radiobroadcasting stations and 14 commercial television stations. The state's first radio station, WKY in Oklahoma City, was licensed in 1921. WKY-TV in Oklahoma City and KOTV in Tulsa, Oklahoma's first commercial television stations, began operations in 1949. The *Cherokee Advocate,* the state's first newspaper, was initially published in Tahlequah in 1844. In the early 1980s Oklahoma had 54 daily newspapers with a total daily circulation of about 837,900. Influential dailies included the *Daily Oklahoman* and the *Oklahoma City Times,* in Oklahoma City; and the *Tulsa Tribune* and the *Tulsa Daily World,* in Tulsa.

GOVERNMENT AND POLITICS

Oklahoma is governed under its original constitution, adopted in 1907, as amended. An amendment to the constitution may be proposed by initiative, a constitutional convention, or the state legislature. To become effective, an amendment must be approved by a majority of the persons voting on the issue in a general election.

Executive. The chief executive of Oklahoma is a governor, who is popularly elected to a 4-year term and who may serve any number of terms but not more than two in a row. The lieutenant governor, who succeeds the governor should the latter resign, die, or be removed from office, may be reelected to any number of 4-year terms.

Other elected executive officials include the attorney general, treasurer, auditor and inspector, and superintendent of public instruction.

Legislature. The bicameral Oklahoma legislature comprises a Senate and a House of Representatives. The 48 members of the Senate are elected to 4-year terms, and the 101 members of the House are elected to 2-year terms.

Judiciary. Oklahoma's highest courts are the supreme court, with nine justices, and the court of criminal appeals, with three justices. Judges of these courts are initially appointed by the governor, but later must run for election (to a 6-year term) at the first general election following 12 months of service. The 6 judges of the intermediate court of appeals are popularly elected to 6-year terms, and the 202 judges of the district courts are popularly elected to 4-year terms.

Local Government. In the early 1980s Oklahoma had 77 counties and 559 incorporated cities and towns. Most counties are governed by a three-member board of commissioners; most cities are run either by the mayor-council or council-manager form of government.

National Representation. Oklahoma elects two senators and six representatives to the U.S. Congress. The state has eight electoral votes in presidential elections.

Politics. In state and local politics, Oklahoma was, until the 1960s, a stronghold of the Democratic party. Since that time Republican candidates for governor and U.S. senator have scored successes, although the Democrats retain a large lead in voter registration. In presidential elections, Oklahoma, which was solidly Democratic through the 1940s, has become one of the nation's most dependably Republican states.

ECONOMY

Homesteaders, settling in Oklahoma in the late 19th century, established an overwhelmingly agricultural economy. Cattle and crops, particularly grains and cotton, were the state's principal products. The discovery of petroleum in the 1920s added a new dimension to the economy, encouraging the growth of commercial activity and related industry. Mineral and agricultural production still dominate the state economy. Although manufacturing is the single largest sector, it is to a large extent based on the processing of raw materials. Other important economic activities are wholesale and retail trade, government, and finance.

Agriculture. Farming accounts for 21% of the annual value of goods produced in Oklahoma. The state has some 72,000 farms, which average 195 ha (481 acres) in size; most of the state's smaller farms are located in the SE. Livestock and livestock products make up about two-thirds of Oklahoma's yearly farm income. Beef cattle are the state's leading agricultural product. Cattle feedlots and ranches are concentrated in the semiarid Panhandle and in the N part of the state. The raising of poultry and hogs is largely limited to the E half of the state.

Crops account for about one-third of Oklahoma's annual agricultural income. The leading crops are wheat, sorghum, cotton, soybeans, peanuts, and alfalfa. Wheat is grown primarily in the N and SW parts of the state; cotton raising is concentrated in the SW. In the more humid E part of Oklahoma, soybeans, pecans, corn, and vegetables are grown.

Forestry. The annual income from forestry in Oklahoma is relatively small. Commercial forests, located primarily in the E, yield quantities of shortleaf and loblolly pines, sweet gum, various oaks, cottonwood, pecan, and walnut.

Mining. The mining industry accounts for 32% of the annual value of goods produced in Oklahoma, and the state ranks as one of the nation's leading producers of minerals. Petroleum and natural gas make up more than 90% of the yearly mineral production by value. The state is also a major producer of gypsum. Other minerals include coal, granite, and limestone.

Manufacturing. Manufacturing enterprises account for 47% of the annual value of goods produced in Oklahoma and employ some 204,200 workers. The yearly value added by manufacturing in the state is rising rapidly. The leading manufactures include nonelectrical machinery, fabricated metal products, food and related products, electric and electronic equipment, transportation equipment, refined petroleum, and apparel. The two major industrial centers, Oklahoma City and Tulsa, account for more than half the state's manufacturing employment. Tulsa, in particular, has experienced rapid industrial growth since the 1960s.

Tourism. Each year, several million out-of-state visitors produce about $2 billion for the Oklahoma economy. Chickasaw National Recreation Area is a popular tourist spot, as are some 76 state parks and recreation areas. Oklahoma's numerous reservoirs also furnish ample recreation opportunities.

Transportation. Tulsa and Oklahoma City are major hubs in a network of about 176,665 km (about 109,775 mi) of federal, state, and local roads that serve Oklahoma. This figure includes six state-maintained turnpikes as well as 1304 km (810 mi) of Interstate Highways. Railroad companies provide service on the 6325 km (3930 mi) of operated track that cross the state.

The state's major waterway, the McClellan-Kerr Navigation System, provides E Oklahoma with access to the Gulf of Mexico by way of the Verdigris, Arkansas, and Mississippi rivers. The principal ports, Catoosa and Muskogee, have transfer facilities for grain, coal, steel, fertilizer, and other commodities.

Oklahoma has about 297 airports. The two busiest are Tulsa International Airport and Will Rogers World Airport (Oklahoma City).

Numerous oil and gas pipelines cross the state. Many of these are gathering lines run to producing fields; some carry oil and gas to other states.

Energy. The electricity-generating plants in Oklahoma have a total capacity of about 11.3 million kw and produce approximately 44.6 billion kwh of electricity per year. About 75% of the state's electricity is generated by plants using natural gas, and some 22% is produced in coal-burning facilities. Almost all the balance is produced by hydroelectric facilities. R.G.Bo.

HISTORY

The Spanish explorer Francisco Vásquez de Coronado was the first European to enter Oklahoma, in 1541. French traders and trappers visited the region in the 16th and 17th centuries. In 1803, as a result of the Louisiana Purchase, all Oklahoma except the Panhandle, the extreme western portion of the present state, became a part of the U.S. In 1817 the federal government began send-

OKLAHOMA

OKLAHOMA

DATE OF STATEHOOD: November 16, 1907; 46th state

CAPITAL:	Oklahoma City
MOTTO:	*Labor omnia vincit* (Labor conquers all things)
NICKNAME:	Sooner State;
STATE SONG:	"Oklahoma!" (words by Oscar Hammerstein II; music by Richard Rodgers)
STATE TREE:	Redbud
STATE FLOWER:	Mistletoe
STATE BIRD:	Scissor-tailed flycatcher
POPULATION (1980):	3,025,290; 26th among the states
AREA:	181,185 sq km (69,956 sq mi); 18th largest state; includes 3370 sq km (1301 sq mi) of inland water
HIGHEST POINT:	Black Mesa, 1516 m (4973 ft)
LOWEST POINT:	87 m (287 ft), along the Little River
ELECTORAL VOTES:	8
U.S. CONGRESS:	2 senators; 6 representatives

POPULATION OF OKLAHOMA SINCE 1890

Year of Census	Population	Classified As Urban
1890	259,000	4%
1900	790,000	7%
1910	1,657,000	19%
1920	2,028,000	27%
1940	2,336,000	38%
1960	2,328,000	63%
1970	2,559,000	68%
1980	3,025,000	67%

POPULATION OF TEN LARGEST CITIES

	1980 Census	1970 Census
Oklahoma City	403,136	368,164
Tulsa	360,919	330,350
Lawton	80,054	74,470
Norman	68,020	52,117
Enid	50,363	44,986
Midwest City	49,559	48,212
Muskogee	40,011	37,331
Stillwater	38,268	31,126
Broken Arrow	35,761	11,018
Moore	35,063	18,761

CLIMATE

	OKLAHOMA CITY	TULSA
Average January temperature range	−3.3° to 8.9° C (26° to 48° F)	−3.3° to 8.3° C (26° to 47° F)
Average July temperature range	21.1° to 33.9° C (70° to 93° F)	21.7° to 33.9° C (71° to 93° F)
Average annual temperature	15.6° C (60° F)	15.6° C (60° F)
Average annual precipitation	787 mm (31 in)	940 mm (37 in)
Average annual snowfall	229 mm (9 in)	229 mm (9 in)
Mean number of days per year with appreciable precipitation	81	90
Average daily relative humidity	67%	69%
Mean number of clear days per year	141	127

NATURAL REGIONS OF OKLAHOMA

GREAT PLAINS
OZARK PLATEAU
Arkansas R.
ARKANSAS VALLEY
OSAGE PLAINS
OUACHITA MTS.
Red R.
WEST GULF COASTAL PLAIN

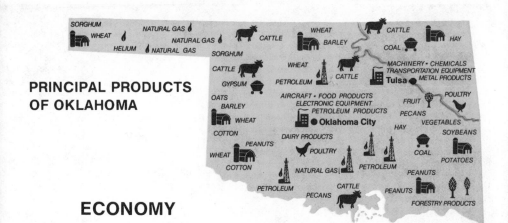

PRINCIPAL PRODUCTS OF OKLAHOMA

ECONOMY

State budget................... revenue $3.4 billion
                          expenditure $3.2 billion
State personal income tax, per capita $116
Personal income, per capita $9116
Assets, commercial banks (489) .... $19.7 billion
Labor force (civilian) 1,337,600
    Employed in services   26%
    Employed in wholesale and retail trade   20%
    Employed in government   18%
    Employed in manufacturing   15%

	Quantity Produced	Value
FARM PRODUCTS		**$3.2 billion**
Crops		**$1.1 billion**
Wheat	5.3 million metric tons	$751 million
Hay	1.0 million metric tons	$80 million
Cotton	45,000 metric tons	$75 million
Sorghum	415,000 metric tons	$51 million
Peanuts	64,000 metric tons	$36 million
Soybeans	82,000 metric tons	$23 million
Livestock and Livestock Products		**$2.1 billion**
Cattle	1.1 million metric tons	$1.5 billion
Milk	489,000 metric tons	$153 million
Hogs	57,000 metric tons	$47 million
Chickens	80,000 metric tons	$47 million
Eggs	839 million	$43 million
MINERALS		**$7.4 billion**
Petroleum	150 million barrels	$4.1 billion
Natural gas	57.2 billion cu m	$2.9 billion
Coal†	4.9 million metric tons	$188 million
Stone	25.7 million metric tons	$76 million

† Value estimated from govt. indications

	Labor and Proprietors' Income
FORESTRY	**$2.7 million**
MANUFACTURING	**$3.7 billion**
Nonelectric machinery	$791 million
Fabricated metal products	$454 million
Motor vehicles and equipment	$277 million
Food and kindred products	$270 million
Petroleum and coal products	$269 million
Electric and electronic equipment	$246 million
Rubber and plastics products	$244 million
Transportation equipment	$236 million
Stone, clay, and glass products	$216 million

OTHER	$12.7 billion
Services	$3.1 billion
Government and government enterprises	$3.5 billion
Transportation and public utilities	$1.7 billion
Finance, insurance, and real estate	$1.0 billion
Wholesale trade	$1.4 billion
Retail trade	$2.0 billion

ANNUAL PRODUCTION OF GOODS BY SECTOR

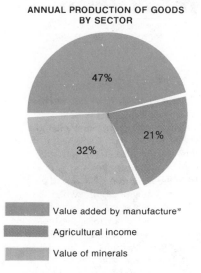

47%

21%

32%

- Value added by manufacture*
- Agricultural income
- Value of minerals

* The value added by an industry is a measure of the value created in its products, not counting such production costs as raw materials and power.

Sources: U.S. government publications

*Cattle cool themselves in a pond on the prairie near Inola, in northeastern Oklahoma.
The raising of livestock is the leading agricultural occupation in the state.*
Shostal Associates

ing the large Indian populations of Alabama, Georgia, Florida, and Mississippi to the region. Oklahoma was divided among the Five Civilized Nations, consisting of the Creek, Cherokee, Chickasaw, Choctaw, and Seminole Indian tribes. In 1834 the region was established as the Indian Territory (q.v.), and the tribal authority of the Indian nations within the territory was assured.

During the American Civil War, the Indians of the territory, many of whom owned slaves, sided with the Confederacy. After the war, by a series of treaties from 1866 to 1883, the Indian nations were forced to cede the western half of the territory to the U.S. as a home for other Indian tribes. Great tracts of land still remained unoccupied, and although whites were forbidden by law to settle on these lands, colonization schemes were developed by various groups; as a result, President Rutherford B. Hayes issued proclamations in 1879 and 1880 forbidding settlement in the territory. Violations occurred frequently, and agita-

tion for the opening of the lands to whites increased to a point at which Congress in 1885 authorized the president to begin negotiations with the Creek and Seminole tribes for the purpose of opening the unoccupied tracts for settlement. The negotiations were successfully concluded in 1889, and at noon on April 22 the land was opened to the public. A race for the best lands and town sites ensued as nearly 50,000 persons flooded the territory the first day. Tent towns were laid out, farms sprang up, and the population of the area increased at an extraordinary rate.

On March 2, 1890, the federal government established the territory of Oklahoma, which consisted of lands in the southern part of the region and the western portion of the Indian Territory, in addition to the Panhandle. Additional lands were opened for settlement up to 1906. On Nov. 16, 1907, the two territories entered the Union as the 46th state.

Until the mid-20th century Oklahoma's economy seesawed dramatically. While oil production became increasingly important, farm prices fell until the demand for farm and fuel products during World War I, and again in World War II, stabilized the economy. The discovery of huge oil and gas deposits in the 1920s was offset by the depression of the 1930s, complicated by drought and crop failures (*see* DUST BOWL). Starting in the 1950s, however, drastic soil-conservation and flood-control measures, and new industries ranging from electronics and space equipment to plastics and mobile-home manufacturing, have led Oklahoma from its former agricultural dependence to an era of industrial stability.

For further information on this topic, see the Bibliography in volume 28, section 1194.

OKLAHOMA, UNIVERSITY OF, state-supported institution of higher learning, in Norman, Okla. Founded in 1890 by an act of the first Oklahoma territorial legislature, the university opened for instruction in 1892. The university has a graduate school; a university college; colleges of arts and sciences, business administration, education, engineering, environmental design, fine arts, law, library science, and pharmacy; an extension division; and, at Oklahoma City, schools of medicine, dentistry, health, and nursing. The university maintains a biological station at Lake Texoma, an earth sciences observatory near Tulsa, and a fisheries research center at Noble. The degrees of bachelor, master, and doctor are conferred.

OKLAHOMA CITY, city, capital of Oklahoma and seat of Oklahoma Co. and also in Canadian, Cleveland, McClain, and Pottawatomie counties, on the Canadian and North Canadian rivers, in the central part of the state; inc. 1890. Covering 1608 sq km (621 sq mi) of land in 1980, it is one of the nation's largest cities in terms of area. Besides being the seat of the state government, Oklahoma City is the state's principal financial, commercial, and transportation center. It also is a major center for producing and refining crude petroleum; other manufactures include fabricated metal, aerospace and electronic equipment, and food products. Cattle and wheat produced in the area are processed and shipped here. The city is served by Will Rogers World Airport, and nearby Tinker Air Force Base, a major aircraft supply and repair depot, is the area's chief single employer.

Among the points of interest in Oklahoma City are the State Capitol (built chiefly of white limestone), the National Cowboy Hall of Fame and

The Oklahoma State Capitol, at Oklahoma City, is unique in having oil-drilling equipment on its grounds.
Oklahoma Planning and Resources Board

Western Heritage Center, the Oklahoma Historical Society museum, the Oklahoma Heritage Association museum, the Oklahoma Museum of Art, and the National Softball Hall of Fame. The city is the seat of Midwest Christian College (1946), Oklahoma Christian College (1950), Oklahoma City University (1901), the University of Oklahoma Health Sciences Center (1900), and two junior colleges. A number of nearby lakes provide outdoor-recreation opportunities.

From early times the Oklahoma City region was inhabited by Indian groups including Cherokee, Chickasaw, Choctaw, Creek, and Seminole Indians. In 1889 the area was opened to settlement with a famous land run for staking out claims. In a single day (April 22) a tent city of nearly 10,000 inhabitants was built at the site of the city. The railroad stop at that site (opened in 1887) may have also encouraged settlement here. By 1910, when Oklahoma City replaced Guthrie as the state capital, it was the largest city in Oklahoma with a population of about 64,000 persons. Only in 1923 did the U.S. postal service officially recognize the city's name, which had been in popular use since 1889. Oklahoma City enjoyed great economic growth after productive oil and gas fields in and near the city were discovered in 1928. Subsequently, the skyline became marked by oil derricks, some situated on the lawns of private homes and near public buildings (notably the Capitol). In the 1970s the center city was renewed according to a plan drawn up by the Chinese-born American architect I. M. Pei. Pop. (1970) 368,164; (1980) 403,213.

OKMULGEE, city, seat of Okmulgee Co., E central Oklahoma; inc. 1900. It is a manufacturing center situated in an agricultural area that also produces petroleum, natural gas, and coal. Major products of the city include refined petroleum, glass, and processed food. The Creek Council House Museum, containing Indian art and artifacts, is here, and Lake Okmulgee is nearby. The site of the city served as the capital of the Creek Indians from 1868 to 1907. It was settled by non-Indians in 1872 and flourished after the discovery of oil deposits in the area in 1904. Pop. (1970) 15,180; (1980) 16,263.

OKRA, also gumbo, an annual herb, *Hibiscus esculentus,* of the family Malvaceae (*see* MALLOW). The okra, which is native to Africa, is extensively cultivated in the southern U.S. and the West Indies for its long, many-seeded pod that, when still young and green, is used to thicken soups and stews and as a cooked vegetable. The okra bears large, yellow flowers, similar in structure to typical *Hibiscus* flowers, and is occasionally planted in flower gardens.

OKUMA SHIGENOBU, Marquess (1838-1922), Japanese statesman, born in Saga. While still a young man he began to oppose Japanese feudalism and championed constitutional government. Okuma became minister of finance in 1869, and during the following 12 years he modernized the fiscal structure of Japan. In 1882 he founded both the Kaishinto (Progressive party) and what is now Waseda University in Tokyo. He served as foreign minister (1888-89, 1896-97) and as prime minister (1898, 1914-16). During Okuma's second premiership, Japan joined the Allies in World War I, flourished economically, and issued the Twenty-one Demands to China, which exacted Japanese territorial, industrial, and transportation privileges in that country.

OLAF GODFREYSON (d. 941), king of Dublin (934-41) and Northumbria (940-41). Olaf was the leader of the non-English forces that battled King Athelstan of England at Brunanburh in 937. Defeated, he fled back to Dublin, but after Athelstan's death two years later, he returned to Northumbria and forced Athelstan's successor, Edmund I, to acknowledge his rule as far south as Mercia. He shared his lordship of Northumbria with his cousin, Olaf Sihtricson. The name is also spelled Olaf Guthfrithson.

Okra, Hibiscus esculentus

OLAF I, full name OLAF TRYGGVASON (968-1000), king of Norway (995-1000). A great-grandson of King Harold I, he was brought up in Russia and later participated in numerous Viking raids along the Baltic and North Sea coasts and in the British Isles. During his last campaign, in England (994) with Sweyn I Forkbeard of Denmark, he was converted to Christianity, and the following year he returned to Norway, where a rebellion had erupted against the pagan Earl Håkon (937?-95). The victorious Olaf founded the city of Nidaros (now Trondheim) as his capital and set out to Christianize the country. Only partly successful in Norway, his efforts contributed to the conversion of Iceland, Greenland, and the Faeroe Islands to Christianity. Olaf's forces were defeated by a coalition consisting of Sweyn Forkbeard, King Olaf of Sweden (d. 1022?), and the two sons of Earl Håkon in the naval Battle of Svold (1000), during which Olaf lost his life.

OLAF II, full name OLAF HARALDSSON, later St. Olaf (995-1030), king of Norway (1015-28). Olaf was a Viking from his early youth and later, while in the service of the exiled King Ethelred II of England, was converted to Christianity in Rouen. He returned to Norway in 1015 and, as a descendant of King Harold I, quickly won recognition, displacing the ruling earls. He introduced a strong central administration, completed the conversion of the Norwegians begun by Olaf I, and built churches throughout the land. Many local chieftains, alienated by Olaf's domineering ways, sided with Canute II, king of Denmark and England, when he invaded Norway in 1028; Olaf was compelled to take refuge with his brother-in-law, Grand Duke Yaroslav of Novgorod (978-1054). Returning with a force to Norway in 1030, he was defeated by a peasant army and killed at the Battle of Stiklestad. Olaf was subsequently worshiped as Norway's patron saint and was canonized in 1164. He was also revered throughout Scandinavia and in England, Germany, and the Baltic countries. His feast day is July 29.

OLAF III, called The Quiet (d. 1093), king of Norway (1066-93), the son of King Harold III Hard Ruler. Olaf brought the Norse fleet to Norway after his father was defeated and killed at the Battle of Stamford Bridge in England in 1066. He ruled jointly with his brother Magnus II Barefoot from 1066 to 1069, and after the death of his brother he ruled alone. His reign was noted for peace and for the continued Christianization of Norway.

OLAF V, original name Alexander Edward Christian Frederik of Glücksburg (1903-), king of Norway (1957-), the son of King Haakon VII, born in Sandringham, England. He went to Great Britain with his father after the German invasion of Norway in 1940, during World War II. Olaf was commander in chief of the Norwegian armed forces fighting with the Allies in 1944-45; he returned to Norway after the defeat of Germany in 1945.

OLAF SIHTRICSON, known in sagas as Olaf the Red (d. 981?), Danish king of Northumbria (940-44, 949-52) and king of Dublin (944-49, 952-80). In 940-41 Olaf ruled Northumbria jointly with his cousin Olaf Godfreyson. He was expelled from his English domain in 944. Thereupon he went to Ireland. He reigned in Dublin until 949, when he regained the Northumbrian throne. After his second expulsion from England in 952, he governed his Irish kingdom until his defeat by fellow Danes at Tara in 980. Soon afterward he died in exile at Iona in the Hebrides Islands.

OLATHE, city, seat of Johnson Co., NE Kansas, near Kansas City; inc. 1868. It is an industrial and distribution center for the surrounding agricultural area. Major manufactures include aircraft parts, batteries, farm machinery, boots, and wood and petroleum products. Olathe is the site of Mid-America Nazarene College (1966), the Kansas School for the Deaf (1866), and a historical museum. The name of the community, established along the Santa Fe Trail in 1857, is derived from a Shawnee Indian term believed to mean "beautiful." Pop. (1970) 17,917; (1980) 37,258.

OLBERS, Heinrich Wilhelm Matthäus (1758-1840), German physician and astronomer, born in Abergen (now part of Bremen), West Germany. He was educated at the University of Göttingen and practiced medicine at Bremen. In 1779 he devised a method, still employed by astronomers, for calculating the orbits of comets. In 1815 he discovered a comet that was named after him. In 1781 he identified Uranus as a planet rather than as a comet, as had previously been assumed. Olbers discovered the asteroids Pallas in 1802 and Vesta in 1807. He also first proposed the hypothesis, later called Olbers' hypothesis, that all asteroids are fragments of a shattered planet that formerly revolved around the sun.

OLD AGE. *See* AGING; GERIATRICS; GERONTOLOGY.

OLD-AGE PENSIONS, provision of annuities for the aged. Old-age pensions, granted by a government to its employees, first appeared in France in the early 19th century and in Great Britain in 1834, and were instituted in newly unified Germany in 1873. The establishment of pensions spread to many other European countries in the first decade of the 20th century.

In the U.S. the railroads remained until 1913 the only important employer group to provide old-age pensions for their employees. Today three principal sources of old-age pensions exist in the U.S. The most important is the social security system established by the Social Security Act of 1935. Under this law, employers and employees contribute to a government fund used to provide monthly allowances to employees past the age of 65; reduced benefits are available starting at the age of 62, or for widows at the age of 60. The second type of old-age pension is one provided directly by many employers, sometimes with the assistance of employee contributions, to people who have been employed by them for specified minimum periods of time; it includes pensions provided by both private employers and government agencies.

Third, the increasing tendency of trade unions to demand improved financial provision for retiring workers in their labor contracts has been important in the enrichment of these programs. Collectively bargained plans are often administered jointly by trustees selected by the employers and unions, implemented with funds contributed by the employers and administered by the unions or by a trustee.

It is often possible for retired employees to receive financial support from two or more sources. Almost all employees, including domestic workers, and the self-employed are now covered by social security. Special provisions in the federal tax laws permit self-employed persons to establish private pension plans, called Keogh accounts, for themselves and their employees, with tax advantages similar to those given to approved corporate pension plans. Other provisions allow individuals who are employed, and have—or are entitled to have—company pension plans, to also establish Individual Retirement Accounts (IRAs) with substantial tax advantages. A frequent supplement to old-age pensions is provided by the veterans' pensions issued to certain classes of war veterans.   A.Tr.

For further information on this topic, see the Bibliography in volume 28, section 307.

OLDCASTLE, Sir John (1377?–1417), titled Baron Cobham after his marriage to lady Joan Cobham in 1408, English leader of the Lollards (a dissident Christian sect) and religious martyr, born probably in Almeley, Herefordshire. In 1401, while serving in the campaign of King Henry IV to put down the Welsh rebel Owen Glendower, he became a close friend of Henry, prince of Wales, later Henry V, king of England. Oldcastle served in the House of Commons in 1404 and in the House of Lords after 1409. Meanwhile, in defiance of royal decrees, he joined the Lollards. In 1413, the year of Prince Henry's accession to the throne, Oldcastle was convicted and condemned to death as a heretic. Henry V granted his old friend a 40-day respite in the hope that he would recant. Oldcastle escaped from imprisonment in the Tower of London and early in 1414 led an abortive revolt of the Lollards against the throne. For almost four years thereafter he continued his Lollardian activities as a fugitive in Herefordshire. Captured on Dec. 14, 1417, Oldcastle was executed the same day by hanging and was burned on the scaffold.

OLD CATHOLICS, Christian denomination organized in Munich in 1871 by Roman Catholics who protested the dogma, proclaimed the previous year by Vatican Council I, of the personal infallibility of the pope in all *ex cathedra* pronouncements (*see* INFALLIBILITY). The Munich protest, by 44 professors under the leadership of the German theologians and historians Johann Joseph Ignaz von Döllinger and Johannes Friedrich (1836–1917), was directed against the binding authority of the Vatican Council. To this protest a number of professors at Bonn, Breslau (now Wrocław, Poland), Freiburg, and Giessen declared their adherence. At Cologne in 1873 the German theologian Joseph Hubert Reinkens (1821–96) was elected bishop of the Old Catholics in the ancient fashion, by "clergy and people," that is, by all the Old Catholic priests and by representatives of the Old Catholic congregations. He was consecrated at Rotterdam by the bishop of Deventer, the Netherlands, and acknowledged by the German states of Prussia, Baden, and Hesse. Döllinger refused to become involved in organized schism and eventually broke with the movement, but he never returned to the Roman Catholic church.

Old Catholics conduct church services in the vernacular. Priests are allowed to marry. Intercommunion with the Church of England was accomplished at a conference in Bonn in July 1931; the concordat was ratified later by the Vienna congress of the Old Catholic church and by the convocations of Canterbury and York of the Church of England. According to recent figures, the Old Catholics number fewer than 250,000. In the U.S. in the mid-1970s, approximately 97,000 were reported.

OLD CHURCH SLAVONIC LANGUAGE. *See* SLAVIC LANGUAGES.

OLDENBURG, city, NW West Germany, in Lower Saxony, on the Hunte R., near Bremen. The city is a road and railroad junction and is linked by inland waterways to the Ruhr R. Manufactures include farm machinery, processed food, and textiles. Among the places of interest in Oldenburg are Lamberti Church (1270) and the Landes-

Old English sheepdog   Evelyn M. Shafer

bibliotek, a library founded in 1792. A university is here.

First mentioned about 1108, Oldenburg was chartered as a town in 1345 and was the seat of the counts of Oldenburg until 1667, when control of the county passed to Denmark. From 1777 to 1918 the city was the residence of the dukes of Oldenburg, and from 1918 to 1945 it was the capital of the former state of Oldenburg. Pop. (1980 est.) 136,400.

OLDENBURG, Claes Thure (1929–   ), American sculptor, who was a pioneer of pop art (q.v.). He was born in Stockholm, where his father was a diplomat. Between 1960 and 1965, Oldenburg conducted a number of so-called happenings, typical of which was *Autobodys* (1964, Los Angeles), which involved automobiles, crowds of people, and quantities of ice cubes in a participational art event. The crudely painted props used in these events formed the basis of much of his later sculpture. In 1961 he opened a store in New York City and sold plastic replicas of hamburgers, sandwiches, sundaes, and other fast-food items. Later versions of these objects were constructed on a gigantic scale from vinyl stuffed with foam rubber. He continued to use similar soft materials, especially vinyl and canvas, in later sculptural series of objects such as bathroom fixtures, fans, and typewriters. These works, called soft sculptures, transform familiar everyday objects into sagging heaps; they are intended both as innovative sensual experiences and as commentary on the social import of the objects portrayed. Oldenburg has also worked in fiberglass and metal;

his huge metal *Geometric Mouse* exists in several versions, adorning plazas in Washington, D.C., Minneapolis, Minn., and Houston, Tex.

OLD ENGLISH. *See* ENGLISH LANGUAGE.

OLD ENGLISH SHEEPDOG, breed of medium-sized working dog used primarily for guarding herds of sheep or cattle. The breed is believed to have developed in western England in the 17th century. The dog can also be trained as a retriever and as a draft animal, and because of its even temper is a good companion for children. The male varies in height from about 53 to 64 cm (21 to 25 in) at the shoulder; the height of the female is somewhat less. The animal has a square-shaped skull, dark eyes, a tapering nose with a blunt end, medium-sized ears lying flat to the sides of the head, straight forelegs and muscular hind legs, and moves with a characteristic rolling gait. Many of the breed have no tail; some have tails that are between 4 to 5 cm (1.5 and 2 in) in length. The coat is profuse, usually either gray or bluish-gray and sometimes with white markings; it is occasionally so shaggy that it conceals the dog's eyes.

OLD GLORY. *See* FLAG OF THE UNITED STATES.

OLDHAM, borough, in the metropolitan county of Greater Manchester, NW England. The borough, enlarged in 1974, lies in a coal-mining region and contains part of Peak District National Park. It is a market and industrial center with a notable cotton-spinning industry. Other manufactures include textile machinery and aircraft parts. Pop. (1981) 219,817.

OLD NORSE LITERATURE. *See* ICELANDIC LITERATURE; NORWEGIAN LITERATURE.

OLDS, Ransom Eli (1864–1950), American automobile manufacturer, born in Geneva, Ohio. A mechanic, Olds began to experiment with horseless carriages in the 1880s. In 1885 he built a successful steam-propelled three-wheeled vehicle. Ten years later he constructed a four-wheeled automobile powered by a gasoline engine. In 1897 he founded the Olds Motor Works, the first automobile factory and the first to use an assembly line. About 12,000 Oldsmobiles were produced between 1902 and 1904, when Olds sold his interest in the company. From 1904 to 1924 Olds was president, and from 1924 to 1936 chairman of the board, of the Reo Motor Car Co. This company produced the Reo, a popular automobile of the 1920s.

OLD SAYBROOK, town, Middlesex Co., S Connecticut, on Long Island Sound, at the mouth of the Connecticut R.; inc. 1854. It is primarily a residential community and a summer resort and has some manufacturing firms. A Dutch trading post was built on the site of the town in 1623, and

Saybrook, the first permanent community in the area, was established in 1635 by a group of English settlers under the leadership of the colonial governor John Winthrop (1606–76). The Collegiate School of America, from which Yale University developed, was founded here in 1701, and in 1775 the American inventor David Bushnell built a submarine here that was used during the American Revolution. Saybrook (now Deep River) and Old Saybrook were separated in 1852. Pop. (1970) 8468; (1980) 9287.

OLD TESTAMENT. *See* BIBLE.

OLDUVAI GORGE, ravine and archaeological site, N Tanzania, in the E Serengeti Plain. It is a steep-sided gorge, about 50 km (about 30 mi) long and nearly 91 m (nearly 300 ft) deep. The gorge was created by earthquake activity, and the deposits exposed in its walls were formed in an ancient lake bed and are more than 2 million years old. Major finds of stone tools, building sites, and bones of early hominids were excavated here by Louis S. B. Leakey, Mary Leakey, and others.

OLD VIC THEATRE, theater in London. Called the Royal Coburg Theatre when it opened in 1818, it was for many years a popular site for the production of melodrama, the most widely performed theatrical fare of the 19th century. In 1833 it was renamed the Royal Victoria Theatre. In 1880 the building was bought by the British social reformer Emma Cons (1838–1912) for the presentation of lectures, concerts, and other offerings for the moral and spiritual enlightenment of the neighborhood. It was then known as the Royal Victorian Music Hall, and later, popularly, as the Old Vic. In 1898 Cons was joined in the management of the music hall by her niece, Lilian Mary Baylis (1874–1937).

In 1914, under Baylis's management, the theater was organized as a nonprofit institution, devoted to the production in repertory of Shakespeare's plays and of opera performed in the English language. By 1923 the Old Vic had produced all of Shakespeare's plays, the first theater in the world to accomplish this feat. From 1946 to 1951 the Old Vic Theatre School, connected with the Old Vic Theatre, flourished under the French director Michel Saint-Denis (1897–   ). The Old Vic Theatre building itself, severely damaged by bombs during World War II, was rebuilt and reopened in 1950. The repertory company appeared from 1946 to 1963, performing in many countries of the world and including many leading actors of the British theater.

In 1943 the Old Vic sent a company to perform at the Theatre Royal in Bristol, England. In 1946 the Bristol Old Vic was established as a permanent repertory company. The National Theatre of Great Britain took over the London Old Vic in 1963, and the Bristol group continued as a separate organization, subsidized by the arts council of Great Britain. The Bristol Old Vic maintained a theater school and a repertory company. In 1970 the National Theater created the experimental Young Vic Theatre; housed in its own London theater, the Young Vic soon became independent. When the National Theatre moved into its own headquarters in 1976, the Old Vic Theatre was closed. It was refurbished and reopened late in 1983.

OLEANDER, species of plants of the family Apocynaceae (*see* DOGBANE). The species are evergreen shrubs with leathery leaves, which are opposite or in threes; the flowers are in terminal branching cymes. The common oleander, *Nerium oleander,* known also as rose laurel, is a native of the Mediterranean region; it has exceedingly poisonous sap.

OLIBANUM. *See* FRANKINCENSE.

OLIGARCHY, in political philosophy, form of government in which the supreme power is vested in a few persons. Political writers of ancient Greece used the term to designate the debased form of an aristocracy, or government by the best citizens. In an oligarchy, the government is controlled by a faction that acts in its own interests to the exclusion of the welfare of the people it is governing.

OLIGOCENE EPOCH, third division of the Tertiary period of the Cenozoic era (qq.v.), spanning an interval from about 40 to 25 million years ago. Like the Eocene epoch, which preceded it, and the Miocene, which followed, the Oligocene (Gr., "little life") was originally defined by the percentage of modern species of shellfish (10–15 percent) found in strata of this age.

Geology. Collisions between the plates of the earth's crust continued unabated from Eocene time (*see* PLATE TECTONICS). In the eastern hemisphere, the Afro-Arabian and Indian remnants of the former supercontinent Gondwanaland, colliding with Eurasia to the north, pinched shut the eastern end of the Tethys Sea, leaving in its place a much shrunken remnant—the Mediterranean. Compressional forces generated by the collision helped to push up an extensive system of mountain ranges, from the Alps in the west to the Himalaya in the east. Meanwhile the Australian plate collided with the Indonesian, and the North American plate had begun to override the Pacific. As a result, the seafloor-spreading process originating at the East Pacific Ridge was diverted to a direction perpendicular to the ridge axis. A great transform fault—the earthquake-producing San Andreas Fault of California—developed to accommodate this shift in motion between the plates. Other effects of the collision included creation of the Basin and Range structure of the southwestern U.S., the continued uplift of the Sierra Navada, and the outpouring of massive basalt flows that built up the Columbia Plateau. The climate remained subtropical and moist throughout North America and Europe, but a gradual, long-term cooling trend had begun that was eventually to culminate in the Pleistocene ice ages.

Life. Mammals were firmly established in the Oligocene as the dominant form of terrestrial life. The horse, a native of North America, continued to evolve there. Three groups of rhinoceroses inhabited both the Old World and the New World; one, now extinct, included *Baluchitherium,* 5.5 m (18 ft) high and 7.6 m (25 ft) long—the largest land mammal of any age. Rhinoceroslike titanotheres, another extinct mammalian tribe, included *Brontotherium,* North America's largest land animal of that time, which stood 2.4 m (8 ft) high at the shoulder. Chalicotheres, which made up still another tribe, were characterized by a horselike skull, a camellike body, and long, narrow claws.

Oligocene camels, which were then the size of sheep, became extinct in North America, but some migrated to South America with the peccaries and tapirs. Meanwhile vast herds of oreodons (piglike cousins of the camel) grazed across the plains of North America, as did the enteledonts (even-toed, giant "pigs") that were also native to that continent; both groups became extinct in the Miocene. The first elephants—short, semiaquatic forms lacking either tusks or trunk—gave rise, in Africa, to the mastodons, which were as yet only a little more than 1.5 m (5 ft) high. Creodonts had by then diverged to form the dogs and cats; the latter comprised two groups, from one of which the saber-toothed cats developed (*see* SABER-TOOTHED TIGER). Rodents were well represented by this time, and primates included the tarsiers and lemurs. Finally, Oligocene strata have yielded bones of the first Old World monkeys, as well as a single species of great ape.

OLINDA, city and port, E Brazil, in Pernambuco State, on the Atlantic Ocean, near Recife. A leading beach resort and art center in an area of sugar plantations, the city has sugar-processing and cigar- and textile-manufacturing industries.

Olinda, long the most important city in N Brazil, was prominent in early colonial history, traces of which are found in the old churches and buildings. The monasteries of São Francisco and São Bento have art collections, and the regional museum, state museum, and sugar museum are of interest. Also in the city are the fort of São Francisco, called the Cheese Fort; the Prefeitura, or government house of the captains general; and the Joaquim Nabuco Institute. Founded in 1535, Olinda was the capital of a Portuguese colonial captaincy until it was succeeded by Recife; from 1630 to 1654 it was under Dutch rule. Pop. (1980 prelim.) 266,392.

OLIVE, common name of the order Oleales, comprising a small group of woody flowering plants, of almost cosmopolitan distribution, that contains several plants of horticultural and economic importance; and of its representative genus, *Olea.* The order contains about 600 species, placed in the single family Oleaceae. In addition to the olive, familiar members of the order include ash (q.v.), *Fraxinus;* lilac (q.v.), *Syringa;* privet (q.v.), *Ligustrum;* jasmine (q.v.), *Jasminum;* *Forsythia* (q.v.); and the fringe tree, *Chionanthus.*

Most members of this order of dicots (q.v.) are shrubs or small trees, although a few are climbers. Nearly all have opposite leaves, which may be simple, as in lilacs and forsythias, or compound (composed of several separate leaflets), as in ashes. Flower structure is rather uniform in the order, but some variation occurs. Typically, flowers have four sepals (outer floral whorls) and four petals (inner floral whorls), two stamens (male flower parts) attached to the inner surface of the petals, and a single ovary (female flower part), which is superior (borne above and free from other flower parts). The fruits, which develop from the ovary after fertilization, vary considerably but usually contain a single seed. Examples of distinctive fruits include those of the olive, which are technically drupes (hard seeds surrounded by fleshy material); those of the ashes, which are indehiscent (remain closed at maturity) and winged and are technically known as samaras; and those of the lilacs, which are dry and dehiscent (splitting at maturity).

The olive genus, *Olea,* contains about 20 species and is widespread in the Old World. A few species produce good timber, for example, the black ironwood, *O. laurifolia,* of southern Africa. The cultivated olive is *O. europaea,* originally native to the eastern Mediterranean region but now widely cultivated throughout that area and in other parts of the world that have Mediterranean-type climates. The olive is cultivated for its fruits, which yield an edible oil and are also pickled for eating. Olive oil, which is derived from fresh, ripe fruits that contain about 20 percent oil, is used in cooking, in canning, and as a table oil. Olives for eating are picked either when un-

Groves of olives in Andalusia, northern Spain, where the warm climate favors their cultivation. Olive oil is a leading export commodity of Spain.   Luis Villota

ripe or when ripe. Unripe olives are green and remain so during pickling; ripe olives are dark bluish when fresh and turn blackish during pickling. The seed, or stone, of the olive is often removed and the cavity stuffed with spicy materials such as sweet red pepper. The wood of the cultivated olive, being hard and variegated, is valued in cabinetry.   M.R.C.

OLIVER, King, real name JOSEPH OLIVER (1885–1938), American cornetist, the earliest indisputably major jazz figure, and the single greatest influence on the jazz trumpeter Louis Armstrong. Born near Abend, La., Oliver formed the Creole Jazz Band in New Orleans, taking them to Chicago in 1918. Armstrong joined the group four years later. In 1923 the group made recordings that are now regarded as the greatest examples of the early New Orleans jazz style. From 1924 Oliver led the Dixie Syncopators. He went to New York City in 1928; thereafter his fortunes declined, and he died in obscurity.

OLIVES, MOUNT OF, also Mt. Olivet, limestone ridge, E of Jerusalem, in an area occupied by Israel in 1967. The ridge, reaching about 823 m (about 2700 ft) at its highest point, is separated from Jerusalem only by the narrow Kidron Valley. Its familiar name is derived from a grove of olive trees that stood on its W flank. The ridge has

three summits. The northernmost is often called Mt. Scopus; it is the site of the Hebrew University of Jerusalem (1918). On the central summit is a village that was once called Olivet and is now named at-Tur (Arab., "the mount"). Around this central summit, generally regarded as the Mt. of Olives proper, many events of Christian history took place. At the top stands a Muslim chapel, on the supposed site of the Ascension of Jesus Christ, as described in Acts 1:2–12. On the slope is the site at which, according to tradition, Jesus wept over Jerusalem (see Luke 19:41–44) during his triumphal entry into the city. High on the slope are a Carmelite church and convent near the site of a church built by St. Helena.

OLIVIER, Laurence Kerr, 1st Baron Olivier of Brighton (1907–   ), English actor, producer, and director, acclaimed as one of the most accomplished of 20th-century actors.

Olivier was born in Dorking, Surrey, on May 22, 1907. Nine years later he made his first stage appearances in amateur performances of plays by Shakespeare. He made his professional debut at Letchworth in 1925. He was a member of the Birmingham Repertory Co. from 1926 to 1928. Olivier made his American theatrical debut in a short-lived melodrama in New York City in 1929. In 1930 and 1931 he appeared in Noel Coward's

Private Lives, in both London and New York City. In 1937 and 1938 he was a member of the Old Vic Shakespearean repertory company in London. Olivier was codirector of the Old Vic company from 1944 to 1949; in 1946 he appeared triumphantly with the company in America. In the theater Olivier played classical roles ranging from Greek tragedy to Restoration comedy, and he also appeared in a wide variety of roles in contemporary plays.

In 1938 he made his first important film, *Wuthering Heights.* In 1946 a film version of Shakespeare's *Henry V* was released; produced, directed by, and starring Olivier, it became a major film classic. He produced, directed, and starred in film versions of Shakespeare's *Hamlet* (1948), for which he received an Academy Award as best actor of the year, and *Richard III* (1956), and he performed the title role in a film version of *Othello* (1966). Among the other films in which he appeared in an astonishing variety of roles are *Rebecca* (1940), *The Entertainer* (1960), *Sleuth* (1972), *Marathon Man* (1976), and *The Boys from Brazil* (1978)—for the last three he received Oscar nominations. He also appeared in the television film *Wagner* in 1982.

A theatrical producer and director as well as actor, Olivier was head of the National Theatre of Great Britain from 1962 until 1973. He was knighted in 1947 and created Baron Olivier in 1970. His marriage to the actor Vivien Leigh (1913–67) ended in divorce. He is married to actor Joan Plowright (1929–   ).

OLIVINE, mineral, magnesium and iron silicate, $(Mg,Fe)_2SiO_4$. It crystallizes in the orthorhombic system (*see* CRYSTAL) and usually occurs in the form of granular masses. The color ranges from olive green or grayish-green to brown. Olivine has a hardness (q.v.) of 6.5 and a sp.gr. from 3 to 4. It exhibits conchoidal fracture, has a glassy luster, and is transparent or translucent. Found principally in ferromanganese igneous rocks, such as basalt and peridotite, it occurs in the lavas of Mount Vesuvius, near Naples, Italy, and in Norway, Germany, and Arizona. A rock called dunite is composed almost entirely of olivine. A transparent, green variety of olivine, called peridot, and a greenish-yellow variety, called chrysolite, are used to some extent as gemstones.

OLMSTED, Frederick Law (1822–1903), major American landscape architect, born in Hartford, Conn., and educated at Yale University. He traveled throughout Europe and the southern U.S., studying landscape gardening and agricultural methods. In 1857 he was appointed superintendent of Central Park in New York City, the first great metropolitan park in the U.S. In collaboration with the American architect Calvert Vaux (1824–95) he drew new plans for the park, which had a pervasive influence on park design

Costumed in faithful reproduction of medieval garb, Sir Laurence Olivier played the title role in the film version (1956) of Shakespeare's Richard III, which the actor also produced and directed.
Janus Films

throughout the U.S. and Canada. Subsequently, he planned a large number of city parks, including Morningside, Prospect, and Riverside parks, New York City; Jackson and Washington parks, Chicago; and the grounds of the Capitol, Washington, D.C. He was the first commissioner of Yosemite National Park, California. Olmsted was one of the first landscape architects in America to preserve the natural features of the terrain and to add naturalistic elements when needed. His experiences are recounted in *Forty Years of Landscape Architecture: Central Park* (1928), edited by F. L. Olmsted, Jr., and T. Kimball. *See* LANDSCAPE ARCHITECTURE.

OLMÜTZ. *See* OLOMOUC.

OLOMOUC, city, central Czechoslovakia, in Severomoravský Region, on the Morava R., near Brno. The trade and industrial center of the fertile Hana Region specializing in dairying and barley, the city has ironworks and steelworks, breweries, and saltworks; products include smoked meats, malt, sugar, chocolate, candy, cement, and machinery. It is a historic Moravian city and contains the Palacký University (1576), the 12th-century Saint Wenceslaus Cathedral, a 13th-century town hall, an archbishop's palace, and other baroque buildings of the 16th and 17th centuries. Founded in 1050, Olomouc was a joint capital of Moravia with Brno until 1640 and alternated after that. In 1242 the Mongols were defeated here, and the city was devastated by the Swedes in 1642. Important treaties effecting European boundary changes were signed in Olomouc in 1478 and 1850. While under Austrian rule, in the 19th century, it was called Olmütz. Pop. (1980 est.) 102,418.

OLSZTYN, city, N Poland, capital of Olsztyn Province, on the Łyna R. An important railroad and industrial center, the city has a large trade in livestock, grain, and leather; it has plants engaged in sawmilling, papermaking, and the production of stoves. Olsztyn was founded about the middle of the 14th century. With the surrounding region, it became a Polish possession in 1466 and passed to Prussian sovereignty in 1772. The city subsequently became part of the Prussian province of East Prussia and was known by its German name of Allenstein. Following World War II it was transferred to Polish control under the provisions of the Potsdam Conference. Pop. (1981 est.) 133,300.

OLYMPIA, ancient site of the Olympian Games (q.v.), which were celebrated every four years by the Greeks. Olympia was situated in a valley in Elis, in western Peloponnesus, through which runs the Alpheus River. It was not a town, but only a sanctuary with buildings associated with games and the worship of the gods. Olympia was a national shrine of the Greeks and contained many treasures of Greek art, such as temples, monuments, altars, theaters, statues, and votive offerings of brass and marble. The Altis, or sacred precinct, enclosed a level space about 200 m (about 660 ft) long by nearly 177 m (nearly 580 ft) broad. In this space were the chief centers of religious worship, the votive buildings, and the buildings associated with the administration of the games.

The most celebrated temple was the Olympieum, dedicated to Olympian Zeus, father of the gods. In this temple was a colossal statue of Zeus made of ivory and gold, the masterpiece of the Athenian sculptor Phidias. Next to the Olympieum ranked the Heraeum, dedicated to Hera, the wife of Zeus. In this temple, probably the oldest Doric building known, stood the table on which were placed the garlands prepared for the victors in the games. The votive buildings included a row of 12 treasure houses and the Philippeum, a circular Ionic building dedicated by Philip II, king of Macedonia, to himself. Outside the Altis, to the east, were the Stadium and the Hippodrome, where the contests took place; on the west were the Palaestra, or wrestling school, and the Gymnasium, where all competitors were obliged to train for at least one month. Explorations conducted from 1875 to 1881, under the auspices of the German government, threw much light upon the plans of the buildings. Many valuable objects were discovered, the most important of which was a statue of Hermes, the messenger of the gods, by Praxiteles.

OLYMPIA, city, capital of Washington State and seat of Thurston Co., a port on Budd Inlet of Puget Sound at the mouth of the Deschutes R., in the W part of the state; inc. 1859. It is a commercial, manufacturing, and shipping center. Major manufactures include wood products, processed food, metal and paper containers, and mobile homes. State and local government activities; tourism; fishing, especially for the famous Olympia oyster; and the Fort Lewis Military Reservation are also important to the city's economy, as is a large brewery in nearby Tumwater. Points of interest in Olympia include the State Capitol Museum, with collections of Indian artifacts, natural-history items, and fine art; Sylvester House (1856), the home of one of the area's first settlers; and the Capitol Group, built between 1911 and 1935, containing the Legislative Building, the Temple of Justice, and four additional government structures overlooking the harbor. Mount Rainier and Olympic national parks are nearby. Evergreen State College (1967), St. Mar-

A view of the handsome capitol building, which was completed in 1935, in Olympia, Wash. Located on an arm of Puget Sound, the city is an important seaport.

Shostal Associates

tin's College (1895), and a junior college are in the area.

Located in a region long inhabited by Nisqually Indians, the community was settled by non-Indians in the late 1840s and called Smithfield. It was laid out about 1850 and renamed Olympia, for the scenic Olympic Mts. that can be viewed from the site. It was made the capital of Washington Territory in 1853 and became the state capital when Washington entered the union in 1889. A branch of the Northern Pacific Railroad reached here in the 1880s. Pop. (1970) 23,296; (1980) 27,447.

OLYMPIAD, in Greek chronology, interval of four years between two successive celebrations of the Olympian Games (q.v.). The use of Olympiads as a convenient system of chronological reckoning appears chiefly in literature, beginning about 300 BC in the writings of the Greek historian Timaeus (c. 356–c. 260 BC). Although the Olympian Games were celebrated in much earlier times, the first Olympiad dates from 776 BC, the year in which the first official list of victors was kept.

OLYMPIAN GAMES, most famous of the four great national festivals of the ancient Greeks, the other three being the Isthmian, Pythian, and Nemean games (*see* GAMES, ANCIENT). The Olympian Games were celebrated in the summer every four years in the sanctuary of Zeus at Olympia. The history of the games dates from 776 BC.

Early in the year of the games, envoys were sent throughout the Greek world to invite the city-states to join in paying tribute to Zeus. The city-states thereupon dispatched deputations to vie with one another in the splendor of their equipment and the proficiency of their athletic feats. The competitions were open only to honorable men of Greek descent.

The order of the events is not precisely known, but the first day of the festival was devoted to sacrifices. The second day began, in all probability, with footraces, for which the spectators gathered in the *stadion,* an oblong area enclosed by sloping banks of earth. On other days wrestling, boxing, and the pancratium, a combination of the two, were held. In the first of these sports the object was to throw the antagonist to the ground three times. Boxing became more and more brutal; at first the pugilists wound straps of soft leather over their fingers as a means of deaden-

365

ing the blows, but in later times hard leather, sometimes weighted with metal, was used. In the pancratium, the most rigorous of the sports, the contest continued until one or the other of the participants acknowledged defeat.

Horse racing, in which each entrant owned his horse, was confined to the wealthy but was nevertheless a popular attraction. After the horse racing came the series of five events known as the pentathlon: sprinting, long jumping, javelin hurling, discus throwing, and wrestling. The exact sequence of the events in this competition, and the method employed to determine the winner, are, however, unknown. The discus was a plate of bronze, probably lens shaped; the javelin was hurled with the aid of a strap, wound about the shaft, thereby producing a rotary motion that secured greater distance and accuracy. The jumping event was always judged for distance, not for height. The last event of the Olympian Games was frequently a race run in armor. On the last day of the festival the victors were awarded crowns of wild olive. Celebrated by poets, they often lived for the remainder of their lives at public expense.

The Olympian Games reached their highest development during the 5th and 4th centuries BC but continued until AD 394, when they were finally suppressed by the Roman emperor Theodosius I. For an account of the modern games, *see* OLYMPIC GAMES.

For further information on this topic, see the Bibliography in volume 28, section 790.

OLYMPIC GAMES, international athletic competition, held every four years at a different site and restricted to amateurs. A modified revival of the Olympian Games (q.v.), one of the great festivals of ancient Greece, the Olympic Games were inaugurated, in 1896, largely as a result of the efforts of the French sportsman and educator Baron Pierre de Coubertin (1863–1937). In 1894, with the help of a few individuals, he succeeded in establishing the International Olympic Committee (IOC). This committee enlisted the aid of sports organizations and individuals of various countries, chiefly European at first. It also drafted plans and policy for the projected games, and selected Athens as an appropriate site of the first Olympic Games. A basic feature of Olympic policy has been that amateur athletes of all nations are eligible to participate.

Organization. The IOC maintains headquarters in Lausanne, Switzerland, and currently recognizes 150 national Olympic committees, such as the U.S. Olympic Committee (USOC), founded in 1900 and with headquarters in Colorado Springs, Colo. The site at which the Olympic

Games are to take place is chosen, usually six years in advance, by the IOC. The 1988 games are scheduled to be held in Seoul, South Korea.

History. The first modern games, held in April 1896, attracted athletes from the U.S., Great Britain, and 11 other nations. Only 42 events in 9 sports were scheduled for these games.

The second Olympic Games (1900) took place in Paris. Saint Louis, Mo., was the site of the games in 1904. (A special Olympic competition, not of the regular cycle, was held in Athens in 1906.) Subsequent sites were London (1908), Stockholm (1912), Antwerp (1920), Paris (1924), Amsterdam (1928), Los Angeles (1932), Berlin (1936), London (1948), Helsinki (1952), Melbourne (1956), Rome (1960), Tokyo (1964), and Mexico City (1968). The Olympic Games scheduled for Berlin in 1916 were canceled because of World War I, and those scheduled for 1940 and 1944 were canceled because of World War II.

Political contentions have increasingly interfered with an avowed aim of the modern Olympics, that of fostering international amity. In the 1936 Berlin Olympics Hitler refused to recognize the achievements of Jesse Owens, a black American who won four gold medals. The 1972 games, held in Munich, West Germany, were marked by a tragedy growing out of political conditions in the Middle East. Members of an Arab guerrilla organization killed two Israeli athletes and took nine hostages, who were later killed, along with five of the guerrillas and a West German policeman, in a gun battle with police at a Munich airport. Olympic activities were suspended for a day to hold memorial services for the murdered Israeli athletes. The 1976 games, held in Montréal, Canada, were also marred by political issues. One involved the athletes of Taiwan. The host Canadian government refused to allow this team to carry its flag or have its national anthem played at the games. The Taiwanese thereupon withdrew. A second political issue involved most of the black African nations. They demanded that New Zealand be excluded from the Olympics because one of its rugby teams had recently played in South Africa, whose racial policies these black African nations opposed. When their demand was refused, 31 nations withdrew their teams from the competition.

The U.S., after much debate, withdrew from the 1980 Olympics held in Moscow, in protest of the Soviet invasion of Afghanistan. About 64 other nations also boycotted the games. The USSR, citing doubts about planned security measures, withdrew from the 1984 games in Los Angeles; 15 other nations followed suit.

Following the games of 1904, which had little

A view from the upper balcony of the Olympic Stadium in Montréal, Canada, during opening ceremonies for the 1976 Olympic Games. Wide World Photos

international significance because the contestants were mainly from the U.S., more and more nations have entered teams in the Olympic Games. The total number of participating athletes has also grown greatly, from the 285 who competed at Athens in 1896 to approximately 7800 who competed in Los Angeles in 1984. A similar development has marked the competitive struggle in many countries among qualified athletes for membership on the Olympic teams. The Olympic tryouts, elimination games conducted for aspirants quadrennially under the auspices of the various national Olympic committees, are increasingly important occasions in the realm of amateur athletics.

Later Developments. Since the first Olympic Games of the modern cycle several significant developments have occurred. One major feature has been the marked increase of Olympic competition among women, notably since 1924. Second, the number of sports and events open to competition at the Olympic Games has increased steadily. Excluding the sports competitions of the Winter Olympics (q.v.), the number of sports at the 1984 Olympics totaled 24: archery, basketball, boxing, canoeing-kayaking, cycling, diving, equestrian sports, fencing, field hockey, gymnastics, judo, modern pentathlon (riding, cross-country running, swimming, shoot-

ing, and fencing), rowing, shooting, soccer, swimming, synchronized swimming, team handball, track and field, volleyball, water polo, weightlifting, wrestling, and yachting. A third development has been the progressively superior performance by successive generations of Olympic athletes.

Olympic Ceremonial. An elaborate ceremony traditionally opens the Olympic Games. The athletes parade into the stadium, always led by the Greek team in honor of the founding of the Olympic Games, and with the host nation bringing up the rear. The Olympic Hymn is then played and the official Olympic flag (five interlocking rings on a white background) is raised. A runner then enters the stadium bearing the Olympic torch, lit by rays of the sun at Olympia, Greece, and carried to the present site by a relay of runners. The ceremony closes with release of doves into flight, symbolizing the spirit of the games.

Scoring. Olympic Games scores are computed according to one of two systems. In the point system of scoring, 10 points are credited for first place in the various events, 5 points for second place, 4 points for third place, 3 points for fourth place, 2 points for fifth place, and 1 point for sixth place. This system has been criticized as favoring populous nations entering teams in a

SUMMER OLYMPIC GAMES OF 1984
Medals Won by Competing Nations

Country	Gold (1st)	Silver (2d)	Bronze (3d)	Total
U.S.	83	61	30	174
West Germany	17	19	23	59
Romania	20	16	17	53
Canada	10	18	16	44
Great Britain	5	10	22	37
China	15	8	9	32
Italy	14	6	12	32
Japan	10	8	14	32
France	5	7	15	27
Australia	4	8	12	24
South Korea	6	6	7	19
Sweden	2	11	6	19
Yugoslavia	7	4	7	18
Netherlands	5	2	6	13
Finland	4	3	6	13
New Zealand	8	1	2	11
Brazil	1	5	2	8
Switzerland	0	4	4	8
Mexico	2	3	1	6
Denmark	0	3	3	6
Spain	1	2	2	5
Belgium	1	1	2	4
Austria	1	1	1	3
Portugal	1	0	2	3
Jamaica	0	1	2	3
Norway	0	1	2	3
Turkey	0	0	3	3
Venezuela	0	0	3	3
Morocco	2	0	0	2
Kenya	1	0	1	2
Greece	0	1	1	2
Nigeria	0	1	1	2
Puerto Rico	0	1	1	2
Algeria	0	0	2	2
Pakistan	1	0	0	1
Colombia	0	1	0	1
Egypt	0	1	0	1
Ireland	0	1	0	1
Ivory Coast	0	1	0	1
Peru	0	1	0	1
Syria	0	1	0	1
Thailand	0	1	0	1
Cameroon	0	0	1	1
Dominican Republic	0	0	1	1
Iceland	0	0	1	1
Taiwan	0	0	1	1
Zambia	0	0	1	1

large number of relatively obscure events. The other scoring system lists the number of medals won by each nation.

See individual articles on sports mentioned above. A.B.

For further information on this topic, see the Bibliography in volume 28, section 790.

OLYMPIC NATIONAL PARK, W Washington, established as a national park in 1938. The park, encompassing most of the Olympic Mts., is one of the finest remaining areas of virgin rain forest in the Pacific Northwest. A noncontiguous section of the park is an 80-km (50-mi) strip of rugged Pacific coast. Mt. Olympus (2424 m/7954 ft), the highest peak of the Olympic Mts., has 6 glaciers on its slopes; a total of about 60 active glaciers are found in the park. Annual precipitation in the region is among the heaviest in the U.S.; in the lower valleys and W slopes, where rainfall averages about 3600 mm (about 142 in) a year, are the noted rain forests, with giant Sitka spruce, dense undergrowths, and deep carpets of moss. At elevations from about 457 to 915 m (1500 to 3000 ft) are stands of Douglas fir, western hemlock, western red cedar, spruce, and pine. At higher altitudes the forests give way to alpine meadows. Wildlife in the park includes the Roosevelt elk, the black-tailed deer, mountain goat, cougar, black bear, and otter. Seal, sea lions, and numerous marine birds inhabit the coastal portion. The park was originally established as Mt. Olympus National Monument in 1909. Area, 3677.5 sq km (1419.9 sq mi).

OLYMPUS, MOUNT, mountain, N Greece, 2917 m (9570 ft) high, the loftiest point in Greece, on the boundary between Thessaly and Macedonia, near the Aegean Sea. In early Greek mythology it was believed to have been the home of the gods. On its summit were the palaces of the gods, which had been built by Hephaestus, god of metalwork. The entrance to Olympus was through a gate of clouds, protected by the goddesses known as the Seasons. Zeus had his throne on Olympus, and the gods feasted on nectar and ambrosia and were serenaded by the Muses.

The 12 major Olympian deities were Zeus and his wife Hera; his brothers Poseidon, god of the sea, and Hades, god of the underworld; his sister Hestia, goddess of the hearth; and his children, Athena, goddess of wisdom, Ares, god of war, Apollo, god of the sun, Artemis, goddess of the moon and of the hunt, Aphrodite, goddess of love, Hermes, messenger of the gods, and Hephaestus. Later Greek writers transferred the home of these deities to a heavenly region free from snow and storm and filled with light.

OLYNTHUS, city of ancient Greece, in Macedonia, on the Chalcidice Peninsula (now Khalkidikí), at the head of the Toronaic Gulf. Founded by the Chalcidians from Euboea, the city became prominent as the result of its leading role during the revolt of the Chalcidians against Athens in the late 5th century BC. For some time, Olynthus headed a powerful confederacy, called the Chalcidic League, but the city was subdued by Sparta in 379 BC and in 348 BC totally destroyed by King Philip II of Macedonia. The Olynthiac orations—three speeches delivered by the famous Greek orator Demosthenes when Philip seized the city—urged the Athenians to aid the citizens of Olynthus.

OMAGUA, South American Indian tribe of the Tupí-Guaraní linguistic family, living in northeastern Peru and western Brazil. Their economy is based on agriculture, hunting, and fishing. At the time of the Spanish conquest of South America in the 16th century, an erroneous report credited the Omagua with having rich stores of gold, and in 1536, 1541, and 1560 unsuccessful attempts were made by the Spanish to conquer their lands. In the 17th century Jesuit missionaries established 40 villages of Omagua converts along the Amazon River; they prospered despite frequent attacks by Portuguese slave hunters. After the expulsion of the Jesuits from the Spanish colonies in 1767 the mission settlements broke up, and the Omagua returned to their former way of life. By the 20th century, the Omagua had been absorbed into the mestizo population in Brazil, while by the turn of the century in Peru the tribe was nearly extinct.

OMAHA, city, seat of Douglas Co., E Nebraska, a port of entry on the Missouri R., opposite Council Bluffs, Iowa; inc. 1857. The largest city in Nebraska, Omaha is a commercial, manufacturing, and transportation center situated in a productive livestock-raising and grain-farming region. It is one of the world's largest livestock markets and meat-packing centers. Other manufactures include railroad and farm equipment, electrical and communications products, refined petroleum, chemicals, metal goods, and clothing. The city also has large insurance, banking, and printing and publishing industries.

Among the institutions of higher education in Omaha are the University of Nebraska at Omaha, Creighton University (1878), the University of Nebraska Medical Center (1869), the College of Saint Mary (1923), Grace College of the Bible (1943), and a community college. Major cultural institutions here are the Joslyn Art Museum; the Western Heritage Museum; the Henry Doorly Zoo, featuring rare and endangered species; and the Union Pacific Historical Museum. The College World Series of baseball is held here each year, and the city supports several performing-arts groups such as Opera/Omaha, the Omaha Ballet, and the Omaha Symphony. Boys Town, a home and school for disadvantaged boys, and Offutt Air Force Base, headquarters of the U.S. Strategic Air Command, are nearby.

The site of Omaha served as the winter quarters for Mormon migrants in 1846–47. The community, named for the Omaha Indians, was laid out in 1854. Its location, close to the geographical center of the U.S., soon made it an important transportation and trading center. The community developed as an outfitting point for overland wagon trains heading W, and its location at the E terminus of the Union Pacific Railroad (completed 1869) helped spur economic growth. Omaha served as the capital of the Nebraska Territory until 1867, when Nebraska became a state. In 1898 a world's fair, the Trans-Mississippi and International Exposition, was held in the city. Pop. (1970) 346,929; (1980) 313,911.

OMAHA INDIANS, North American Indian tribe of the Siouan branch of the Hokan-Siouan linguistic stock, closely related to the Kansa, Osage, Quapaw, and Ponca tribes. They formerly inhabited an extensive territory on the west side of the Missouri River, between the Platte and Niobrara rivers, within the present boundaries of Nebraska. The Omaha followed an economy based on the cultivation of corn and vegetables and the hunting of buffalo. Their dwellings were generally earth-covered lodges, but they also built bark lodges and carried skin tepees with them on their hunting expeditions. In 1802 the Omaha were greatly reduced in number by an epidemic of smallpox. Subsequently, they were even further reduced by incessant warfare with the Sioux, which was terminated through the intervention of the U.S. government. In 1854 the tribe ceded a large part of their territory to the U.S.; the remainder was retained as a reservation, part of which was later sold to the government as a reservation for the Winnebago tribe. In 1882 the Omaha were granted the right to hold land individually. Today the tribe has a total of about 1800 members.

OMAN, independent state, extending about 1610 km (about 1000 mi) along the SE coast of the Arabian Peninsula, bordered on the N by the Gulf of Oman, on the E and S by the Arabian Sea, on the SW by the People's Democratic Republic of Yemen, on the W by the Rub al-Khali (Empty Quarter) of Saudi Arabia, and on the NW by the United Arab Emirates. The country's territory also includes the N tip of the strategic Ras (cape) Musandam, which juts between the Persian Gulf and the Gulf of Oman; this portion is separated from the rest of the country by territory of the United Arab Emirates. The country's interior boundaries are undemarcated. Oman has an area of about 212,450 sq km (about 82,030 sq mi).

Land and Resources. Oman falls naturally into three physical divisions: a narrow coastal plain, ranges of mountains and hills, and an interior plateau. The coastal plain along the Gulf of Oman is known as al-Batinah and is the country's principal agricultural region. Inland from the plain lies al-Jabal al-Akhdar (Green Mts.), where some peaks reach elevations in excess of 3000 m (9843 ft). The coastal plain extending S along the Arabian Sea is largely barren, although some cultivation takes place in the Dhofar region of the extreme SW. The climate is generally hot and arid; however, the humidity along the coast is high. The average annual temperature is about 28.3° C (about 83° F). The average annual rainfall is generally less than 102 mm (less than 4 in). The principal natural resource is petroleum. Other

OMAN

OMAN
0 50 100 200 MI.
0 50 100 200 KM.
© HAMMOND INC., Maplewood, N. J.

A   52° Longitude East of Greenwich 56°   C   60° D

INDEX TO MAP OF OMAN

Cities and Towns

Adam	C 2
Bilad Manah	C 2
Buraymi, al-	B 1
Dank	B 2
Fujayrah, al-	C 1
Ibra	C 2
Ibri	B 2
Jawarah, al-	C 3
Kamil, al-	C 2
Khaluf	C 2
Khasab, al-	B 1
Masqat (cap.)	C 2
Matrah	C 2
Mina al-Fahl	C 2
Mirbat	B 3
Muscat (Masqat) (cap.)	C 2
Nazwa	C 2
Qurayyat	C 2
Raysut	B 3
Salalah	B 3
Sarur	C 2
Shinas	C 1
Suhar	C 1
Sur	C 2
Suwayq, as-	C 2

Other Features

Akhdar, al-Jabal al- (range)	C 2
Arabian (sea)	C 3
Batinah, al- (reg.)	C 1
Dhofar (reg.)	B 3
Hadd, Ras al- (cape)	C 2
Hallaniyah, al- (island)	C 3
Jibsh, Ras (cape)	C 2
Khuriya Muriya (Kuria Muria) (islands)	C 3
Kuria Muria (islands)	C 3
Madrakah, Ras al- (cape)	C 3
Masirah (gulf)	C 3
Masirah (island)	C 2
Musandam, Ras (cape)	B 1
Naws, Ras (cape)	B 3
Oman (gulf)	C 1
Oman (reg.)	C 2
Ruus al-Jibal (district)	C 1
Sawqirah (bay)	C 3
Sawqirah, Ras (cape)	C 3
Sham, Jabal (mt.)	C 2
Sharbatat, Ras ash- (cape)	C 3

known mineral resources include copper, asbestos, and marble.

Population. The total population of Oman (1981 UN est.) was 920,000. The overall population density was only about 4 persons per sq km (about 11 per sq mi). The capital is Masqat (Muscat); the adjacent town of Matrah is a leading port (combined pop., 1980 est., 25,000). The population is overwhelmingly Arab, but significant minorities of Indians, Pakistanis, and East Africans are found in the principal ports. The majority of the population is Ibadhi Muslim; Sunni

Muslims form the other major religious group. Arabic is the official language. It is estimated that more than half the population is nomadic. The national educational program expanded rapidly during the 1970s; in 1980 about 100,000 students attended some 372 schools.

Economy and Government. In the early 1980s estimated annual national budget figures showed $2.88 billion in revenue and $2.81 billion in expenditure. Agriculture is dominated by the cultivation of export crops, primarily dates and limes. Some grains and vegetables are grown for local consumption, but most food must be imported. In the early 1980s petroleum production totaled about 14 million metric tons annually. Reserves are relatively small, but new fields, notably in Dhofar, are being explored. A road-building program was undertaken in the 1970s, and most settlements are now linked by a network of graded roads. New port facilities were completed at Matrah in the 1970s; Mina al-Fahl is the leading oil terminal. The country's unit of currency is the rial Omani (0.345 RO equals U.S.$1; 1982).

Oman is ruled by a sultan, who is advised by an appointed cabinet. The country has no constitution, legislature, or political parties. The judicial system is based on Islamic law. A chief court and court of appeals are located in Masqat.

History. In ancient times the Dhofar region was famous for its incense, which was sold throughout the Old World. In the early 3d century AD an Arab chief from Hira in Mesopotamia founded a kingdom in Oman that retained its independence until the first caliphate. The Omanis accepted Islam in the 7th century and elected their first imam in 751. In the 10th century the Qarmatians conquered the country, and it was later occupied by the Seljuks.

The Portuguese in 1507 were the first Europeans to arrive. They subsequently captured Muscat (Masqat) but were contested by the British, the Dutch, and the Iranians. The Portuguese were driven out of Muscat in 1650, and in 1741 Imam Ahmed bin Said (d. 1783), founder of the present dynasty, expelled the Iranians. In 1861 the ruler took the title of sultan. Special relations with Great Britain were established in the late 19th century.

In 1913 rivalry between imam and sultan broke out in rebellion by inland tribes supporting the imam. Peace was restored in 1920 and lasted until 1954, when a succeeding imam began a new rebellion, aided by Egypt and Saudi Arabia. With British help, however, the sultan's forces put down the rebellion by 1959.

The ruling sultan, Said bin Taimur (1910–72), who acceded to the throne in 1932, was overthrown by his son, Qabus bin Said (1940–), in a palace coup in 1970. The new ruler liberalized the regime and increased spending on development. He changed the name of the country from Muscat and Oman to Oman to symbolize its unity, but was long plagued by a divisive guerrilla war by Marxist rebels in the Dhofar. Concerned about the country's safety after the Iranian revolution and the Soviet invasion of Afghanistan in 1979, and faced with growing Soviet influence in the area, the sultan in 1980 signed an agreement with the U.S. providing for military assistance in return for U.S. access to Omani bases. Defense agreements with neighboring Arab states were made in 1982.

OMAR KHAYYAM (d. 1122?), Persian mathematician, astronomer, and author of one of the world's best-known works of poetry. He was born in Nishapur (now in Iran); his name means Omar the Tentmaker. As astronomer to the royal court, he was engaged with several other scientists to reform the calendar; their work resulted in the adoption of a new era, called the Jalalian or the Seljuk. As a writer on algebra, geometry, and related subjects, Omar was one of the most notable mathematicians of his time. He is, however, most famous as the author of the *Rubáiyát*. About 1000 of these epigrammatic four-line stanzas, which reflect upon nature and humanity, are ascribed to him. The English poet and translator Edward FitzGerald was the first to introduce Omar to the West through a version (1859) of 100 of the quatrains. This version is a paraphrase, often very close, that despite its flowery rhymed verse captures the spirit of the original.

OMDURMAN, city, central Sudan, opposite Khartoum, near the junction of the White and Blue Nile rivers. It is a marketing center for the surrounding agricultural area with trade in cotton, grain, and handicrafts. In 1898 the forces of the political and religious leader Abd Allah (1846–99) were defeated decisively at Omdurman by Anglo-Egyptian troops. Pop. (est.) 299,400.

OMIYA, city, Japan, in Saitama Prefecture, S Honshu Island, near Tokyo. A rail junction on the Tohoku Line, the city is the trade center of an agricultural area producing rice, silk, and wheat and has workshops of the National Railways. It is the site of the Hikawa Shrine, founded in the 5th century BC. Omiya Park has sports facilities. Pop. (1980 prelim.) 354,082.

OMSK, city, capital of Omsk Oblast, Russian SFSR, in SW Siberian USSR, at the confluence of the Irtysh and Om rivers. The city is a major commercial and industrial center of the steppe region and is served by the Trans-Siberian Railroad.

Manufactures include processed grain, refined petroleum, forest products, agricultural machinery, and textiles. Omsk was founded in 1716 as a Russian fortress. Following the Russian Revolution of 1917, it was the headquarters of the forces of Adm. A. V. Kolchak, the anti-Bolshevik leader. Pop. (1980 est.) 1,028,000.

OÑATE, Juan de (c. 1550–c. 1630), Spanish-American explorer and administrator, founder of New Mexico (1598). Born in New Spain (now Mexico) he was related by marriage to Hernán Cortés and to the Aztec ruler Montezuma II. In 1595 he attained the governorship of New Mexico, an unexplored region. In 1598, with 400 settlers, he founded San Juan de los Caballeros, near present-day Santa Fe. He subsequently led two fruitless searches for gold, one as far as modern Kansas (1601) and the other to the Gulf of California (1605). Relieved as governor in 1609, Oñate later (1614) was convicted of misconduct in office.

ONCOLOGY. See CANCER.

ONEGA, LAKE, NW European USSR, in the Russian SFSR. After Lake Ladoga, which lies to the SW, it is the largest lake in Europe, about 97 km (about 60 mi) at its greatest breadth and about 240 km (150 mi) in length; its maximum depth is about 110 m (about 360 ft). It is about 1989 sq km (about 768 sq mi) in area. The lake is fed by numerous rivers but its only outlet is the river Svir, which flows into Lake Ladoga.

ONEIDA, North American Indian tribe belonging linguistically to the Iroquoian family and forming part of the Iroquois Confederacy. The name by which the tribe is known is a corruption of an Indian word meaning "standing rock" and referring to a boulder sacred to the tribe and situated near the site of their ancient village on Lake Oneida, N.Y. Their territory included the region surrounding the lake and later extended south to the Susquehanna River. The tribe was friendly toward the French colonists and Jesuit missionaries, although most members of the confederacy were hostile to the outsiders. During the American Revolution the Oneida sided with the colonists and were obliged to take refuge within the American settlements when their fellow tribes took the side of the British. After the war most of the Oneida returned to Canada and settled in the region of the Thames River, Ont., where their descendants still remain. Between 1820 and 1835, most of the Oneida who had returned to their homes in New York State sold their land and moved to a reservation near Green Bay, Wis. The Oneida number about 3500.

ONEIDA COMMUNITY, utopian society established at Oneida, N.Y., in 1848 and dissolved about 1880. The community was a religious and social experiment based on communistic principles. It was founded originally at Putney, Vt., by the American religious leader John Humphrey Noyes in the late 1830s. The members of the community, who were called Perfectionists, believed that freedom from sin could be obtained on earth by communion with God, followed by a renunciation of personal property and of binding personal relationships, including marriage.

After being expelled from Putney, where the group's practices had aroused opposition, the members settled at Oneida and established several successful manufacturing enterprises there. All properties, including farms and industries, were held in common; the community government was conducted by committees that met weekly in public sessions. Women had equal rights with men in the society. Cohabitation was permitted, but conception was directed, theoretically, by the community leaders, who attempted to impose eugenic principles in order to produce healthy and intelligent offspring. Children were reared by the community, which in many cases provided them with professional and technical training.

Because of outside antagonism to the system of "complex marriage," whereby all adults in the community were considered married to one another, the system was abandoned in 1879. Soon afterward, the members also abolished their communal property system, thus ending the utopian experiment. A joint-stock company, known as Oneida Community, Ltd., was formed to carry on the various manufacturing establishments, which had become profitable endeavors. The company still exists; but it has gradually narrowed its activities from the manufacture of steel traps and silk and the canning of fruits and vegetables to the manufacture of fine plated and sterling silverware, for which it is now known.

See also COMMUNAL LIVING; COOPERATIVES.

ONEIDA LAKE, lake, central New York, near Syracuse. It is about 35 km (about 22 mi) long and has a maximum width of 8 km (5 mi). The Oneida and Fish rivers are the chief affluents. A canal connects it with Lake Ontario on the N and with the New York State Barge Canal on the E.

O'NEILL, Eugene Gladstone (1888-1953), American dramatist, who is considered the most important writer in the American theater.

O'Neill was born in New York City, Oct. 16, 1888, the son of the Irish-American actor James O'Neill (1847-1920). He accompanied his father on theatrical tours during his youth, attended Princeton University for one year (1906-07), and worked subsequently as a clerk in New York City. From 1909 to 1912 he prospected for gold in Honduras, served as assistant manager of a theatrical troupe organized by his father, went to South America and South Africa as a seaman, toured as an actor with his father's troupe, and worked as a newspaper reporter in New London, Conn. Having contracted a mild case of tuberculosis, in 1912 he went to a sanatorium, where he wrote his first plays. After leaving the sanatorium, he studied (1914-15) the techniques of playwriting at Harvard University under the famous theater scholar George Pierce Baker.

During most of the next ten years O'Neill lived in Provincetown, Mass., and New York City, where he was associated both as a dramatist and as a manager with the Provincetown Players. This experimental theatrical group staged a number of his one-act plays, beginning with *Bound East for Cardiff* (1916), and several long plays, including *The Hairy Ape* (1922). *Beyond the Horizon* (1920; Pulitzer Prize, 1921), a domestic tragedy in three acts, was produced successfully on the Broadway stage, as was *The Emperor Jones* (1920), a study of the disintegration of the mind of a black dictator under the influence of fear. In the nine-act play *Strange Interlude* (1927; Pulitzer Prize, 1928) O'Neill sought to portray the way in which hidden psychological processes impinge upon outward actions. His most ambitious work, the trilogy *Mourning Becomes Electra* (1931), was an attempt to re-create the power and profundity of the ancient Greek tragedies by setting the themes and plot of the *Oresteia* by Aeschylus

Eugene O'Neill Random House

in 19th-century New England. *Ah, Wilderness* (1932), written in a relatively light vein, was highly successful.

O'Neill's other dramas include *Moon of the Caribbees* (1918), *Anna Christie* (1921; Pulitzer Prize, 1922), *All God's Chillun Got Wings* (1924), *Desire Under the Elms* (1924), *The Great God Brown* (1926), *Lazarus Laughed* (1926), *Marco Millions* (1928), *Dynamo* (1929), and *Days Without End* (1934).

From 1934 until his death O'Neill suffered from a crippling illness. During this entire period he worked intermittently on a long cycle of plays concerning the history of an American family but completed only *A Touch of the Poet* (produced 1958) and *More Stately Mansions* (U.S. production 1967). After 1939 he wrote three other plays unrelated to the cycle: *The Iceman Cometh* (1946), which portrays a group of social misfits unable to live without illusions, and two tragedies dealing with his family, *Long Day's Journey into Night* (produced 1956) and *A Moon for the Misbegotten* (produced 1957). O'Neill was awarded the 1936 Nobel Prize in literature. He died in Boston, on Nov. 27, 1953.

Many of O'Neill's dramas are marked by new theatrical techniques and symbolic devices that express religious and philosophical ideas and give his characters psychological depth. He employed the sound of tom-toms gradually increasing in volume to mark an increase in tension, masks to indicate shadings of personality, lengthy asides in which his characters voice their thoughts, and choruses used as in ancient Greek tragedies to comment on the play's action.

Throughout his career O'Neill attempted to grapple with fundamental human problems seriously and with integrity. His best works convey forcibly his vision of modern humans, victims of circumstances who cannot believe in God, destiny, or free will and who therefore blame impersonal causes for their misery and punish themselves for their own sin and guilt. Despite the seriousness and theatrical brilliance of many of O'Neill's plays, much of his symbolism is obscure, and his innovations in stagecraft often do not achieve the desired effects. In addition, the language of his characters has been criticized for lapses into banality or bathos at many of the most compelling moments of his plays. By bringing psychological realism, philosophical depth, and poetic symbolism into the American theater, however, O'Neill's work raised the standards of most later American dramatists.

For further information on this person, see the section Biographies in the Bibliography in volume 28.

O'NEILL, Hugh, 2d Earl of Tyrone (1540?-1616), Irish national hero. He succeeded as chieftain of the O'Neills in 1593 and having secured a pledge of support from Spain, raised an army to fight the English power in Ireland. His initial successes led to a truce with the English in 1599, but hostilities were soon renewed, and in 1601, as he was marching to meet the Spanish army that had landed in Ireland, he was defeated by an English force at Kinsale. In 1603, he was forced to make a formal submission. He was pardoned by James I, king of England, but in 1607, suspecting the English of duplicity, O'Neill fled to Rome, where he lived for the rest of his life.

O'NEILL, Peggy, also known as Margaret Eaton (1796-1879), wife of John Henry Eaton (1790-1856), secretary of war in the cabinet of U.S. President Andrew Jackson. She was originally named Margaret O'Neale, or O'Neill, the daughter of a Washington, D.C., tavernkeeper, and was noted for her beauty and wit. About 1823 she married a U.S. Navy purser named John B. Timberlake, who died in 1828, while on duty in the Mediterranean. In 1829 she married Eaton, who in the same year became secretary of war. Because of rumors regarding her relations with Eaton while she was still Mrs. Timberlake, Mrs. Eaton was ostracized by the wives of other cabinet members and by Washington society in general. President Jackson, an old friend of the Eatons, tried to break down the opposition to her, and it was partly for this reason that he replaced certain men in his cabinet. Among Mrs. Eaton's supporters was Martin Van Buren, who thereafter became more closely associated with Jackson; Van Buren was assured of the nomination for the presidency in 1836 in preference to the former vice-president John C. Calhoun, whose wife had opposed Mrs. Eaton. In later years, while her husband was minister to Spain, Mrs. Eaton became popular in the society of Madrid. Some time after the death of Eaton, she married an Italian dancing master, then about 20 years old, from whom she was subsequently divorced.

ONE-STEP. *See* Castle, Vernon and Irene; Fox-Trot.

ONION, common name applied to any biennial herb of the genus *Allium* of the family, Liliaceae (*see* Lily), especially *A. cepa,* native to Asia but cultivated in temperate and subtropical regions for thousands of years. The true onion is a bulb-bearing plant; its long, hollow leaves with thickened bases make up most of the bulb. The white or pink flowers, which are borne in umbels, have six sepals, six petals, six stamens, and a solitary pistil. In the varieties known as top onions, the flowers are supplanted by bulblets, that may be grown to obtain new plants. The plant contains sulfurous, volatile oils that give it a characteristic pungent taste; one component readily dissolves in water to produce sulfuric acid, which may be produced in the eyes and induce tears.

Onions are one of the most versatile vegetables. They are eaten raw in salads, are cooked or pickled in a variety of ways, and are used as a flavoring or seasoning. Dehydrated onion products provide popular flavorings for soups and stews.

Onions raised in warm areas are planted as winter crops and are milder in taste and odor than onions planted during the summer in cooler regions. Yellow Bermuda and white Spanish onions are among the mildest cultivated onions.

Onions are easily grown from seed that may be either field-grown directly or planted in beds to produce small bulbs, or sets. These are commonly dried, shipped, and planted by gardeners or commercial onion growers.

Onions are highly adaptable to temperature and can be planted at any time of the year as long as the soil is rich and moist. They are usually sown four to six weeks before the last frost in the spring or are planted in late summer for a fall crop.

The crop is allowed to ripen in the field until tops begin to bend and break. The bulbs are then

Wild onion, Allium cernuum

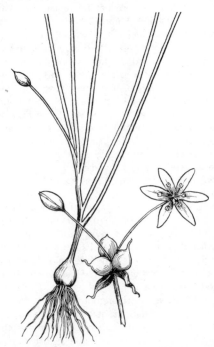

pulled up and spread or hung in a dry area to cure. Once dry, they are normally stored and shipped in slotted or open-mesh bags to keep them dry enough to prevent sprouting. U.S. production of onions in the early 1980s reached 1,450,000 metric tons a year.

Other plants in the genus *Allium* that are also called onions include the wild onion, *A. cernuum;* the shallot, *A. ascalonicum;* the chive, *A. schoenoprasum;* and the green onion, or common leek, *A. porrum.* Both the shallot and the green onion, which have small bulbs, are also known as scallions.

See also CROP FARMING; GARLIC.   W.D.P.

ONITSHA, city, SE Nigeria, in Anambra State, on the Niger R., near Enugu. Palm products, corn, nuts, vegetables, and fruits are traded here, and petroleum products, tires, bearings, and nails are manufactured; and the city is a source of mineral water. A teachers college for women and a leper colony are in Onitsha; the city is also the residence of the Obi of Onitsha, an Ibo leader. In 1966 it was connected to Asaba by the longest road bridge in the country. Pop. (est.) 220,000.

ONNES, Heike Kamerlingh. *See* KAMERLINGH ONNES, HEIKE.

ONONDAGA, North American Indian tribe belonging linguistically to the Iroquoian family and also to the Iroquois Confederacy. The territory they occupied centered about Onondaga Lake in central New York State and extended north to Lake Ontario and south to the Susquehanna River. Their principal village was called Onondaga or Onondaga Castle. This village served as the capital of the Iroquois Confederacy, and the Onondaga were the official guardians of the council fire of the league. The tribe ranked as the chief member of the confederacy. During the American Revolution the Onondaga sided with the British, and after the war most of the tribe immigrated to a reservation on the Grand River, in Canada, where their descendants still live. The rest of the tribe was placed on reservations in the region of their former territory in Onondaga Co., N.Y.

ONTARIO, city, San Bernardino Co., S California; inc. 1891. It is a residential, transportation, and industrial center. Among its diverse manufactures are citrus products, steel, electrical appliances, plastics, rubber items, aircraft equipment, and trucks. The city has an international airport that serves the E areas of metropolitan Los Angeles and a large motor speedway. The community was laid out in 1882 by brothers from Ontario, Canada, who developed it as an irrigated farming center. It was reached by railroad in 1887. Pop. (1970) 64,118; (1980) 88,820.

Vacationers at Recollet Falls on the French River in southeastern Ontario. Some 96.5 km (60 mi) long, the river was once part of the route taken by early fur traders making their way westward from the Ottawa River by canoe.

Annan Photo Services

ONTARIO, province of Canada, bordered on the N by Hudson Bay and James Bay, on the E by Québec Province, on the SE by New York, on the S by Lakes Ontario, Erie, Huron, and Superior and the state of Michigan, on the SW by Minnesota, and on the W by Manitoba. The Ottawa R. forms part of the E boundary, the Saint Lawrence and Niagara rivers part of the SE boundary, the Saint Mary's, Saint Clair, and Detroit rivers part of the S boundary, and the Rainy R. part of the SW boundary.

Ontario became part of the Canadian Confederation on July 1, 1867, as one of the four original provinces. It had previously been known as Upper Canada (1791–1841) and Canada West (1841–67). In the early 1980s Ontario had great manufacturing, mining, farming, financial, and tourist industries and played a leading role in the economy of Canada. The name of the province is derived from an Iroquois Indian term perhaps meaning "beautiful lake," a reference to Lake Ontario, or "rocks standing by the water," a reference to Niagara Falls. Ontario is sometimes called the Heartland Province.

LAND AND RESOURCES

Ontario is the second largest province in Canada; only Québec Province is larger. It covers 1,068,582 sq km (412,582 sq mi), of which 177,388 sq km (68,490 sq mi) are inland water surface. About 0.3% of the total area is owned by the federal government. The extreme dimensions of Ontario are about 1610 km (about 1000 mi) from E to W and about 1690 km (about 1050 mi) from N to S. The highest elevation in the province is 693 m (2275 ft), near Haileybury; the lowest elevation, sea level, occurs at James Bay and at Hudson Bay. Ontario has a shoreline of some 7600 km (some 4725 mi) along four of the five Great Lakes and of some 1210 km (some 752 mi) along Hudson and James bays.

Physical Geography. Ontario can be divided into four geographic regions that are of unequal size—the Canadian Shield, the Hudson Bay Lowland, the Great Lakes Lowland, and the St. Lawrence Lowland.

The Canadian Shield region covers about two-thirds of the province. It is underlain by ancient Precambrian igneous and metamorphic rocks, which are the source of most of the mineral wealth of Ontario. These rocks help form a monotonous landscape of flat plateaus and low, rounded hills, interrupted by numerous steep-sided river valleys and lake basins. Widespread deposits of glacial sand, gravel, and clay also help flatten the relief, such as in the fertile Clay Belt area around Hearst and Cochrane. The average elevation in the Canadian Shield region is about 305 m (about 1000 ft), but peaks reach above 660 m (2165 ft) in the rugged area N and E of Sault Ste. Marie. The region slopes gently to the N,

375

Toronto's lakefront area. Dominating the skyline is the CN Tower. In the foreground is Ontario Place, a recreation complex. Convention & Tourist Bureau of Metropolitan Toronto

where it is overlain by flat-lying sedimentary rocks of the Hudson Bay Lowland. Few of these Paleozoic rocks are visible on the surface, because much of the poorly drained area is covered by vast muskegs and swampy forests.

A SE extension of the Canadian Shield separates the St. Lawrence and the Great Lakes lowlands, both of which are underlain by flat sedimentary Paleozoic limestones, shales, and sandstones. The St. Lawrence Lowland is less than 91 m (300 ft) high and is part of the sand and clay plains that extend along the St. Lawrence R. into Québec Province. In Ontario, the region contains several areas of fertile soil. The most dramatic features of the Great Lakes Lowland are the east-facing cliffs of the Niagara escarpment, which extends from Niagara Falls through the Bruce Peninsula to Manitoulin Island. Much of the region is covered with fertile soil, and some of the province's most productive farms are here.

Rivers and Lakes. The rivers and lakes of Ontario form two large drainage systems—one trending N to Hudson and James bays and one S to the Great Lakes and the St. Lawrence R. In addition, a smaller region in the W drains into Manitoba. Among the major rivers that drain the Canadian Shield and the Hudson Bay Lowland toward the N are the Severn, Winisk, Attawapiskat, Albany,

and Abitibi. Major components of the Great Lakes-St. Lawrence drainage basin include the Ottawa, French, Grand, and Thames rivers. The Niagara R., between Lakes Erie and Ontario, flows over the scenic Niagara Falls. Many of Ontario's rivers are used to produce hydroelectricity.

Besides parts of four of the Great Lakes, Ontario contains thousands of other lakes, many of which are located in the W. Among the big lakes, some extending beyond the province's boundaries, are Lake Nipigon, Lake of the Woods, Lac Seul, Lake Abitibi, Lake Nipissing, Lake Simcoe, Rainy Lake, and Big Trout Lake.

Climate. Ontario covers a large area and has a wide range of climates, which can be grouped into two main regions—an arctic and subarctic climate area in the N and a humid continental zone in the S. The former region is affected by very cold air from the Arctic and the Canadian prairies, and the climate of the latter region is moderated by winds from the Great Lakes. Thus, Trout Lake, in the N, has a mean January temperature of −24.1° C (−11.4° F) and a mean July temperature of 15.9° C (60.6° F), and Toronto, in the SE, has a mean January temperature of −4.4° C (24° F) and a mean July temperature of 21.8° C (71.2° F). The recorded temperature in the province has ranged from −58.3° C (−73° F), in 1935 at Iroquois Falls, to 42.2° C (108° F), in 1936 at

INDEX TO MAP OF ONTARIO

Cities and Towns

Atikokan	A 3
Attawapiskat	C 2
Belleville	D 4
Brantford	C 4
Britt	C 3
Chapleau	C 3
Chatham	C 4
Cochrane	C 3
Cornwall	D 3
Dryden	A 3
Fort Frances	A 3
Fort Severn	B 1
Fraserdale	C 3
Geraldton	B 3
Guelph	C 4
Haileybury	C 3
Hamilton	D 4
Iroquois Falls	C 3
Kapuskasing	C 3
Kenora	A 3
Kingston	D 4

Kirkland Lake	C 3
Kitchener	C 4
London	C 4
Michipicoten River	B 3
Moose Factory	C 2
Moosonee	C 2
Niagara Falls	D 4
North Bay	D 3
Oshawa	D 4
Ottawa (cap. of Canada)	D 3
Owen Sound	C 4
Pembroke	D 3
Peterborough	D 4
Pickel Lake	A 2
St. Catharines	D 4
Saint Thomas	C 4
Sarnia	C 4
Sault Ste. Marie	C 3
Stratford	C 4
Sudbury	C 3
Thunder Bay	B 3
Timmins	C 3

Toronto (cap.)	D 4
Welland	D 4
Windsor	C 4
Woodstock	C 4

Other Features

Abitibi (lake)	C 3
Abitibi (river)	C 2
Albany (river)	C 2
Attawapiskat (river)	B 2
Big Trout (lake)	B 2
Ekwan (river)	C 2
Fawn (river)	B 2
Georgian (bay)	C 3
Henrietta Maria (cape)	C 1
Hurd (cape)	C 3
Kapuskasing (river)	C 3
Kenogami (river)	B 2
Kesagami (lake)	C 2
Lake Superior Prov. Park	C 3

Lake of the Woods (lake)	A 3
Long (lake)	B 3
Long (point)	C 4
Manitoulin (island)	C 3
Mattagami (river)	C 2
Mille Lacs (lake)	A 3
Nipigon (lake)	B 3
Nipissing (lake)	C 3
North (chan.)	C 3
North Caribou (lake)	A 2
Pigeon (river)	A 3
Polar Bear Prov. Park	C 2
Pukaskwa Nat'l Park	B 3
Quetico Prov. Park	A 3
Sachigo (river)	A 2
Saint Joseph (lake)	A 2
Sandy (lake)	A 2
Seul (lake)	A 2
Severn (river)	B 2
Wabuk (point)	C 1
Winisk (river)	B 2
Woods (lake)	A 3

Atikokan and Biscotasing. The SE part of Ontario gets about 915 mm (about 36 in) of precipitation per year, and the remainder of the province gets up to about 635 mm (about 25 in) annually. Much of Ontario gets considerable snow each year, with particularly big annual snowfalls at Kapuskasing (about 3225 mm/127 in) and at Parry Sound (about 2970 mm/117 in).

Plants and Animals. The vegetation of Ontario may be grouped into five main areas. Along the shore of Hudson Bay is a narrow strip of arctic tundra, made up of low shrubs, mosses, and lichens underlain by permafrost. A wide subarctic transitional zone covers most of the Hudson Bay Lowland and the N half of the Canadian Shield region. Black spruce is the dominant tree species here. Drainage is poor, and swamps and muskegs are widespread. A third area, part of the Boreal forest, covers the central section of the Shield and is the main resource area for pulpwood. Black spruce abounds, and white spruce, jack pine, and balsam fir occur on drier sites. The Great Lakes and St. Lawrence forests also are major sources of timber. This area extends from the S part of the shield, where the Boreal softwoods as well as red spruce and hemlock occur, to SE Ontario between Lakes Huron and Ontario, where hardwoods such as maple, beech, oak, basswood, and walnut dominate. Along the shores of Lakes Erie and Ontario is the fifth area, made up mainly of S broadleaf forest, which includes such trees as beech, hickory, and oak. Altogether, forest covers about half of Ontario.

The animal life of Ontario is rich and varied. Polar bear, white whale, seal, walrus, and caribou are common in the arctic area along Hudson Bay. The swampy N areas and the countless lakes of the Canadian Shield region provide ideal habitats for many furbearing animals such as beaver, muskrat, marten, mink, fox, wolverine, and raccoon. In the Boreal and Great Lakes forests are black bear, skunk, deer, moose, wolf, weasel, and smaller animals such as squirrel, rabbit, and woodchuck. Common game birds of Ontario include duck, goose, and ruffed grouse, and many other birds, such as heron, loon, woodpecker, warbler, and finch, live in the province. Ontario's lakes and streams abound in trout, pickerel, pike, perch, whitefish, muskellunge, and bass.

Mineral Resources. Ontario has great mineral resources, some of the most important of which are situated in the Canadian Shield region. In the area around Sudbury, Timmins, and Wawa are vast deposits of nickel, copper, and iron ore as well as substantial resources of gold, silver, platinum metals, cobalt, lead, and zinc. The sedimentary beds of S Ontario yield construction materials such as stone, sand and gravel, lime,

Interior of a copper smelter at Sudbury, Ont., which is located in one of the most important copper-producing areas in Canada. National Film Board of Canada

INDEX TO MAP OF ONTARIO

Cities and Towns

Ailsa Craig ....C 4
Ajax ....E 4
Alban ....D 1
Alcona Beach ....E 3
Alexandria ....K 2
Alfred...............K 2
Alliston.............E 3
Alma ....D 4
Almonte..............H 2
Alvinston............B 5
Amherstburg..........A 5
Amherst View.........H 3
Ancaster ....D 4
Angus ....E 3
Apsley ....F 3
Arkona...............C 4
Armstrong............H 4
Arnprior.............H 2
Aroland..............H 4
Arthur ....D 4
Astorville ....E 1
Athens ....J 3
Atherley ....E 3
Atikokan ....G 5
Atwood ....D 4
Auden ....H 4
Aurora ....J 3
Avonmore ....K 2
Aylmer...............C 5
Ayr ....D 4
Ayton ....D 3
Baden ....D 4
Bala ....E 2
Bancroft ....G 2
Barrie ⊙ ....E 3
Barry's Bay..........G 2
Batawa ....G 3
Bath ....H 3
Bayfield ....C 4
Bayside ....G 3
Beachburg ....H 2
Beachville ....D 4
Beardmore ....H 5
Beaverton ....E 3
Beeton ....E 3
Belle River..........B 5
Belleville ⊙ ....G 3
Belmont..............C 5
Bethany ....F 3
Bewdley..............F 3
Binbrook ....E 4
Blackstock ....F 3
Blenheim.............C 5
Blind River..........J 5
Bloomfield...........G 4
Blyth ....C 4
Bobcaygeon ....F 3
Bonfield.............E 1
Bothwell ....C 5
Bourget ....J 2
Bracebridge ⊙ ....E 2
Bradford ....E 3
Braeside ....H 2
Brampton ⊙ ....J 4
Brantford ⊙ ....D 4
Brechin ....E 3
Bridgenorth ....F 3
Brigden ....B 5
Brighton ....G 3
Brights Grove ....B 4
Britt ....D 2
Brockville ⊙ ....J 3
Bruce Mines ....J 5
Brussels ....C 4
Burford ....D 4
Burgessville.........D 4
Burk's Falls ....E 2
Burlington ....E 4
Cache Bay............D 1
Caesarea ....F 3
Calabogie ....H 2
Caledon..............E 4
Callander ....E 1
Cambridge ....D 4

Campbellford ....G 3
Cannington ....E 3
Capreol ....K 5
Caramat...............H 5
Cardinal ....J 3
Carleton Place ....H 2
Carlisle ....D 4
Carlsbad Springs .....J 2
Carp..................H 2
Cartier ....J 5
Casselman ....J 2
Castleton ....F 3
Cedar Springs.........B 5
Chalk River...........G 1
Chapleau ....J 5
Charing Cross.........B 5
Chatham ⊙ ....B 5
Chatsworth ....D 3
Cherry Valley ....G 4
Chesley ....C 3
Chesterville ....J 2
Chute-à-Blondeau .....K 2
Clarence Creek ....J 2
Clarksburg ....D 3
Clifford..............D 4
Clinton...............C 4
Cobalt ....K 5
Cobden ....H 2
Coboconk ....F 3
Cobourg ⊙ ....F 4
Cochrane ⊙ ....K 5
Codes Corner ....H 3
Colborne ....G 4
Colchester............B 6
Coldwater ....E 3
Collingwood ....D 3
Collins Bay ....H 3
Comber ....B 5
Consecon ....G 3
Cookstown ....E 3
Cornwall ⊙ ....K 2
Corunna ....B 5
Cottam ....B 5
Courtland ....D 5
Coverdale ....F 4
Crediton ....C 4
Creemore ....D 3
Crysler ....J 2
Cumberland...........J 2
Cumberland Beach.....E 3
Dashwood..............C 4
Deep River ....G 1
Delaware ....C 5
Delhi ....D 5
Delta ....H 3
Denbigh ....G 2
Deseronto ....G 3
Dorchester ....C 5
Douglas...............H 2
Drayton ....D 4
Dresden ....B 5
Drumbo ....D 4
Dryden ....G 4
Dublin ....C 4
Dubreuilville.........J 5
Dundalk...............D 3
Dundas ....D 4
Dunnville ....E 5
Durham ....D 3
Dutton ....C 5
Earlton...............K 5
Eastwood ....D 4
East York ....J 4
Echo Bay ....J 5
Eden Mills ....D 4
Eganville.............G 2
Egmondville...........C 4
Elgin ....H 3
Elk Lake ....K 5
Elliot Lake ....B 1
Elmira ....D 4
Elmvale ....E 3
Elmwood ....C 3
Elora ....D 4
Embro ....D 4
Embrun ....J 2
Emo ....F 5
Englehart ....K 5

Enterprise ....H 3
Erieau ....C 5
Erie Beach ....B 5
Erin ....D 4
Espanola ....J 5
Essex.................B 5
Etobicoke.............J 4
Everett...............E 3
Exeter ....C 4
Fauquier..............J 5
Fenelon Falls.........F 3
Fergus ....D 4
Field.................E 1
Finch.................J 2
Fitzroy Harbour.......H 2
Flesherton............D 3
Foleyet...............J 5
Fordwich..............C 4
Forest ....C 4
Formosa ....C 3
Fort Erie ....E 5
Fort Frances ⊙ ....F 5
Foxboro...............G 3
Frankford ....G 3
Fraserdale ....J 5
Freelton..............D 4
French River..........D 1
Gananoque ....H 3
Garden Village ....E 1
Geraldton ....H 5
Glencoe...............C 5
Glen Miller ....G 3
Glen Robertson ....K 2
Glen Walter ....K 2
Goderich ⊙ ....C 4
Gogama ....J 5
Goodwood..............D 3
Gore Bay ⊙ ....B 2
Gorrie ....C 4
Grafton ....G 4
Grand Bend ....C 4
Grand Valley ....D 4
Gravenhurst ....E 3
Greely................J 2
Green Valley ....K 2
Grimsby ....E 4
Guelph ⊙ ....D 4
Haileybury ⊙ ....K 5
Haldimand ....E 5
Haliburton ....F 2
Halton Hills ....E 4
Hamilton ⊙ ....E 4
Hanover...............C 3
Harriston ....D 4
Harrow................B 5
Harrowsmith ....H 3
Harwood ....F 3
Hastings ....G 3
Havelock ....G 3
Hawkesbury ....K 2
Hawkestone ....E 3
Hawk Junction.........J 5
Hearst................J 5
Hensall ....C 4
Hepworth ....C 3
Heyden................J 5
Highgate ....C 5
Hillsburgh ....D 4
Hillsdale.............E 3
Holland Landing ......E 3
Honey Harbour ....E 3
Hornepayne...........J 5
Hudson ....G 4
Huntsville............E 2
Huron Park ....C 4
Ignace ....G 5
Ilderton ....C 4
Ingersoll ....C 4
Ingleside ....J 2
Innerkip..............D 4
Inverhuron ....C 3
Iron Bridge ....A 1
Iroquois ....J 3
Iroquois Falls ....J 5
Jasper................H 3
Johnstown ....J 3
Kakabeka Falls........G 5
Kaladar ....H 3

Kanata ....J 2
Kapuskasing ....J 5
Kars ....J 2
Kearney...............E 2
Keene.................F 3
Keewatin ....F 5
Kemptville ....J 2
Kenora ⊙ ....F 4
Keswick ....E 3
Killaloe Station .....G 2
Killarney ....C 2
Kincardine............C 3
King City ....J 3
Kingston ⊙ ....H 3
Kingsville............B 6
Kinmount..............F 3
Kiosk.................F 1
Kirkland Lake ....K 5
Kitchener ⊙ ....D 4
Komoka ....C 5
Lakefield ....F 3
Lambeth ....C 5
Lanark................H 2
Lancaster ....K 2
Langton...............D 5
Lansdowne ....H 3
Larder Lake...........K 5
Latchford ....K 5
Leamington ....B 5
Lefroy ....E 3
Limoges ....J 2
Lincoln...............E 4
Linden Beach ....B 6
Lindsay ⊙ ....F 3
Linwood ....D 4
Lion's Head...........C 2
Lisle ....E 3
Listowel..............D 4
Little Britain........F 3
Little Current........B 2
London ⊙ ....C 5
Longlac...............H 5
Long Sault............K 2
L'Orignal ⊙ ....K 2
Lucan ....C 4
Lucknow ....C 4
Lyn ....J 3
Lynden ....D 4
Lynhurst ....C 5
Macdiarmid ....H 5
McGregor ....B 5
MacGregor's Bay ......G 2
McKellar ....D 2
McKerrow ....C 1
MacTier ....E 2
Madawaska ....F 2
Madoc.................G 3
Maitland ....J 3
Mallorytown ....J 3
Manitouwadge ....H 5
Manitowaning ....C 2
Manotick ....J 2
Marathon..............H 5
Markdale..............D 3
Markham ....K 4
Markstay ....D 1
Marmora...............G 3
Martintown ....K 2
Massey ....C 1
Matachewan ....J 5
Matheson ....K 5
Mattawa ....F 1
Mattice ....J 5
Maxville ....K 2
Maynooth ....G 2
Meaford...............D 3
Melbourne.............C 5
Merlin................B 5
Merrickville ....J 3
Metcalfe ....J 2
Midhurst ....E 3
Midland...............D 3
Mildmay...............C 3
Milford Bay ....E 2
Millbank..............D 4
Millbrook ....F 3
Milton ⊙ ....E 4
Milverton.............D 4

⊙ County seat

ONTARIO

Index to Map of Ontario

Mindemoya . . . . B 2
Minden ⊙ . . . . F 3
Mississauga . . . . J 4
Mitchell . . . . C 4
Monkton . . . . C 4
Moonbeam . . . . J 5
Moorefield . . . . D 4
Moose Creek . . . . K 2
Morewood . . . . J 2
Morpeth . . . . C 5
Morrisburg . . . . J 3
Morriston . . . . D 4
Mount Albert . . . . E 3
Mount Brydges . . . . C 5
Mount Elgin . . . . D 5
Mount Forest . . . . D 4
Mount Hope . . . . E 4
Mount Pleasant . . . . D 4
Munster . . . . J 2
Nairn . . . . C 1
Nakina . . . . H 4
Nanticoke . . . . E 5
Napanee ⊙ . . . . G 3
Navan . . . . J 2
Neustadt . . . . D 3
Newboro . . . . H 3
Newburgh . . . . H 3
Newbury . . . . C 5
Newcastle . . . . F 4
New Hamburg . . . . D 4
Newington . . . . K 2
New Liskeard . . . . K 5
New Lowell . . . . E 3
Newmarket ⊙ . . . . E 3
Niagara Falls . . . . E 4
Niagara-on-the-Lake . . . . E 4
Nickel Centre . . . . D 1
Nipigon . . . . H 5
Nobel . . . . D 2
Nobleton . . . . J 3
Noelville . . . . D 1
North Bay . . . . E 1
North Brook . . . . G 3
North Gower . . . . J 2
North York . . . . J 4
Norwich . . . . D 5
Norwood . . . . F 3
Nottawa . . . . D 3
Oakville . . . . E 4
Oakwood . . . . F 3
Odessa . . . . H 3
Oil Springs . . . . B 5
Omemee . . . . F 3
Onaping Falls . . . . J 5
Opasatika . . . . J 5
Orangeville ⊙ . . . . D 4
Orillia . . . . E 3
Orleans . . . . J 2
Osgoode . . . . J 2
Oshawa . . . . F 4
Ottawa (cap. of
  Canada) ⊙ . . . . J 2
Otterville . . . . D 5
Owen Sound ⊙ . . . . D 3
Paincourt . . . . B 5
Painswick . . . . E 3
Paisley . . . . C 3
Pakenham . . . . H 2
Palmerston . . . . D 4
Paris . . . . D 4
Parkhill . . . . C 4
Parry Sound ⊙ . . . . E 2
Pefferlaw . . . . E 3
Pelham . . . . E 4
Pembroke ⊙ . . . . G 2
Penetanguishene . . . . . . D 3
Perkinsfield . . . . E 3
Perth ⊙ . . . . H 3
Petawawa . . . . G 2
Peterborough ⊙ . . . . F 3
Petrolia . . . . B 5
Pickering . . . . K 4
Picton ⊙ . . . . G 3
Plantagenet . . . . K 2
Plattsville . . . . D 4

Point Edward . . . . B 4
Pontypool . . . . F 3
Port Burwell . . . . D 5
Port Carling . . . . E 2
Port Colborne . . . . E 5
Port Elgin . . . . C 3
Port Hope . . . . F 4
Port Lambton . . . . B 5
Portland . . . . H 3
Port McNicoll . . . . E 3
Port Perry . . . . E 3
Port Rowan . . . . D 5
Port Stanley . . . . C 5
Pottageville . . . . J 3
Powassan . . . . E 1
Prescott ⊙ . . . . J 3
Princeton . . . . D 4
Providence Bay . . . . B 2
Rainy River . . . . F 5
Ramore . . . . K 5
Rayside-Balfour . . . . K 5
Red Lake Road . . . . G 5
Red Rock . . . . H 5
Renfrew . . . . H 2
Richards Landing . . . . . . J 5
Richmond . . . . J 2
Richmond Hill . . . . J 4
Ridgetown . . . . C 5
Ripley . . . . C 3
Rockcliffe Park . . . . J 2
Rockland . . . . J 2
Rockwood . . . . D 4
Rodney . . . . C 5
Rolphton . . . . G 1
Rosseau . . . . E 2
Rosslyn Village . . . . G 5
Russell . . . . J 2
Ruthven . . . . B 6
Saint Albert . . . . J 2
St. Catharines ⊙ . . . . . . E 4
Saint Charles . . . . D 1
Saint Clair Beach . . . . . . B 5
Saint Clements . . . . D 4
Saint George . . . . D 4
Saint Isidore de
  Prescott . . . . K 2
Saint Jacobs . . . . D 4
Saint Mary's . . . . C 4
Saint Thomas ⊙ . . . . . . C 5
Saint Williams . . . . D 5
Salem . . . . D 4
Sarnia ⊙ . . . . B 5
Sauble Beach . . . . C 3
Sault Ste. Marie ⊙ . . . J 5
Scarborough . . . . K 4
Schomberg . . . . J 3
Schreiber . . . . H 5
Scotland . . . . D 4
Seaforth . . . . C 4
Sebringville . . . . C 4
Seeleys Bay . . . . H 3
Shakespeare . . . . D 4
Thorndale . . . . C 4
Thornton . . . . E 3
Thorold . . . . E 4
Thunder Bay ⊙ . . . . H 5
Tilbury . . . . B 5
Tillsonburg . . . . D 5
Timagami . . . . K 5
Timmins . . . . J 5
Tiverton . . . . C 3
Tobermory . . . . C 2
Toronto (cap.) ⊙ . . . . . . K 4
Torrance . . . . E 3
Tottenham . . . . E 3
Trenton . . . . G 3
Trout Creek . . . . E 2
Turkey Point . . . . D 5
Tweed . . . . G 3
Udora . . . . E 3
Union . . . . C 5
Uxbridge . . . . E 3
Valley East . . . . J 5
Vanier . . . . J 2
Vankleek Hill . . . . K 2
Vars . . . . J 2

Vaughan . . . . J 4
Vermilion Bay . . . . G 4
Verner . . . . D 1
Vernon . . . . J 2
Verona . . . . H 3
Victoria Harbour . . . . . . E 3
Victoria Road . . . . F 3
Vienna . . . . D 5
Virginiatown . . . . K 5
Vittoria . . . . D 5
Wabigoon . . . . G 5
Walden . . . . J 5
Walkerton ⊙ . . . . C 3
Wallaceburg . . . . B 5
Wallacetown . . . . C 5
Wardsville . . . . C 5
Warkworth . . . . G 3
Warren . . . . D 1
Warsaw . . . . F 3
Wasaga Beach . . . . D 3
Washago . . . . E 3
Waterdown . . . . D 4
Waterloo . . . . D 4
Watford . . . . C 5
Waubaushene . . . . E 3
Wawa . . . . J 5
Webbwood . . . . C 1
Welland . . . . E 5
Wellandport . . . . E 4
Wellesley . . . . D 4
Wellington . . . . G 4
Wendover . . . . J 2
West Lorne . . . . C 5
Westmeath . . . . H 2
Westmount . . . . H 2
Westport . . . . H 3
Wheatley . . . . B 5
Whitby ⊙ . . . . F 4
Whitchurch-Stouffville . . J 3
White River . . . . J 5
Whitney . . . . F 2
Wiarton . . . . C 3
Wikwemikong . . . . C 2
Wilberforce . . . . F 3
Williamsburg . . . . J 3
Williamsford . . . . D 3
Williamstown . . . . K 2
Winchester . . . . J 2
Windsor ⊙ . . . . B 5
Wingham . . . . C 4
Wolfe Island . . . . H 3
Woodstock ⊙ . . . . D 4
Woodville . . . . F 3
Wroxeter . . . . C 4
Wyoming . . . . B 5
Yarker . . . . H 3
York . . . . J 4
Zephyr . . . . E 3
Zurich . . . . C 4

Other Features

Abitibi (river) . . . . J 5
Algonquin Prov. Park . . . F 2
Amherst (island) . . . . . . H 3
Balsam (lake) . . . . F 3
Barrie (island) . . . . B 1
Bays (lake) . . . . F 2
Black (river) . . . . E 3
Bruce (pen.) . . . . C 2
Buckhorn (lake) . . . . F 3
Burnt (river) . . . . F 3
Cabot (head) . . . . C 2
Charleston (lake) . . . . . . J 3
Christian (island) . . . . . . D 3
Clear (lake) . . . . F 3
Cockburn (island) . . . . . A 2
Couchiching (lake) . . . . . E 3
Croker (cape) . . . . D 3
Don (river) . . . . J 4
Doré (lake) . . . . G 2
Douglas (point) . . . . C 3
Duck (islands) . . . . A 2
Erie (lake) . . . . E 5
Fitzwilliam (island) . . . . . C 2
Flowerpot (island) . . . . C 2
French (river) . . . . D 1

Georgian (bay) . . . . D 2
Georgian Bay Is. Nat'l
  Park . . . . C 2, D 3
Georgina (island) . . . . . . E 3
Grand (river) . . . . D 4
Humber (river) . . . . J 3
Hurd (cape) . . . . C 2
Huron (lake) . . . . B 3
Ipperwash Prov. Park . . . C 4
Joseph (lake) . . . . E 2
Killarney Prov. Park . . . . C 1
Killbear Point Prov.
  Park . . . . D 2
Lake Superior Prov.
  Park . . . . J 5
Lake of the Woods
  (lake) . . . . F 5
Lonely (island) . . . . C 2
Long (point) . . . . D 5
Long Point (bay) . . . . . . D 5
Madawaska (river) . . . . . G 2
Magnetawan (river) . . . . D 2
Main (chan.) . . . . C 2
Manitou (lake) . . . . C 2
Manitoulin (island) . . . . . B 2
Mattagami (river) . . . . . . J 5
Mazinaw (lake) . . . . G 3
Michipicoten (island) . . . . H 5
Missinaibi (river) . . . . . . J 5
Mississagi (river) . . . . . . A 1
Mississippi (lake) . . . . . . H 2
Muskoka (lake) . . . . E 2
Niagara (river) . . . . E 4
Nipigon (lake) . . . . H 5
Nipissing (lake) . . . . E 1
North (chan.) . . . . A 1
Nottawasaga (bay) . . . . . D 3
Ogidaki (mt.) . . . . J 5
Ontario (lake) . . . . G 4
Opeongo (lake) . . . . F 2
Ottawa (river) . . . . H 2
Owen (chan.) . . . . C 2
Owen (sound) . . . . D 3
Panache (lake) . . . . C 1
Parry (island) . . . . D 2
Parry (sound) . . . . D 2
Pelee (point) . . . . B 6
Petawawa (river) . . . . . . G 2
Petre (point) . . . . G 4
Pins (point) . . . . C 5
Point Pelee Nat'l Park . . B 5
Presqu'ile Prov. Park . . . G 4
Pukaskwa Nat'l Park . . . H 5
Quetico Prov. Park . . . . G 5
Rainy (lake) . . . . G 5
Rice (lake) . . . . F 3
Rideau (lake) . . . . H 3
Rondeau Prov. Park . . . . C 5
Rosseau (lake) . . . . E 2
Saint Clair (lake) . . . . . . B 5
Saint Clair (river) . . . . . . B 5
Saint Lawrence (lake) . . K 3
Saint Lawrence (river) . . J 3
Saint Lawrence Is.
  Nat'l Park . . . . J 3
Saugeen (river) . . . . C 3
Scugog (lake) . . . . F 3
Seul (lake) . . . . G 4
Severn (river) . . . . E 3
Sibley Prov. Park . . . . . . H 5
Simcoe (lake) . . . . E 3
South (bay) . . . . C 2
Spanish (river) . . . . C 1
Stony (lake) . . . . G 3
Superior (lake) . . . . H 5
Sydenham (river) . . . . . . B 5
Thames (river) . . . . B 5
Theano (point) . . . . J 5
Thousand (islands) . . . . . H 3
Timagami (lake) . . . . K 5
Trout (lake) . . . . E 1
Vernon (lake) . . . . E 2
Walpole (island) . . . . . . B 5
Wanapitei (river) . . . . . . D 1
Welland (canal) . . . . E 5
Weslemkoon (lake) . . . . . G 2
Woods (lake) . . . . F 5

⊙ County seat

and clay. Other important mineral resources of Ontario include salt, gypsum, petroleum, natural gas, nepheline syenite, sulfur, and uranium.

R.N.D.

POPULATION

According to the 1981 census, Ontario had 8,625,107 inhabitants, an increase of 12% over 1971. The overall population density in 1981 was 8 persons per sq km (21 per sq mi); the distribution of population, however, was extremely uneven, with the majority concentrated in the SE corner of the province. English was the first language of about 78% of the people; slightly less than 6% had French as their native language. Some 65,000 American Indians lived in Ontario, more than in any other province; the majority of these lived on the province's 170 reserves. Roman Catholics formed the largest single religious group; other churches with large memberships were the United Church of Canada, the Anglican Church of Canada, and the Baptist Church. Ontario is the most urbanized of Canada's provinces; about 81% of all Ontarians lived in areas defined as urban, and the rest lived in rural areas. The province's biggest cities were Toronto, the provincial capital and second largest city in the country; North York; Mississauga; Hamilton; Ottawa, the national capital; London; and Windsor.

EDUCATION AND CULTURAL ACTIVITY

Ontario is served by a comprehensive educational system and has a wide variety of notable cultural institutions and places of historical and recreational interest.

Education. The first elementary (common) school in Ontario was founded in the late 1780s, and in 1816 the government provided for elementary schools to be established throughout the province. It was not until the 1870s, however, that all elementary and secondary schools were made free. Tax-supported elementary schools today include public (nondenominational) and separate (Roman Catholic) schools. In the early 1980s Ontario's public and separate elementary and secondary schools had a combined annual enrollment of about 1.8 million students.

King's College, the first institution of higher education in Ontario, was established by a royal charter in 1827 and became the University of Toronto in 1850. In the early 1980s Ontario had some 50 institutions of higher education with a total yearly enrollment of more than 236,700 students. Besides the University of Toronto, notable schools included Queen's University (1841) and the Royal Military College of Canada (1876), in Kingston; Brock University, in St. Catharines; McMaster University (1887), in Hamilton; the University of Ottawa (1848) and Carleton University

(1942), in Ottawa; Ryerson Polytechnical Institute (1948), in Toronto; Trent University (1963), in Peterborough; York University (1959), in Downsview (near Toronto); the University of Windsor (1857), in Windsor; the University of Western Ontario (1878), in London; Laurentian University of Sudbury (1960), in Sudbury; Wilfrid Laurier University (1911) and the University of Waterloo (1956), in Waterloo; and the University of Guelph (1964), in Guelph.

Cultural Institutions. Ontario contains a number of excellent museums and other cultural facilities. Toronto is the site of the Art Gallery of Ontario, the Royal Ontario Museum, and the Ontario Science Centre. Located in Ottawa are the National Gallery of Canada, the National Museum of Science and Technology, the National Museum of Man, and the National Museum of Natural Sciences. Also in Toronto are Ontario Place, a cultural and recreational complex; two centers for the performing arts, the O'Keefe Centre and St. Lawrence Centre; and Massey Hall, home of the Toronto Symphony Orchestra. The National Arts Centre in Ottawa, another performing-arts complex, contains an opera house and a theater. Also of note are the Art Gallery of Hamilton, in Hamilton; the Agnes Etherington Art Centre, in Kingston; the Art Gallery of Windsor, in Windsor; the Ontario Agricultural Museum, in Milton; and the Oil Museum of Canada, in Oil Springs, located on the site of North America's first commercial petroleum well. Two major annual cultural events in Ontario are the Stratford Festival, in Stratford, featuring productions of plays by Shakespeare, and the George Bernard Shaw Festival, in Niagara-on-the-Lake, with productions of works by Shaw and other 20th-century playwrights.

Historical Sites. Ontario's places of historical interest include Fort Malden National Historic Park in Amherstburg, containing the remains of a British military post founded in the 1790s; Fort George National Historic Park, in Niagara-on-the-Lake, encompassing a reconstruction of a British fort used in the War of 1812; and Fort Wellington National Historic Park, in Prescott, with a restored British fort erected in 1838–39. Also of note are Fanshawe Pioneer Village, near London, a re-creation of a mid-19th century community; the Bell Homestead, near Brantford, including a home of the inventor Alexander Graham Bell; and Bellevue House, in Kingston, a residence of Sir John A. Macdonald, Canada's first prime minister.

Sports and Recreation. Ontario's parks, forests, extensive shoreline, and numerous lakes and rivers provide excellent conditions for swimming,

ONTARIO

Officers of the Royal Canadian Mounted Police on duty near the Parliament buildings on Parliament Hill in Ottawa, the federal capital of Canada.   Malak–Shostal Associates

boating, fishing, hunting, camping, hiking, skating, ice hockey, and skiing. Professional sports events attract many spectators. The Hockey Hall of Fame is in Toronto, and the Canadian Football Hall of Fame is in Hamilton.

Communications. In the early 1980s Ontario had approximately 181 radiobroadcasting stations and 36 television stations. The first radio station in the province, CKOC in Hamilton, began operation in 1922. CBLT in Toronto, Ontario's first television station, went on the air in 1952. The Upper Canada Gazette and American Oracle, the first newspaper printed in Ontario, was initially published in Newark (now Niagara-on-the-Lake) in 1793. In the early 1980s Ontario had 48 daily newspapers with a total circulation of about 2.2 million. Influential newspapers included the *Spectator* of Hamilton; the *London Free Press;* the *Citizen* and *Le Droit* of Ottawa; the *Globe and Mail* and the *Toronto Star* of Toronto; and the *Windsor Star.* Toronto is also one of the leading book and magazine publishing centers in Canada.

GOVERNMENT AND POLITICS

Ontario has a parliamentary form of government.
Executive. The chief executive of Ontario is a lieutenant governor, who is appointed by the Canadian governor-general in council to a term of five years. The lieutenant governor, representing the British sovereign, holds a position that is largely honorary. The premier (called the prime minister until 1972), who is usually the leader of the majority party in the Ontario legislature, is the actual head of the provincial government and presides over the executive council or cabinet. In addition to the premier, the executive council includes the treasurer, minister of economics, minister of education, minister of energy, minister of health, and about 20 other officials. The premier and the members of the executive council must resign their posts if they lose the support of a majority in the legislature of Ontario.

Legislature. The unicameral Ontario Legislative Assembly contains 125 seats, including those of the premier and the members of the executive

384

council. Members of the legislature are popularly elected to a term of up to five years. The lieutenant governor, on the advice of the premier, may call for new elections before the 5-year term has been completed.

Judiciary. Ontario's highest tribunal, the supreme court, is composed of the court of appeal, with about 15 full-time justices, and the high court of justice, with about 42 full-time justices. All these judges are appointed by the Canadian governor-general in council. Ontario also has provincial criminal and family courts, county and district courts, and magistrates' courts.

Local Government. In the early 1980s the populous S part of Ontario was divided into 31 counties, 10 regional municipalities, and the Municipality of Metropolitan Toronto, which included two cities and four boroughs. The rest of the province was divided into 10 districts and one district municipality. Altogether, Ontario had 45 cities, 143 towns, and 119 villages. Many of the cities and towns were governed by a mayor and council.

National Representation. Ontario is represented in the Canadian Parliament by 24 senators, appointed by the Canadian governor-general in council, and by 95 members of the House of Commons, popularly elected to terms of up to five years.

Politics. Since becoming part of the Canadian Confederation in 1867, Ontario has been governed by three political parties. The Liberal party controlled the office of prime minister from 1867 to 1905 and again from 1934 to 1943; the United Farmers of Ontario were in power from 1919 to 1923; and the Conservative party (called the Progressive Conservative party beginning in 1943) governed Ontario from 1905 to 1919, from 1923 to 1934, and from 1943 into the early 1980s. The New Democratic party gained considerable strength in the 1970s.

ECONOMY

In the 19th century the economy of Ontario was dominated by agriculture, forestry, mining, and trapping. These activities continued to be important in the 20th century, but manufacturing became by far the leading economic sector. Commerce, banking, insurance, tourism, and government operations were other major aspects of the Ontario economy in the early 1980s. The province benefited from the proximity of such major U.S. industrial centers as Buffalo, N.Y.; Cleveland, Ohio; and Detroit.

Agriculture. Ontario is the leading agricultural province of Canada; its cash receipts from farming totaled about Can.$4.2 billion annually in the early 1980s. About 64% of the income usually is generated by sales of livestock and livestock

Harvesting winter wheat on the plains of Ontario, near Lake Simcoe. Canada is a major wheat-producing country. Photo Researchers, Inc.

ONTARIO

JOINED THE CANADIAN CONFEDERATION:
July 1, 1867, one of the four original provinces

CAPITAL:	Toronto
MOTTO:	*Ut incepit fidelis sic permanet* (Loyal she began, loyal she remains)
FLORAL EMBLEM:	White trillium
POPULATION (1981):	8,625,107
AREA:	1,068,582 sq km (412,582 sq mi), includes 177,388 sq km (68,490 sq mi) of inland waters; 3d largest among the provinces and territories
COASTLINE:	1210 km (752 mi)
HIGHEST POINT:	693 m (2274 ft)
LOWEST POINT:	Sea level, along Hudson and James bays
PRINCIPAL RIVERS:	Albany, Severn, Ottawa, Attawapiskat
PRINCIPAL LAKES:	Nipigon, Lake of the Woods, Seul, Nipissing, Abitibi, Simcoe
CANADIAN PARLIAMENT:	24 members of the Senate; 95 members of the House of Commons

POPULATION OF ONTARIO SINCE 1851

Year of Census	Population	Percentage of Total Can. Pop.
1851	952,004	39.1%
1871	1,620,851	43.9%
1891	2,114,321	43.7%
1911	2,527,292	35.1%
1921	2,933,662	33.4%
1931	3,431,683	33.1%
1951	4,597,542	32.8%
1961	6,236,092	34.2%
1971	7,703,106	35.7%
1981	8,625,107	35.4%

POPULATION OF TEN LARGEST COMMUNITIES

	1981 Census	1971 Census
Toronto	599,217	712,786
North York	559,521	504,150
Mississauga	315,056	172,042
Hamilton	306,434	309,173
Ottawa	295,163	302,341
London	254,280	223,222
Windsor	192,083	203,200
Kitchener	139,734	116,966
St. Catharines	124,018	109,722
Oshawa	117,519	94,994

CLIMATE

	TORONTO	OTTAWA
Average January temperature range	−7.8° to −0.6° C (18° to 31° F)	−16.1° to −6.1° C (3° to 21° F)
Average July temperature range	16.1° to 27.2° C (61° to 81° F)	14.4° to 26.7° C (58° to 80° F)
Average annual temperature	7.8° C (46° F)	5.6° C (42° F)
Average annual precipitation	790 mm (31 in)	851 mm (34 in)
Average annual snowfall	1410 mm (56 in)	2156 mm (85 in)
Average number of days per year with appreciable precipitation	134	152
Average dates of freezing temperatures (0° C/32° F or less):		
Last in spring	April 20	May 11
First in autumn	Oct. 30	Oct. 1

HUDSON BAY
LOWLAND

Albany R.

CANADIAN SHIELD

ST. LAWRENCE
LOWLAND

NATURAL REGIONS OF ONTARIO

GREAT LAKES
LOWLAND

PRINCIPAL PRODUCTS
OF ONTARIO

ECONOMY

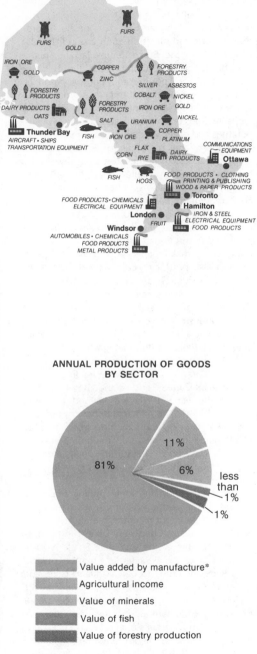

Province budget. . . . . revenue $15.2 billion
expenditure $15.8 billion
Provincial gross domestic product . . . . . . $111.7 billion
Personal income, per capita. $10,614
Labor force (civilian) 4,367,000
   Employed in agriculture   3%
   Employed in manufacturing   25%
   Employed in services   28%

	Quantity Produced	Value
FARM PRODUCTS		**$4.2 billion**
CROPS		**$1.5 billion**
Corn	179,000 metric tons	$357 million
Vegetables	882,000 metric tons	$201 million
Tobacco	98,400 metric tons	$196 million
Floriculture and nursery products		$144 million
Livestock and Livestock Products		**$2.7 billion**
Cattle	994,000	$1.0 billion
Dairy prod.	849,000 kiloliters	$710 million
Hogs	4.0 million	$467 million
Poultry	140,000 metric tons	$237 million
MINERALS		**$4.7 billion**
Nickel	156,000 metric tons	$1.3 billion
Copper	234,000 metric tons	$611 million
Uranium	4300 metric tons	$413 million
Gold	18,400 kg	$388 million
Silver	450,000 kg	$354 million
FISHING	**26,700 metric tons**	**$24 million**
FORESTRY		**$668 million**

	Value of Shipments
MANUFACTURING	**$81.6 billion**
Food and beverage products	$11.4 billion
Primary metal products	$7.8 billion
Chemicals and chemical products	$6.5 billion
Fabricated metal products	$6.2 billion
Electrical and electronic products	$5.0 billion
Petroleum and coal products	$4.9 billion
Nonelectric machinery	$4.6 billion
Paper and allied products	$4.4 billion
Printing and publishing	$2.7 billion
Textiles	$2.0 billion
Nonmetallic mineral products	$2.0 billion

	Wages and Salaries
OTHER	**$78.4 billion**
Construction	$3.8 billion
Transportation, communications, and other utilities	$5.3 billion
Trade	$7.2 billion
Finance, insurance, and real estate	$4.6 billion
Service	$52.5 billion
Public administration	$5.0 billion

ANNUAL PRODUCTION OF GOODS BY SECTOR

81%
11%
6%
less than 1%
1%

Value added by manufacture*
Agricultural income
Value of minerals
Value of fish
Value of forestry production

*The value added by an industry is a measure of the value created in its products, not counting such production costs as raw materials and power.

Sources: Canadian Government Publications
(All figures are in Canadian dollars)

products, and the rest is derived from the sale of crops. The province has about 77,000 farms. Livestock and livestock products include beef cattle, raised especially along the SE shore of Lake Huron and near Georgian Bay; dairy products, produced particularly in the region around the city of London, in the Bruce Peninsula, and in the area bordering Lake Ontario and the St. Lawrence R.; sheep; poultry and poultry products; and hogs. A big portion of the crops produced in Ontario is used as fodder for livestock. The major crops include corn, wheat, oats, barley, soybeans, potatoes and other vegetables, hay, and tobacco. In addition, large quantities of apples, cherries, grapes, peaches, and other fruit are grown in the Niagara Peninsula. Maple syrup, flowers, and nursery plants are also significant products.

Forestry. Ontario has a substantial forestry industry, and about 18 million cu m (about 635 million cu ft) of wood are typically cut yearly. Softwoods harvested in the N part of the province are used primarily to make paper, especially newsprint. Ontario also produces much sawed lumber for use in construction as well as hardwoods and softwoods for furniture making.

Fishing. Ontario's relatively small commercial fishing industry is concentrated in the Great Lakes, especially Lake Erie. The principal species landed are yellow perch, lake whitefish, smelt, pickerel, white bass, pike, lake trout, and herring.

Mining. Ontario is one of the leading mining provinces of Canada, and its annual mineral output in the early 1980s was valued at about Can.\$4.7 billion. The principal minerals produced are nickel, copper, uranium, zinc, iron ore, gold, silver, platinum metals, salt, nepheline syenite, asbestos, gypsum, quartz, sulfur, cobalt, and such construction materials as sand and gravel, stone, and lime.

The most important single mining region in Ontario is the Sudbury Basin, in which copper, iron ore, nickel, and platinum metals are mined. North of Sudbury, between Lake Timiskaming and the N edge of the Canadian Shield, cobalt, gold, and silver are extracted in a number of mining towns, including Cobalt, Kirkland Lake, and Timmins. Ontario has several important iron-ore regions, notably the Michipicoten Range, a continuation of the famous iron-bearing ranges of Minnesota and Wisconsin, and Steep Rock Lake, both in W Ontario. Major uranium mines are located in the Elliot Lake region N of Lake Huron. Of the nonmetallic minerals, salt is produced in the S, and asbestos and nepheline syenite are produced in the Canadian Shield area. Structural materials, such as clay, gravel and sand, and lime, are produced mostly in the S.

Manufacturing. The most important economic sector of Ontario is manufacturing, and the province leads Canada in this activity. Ontario's chief fabricated goods are transportation equipment, especially motor vehicles; packed meat and other processed food; beverages; primary metals and metal products; chemicals; electrical and electronic equipment; and machinery. Other major manufactures include tobacco products, rubber and leather goods, textiles, clothing, furniture, paper and paper items, refined petroleum, and printed materials. The province's main manufacturing center is Toronto; it is part of the Golden Horseshoe industrial region that extends along the shore of Lake Ontario from Oshawa to the Niagara Falls area. In addition, the Ottawa area contains many firms producing electronic equipment, Windsor has big motor-vehicle assembly plants, Sault Ste. Marie produces much steel, Sarnia has large oil refineries, Thunder Bay has major paper factories, and Sudbury has important mineral-processing facilities.

Tourism. Each year Ontario attracts some 30 million visitors, many of whom are lured by the cultural offerings of the province's cities (especially Toronto and Ottawa) and by the wide variety of vacation and outdoor-recreation opportunities. Niagara Falls is a popular tourist spot, and other favorite areas include Ontario's four national parks (Georgian Bay Islands, Point Pelee, Pukaskwa, and St. Lawrence Islands), several national historic parks and sites, and more than 120 provincial parks, including the large Algonquin Provincial Park. Many summer vacationers visit the lake region SE of Georgian Bay and the Thousand Islands region of the St. Lawrence R.

Transportation. Ontario is well served by all modes of transportation, with a dense concentration of facilities in the heavily populated S part of the province and an adequate network in the less populous N. Ontario is served by lengthy sections of the Trans-Canada Highway; by two transcontinental rail lines; by a busy international airport near Toronto; by the Great Lakes-St. Lawrence Seaway system, which gives most of the S part of the province access to the Atlantic Ocean; and by major crude-petroleum and natural-gas pipelines from W Canada. Altogether, Ontario has about 155,700 km (about 96,750 mi) of roads and about 15,800 km (about 9820 mi) of operated mainline railroad track. Major ports include Thunder Bay (which mainly handles grain and iron-ore concentrates), Hamilton (iron ore, iron-ore concentrates, and coal), Sarnia (petroleum products), and Toronto (various commodities). An important artificial waterway, in addition to those forming parts of the Great

The City Hall of Stratford, Ont., on the banks of the Avon River. Stratford is famous as the site of an annual theater festival.

Lakes-St. Lawrence Seaway system, is the Trent Canal system, which links Georgian Bay and Lake Ontario.

Energy. Ontario has an installed electricity-generating capacity of about 25.7 million kw, and annual output is approximately 102.2 billion kwh. About 38% of the electricity is produced in hydroelectric installations, about 29% in nuclear power plants, and about 25% in thermal facilities burning coal. Major hydroelectric developments are situated on the Niagara, Ottawa, and St. Lawrence rivers.   A.M.Bl.

HISTORY

The first explorer to visit parts of what is now Ontario was the Frenchman Étienne Brûlé, who ascended the Ottawa River in 1610–11 and again in 1615 with the French explorer Samuel de Champlain; in the latter year they penetrated to Georgian Bay. A Jesuit mission was established among the Huron Indians soon afterward; it was destroyed when the Huron were attacked by the Iroquois in 1649. The French constructed a number of forts and trading posts but made no attempts to colonize the region. The earliest English settlement in present Ontario was Moose Factory, a Hudson Bay post established in 1671. Rivalry, often bloody, developed between the British and French over the lucrative fur trade. Under the terms of the Treaty of Paris in 1763 at the conclusion of the French and Indian War between France and Great Britain, the region was established as British territory. In 1774 the area that is now Ontario, as well as much territory now part of the U.S., was attached to the British colony of Québec.

After the American Revolution thousands of Tories, who called themselves United Empire Loyalists, settled in the southern part of the region; they were followed by other Americans who wanted to buy good land cheaply. The region was under French civil law during this period and had no representative government. The English-speaking pioneers expressed dissatisfaction with the governmental and legal system. As a result of their insistence the Ontario region was established in 1791 as a separate colony called Upper Canada, and Québec became Lower Canada. The small degree of local autonomy granted to Upper Canada did not satisfy the inhabitants, however, and in 1837 the Upper Canadians rose in rebellion. Upper Canada and Lower Canada were reunited in 1841 by the British authorities in the hope that the merger would lead eventually to the Anglicization of the French Catholic population of Lower Canada. This hope was not realized, however, and a paralyzing political deadlock ensued. It was broken in 1867 by the creation of the Canadian Confederation, in which the former regions of Upper and Lower Canada became the separate provinces of Ontario and Québec.

At the time of confederation, Ontario was predominantly agricultural and rural. Under the protectionist policies of the new federal government, encouraged by the provincial government, Ontario gradually became industrialized and urban. This process was aided by the building of railways to the west and the development of hydroelectric power from the Saint Lawrence River and Niagara Falls in the late 19th century and by mining in the Canadian Shield in the early 20th century. Pulp and paper industries have also been important in northern Ontario. In the 1950s, as the last new sources of hydroelectric power were tapped, Ontario began to develop nuclear power as an alternative source of energy; oil and natural gas also were piped in from western Canada. Industrialization has greatly increased Ontario's wealth. Since the 1920s Toronto has succeeded Montréal as Canada's major financial center.

Ontario's economic development has been accompanied by great changes in the population. Formerly inhabited chiefly by Protestants of British descent, Ontario has attracted large numbers of immigrants of different nationalities and religions, most of them seeking economic opportunity. In the late 19th century many French-Canadians came to work as lumberers, farmers, and railway laborers, In the early 20th century many southern and eastern Europeans arrived. Since World War II almost 2 million immigrants, chiefly from Europe, have settled in Ontario, giving its cities, once British in character, a more cosmopolitan atmosphere.

From the era of confederation to 1905 Ontario was governed by the Liberal party and from 1905 to 1919 by the Conservatives. Both parties favored industry. The farmers, dissatisfied with their lot, formed their own United Farmers party, which governed ineffectively from 1919 to 1923. The Conservatives returned to power in 1923 but, undermined by unrest during the Great Depression, were displaced by the Liberals from 1934 to 1943. Since then Ontario has had only Conservative governments. The New Democratic party, formed in 1961, represents socialist and trade union interests. In the 1970s the government was preoccupied with educational policy and environmental questions, including the implementation of a 1972 agreement with the U.S. to clean up the Great Lakes. The government was also anxious to induce Québec to remain within the Confederation. R.Bw.

For further information on this topic, see the Bibliography in volume 28, section 1114.

ONTARIO, LAKE, lake of North America, bordered by Ontario, Canada, on the N and by New York on the S. About 310 km (about 190 mi) long and up to about 85 km (about 53 mi) wide, the lake covers an area of 19,011 sq km (7340 sq mi), slightly more than half of which is in Canada. It is the smallest and most easterly of the five Great Lakes.

Lake Ontario is fed by several rivers, including the Niagara R., which flows N from Lake Erie; the Genesee, Oswego, and Black rivers, which enter from New York; and the Trent and Humber rivers, which enter from Ontario. The lake discharges into the Saint Lawrence R. to the NE. A major shipping route, it is an important component of the Saint Lawrence Seaway, and is linked with Lake Erie by the Welland Ship Canal and with Lake Huron by the Trent Canal system. In addition, Lake Ontario is connected with the Ottawa R. by the Rideau Canal and with the Hudson R. by the New York State Barge Canal system. Major ports on the lake include Oswego and Rochester, in New York, and Hamilton, Kingston, and Toronto, in Ontario. During the winter months the area near the shore freezes over, and many harbors on the lake are icebound from about mid-December to mid-April.

ONTOLOGY. *See* METAPHYSICS.

ONYX, mineral (SiO_2), composed of alternating bands of chalcedony and opal (qq.v.). The bands, straight, parallel, and usually colored black and white in alternating layers, are used as a gemstone often for cameos. *Compare* AGATE.

OOMYCETES. *See* FUNGI: *Classification: Oomycota.*

OOSTENDE, also Ostend, town and port, NW Belgium, in West Flanders Province, on the North Sea, near Bruges. It is a leading Belgian port and has important fishing and shipbuilding industries.

Oostende, now a popular seaside resort, was founded as a fishing village in the 9th century. A wall was built around it in 1445, and it was fortified by Prince William I of Orange in 1583. Oostende was the last Dutch stronghold in Belgium. Between 1601 and 1604 the town heroically resisted a Spanish siege, in which 40,000 Spanish were killed, and the Flemish surrendered only after the town had been reduced to ruins. The Ostend Manifesto (q.v.) was drawn up in Oostende in 1854. During World War II the Germans used the town as an important submarine base until the British sealed the harbor by sinking a ship at its entrance. Pop. (1981 est.) 69,678.

OPAL, mineral consisting of hydrated silica ($SiO_2 \cdot NH_2O$), in the gel state. Opal has a hardness of between 5.5 and 6.5 and a sp.gr. of 1.9 to 2.3. The fracture of the mineral is conchoidal, and its luster varies from glassy to dull. The opal also shows extreme variations in color from white to black and in transparency from transparent to opaque.

One of the chief characteristics of the opal is the brilliant play of colors that may be seen in superior stones. These colors result from the formation of minute fissures in the stone as it hardens and the deposition of additional opal in the fissures. The indices of refraction of the original stone and the additional deposits are frequently different and result in light interference causing a play of colors. Opal has been used as a gemstone for many centuries in spite of a superstition that the gem brings bad luck to its owners.

A large number of different types of opal are known, but usually only the transparent or translucent varieties are used as gems. Gem opals include white opals; black opals; fire opals, which are yellow to red in color; girasol, which has a bluish-white opalescence; harlequin opals, which show uniform patches of contrasting colors; and lechosa opals, which have a deep green play of color within the stone. Other types of opal include moss opal, which has inclusions of foreign material resembling moss; hydrophane, a porous, white opal that is cloudy when dry and transparent when the pores are filled with watrer; and hyalite, a glasslike, transparent form of opal.

The finest opals are found chiefly in Australia, Wales, and Mexico.

OPARIN, Aleksandr Ivanovich (1894–1980), Russian biochemist, who pioneered in developing biochemical theories of how life originated on earth. Oparin graduated from Moscow University in 1917, became a professor of biochemistry there in 1927, and from 1946 until his death was director of Moscow's A. N. Bakh Institute for biochemistry. Strongly influenced by Charles Darwin's evolutionary theory, he sought to account for the origin of life in terms of chemical and physical processes. He hypothesized that life developed, in effect, by chance, through a progression from simple to complex self-duplicating organic compounds. His proposal initially met with strong opposition but has since received experimental support and has been accepted as a legitimate hypothesis by the scientific community (see LIFE). Oparin's major work is *The Origin of Life on Earth* (1936).

OP ART. *See* MODERN ART AND ARCHITECTURE.

OPEN DOOR POLICY, doctrine of diplomacy, advocating equal trading rights in the nation to which it is applied for all other nations. The Open Door Policy was first enunciated by the U.S. with respect to China at the end of the 19th century. The major European powers had at that time already obtained control of important areas of China, and it appeared that the country would soon be divided into spheres of influence into which other trading nations would have no access. The U.S. was unwilling to compete for territory, but desired access to China for trading purposes. Accordingly, in 1899 and 1900 U.S. Secretary of State John Milton Hay negotiated an agreement with Great Britain, France, Germany, Russia, Italy, and Japan that guaranteed "equal and impartial trade with all parts of the Chinese Empire" and preservation of "Chinese territorial and administrative" integrity.

The open door agreement remained the basis of U.S. policy toward China until the establishment of the Communist regime there in 1949. Japan's violations of it caused friction between that country and the U.S. before World War II.

OPEN-HEARTH PROCESS. *See* IRON AND STEEL MANUFACTURE.

OPEN SHOP, in labor relations, business establishment or factory in which workers may be employed without regard to their membership or nonmembership in a trade union. The abolition of the open shop is usually one of the primary demands made by labor unions when they engage in collective bargaining with employers because the freedom of employers to hire and retain nonunion help generally makes all attempts at unionization ineffective. The alternatives to the open shop are the closed shop and the union shop.

OPERA, drama in which all or part of the dialogue is sung, and which contains instrumental overtures, interludes, and accompaniments. Types of musical theater closely related to opera include musical comedy and operetta.

Origins. Opera began in Italy in the late 16th and early 17th centuries. Among its precedents were many Italian madrigals of the time, in which scenes involving dialogue, but no stage action, were set to music. Other precursors were masques, ballets de cour, intermezzi, and other Renaissance court spectacles of pageantry, music, and dance. Opera itself was developed by a group of musicians and scholars who called themselves the Camerata (Ital., "salon"). The Camerata had two chief goals: to revive the musical style used in ancient Greek drama and to develop an alternative to the highly contrapuntal music of the late Renaissance. Specifically, they wanted composers to pay close attention to the texts on which their music was based, to set these texts in a simple manner, and to make the music reflect, phrase by phrase, the meaning of the text. These goals were probably characteristic of ancient Greek music, although detailed information about Greek music was not available to the Camerata (nor is it today).

The Camerata developed a style of vocal music called monody (Gr., "solo song"). It consisted of simple melodic lines with contours and rhythms that followed the spoken inflections and rhythms of the text. The melody was accompanied by basso continuo, that is, a series of chords on a harpsichord or other instrument, supported by a bass melody instrument. Two members of the Camerata, Giulio Caccini (1546–1618) and Jacopo Peri (1561–1633), realized that monody could be used for soliloquies and dialogues in a staged drama. In 1597 Peri made use of this insight by writing the first opera, *Dafne*. In 1600 an opera called *Euridice* was performed in Florence, incorporating music by both Peri and Caccini.

The first composer of genius to apply himself to opera was the Italian Claudio Monteverdi. His operas made use not only of the word-centered monodic style but of songs, duets, choruses, and instrumental sections. The nonmonodic pieces had a coherent shape based on purely musical relationships. Monteverdi thus demonstrated that a wide variety of musical procedures and styles could be used in opera to enhance the drama.

Opera spread quickly throughout Italy. The principal Italian opera center during the middle and late 17th century was Venice. The next most important was Rome, where a clear differentiation was made for the first time between the singing styles of aria (used for emotional reflection) and recitative (derived from monody and used for plot information and dialogue). Monody died out as a genre; its principle remained influential. The chief Roman composers were Stefano Landi (c. 1590–c. 1655) and Luigi Rossi (1597–1653). Venetian audiences liked lavish stage settings and spectacular visual effects, such as storms and descents of the gods from heaven. The leading early composers in Venice were Monteverdi, Pier Francesco Cavalli (1602–76), and Marc'Antonio Cesti (1623–69).

Neapolitan Style. Alessandro Scarlatti developed a new kind of opera in Naples in the late 17th century. Neapolitan audiences liked solo singing, and Neapolitan composers began to differentiate further between various kinds of singing. They developed two kinds of recitative: *recitativo secco* (Ital., "dry recitative"), which was accom-

The prison scene from John Gay's ballad opera The Beggar's Opera *(1728), a lighthearted satire and burlesque of operatic form.*   Bettmann Archive

panied only by basso continuo, and *recitativo accompagnato* (Ital., "accompanied recitative"), which was used for tense situations and accompanied by the orchestra. They also introduced arioso, a style that combined arialike melodic contours with the conversational rhythms of a recitative.

By the beginning of the 18th century, the Neapolitan style, with its emphasis on tuneful, entertaining music, had been established in most parts of Europe. The only country where this did not happen was France. There, an Italian-born composer, Jean Baptiste Lully, founded a French school of opera. Lully's patron was Louis XIV, king of France, and the pomp and splendor of the French court find echoes in the massive, slow-moving choral and instrumental episodes of Lully's operas. Ballet was more prominent in Lully's French operas than in Italian operas. His librettos was based on classical French tragedy, their melodic lines following the distinctive inflections and rhythms of the French language. Another of Lully's contributions was the establishment of the first standardized overture type, known as the French overture (*see* OVERTURE).

Wide Popularity. In the late 17th and early 18th centuries, the infant German style of opera was overwhelmed by Italian opera. The most important German operatic center was Hamburg, where an opera house was opened in 1678. Reinhard Keiser (1674–1739) composed more than 100 works there. After Keiser's death Italian composers and singers dominated all the opera houses in Germany.

Italian opera was extremely popular in England. Nevertheless, two operas written about 1700 by English composers were frequently performed there: *Venus and Adonis* by John Blow (1649–1708) and *Dido and Aeneas* by Henry Purcell. These works were an outgrowth of the English courtly stage spectacle, the masque. They incorporated French and Italian elements, particularly the instrumental writing of Lully and the emotional recitatives and arias of the Italians. The German-born composer George Frideric Handel had his greatest successes in England. He wrote 40 operas in the Italian style there during the 1720s and 1730s, after which he gave up opera and turned to the oratorio.

By the 18th century opera had moved away from the ideals of the Camerata and adopted a large number of artificialities. Many Italian boys, for instance, were castrated so that their voices would not change but would remain in a high range. The combination of the voice of a boy and the chest development of a man resulted in a piercing quality and agile technique that was extremely popular. Singers of this type, who played the roles of women, were called castrati. They, along with all other singers, were valued more for their beautiful voices and virtuoso singing than for their acting. Operas came to consist of little more than a series of spectacular arias. The arias themselves followed a single formal scheme, A-B-A, called da capo (Ital., "from the beginning") form; it featured variations that were improvised by the singer when the A section was repeated.

Preclassical and Classical Periods. Several composers in the mid-18th century tried to change operatic practices. They introduced forms other than the da capo for arias and made greater use of choral and instrumental music. The most important of the composers who introduced these reforms was the German-born Christoph Willibald Gluck. A parallel 18th-century development that helped to reform operatic practices was the growth of comic opera, which was known under various names. In England it was called ballad opera; in France, *opéra comique;* in Germany, *Singspiel;* and in Italy, *opera buffa.* All these were lighter in style than the traditional *opera seria* (Ital., "serious opera"). Some of the dialogue was spoken rather than sung, and the plots concerned everyday people and places rather than mythological characters. These traits were clearly seen in the work of the first Italian master of comic opera, Giovanni Battista Pergolesi. Because comic operas emphasized naturalness and good acting, they showed composers of serious opera some ways by which their own works could be made more realistic.

The composer who transformed Italian *opera buffa* into a serious art was Wolfgang Amadeus Mozart, who wrote his first opera *La finta semplice* (The Simple Pretense) at the age of 12. His three Italian-language masterpieces—*The Marriage of Figaro* (1786), *Don Giovanni* (1787), and *Così fan tutte* (1790)—display a genius for musical characterization, and *Don Giovanni* created one of the first great romantic roles. Mozart's German-language *singspiels* range from the comic, in *The Abduction from the Seraglio* (1782), to the ethically symbolic, in *The Magic Flute* (1791).

Romantic Period. France, Germany, and Italy developed characteristic operatic styles during the 19th century, all reflective of the romantic movement. Paris was the birthplace of grand opera—a lavish combination of stage spectacle, action, ballet, and music, much of which was written by foreign composers who settled in France. Early examples were *La vestale* (The Vestal, 1807) by Gasparo Spontini (1774–1851) and *Lodoïska*

The final scene of Wolfgang Amadeus Mozart's famous opera, Così fan tutte, as performed by the Metropolitan Opera in New York City.   Louis Mélancon

(1791) by Luigi Cherubini, both Italians; and *Masaniello,* or *La muette de Portici* (The Mute Girl of Portici, 1822) by Daniel Auber (1782–1871). The style reached its climax in the huge works of the Berlin-born Giacomo Meyerbeer, such as *Robert le diable* (Robert the Devil, 1831) and *Les Huguenots* (1836). The authentically French *Les Troyens* (1856–59) by Hector Berlioz, a setting of the Dido and Aeneas story, was largely ignored in his own country; indeed, it was not performed in its monumental entirety during the composer's lifetime. *Faust* (1859), by Charles Gounod, based on Goethe's poem, was one of the most popular mid-19th-century French operas.

German opera's first great 19th-century work was Ludwig van Beethoven's *Fidelio* (1805; rev. 1806, 1814), a dramatic *singspiel* for which the composer wrote four different overtures. It uses the theme of rescue of an unjustly held captive, a kind of plot that became popular during the French Revolution. Carl Maria von Weber created German romantic opera in Der Freischütz (The Free Shooter, 1821), with its famous supernatural "Wolf's Glen" scene, and in the equally fanciful *Euryanthe* (1823) and *Oberon* (1826).

The summit of German opera was reached by Richard Wagner, who devised a new form of "music drama" in which text (written by him-

Act 1 of Richard Wagner's Lohengrin, from a performance by the Metropolitan Opera in New York City.
Louis Mélancon

Beverly Sills sings the role of Elizabeth I in Roberto Devereux, an opera by Gaetano Donizetti based on the historic events surrounding the execution of the 2d earl of Essex, who had fallen from the queen's favor. Beth Bergman

self), score, and staging were all inextricably blended. His earlier operas, such as *The Flying Dutchman* (1843), *Tannhäuser* (1845), and *Lohengrin* (1850), retained elements of the old style, including arias and choruses. But in subsequent works such as *Tristan und Isolde* (1865) and the mighty tetralogy *Der Ring des Nibelungen* (1869–76), based on Nordic myth, Wagner abandoned previous conventions and wrote in a continuous flowing style, with the orchestra rather than the stage characters often serving as the dramatic protagonist. *Die Meistersinger von Nürnberg* (1868) was a depiction of the medieval guilds, and *Parsifal* (1882), an expression of religious mysticism. In virtually all his works Wagner made extensive use of the leitmotiv (leading theme), a musical label that identifies a particular personage or idea and that recurs in the orchestra, often illuminating the action psychologically. The Festival Theater at Bayreuth was opened in 1876 expressly as a Wagnerian shrine. In his new operatic concepts, both of composition and staging, Wagner exerted enormous influence on musicians of all countries for many years.

Italian opera continued to place primary emphasis on the voice. Gioacchino Rossini composed comic operas, such as *The Barber of Seville* (1816) and *La Cenerentola* (Cinderella, 1817), which have outlasted his more dramatic works; *William Tell* (1829), for example, is known today mainly for its overture. The *bel canto* ("beautiful singing") style, characterized by smooth, expressive, and often spectacular vocalism, also flowered in such works as Vincenzo Bellini's *Norma* (1831), *La sonnambula* (The Sleepwalker, 1831), and *I Puritani* (1835); and in Gaetano Donizetti's *Lucia di Lammermoor* (1835), with its celebrated "mad scene," and his comedies *L'elisir d'amore* (Elixir of Love, 1832) and *Don Pasquale* (1843).

The man who embodied Italian opera, however, was Guiseppe Verdi. He infused his works with unprecedented dramatic vigor and rhythmic vitality. To the rough power of the early *Nabucco* (1842) and *Ernani* (1844) were added the more subtle characterizations of *Rigoletto* (1851), *Il trovatore* (1853), *La traviata* (1853), *Un ballo in maschera* (A Masked Ball, 1859) and *La forza del destino* (1862). *Aïda* combines the visual splendors of grand opera and the musical intimacies of a tragic love story. Verdi's last two operas, *Otello* (1887) and *Falstaff* (1893), composed in his old age, adapted Shakespearean plays to the operatic stage with a dramatic and musical continuity that led some critics to charge him with imitating Wagner. Nevertheless, Verdi's operas remained Italian to the core, with the human voice their basic expressive means and human passions their basic subject.

Russian opera developed its own nationalist

school, starting with *A Life for the Tsar* (1836) by Mikhail Glinka and including *Prince Igor* (produced posthumously, 1890) by Aleksandr Borodin, *Le coq d'or* (The Golden Cockerel, 1909) by Nikolay Rimsky-Korsakov, and the supreme masterpiece of the genre, *Boris Godunov* (1874) by Modest Mussorgsky. Peter Ilich Tchaikovsky's most notable operas are *Eugene Onegin* (1879) and *Pique dame,* or *The Queen of Spades* (1890).

Late 19th and Early 20th Centuries. *Carmen* (1875) by the Frenchman Georges Bizet was viewed by the German philosopher Friedrich Nietzsche as bringing a Mediterranean clarity that dispelled "all the fog of the Wagnerian ideal." Originally an *opéra comique* (which by the 19th century referred to French opera with spoken dialogue, whether serious or comic), *Carmen* created an alluring character in its title role and gave opera a new realistic thrust. Bizet's premature death at the age of 36 cut short a promising career. The most productive French composer of the latter part of the century was Jules Massenet, who composed *Manon* (1884), *Werther* (1892), *Thaïs* (1894), and similar sentimental but stageworthy operas. Other characteristic works of the period were *Mignon* (1866) by Ambroise Thomas, *Lakmé* (1883) by Léo Délibes, *Samson et Dalila* (1877) by Camille Saint-Saëns, and *The Tales of Hoffmann* (produced posthu-

Violetta, the heroine of Guiseppe Verdi's La Traviata, *as portrayed by the soprano Amelita Galli-Curci.*
Brown Brothers

In the triumphal scene of Giuseppe Verdi's Aïda, *the returning hero Radames is welcomed by the king, shown in a production by the Metropolitan Opera Company in New York City.* Metropolitan Opera Guild

The American mezzo-soprano Joy Davidson sings the title role of Carmen, by Georges Bizet, in a New York City Opera Company production. Metropolitan Opera Guild

mously, 1881) by Jacques Offenbach, a German-born Parisian who had previously proved a master of 19th-century French comic opera, called *opéra bouffe*. At the turn of the century Gustave Charpentier composed *Louise* (1900), a realistic opera with a Parisian working-class background, and Claude Debussy adapted the techniques of impressionism to produce in *Pelléas et Mélisande* (1902) vocal music that reflected the contours and shadings of the French language itself.

Realism in Italian opera became known by the name *verismo*, from the Italian word for "truth." Its two foremost exemplars were *Cavalleria rusticana* (Rustic Chivalry, 1890) by Pietro Mascagni and *I pagliacci* (The Clowns, 1892) by Ruggero Leoncavallo, short but searing melodramas about passion and murder in sunbaked southern Italian villages. The true successor to Verdi was Giacomo Puccini, who composed such unfailingly melodic, frankly emotional, and eminently singable operas as *Manon Lescaut* (1893), *La Bohème* (1896), *Tosca* (1900), *Madama Butterfly* (1904), and the unfinished *Turandot* (produced posthumously, 1926). Other successful post–Verdi operas include *La gioconda* (The Ballad Singer, 1876) by Amilcare Ponchielli (1834–86), *Andrea Chenier* (1896) by Umberto Giordano (1867–1948), and *La Wally* (1892) by Alfredo Catalani (1854–93).

In Germany Wagner's influence pervaded virtually all subsequent operas, including Engelbert Humperdinck's setting of the children's tale *Hänsel und Gretel* (1893). The dominant figure was Richard Strauss, who used a Wagnerian-scale orchestra and similar vocal techniques in *Salome* (1905) and *Elektra* (1909), both short, sensational works with an undercurrent of morbid psychology. Strauss's *Der Rosenkavalier* (The Cavalier of the Rose, 1911), a comedy, became his most popular work. That opera was followed by *Ariadne auf Naxos* (1912), *Die Frau ohne Schatten* (The Woman Without a Shadow, 1919), and *Arabella* (1933).

Other middle-European countries produced operas with national flavoring that entered the international repertoire. From Czechoslovakia came Bedřich Smetana's village comedy *The Bartered Bride* (1866), Antonin Dvořák's *Rusalka* (1901), and Leoš Janáček's *Jenufa* (1904) and *The Makropoulos Affair* (1926). Hungary produced Zoltán Kodály's *Háry János* (1926) and Béla Bartók's *Bluebeard's Castle* (1918).

Arnold Schoenberg and his pupil Alban Berg introduced atonality and the twelve-tone system. Schoenberg's unfinished *Moses und Aron* (produced posthumously, 1957) and Berg's *Wozzeck* (1925) and also his unfinished *Lulu* (produced posthumously, 1937; complete version produced

OPERA

The death of Scarpia, a scene from Tosca, *by Giacomo Puccini, is in the style of the Italian opera seria, which usually has a tragic mood.*   John G. Ross–UPI

1979) made use of *Sprechstimme* or *Sprechgesang* ("speech voice" or "speech song"), a kind of declamation midway between speech and song. *Wozzeck,* a nightmarish portrayal of the degradation of an army private, was soon recognizd as a modern masterpiece.

Modern Trends. As the 20th century developed, operatic styles reflected both persistent national approaches and the growing internationalism represented by the atonal and serial techniques. The Russian Sergey Prokofiev wrote the piquant *Love for Three Oranges* while traveling through the American West; it was first given in Chicago in 1921. Before his death he composed the massive *War and Peace* (1946, rev. 1955). Dimitri Shostakovich fell out of favor with the Soviets for his *Lady Macbeth of Mtsensk* (1934), and it was later revised under the title *Katerina Ismailova* (1963).

Most modern composers tended to incorporate not only symphonic techniques but also folk, popular, or jazz styles into their works. French operas reflecting some of these influences include Maurice Ravel's *L'heure Espagnole* (The Spanish Hour, 1911) and *L'enfant et les sortilèges* (The Bewitched Child, 1925), as well as Francis Poulenc's *Les mamelles de Tirésias* (The Breasts of Tiresias, 1947) and *Les dialogues des Carmélites* (1957). Spain produced Manuel de Falla's *La vida breve* (Life Is Short, 1913), and Ger-

many *Mathis der Maler* (Matthias the Painter, 1938) by Paul Hindemith, as well as the satiric, cabaret-style *Aufstieg und Fall der Stadt Mahagonny* (1929; Mahagonny, 1970) and *Die Dreigroschenoper* (1928; The Threepenny Opera, 1954) by Kurt Weill, text by the German dramatist Bertolt Brecht. The Russian expatriate Igor Stravinsky utilized a neoclassical style in *The Rake's Progress* (1951).

Italian opera, although producing relatively conservative melodic scores by Italo Montemezzi (1875–1952) and Ermanno Wolf-Ferrari, also followed more radical approaches in such works as *Assassino nella cattedrale* (Murder in the Cathedral, 1958) by Ildebrando Pizzetti (1880–1968), *Il prigionero* (The Prisoner, 1950) by Luigi Dallapiccola, and *Intolleranza* (1960) by Luigi Nono, the last two having a musical structure based on Schoenberg's twelve-tone system. Other notable post–World War II operas have been written by the Germans Boris Blacher (1903–75), Werner Egk (1901–83), Hans Werner Henze, and Carl Orff; the Austrian Gottfried von Einem (1918–   ); and the Argentine Alberto Ginastera. The British composers Frederick Delius and Ralph Vaughan Williams also produced distinctive works. English opera found its authentic voice, however, in 1945 with Benjamin Britten's *Peter Grimes,* a grim depiction of life in a village of seafarers. Britten later composed such notable works as *Albert Herring* (1947), *The Turn of the Screw* (1954), *A Midsummer Night's Dream* (1960), and *Death in Venice* (1973).

The first American grand opera was *Leonora* (1845) by William Henry Fry (1813–64). Most subsequent works, such as *The Scarlet Letter* (1896) by Walter Damrosch, were European in style. Among operas produced at the Metropolitan Opera House in New York City were *The Pipe of Desire* (1910) by Frederick S. Converse (1871–1940), *Cleopatra's Night* (1920) by Henry K. Hadley, and *Peter Ibbetson* (1931) by Deems Taylor (1885–1966). Genuine American influences asserted themselves only in the 20th century. The influence of American blacks was notable in works from *Treemonisha* (produced posthumously, 1974), by the ragtime composer Scott Joplin, to *Porgy and Bess* (1935), by George Gershwin. Virgil Thomson's *Four Saints in Three Acts* (1934) and *The Mother of Us All* (1947) and Marc Blitzstein's masterpiece *Regina* (1949) used elements of folk and popular music. American subjects were dramatized in *The Ballad of Baby Doe* (1956) by Douglas Moore (1893–1969), *Susannah* (1955) by Carlisle Floyd (1926–), and *Lizzie Borden* by Jack Beeson (1921–). The most popular "American" operas, however, were those of the Italian-born Gian-Carlo Menotti, composer of *The Medium* (1946), *The Telephone* (1947), *The Consul* (1950), and *Amahl and the Night Visitors* (1951).

Operatic Production. Opera has always been vocal. The prima donna traditionally has been the pivot of a successful production. In the 20th century, however, emphasis has also been placed on the operatic ensemble, with the conductor, the scenic designer, and the stage director assuming roles at least coequal with the singers. In the U.S. stage directors such as Frank Corsaro (1924–) and Sarah Caldwell (1928–) have left a personal imprint upon operatic staging.

A growth in multimedia production techniques has paralleled the increase in electronic and synthesizer music by modern composers. Leonard Bernstein's *Mass* (1971), while not strictly an opera, blended operatic elements into a mixed media format in which dance, electronic music, and novel stage techniques all played a part. Slide projections and film were used to great effect in the New York City Opera Company's productions of *A Village Romeo and Juliet* (1907) by Delius and *Die Tote Stadt* (The Dead City, 1920) by Erich Wolfgang Korngold, both directed by Frank Corsaro. The Center Opera of Minneapolis utilized striking lighting and film effects in *Faust Counter Faust*, a concoction of

original music interspersed with tape recordings of previous Faust operas. Such rock operas as *Jesus Christ Superstar* (New York City, 1971) emphasized multimedia stage techniques, although the work itself was more a pop culture phenomenon than an esthetic creation. In both standard theaters and experimental workshops, opera seemed to be regaining the place it had held in the 17th century as a scenic innovator and staging pioneer.

Technology also contributed to the development of new audiences, especially through the proliferation of complete recordings made possible by the invention of the long-playing record. Weekly radio broadcasts from the Metropolitan Opera stage commenced with *Hänsel und Gretel* in 1931 and have continued ever since. Several operas have been written expressly for broadcast, such as Menotti's *Amahl* and Britten's *Owen Wingrave* (1971), both conceived for television. Ingmar Bergman's version of Mozart's *The Magic Flute* achieved a high level of artistry in cinematic opera.

As it entered the last quarter of the 20th century, opera was thriving both from the artistic and the technological standpoints, but it faced a financial crisis because of rising production costs and union pay scales. Abroad, most companies are substantially subsidized by the state, but in the U.S., where government support is considerably less, the main source of support continues to be private foundations, commercial enterprises, and individual patrons.

For additional information on individual composers and other figures, see biographies of those whose names are not followed by dates.

H.Ku.

For further information on this topic, see the Bibliography in volume 28, sections 736–37.

OPERETTA, stage play with songs and dance interspersed with dialogue. In the 18th century, the term meant a short opera, but in the 19th and 20th centuries it came to mean a play with music of light character and popular appeal. The French operetta developed in small theaters such as the Bouffes Parisiens, founded by the composer Jacques Offenbach. The form, originally a one-act piece, later grew into a three-act or four-act play that approached the opéra comique. Offenbach's 90-odd operettas include *Orpheus in the Underworld* (1858) and *Tales of Hoffman* (1881). For these works, he and his countryman Charles Lecocq (1832–1918), composer of *La fille de Madame Angot* (1872), used the term *opéra bouffe*.

The roots of the Viennese operetta lay in the singspiel and the local farce (*see also* OPERA). Suppé helped establish this form and excelled in it, producing such works as *The Beautiful Gala-tea* (1865), *Light Cavalry* (1866), and *Boccaccio* (1879). With Johann Strauss, Jr., Viennese oper-etta reached international repute. His younger contemporary Karl Millöcker (1842–99) produced *The Beggar Student* (1882) to acclaim in Great Britain and the U.S. The waltz was an essential element in the operetta of the younger Strauss, and with *Die Fledermaus* (1874) he introduced a significant quality of sentimentality and operatic seriousness, which became an important musical facet of the typical Viennese second act finale. Other Viennese composers of operettas were Franz Lehár, who wrote *The Merry Widow* (1905); Robert Stolz (1880–1975), known for his *White Horse Inn* (1936); Oscar Straus (1870–1954), composer of *The Chocolate Soldier* (1909); and Emmerich Kalman (1882–1953), composer of *Countess Maritza* (1924).

The English operetta developed from the short ballad opera to more extended works, of which the best known, *Clari, or the Maid of Milan* (1823), by Sir Henry Bishop, is remembered for the tune "Home, Sweet Home." The develop-ment reached a climax in the light operas of Sir Arthur Sullivan and Sir William S. Gilbert, among them *H.M.S. Pinafore* (1878) and *The Mikado* (1885). A late example is *Bitter Sweet* (1929), with libretto and music by Sir Noel Coward.

The outstanding American operetta composer was the Irish-born Victor Herbert, whose 40 op-erettas included *The Red Mill* (1906) and *Naughty Marietta* (1910). Among other noted Americans in this field were Reginald De Koven (1859–1920), the Czech-born Rudolf Friml, and the Hungarian-born Sigmund Romberg. Ameri-can operettas that achieved considerable success include De Koven's *Robin Hood* (1890), Friml's *Rose Marie* (1924) and *Vagabond King* (1925), and Romberg's *Student Prince* (1924) and *Desert Song* (1926). After 1930, operetta, at least in the U.S., gradually evolved into the musical or musi-cal comedy.

OPHIOLITE, any of the mixed metamorphic rocks produced along the line of collision be-tween an oceanic plate and a continental plate of the earth's crust (*see* PLATE TECTONICS). Ophio-lites form in subduction zones—convergent plate boundaries where the basaltic seafloor plunges (is subducted) beneath the continent and is melted and consumed—such as, for exam-ple, along the west coast of South America. The ophiolites created in these zones consist of de-tached slices of seafloor basalts altered to green-stone schists (*see* SCHIST) and serpentine (q.v.), interlayered with other metamorphosed rocks. Many of today's high mountain ranges, including the South American Andes, consist partly of ophiolitic rocks and thus mark former junctures of seafloor and continent.

OPHITES (Gr. *ophis,* "serpent"), a group of Gnostic sects that flourished in the Roman Em-pire during the 2d century AD. Like other Gnos-tics, they believed that the human soul is imprisoned in the body and the material universe and can be saved through gnosis, or revealed knowledge of the soul's transcendent origin (*see* GNOSTICISM). The Ophites revered the serpent as a symbol of spirituality and wisdom, holding that the serpent in the Garden of Eden imparted gno-sis to Adam and Eve, who were therefore pun-ished by God. (Gnostics in general identified the God of the Old Testament with the evil deity who, they believed, created the material world, and they venerated all those who defied him.) Most Ophites were nominally Christian, but they repudiated the human Jesus, as opposed to the spiritual Christ who temporarily inhabited his body and who taught the esoteric wisdom of gnosis. They were therefore considered heretics (*see* HERESY) and eventually succumbed to the persecution of the early church.

OPHTHALMOLOGY (Gr. *ophthalmos,* "eye"), branch of medicine concerned with the study of the eyes—their physiology and structure and the diseases and conditions affecting them (*see* EYE). Unlike optometrists (*see* OPTOMETRY), ophthal-mologists are required to have a medical degree. In addition to eye infections and other disorders, ophthalmologists are concerned with refraction, orthoptics (the treatment of defective visual hab-its), the prevention of blindness, and the care of the blind.

OPIUM, narcotic drug produced from the drying resin of unripe capsules of the opium poppy (q.v.), *Papaver somniferum.* Opium is grown mainly in Turkey and India. The legitimate world demand for opium amounts to about 680 metric tons a year, but many times that amount is dis-tributed illegally.

In its commercial form, opium is a chestnut-colored globular mass, sticky and rather soft, but hardening from within as it ages. It is processed into the alkaloid morphine which has long served as the chief painkiller in medical practice, although synthetic substitutes such as meperi-dine (trade name Demerol) are now available. Heroin, a derivative of morphine, is about three times more potent. Codeine (q.v.) is another im-portant opium alkaloid.

The molecules of opiates have painkilling properties similar to those of compounds called endorphins or enkephalins produced in the body. Being of similar structure, the opiate molecules occupy many of the same nerve-receptor sites and bring on the same analgesic effect as the body's natural painkillers. Opiates first produce a feeling of pleasure and euphoria, but with their continued use the body demands larger amounts to reach the same sense of well-being. Withdrawal is extremely uncomfortable, and addicts typically continue taking the drug to avoid pain rather than to attain the initial state of euphoria. Malnutrition, respiratory complications, and low blood pressure are some of the illnesses associated with addiction.

As long ago as 100 AD, opium had been used as a folk medicine, taken with a beverage or swallowed as a solid. Only toward the middle of the 17th century, when opium smoking was introduced into China, did any serious addiction problems arise. In the 18th century opium addiction was so serious there that the Chinese made many attempts to prohibit opium cultivation and opium trade with Western countries. At the same time opium made its way to Europe and North America, where addiction grew out of its prevalent use as a painkiller.

With the invention of the hypodermic syringe during the American Civil War, the injection of morphine became indispensable in treating patients who had to undergo some of the newly developed surgical operations. Physicians of that time hoped that injecting morphine directly into the blood stream would avoid the addictive effects of smoking or eating opium, but instead it proved more addictive. With the discovery of heroin in 1898 came a similar hope that it would prevent addiction, but this more potent drug created a much stronger dependency than opium or morphine.

Today opium is sold on the street as a powder or dark brown solid and is smoked, eaten, or injected. Heroin addicts in the U.S. number close to half a million people. Although the synthetic narcotic methadone has been used to offer addicts some relief from opiates, it is itself addictive. Complete recovery from opiate addiction is acknowledged to require years of social and psychological rehabilitation. See DRUG DEPENDENCE; NARCOTICS.

OPIUM WAR, war between Great Britain and China, 1839–42, resulting from the attempt of the Chinese government to prevent the importation of opium into China by British merchants. By the Treaty of Nanking, which ended the war, China opened certain ports of British trade and ceded Hong Kong to Great Britain.

OPOLE (Ger. *Oppeln*), city and port, S Poland, capital of Opole Province, on the Odra R., near Wrocław. The city is a rail junction and grain-

trade center in a quartz-quarrying region, and its manufactures include machinery, textiles, cement, lime, lumber and wood products, tile, and flour. Capital of a duchy from 1163 to 1532, Opole passed to the Habsburgs and, in 1742, to Prussia. As a part of Germany, the city was the capital of the Prussian province of Upper Silesia from 1919 to 1945. Pop. (1981 est.) 116,700.

OPORTO, also Porto, city, NW Portugal, capital of Oporto District, mostly on the steep N bank of the Douro R., near the Atlantic Ocean. With Lisbon, it is one of Portugal's chief economic centers and the focus of a large metropolitan area. Suburbs include the deepwater port of Leixões, located to the NW; and Vila Nova de Gaia, located on the S bank of the Douro and the principal site of the region's famed wine storage warehouses. Port wine (named for the city) is Oporto's most noted manufacture and export; other products include processed fish, textiles, and clothing. Among the points of interest of the city are the old quarter, with narrow, cobbled streets; the cathedral (12th–18th cent.); and the 18th-century Torre dos Clérigos (Tower of the Clerics), a granite structure 75 m (246 ft) high. Also here are the University of Oporto (1911), the Higher School of Fine Arts (1836), and the National Museum of Soares dos Reis, containing a collection of paintings and antiquities.

Cale, a pre-Roman settlement on the S bank of the Douro R., was occupied by the Romans and became known as Portus Cale. The Visigoths held the city from around 540 until 716, when the Moors gained control. The Moors relinquished Oporto in the late 11th century. The city developed as an exporting center of port wine in the late 17th century. The construction in 1890 of an artificial harbor at Leixões contributed to Oporto's later growth. Pop. (1978 est.) 333,300.

OPOSSUM, a common name of the marsupial animals in the family Didelphidae, which is made up of 12 genera and about 65 species. Opossums, found only in the western hemisphere, range in length from 15 to 76 cm (6 to 30 in), including the long, naked prehensile tail, which is from 5 to 25 cm (2 to 10 in) long. The common Virginia opossum, *Didelphis marsupialis*, is the largest of the opossums, measuring 76 cm, of which one-third is the tail. The front feet have five toes with claws; on the hind feet the outer four toes bear claws, and the inmost is opposable, like a thumb, and nailless. The Virginia opossum is covered with long, sleek, white hair and an undercoating of soft, woolly fur. It has a pointed, slender face and large, broad, naked ears. An opossum has 50 teeth. Most species are omnivorous, usually preferring a diet of insects

Virginia opossum, Didelphis marsupialis. *Female opossum and young.* Gordon S. Smith–National Audubon Society

and already dead animals. They are nocturnal, sleeping in a burrow during the day and hunting food at night; most are arboreal. The yapock, *Chironectes,* of South America is aquatic, having webbed hind feet for swimming. One of the best-known characteristics of opossums, their habit of feigning death when surprised, has given rise to the expression "playing possum."

Most species have the abdominal pouch characteristic of marsupials; however, in some South American species this pouch is rudimentary or absent. A female opossum may have as many as 19 nipples within the pouch, but 12 to 14 is the usual number. Of the 4 to 24 young that may be born in a litter, only 8 or 9 usually survive. The gestation period is about 13 days, and the newborn opossums, about 1 cm (less than 0.5 in) long and weighing about 0.33 g (0.12 oz), are quite undeveloped. They must spend about two months in the mother's pouch attached to the nipples before they are able to move about.

The Virginia opossum, found throughout the eastern U.S. and occasionally in the western states, is edible and considered a delicacy in the South; it is hunted with the aid of dogs and, when treed, is captured with a forked stick. Opossum fur formerly had commercial value but is little used now. The name opossum is frequently shortened to possum.

OPPENHEIMER, J. Robert (1904-67), American physicist and government adviser, who directed the development of the first atomic bombs.

Oppenheimer was born in New York City on April 22, 1904, and was educated at Harvard University and the universities of Cambridge and Göttingen. After serving with the International Education Board (1928-29), he became a profes-

sor of physics at the University of California and the California Institute of Technology (1929-47), where he built up large schools of theoretical physics. He was noted for his contributions relating to the quantum theory, the theory of relativity, cosmic rays, positrons, and neutron stars.

During a leave of absence (1943-45), Oppenheimer served as director of the atomic bomb project at Los Alamos, N.Mex. His leadership and organizational skills earned him the Presidential Medal of Merit in 1946. In 1947 he became direc-

Dr. J. Robert Oppenheimer, in 1948, as chairman of the General Advisory Committee of the Atomic Energy Commission. UPI

tor of the Institute for Advanced Studies in Princeton, N.J., serving there until the year before his death. He was also chairman of the General Advisory Committee of the Atomic Energy Commission (q.v.), or AEC, from 1947 to 1952 and served thereafter as an adviser. In 1954, however, he was suspended from this position on charges that his past association with Communists and so-called fellow travelers made him a poor security risk. This action reflected the political atmosphere of the time, as well as the dislike of some politicians and military figures for Oppenheimer's opposition to development of the hydrogen bomb and his support of arms control; his loyalty was not really in doubt. Subsequently, efforts were made to clear his name, and in 1963 the AEC conferred on him its highest honor, the Enrico Fermi Award. Oppenheimer devoted his final years to study of the relationship between science and society; he died in Princeton on Feb. 18, 1967. His writings include *Science and the Common Understanding* (1954) and *Lectures on Electrodynamics* (pub. posthumously 1970).

OPPER, Frederick Burr (1857–1937), American illustrator and cartoonist, born in Madison, Ohio. He was associated with the New York *Journal* and the weekly *Puck* from 1880 to 1899. Noted for his sharp, witty drawings, he illustrated books by Bill Nye (1850–96), Mark Twain, and Finley Peter Dunne, author of the *Mr. Dooley* series. Opper created the comic-strip characters Happy Hooligan and Alphonse and Gaston.

OPPIAN, name of two Greek didactic poets of antiquity. One poet was born in Cilicia (fl. 2d cent. AD). He composed a work on fishing in five books, entitled *Halieutica*. The poem, which is extant, was written in ornate and artificial hexameters. The other poet was the author of an extant poem, also in hexameters, on the subject of hunting; this work, entitled *Cynegetica,* was in four books, and was probably composed early in the 3d century AD. The second Oppian spoke of his home as Apamea, in Syria.

OPTICAL FIBERS. See FIBER OPTICS.

OPTICS, branch of physical science dealing with the propagation and behavior of light (q.v.). In a general sense, light is that part of the electromagnetic spectrum that extends from X rays to microwaves and includes the radiant energy that produces the sensation of vision (*see* ELECTROMAGNETIC RADIATION; ENERGY; SPECTRUM; X RAY). The study of optics is divided into geometrical optics and physical optics, and these branches are discussed below.

NATURE OF LIGHT

Radiant energy has a dual nature and obeys laws that may be explained in terms of a stream of particles, or packets of energy, called photons, or in terms of a train of transverse waves (*see* PHOTON; RADIATION; WAVE MOTION). The concept of photons is used to explain the interactions of light and matter that result in a change in the form of energy, as in the case of the photoelectric cell or luminescence (q.v.). The concept of transverse waves is usually used to explain the propagation of light through various substances and some of the phenomena of image formation. Geometrically, a simple transverse wave may be described by points that oscillate in the same plane back and forth across an axis perpendicular to the direction of oscillation such that at any instant of time the envelope of these points is, for example, a sine function that intersects the axis (*see* GEOMETRY; TRIGONOMETRY). The wave front progresses, and the radiant energy travels along the axis. The oscillating point may be considered to describe the vibration of the electric component, or vector (q.v.), of the light wave. The magnetic component vibrates in a direction perpendicular to that of the electric vector and to the axis. The magnetic component is ineffective and may be ignored in the study of visible light. The number of complete oscillations, or vibrations (*see* OSCILLATION), per second of a point on the light wave is known as the frequency (q.v.). The wavelength is the linear distance parallel to the axis between two points in the same phase, or occupying equivalent positions on the wave, for example, the distance from maximum to maximum in the case of a sine function representation. Differences in wavelength manifest themselves as differences in color (q.v.) in the visible spectrum. The visible range extends from about 350 nanometers (violet) to 750 nanometers (red), a nanometer being equal to a billionth of a meter, or 4×10^{-8} in. White light is a mixture of the visible wavelengths. No sharp boundaries exist between wavelength regions, but 10 nanometers may be taken as the low wavelength limit for ultraviolet radiation. Infrared radiation (q.v.), which includes heat energy, includes the wavelengths from about 700 nanometers to approximately 1 mm. The velocity of an electromagnetic wave is the product of the frequency and the wavelength. In a vacuum this velocity is the same for all wavelengths. The velocity of light in material substances is, with few exceptions, less than in a vacuum. Also, in material substances this velocity is different for different wavelengths, as a result of dispersion. The ratio of the velocity of light in vacuum to the velocity of a particular wavelength of light in a substance is known as the index of refraction of that substance for the given wavelength. The index of refraction of a vacuum is equal to 1; that of air is 1.00029, but for most applications it is also taken to be 1.

The laws of reflection and refraction of light are usually derived using the wave theory of light introduced by the Dutch mathematician, astronomer, and physical scientist Christiaan Huygens. Huygens's principle states that every point on an initial wave front may be considered as the source of small, secondary spherical wavelets that spread out in all directions from their centers with the same velocity, frequency, and wavelength as the parent wave front. When the wavelets encounter another medium or object, each point on the boundary becomes a source of two new sets of waves. The reflected set travels back into the first medium, and the refracted set enters the second medium. It is sometimes simpler and sufficient to represent the propagation of light by rays rather than by waves. The ray is the flow line, or direction of travel, of radiant energy, and the assumption is made that light does not bend around corners. In geometrical optics the wave theory of light is ignored and rays are traced through an optical system by applying the laws of reflection and refraction.

GEOMETRICAL OPTICS

This area of optical science concerns the application of laws of reflection and refraction of light in the design of lenses (see Lenses below) and other optical components of instruments. If a light ray that is traveling through one homogeneous medium is incident on the surface of a second homogeneous medium, part of the light is reflected and part may enter the second medium as the refracted ray and may or may not undergo absorption in the second medium.

Reflection and Refraction. The amount of light reflected depends on the ratio of the refractive indexes for the two media. The plane of incidence contains the incident ray and the normal (line perpendicular) to the surface at the point of

incidence (see Fig. 1). The angle of incidence (reflection or refraction) is the angle between the incident (reflected or refracted) ray and this normal. The laws of reflection state that the angle of incidence is equal to the angle of reflection and that the incident ray, the reflected ray, and the normal to the surface at the point of incidence all lie in the same plane. If the surface of the second medium is smooth or polished it may act as a mirror (q.v.) and produce a reflected image. If the mirror is flat, or plane, the image of the object appears to lie behind the mirror at a distance equal to the distance between the object and the surface of the mirror. The light source in Fig. 2 is the object A, and a point on A sends out rays in all directions. The two rays that strike the mirror at B and C, for example, are reflected as the rays BD and CE. To an observer in front of the mirror, these rays appear to come from the point F behind the mirror. It follows from the laws of reflection that CF and BF form the same angle with the surface of the mirror as do AC and AB. If the surface of the second medium is rough, then normals to various points of the surface lie in random directions. In that case, rays that may lie in the same plane when they emerge from a point source nevertheless lie in random planes of incidence, and therefore of reflection, and are scattered and cannot form an image.

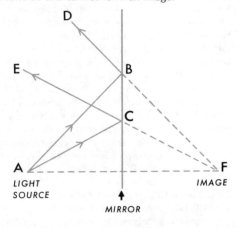

Fig. 2. Reflection from a plane mirror.

Snell's law. This important law, named after the Dutch mathematician Willebrod Von Roijen Snell (1591–1626), states that the product of the refractive index and the sine of the angle of incidence of a ray in one medium is equal to the product of the refractive index and the sine of the angle of refraction in a successive medium. Also, the incident ray, the refracted ray, and the normal to the boundary at the point of incidence

Fig. 1. Fundamental laws of reflection.

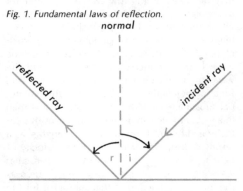

r = angle of reflection   i = angle of incidence

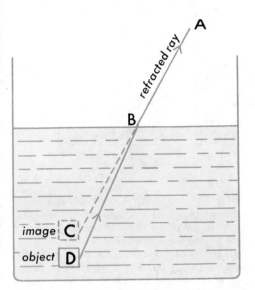

Fig. 3. As a result of refraction, object in water appears closer to the water's surface.

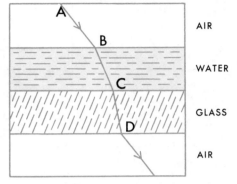

Fig. 4. Refracted ray passing through three media.

all lie in the same plane. Generally, the refractive index of a denser transparent substance is higher than that of a less dense material; that is, the velocity of light is lower in the denser substance. If a ray is incident obliquely, then a ray entering a medium with a higher refractive index is bent toward the normal, and a ray entering a medium of lower refractive index is deviated away from the normal. Rays incident along the normal are reflected and refracted along the normal. In making calculations, the optical path, which is defined as the product of the distance a ray travels in a given medium and the refractive index of that medium, is the important consideration. To an observer in a less dense medium such as air, an object in a denser medium appears to lie closer to the boundary than is the actual case. A common example, that of an object lying underwater observed from above water, is shown in Fig. 3. Oblique rays are chosen only for ease of illustration. The ray DB from the object at D is bent away from the normal to A. The object, therefore, appears to lie at C, where the line ABC intersects a line normal to the surface of the water and passing through D.

The path of light passing through several media with parallel boundaries is shown in Fig. 4. The refractive index of water is lower than that of glass. Because the refractive index of the first and last medium is the same, the ray emerges parallel to the incident ray AB, but it is displaced.

Prism. If light passes through a prism, a transparent object with flat, polished surfaces at angles to each other, the exit ray is no longer parallel to the incident ray. Because the refractive index of a substance varies for the different wavelengths, a prism can spread out the various wavelengths of light contained in an incident beam and form a spectrum. In Fig. 5, the angle CBD between the path of the incident ray and the path of the emergent ray is the angle of deviation. If the angle the incident ray makes with the normal is equal to the angle made by the emergent ray, the deviation is at a minimum. The refractive index of the prism can be calculated by measuring the angle of minimum deviation and the angle between the faces of the prism.

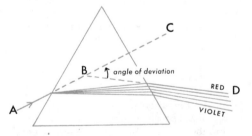

Fig. 5. Refraction of light by a prism.

Critical angle. Given that a ray is bent away from the normal when it enters a less dense medium, and that the deviation from the normal increases as the angle of incidence increases, an angle of incidence exists, known as the critical angle, such that the refracted ray makes an angle of 90° with the normal to the surface and travels along the boundary between the two media. If the angle of incidence is increased beyond the critical angle, the light rays will be totally reflected back into the incident medium. Total reflection cannot occur if light is traveling from a less dense medium to a denser one. The three drawings in Fig. 6 show ordinary refraction, refraction at the

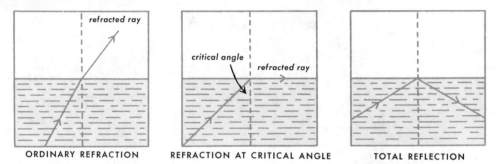

ORDINARY REFRACTION   REFRACTION AT CRITICAL ANGLE   TOTAL REFLECTION

Fig. 6. Critical angle of refraction.

critical angle, and total reflection. In recent years, a new, practical application of total reflection has been found in the use of fiber optics (q.v.). If light enters a solid glass or plastic tube obliquely, the light can be totally reflected at the boundary of the tube and, after a number of successive total reflections, emerge from the other end. Glass fibers can be drawn to a very small diameter, coated with a material of lower refractive index, and then assembled into flexible bundles or fused into plates of fibers used to transmit images. The flexible bundles, which can be used to provide illumination as well as to transmit images, are valuable in medical examination, as they can be inserted into various openings.

Spherical and Aspherical Surfaces. Traditionally, most of the terminology of geometrical optics was developed with reference to spherical reflecting and refracting surfaces. Aspherical surfaces, however, are sometimes involved. The optic axis is a reference line that is an axis of symmetry. If the optical component is spherical, the optic axis passes through the center of a lens or mirror and through the center of curvature. Light rays from a very distant source are considered to travel parallel to one another. If rays parallel to the optic axis are incident on a spherical surface, they are reflected or refracted so that they intersect or appear to intersect at a point on the optic axis. The distance between this point and the vertex of a mirror or a thin lens is the focal length. If a lens is thick, calculations are made with reference to planes called principal planes, rather than to the surface of the lens. A lens may have two focal lengths, depending on which surface (if the surfaces are not alike) the light strikes first. If an object is at the focal point, the rays emerging from it are made parallel to the optic axis after reflection or refraction. If rays from an object are converged by a lens or mirror so that they actually intersect in front of a mirror or behind a lens, the image is real and inverted, or upside down. If the rays diverge after reflec-

tion or refraction so that the light only appears to converge, the image is virtual and erect. The ratio of the height of the image to the height of the object is the lateral magnification.

If it is understood that distances measured from the surface of a lens or mirror in the direction in which light is traveling are positive and distances measured in the opposite direction are negative, then if u is the object distance, v the image distance, and f is the focal length of a mirror or of a thin lens, the equation

$$\frac{1}{v} + \frac{1}{u} = \frac{1}{f}$$

applies to spherical mirrors, and the equation

$$\frac{1}{v} - \frac{1}{u} = \frac{1}{f}$$

applies to spherical lenses. If a simple lens has surfaces with radii r_1 and r_2, and the ratio of its refractive index to that of the medium surrounding it is n, then

$$\frac{1}{f} = (n - 1)\left(\frac{1}{r_1} - \frac{1}{r_2}\right)$$

The focal length of a spherical mirror is equal to half the radius of curvature. As is shown in Fig. 7, rays parallel to the optic incident on a concave mirror with its center of curvature at C are reflected so that they intersect at B, halfway between A and C. If the object distance is greater than the distance AC, and image is real, inverted, and diminished. If the object lies between the center of curvature and the focal point, the image is real, inverted, and enlarged. If the object is located between the surface of the mirror and the focus, the image is virtual, upright, and enlarged. Convex mirrors form only virtual, erect, and diminished images.

Lenses. Lenses made with surfaces of small radii have the shorter focal lengths. A lens with two convex surfaces will always refract rays parallel to

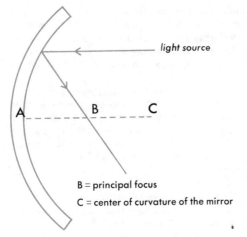

B = principal focus

C = center of curvature of the mirror

Fig. 7. Reflection from a concave spherical mirror.

the optic axis so that they converge to a focus on the side of the lens opposite to the object. A concave lens surface will deviate incident rays parallel to the axis away from the axis, so that even if the second surface of the lens is convex, the rays diverge and only appear to come to a focus on the same side of the lens as the object. Concave lenses form only virtual, erect, and diminished images. If the object distance is greater than the focal length, a converging lens forms a real and inverted image. If the object is sufficiently far away, the image is smaller than the object. If the object distance is smaller than the focal length of this lens, the image is virtual, erect, and larger than the object. The observer is then using the lens as a magnifier or simple microscope (q.v.). The angle subtended at the eye by this virtual enlarged image is greater than would be the angle subtended by the object if it were at the normal viewing distance. The ratio of these two angles is the magnifying power of the lens. A lens with a shorter focal length would cause the angle subtended by the virtual image to increase and thus cause the magnifying power to increase. The magnifying power of an instrument is a measure of its ability to bring the object apparently closer to the eye. This is distinct from the lateral magnification of a camera (*see* PHOTOGRAPHY) or telescope (q.v.), for example, where the ratio of the actual dimensions of a real image to those of the object increases as the focal length increases. *See* LENS.

The amount of light a lens can admit increases with its diameter. Because the area occupied by an image is proportional to the square of the focal length of the lens, the light intensity over the image area is directly proportional to the diameter of the lens and inversely proportional to the square of the focal length. The image produced by a lens of a 1-in. diameter and 8-in. focal length would be one-fourth as bright as the image formed by a lens of a 1-in. diameter and 4-in. focal length. The ratio of the focal length to the effective diameter of a lens is its focal ratio or the so-called *f*-number. The reciprocal of this ratio is called the relative aperture. Lenses having the same relative aperture have the same light-gathering power, regardless of the actual diameters and focal lengths.

Aberration. Geometrical optics predicts that rays of light emanating from a point are imaged by spherical optical elements as a small blur. The outer parts of a spherical surface have a different focal length than does the central area, and this defect would cause a point to be imaged as a small circle (q.v.). The difference in focal length for the various parts of the spherical section is called spherical aberration. If, instead of being a portion of a sphere, a concave mirror is a section of a paraboloid (*see* PARABOLA) of revolution, parallel rays incident on all areas of the surface are reflected to a point without spherical aberration. Combinations of convex and concave lenses can help to correct spherical aberration, but this defect cannot be eliminated from a single spherical lens for a real object and image.

The manifestation of differences in lateral magnification for rays coming from an object point not on the optic axis is called coma. If coma is present, light from a point is spread out into a family of circles that fit into a cone, and in a plane perpendicular to the optic axis, the image pattern is comet shaped. Coma may be eliminated for a single object-image point pair, but not for all such points, by a suitable choice of surfaces. Corresponding or conjugate object and image points, free from both spherical aberration and coma, are known as aplanatic points, and a lens having such a pair of points is called an aplanatic lens. Astigmatism is the defect in which the light coming from an off-axis object point is spread along the direction of the optic axis. If the object is a vertical line, the cross section of the refracted beam is an ellipse (q.v.) that collapses first into a horizontal line, spreads out again, and later becomes a vertical line. If a flat object has any extent, the surface of best focus is curved, or curvature of field results. Distortion arises from a variation of magnification with axial distance and is not caused by a lack of sharpness in the image. Because the index of refraction varies with wavelength, the focal length of a lens also varies and causes longitudinal or axial chromatic aberration. Magnification of different image sizes by various wavelengths is known as lateral chromatic aberration. Converging and diverging lenses grouped together, and combinations of glasses with different dispersions, help to minimize chromatic aberration. Mirrors are free of this defect. In general, achromatic lens combinations are corrected for chromatic aberration for two or three colors.

PHYSICAL OPTICS

This branch of optical science concerns the study of the polarization of light, interference and diffraction, and the spectral emission, composition, and absorption of light.

Polarization of Light. The atoms in an ordinary light source emit pulses of radiation of extremely short duration. Each pulse from a single atom is a nearly monochromatic (consisting of a single wavelength) wave train. The electric vector corresponding to the wave does not rotate about the axis across which it oscillates as the wave travels through space, but keeps the same angle, or azimuth, with respect to the direction of travel. The initial azimuth can have any value. When a large number of atoms are emitting light, these azimuths are randomly distributed, the properties of the light beam are the same in all directions, and the light is said to be unpolarized. If the electric vectors for each wave all have the same azimuth angle (or all the transverse waves lie in the same plane), the light is plane, or linearly, polarized. The equations that describe the behavior of electromagnetic waves involve two sets of waves, one with the electric vector vibrating perpendicular to the plane of incidence and the other with the electric vector vibrating parallel to the plane of incidence, and all light can be considered as having a component of its electric vector vibrating in each of these planes. A certain synchronism of phase difference may persist in time between the two vibrations of the component, or the phase differences may be random. If light is linearly polarized, for example, this phase difference becomes zero or 180°. If the phase relationship is random, but more of one component is present, the light is partially polarized. When light is scattered by dust particles, for instance, the light scattered 90° to the original path of the beam is plane polarized, explaining why skylight from the zenith is markedly polarized. At angles other than zero or 90° of incidence, the reflectance at the boundary between two media is not the same for those two components of vibrations. Less of the component that vibrates parallel to the plane of incidence is reflected. If light is incident on a nonabsorbing medium at the so-called Brewster's angle, named after the British physicist David Brewster (1781–1868), the reflectance of the component vibrating parallel

to the plane of incidence is zero. At this angle of incidence, the reflected ray would be perpendicular to the refracted ray, and the tangent of this angle of incidence is equal to the refractive index of the second medium if the first medium is air.

Certain substances are anisotropic, or display properties with different values when measured along axes in different directions, and the velocity of light in them depends on the direction in which the light is traveling. Some crystals are birefringent, or exhibit double refraction (*see* CRYSTAL). Unless light is traveling parallel to an axis of symmetry with respect to the structure of the crystals (the optic axis of the crystal), it is separated into two parts that travel with different velocities. A uniaxial crystal has one axis. The component with the electric vector vibrating in a plane containing the optic axis is the ordinary ray; its velocity is the same in all directions through the crystal, and Snell's law of refraction holds. The component vibrating perpendicular to the plane of the optic axis forms the extraordinary ray, and the velocity of this ray depends on its direction through the crystal. If the ordinary ray travels faster than the extraordinary ray, the birefringence is positive; otherwise the birefringence is negative.

If a crystal is biaxial, no component exists for which the velocity is independent of the direction of travel. Birefringent materials can be cut and shaped to introduce specific phase differences between two sets of polarized waves, to separate them, or to analyze the state of polarization of any incident light. A polarizer transmits only one component of vibration either by reflecting away the other by means of properly cut prism combinations or by absorbing the second component. A material that preferentially absorbs one component of vibration exhibits dichroism, and Polaroid is an example of this. Polaroid consists of many small dichroic crystals embedded in plastic and identically oriented. If light is unpolarized, Polaroid absorbs approximately half of it. Because light reflected from a large flat surface such as water or a wet road is partially polarized, properly oriented Polaroid can absorb more than half of this reflected glare light. This explains the effectiveness of Polaroid sunglasses. The so-called analyzer may be physically the same as a polarizer. If a polarizer and analyzer are crossed, the analyzer is oriented to allow transmission of vibrations lying in a plane perpendicular to those transmitted by the polarizer, and blocks or extinguishes the light passed by the polarizer. Substances that are optically active rotate the plane of linearly polarized light.

Either a crystal or a solution of sugar, for example, may be optically active. If a solution of sugar is placed between a crossed polarizer and analyzer, the light is able to pass through. The amount of rotation of the analyzer required to restore extinction of the light determines the concentration of the solution. The polarimeter is based on this principle.

Some substances, such as glass and plastic, that are not normally doubly refracting, may become so if subjected to stress. If such stressed materials are placed between a polarizer and analyzer, the bright and dark areas that are seen give information about the strains. The technology of photoelasticity is based on double refraction produced by stresses.

Birefringence can also be introduced in otherwise homogeneous materials by magnetic and electric fields. The Faraday effect, named after the British physicist and chemist Michael Faraday, refers to the fact that a strong magnetic field across a liquid may cause it to become doubly refracting, a phenomenon known as the Kerr effect, after the British physicist John Kerr (1824–1907). If an appropriate material is placed between a crossed polarizer and analyzer, light is transmitted depending on whether the electric field is on or off. This can act as a very rapid light switch or modulator.

Interference and Diffraction. When two light beams cross, they may interfere or interact in such a way that the resultant intensity pattern is affected (*see* INTERFERENCE). The degree of coherence, or waves in phase and of one wavelength, is related to the ability of waves to produce a steady state that depends on the phase relationships of successive wave fronts remaining constant with time. If the phase relationship changes rapidly and randomly, two beams are incoherent. If two wave trains are coherent and if the maximum of one wave coincides with the maximum of another, the two waves combine to produce a greater intensity in that place than if the two beams were present but not coherent. If coherence exists and the maximum of one wave coincides with the minimum of another wave, the two waves will cancel each other in part or completely, thus decreasing the intensity. A dark and bright pattern consisting of interference fringes may be formed. To produce a steady interference pattern the two wave trains must be polarized in the same plane. Atoms in an ordinary light source radiate independently, so a large light source usually emits incoherent radiation. To obtain coherent light from such a source, a small portion of the light is selected by means of a pinhole or slit. If this portion is then again split

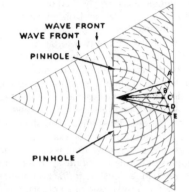

Fig. 8. Interference of light caused by passage through two pinholes.

by double slits, double mirrors, or double prisms, and the two parts made to travel definite but different paths before they are combined again, an interference pattern results. Devices that do this are called interferometers; they are used in measuring such things as diameters of stars, distances or thicknesses, and deviations of an optical surface from the required shape in terms of wavelengths of light (*see* INTERFEROMETER). Such an interference pattern was first demonstrated by the British physicist Thomas Young in the experiment illustrated in Fig. 8. Light that had passed through one pinhole illuminated an opaque surface that contained two pinholes. The light that passed through the two pinholes formed a pattern of alternately bright and dark circular fringes on a screen. Wavelets are drawn in the illustration to show that at points such as A, C, and E (intersection of solid line with solid line) the waves from the two pinholes arrive in phase and combine to increase the intensity. At other points, such as B and D (intersection of solid line with dashed line), the waves are 180° out of phase and cancel each other.

Light reflected at each surface of an extremely thin transparent film on a smooth surface can interfere. The rainbow colors of a film of oil on water are a result of interference, and they demonstrate the importance of the ratio of film thickness to wavelength. A single film or several films of different material can be used to increase or decrease the reflectance of a surface. Dichroic beam splitters are stacks of films of more than one material, controlled in thickness so that one band of wavelengths is reflected and another band of wavelengths is transmitted. An interference filter made of such films transmits an extremely narrow band of wavelengths and reflects the remainder. The shape of the surface of an optical element can be checked by touching it to a master lens, or flat, and observing the fringe pattern formed because of the thin layer of air remaining between the two surfaces.

Light incident on the edge of an obstacle is bent or diffracted, and the obstacle does not form a sharp geometric shadow. The points on the edge of the obstacle act as a source of coherent waves, and interference fringes, called a diffraction pattern, are formed. The shape of the edge of the obstacle is not exactly reproduced because part of the wave front is cut off. Because light passes through a finite aperture when it goes through a lens, a diffraction pattern is formed around the image of an object. If the object is extremely small, the diffraction pattern appears as a series of concentric bright and dark rings around a central disk called the Airy disk, after the British astronomer George Biddell Airy (1801–92). This is true for an aberration-free lens. If two particles are so close together that the two diffraction patterns overlap and the bright rings of one pattern fall on the dark rings of the second pattern, the two particles appear to merge, or cannot be resolved. The German physicist and optician Ernst Karl Abbe (1840–1905) first explained image formation by a microscope with a theory based on the interference of diffraction patterns of various points on the object.

Fourier analysis is a mathematical treatment, named after the French mathematician Jean Fourier, that assigns a frequency spectrum to an object and permits the calculation of the diffraction pattern of an object at some plane intermediate between the object plane and image plane, allowing the appearance of the image to be calculated. This is possible because a complex wave can be considered to consist of a combination of simple waves. Optical systems are sometimes evaluated by choosing an object of known Fourier components and then evaluating the Fourier components present in the image. Such procedures measure the optical transfer function. Extrapolations of these techniques sometimes allow extraction of information from poor images. Statistical theories have also been included in analyses of the recording of images.

A diffraction grating (q.v.) consists of several thousand slits that are equal in width and equally spaced (formed by ruling lines on glass or metal with a fine diamond point). Each slit gives rise to a diffraction pattern, and the many diffraction patterns interfere. If white light is incident, a continuous spectrum is formed. Prisms and gratings are used in instruments such as monochromators, spectrographs, or spectrophotometers to provide nearly monochromatic light or to analyze the wavelengths present in the incident light (see MASS SPECTROGRAPH; SPECTROHELIOGRAPH).

Stimulated Emission. The atoms in common light sources, such as the incandescent lamp, fluorescent lamp, and neon lamp (q.v.), produce light by spontaneous emission, and the radiation is incoherent. If a sufficient number of atoms have absorbed energy so that they are excited into appropriate states of higher energy, stimulated emission can occur. Light of a certain wavelength can produce additional light that has the same phase and direction as the original wavelength, and it will be coherent. Stimulated emission amplifies the amount of radiation having a given wavelength, and this radiation has a very narrow beam spread and a long coherence path. The material that is excited may be a gas or solid, but it must be contained or shaped to form an interferometer in which the wavelength being amplified is reflected back and forth many times. A small fraction of the excited radiation is transmitted by one of the mirrors of the interferometers. Maser (q.v.) is an acronym for microwave amplification by stimulated emission of radiation (see ELECTRONICS). If optical frequencies are being amplified by stimulated emission, the term *laser* (q.v.), an acronym for light amplification by stimulated emission of radiation, is commonly used. Energizing a large number of atoms to be in the appropriate upper state is called pumping. Pumping may be optical or electrical. Because lasers can be made to emit pulses of extremely high energy that have a very narrow beam spread, laser light sent to the moon and reflected back to the earth can be detected. The intense narrow beam of the laser has found practical application in surgery and in the cutting of metals.

The Hungarian-born British physicist and electrical engineer Dennis Gabor first noted that if the diffraction pattern of an object could be recorded and the phase information also retained, the image of the object could be reconstructed by coherent illumination of the recorded diffraction pattern. Illuminating the diffraction pattern with a wavelength longer than that used to produce the diffraction pattern would result in magnification. Because the absolute phase of a light wave cannot be directly detected physically, it was necessary to provide a reference beam coherent with the beam illuminating the object to interfere with the diffraction pattern and provide phase information. Before the development of the laser, the Gabor scheme was limited by the lack of sufficiently intense coherent light sources.

A hologram is a photographic record of the in-

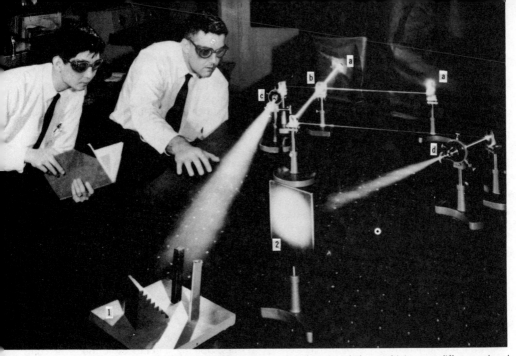

A hologram of three objects (1) is being made by combining two different-colored laser beams (a) into a single beam (b). This beam is then split, one part (c) being directed onto the objects, the other part (d) onto a photographic plate (2). When the plate is developed and illuminated by laser, a multicolor, three-dimensional image of the objects will be visible.   Bell Telephone Laboratories

terference between a reference beam and the diffraction pattern of the object. Light from a single laser is separated into two beams. The reference beam illuminates the photographic plate, perhaps via a lens and mirror, and the second beam illuminates the object, which forms a diffraction pattern on the photographic plate. If the processed hologram is illuminated by coherent light, not necessarily of the same wavelength that was used to make the hologram, the image of the object is reconstructed, and a three-dimensional image of the object can be obtained. Holograms of a theoretical object can be produced by computing machines, and the image of these objects can then be reconstructed (*see* HOLOGRAPHY).

Intense, coherent laser beams permit the study of new optical effects that are produced by the interaction of certain substances with electric fields and that depend on the square or third power of the field strength. This is called nonlinear optics, and the interactions being studied affect the refractive index of the substances. The Kerr effect, mentioned earlier, belongs to this group of phenomena.

Harmonic generation of light has been observed. Infrared laser light of wavelength 1.06 microns, for example, can be changed to green light with a wavelength of 0.53 microns in a crystal of barium sodium niobate. Broadly tunable sources of coherent light in the visible and near infrared ranges can be produced by pumping with light or shorter wavelengths. A lithium niobate crystal can be made to fluoresce in red, yellow, and green by pumping it with laser light having a wavelength of 488 nanometers. Certain scattering phenomena can be stimulated by a single laser to produce a source of intense, pulsed, monochromatic wavelengths at a wide variety of wavelengths. One of the phenomena observed in high-power optical experiments is a self-focusing effect that produces extremely short-lived filaments as small as 5 microns in diameter. Nonlinear optical effects are applied in developing efficient broadband modulators for communication systems (*see* RADIO: *Modulation*).   H.J.

For further information on this topic, see the Bibliography in volume 28, sections 395–397.

OPTOMETRY, profession concerned with vision problems. Optometrists conduct eye tests and prescribe corrective lenses (*see* EYEGLASSES). In the U.S. practitioners are required to pass a state licensing examination after graduation from a 4-year school that offers the doctor of ophthalmology (D.O.) degree. *See also* OPHTHALMOLOGY; VISION.

ORACLE, response delivered by a deity or supernatural being to a worshiper or inquirer; also, the

411

place where the response was delivered. The responses were supposed to be given by divine inspiration and were manifested through the medium of human beings; through their effect on certain objects, as in the tinkling, at the ancient Greek town of Dodona, of a cauldron when hit by a chain impelled by the wind; or by the actions of sacred animals. Oracles date from the greatest antiquity. Among the ancient Egyptians all the temples were probably oracular. In later days one of the most renowned oracles was that of Amon, in the oasis of Siwa, Egypt. Oracles were used by the Hebrews, as in the consultation of the Urim and Thummin by the high priest. The oracles in Phoenicia were associated with the deities Baalzebub and other Baalim. Oracles were also common throughout Babylonia and Chaldea. The most renowned Greek oracle was that of Apollo at Delphi. In Asia Minor the most celebrated was the one at Didyma, near Miletus.

ORADEA (Hung. *Nagyvárad*), city, NW Romania, on the Crişul Repede R., near the Hungarian border. It is a railway junction, the commercial center of an important grape-growing area, and an industrial center with factories producing textiles, shoes, clothing, processed food, glass, tools, and agricultural machinery. Among the noteworthy features in the city are several churches, such as the parish church containing the remains of Ladislaus I, king of Hungary (1040?–95), who made the city a Roman Catholic bishopric in 1080. Oradea was ceded by Hungary to Romania following World War I. Occupied by Hungarian forces during World War II, it again passed to Romanian control after 1945. Pop. (1980 est.) 184,871.

ORAN, also Wahran, city, NW Algeria, capital of Oran Department, on the Gulf of Oran (an arm of the Mediterranean Sea). It is one of the nation's busiest ports and a commercial and manufacturing center. Products include plastic items, chemicals, wine, and processed food. A pipeline carries natural gas to the city from the Sahara. Points of interest here include the large citadel of Santa Cruz, begun by the Ottoman Turks; the Great Mosque (1796); and the Casbah. The University of Oran (1965), the University of Science and Technology of Oran (1975), and institutes of music, dramatic arts, meteorology, and telecommunications are in the city.

Oran was probably founded in the early 10th century as a center for trade between N Africa and Moorish-held S Spain. The settlement declined after the Moors began to leave Spain in 1492, and it subsequently became a base for pirates. During the 18th century it was held at times by the Ottoman Turks and the Spanish.

The community experienced renewed economic growth after being annexed in 1831 by the French. Many French settled here, but most of the European population left Oran during the Algerian struggle for independence (1954–62). Pop. (1978) 491,900.

ORANGE, city, Orange Co., SW California; inc. 1888. It is a transportation hub located in a citrus-growing area. Manufactures include oil-field equipment, industrial furnaces, and rubber products. Chapman College (1918) and West Coast University Orange County Center (1963) are here. The community was founded in 1869 by two lawyers who accepted the land, which was part of the Rancho Santiago de Santa Ana, as payment for legal services. Originally known as Richland, it was renamed in 1875 for its orange trees. Pop. (1970) 77,365; (1980) 91,450.

ORANGE, city, Essex Co., NE New Jersey, near Newark; inc. as a city 1872. It is a residential and industrial center; manufactures include pharmaceuticals, electrical equipment, office machines, textiles, clothing, and processed food. The community, located in an area settled by whites in the late 1660s, was named Mountain Plantations in 1678 and subsequently was renamed Orange in honor of William, prince of Orange (later William III of England). It was part of Newark until 1806, and was separated from East Orange, South Orange, and West Orange in the 1860s. Pop. (1970) 32,566; (1980) 31,136.

ORANGE, city, seat of Orange Co., E Texas, a deepwater port on the Sabine R. and the Gulf Intracoastal Waterway; founded 1836, inc. 1858. It is an industrial center located in a natural-gas and petroleum-producing area. Manufactures include petrochemicals, metal products, ships, processed food, and lumber. Industrialization of the city was spurred after its harbor was improved in 1914. The city, a naval station during World War II, probably is named for the orange trees that once grew here. Pop. (1970) 24,457; (1980) 23,628.

ORANGE, river, S Africa, rising on the W slope of the Drakensberg range in Lesotho. It flows generally SW through Lesotho and enters South Africa, where, turning NW, it forms the boundary between the provinces of the Orange Free State and the Cape of Good Hope. The Orange continues on a W course through the N part of the Cape of Good Hope, finally forming the border between that province and Namibia. The Orange empties into the Atlantic Ocean at Alexander Bay. The Orange R. is about 2090 km (about 1300 mi) long; its chief tributary is the Vaal R.

ORANGE, fruit of several trees of the genus *Citrus*, especially the sweet orange, *C. sinensis;* the

Harvesting Florida oranges for processing. The fruit is loaded into a container capable of holding 408 kg (900 lb) and then lifted into the "grove goat." The vehicle is so called because it can maneuver through the deep sandy soil of the orange groves.
Florida Department of Citrus

sour orange, *C. aurantium;* and the mandarin orange, or tangerine, *C. reticulata.* The fruit is technically a hesperidium, a kind of berry. It consists of several easily separated carpels, or sections, each containing several seeds and many juice cells, covered by a leathery exocarp, or skin, containing numerous oil glands. Orange trees are evergreens, seldom exceeding 9 m (30 ft) in height; the leaves are oval and glossy and the flowers are white and fragrant. Three different essential oils are obtained from oranges: oil of orange, obtained from the rind of the fruit and used principally as a flavoring agent; oil of petigrain, obtained from the leaves and twigs and used in perfumery; and oil of neroli, obtained from the blossoms and used in flavorings and perfumes.

Oranges, of great commercial importance, are cultivated in warm regions although native to southeastern Asia. The sour orange was introduced to the Mediterranean region by the Arabs about the 10th century, and the sweet orange was introduced by Genoese traders in the 15th century.

In the U.S. the principal orange-producing states are Florida (the orange blossom is the official state flower of Florida), California, Texas, and Arizona. In 1979-80 the yield of oranges in the U.S. was about 11 million metric tons. The principal varieties of the sweet orange cultivated by orange growers of the eastern U.S. are the Hamlin and Parson Brown, both early-maturing, seedy varieties with thin, russet skin and juicy pulp.

Both eastern and western growers cultivate the Valencia, a late variety that is commercially "seedless," having two to five seeds. The principal crops of the western growers consist of the Valencia and the Bahia or Washington navel orange, imported from Bahia, Brazil, in 1870, and developed in Washington, D.C., by the U.S. Department of Agriculture. The navel orange is a seedless orange, with medium-thick rind, in which a second small, or abortive, orange grows. A variety of the Washington navel orange is the principal orange product of Texas. The bitter orange is cultivated to a limited extent for marmalade and to provide rootstock for less vigorous strains. About 20 percent of the total crop of oranges is sold as whole fruit; the remainder is used in preparing frozen and canned orange juice, extracts, and preserves.

ORANGE, Prince of. *See* WILLIAM I, called William the Silent; WILLIAM III, king of England.

ORANGE FREE STATE, also Oranje Vrystaat, province, E central South Africa, separated from Transvaal Province on the N by the Vaal R., bordered on the E and SE by Natal Province and Lesotho, and on the S and SW by the Cape of Good Hope Province. The Orange R. forms the S border. The capital and largest city is Bloemfontein. The province is largely a plateau, lying between about 1219 and 1524 m (about 4000 and 5000 ft) above sea level. Mountains in the E descend gradually to great plains, with very few trees.

The Orange Free State is primarily pastoral, and cattle, horses, goats, and sheep are raised in

413

huge herds. Farming districts are chiefly in the E; crops include wheat, corn, oats, potatoes, tobacco, apples, plums, and kafir. Gold, diamonds, and coal are mined in the province. Industries include the processing of oil from coal and the manufacture of fertilizer, agricultural tools, blankets and woolens, clothing, hosiery, cement, and pharmaceuticals. A government-owned railroad extends for some 2670 km (some 1660 mi) through the province. Education is free and compulsory for children between the ages of 7 and 16. The University of the Orange Free State (1855) is at Bloemfontein. Both English and Afrikaans are official languages.

The first European settlements in the region were made between 1810 and 1820. In 1836 the great emigration, called the "great trek," of Boers from the Cape Colony, where they were dissatisfied with the British government, occurred in this area. The Boers created a republic that was annexed (1848) by force by the British, who named it the Orange River Sovereignty. Six years later Great Britain relinquished the territory, which then became known as the independent Orange River Free State. In 1899 the state joined with the Transvaal in the South African War against Great Britain. In 1900 the area was occupied and annexed by Great Britain as the Orange River Colony. During the settlement of peace terms in 1902, the state acknowledged British sovereignty.

In 1907 the colony was granted responsible government similar to that of the Transvaal. In 1910, as the Province of the Orange Free State, the region was incorporated into the Union of South Africa (since 1961, the Republic of South Africa). Area, 129,152 sq km (49,866 sq mi); pop. (1980) 1,833,216.

ORANGEMEN, members of the Orange Society (later known as the Orange Order), which was formed in 1795 by Protestants in county Armagh, Ireland, to work for the continuation of British rule and Protestant supremacy in Ireland. It was named for King William III of England—known as William of Orange—who destroyed the political power of Irish Roman Catholics. The Orangemen were, however, charged with anti-Roman Catholic bigotry and were forced by British authorities to suspend their activities in Ireland in 1836. When British Prime Minister William Ewart Gladstone declared in favor of Irish home rule in 1885, the Orange Order revived, became a center of resistance, and gained many new members, especially in Ulster. In the 1980s the Orangemen remained influential among farmers, skilled workers, and professional men in Northern Ireland, and had lodges for women as well. The most important holiday of the society is celebrated on July 12, the anniversary of the Battle of the Boyne, in which William III won control of Ireland.

A panoramic view of the rolling terrain of Orange Free State. Pastoral agriculture is the mainstay of the state's economy.　　　South African Tourist Corporation

The history of the oratorio began in the mid-16th century, when the Italian priest St. Philip Neri organized devotional services in the oratory, or prayer hall, of a church in Rome. The services included sermons, prayers, hymn singing, and devotional music. After opera spread from Florence to Rome in the early 17th century, some of its characteristics, including the recitativelike vocal style called monody, and the use of a dramatic libretto, were incorporated into music written for the oratory services. Works of this type were called oratorios. Some of the early oratorios were performed as operas, with scenery, costumes, and staged action. Soon, however, a narrator (*testo*) sang descriptions of settings and actions. By the mid-17th century, the oratorio was easily distinguishable from opera in its use of a *testo,* its lack of staged action, its generally contemplative tone, and its emphasis on music for chorus rather than for solo voices. The early composers of oratorios included the Italian Giacomo Carissimi, his student, the Frenchman Marc-Antoine Charpentier (1634–1704), and the Italian opera composers Alessandro Stradella and Alessandro Scarlatti. In Germany oratorios were written by a great number of composers, the most prominent of which were Heinrich Schütz and Johann Sebastian Bach. Bach's oratorios include his great settings of the biblical passion story, *St. John* (1723) and *St. Matthew* (1729). With works such as *Messiah* (1724), the German-born British composer George Frideric Handel created the British oratorio.

During the later 18th and 19th centuries, most major composers wrote oratorios with musical styles borrowed from their operas, symphonies, and other secular music. These composers included the Austrian Joseph Haydn and the German Felix Mendelssohn, the Hungarian Franz Liszt, the Englishman Sir Edward Elgar, the Frenchmen Hector Berlioz and Charles Gounod, and the Belgian-French César Franck. Oratorios were very popular in the U.S., especially those by 19th-century composers in New England, most notably Horatio Parker.

The composition of oratorios has decreased markedly in the 20th century. The most notable examples have been written by the Englishman Sir William Walton, the Frenchman Arthur Honegger, the Russian-born Igor Stravinsky, the German-born Paul Hindemith, the Austrian-born Arnold Schoenberg, and the Hungarian Zoltán Kodály. Oratorios do, however, continue to be performed frequently.

ORATORY. *See* RHETORIC.

ORATORY, CONGREGATION OF THE, name of two Roman Catholic religious associations.

Orangutan, Pongo pygmaeus
Arthur W. Ambler–National Audubon Society

ORANGUTAN (Malay *orang,* "man"; *hutan,* "forest"), anthropoid ape (q.v.), *Pongo pygmaeus,* of the family Pongidae, native to the forests of Borneo and Sumatra. The male adult attains a height of about 1.4 m (about 4.5 ft) and a weight of about 70 kg (about 150 lb), becoming corpulent with age. Twice the size of the female, the male has an air sac hanging down from its throat, which it inflates and uses to make the "long call," a throaty scream easily heard a kilometer away. Both the male and the female of the species have reddish-brown hair, which is luxuriant on the arms and thighs, and a humanlike facial structure.

Orangutans are exclusively arboreal, with limbs adapted to swinging through trees; the extremely long arms reach a span of about 2 m (about 7 ft), but the legs are short. The animals travel in small groups during the day, feeding on leaves and fruit. At night they nest in the forks of tall trees on individual platforms built of branches and leaves. Adult males frequently live alone, and many groups are composed solely of females and young. Human incursions into its habitat have made the orangutan an endangered species.

ORATORIO, large-scale musical composition for voices and instruments, of a dramatic or contemplative nature, and usually on a religious subject. Although the libretto may contain dramatic incidents, as in opera, oratorios are usually performed in concert without scenery or costumes.

ORBIT

The original Congregation of the Oratory was founded in Rome in 1575 by the Italian priest St. Philip Neri. Its rules were codified under the Italian prelate Caesar Baronius and approved by Pope Paul V in 1612. Its essential constitution is that of a body of priests living in community but without monastic vows. The British religious leader Cardinal John Henry Newman introduced the Oratorians to England in 1849. The houses are independent. In 1942, however, they formed a confederation known as the Institute of the Oratory of Saint Philip Neri. They are represented by several houses in the U.S.

The other oratory was founded along the same lines in France by the French religious leader Cardinal Pierre de Bérulle (1575–1629) in 1611. It is a distinct institution with its own superior general. Suppressed during the French Revolution, it was reconstituted in 1852 as the Oratory of Jesus and Mary.

ORBIT, path or trajectory of a body through space. A force of attraction or repulsion from a second body usually causes the path to be curved. A familiar type of orbit occurs when one body revolves around a second, strongly attracting body. In the solar system the force of gravity causes the moon to orbit about the earth and the planets to orbit about the sun, whereas in an atom electrical forces cause electrons to orbit about the nucleus. In astronomy, the orbits resulting from gravitational forces, which are discussed here, are the subject of the scientific field of celestial mechanics.

An orbit has the shape of a conic section (see GEOMETRY: *Conic Sections*)—a circle, ellipse, parabola, or hyperbola—with the central body at one focus of the curve. When a satellite traces out an orbit about the center of the earth, its most distant point is called the apogee and its closest point the perigee. The perigee or apogee height of the satellite above the earth's surface is often given, instead of the perigee or apogee distance from the earth's center. The ending -*gee* refers to orbits about the earth; perihelion and aphelion refer to orbits about the sun; the ending -*astron* is used for orbits about a star; and the ending -*apsis* is used when the central body is not specified. The so-called line of apsides is a straight line connecting the periapsis and the apoapsis.

Laws of Motion. Early in the 17th century, the German astronomer and natural philosopher Johannes Kepler deduced three laws that first described the motions of the planets about the sun: (1) The orbit of a planet is an ellipse (q.v.). (2) A straight line from the planet to the center of the sun sweeps out equal areas in equal time intervals as it goes around the orbit; the planet moves faster when closer to the sun and slower when distant. (3) The square of the period (in years) for one revolution about the sun equals the cube of the mean distance from the sun's center, measured in astronomical units (see ASTRONOMICAL UNIT).

The physical causes of Kepler's three laws were later explained by the English mathematician and physicist Isaac Newton as consequences of Newton's laws of motion (see MECHANICS) and of the inverse square law of gravity. Kepler's second law, in fact, expresses the conservation of angular momentum. Moreover, Kepler's third law, in generalized form, can be stated as follows: The square of the period (in years) times the total mass (measured in solar masses) equals the cube of the mean distance (in astronomical units). This last law permits the masses of the planets to be calculated by measuring the size and period of satellite orbits.

Orbital Elements. Six orbital elements describe an orbit. Two of these, the size and elongation of the orbit, are given by the periapsis distance (SP) and the eccentricity (e), which for the ellipse in the accompanying figure is the ratio CS/CP, where S is the focus and C the center of the ellipse. For elliptical orbits, e is greater than 0, but less than 1; for circular orbits, e is exactly 0; and for parabolic orbits, e is exactly 1. A body in a hyperbolic orbit—that is, when e is greater than 1—makes a single close passage to a central body and escapes along a so-called open orbit, never to return.

The next three orbital elements are concerned with orientation, which must first be explained. An orbit is oriented with respect to a reference plane—the plane of the equator for earth satellites, or the earth's orbital plane (ecliptic) for orbits around the sun—and a direction called the equinox (γ), which is the northbound intersection of the ecliptic on the equator. The northbound intersection of the orbital plane on the reference plane—that is, the plane of the equator or the plane of the ecliptic—is the ascending node (N). The three orbital elements of orientation, then, are the right ascension (or ecliptic longitude) of the ascending node, which is the angle (Ω), along the equator (or ecliptic) from the equinox to the ascending node; the argument of periapsis, which is the angle (ω) along the orbital plane from the ascending node to the line of apsides (AP'); and the inclination, the angle (i) between the orbit and the reference plane. The sixth orbital element is the time when the celestial body in question passes through periapsis (P).

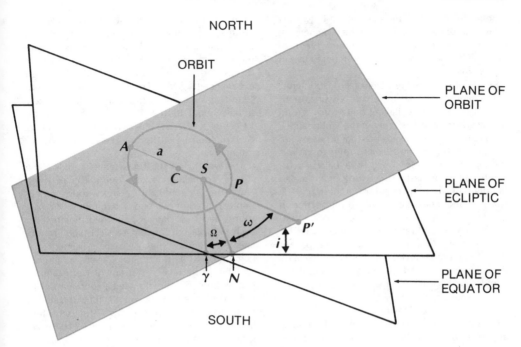

NORTH

ORBIT

PLANE OF ORBIT

PLANE OF ECLIPTIC

A a

C S P

Ω ω P'

i

γ N

PLANE OF EQUATOR

SOUTH

An orbit can also be described in terms of its semimajor axis (AC, CP, or a). This axis is half the long axis (AP) of the ellipse, or half the distance between the points of periapsis (P) and the apoapsis (A). The semimajor axis is longer than the periapsis distance (SP) and shorter than the apoapsis distance (AS), by an amount (CS) that is equal to the product of the semimajor axis and the eccentricity:

$$CS = e(AC) = e(CP) = ea$$

Perturbations. An orbit is perturbed when the forces are more complex than those between two spherical bodies. (Kepler's laws are exact only for unperturbed orbits.) The attraction between planets causes their elliptical orbits to change with time. The sun, for example, perturbs the lunar orbit by several thousand kilometers. Atmospheric drag causes the orbit of an earth satellite to shrink, and the oblate shape of the earth causes the direction of its node and perigee to change. Albert Einstein's relativity theory explains an observed perturbation in the perihelion of the planet Mercury. *See* RELATIVITY.   J.G.Wi.

ORCAGNA, Andrea, real name ANDREA DI CIONE (c. 1308–c. 1368), Italian painter, sculptor, mosaicist, and architect, born in Florence, the son of a goldsmith. He entered the painters' guild in 1343 and the stone masons' guild in 1352. Influenced both by the traditional, hieratic Byzantine style and by the new naturalism of Giotto and Andrea

Pisano, Orcagna was regarded as the leading master of his day. He often collaborated with his three brothers, Nardo, Matteo, and Jacopo. The only painting solely by Orcagna is an elaborate altarpiece, *The Redeemer* (1357), for the Strozzi Chapel in Santa Maria Novella, Florence. In this work the expressive monumental figures stand out boldly from the gold Byzantine background. Remnants of frescoes by Orcagna adorn Santa Croce, Florence.

In 1355 Orcagna began work on the famous sculptured tabernacle for Or San Michele, Florence; it is an elaborate structure decorated in late Gothic style but with strong modeling and an emotional expressiveness that foreshadowed the Renaissance. From 1359 to 1362 he directed the construction of Orvieto Cathedral and made mosaics for its facade. From 1364 to 1367 he directed the building of Florence Cathedral.

ORCHARD, a stand of fruit-bearing trees arranged and maintained to yield crops of maximum size and quality. The chief orchard trees are apple, peach, pear, and apricot, which once grew in small home orchards of nearly every American farm. With the ability to store, transport, and market entire crops, fruit growers now carefully select large orchard sites where trees receive optimum sunlight, nourishment, soil drainage, and air currents. Hill sites, for example, avoid the early and late frosts that settle in river valley sites. By improving soils with nitrogen-fixing legumes, pruning to increase fruit size, and using insect sprays and better tree strains, orchard owners are able to produce and package uniform, blemish-free fruit; this kind of fruit is now standard fare in supermarkets.

ORCHESTRA, ensemble of musical instruments; in the narrowest sense, the characteristic ensemble of Western music, having as its core a group of bowed-string instruments of the violin family, augmented by woodwind, brass, and percussion instruments. *Orchestra* can also refer to various specialized ensembles, such as a balalaika orchestra, a jazz orchestra (*see* BAND), or a gamelan (Indonesian tuned-percussion orchestra). The word *orchestra* originally signified the section in ancient Greek theaters between the stage and the audience that was used by dancers and instrumentalists. In a modern theater the part of the auditorium reserved for musicians is called the orchestra pit, and the term orchestra often also designates the part of the ground floor used for audience seating.

Sections of the Orchestra. The string section, which forms the backbone of orchestral sound, is divided into four parts, much like a vocal choir: first violins, second violins, violas, and cellos and double basses. The double basses often duplicate the cello part an octave lower, but sometimes the music calls for an independent bass part, which results in a five-part texture. The number of players in a modern orchestra can vary from about two dozen or fewer to well over 100. Of these, the woodwind and brass sections each constitute about 10 to 20 percent of the orchestra, and the percussion about 10 percent. For the strings, certain proportions have proved through experience to give the most effective balance of sound; an orchestra with 20 first violins is likely to have about 18 to 20 second violins, 14 violas, 12 cellos, and 8 double basses; these numbers vary, of course, but they can be considered representative.

The woodwind and brass sections, unlike the strings, normally have only one player per part. Until the late 19th century, the woodwind section consisted of two oboes, two flutes, two bassoons, and two clarinets; the two members of each pair played different musical parts. By the late 19th century three of each instrument was common, with the third player sometimes switching to a related instrument (for example, English horn, piccolo, double bassoon, bass clarinet). The brass section, in its fully developed form, typically consists of two trumpets, four horns, three trombones, and a tuba. These are sometimes augmented by other brass instruments, such as the bass trombone or the Wagner tuba designed by the German composer Richard Wagner and used in his scores. The percussion section employs one or two (rarely, more) players, each of whom covers several instruments. The basic percussion group consists of a pair of

A modern symphony orchestra has four sections of instruments: strings (violins and violas at left, cellos and basses at right); woodwinds (front center); brass (middle center); and percussion (rear center).   Philadelphia Orchestra

timpani (kettledrums), a side drum (snare drum), a bass drum, cymbals, and a triangle. Individual compositions may call for additional instruments such as the Chinese wood block, glockenspiel, or xylophone. In addition to these four groups (bowed string, woodwind, brass, and percussion), most orchestras have a harp and a piano.

Seating Arrangement. The seating of the orchestra is determined by the conductor, who directs the orchestra in performance (*see also* CONDUCTING). The first and second violins are usually placed to the left of the conductor, the violas and cellos to the right. The woodwinds and brass are typically in front of the conductor but behind the strings, and the percussion are placed farthest back.

Kinds of Orchestras. Opera and ballet orchestras share with symphony orchestras the size and structure described above; they differ in their ancestry and function. The symphony orchestra performs symphonies, concerti, and other concert music and is normally placed on a stage. Opera and ballet orchestras are part of theatrical performances and are seated in the orchestra pit of a theater. A chamber orchestra is one consisting usually of 25 or fewer players. Virtually all orchestras before 1800 were of this size, and many 20th-century composers call for chamber orchestras. A string orchestra, which may be of chamber-orchestra size or may be quite large, consists of the standard orchestral string section, with no added wind or percussion instruments.

History. The development and standardization of the modern orchestra took place between about 1600 and about 1750. In the first major opera, *Orfeo* (1607), the Italian composer Claudio Monteverdi used an orchestra having a central string section augmented by other instruments and bound together harmonically by basso continuo (bass melody instrument, such as cello or bassoon, plus harmony instrument, such as harp or organ). During the 1600s, orchestras became common not only in opera performances but as ensembles maintained by noble families for private concerts. By the early 18th century the combination of first and second violins, violas, cellos, and double basses had become standard for the strings; and a pair of oboes or flutes or both and a bassoon were usually added. A harpsichord or an organ normally supplied chords for the basso continuo part. The newly invented clarinet was added to the orchestra about the middle of the 18th century, and pairs of flutes, oboes, bassoons, and clarinets became common. The coiled hunting horn also entered the orchestra, used to evoke an atmosphere of the hunt and to give added volume and richness. Trumpets and tim-

pani, previously the prerogative of the nobility, were sometimes used when an opera or cantata text alluded to royalty; later, trumpets were added for brilliance. Trombones, used for centuries in church music and municipal bands, entered the opera orchestra in the late 18th century and the symphony orchestra in the early 19th century. In the late 18th century the basso continuo fell out of use and the keyboard instrument dropped out. Its role in filling in the harmonies was taken by the horns. A vogue for imitating Turkish military music introduced the triangle, cymbals, and bass drum. The tuba entered the orchestra only in the 19th century, a result of technological experimenting with brass instruments. Its predecessors had been the serpent (an S-shaped wood horn with fingerholes) and the ophicleide (keyed bass bugle). Until the late 18th century, orchestras tended to have 20-30 members. During the lifetime of Ludwig van Beethoven the size increased to 30 to 40 players. As 19th-century composers sought new, dramatic ways to express themselves in music, orchestras became larger and by the early 20th century about 100 players was considered optimal.

For further information on this topic, see the Bibliography in volume 28, section 743.

ORCHESTRATION, the art of combining musical instruments in orchestral compositions. Orchestration is a complex instance of instrumentation, the assigning of instruments in music for an ensemble of any size.

Techniques. Besides a knowledge of the ranges of the instruments to be used, orchestrating a work requires an understanding of each instrument's idiosyncrasies. A certain passage may be playable on a clarinet only with an awkward fingering, for example, or it may require the harpist to carry out an ungainly ineffective series of changes of pedals, which control the available notes. Violins and trumpets must be given a few measures' rest if the players are to add or remove mutes. Although such information can be obtained from books, it is most thoroughly learned by working closely with players. Conducting provides invaluable experience with effective instrumental combinations, which can be augmented by careful analysis of musical scores. Orchestrating a work that was composed for another medium requires an aesthetic sense attuned to preserving the style of the original and to clarifying its structure.

History. Before the 17th century performers usually worked out the instrumentation of a piece in rehearsal. About 1600 composers began assigning specific instruments to various parts. The development and standardization of the orchestra

(c. 1600–c. 1750) made possible the early 18th-century conventions of orchestration. The strings usually were scored in three parts—two treble parts played by violins and a bass part played by cellos and double basses. The viola generally doubled (followed) one of the other parts. A pair of oboes or flutes, or both, plus a bassoon, reinforced and enriched the sound of the string parts. Harmonic cohesiveness was provided by the basso continuo (the bass line plus harmonies provided by a harpsichord or organ). Trumpets and timpani appeared occasionally, and, after the mid-18th century, the clarinet and horn were added. Trombones became common a few decades later. Instruments were often used for their symbolic or nonmusical associations (the oboe, pastoral; trumpets and timpani, royal; the trombone, solemn or sacred; the French horn, the hunt; the triangle, cymbals, and bass drum, Turkish or exotic).

By the late 18th century the basso continuo was no longer used, and the harmonies were largely filled in by the French horns. The trend was toward a texture in which short phrases were fragmented and developed by the different instrument sections; the winds thus provided many hues and flashes of color. Ludwig van Beethoven gave prominent, independent parts to the viola and experimented with the use of piccolos and trombones, and he was among the first to exploit the soloistic capabilities of the French horn.

In the romantic era (c. 1820–c. 1900) composers tended more than in the past to conceive their works directly in terms of orchestral colors, and they explored the capability of two or more instruments being played at the same pitch to yield a tone quality unlike that of any single instrument. Composers such as Hector Berlioz, a Frenchman, Nikolay Rimsky-Korsakov, a Russian, and Richard Wagner, a German, used technically improved wind instruments in increasingly varied ways, both in massive and delicate sonorities. Much orchestral music of the late 19th century, such as that of the Austrian composer Gustav Mahler, required orchestras of great size and complex instrumentation.

In the 20th century, French composers such as Claude Debussy and Maurice Ravel emphasized the sensuous and pictorial color effects available to the modern orchestra. The Russian-born composer Igor Stravinsky often broke with classical tradition, giving the melody to the brass section and transferring the percussive function to the strings. Percussion instruments were increasingly drawn on to provide new colors, and new techniques were applied to many instruments (for example, using the wood body of a violin for percussion). Electronic musical instruments and sound synthesizers made a new palette of sounds available to composers.

See also ORCHESTRA. For jazz orchestras or big bands, *see* JAZZ.

ORCHID, common name of the order Orchidales, comprising one of the largest groups of flowering plants. The order contains the single family Orchidaceae and is worldwide in distribution, being absent only from Antarctica and some of the most arid desert zones of the Old World. The greatest diversity of genera and species occurs in tropical regions that remain poorly explored. For this reason, and because of the complexity of the family, estimates of the number of orchid species vary from 15,000 to 35,000, and the number of genera from 400 to 800.

Orchids, which are monocots, are distinguished from other orders of flowering plants by a combination of floral characteristics rather than by a single characteristic unique to the group. Orchid flowers are borne on stalks called pedicels, as are other flowers. During the growth and development of the flower, however, the pedicel rotates 180°, so that the mature orchid flower is borne upside down. Of the flower's three sepals

A Brazilian cattleya orchid, Cattleya amethystoglossa. *Cattleya orchids are native to tropical America and are the ancestors of modern florists' corsage orchids.*
Dr. E. R. Degginger

An epidendrum orchid hybrid. Epidendrum orchids, a large tropical genus of more than 1000 species, range from miniature plants to 3-m (10-ft) tree-dwelling epiphytes.
Dr. E. R. Degginger

surrounded by pedicel tissue. Tripartite, it contains numerous ovules (egg-bearing structures) that mature into seeds. The seeds are small, with only an undifferentiated embryo; as many as 2 million seeds may be produced from a single orchid seedpod. Unlike most other flowering plants, orchids have no food-storage tissue.

Orchid flowers are pollinated by a great variety of flying animals, and their great diversity in floral structure has resulted from adaptations to various pollinators. About half the orchid species are pollinated by bees; moths, butterflies, flies, birds, and other agents pollinate the rest. Many orchid flowers are adapted for pollination by a single species of insect.

Although orchids do not vary as much vegetatively as they do in floral structure, a great variety of forms does exist, reflecting the wide range of habitats they occupy. About half are epiphytic, growing on other plants for support only, but some are parasitic and others saprophytic (living on decaying vegetation). A few Australian species complete their life cycles entirely underground.

Apart from their phenomenal popularity among horticulturists, orchids have little economic importance, although vanilla flavoring is obtained from fruits of *Vanilla planifolia,* widely

Spider orchid, Arachnis flos-aeris
M. P. L. Fogden–Bruce Coleman, Inc.

(outer floral whorls) and three petals (inner floral whorls), all the sepals and the two lateral petals are usually similar to one another in color and shape. The remaining petal, always distinct from them, is called the labellum, or lip; it is usually larger and different in color and shape, often being lobed or cupped. The labellum, which often acts as a landing platform for the orchid pollinator, may attract the pollinator to the flower through particular color patterns and shapes to which the pollinator responds in particular ways.

The sexual organs (pistil and stamens) of the orchid flower are fused together into a structure called the column, which lies opposite the lip. Orchids have only one stamen (male floral organ), and in most orchids it bears only one anther (pollen-producing structure); in a few orchids, however, two anthers are produced. The pollen is not granular, as it is in most flowering plants, but is aggregated together in a number of masses, or sacs, that vary in texture from mealy to horny. Three stigmatic lobes (pollen-receptive areas) are usually present and located near the anther, although usually only two are functional. The ovary is below the other flower parts and is

grown in tropical areas. Not satisfied with the tremendous natural variety of orchid flowers, growers have produced thousands of new forms through hybridization. M.R.C.

ORDEAL, practice of referring disputed questions to the judgment of God, determined either by lot or by certain trials.

Throughout Europe the ordeal existed in various forms under the sanction of law and was closely related to the oath. The most prevalent kinds of ordeal were those of fire, water, and the wager of battle. Fire ordeal was allowed only to persons of high rank. The accused had to carry a piece of red-hot iron in the hand some distance or walk barefoot and blindfolded across red-hot plowshares. The hand or foot was bound up and inspected three days afterward. If the accused had escaped unhurt, the person was pronounced innocent; if hurt, the person was guilty. Water ordeal was the usual mode or trial allowed to members of the lower classes and was of two kinds, the ordeal of boiling water and of cold water. The ordeal of boiling water, according to the laws of Athelstan, the first king of England, consisted of lifting a stone out of boiling water, where the hand had to be inserted as deep as the wrist; the triple ordeal deepened the water to the elbow. The person allowed the ordeal of cold water, the usual mode of trial for witchcraft, was flung into a pool. If the accused floated he or she was guilty; if the accused sank he or she was acquitted. In the wager of battle the defeated party was allowed to live as a "recreant," that is, on retracting the perjury that had been sworn.

By the middle of the 13th century the ordeal had died out in England and on the Continent.

ORDERS, HOLY, the several different degrees of ordained ministries recognized by the Orthodox, Roman Catholic, and Anglican churches. For Orthodoxy and Roman Catholicism, holy orders rank among the seven sacraments. Anglicans regard ordination as a "sacramental rite," or as "commonly called a sacrament" (see SACRAMENT). The outward and visible sign of the sacrament is the imposition of hands by a bishop, sometimes accompanied by the transmission of an object or objects associated with the order, such as a chalice and paten for a priest. The sacramental inward grace conferred by ordination is the spiritual power and authority proper to the respective orders.

Origin. Like Jewish synagogues, early Christian congregations were organized under the leadership of elders (Gr. *presbyteroi;* see Acts 14:23). In the New Testament, the terms *elder* and *bishop* are interchangeable (see Titus 1:5-9). Although mentioned rarely, deacons (*see* DEACON) are al-

ways referred to in association with bishops, whose assistants they were (see Phil. 1:1; 1 Tim. 3:8-13). The early church may have recognized only these two orders, as most Protestants argue. The emergence of a third order can perhaps be identified, however, in the figures of Timothy and Titus, recipients of the letters that bear their names, who had authority over bishops and deacons. The process of establishing a threefold ministry probably varied in different localities, but three distinct orders were recognized by the 2d century; these orders were bishops, presbyters, and deacons.

Priesthood. Individual Christian ministers were not called priests until the 3d century, when the terms was first applied to bishops because of their role as celebrants of the Eucharist (q.v.). The term *priest* (Lat. *sacerdos*) implies a sacrificial ministry, and the Eucharist was regarded as sacrificial because of its mystical relation to the sacrifice of Christ. When presbyters were authorized to celebrate the Eucharist in the 4th century, they too were called priests. Today, the Orthodox, Roman Catholic, and Anglican churches regard bishops, priests, and deacons as constituting holy orders. Because both bishops and presbyters function as priests, the Roman Catholic church, until the Second Vatican Council (*see* VATICAN COUNCIL, SECOND), considered priests (including bishops and presbyters), deacons, and subdeacons as the three orders.

Minor Orders. In addition to the three major orders, Orthodox churches also acknowledge minor orders, such as subdeacon and lector (reader), having subordinate roles in the liturgy. The Roman Catholic church abolished minor orders at the Second Vatican Council.

Character. Holy orders, like baptism and confirmation, are considered to have character; that is, the power conferred at ordination is regarded as permanent. It may become latent if the ordained person fails to act as the church intends, but it is not lost. In this respect, holy orders are to be distinguished from functional ministries, such as dean or archdeacon, or honorary titles, such as patriarch or monsignor. Authority for such roles is conveyed nonsacramentally and is withdrawn when the holder leaves office.

See also BISHOP; CHURCH OF ENGLAND; ORTHODOX CHURCH; PRIEST; ROMAN CATHOLIC CHURCH. C.P.P.

ORDERS, RELIGIOUS. See RELIGIOUS ORDERS AND COMMUNITIES.

ORDERS OF ARCHITECTURE. See COLUMN.

ORDOVICIAN PERIOD, second division of the Paleozoic era (q.v.) of the geologic time scale (*see* GEOLOGY), spanning a period from about

500 million to 430 million years ago. It was named for an ancient Welsh tribe, rocks of this age having first been studied systematically in Wales.

North America and Europe, separated by water during the preceding Cambrian period, collided in Ordovician time, crumpling between them a great thickness of sediments that had been accumulating in the Appalachian geosyncline (q.v.) and lifting these rocks to form a new mountain range, the Taconics, remnants of which are visible today in eastern New York State. Shallow seas that covered much of North America at the beginning of the period withdrew, leaving behind thick deposits of limestone; returning later in the Ordovician, the seas deposited thick blankets of quartz sand and additional limestone. Europe and Asia were separated by a long, narrow sea in which sediments of the Uralian geosyncline accumulated. Asia itself was fragmented, with Siberia and China separated by marine waters. In the southern hemisphere, the supercontinent of Gondwanaland, encircled by a belt of geosynclines, encompassed South America, Antarctica, Africa, India, and Australia, as well as portions of continental crust—Mexico and Florida—that would not become attached to North America until the Carboniferous period. See PLATE TECTONICS.

The climate of Ordovician time was warm and humid throughout much of present-day North America and Eurasia but colder in the southern continents, the South Pole of the time being centered in present-day Algeria. Marine invertebrates were still the predominant life forms; no animals and few plants had appeared on land, and only a few primitive species of fish with bony armor plates swam in the seas. Graptolites (extinct colonial organisms), corals, crinoids, bryozoans, and clams first made their appearance in this period. See PALEONTOLOGY.

ORDZHONIKIDZE, city, capital of North Ossetian ASSR, Russian SFSR, in SE European USSR, on the Terek R. Located at the N foot of the Caucasus Mts., the city is an industrial and transportation center. Manufactures include processed zinc and lead, machinery, chemicals, clothing, and food products. The city was founded in 1784 as the fortress of Vladikavkaz, located at the N entrance of the Georgian Military Road to Tbilisi. The city was known as Ordzhonikidze from 1933 to 1944 and as Dzaudzhikau from 1944 to 1954, when its present name was readopted. Pop. (1980 est.) 283,000.

ORE. See MINING.

OREADS, in Greek mythology, nymphs of grottoes and mountains. One of the most famous

Oreads was Echo, who was deprived by the goddess Hera of the power of speech and could only repeat the last words that were said to her.

ÖREBRO, city and port, S Sweden, capital of Örebro Co., near Lake Hjälmaren. The major industry of the city is the manufacture of shoes. Minerals obtained from the neighboring zinc, copper, and iron mines are conveyed to Göteborg and Stockholm by means of the extensive system of canals that connects the lakes of the interior with the maritime ports. The University of Örebro (1967) is here. Örebro is one of the oldest settlements in Sweden. The modern city, rebuilt after the fire of 1854, has a number of medieval structures. At the Diet of Örebro, held in 1529, Lutheranism was established as the state religion of Sweden. Pop. (1980 est.) 116,969.

OREGON, one of the Pacific states of the U.S., bounded on the N by Washington, on the E by Idaho, on the S by Nevada and California, and on the W by the Pacific Ocean. The Columbia R. forms much of the N boundary.

Oregon entered the Union on Feb. 14, 1859, as the 33d state. Encompassing a land area of great topographic diversity and scenic beauty, Oregon has traditionally had an economy based on agriculture and the exploitation of its vast forests. In the early 1980s manufacturing and service industries also were very important. The origin of the state name is uncertain. It may, however, be derived from the French *ouragan,* meaning "hurricane," a name formerly applied to the Columbia R. Oregon is called the Beaver State.

LAND AND RESOURCES

Oregon, with an area of 251,418 sq km (97,073 sq mi), is the tenth largest state in the U.S.; 52.4% of the land area is owned by the federal government. The state is roughly rectangular in shape, and its extreme dimensions are about 475 km (about 295 mi) from N to S and about 605 km (about 376 mi) from E to W. Elevations range from sea level to 3424 m (11,233 ft) atop Mt. Hood. The approximate mean elevation is 1006 m (3300 ft). Oregon's coastline along the Pacific Ocean is 476 km (296 mi).

Physical Geography. Oregon has considerable physiographic diversity. Along much of the Pacific coast lie the Coast Ranges. Lower than the coastal mountains of California or Washington, they have a maximum elevation of about 1219 m (about 4000 ft). To the S lies a small portion of the granitic Klamath Mts. Both of these regions are well covered with forest and undergrowth and have inhibited E-W travel, except along such stream canyons as those of the Columbia, Umpqua, and Rogue rivers. Inland, to the N, lies the Willamette Valley. A southern extension of the

Mt. Hood, in the eastern portion of Oregon's Cascade Range, is one of a series of volcanic peaks. At 3417 m (11,239 ft), it is the highest point in the state. Bob & Ira Spring

Puget Trough, this region is an alluvial plain, its rich soils having been deposited by the Willamette R. and its tributaries. To the E lies the Oregon portion of the Cascade Range (q.v.). This region consists of a sloping volcanic tableland, capped by a series of presently dormant volcanoes, including Mt. Hood, the Three Sisters, and Mt. McLoughlin.

Covering much of the E half of the state is the Columbia Plateau (q.v.). Much of this area is covered to great depths by basaltic (lava) flows. Streams, such as the John Day R., have cut canyons in the surface. A unique portion of this region is the Blue Mts.; with elevations exceeding 2743 m (9000 ft), the mountains are sufficiently high to have experienced local glaciation during the Pleistocene epoch. To the S of the Columbia Plateau lies a portion of the Great Basin (q.v.). A region of basins separated by low-lying mountains, the Great Basin is internally drained.

Rivers and Lakes. The Columbia R., forming most of the Oregon-Washington boundary, is the principal river of the state. It is sufficiently deep so

that oceangoing ships may reach The Dalles. Its major tributary, the north-and-west flowing Snake R., forms part of the state's NE boundary and joins the Columbia R. in Washington. Both of these rivers cut deep canyons along their courses in Oregon. Two other north-flowing tributaries of the Columbia R.—the Willamette and Deschutes—drain much of Oregon's Cascade Range. Other streams rising in the Cascade Range, but flowing W to the Pacific Ocean, include the Rogue, Umpqua, and Klamath rivers.

The state has numerous natural lakes, especially in the Cascade Range, although none of these is large. Beautiful Crater Lake, the most famous, lies in the crater of an ancient extinct volcano. To the SE is the larger Klamath Lake, and to the E are the shallow Harney and Malheur lakes.

Climate. Western Oregon has an equable, humid climate, dominated by marine influences; E of the Cascade Range the climate is dry and continental, characterized by greater daily and seasonal temperature extremes. In coastal areas the coldest month is only 8.3° C (15° F) lower than that of the warmest month; in the Columbia Plateau the difference is 22.2° C (40° F). The recorded temperature has ranged from −47.8° C (−54° F) in 1933 to 48.3° C (119° F) in 1898. Annual precipitation along the coast averages 1778 to 2286 mm (70 to 90 in). The upper W slopes of the Coast Range receive 5080 mm (200 in) of precipitation annually; the Willamette Valley to the E receives about 1016 mm (about 40 in). The Cascades also receive heavy precipitation and are high enough to prevent moist air masses from moving inland; E Oregon is therefore semiarid, receiving only 203 to 508 mm (8 to 20 in) of precipitation a year. In all areas precipitation is concentrated in the winter months. Although the W is cool, humid, and cloudy, summers there are relatively dry. The W slopes of the Cascades receive 7620 to 12,700 mm (300 to 500 in) of snow a year.

Plants and Animals. Oregon has more standing commercial timber than any other state. Forest, primarily in the W, covers 48% of the total land area. Conifers are predominant. Near the Pacific coast is a tall forest dominated by spruce, cedar, and western hemlock. Inland, over much of the Coast Range, are forests of Douglas fir. The Willamette Valley also has Douglas fir groves, as well as remnants of oak woods. In the Cascade Range are forests of silver and Douglas fir. North of Klamath Lake is a sizable area of open ponderosa pine forest with a grassy undergrowth. Farther N this grades into a juniper woodland with shrubs and grasses. In the drier E half of Oregon the vegetation is relatively scanty, dominated by grasses and sagebrush, with saltbush and greasewood in alkaline areas. The Blue Mts. region, which contains fir forests, is an exception to this pattern.

The forests of W Oregon contain a diversity of wildlife, including Roosevelt elk, cougar, fox, beaver, muskrat, otter, and mink. Seals and sea lions frequent the state's Pacific coast. Salmon, steelhead and rainbow trout, and bass are found in the rivers and lakes. In the E, wildlife includes pronghorn, deer, coyote, jackrabbit, and rattlesnake.

Mineral Resources. Although gold was recovered near Jacksonville in the 19th century, Oregon lacks the rich mineral resources of neighboring California, Nevada, and Idaho. The principal mineral products are sand and gravel and limestone. Other minerals found include nickel, clay, diatomite, and pumice.   D.W.L.

POPULATION

According to the 1980 census, Oregon had 2,633,149 inhabitants, an increase of 25.9% over 1970. Between 1970 and 1979 Oregon experienced a net in-migration of about 300,000 peo-

These fish ladders at Bonneville Dam, on the Columbia River, enable salmon and other migratory fish to move upstream to their spawning grounds, bypassing the obstacle presented by the dam. Greater Portland Convention and Visitors Association, Inc.

INDEX TO MAP OF OREGON

Cities and Towns

Agate Beach .... A 2
Albany .... B 2
Altamont .... C 3
Amity .... A 2
Arlington .... C 2
Ashland ⊙ .... B 3
Astoria ⊙ .... B 1
Athena .... D 2
Baker ⊙ .... E 2
Bandon .... A 3
Bates .... D 2
Bay City .... B 2
Beaverton .... A 2
Bend ⊙ .... C 2
Bly .... A 3
Brookings .... A 3
Brownsville .... B 2
Burns ⊙ .... D 3
Canby .... A 2
Canyon City ⊙ .... D 2
Canyonville .... B 3
Carlton .... B 2
Cascade Locks .... B 2
Central Point .... B 3
Chiloquin .... C 3
Clatskanie .... B 1
Condon ⊙ .... C 2
Coos Bay .... A 3
Coquille ⊙ .... A 3
Corvallis ⊙ .... B 2
Cottage Grove .... B 3
Creswell .... B 3
Dallas ⊙ .... A 2
Drain .... B 3
Dufur .... C 2
Eagle Point .... B 3
Eastside .... A 3
Elgin .... D 2
Elmira .... B 2
Enterprise ⊙ .... E 2
Estacada .... B 2
Eugene ⊙ .... B 2
Falls City .... B 2
Florence .... A 1
Forest Grove ⊙ .... C 2
Fossil ⊙ .... C 2
Garibaldi .... B 1
Gearhart .... A 2
Gladstone .... B 2
Glendale .... A 2
Gold Beach ⊙ .... A 3
Grants Pass ⊙ .... B 3
Gresham .... A 2
Halfway .... E 2
Harrisburg .... B 2
Hayesville .... A 2
Heppner ⊙ .... D 2
Hermiston .... D 2
Hillsboro ⊙ .... B 2, D 3
Hines .... D 3
Hood River ⊙ .... C 2
Huntington .... E 2
Independence .... B 2
Jacksonville .... B 3
Jefferson .... B 2
John Day ⊙ .... D 2
Jordan Valley .... E 3
Joseph .... E 2
Junction City .... B 2
Keizer .... A 2
Kerby .... B 3
Klamath Falls ⊙ .... C 3
La Grande ⊙ .... E 2
Lake Oswego .... A 2
Lakeside .... A 3
Lakeview ⊙ .... C 3
La Pine .... C 2
Lebanon .... B 2
Lincoln City .... A 2
McMinnville ⊙ .... B 2, A 2
Madras ⊙ .... C 2
Malin .... C 3
Mapleton .... B 2
Maupin ⊙ .... C 2
Medford ⊙ .... B 3
Merrill .... C 3
Metzger .... A 2
Mill City .... B 2
Milton-Freewater .... D 2
Milwaukie .... A 2
Molalla .... A 2
Monmouth .... B 2
Moro ⊙ .... C 2
Mount Angel .... A 2
Mount Vernon .... D 2
Myrtle Creek .... B 3
Myrtle Point .... A 3
Netarts .... B 2
Newberg .... A 2
Newport ⊙ .... A 2
North Bend .... A 3
Nyssa .... E 3
Oakland .... B 3
Oakridge .... B 3
Ontario ⊙ .... E 3
Oregon City ⊙ .... B 2, A 2
Pacific City .... A 2
Pendleton ⊙ .... D 2
Philomath .... B 2
Pilot Rock .... D 2
Portland ⊙ .... B 2, A 1
Port Orford .... A 3
Powers .... A 3
Prairie City .... D 2
Prineville ⊙ .... C 2
Prospect .... B 3
Rainier .... B 1
Redmond .... C 2
Reedsport .... A 3
Riddle .... B 3
Roseburg ⊙ .... B 2
Saint Helens ⊙ .... A 2
Salem (cap.) ⊙ .... B 2, A 2
Sandy .... C 2
Scappoose .... B 2
Seaside .... B 2
Shady Cove .... B 3
Sheridan .... B 2
Silverton .... A 2
Sisters .... C 3
Springfield .... B 2
Stayton .... B 2
Sutherlin .... C 2
Sweet Home .... B 2
The Dalles ⊙ .... C 2
Tigard .... A 2
Tillamook ⊙ .... B 2
Toledo .... B 2
Union ⊙ .... D 2
Vale ⊙ .... E 2
Valsetz .... B 2
Vernonia .... A 2
Waldport .... A 2
Wallowa .... A 3
Warm Springs .... E 3
Warrenton .... A 1
Wasco .... C 2
West Linn .... A 2
Weston .... D 2
Willamina .... B 2
Winston .... B 3
Woodburn .... B 2
Wood Village .... A 1

Other Features

Abert (lake) .... C 3
Alvord (desert) .... D 3
Alvord (lake) .... D 3
Antelope (res.) .... E 3
Blanco (cape) .... A 3
Blue (mts.) .... D 2
Blue-Joint (lake) .... D 3
Bonneville (dam) .... B 2
Bowman (dam) .... C 2
Butte (creek) .... A 2
Calapooya (mts.) .... B 2
Cascade (mt. range) .... B 3
Coast (mt. range) .... B 3
Columbia (river) .... B 1
Crane Prairie (res.) .... C 3
Crater (lake) .... B 2
Crater Lake Nat'l Park .... B 3
Crescent (lake) .... C 2
Crooked (river) .... C 2
Crump (lake) .... D 3
Deschutes (river) .... C 2
Detroit (lake) .... B 2
Donner und Blitzen (river) .... D 3
Drews (res.) .... C 3
Fern Ridge (lake) .... B 2
Flagstaff (lake) .... D 3
Fort Clatsop Nat'l Mem. .... A 1
Gerber (res.) .... C 3
Goose (lake) .... C 3
Grande Ronde (river) .... E 2
Harney (lake) .... D 3
Hart (lake) .... C 2
Hells Canyon (dam) .... E 2
Hells Canyon Nat'l Rec. Area. .... E 2
High (desert) .... C 3
High Mt. Sheep (res.) .... E 2
Hills Creek (lake) .... B 3
Hood (mt.) .... C 2
Jefferson (mt.) .... C 2
John Day (river) .... C 2
John Day Fossil Beds Nat'l Mon. .... D 2
Kincheloe (point) .... C 2
Klamath (mts.) .... A 3
Klamath (river) .... B 3
Lookout (cape) .... A 2
Lookout Point (lake) .... B 3
Lost (river) .... C 3
McLoughlin House Nat'l Hist. Site .... A 2
McNary (dam) .... D 2
Malheur (lake) .... D 3
Malheur (river) .... E 3
Middle Fork (Willamette) (river) .... B 3
Molalla (river) .... A 2
Nehalem (river) .... B 3
North Umpqua (river) .... B 3
Oregon Caves Nat'l Mon. .... B 3
Oregon Dunes Nat'l Rec. Area. .... A 3
Owyhee (lake) .... E 3
Owyhee (river) .... E 3
Powder (river) .... E 2
Prineville (res.) .... C 2
Pudding (river) .... A 2
Rogue (river) .... B 3
Sacajawea (peak) .... E 2
Silver (creek) .... C 3
Silver (lake) .... C 3
Silver (river) .... D 3
Silvies (river) .... D 3
Snake (river) .... E 2
Sprague (river) .... C 3
Steens (mts.) .... D 3
Strawberry (mt.) .... D 2
Summer (lake) .... C 3
Thielsen (mt.) .... C 3
Three Sisters (mt.) .... C 2
Umatilla Ind. Res. .... D 2
Umpqua (river) .... B 3
Upper Klamath (lake) .... B 3
Waldo (lake) .... B 3
Wallowa (mts.) .... D 1
Wallula (lake) .... D 1
Warm Springs (res.) .... D 3
Warm Springs Ind. Res. .... C 2
Warner (valley) .... C 3
Wickiup (res.) .... C 3
Willamette (river) .... B 2

⊙ County seat

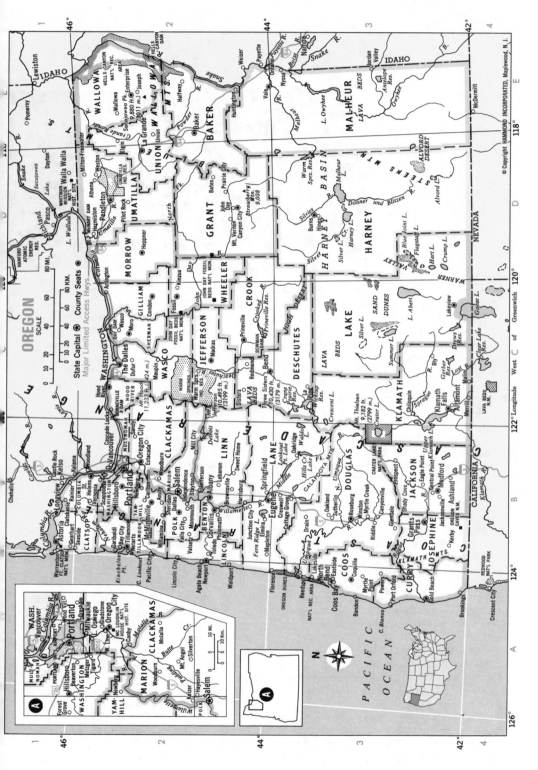

OREGON

SCALE

MI.
0 10 20 30 40 50 60 70 80 MI.

KM.
0 10 20 30 40 50 60 70 80 KM.

● State Capital ⊛ County Seats

Major Limited Access Hwys.

The golden statue The Pioneer can be seen atop Oregon's white marble capitol in Salem, overlooking a green mall and other modern buildings in the capitol group.

Oregon State Highway Commission

ple. The average population density in 1980 was 10.5 people per sq km (27 per sq mi). Whites made up 94.6% of the population and blacks 1.4%; additional population groups included some 26,590 American Indians, 8430 persons of Japanese background, 8035 persons of Chinese descent, 5565 persons of Vietnamese extraction, 4430 persons of Korean ancestry, and 4255 persons of Filipino origin. Approximately 65,835 persons were of Hispanic background. American Indian groups included the Klamath, Wasco, Walla Walla, Paiute, Umatilla, and Cayuse. Although a majority of the Oregon population in 1980 was Protestant, the largest single religious group was the Roman Catholic church, with some 320,315 adherents. Principal Protestant groups included Baptists, Disciples of Christ, Episcopalians, Lutherans, and Methodists. Oregon also had a substantial community of Mormons. In 1980 about 68% of all persons in Oregon lived in areas defined as urban, and the rest resided in rural areas. The major area of population concentration was in the W, especially in the Willamette R. valley of the NW. The largest cities in the state were Portland; Eugene; Salem, the capital; Springfield; Corvallis; and Medford.

EDUCATION AND CULTURAL ACTIVITY

Oregon has a comprehensive statewide public educational system and a number of prominent cultural institutions, concentrated for the most part in Portland.

Education. In 1849 the territory of Oregon was officially organized, and the passage of the Nathan Dane Act provided for funds to establish an educational system; Oregon's first public school was opened in 1851. In the early 1980s the state had 1003 public elementary and secondary schools with a combined annual enrollment of about 319,100 elementary pupils and 145,500 secondary students. Some 28,200 students attended private schools. In the same period Oregon had 45 institutions of higher education with a total yearly enrollment of about 157,500 students. Among the most notable of these schools were Willamette University (1842), the oldest institution of higher education in the Far West, in Salem; Lewis and Clark College (1867), Reed College (1909), Portland State University (1946), the University of Portland (1901), and Pacific Northwest College of Art (1909), all in Portland; Linfield College (1849), in McMinnville; the University of Oregon (1876), in Eugene; Oregon State University (1850), in Corvallis; and Pacific University (1849), in Forest Grove.

Cultural Institutions. Three of Oregon's most important museums—the Portland Art Museum (containing the Rasmussen collection of Indian artifacts), the Oregon Historical Society Museum, and the Oregon Museum of Science and Industry—are located in Portland. Portland is also the home of the Oregon Symphony Orchestra, the Portland Opera Association, and the Portland Symphony Orchestra. Other museums of note are the University of Oregon Museum of Art, in Eugene; the Butler Museum of American Indian Art, also in Eugene; and the Favell Museum of Western Art and Indian Artifacts, in Klamath Falls. Two prominent cultural events of the summer are the Oregon Shakespearean Festival, which takes place in Ashland, and the Peter Britt Music Festival, held in Jacksonville.

Historical Sites. The heritage of the Old West is commemorated in a number of Oregon's historical sites, such as Pioneer Village, in Jacksonville, and Astoria Column and Fort Clatsop National Memorial, both in Astoria. Period houses in the state include the McLoughlin House National Historic Site (1846) and the Capt. John C. Ainsworth House (1850), in Oregon City; Bush House (1877), in Salem; and the Bybee Howell House (1856) in Portland.

Sports and Recreation. Oregon's national forests, which cover much of the state, together with its scenic ocean shoreline, mountains, rivers, and lakes, furnish ideal conditions for such outdoor activities as swimming, boating, fishing, hiking, camping, mountain climbing, and hunting. Golfing and horseback riding are popular sports, as is skiing, with major ski areas located around Mt. Hood, Mt. Bachelor, and Mt. Ashland.

Communications. In the early 1980s Oregon had 80 AM and 37 FM commercial radiobroadcasting stations and 12 commercial television stations. The state's first radio station, KGW in Portland, was licensed in 1922. KPTV in Portland, Oregon's first commercial television station, went on the air in 1953. The *Oregon Spectator,* Oregon's first newspaper and the first newspaper published W of the Rocky Mts., began publication in Oregon City in 1846. In the early 1980s Oregon had 21 daily newspapers with a combined daily circulation of about 702,500. Major dailies included the *Oregonian* and the *Oregon Journal,* in Portland; the *Eugene Register-Guard,* in Eugene; and the *Statesman-Journal,* in Salem.

GOVERNMENT AND POLITICS

Oregon is governed under its original constitution adopted in 1857, as amended. Amendments to the constitution may be proposed by the legislature, by initiative, or by a constitutional convention. An amendment proposed by the legislature or by initiative must be approved by a majority of the persons voting on the issue in a general election.

Executive. The chief executive of Oregon is a governor, who is popularly elected to a 4-year term and who is limited to a maximum of two terms in any 12-year period. The same regulations apply to the secretary of state, who succeeds the governor should the latter resign, die, or be removed from office. Other elected executive officials include the attorney general, treasurer, superintendent of public instruction, and labor commissioner.

Legislature. The bicameral Oregon legislative assembly comprises a Senate and a House of Representatives. The 30 members of the Senate are elected to serve 4-year terms, and the 60 members of the House are elected to 2-year terms.

Judiciary. Oregon's highest tribunal, the supreme court, is composed of a chief justice and 6 associate justices. The intermediate court of appeals has 10 judges, and the major trial courts, the circuit courts, have a total of 85 judges. All judges except municipal judges are elected on nonpartisan ballots to 6-year terms.

Local Government. In the early 1980s Oregon had 36 counties and about 240 municipalities. Most of the counties were governed by a county judge and several commissioners, and cities generally operated under the mayor-council form of government.

National Representation. Oregon elects two senators and five representatives to the U.S. Congress. The state has seven electoral votes in presidential elections.

Politics. Although the Democrats hold an advantage in party registration, Oregon has a well-established tradition of political independence, and Republican candidates usually come out ahead in presidential elections. In the early 1980s Republicans held the governorship and both of Oregon's seats in the U.S. Senate, but Democrats controlled the state legislature.

ECONOMY

From its earliest settlement, Oregon has had an economy dominated by the exploitation of natural resources, particularly forest and agricultural resources. Since World War II, however, the state's economy has diversified with the growth of manufacturing and service industries. By the early 1980s some 27% of Oregon's labor force was employed in service industries, and about 18% in manufacturing. Only 4% was employed in farming, forestry, fishing, and mining together.

Agriculture. Farming accounts for 15% of the annual value of goods produced in Oregon. The state has some 35,000 farms, which average 209 ha (517 acres) in size. Livestock and dairy products make up about 34% of Oregon's yearly farm income. Beef cattle is the leading livestock product; cattle ranching is concentrated E of the Cascade Range. Dairy farming and poultry and hog raising are important in the W. Sheep are raised in both the W and E parts of the state.

Crops account for 66% of Oregon's annual agricultural income. The leading crop, wheat, is grown in the relatively dry E part of the state. Other crops grown in this region include potatoes, barley, oats, and—under irrigation—vegetables and sugar beets. The state's most productive agricultural areas, the Willamette Valley and the narrow valleys W of the Cascade Range, are known for their vegetables and fruits. Major crops here include pears, cherries, strawberries,

STATE OF OREGON
1859

OREGON
(1925)

OREGON

DATE OF STATEHOOD: February 14, 1859; 33d state

CAPITAL:	Salem
MOTTO:	The Union
NICKNAME:	Beaver State
STATE SONG:	"Oregon, My Oregon" (words by J. A. Buchanan; music by Henry B. Murtagh)
STATE TREE:	Douglas fir
STATE FLOWER:	Oregon grape
STATE BIRD:	Western meadowlark
POPULATION (1980):	2,633,149; 30th among the states
AREA:	251,418 sq km (97,073 sq mi); 10th largest state; includes 2302 sq km (889 sq mi) of inland water
COASTLINE:	476 km (296 mi)
HIGHEST POINT:	Mount Hood, 3424 m (11,233 ft)
LOWEST POINT:	Sea level, at the Pacific coast
ELECTORAL VOTES:	7
U.S. CONGRESS:	2 senators; 5 representatives

POPULATION OF OREGON SINCE 1850

Year of Census	Population	Classified As Urban
1850	12,000	0%
1870	91,000	9%
1880	175,000	15%
1900	414,000	32%
1920	783,000	50%
1940	1,090,000	49%
1960	1,769,000	62%
1970	2,092,000	67%
1980	2,633,000	68%

POPULATION OF TEN LARGEST CITIES

	1980 Census	1970 Census
Portland	366,383	379,967
Eugene	105,624	79,028
Salem	89,233	68,725
Springfield	41,621	26,874
Corvallis	40,960	35,056
Medford	39,603	28,973
Gresham	33,005	10,030
Beaverton	30,582	18,577
Hillsboro	27,664	14,675
Albany	26,678	18,181

CLIMATE

	PORTLAND	PENDLETON
Average January temperature range	0.6° to 6.7° C (33° to 44° F)	−3.9° to 3.9° C (25° to 39° F)
Average July temperature range	12.8° to 26.1° C (55° to 79° F)	15° to 31.1° C (59° to 88° F)
Average annual temperature	11.7° C (53° F)	11.1° C (52° F)
Average annual precipitation	965 mm (38 in)	305 mm (12 in)
Average annual snowfall	178 mm (7 in)	457 mm (18 in)
Mean number of days per year with appreciable precipitation	152	99
Average daily relative humidity	66%	52%
Mean number of clear days per year	69	107

WILLAMETTE VALLEY
Columbia R.
COAST RANGES
Willamette R.
Snake R.
COLUMBIA PLATEAU
CASCADE RANGE
KLAMATH MTS.
GREAT BASIN

NATURAL REGIONS OF OREGON

PRINCIPAL PRODUCTS OF OREGON

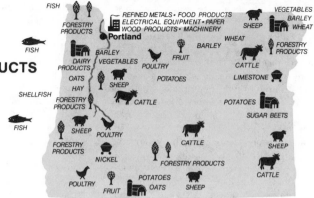

ECONOMY

State budget................... revenue $4.0 billion
                              expenditure $3.5 billion
State personal income tax, per capita $319
Personal income, per capita $9317
Assets, commercial banks (75)......... $12.3 billion
Labor force (civilian) 1,238,500
   Employed in services   27%
   Employed in wholesale and retail trade   21%
   Employed in manufacturing   18%
   Employed in government   15%

	Quantity Produced	Value
FARM PRODUCTS		**$1.6 billion**
Crops		**$1.1 billion**
Wheat	2.1 million metric tons	$310 million
Hay	2.6 million metric tons	$221 million
Vegetables	791,000 metric tons	$126 million
Potatoes	896,000 metric tons	$91 million
Pears	181,000 metric tons	$43 million
Livestock and Livestock Products		**$537 million**
Cattle	237,000 metric tons	$312 million
Milk	510,000 metric tons	$158 million
Eggs	638 million	$27 million
Chickens	36,000 metric tons	$24 million
MINERALS		**$160 million**
Stone	19.7 million metric tons	$56 million
Sand, gravel	13.3 million metric tons	$39 million
Pumice	694,000 metric tons	$2 million
FISHING	57,300 metric tons	**$55.7 million**

	Labor and Proprietor's Income
FORESTRY	**$46.4 million**
MANUFACTURING	**$4.6 billion**
Lumber and wood products	$1.6 billion
Food and kindred products	$407 million
Nonelectric machinery	$404 million
Instruments and related products	$374 million
Primary metals	$316 million
Paper and allied products	$285 million
Fabricated metal products	$264 million
Electric and electronic equipment	$183 million
Printing and publishing	$171 million

OTHER .... **$12.2 billion**
Services............................ $3.0 billion
Government and government enterprises $3.0 billion
Transportation and public utilities....... $1.5 billion
Finance, insurance, and real estate ..... $1.2 billion
Wholesale trade .... $1.4 billion
Retail trade .... $2.1 billion

ANNUAL PRODUCTION OF GOODS BY SECTOR

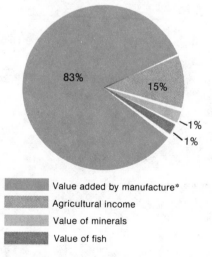

Value added by manufacture*

Agricultural income

Value of minerals

Value of fish

*The value added by an industry is a measure of the value created in its products, not counting such production costs as raw materials and power.

Sources: U.S. government publications

beans, peas, peaches, plums, and nuts. Flower bulbs and other horticultural products are also grown in these areas.

Forestry. Forestry is an important sector of the Oregon economy; processed forestry products account for nearly 30% of the state's total value added by manufacturing. Oregon is a leading state in its output of forestry products, supplying more than 17% of all saw timber, 25% of all lumber, and almost 70% of all plywood manufactured in the U.S. Major commercial species are the Douglas fir and hemlock in the W and the ponderosa pine in the E. Logging occurs in almost every county of the state but is concentrated in the Cascade Range.

Fishing. The fishing industry accounts for about 1% of the value of goods produced each year in Oregon. Chinook, coho (silver), and other varieties of salmon constitute nearly half the annual catch; tuna, crab, and shrimp make up much of the varied remainder. Most commercial fishing takes place along the continental shelf, but a minor amount is conducted on the Columbia R. and other inland waterways.

Mining. The mining industry accounts for about 1% of the annual value of goods produced in Oregon. Sand and gravel account for about one-quarter of the total mineral value and are mined in nearly every county. Limestone and other stone make up one-third of the value and occur widely throughout the state. Other mineral products include clay, diatomite, pumice, chalk, and nickel.

Manufacturing. Manufacturing enterprises account for 83% of the value of goods produced annually in Oregon and employ about 226,100 workers. The leading manufactures are lumber, wood, and paper products; these related industries employ approximately two-fifths of the state's manufacturing labor force. The other leading industries include food processing and the manufacture of nonelectrical machinery, instruments, primary and fabricated metal, and electrical and electronic equipment. The last named, which includes the manufacture of such products as computers, has expanded significantly and now employs about one-sixth of the manufacturing labor force. Other important manufactures include transportation equipment and printed materials. Portland and Eugene are the principal industrial centers in Oregon and have attracted much of the state's new high-technology industry.

Tourism. Each year several million visitors to the state produce about $2 billion for the Oregon economy. Crater Lake National Park is the out-

Logs going into a mill at Bend, Oreg. Oregon is one of the leading states in timber production.
American Forest Products Industries, Inc.

Crater Lake, the most famous of Oregon's many lakes, and Wizard Island in Crater Lake National Park. The lake is situated in the crater of the extinct Mt. Mazama.
Oregon Travel Information

standing attraction among the areas administered in Oregon by the National Park Service. In addition, Oregon maintains a system of about 235 state parks and recreation areas, some 70 of which have frontage on the Pacific Ocean.

Transportation. Portland is the principal hub within a network of about 208,410 km (about 129,500 mi) of federal, state, and local roads that serve all sections of Oregon. This includes 1130 km (702 mi) of Interstate Highways that cross the state from N to S and E to W. The 4738 km (2944 mi) of operated railroad track extend mainly in a N-S direction, with secondary E-W connections. The state has 18 marine and river ports, of which Portland and Coos Bay are the most important. Oceangoing barges and river craft are able to navigate the Columbia R. as far inland as The Dalles. The Portland International Airport is by far the most important of the 318 airports in the state.

Energy. The electricity-generating plants in Oregon have a total installed capacity of about 8.5 million kw and produce some 36.6 billion kwh of electricity each year. Approximately four-fifths of all electricity is generated by hydroelectric projects, primarily from major dams located at The Dalles, Bonneville, and other sites on the Columbia and Snake rivers. Since the mid-1970s, when all major dam sites had been developed, the state has turned increasingly to thermal electricity. The Trojan plant, near Rainier, is a major source of nuclear energy.   R.S.Th.

HISTORY

Among the early inhabitants of Oregon were the Chinook, Yakima, Cayuse, Modoc, and Shoshoni Indians. In 1542–43 a Spanish navigator, Bartolomé Ferrelo, sailed from Mexico to a point near southern Oregon. In 1602–03 his exploit was duplicated by another Spanish mariner, Sebastián Vizcaíno. In 1579 the English navigator Sir Francis Drake sailed along the Pacific coast, possibly as far north as Oregon. Other Spanish explorers made voyages to Oregon coastal waters during the 17th and 18th centuries. In 1775 the Spanish navigator Bruno Heceta sailed to the mouth of the Columbia River. In 1778 the British sea captain James Cook saw the Oregon coast near the mouth of the Alsea River. Within the next decade various British and American vessels frequented the northern Pacific coast. In 1788 occurred the first known landing of whites on the Oregon coast, by seamen of the American vessel *Lady Washington,* commanded by Capt. Robert Gray. On a second voyage, in 1792, Capt. Gray discovered the great river, which he named the Columbia, after his ship; the U.S. later claimed the entire region drained by the Columbia, basing its claim on Gray's voyage. George Vancouver, a British captain, was at this time exploring Puget Sound. Fur traders entered a region in 1793. The immense wilderness, inhabited only by Indian tribes, was explored in 1804–05 by the Americans Meriwether Lewis and William Clark.

Oregon's Fur Trade. A trading post in the Columbia River region was established in 1811 by the Pacific Fur Co. of John Jacob Astor at Astoria. After the declaration of the War of 1812 between Great Britain and the U.S., Astoria was sold to the British North West Co. and renamed Fort George.

Negotiations in 1818 led to the establishment of the 49th parallel as the boundary between the U.S. and British possessions as far west as the Rocky Mountains. Because an agreement could not be reached regarding the boundary west of the Rocky Mountains and north of the 42d parallel, the two countries agreed to a 10-year period of joint occupancy. In 1819 Spain, which also had laid claim to the Oregon country, relinquished its

The 19th-century explorer and fur trader Dr. John McLoughlin, called the Father of Oregon, overlooks the Willamette River from his vantage point near U.S. Highway 99E at Oregon City. Oregon State Highway Commission

claim to all Pacific coast territory north of the 42d parallel; and in 1824 and 1825, by treaties with the U.S. and Great Britain, Russia relinquished claim to territory south of the parallel 54° 40′. The Anglo-American convention was extended in 1827.

The rich Oregon fur trade was controlled by the British Hudson's Bay Co., which had absorbed the North West Co. During the 1840s organized American immigration to the Oregon territory began, and the "Oregon question" became a matter of concern.

A Question of Sovereignty. By 1843 Americans were demanding that Great Britain relinquish all jurisdiction south of 54° 40′ latitude; in 1844 the Democratic party slogan, on which James Polk was elected president of the U.S., was "Fifty-four forty, or fight." At length, in 1846, the two countries agreed, in the Oregon Treaty, on the 49th parallel as the boundary from the Rockies to the coast, and a line along the midchannel between Vancouver Island and the mainland to the Pacific Ocean. In 1848 Oregon was established as a territory; as originally established, it covered all the area between the 42d and 49th parallels, from the Rocky Mountains to the Pacific Ocean, and included present-day Washington and parts of Idaho, Montana, and Wyoming. Many Oregon settlers left for California after the discovery of gold there in 1849, but the depopulation was more than compensated for after the passage by Congress of the Donation Land Act in 1850, giving large tracts of land free to settlers in Oregon. The increase of population and prosperity prompted the settlers to hold a convention in 1857 and request statehood, which was granted in 1859. Indian rebellions and wars became increasingly serious after the American Civil War. The Modoc War (1864–73) and the Shoshoni War (1866–68) were marked by fierce battles and widespread destruction. Many Indian engagements were fought in the 1870s, when the tribes were being forced to move to reservations.

Progressive Growth. Between 1869, when the Union Pacific Railroad was completed, and 1900, Oregon's population more than quadrupled. An early leader in governmental reform, Oregon was among the first states to enact the initiative and referendum (1902), the direct primary (1904), recall (1908), and woman suffrage (1912).

From the beginning, lumber and agriculture played a central role in the state's economy. Both industries have been greatly aided by irrigation water and low-cost electric power supplied since the 1930s by several dam projects. Oregon's various World War II defense efforts led to enormous expansion. In 1956 the introduction of

The Portland Building (1979-82), designed by Michael Graves, might be seen as embodying Oregon's forward-looking spirit. This multicolored office building housing Portland city agencies is one of only a handful of nonresidential structures to be built in the controversial postmodern style. Proto-Acme Photo

natural gas brought about further industrial and attendant population growth.

Since the 1960s the lumber industry has undergone many changes. New ways have also been found to utilize logging by-products and strong reforestation programs designed to reduce waste and conserve timber resources.

For further information on this topic, see the Bibliography in volume 28, section 1225.

OREGON CAVES NATIONAL MONUMENT. See NATIONAL PARK SERVICE (table).

OREGON QUESTION. See NORTHWEST BOUNDARY DISPUTE; OREGON.

OREGON TRAIL, overland pioneer route to the northwestern U.S. About 3200 km (about 2000 mi) long, the trail extended from Independence, Mo., to the Columbia River in Oregon. The first part of the route followed the Platte River for 870 km (540 mi) through what is now Nebraska to Fort Laramie in present-day Wyoming. The trail continued along the North Platte and Sweetwater rivers to South Pass in the Wind River Range of the Rocky Mountains. From there the main trail went south to Fort Bridger, Wyo., before turning into the Bear River valley and north to Fort Hall in present-day Idaho. A more direct route from the South Pass to the Bear River was Sublette's Cutoff, which was 85 km (53 mi) shorter but more arid than the main trail. In Idaho the Oregon Trail followed the Snake River to the Salmon Falls and then went north past Fort Boise (now Boise). The route entered what is now Oregon, passed through the Grande Ronde River valley, crossed the Blue Mountains and followed the Umatilla River to the Columbia River.

Originally, like many of the main roads of the country, sections of the Oregon Trail had been crossed by the Indians and trappers. As early as 1742-43, part of the trail in Wyoming had been blazed by the Canadian explorer Pierre Gaultier de Varennes, sieur de la Vérendrye; the Lewis and Clark expedition, between 1804 and 1806, made more of it known. The German-American fur trader and financier John Jacob Astor, in establishing his trading posts, dispatched a party overland in 1811-12 to follow in the trail of these explorers. Later, mountain men such as James Bridger, who founded (1843) Fort Bridger, contributed their knowledge of the trail and often acted as guides. The first emigrant wagon train, headed by the American pioneer physician Elijah White (1806-79), reached Oregon in 1842. The trip took the early pioneers some five or six months, a journey fraught with much hardship resulting from poor equipment, illness, and attack by the Indians, for whom the growing number of pioneers on the trail was an ever-constant threat. At first, the termination point of the Ore-

ORËL

gon Trail was Astoria, Oreg.; later, it was extended into southern Oregon to the fertile and valuable land in the Willamette Valley.

ORËL, also Oryol, city, capital of Orël Oblast, Russian SFSR, in central European USSR, on the Oka R. The city is a road and railroad junction and a center of agricultural trade. Manufactures include machinery, clothing, flour, and beer. The childhood home here of the writer I. S. Turgenev is now a museum. Orël was founded in 1564 by Ivan IV as a defense post against Tatar invasions. The city suffered extensive damage during World War II. Pop. (1980 est.) 309,000.

ORELLANA, Francisco de (1500?–45), Spanish explorer and soldier, born in Trujillo. He went to Peru in 1535. In 1540 he accompanied the Spanish explorer Gonzalo Pizarro (1506?–48) as second-in-command on an expedition across the Andes Mountains into the country to the east, which was reported to abound in gold, silver, and cinnamon.

After many misfortunes the expedition reached the Napo River. After the supplies were exhausted, Orellana was ordered (1541) to sail down the Napo River with 50 men to search for provisions and signs of treasure. He descended the stream to its junction with the Amazon River, in present-day northeastern Peru; instead of returning, he proceeded down the river to the Atlantic Ocean. The voyage to the mouth of the Amazon lasted nearly eight months. From the mouth of the river he sailed to Spain, relating descriptions of a marvelous race of female warriors who he renamed after the classical Amazons. Orellana was granted permission by the Spanish government to explore the land he had discovered, and he set forth in 1544 with an expedition. He died in the new territory within a year.

OREM, city, Utah Co., N Utah, just N of Provo, at the foot of Mt. Timpanogos; inc. 1919. It has manufactures that include steel and electronic equipment, and it is also a shipping center for the fruit, grain, poultry, and dairy items produced in the surrounding region. Settlement began in 1861; a small canal from the Provo R. was built in 1863 and encouraged farming of the arid land. In 1919 the city was named for Walter C. Orem (1873–1951), president of a local railroad company. Pop. (1970) 25,729; (1980) 52,399.

ORENBURG, formerly CHKALOV, city, capital of Orenburg Oblast, Russian SFSR, in E European USSR, on the Ural R. The city, an industrial and transportation center, has railroad repair shops, petroleum refineries, and factories producing machinery and leather goods. Originally established in 1735 at the site of modern Orsk, Oren-

burg was moved to its present location in 1743 and subsequently served as a center of Russian trade with Kazakhstan. The city was known as Chkalov from 1938 to 1957, when its current name was readopted. Pop. (1980 est.) 471,000.

ORENSE, city, NW Spain, capital of Orense Province, on the Miño R., in Galicia. The city, at the center of an agricultural region, has some light industry. Its hot sulfurous springs, from which its name is derived, have been used since Roman times, when it was called Aquae Originis or Urentae. Orense has a handsome bridge and a Gothic cathedral, both dating from the 13th century. The city reached its peak as capital of the Suevi Kingdom in the 6th and 7th centuries. Pop. (1981 est.) 86,951.

ORESTES, in Greek mythology, son of Agamemnon, king of Mycenae, and Clytemnestra. He was still a boy when his mother and her lover, Aegisthus, murdered Agamemnon. Orestes' older sister Electra, fearing for the boy's life, sent him to live with their uncle Strophius, king of Phocis. There he grew up with Pylades, son of Strophius, who became his lifelong companion. When he reached maturity, Orestes realized that he had a sacred duty to avenge the death of his father, but the crime of matricide was abhorrent to him. He consulted the oracle at Delphi and was advised to kill the two who had murdered his father. With Pylades he returned to Mycenae and avenged Agamemnon's death. Pursued by the avenging goddesses the Erinyes, Orestes wandered through many lands. Finally, at the command of the god Apollo, he went to Athens to plead his cause before the goddess Athena and a council of nobles, the Areopagus. Orestes declared himself guilty of matricide, but stated that he had been cleansed of guilt through suffering. The court, accepting the plea, acquitted Orestes.

According to the dramas of the Greek playwright Euripides, some of the Erinyes refused to accept the verdict and continued to pursue Orestes. In despair he again consulted the Delphic oracle. He was advised to go to the land of the Taurians (modern Crimea) and steal the sacred image of Artemis from the temple of the goddess. With Pylades he went to the temple and discovered that the priestess was his sister Iphigenia, whom he had thought to be dead. With her help they stole the sacred statue and returned with it to Mycenae. Thereafter the Erinyes let Orestes live in peace.

ØRESUND (Eng. *The Sound*), strait connecting the strait of Kattegat on the N with the Baltic Sea on the S, and separating Sweden on the E from the Danish island of Sjaelland on the W. Øresund forms part of the usual shipping passage

436

between the North and Baltic seas. It is 105 km (65 mi) long, varies in width from about 48 km to 3 km (about 30 mi to 2 mi), and has a minimum depth of 7 m (23 ft). The most important seaports on the strait are Copenhagen, Denmark, and Malmö, Sweden.

ORFF, Carl (1895–1982), German composer known for his educational and theatrical music. Born July 10, 1895, in Munich, where he studied music, he conducted in various German theaters and in 1924, with the dancer Dorothea Günther, he founded the Günther School to train children in music, dance, and gymnastics. His *Schulwerk* (*Music for Children*, 1930–33, rev. 1950–54) begins with simple rhythmic patterns and progresses to sonorous ensemble pieces for xylophones, glockenspiels, and other percussion instruments. In his famous oratorio-mime *Carmina burana* (1937) he set 13th-century secular poetry to concentrated, deliberately simple music structured around vigorous, pulsating rhythms and rich sonorities. His other works include the fairy-tale opera *Die Kluge* (The Clever Woman, 1943) and the austere musical play *Antigonae* (1949).

ORGAN, keyboard musical instrument in which compressed air vibrates within tuned pipes to produce sound. An organ consists of flue pipes and/or reed pipes, an air supply, and the keys and other controls.

Pipes. Flue pipes are made of metal or wood, and they work much like whistles. Air enters at the foot of the pipe, moves as a sheet against a narrow slit or flue, and begins to vibrate as it passes across a sharp lip set in the pipe above the flue. This initial vibration causes all the air in the pipe to vibrate, producing a musical tone. The pitch of the tone depends on the length of the pipe; the shape and material of the pipe influence the color or quality of the tone. Some flue pipes are closed at the top; "stopped" pipes produce pitches an octave lower than open pipes of the same length.

In reed pipes, the reed and the metal trough against which it beats (called a shallot) are encased in a pipe into which air is released from the air supply. The incoming air causes the curved end of the reed to beat against the shallot and set the surrounding air into vibration. The musical pitch produced is low for long reeds, high for short reeds. The shallot is connected to a pipelike resonator, the shape of which affects the color of the sound.

A set of pipes all having the same tone quality is called a rank. The most characteristic organ sound is produced by metal flue pipes called diapasons or principals; pipes of this kind form the central core of classic organ sound. Because the lowest note on most organs (two octaves below middle C) is produced by an open diapason pipe about 8 ft long, ranks of pipes at normal pitch are spoken of as 8-ft ranks. Ranks sounding an octave lower than normal are called 16-ft ranks, and those sounding an octave higher, 4-ft ranks. Mutations are ranks of pipes sounding at pitches other than octaves above normal pitch, such as an octave and a fifth above normal (for example, two G's above a C). Mixtures are ranks of pipes of different pitches operated as a single unit (by a single stop). Mixtures often contain ranks sounding several octaves above 8-ft pitch as well as mutation ranks. The high pitches of mutations and mixtures blend together to produce the incisive, bright quality that is associated with organ sound.

On large organs the ranks are grouped together into several divisions, each controlled by a separate keyboard, or manual, and having one or more wind chests, airtight boxes that act as air reservoirs. The main division is called the Great Organ; the other most common divisions are the Choir Organ, the Swell Organ, and the Pedal Organ. The pipes of the Swell Organ are enclosed in a "swell box," a chamber having a slat-covered opening similar to a venetian blind. The slats can be opened and closed by a pedal lever, allowing gradual changes in volume.

Air Supply. The air for the pipes is supplied from a wind chest, on which the pipes are mounted. Air, which is produced by bellows or by an electrical blower, enters the wind chest at a constant pressure.

Controls. When a key is depressed, small valves open to allow air from the wind chest to enter the pipes and cause them to sound. A "stop" mechanism allows any rank of pipes to be prevented from sounding. The ranks are controlled by knobs or switches (called stops) set near the keyboard. By extension, the ranks of pipes they control are sometimes called stops.

Until the 19th century the connections linking the keys and pipe valves—including mechanisms to couple keyboards so that ranks of pipes may be multiply controlled—were achieved mechanically by a system of levers and cranks connected by strips of wood called trackers and stickers. Builders in the 19th century began to devise electrical and pneumatic actions to make the key-to-valve and stop connections. Because many organists believe these actions to be less responsive and sensitive than direct mechanical linkages, in the 20th century organs were again being built with the traditional tracker action.

The keyboards, wind chest, and pipes of small

organs are contained in one unit. In large organs the keyboards and other controls are built in a separate unit called the console. Many organ consoles have a number of controls, called pistons, which allow the organist to bring into play at one stroke a combination of several ranks or stops.

Each organ is unique in that it must suit the acoustics and architecture of the room that houses it. The room itself has an intimate acoustic relation to the organ, profoundly influencing the sound of the organ by the amount of reverberation it allows.

History. The earliest organ, the hydraulis, was developed by the Greek inventor Ctesibius (fl. 3d cent. BC). It utilized a large chamber partly filled with water. The wide mouth of a funnellike extension from the wind chest was set in the top of the water; as air pressure in the wind chest fell, water rose in the funnel and compressed the air, thus keeping the air pressure constant. The hydraulis was used for public entertainments in an-

Antique positive organ (Vesterheim Museum, Decorah, Iowa). The keyboard, wind chest, and pipes are contained in one movable unit and linked mechanically by a system of levers, cranks, and wooden strips called trackers.   Dale Rosene–Bruce Coleman, Inc.

cient Rome and Byzantium. Bellows-type organs were also known to the ancient world. This was the organ that reappeared in Europe in the 8th and 9th centuries, imported from Byzantium and from Arabs who had discovered ancient Greek treatises. Although some ancient organs had a stop mechanism, this device was forgotten, and on early medieval organs all ranks sounded at once, creating a formidable effect. By the 15th century the stop mechanism had been reinvented, pedal keyboards came into common use, and reed stops (not found on ancient organs) were developed. Smaller organs had also become common: the portative organ, carried by a strap around the player's neck, which had only one rank of pipes and was supplied with wind by a small bellows pumped by the player; the positive organ, self-contained and portable; and the regal, a small instrument with one rank of nasal-sounding reed pipes.

Between 1500 and 1800, various national styles of organ building developed, each distinguished by characteristic-sounding ranks. German organs of the 17th and 18th centuries were particularly outstanding, and it was for such organs that the music of Johann Sebastian Bach was written.

Organ builders in the 19th century devoted much effort to developing pipes that imitated the sound of orchestral instruments. About the same time, the swell box came into use. These innovations, which the best builders integrated with the traditional features of earlier organs, stimulated the organ works of such composers as the Hungarian Franz Liszt, the Belgian César Franck, the German Max Reger, and, in the 20th century, the French composer Olivier Messiaen. Many 19th-century organs, however, concentrated principally on stops imitating the orchestra and were used for music that was basically orchestral in origin or conception. In the 20th century a movement occurred to revive 18th-century instruments, often incorporating the best of the 19th-century innovations.

Electronic Organs. Electronic and electric organs, developed in the 20th century, are not organs in the strict sense, for they do not produce sound by air vibrating in a pipe; rather, they are instruments in their own right. One kind, invented in 1935 by an American, Laurens Hammond (1895–1973), utilizes electrical circuits and amplifiers to produce and enlarge the sound. Another kind uses electronic devices such as vacuum tubes. Although such instruments are often designed to imitate the tone qualities of pipe organs, they are frequently criticized for a pinched or artificial-seeming sound. Electronic organs were widely used in the rock bands of the 1960s and after. In such bands, which use extensive electrical sound amplification and manipulation, the distinctive qualities of electronic-organ sound are exploited for their own sake.

Reed Organs. Keyboard instruments in which the wind supply is directed toward free metal reeds like those of a harmonica or accordion are called reed organs. They include the melodeon, developed in the U.S. about 1825, and the harmonium, developed in Germany about 1810. G.V.

For further information on this topic, see the Bibliography in volume 28, section 747.

ORGANIC CHEMISTRY. *See* CHEMISTRY, OR- GANIC.

ORGANIZATION OF AFRICAN UNITY (OAU), regional organization of independent African states (excluding South Africa). Its purposes are to promote unity, to coordinate political, economic, cultural, medical, scientific, and defense policies, to defend the independence and territorial integrity of the member states, and to eliminate colonization on the continent. Headquarters is in Addis Ababa, Ethiopia.

Structure. The policymaking body of the organization is the Assembly of Heads of State and Government, consisting of the leaders of the member nations or their representatives. The assembly, at its annual meetings, approves decisions made, at periodic conferences, by the Council of Ministers, which consists of the foreign ministers of the member countries. Peacekeeping efforts are made through the Commission of Mediation, Conciliation, and Arbitration and through ad hoc committees. Aid for groups opposing colonial rule is channeled through its Coordination Committee for the Liberation of Africa. Technical research, mainly in agriculture, is conducted through a scientific and research commission.

The permanent administrative body of the organization is the General Secretariat. It is headed by a secretary-general, aided by four assistant secretaries as heads of divisions. The secretariat carries out the resolutions and decisions of the assembly, keeps archives, and conducts the organization's public relations.

History. The OAU is an outgrowth of pan-African sentiment dating from 1900, when the First Pan-African Congress met in London. Between 1900 and 1927 five congresses met to promote black solidarity and protest colonization, but the delegates were primarily from the U.S. and the West Indies. During the 1930s the movement was almost nonexistent, but in 1944 several black organizations founded the Pan-African Federation, and the Sixth Pan-African Congress was organized in 1945. Africans, who now were in the

majority, sponsored resolutions demanding political independence in the 1950s, and new African states formed various political and economic organizations. The first conference of independent African states met in Ghana in 1958. In the early 1960s two blocs emerged. One, the Casablanca Group, consisting of the more "radical" states, was created in January 1961. Under the leadership of Kwame Nkrumah of Ghana, it argued for rapid political unity. The Monrovia Group, including the more "conservative" states, met in May 1961 and outlined a program of gradual economic unity. Primarily through the efforts of Emperor Haile Selassie I of Ethiopia, Sir Abubakar Tafawa Balewa, prime minister of Nigeria, and Sékou Touré, president of Guinea, representatives from most independent African states met at Addis Ababa in 1963, and on May 25 the OAU was founded by 30 states. By 1980 the membership had increased to 50 states.

The OAU Charter, as signed at Addis Ababa, reflected a compromise between the prevailing views among the Casablanca and Monrovia groups, envisaging a unity "that transcends ethnic and national differences." After the formation of the OAU, the two groups disbanded.

ORGANIZATION OF AMERICAN STATES (OAS), regional alliance comprising the U.S. and 27 nations of Central and South America, including the Caribbean. It was established April 30, 1948, by 21 nations at the Ninth Inter-American Conference, held at Bogotá, Colombia. The organization is an outgrowth of the International Union of American Republics, created in 1890 at the First International Conference of American States, held in Washington, D.C.

Purposes. The basic purposes of the OAS, as described in the charter, are "(1) to strengthen the peace and security of the continent; (2) to prevent possible causes of difficulties and to ensure the pacific settlement of disputes that may arise among the Member States; (3) to provide for common action on the part of those States in the event of aggression; (4) to seek the solution of political, juridical, and economic problems that may arise among them; and (5) to promote, by cooperative action, their economic, social, and cultural development."

Within two decades after its adoption, the charter of the OAS proved too limited in scope and structure to deal effectively with pressing socioeconomic problems arising from change and growth in the western hemisphere. In order to strengthen the structure of the organization, the Protocol of Amendment to the Charter of the OAS, known as the Protocol of Buenos Aires, was signed on Feb. 27, 1967. The amendments became effective on Feb. 27, 1970, on ratification of the protocol by two-thirds of the member nations. The most important amendments were designed to raise living standards, to ensure social justice, and to achieve economic development and integration among the nations of the western hemisphere.

Structure. Under the amendments, the OAS functions through eight major organs, replacing the six organs of the original charter. They are (1) the General Assembly, which meets annually (replacing the Inter-American Conference); (2) the Meeting of Consultation of Ministers of Foreign Affairs; (3) the councils of the organization (the Permanent Council; the Inter-American Economic and Social Council; and the Inter-American Council for Education, Science, and Culture); (4) the Inter-American Juridical Committee; (5) the Inter-American Commission on Human Rights; (6) the General Secretariat; (7) the specialized conferences, called to deal with specific instances of international cooperation or technical problems; and (8) the specialized organizations, established among member nations to deal with specific needs in specific areas, such as health, history and geography, agricultural sciences, and the problems of Indians, women, and children.

The central organ of the OAS is the General Secretariat, formerly known as the Pan-American Union, which is presided over by the secretary-general. It is divided into nine departments, covering economics, social problems, legal matters, cultural affairs, administration, science, technical cooperation, statistics, and public information. Headquarters of the secretariat and the OAS is in the Pan American Union Building in Washington, D.C., donated by the American industrialist and philanthropist Andrew Carnegie, who was a delegate to the First Inter-American Conference. The secretariat also has offices in capital cities of the member nations and an office in Europe.

Membership. The 28 member nations of the OAS are Argentina, Barbados (admitted 1967), Bolivia, Brazil, Chile, Colombia, Costa Rica, Cuba, Dominica (admitted 1979), the Dominican Republic, Ecuador, El Salvador, Grenada (admitted 1975), Guatemala, Haiti, Honduras, Jamaica (admitted 1969), Mexico, Nicaragua, Panama, Paraguay, Peru, Saint Lucia (admitted 1979), Suriname (admitted 1977), Trinidad and Tobago (admitted 1967), Uruguay, and Venezuela, besides the U.S. The Communist-oriented government of Cuba, however, has been excluded from active participation. Each member nation of the OAS shares the expenses of the organization in proportion to its economic capacity.

ORGANIZATION FOR ECONOMIC COOPERATION AND DEVELOPMENT (OECD), international body composed of 24 countries, most of which are in Europe, participating in a permanent cooperation designed to coordinate the policies of the member nations. The OECD makes available all information relevant to the formulation of national policy in every major field of economic activity. Its principal goals are (1) to promote employment, economic growth, and a rising standard of living in member countries, while maintaining stability; (2) to contribute to sound economic expansion of both member and nonmember nations in the process of development; and (3) to further the expansion of world trade on a multilateral, nondiscriminatory basis in accord with international obligations. Policies are formulated and ideas shared at meetings held throughout the year.

This form of cooperation, rooted in the growing interdependence of national economies, began in April 1948, when a group of 16 European countries founded the Organization for European Economic Cooperation (OEEC) to allocate aid under the European Recovery Program and to work together for postwar recovery. The OECD, succeeding the OEEC, was established on Sept. 30, 1961 in order to broaden the scope of cooperation. The nations that signed the Convention of the OECD on Dec. 14, 1960 were Austria, Belgium, Canada, Denmark, France, Great Britain, Greece, Iceland, Ireland, Italy, Luxembourg, the Netherlands, Norway, Portugal, Spain, Sweden, Switzerland, Turkey, the U.S., and West Germany. Japan, Finland, Australia, and New Zealand joined later. Yugoslavia, although not a member, participates in some of the organization's activities.

The principal organ of the OECD is its council, made up of representatives from all member nations. The council elects the 14-member executive committee and establishes subsidiary committees to investigate and deal with common economic concerns. OECD headquarters is in Paris.

ORGANIZATION OF PETROLEUM EXPORTING COUNTRIES (OPEC), international organization primarily concerned with coordinating the crude-petroleum policies, especially prices, of its members. By 1981 OPEC had 13 members—Algeria, Ecuador, Gabon, Indonesia, Iran, Iraq, Kuwait, Libya, Nigeria, Qatar, Saudi Arabia, United Arab Emirates, and Venezuela. Headquarters is in Vienna. The organization's supreme authority is the Conference, made up of high-level representatives of the member governments, which meets twice a year. The board of governors implements resolutions of the Conference and manages the organization.

Founded in 1960 to counteract falling petroleum prices, OPEC was not of great importance until the early 1970s, when increased international demand made oil a relatively scarce commodity. In 1973-74 OPEC brought about a fourfold increase in the international price of crude petroleum; further increases took place throughout the 1970s. The rises in the price of oil generated by OPEC have been a major cause of the chronic inflation that has plagued the nations of the world in the 1970s and early '80s. Efforts are under way in many industrial countries to establish programs of energy conservation in response to threats of increasing oil prices.

ORGAN PIPE CACTUS NATIONAL MONUMENT. See NATIONAL PARK SERVICE (table).

ORIBE, Manual Ceferino (1792-1857), Uruguayan independence leader and president (1835-38), who founded the Blanco party. Born in Montevideo, he joined the fight for independence at its outset in 1811. After the fall of Montevideo to the Portuguese in 1817 he served in different forces until 1825, when he landed in Uruguay as one of the so-called immortal 33; he subsequently took part in all the major battles of the Cisplatine War (1825-28). Made minister of war in President Fructuoso Rivera's government, he succeeded him in 1835, but Rivera's ensuing revolt forced him to resign in 1838. This conflict and the following 11-year armed struggle between the two men shaped Oribe's Blanco and Rivera's Colorado parties, which have since dominated Uruguayan politics. Oribe led an army into Uruguay in 1843 and began a 9-year unsuccessful siege of Montevideo. He returned to private life in 1851 without regaining office, but continued to wield influence in Uruguayan affairs.

ORIENTAL DRAMA. See CHINESE LITERATURE; DRAMA AND DRAMATIC ARTS; JAPANESE DRAMA.

ORIGEN, also Origenes, surnamed Adamantius (c. 185-c. 254), celebrated Christian writer, teacher, and theologian of antiquity.

Origen was born in Alexandria, Egypt. According to standard church histories, he was a student of Clement of Alexandria. Origen taught in the city for about 28 years, instructing Christians and pagans. He composed his major dogmatic treatises there and began his many critical works.

Visiting in Palestine in 216, Origen, a layperson, was invited by the bishop of Jerusalem and the bishop of Caesarea to lecture in the churches on the Scriptures. About 230 the same bishops ordained him a presbyter without consulting Origen's own bishop, Demetrius of Alexandria (189-

231). Demetrius objected, and two synods were held at Alexandria, the first forbidding Origen to teach there and the second depriving him of his priesthood.

Origen then settled at Caesarea and founded a school of literature, philosophy, and theology. During the persecutions of the Christians in 250 under Emperor Decius, Origen was imprisoned and tortured. Released in 251, but weakened by injuries, he died about 254, probably in Tyre.

Origen may well have been the most accomplished biblical scholar of the early church. His accomplishments as an exegete and student of the text of the Old Testament were outstanding. He was a voluminous writer whose works include letters, treatises in dogmatic and practical theology, apologetics, exegeses, and textual criticism. *Contra Celsum* (Against Celsus) is a closely reasoned long apologetic work refuting arguments advanced by the philosopher Celsus, an influential 2d-century Platonist of Alexandria and perhaps the first serious critic of Christianity.

In addition, Origen is regarded as the father of the allegorical method of scriptural interpretation. He taught the principle of the threefold sense, corresponding to the threefold division of the person into body, spirit, and soul, which was then a common concept. He was a Platonist and endeavored to combine Greek philosophy and the Christian religion. He developed the idea of Christ as the Logos, or Incarnate Word, who is with the Father from eternity, but he taught also that the Son is subordinate to the Father in power and dignity. This latter doctrine and others, such as that of the preexistence of the soul, were severely criticized by many of Origen's contemporaries and by subsequent writers. Theories that were developed from his doctrines became the subject of considerable theological controversy during the Middle Ages.

ORIGINAL SIN, in Christian theology, the universal sinfulness of the human race, traditionally ascribed to the first sin committed by Adam. Sin (q.v.), in Christian doctrine, is considered a state of alienation or estrangement from God.

Scriptural Foundation. The term *original sin* is not found in the Bible. Theologians who advocate the doctrine of original sin argue, however, that it is strongly implied by Paul (see Rom. 7), by John (see 1 John 5:19), and even by Jesus himself (see Luke 11:13). Behind this New Testament teaching lies the world view of late Jewish apocalyptic writings (q.v.). Some of these writings attribute the corrupt state of the world to a prehistoric fall of Satan, the subsequent temptation of Adam and Eve, and the immersion of human history thereafter in disorder, disobedience, and pain (see 2 Esdras 7). In this apocalyptic framework, Paul and other New Testament writers interpreted the work of Christ as overcoming the tremendous power of inherited sin and evil once and for all, reconciling humanity to God, and thus making peace.

St. Augustine. The decline and fall of Rome in the late 4th and early 5th centuries produced a similar apocalyptic atmosphere of crisis and despair. In his controversy with the Romano-British monk Pelagius (c. 354–after 418) over the nature of sin and grace (q.v.), Augustine was able to appeal powerfully and effectively to the Pauline-apocalyptic understanding of the forgiveness of sin (see PELAGIANISM). In his elaboration of the doctrine, however, Augustine imported an idea foreign to the Bible: the notion that the taint of sin is transmitted from generation to generation by the act of procreation. He took this idea from the 2d-century theologian Tertullian, who actually coined the phrase *original sin.*

Subsequent Theology. Medieval theologians retained the idea of original sin, with certain qualifications. It was asserted again in a more recognizably Augustinian form by 16th-century Protestant reformers, primarily Martin Luther and John Calvin. In subsequent Protestant thought, the doctrine was diluted or circumvented. Liberal Protestant theologians developed an optimistic view of human nature that was essentially incompatible with the idea of original sin. The extended crisis of Western civilization that began with World War I, however, has aroused renewed interest in the original, basically apocalyptic outlook of the New Testament and in the doctrine of original sin. Such neoorthodox or postliberal theologians as Karl Barth, Reinhold Niebuhr, and Paul Tillich, however, were unwilling to attribute the transmission of sin to procreation, instead attributing it to an already corrupt society.   C.P.P.

ORINOCO, one of the longest rivers of South America, about 2736 km (about 1700 mi) long. The source of the Orinoco is in the Guiana Highlands, on the slopes of the Sierra Parima, in extreme SE Venezuela, on the border of Brazil. It flows NW to a point near La Esmeralda, where it divides. One arm, the Brazo Casiguiare R., goes S and after a course of 290 km (180 mi) enters the Río Negro, a tributary of the Amazon R. The main branch continues NW to the town of San Fernando de Atabapo, where it receives the Guaviare R. and, flowing generally N, forms the border between Venezuela and Colombia. After passing over the Maipures and Atures rapids and receiving the Meta R. on the left, it meets the Apure R. The Orinoco R. then turns NE and traverses the

Llanos, or plains, of Venezuela before emptying into the Atlantic Ocean.

The Orinoco, which averages 6 km (4 mi) in width, is augmented from the right by several rivers, including the Caura and the Caroni. The delta of the river, with an area of about 20,700 sq km (about 8000 sq mi), begins about 190 km (about 120 mi) from the Atlantic. The total area of the drainage basin is approximately 1,165,500 sq km (about 450,000 sq mi). The Orinoco is navigable for oceangoing ships for some 420 km (some 260 mi), from the mouth to the city of Ciudad Bolívar, the major commercial and communications center for the drainage basin. It is navigable for smaller craft for a distance of about 1610 km (about 1000 mi).

The Orinoco was sighted in 1498 by Christopher Columbus and was first explored (1530–31) to the confluence with the Meta R. Members of an expedition led by the American physician and explorer Herbert Spencer Dickey (1876–1948) claimed to have reached the headwaters of the Orinoco in 1931. Several Brazilian and Venezuelan expeditions made in 1944 and in the 1950s further penetrated the region to the site that is now accepted as the headwaters of the Orinoco.

ORIOLE, common name applied to approximately 35 species of passerine birds of the family Oriolidae, especially the 31 species in the genus *Oriolus,* confined entirely to the Old World. The members of the family are generally of a bright

Golden oriole, Oriolus oriolus

yellow or golden color, which is set off by the black of the wings. They are swift fliers, and some species are good mimics. The birds are insectivorous but also eat fruit.

The best-known Old World oriole is the golden oriole, *O. oriolus*. The adult male is about 23 cm (about 9 in) long and in general color is a rich golden yellow. The bill is dull orange-red with a black streak reaching from its base to the eye, the iris of which is blood red. The wings are black, with markings and a conspicuous wing spot of yellow. The two middle feathers of the tail are black, shaded to olive at the base, the very tips yellow, the basal half of the others black, the distal half yellow. The legs, feet, and claws are dark brown. In certain areas of central and southern Europe, the bird is common in summer; it is common in Iran, and ranges throughout Central Asia as far as Irkutsk, in the southern Soviet Union. It winters in South Africa. The birds build a cup-shaped nest in which two to five eggs are laid.

The orioles of North America belong to the family Icteridae, commonly known as the blackbird (q.v.) family, which includes the Baltimore oriole (q.v.).

ORION, in Greek mythology, handsome giant and mighty hunter, the son of Poseidon, the god of the sea, and Euryale, the Gorgon. Orion fell in love with Metrope, the daughter of Oenopion, king of Chios, and sought her in marriage. Oenopion, however, constantly deferred his consent to the marriage, and Orion attempted to gain possession of the maiden by violence. Incensed at his behavior, her father, with the aid of the god Dionysus, threw him into a deep sleep and blinded him. Orion then consulted an oracle, who told him he could regain his sight by going to the east and letting the rays of the rising sun fall on his eyes. His sight restored, he lived on Crete as the huntsman of the goddess Artemis. The goddess eventually killed him, however, because she was jealous of his affection for Aurora, goddess of the dawn. After Orion's death, Artemis placed him in the heavens as a constellation.

ORION, constellation located on the celestial equator east of Taurus. It is an oblong configuration with three stars in line near its center. It is represented on pictorial charts as the figure of Orion, the hunter in Greek mythology, standing with uplifted club. Three bright stars represent his belt and three fainter stars aligned south of the belt represent his sword. Alpha (α) Orionis, or Betelgeuse, is located in the left corner of the oblong, corresponding to Orion's shoulder. Beta (β) Orionis, or Rigel, is diagonally opposite Betelgeuse. A nebula surrounding the three stars

marking Orion's sword is one of the most conspicuous bright nebulas in the heavens.

ORISKANY, BATTLE OF, military engagement of the American Revolution. It was fought near Oriskany, N.Y., on Aug. 6, 1777, between a force of Loyalists led by the British colonial administrator Sir John Johnson (1742–1830) and the Mohawk Indian chief Joseph Brant, both under the command of the British officer Barry St. Leger (1737–89), on one side; and Americans under Gen. Nicholas Herkimer, on the other. Herkimer was mortally wounded in the battle, and more than a third of the forces on each side were killed or wounded. The British were forced to retreat, thus ending hopes for a British victory at Saratoga. A monument that was erected in 1880 marks the site of the battleground, which is now a public park.

ORISSA, state E India, bordered on the N by Bihar State and West Bengal State, on the E by the Bay of Bengal, on the S by Andhra Pradesh State, and on the W by Madhya Pradesh State. The capital of Orissa is Bhubaneswar. The coastline is largely smooth, indented, and lacks good ports. The coastal strip is narrow, level, and extremely fertile. Most of the population is engaged in raising rice. Other agricultural products are pulses, cotton, tobacco, sugarcane, and turmeric. Among the livestock raised are buffalo and other cattle, sheep, and goats. The state has a large export trade in fish. Industries include the production of pig iron and steel, the manufacture of textiles, cement, paper, glass, aluminum, flour, and soap, and the processing of sugar and oil. Handloom weaving and the making of baskets, wooden articles, hats, nets, and silver filigree works are carried on.

Orissa came under British control in 1803. In 1912 it was united as a province with Bihar, but it became a separate province in 1936. In 1949 it became a state, with the addition of some small native states. The boundaries were unchanged with the States Reorganization Act of 1956.

Area 155,782 sq km (60,148 sq mi); pop. (1981 prelim.) 26,272,054.

ORIZABA, city, E Mexico, in Veracruz State. It lies in a fertile garden region of sugar plantations, about 1230 m (about 4030 ft) above the sea. It is a tourist resort and an industrial city, containing textile mills, breweries, and sugar refineries. The Regional Technological Institute of Orizaba (1957) is here. The city was damaged by an earthquake in 1973. Nearby is Citlaltépetl (Orizaba), the highest peak in Mexico. Pop. (1978 est.) 118,354.

ORKNEY ISLANDS, group of about 90 islands and islets, N Scotland, constituting Orkney Island

Area (an administrative region), separated from the N coast of the Scottish mainland by the Pentland Firth. The administrative center and largest town is Kirkwall, on Mainland (or Pomona), the largest of the islands. Other major islands include Hoy, Sanday, Westray, Stronsay, and South Ronaldsay. The islands are generally low lying and treeless, and fewer than 30 are inhabited. Soils are fertile, and agriculture, the chief economic activity, is productive. Many of the islands have brochs (Pictish stone towers) and other relics of prehistoric habitation. *See also* SCAPA FLOW. Area, 905 sq km (349 sq mi); pop. (1981) 18,906.

ORLANDO, city, seat of Orange Co., central Florida, in a citrus-fruit–growing area, near Winter Park; inc. as a city 1875. It is a winter resort and a tourist center, situated in a region with many lakes. Walt Disney World and the Epcot Center, large theme parks located nearby, are tourist attractions. Electronic and aerospace equipment are manufactured in the city, and citrus fruit products are processed here. Orlando is the site of the University of Central Florida (1963), Jones College Orlando (1918), a junior college, a large U.S. naval training center, and McCoy Air Force Base. Orlando was settled in 1843. The community is named for Orlando Reeves, a soldier who was killed during the Second Seminole War. Citrus production began in Orlando in 1870, and the railroad arrived here ten years later. Pop. (1970) 99,006; (1980) 128,291.

ORLANDO, Vittorio Emanuele (1860–1952), Italian statesman, born in Palermo, Sicily, and educated at the University of Palermo. He served as minister of education from 1903 to 1905, minister of justice from 1907 to 1909 and again from 1914 to 1916, and minister of the interior from 1916 to 1917. He favored the entry of Italy into World War I on the side of the Allies, and in 1917 he was elected prime minister. Orlando headed the Italian delegation to the Paris Peace Conference in 1919. His failure to obtain the territorial concessions that had been secretly promised to Italy by the Allies in 1915 under the Treaty of London caused the downfall of his ministry in June 1919. Six months later he was elected president of the chamber of deputies. He was at first a supporter of the Fascist government established by Benito Mussolini in 1922, but after the Fascists killed the Socialist leader Giacomo Matteotti (1885–1924), Orlando withdrew his support. Three years later he resigned from the chamber. From 1944 to 1946 he was again president of the chamber of deputies and served thereafter in the constituent assembly. Orlando's writings include more than 100 works on juridical subjects.

ORLÉANS, cadet or younger branch of the Valois and Bourbon royal dynasties of France. In 1344 the Valois king Philip VI created the title duc d'Orléans for his son, Philippe (1336–75), and it was thereafter frequently used by members of the royal family. Among the more prominent ducs d'Orléans were Charles d'Orléans (1391–1465), a distinguished poet; Gaston d'Orléans, brother of King Louis XIII; Philippe I d'Orléans (1640–1701), brother of Louis XIV; Philippe II d'Orléans, regent during the minority of Louis XV; Louis Philippe Joseph d'Orléans, a cousin of Louis XVI who supported the French Revolution and was known as Philippe Égalité; and Louis Philippe, son of Philippe Égalité, who became king of France when the Bourbon Charles X was deposed by the Revolution of 1830, and was himself overthrown by the Revolution of 1848. In the late 19th century, those who supported the restoration of Louis Philippe's descendants were known as Orléanists.

ORLÉANS, city, N central France, capital of Loiret Department, on the Loire R. It is a transportation and commercial center. Major manufactures include chemicals, processed foods, textiles, and machinery. Tourism is also important to the city's economy; the Sainte-Croix Cathedral, destroyed by the Huguenots in 1567 and rebuilt by Henry IV and his successors, is a principal attraction. The University of Orléans (1971) is in the city.

Orléans is located on the site of Genabum, the Celtic town burned in 52 BC by the Roman general Gaius Julius Caesar. It was rebuilt by the Roman emperor Lucius Domitius Aurelian and named Aurelianum, whence its modern name. In the 6th century and early 7th centuries Orléans was the capital of a Frankish kingdom, after which it became a favored residence of the kings of France. In 1428–29 the city was besieged by the English during the Hundred Years' War, but was liberated by the French heroine Joan of Arc, also known thereafter as the Maid of Orléans. The town was a headquarters for the Huguenots during the Wars of Religion of the 16th century. In 1870, during the Franco-Prussian War, it was occupied by the Germans, and during World War II it suffered bombings. Pop. (1982) 105,589.

ORLÉANS, Gaston, Duc d' (1608–60), brother of Louis XIII of France, best known for his incessant and bloody, but fruitless, intrigues against his brother's chief minister, Cardinal Richelieu. During the minority of Louis XIV he placed himself at the head of the Fronde, the movement in opposition to the administration of Cardinal Jules Mazarin, but soon betrayed his friends and came to terms with the court. After Mazarin's final triumph, Orléans was exiled to Blois.

ORLÉANS, ÎLE D' (Eng. *Island of Orléans*), island, S Québec Province, Canada, in the Saint Lawrence R., near Québec City. It is about 34 km (about 21 mi) long and has an area of 186 sq km (72 sq mi). The island retains an old French rural character and is a popular summer resort. Its chief products are potatoes, strawberries, dairy goods, and poultry. British troops camped here during the siege of Québec City in 1759. Pop. (1981) 6436.

ORLÉANS, Louis Philippe Joseph, Duc d' (1747–93), French nobleman, cousin of King Louis XVI, who during the French Revolution adopted the name Philippe Égalité. Before the Revolution, he distributed books and papers throughout France advocating liberal ideas. In June 1789, during the meeting of the Estates-General summoned by the king, he led the 47 nobles who seceded from their own order to join the revolutionary third estate. He was elected to the National Convention and voted for the death of Louis XVI. In 1793, during the Reign of Terror, he was guillotined. His son Louis Philippe became king of France in 1830.

ORLÉANS, Philippe II, Duc d' (1674–1723), regent of France during the minority of King Louis XV, a period known as the Régence. A nephew of Louis XIV, Orléans came to power after his uncle's death in 1715, replacing the piety and rigid ceremony of Louis XIV's court with an atmosphere of informality, moral license, and religious skepticism. At home he restored the influence of the parlements (courts that claimed the right to restrict royal power) and tried unsuccessfully to revive the political power of the great nobles. In foreign affairs he and his minister Guillaume Dubois (1656–1723) formed an alliance with Louis XIV's enemies, Great Britain, Austria, and the Netherlands, and fought a successful war against Spain (1718–20). The object of his foreign policy was to gain support for his own succession to the throne in the event of Louis XV's death. In 1719 Orléans made John Law, a Scottish financier, comptroller general of France. The regent was discredited when the Compagnie de la Louisiane, a trading company formed by Law to colonize Louisiana, went bankrupt (1720), causing great losses to its many investors.

A statue of Joan of Arc marks a central square in Orléans. Joan of Arc became known as the Maid of Orléans after she liberated the city from the English in 1429.
French Tourist Office

ORMANDY, Eugene, professional name of Eugene Blau (1899–), American conductor,
born in Budapest, Hungary. A child prodigy on
the violin, he taught in Budapest until 1921,
when he settled in the U.S. During the 1920s and
early '30s he frequently conducted theater and
radio orchestras. From 1931 until 1936 Ormandy
conducted the Minneapolis Symphony Orchestra. He joined the Philadelphia Orchestra in 1936
and was its permanent conductor and music director from 1938 until 1980. Under his direction
the orchestra became known for its rich sound,
particularly that produced by its strings. In 1973,
in Peking, he conducted the Philadelphia Orchestra in the first concerts by an American orchestra in the People's Republic of China.

ORMOC, city and port, central Philippines, in
Leyte Province, on Leyte Island, on Ormoc Bay
(an arm of the Camotes Sea), near Tacloban. A
port and market center in an area of chiefly rice
and sugar production, the city has milling industries. It was one of the chief ports of supply for
the Japanese during World War II until it was
captured by American troops in 1944. The city
was briefly renamed MacArthur after 1950 in
honor of the American general Douglas MacArthur, who helped to liberate the country. Pop.
(1980 prelim.) 104,912.

**ORMONDE, James Butler, 12th Earl and 1st Duke
of** (1610–88), Irish statesman and soldier, born in
London. A strong supporter of Lord Wentworth's
regime in Ireland during the 1630s, Ormonde
backed the English in the Irish rebellion of 1641.
In 1642 he was created a marquis and two years
later was named lord lieutenant of Ireland by
King Charles I of England. In 1649 he concluded
a peace granting the Irish free exercise of the
Catholic religion. With the conquest of Ireland
by Oliver Cromwell in 1650, Ormonde fled to
France. After the Restoration he returned, and in
1661 he received the title duke of Ormonde in
the Irish peerage and again was named lord lieutenant of Ireland. In the latter position he encouraged learning and manufacturing in Ireland,
upholding the Cromwellian seizure of Catholic
land. In 1669, having lost the king's favor, he was
dismissed and became chancellor of the University of Oxford. Shortly afterward an attempt was
made on his life by Thomas Blood, an Irish adventurer. Ormonde was restored as lord lieutenant in 1677 and served in that position until 1682,
when he was raised to the English peerage as
duke of Ormonde.

ORNITHOLOGY, the scientific study of birds; a
branch of zoology (q.v.). Ornithologists examine
both wild and domestic birds, investigating their
anatomy, behavior, evolutionary development,

ecology, classification, and species distribution.
Much of today's knowledge of birds also comes
from amateur bird-watching, which is not only
an enjoyable hobby but has also contributed
valuable data on the behavior and migration of
birds. As a result of such activities, many organizations have been formed to educate the public
in the protection and consideration of bird life,
including the Royal Society for the Protection of
Birds in Great Britain and the National Audubon
Society (q.v.) in the U.S. The International Orni-
thological Congress, which originated in Vienna
in 1884, is held every four years for amateur bird-
watchers and professionals alike. See Bird.

ORONTES (Arab. 'Asi; Turk. Asi), river, SW Asia,
forming part of the border between Lebanon and
Syria and between Syria and Turkey. It rises near
the city of Baalbek, Lebanon, and flows in a
northerly direction between the Lebanon and
Anti-Lebanon mountains into Syria. It flows N to
the city of Antakya (Antioch), Turkey, and then
W to the Mediterranean Sea, through a total
course of about 400 km (about 250 mi). The dam-
ming of the Orontes R. in Syria provides irrigation water for the rich river valley. In ancient
times the valley of the Orontes R. formed a corridor between Asia Minor and Egypt.

OROZCO, José Clemente (1883–1949), Mexican
painter, who contributed to the revival of fresco
technique, design, and subject matter, and who
is regarded as one of the foremost mural painters
in the western hemisphere.

Orozco was born in Zapotlán del Rey, Jalisco
State, on Nov. 22, 1883, and educated at the National Autonomous University of Mexico. In 1922
he became one of the leaders of the Syndicate of
Painters and Sculptors that sought to revive the
art of fresco painting, under the patronage of the
Mexican government. Orozco's most important
early work was a series of frescoes for the National Preparatory School in Mexico City, commemorating the revolutionary uprisings of
peasants and workers in Mexico. Between 1927
and 1934 he worked in the U.S. There he executed a set of murals entitled The Dispossessed
at the New School for Social Research in New
York City. In Pomona College, Claremont, Calif.,
he painted a fresco on the theme of the Greek
hero Prometheus. His mural panels for the Baker
Library at Dartmouth College depict the history
of America in the Coming of Quetzalcoatl, the
Return of Quetzalcoatl, and Modern Industrial
Man. In the 1930s he painted his great murals in
Mexico City and Guadalajara, and in the 1940s he
explored on canvas the unique style, marked by
diagonals and neutral color, that he already had
conveyed in his murals. In his later years, Oroz-

Scene from The Dispossessed, *a set of murals painted by José Clemente Orozco, at the New School for Social Research in New York City.*   New School for Social Research

co's simple, dramatic style became more expressionistic; his subject matter remained the suffering of humanity.

Orozco died in Mexico City on Sept. 7, 1949.

ORPHAN, a minor who has lost one or both parents. In ancient times the care of orphans was a purely private matter. The responsibility of the community for the care of orphans was recognized by the early Christians, and collections to raise funds were taken among the members of congregations. Later church charity provided for the establishment of orphan asylums as well as for the care of orphans in monasteries. The duty of the state to provide for orphans was first recognized in the early 17th century, in England, where they were frequently placed in institutions known as workhouses. The abuses of the workhouse system led in the 18th century to the establishment by the government of separate residential schools, called barrack schools, for the housing and instruction of orphans, and to a substantial growth in the number of orphan asylums founded by private groups. Orphanages became favorite objects of philanthropy in the 19th century as concern mounted over the mistreatment of children. In recent years, as the negative effects of institutional regimentation on the personalities of children have been better understood, the emphasis has shifted to care in foster homes.

In most countries, including Great Britain and the U.S., orphans are recognized as wards of the state, and governmental provision is made for their care. In the U.S. both state and federal legislation provides for aid to orphans in various forms, including their total support in orphanages and foster homes, when necessary. Orphanages in the U.S. are maintained by religious organizations, by social or fraternal organizations, by private endowment, as well as by government institutions.

A recent tendency has been toward organizing orphanages on the so-called cottage system, in which children live together in small groups under the care of a house mother. In these groups efforts are made to integrate the lives of the children with the life of the community. All Jewish institutions and most Protestant institutions, for example, provide for the education of their charges in public schools in which they can meet and associate with other children. In addition, increasing emphasis is given to securing qualified supervisory personnel; and increasingly high salaries are offered by most institutions to attract people with medical, psychiatric, dietary, and social work training. *See also* ADOPTION.

ORPHEUS, in Greek mythology, poet and musician, the son of the muse Calliope (*see* MUSES) and Apollo, god of music, or Oeagrus, king of Thrace. He was given the lyre by Apollo and became such an excellent musician that he had no rival among mortals. When Orpheus played and sang, he moved everything animate and inanimate. His music enchanted the trees and rocks and tamed wild beats, and even the rivers turned in their course to follow him.

Orpheus is best known for his ill-fated marriage to the lovely nymph Eurydice. Soon after the wedding the bride was stung by a viper and died. Overwhelmed with grief, Orpheus determined to go to the underworld and try to bring her back, something no mortal had ever done.

Hades, the ruler of the underworld, was so moved by his playing that he gave Eurydice back to Orpheus on the one condition that he not look back until they reached the upperworld. Orpheus could not control his eagerness, however, and as he gained the light of day he looked back a moment too soon, and Eurydice vanished. In his despair, Orpheus forsook human company and wandered in the wilds, playing for the rocks and trees and rivers. Finally a fierce band of Thracian women, who were followers of the god Dionysus, came upon the gentle musician and killed him. When they threw his severed head in the river Hebrus, it continued to call for Eurydice, and was finally carried to the shore of Lesbos, where the Muses buried it. After Orpheus's death his lyre became the constellation Lyra.

For the importance of Orpheus in Greek religious history, *see* ORPHISM.

ORPHISM, in classical religion, mystic cult of ancient Greece, believed to have been drawn from the writings of the legendary poet and musican Orpheus. Fragmentary poetic passages, including inscriptions on gold tablets found in the graves of Orphic followers from the 6th century BC, indicate that Orphism was based on a cosmogony that centered on the myth of the god Dionysus Zagreus, the son of the deities Zeus and Persephone. Furious because Zeus wished to make his son ruler of the universe, the jealous Titans dismembered and devoured the young god. Athena, goddess of wisdom, was able to rescue his heart, which she brought to Zeus, who swallowed it and gave birth to a new Dionysus. Zeus then punished the Titans by destroying them with his lightning and from their ashes created the human race. As a result, humans had a dual nature: the earthly body was the heritage of the earth-born Titans; the soul came from the divinity of Dionysus, whose remains had been mingled with that of the Titans.

According to the tenets of Orphism, people should endeavor to rid themselves of the Titanic or evil element in their nature and should seek to preserve the Dionysiac or divine nature of their being. The triumph of the Dionysiac element would be assured by following the Orphic rites of purification and asceticism. Through a long series of reincarnated lives, people would prepare for the afterlife. If they had lived in evil, they would be punished, but if they had lived in holiness, after death their souls would be completely liberated from Titanic elements and reunited with the divinity.

ORR, John Boyd. *See* BOYD, ORR, JOHN, 1ST BARON BOYD ORR.

ORRISROOT. *See* IRIS.

ORSK, city, Russian SFSR, in E European USSR, at the confluence of the Ural and Or rivers. The city is the transportation and processing center of a region rich in minerals. It has plants processing iron and steel, nickel, aluminum, and petroleum; food products and machinery are also manufactured. In 1735 the fortress of Orenburg was built here; it was relocated to its present site in 1743. In the 19th century Orsk was known for its cattle market; major industrialization began in the late 1930s. Pop. (1980 est.) 252,000.

ORTEGA Y GASSET, José (1883–1955), Spanish writer and philosopher, noted for his humanistic criticism of modern civilization. He was born in Madrid, and educated at the universities of Madrid and Marburg. In 1910 he was appointed professor of metaphysics at the University of Madrid. His articles, lectures, and essays on philosophical and political issues contributed to a Spanish intellectual renaissance in the first decades of the 20th century and to the fall of the Spanish monarchy in 1931. He was a member from 1931 to 1933 of the Cortes (Spanish parliament) that promulgated the republican constitution. After the outbreak of the Spanish civil war in 1936 he lived abroad, returning to Spain in the late 1940s. His reflections on the problems of modern civilization are contained in *The Revolt of the Masses* (1930; trans. 1932), a work that earned him an international reputation. In it he decries the destructive influence of mass-minded, and therefore mediocre, people, who, if not directed by the intellectually and morally superior minority, encourage the rise of totalitarianism. His writings include *The Modern Theme* (1923; trans. 1933), *Invertebrate Spain* (1921; trans. 1937), *The Dehumanization of Art* (1925; trans. 1948), and *Some Lessons in Metaphysics* (posthumously pub., 1970; trans. 1970).

ORTELIUS, Abraham (1527–98), Flemish geographer, who produced the first modern atlas, *Theatrum Orbis Terrarum* (1570), which contained 70 maps, the largest collection of the time. Although many of his maps were copies, and some were inaccurate, they were the best available. In 1575 he became geographer to the court of Philip II of Spain, where he continued to publish studies of ancient geography and travel accounts. Ortelius was also a collector and dealer in rare antiquities and maps.

ORTHODONTICS. *See* DENTISTRY.